Cultural Landscapes of Universal Value

Cover photos

Uluru Kata National Park (Australia) (Photo: Jim Thorsell, IUCN)

Mediterranean cultural landscape; Orvieto, Umbria, Italy (Photo: Harald Plachter)

Mount Huangshan (China) (Photo: Mechtild Rössler, UNESCO)

Terraced rice landscape of the Ifugo region; Batad, Northern Luzon, Philippines (Photo: Harald Plachter)

Financial support:

Edited by
Bernd von Droste,
Harald Plachter,
Mechtild Rössler

With contributions of
42 scientists

Cultural Landscapes of Universal Value

-Components of a Global Strategy-

87 Figures, 16 Boxes and
5 Tables

Gustav Fischer Verlag Jena • Stuttgart • New York
in cooperation with UNESCO

Dr. Bernd von Droste zu Hülshoff
Dr. Mechtild Rössler
UNESCO – World Heritage Centre
7, place de Fontenoy, F-75700 Paris

Prof. Dr. Harald Plachter
Universität Marburg
FB Biologie, Fachgebiet Naturschutz,
D-35032 Marburg

with technical assistance from Alison Semple, Lisa Lundby and Kerstin Balthasar

The designations employed and the presentation of the material in this publication do not imply the expression of any opinion whatsoever on the part of the publishers concerning the legal status of any country or territory or of its authorities, or concerning the frontiers of any country or territory.
The authors are responsible for the choice and the presentation of the facts contained in this book and for the opinions expressed therein which are not necessarily those of UNESCO and do not commit the organization.
No part of this publication may be reproduced in any form without written permission from the publishers except for the quotation of brief passages for the purpose of review.

Die Deutsche Bibliothek – CIP-Einheitsaufnahme
Cultural landscapes of universal value : components of a global strategy ; 5 tables / in cooperation with UNESCO. Ed. by Bernd von Droste: With contributions of 42 scientists. – Jena ; Stuttgart ; New York : G. Fischer, 1995
   ISBN 3-334-61022-5 (Fischer)
   ISBN 1-56081-434-9 (VCH)
NE: Droste zu Hülshoff, Bernd von

Published jointly by:
Gustav Fischer Verlag
220 East 23rd Street, Suite 909, New York 10010, USA

Gustav Fischer Verlag
Villengang 2, D - 07745 Jena, Federal Republic of Germany

For orders from USA and Canada:
VCH Publishers Inc., 303 N.W. 12th Avenue, Deerfield Beach, Florida 33442-1705, USA
© Gustav Fischer Verlag · Jena · Stuttgart · New York · 1995
This work with all its parts is protected by copyright. Any use beyond the strict limits of the copyright law without the consent of the publisher is inadmissible and punishable. This refers especially to reproduction of figures and/or text in print or xerography, translations, microforms and the data storage and processing in electronical systems.

Setting: SATZREPROSERVICE GmbH Jena
Printed/Bound: Druckerei zu Altenburg GmbH
Printed in Germany

Preface by the Director-General of UNESCO

The splendid cultural landscapes of Machu Picchu in Peru and the outstanding natural beauty of Ayers Rock in the Uluru-Kata Tjuta National Park, in Australia, are just two examples of the many masterworks of nature and culture included in UNESCO's World Heritage List in recognition of their unique significance and the need for international protection.

With the decision of the World Heritage Committee to include outstanding cultural landscapes in the World Heritage List, a new era has begun. Now, nature and culture can be seen and protected together, and more effectively. The identification, recognition and conservation of cultural landscapes is one of the tasks for all nations and all cultures of the world. Moreover, it opens the World Heritage List for a type of non-monumental cultural property which was not acknowledged before. The World Heritage Convention is the first international legal instrument to recognize and to protect cultural landscapes.

The aim of this book is to guide the community in the identification and nomination of cultural landscapes and to promote the safeguarding of our common heritage for the benefit of present and future generations.

8 August 1995   Federico Mayor

List of Contributors

Prof John Aitchison
International Centre for Protected
Landscapes
University College of Wales
Science Park
Aberystwyth
Dyfed SY23 3AH
Wales
United Kingdom

Dr Boakye Amoako-Atta
Chief Project Coordinator
P.O. Box 16496
Accra Airport
Ghana

Mr Jeffery Bentley
Casilla 2695
Cochabamba
Bolivia

Dr Peter Bridgewater
Mr Theo Hooy
Australian Nature Conservation Agency
GPO Box 636
Canberra ACT 2601
Australia

Prof Susan Buggey
Canadian Park Service
3rd Floor
10 Wellington Street
Hull
Quebec K1A OH3
Canada

Dr Hans Caspary
Landesamt für Denkmalpflege
Rheinland-Pfalz
Göttelmannstr. 17
D-55130 Mainz
Germany

Ms Silvia Chalukian
Department Natural Resources
& Conservation Biology
Zamorano
P.O. Box Tegucigalpa
Honduras

Dr Henry Cleere
Acres Rise
Lower Platts
Ticehurst
Wadhurst TN5 7DD
United Kingdom

Dr Almo Farina
Museo di Storia Naturale
Fortezza della Brunella
I-54011 Aulla
Italy

Ms Carmen Añon Feliu
Ulises, 114
E-28043 Madrid
Spain

Prof P. J. Fowler
Department of Archaeology
The University
Newcastle upon Tyne
NE1 7RN
United Kingdom

Prof Bryn Green
Wye College
University of London
Wye
Ashford
Kent TN25 5AH
United Kingdom

Prof Wolfgang Haber
Lehrstuhl für Landschaftsökologie
TU München
D-85354 Freising
Germany

Ms Jelka Habjan
Institute for Conservation of
Natural and Cultural Heritage
Plecnikov trg. 2
61000 Ljubljana
Slovenia

Ms Tonte Hegard
Riksantikvaren
Postboks 8196 Dep.
N-0034 Oslo
Norway

Dr Eberhard Henne
LAG, Land Brandenburg
Am Stadtsee, PSF 100526
D-16225 Eberswalde
Germany

Mr Tumu Te Heuheu
Department of Conservation
GPO Box 19-420
Wellington
New Zealand

Mr David Jacques
ICOMOS Landscapes Working Group
Sugnall
Stafford ST21 6NF
United Kingdom

Dipl.-Ing. Hans P. Jeschke
Amt der Oberösterreichischen
Landesregierung
Kulturgüterkataster
A-4020 Linz
Austria

Ms Vesna Kolar-Planinšič
Agency for Natural and Cultural Heritage
Conservation
Tomšičeva 44
64000 Kranj
Slovenia

Prof Robert Layton
Department of Anthropology
University of Durham
43 Old Elvet
Durham DH1 3HN
United Kingdom

Mr Yves Luginbühl
5, rue Leon Delhomme
F-75015 Paris
France

Dr Jeffrey A. McNeely
Mr William S. Keeton
IUCN
rue Mauverney 28
CH-1196 Gland
Switzerland

Mr Alain Megret
Mr Gérard Collin
Ministère de l'Environnement
Direction de la Nature et des Paysages
20, avenue de Ségur
F-75302 Paris 07 SP
France

Ms Nora Mitchell
Cultural Landscape Preservation
Program Manager
National Park Service
North Atlantic Region
15 State Street
Boston Massachusetts 02109-3572
United States of America

Prof Nobukazu Nakagoshi
Dept. of Environmental Studies
Faculty of Integrated Arts and Sciences
Hiroshima University
1-7-1 Kagamiyama
Higashi-Hiroshima 730 724
Japan

Ms Patricia O'Donnell
LANDSCAPES
Box 2425 Saugatuck Station
Westport
Connecticut 06880-0425
United States of America

Dr Adrian Phillips
2, The Old Rectory
Dumbleton near Eveshawn
WR II 6T9
United Kingdom

Prof Harald Plachter
University of Marburg
Fachbereich Biologie
Fachgebiet Naturschutz
Lahnberge
D-35032 Marburg
Germany

Ms Kerstin Riessen
Vikingatan 11
S-11342 Stockholm
Sweden

Dr Mechtild Rössler
UNESCO
World Heritage Centre
7, place de Fontenoy
F-75700 Paris
France

Ms Alison Semple
25 Canonbury Square
London N1 2AL
United Kingdom

Prof Ken Taylor
Faculty of Environmental Design
University of Canberra
P.O. Box 1
Belconnen ACT 2616
Australia

Ms Sarah Titchen
Department of Archaeology
and Anthropology
The Faculties
The Australian National University
Canberra ACT 0200
Australia

Ms Dominique Verdugo
Ms Jalila Kadiri Fakir
12, zankat Al Yamama
10 000 Rabat
Marocco

Mr Augusto F. Villalon
Commissioner for Cultural Heritage
107 Wilson Circle
San Juan
M. Manila 1500
Philippines

Dr Bernd von Droste zu Hülshoff
UNESCO
World Heritage Centre
7, place de Fontenoy
F-75700 Paris
France

Dr Ying Yang Petersen
764 Alderwood Dr.
Newport Beach
CA 92660
United States of America

Dr Jonathan Wager
19 Langham Road
Bowdon
Cheshire WA14 2HX
United Kingdom

Contents

Preface
0 F. Mayor 5

Introduction
1 Cultural Landscapes: Reconnecting Culture and Nature 15
   Harald Plachter and Mechtild Rössler

Conceptual Framework
2 Cultural Landscapes in a Global World Heritage Strategy 20
   Bernd von Droste
3 The Interaction between Biological and Cultural Diversity 25
   Jeffrey A. McNeely and William S. Keeton
4 Concept, Origin and Meaning of "Landscape" 38
   Wolfgang Haber
5 UNESCO and Cultural Landscape Protection 42
   Mechtild Rössler
6 The Evaluation of Cultural Landscapes: The Role of ICOMOS 50
   Henry Cleere
7 Cultural Landscapes and Fauna 60
   Almo Farina

Cultural Landscapes of the World
Africa and Arab States
8 Sacred Groves in Ghana 80
   Boakye Amoako-Atta
9 Cultural Landscapes: Maraboutic sites in Morocco 96
   Dominique Verdugo and Jalila Kadiri Fakir

Asia

10	The Cultural Lancscape of the Rice Terraces of the Philippine Cordilleras *Augusto F. Villalon*	108
11	Mt. Huangshan and Mt. Taishan, Outstanding Cultural Landscapes in China... *Ying Yang*	114
12	Changing Cultural Landscapes in Japan .... *Nobukazu Nakagoshi*	128
13	Cultural Landscapes of Angkor Region, Cambodia. A Case Study of Planning for a World Heritage Site – The Zoning and Environmental Management Plan for Angkor (ZEMP) .... *Jonathan Wager*	139
14	The Cultural Landscape of Sagarmatha National Park in Nepal........ *Hans Caspary*	154

Australia and the Pacific

15	Outstanding Cultural Landscapes in Australia, New Zealand and the Pacific: the Footprint of Man in the Wilderness .... *Peter Bridgewater and Theo Hooy*	162
16	A Sacred Gift: Tongariro National Park, New Zealand .... *Tumu Te Heuheu*	170
17	Uluru: An Outstanding Australian Aboriginal Cultural Landscape .... *Robert Layton and Sarah Titchen*	174
18	Australian Colonial Landscapes .... *Ken Taylor*	182

The Americas

19	Cultural Landscapes in Honduras: the Mosquitia .... *Silvia C. Chalukian and Jeffery W. Bentley*	202
20	Cultural Landscapes in North America: an Overview of Status in the United States and Canada .... *Patricia M. O'Donnell*	210
21	Cultural Landscapes in the United States .... *Nora J. Mitchell*	234
22	Cultural Landscapes in Canada .... *Susan Buggey*	252

Europe

23	Cultural Landscapes in Europe: A Geographical Perspective .... *John Aitchison*	272
24	On the Traces of the Mediterranean Landscape .... *Yves Luginbühl*	289
25	Aranjuez: Nature, Agriculture and the Art of the Landscape .... *Carmen Añon Feliu*	295
26	Cultural Landscapes in France .... *Alain Megret* and *Gérard Collin*	307
27	Slovenian Cultural Landscapes and the Triglav National Park .... *Jelka Habjan* and *Vesna Kolar-Planinšič*	316
28	Austrian Cultural Landscapes: Methodological Aspects for an Inventory *Hans Peter Jeschke*	324
29	The Schorfheide-Chorin Biosphere Reserve, Germany: Unique Species Diversity in a Centuries-Old Cultivated Landscape .... *Eberhard Henne*	333
30	Cultural Landscapes in Britain .... *Peter Fowler* and *David Jacques*	350
31	The Cultural Landscape of Markim/Orkesta .... *Kerstin Riessen*	364
32	Nature and Culture – Two Aspects of the Same Story. Norwegian Landscape Management in the 1990s .... *Tonte Hegard*	374

Conserving Cultural Landscapes: Elements for a Strategy of Protection through Development

33	Cultural Landscapes: an IUCN Perspective .... *Adrian Phillips*	380
34	Functional Criteria for the Assessment of Cultural Landscapes .... *Harald Plachter*	393
35	Principles for Protecting Endangered Landscapes: The Work of the IUCN-CESP Working Group on Landscape Conservation .... *Bryn H. Green*	405
36	Conservation of Landscapes in Post-Industrial Countries .... *David Jacques* and *Peter Fowler*	412
37	Tentative Lists as a Tool for Landscape Classification and Protection .. *Sarah M. Titchen* and *Mechtild Rössler*	420

Annexes

I	Action Plan for the Future (Cultural Landscapes) adopted by the seventeenth session of the World Heritage Committee in December 1993	430
II	Extract of the Operational Guidelines for the Implementation of the World Heritage Convention	431
III	Extract from the report of the expert meeting on "Heritage Canals" (Canada, September 1994)	433
IV	Extract from the report of the expert meeting on "Routes as Part of Our Cultural Heritage" (Spain, November 1994)	436
V	Extract from the report of the "Regional Thematic Study Meeting on Asian Rice Culture and its Terraced Landscapes" (Philippines, March/April 1995)	441
VI	Extract from the report of the "Asia-Pacific Regional Workshop on Associative Cultural Landscapes" (Australia, April 1995)	447
VII	World Heritage Convention (1972)	456

Chapter 1 · Introduction

Cultural Landscapes:
Reconnecting Culture and Nature

Harald Plachter and Mechtild Rössler

Cultural landscapes reflect the interactions between people and their natural environment over space and time. Nature, in this context, is the counterpart to human society; both are dynamic forces, shaping the landscapes. In some regions of the world, cultural landscapes stand out as models of interaction between people, their social system and the way they organize space. A cultural landscape is a complex phenomenon with a tangible and an intangible identity. The intangible component arises from ideas and interactions which have an impact on the perceptions and shaping of a landscape, such as sacred beliefs closely linked to the landscape and the way it has been perceived over time. Cultural landscapes mirror the cultures which created them.

At least since the beginning of the Industrial Revolution in the first half of the nineteenth century, nature and culture have often been conceived of as extreme opposites in Western thought. Nature was seen not as the counterpart of culture, but above all as an "enemy" to be controlled and dominated, with the assistance of technology. Technological achievements were seen in the industrial nations as a way protecting and insulating people from nature. The structure of nature was regarded as if it were similar to that of a machine: to be analyzed, used and altered as far as possible and controllable. This approach to nature is still reflected in many scientific disciplines.

Through political and socio-economic developments during the last two centuries, this approach was introduced into other geo-cultural regions of the world. The community of nations has not found a single language. But seemingly this world today is dominated by the priority placed on technological development, independent from natural conditions, the belief in progress promoted by technological development and a profound disconnection and confrontation of nature and culture.

This thinking, the confidence in technological developments and modern science and a cultural identification with it, reached a peak in the early 1970s. This was also the time of a major environmental movement, demonstrated at the First United Nations Conference on the Human Environment in Stockholm. At that time UNESCO established the Interational Convention for the Protection of the World's Cultural and Natural Heritage. It was based on scientific understanding, as well as on the urge for an international effort: who would question the need to protect Abu Simbel or the Great Wall, Victoria Falls or the Everglades? To cover this by a single instrument was quite innnovative and encouraging. However, a substantive connection between nature and culture was not automatically implied by the World Heritage Convention.

In implementing the World Heritage Convention, the World Heritage Committee tried to avoid the separation between nature and culture. But despite these efforts the gap could terraced landscapes as well as associative cultural landscapes in the Asia-Pacific region. The extracts of the Operational Guidelines and the text of the World Heritage Convention itself complete this volume. It should be emphasized that this is only the first step of a major initiative for both the natural and cultural heritage field, to enhance the protection of cultural landscapes on the local, regional and international levels.

We would like to take this opportunity to thank the Governments who hosted expert meetings for their generous support, the World Heritage Committee for their efforts to make the World Heritage Convention the first international legal instrument to protect cultural landscapes, all those who contributed to this book, and especially people living in and maintaining cultural landscapes for sharing their knowledge with us, and - last but not least - the "Deutsche Bundesstiftung Umwelt" for their financial support.

Harald Plachter has a MA in biology and a Ph.D. in natural sciences. He ist professor for nature conservation at the University of Marburg, Germany. He is member of the German delegation for the World Heritage Convention since 1992.

Mechtild Rössler has a MA in cultural geography and a Ph.D. in natural sciences. She has worked in the UNESCO World Heritage Centre since its creation in 1992 and is responsible for natural sites and cultural landscapes.

Conceptual Framework

Cultural Landscapes in a Global World Heritage Strategy
Bernd von Droste

The Interaction between Biological and Cultural Diversity
Jeffrey A. McNeely and William S. Keeton

Concept, Origin and Meaning of "Landscape"
Wolfgang Haber

UNESCO and Cultural Landscape Protection
Mechtild Rössler

The Evaluation of Cultural Landscapes: The Role of ICOMOS
Henry Cleere

Cultural Landscapes and Fauna
Almo Farina

Chapter 2

Cultural Landscapes in a Global World Heritage Strategy

Bernd von Droste

More than 140 States Parties have adhered to the World Heritage Convention which therefore is the world's most universal legal instrument in the field of conservation. Most of the 440 properties on the World Heritage List are monuments and other cultural sites.

From the examination of the distribution of the properties, it becomes obvious that there is (a) a serious imbalance in the World Heritage List between cultural and natural sites, (b) cultural landscapes and its notion is a latecomer to the World Heritage List and (c) an asymmetry with respect to the representation of the different cultural regions of the world, types of properties and periods represented.

"Cultural landscape is a transformed part of free nature resulting from man's intervention to shape it according to particular concepts of culture. There are many types of landscape, which are historically dependent on the culture of a given time and on the original space" (Svobodova 1990, 24).

I will therefore address the inclusion of cultural landscapes in the World Heritage List from two angles: (1) the global strategy approach and (2) with respect to the results of the authenticity meeting in Nara, Japan, November 1994.

The Global Strategy for a representative World Heritage List

For several years now, the Committee has constantly stressed the importance of completing the identification of World Heritage and ensuring a truly representative List, and thus its credibility. Consequently, it has also stressed the necessity of implementing the "Global Study" of the List and the associated thematic studies on the different types of cultural properties which could be proposed for inscription, including those which are at present little or not at all represented.

During its seventeenth session at Cartagena (Colombia), the Committee requested the World Heritage Centre and ICOMOS to continue their efforts in this direction. The World Heritage Centre and ICOMOS therefore jointly organized a first expert meeting at UNESCO Headquarters from 20 to 22 June 1994, representing the different regions of the world and the different disciplines concerned (cultural heritage specialists, anthropologists, art and architecture historians, archaeologists, etc.) with the objective of reviewing the issues and considering all the different approaches, and especially all the work and contributions made to date, in an attempt to define a conceptual framework, a methodology and common goals.

The principal objectives of the meeting were to:
- examine the present representative structure of the World Heritage List with regard to cultural properties;
- carry out an in-depth study of all the studies and earlier contributions to the "Global Study" and in particular the proposals presented by ICOMOS and in Mr. Léon Pressouyre's publication *La Convention du Patrimoine mondial, vingt ans après;*
- integrate the international scientific community's most recent findings and ideas on the content and concept of cultural heritage over the past twenty years.

The experts were in full agreement on the following points:
1) that there is a serious imbalance in cultural heritage on the World Heritage List in its present form with regard to regions of the world, types of properties and the periods represented. Living cultures, especially those of "traditional" societies, are largely under-represented;
2) earlier proposals and the work carried out from 1984 to 1993 on the "Global Study", in particular the three-dimensional space-time-human achievement grid, have been found invaluable to the process of reflection in this complex and difficult domain. Thus, they were indispensable steps towards the new anthropological and multidimensional approach proposed by the experts in the more dynamic, continuous and evolutive form of a "global strategy";
3) the development of knowledge and the process of reflection within the international scientific community over the past twenty years has led to an evolution in the content and the extension of the concept of cultural heritage, and to the abandon of a basically "monumental" vision for a far more anthropological and global conception of material evidence of the different cultures of the world. This material evidence is no longer considered out of context, but in its multiple relationships to its physical and non-physical environment.

The conclusions of the expert meeting were formulated in seven recommendations which were proposed to the World Heritage Committee at its eighteenth session. The Committee examined the proposals for revision of certain of the cultural criteria of the Operational Guidelines. It furthermore asked to make full use of certain thematic and regional meetings, which were held in 1994, such as the **Heritage Canals** and the meeting on **Routes as a part of our Cultural Heritage** (Madrid), as well as meetings organized in 1995, in particular the meeting on Rice Terraces Cultural Landscapes (Philippines) and the thematic study meeting on associative cultural landscapes (Australia); also to communicate the problematic of the Global Strategy, place the discussions in the wider framework of current scientific thought concerning the concept of cultural heritage, and identify potential partners for future regional meetings of a specific nature.

In 1995, a first regional scientific meeting to discuss the place of African cultural heritage within the World Heritage Convention was organized. Presently, African cultural heritage is very under-represented on the List (17 inscribed sites under at least one cultural criterion, located in eight States Parties, several of which having only an indirect relation with the traditional African cultures themselves), in spite of its vast archaeological, technical, architectural and spiritual wealth, its modes of occupying and using the land and space, its networks of exchange for commerce and ideas, etc. This meeting could associate about thirty States Parties or not yet Party to the Convention, with members of the international scientific community.

Furthermore, at the 18th Committee session there was a discussion of the widening of the global strategy approach for natural heritage and to pursue, with ICCROM, ICOMOS and IUCN and the other partners, the improvement of theoretical and methodological frameworks. The first step for a representative World Heritage list for natural heritage will be to contribute to the preparation of a report on selective geological sites which would meet World Heritage criteria with a view to much stricter application of World Heritage criteria. Furthermore, a workshop on the notion of "integrity" for natural heritage will be scheduled, as the Nara conference widened the approach of "authenticity" for cultural heritage. Let me discuss this notion in the following with regard to cultural landscapes:

Authenticity

Authenticity is a basic requirement for new nominations to the World Heritage List. Cultural properties will be included in the World Heritage List only if they meet the test of authenticity, which remained an essential criterion for the World Heritage Committee. The original intention to require that "each property should meet the test of authenticity", was obviously to ensure that cultural World Heritage properties responded to the concept of authenticity in a historical sense as well as in a material sense. Apparently this was done to exclude copies or reconstructions and would ensure that the hypothetical number of nominated and actually inscribed cultural heritage properties would remain limited.

The 16th session of the World Heritage Committee held in Santa Fe became a major turning point for the future of the World Heritage Convention. At this session, the World Heritage Committee, amended the Operational Guidelines not only to include cultural landscapes, but also:

Each cultural property has to meet the test of authenticity in design, material, workmanship or setting and in the case of cultural landscapes their distinctive character and components. In this connection, the Committee stressed that reconstruction is acceptable only if it is carried out on the basis of complete and detailed documentation on the original and to no extent on conjecture. (Paragraph 24 in the Operational Guidelines for the Implementation of the World Heritage Convention.)

The strategic orientations call for actions to ensure the continued representativity and credibility of the World Heritage List. This implies to redefine and update criteria for the evaluation of natural and cultural properties nominated for the World Heritage List.

More specifically, two recommendations were adopted at Santa Fé. The first one, asks the World Heritage Centre to convene a group of experts to address the deficiencies of the World Heritage List and identify ways of correcting them in order to make the World Heritage List more representative. This issue was dealt with by a group of experts who met at the UNESCO Headquarters in June this year. The experts urged to abandon a basically monumental vision of cultural heritage in favor of more anthropological and global conception. The experts also proposed to modify cultural criteria for the World Heritage List. These proposals are based on a number of shortcomings in the World Heritage List such as the over-representation of European cultural properties; of historic centres; of religious properties; particularly of Christian properties, under-representation of pre-historic properties and of contemporary 20th century properties. In particular the absence of cultural expressions of living, traditional cultures on the World Heritage List was stated. The obvious bias which can be observed in examining the World Heritage List in favor of societies with a monumental culture was severely criticized.

This meeting was followed one month later by an expert gathering on World Heritage Canals which was hosted by Canada. At this meeting the question of authenticity of World Heritage Canals formed part of the debate.

The Nara Conference on authenticity is therefore inscribed in the overall process of giving a new dynamic to the World Heritage Convention, to make it more relevant to the diversity of world culture and to elaborate a conservation concept better adapted increased insight into cultures of other parts of the world and to conservation needs of the present and the future: from that perspective, authenticity needs to be seen as an open, flexible concept which has to be applied on case by case basis and in a finely tuned way, with full understanding of the socio-economic, ecological, cultural and historical context.

In order to illustrate the problems that may arise from efforts to once and for all fix the meaning of the concept of authenticity would like to give few examples showing how complex the "test of authenticity" - might be with certain types of properties which are already present on the World Heritage List.

As we are all aware, the majority of the buildings of the world are not monumental, at least not in the European, or colonial sense of the concept. In the indigenous cultures of the Americas, Africa, Australia and the Pacific most of the architectural achievements might be classified as vernacular even though they were often built for "monumental" reasons. Their vernacularity, then, stems more from the aspects of design, material and technique, than from those of function and spirit. However, as pointed out in the proceedings of the Bergen Conference, there exists no distinct dividing-line between the monumental and the vernacular architecture.

The following examples from the World Heritage List illustrate a different set of problems, which suggest a more flexible application of the concept of authenticity: an example of vernacular architecture is the native site of Ninstints or Anthony Island, Canada (inscribed on the World Heritage List in 1981), which offers a unique view of the activity of the Haida people and fishermen who once lived on the North Pacific coast. The main elements of the site consisted of wooden structures, houses and different types of totem poles which have seriously deteriorated over the course of time. Because of this, a totem pole rescue project was organized in the middle of the 1950's. However, from an "eurocentric" point of view it is interesting to learn that the ethnic group of people who were the original inhabitants, the Haidas, give a somewhat different meaning to authenticity, in emphasizing culture and tradition more than the material aspects.

In the end, this will facilitate the emergence of a new and multicultural concept of the World Heritage with composite authentic elements. Let us try to make the concept of authenticity evolve into a concept which encompasses all the different, cultural architectural expressions and manifestations of the world, monumental and vernacular - built not only of stone, but also of wood, earth or straw or other materials. In this way we could move on from a concept of authenticity focused on material and technique only, to one, including also the know-how, the context of the natural and social environment, which would safeguard also the context and spirit of the original builder or culture. Such a concept would increase the prospects for a universal dialogue, incorporating all the different cultures of the world, and result in a more balanced and equitable World Heritage List which would include nature and culture and thus cultural landscapes.

References

Conventions and Recommendations of UNESCO Concerning the Protection of the Cultural Heritage (1985). UNESCO. Paris.

Feilden, B.M. and Jokilehto, J. (1993). *Management Guidelines for World Cultural Heritage Sites*. ICCROM, UNESCO, ICOMOS. Rome.

Global strategy for a Representative World Heritage List, in relation with the Convention for the Protection of the World Cultural and Natural Heritage (1994). Bureau of the World Heritage Committee. Eighteenth session. UNESCO. Headquarters. Paris, 4–9 July 1994. Report of the Rapporteur. pp. 53 - 57. UNESCO. Paris.

International Charter for the Conservation and Restoration of Monuments and Sites (1966). ICOMOS. Paris.

Larsen, K.E. and Marstein N. (ed.), *Conference on Authenticity in relation to the World Heritage Convention*. Preparatory Workshop (1994). Riksantikvaren (Directorate for Cultural Heritage), Bergen, Norway.

Larsen, K.E. and Marstein N. (ed). *ICOMOS International Wood Committee*, 8th international symposium. Kathmandu, Patan and Bhaktapur, Nepal (1994), ICOMOS, UNESCO and Riksantikvaren. Norway.

Operational Guidelines for the Implementation of the World Heritage Convention (1995), UNESCO, Paris.

Pressouyre, L. (1992). *La Convention du Patrimoine mondial, vingt ans après*. Paris: UNESCO.

Revision of the Guidelines for the Implementation of the World Heritage Convention Concerning the Protection of the World Cultural and Natural Heritage. World Heritage Committee, Sixteenth Session, Santa Fe. United States of America (7 - 14 December 1992). Report (1992). UNESCO. Paris.

Sites inscribed on the World Heritage List. Brief descriptions. World Heritage Centre (1995). UNESCO. Paris.

Svobodova, H. (1990). *Some remarks on the phenomenological categories of the cultural aspects of landscape*. In: Svobodova, H. (ed.), *Cultural aspects of landscape,* Wageningen, Pudoc.

Bernd von Droste zu Hülshoff is the Director of the UNESCO World Heritage Centre, Paris.

Chapter 3

The Interaction between Biological and Cultural Diversity

Jeffrey A. McNeely and William S. Keeton

"Variety is the spice of life" takes on new meaning in a time when consumers in Bangkok, Bogota, Bangui, Boston, Brisbane and Belfast are eating the same Big Macs, drinking the same Pepsi, watching the same Bill Cosby programme, smoking the same Marlboros, and wearing the same Levis jeans. Does the global consumer culture mean the death of the world 's rich diversity of peoples and cultural traditions? If so, what are we losing? And what does the loss of cultural diversity mean to the natural environment?

Introduction

Throughout history, local societies have ebbed and flowed as their wisdom was tested against the criterion of sustainability. Those societies that were able to develop the wisdom, technology, and knowledge to live within the limits of their environments were able to survive. Others over-exploited their resources, so they flourished only briefly, giving up sustainability and adaptability for a flash-in-the-pan flush of immediate wealth.

Over the past several generations, the highly diverse and often localized adaptations to local environmental conditions have been replaced in most places by a world culture increasingly characterized by very high levels of material consumption, at least for a privileged minority. Economic growth based on the use of fossil fuels as an energy source, greatly expanded international trade, and improved public health measures have spurred such a rapid expansion of human numbers and consumption that new approaches to resource exploitation have been required.

These approaches, often involving powerful machinery, sophisticated technology, and arcane economic instruments, have overwhelmed the conservation measures that local communities have developed from long experience. Cultural controls on over-exploitation, such as self, imposed restrictions on hunting certain species of animals or females during calving seasons, ownership of grazing rights and forest resources, rotation of hunting zones, taboos on hunting certain species, limitations on forest clearance, and protection of special groves of trees for religious reasons, often have not been able to stand up to the seductions of the market economy, especially when harvesting rights are given to outsiders by governments who disregard traditional land rights.

In Colombia, the forests of the north-west Amazon basin harbour a bewildering array of plants and animals. This region is often considered part of the world's greatest remaining tropical wilderness. But for the Tukano people who live there, it is not a wilderness, it is home, and they have developed a detailed knowledge about how to wrest a living from this seemingly inhospitable environment. The Tukano perceive their "wilderness" environment to be man-made, transformed and structured in the past by the symbolic meaning their ancestors gave to resources and the knowledge they obtained of plants and animals that enabled people to survive. Their forest is a system of resources in which the energy produced is directly proportional to the amount of energy it receives. They know that they cannot harvest more than the forest can produce, and they call on a sophisticated knowledge of individual species and their uses. Their long tradition of constant observation of animal behaviour, acquired as part of their daily struggle to survive, provides guidance on what adaptations are possible. Their myths tell of animal species that were punished by the spirits for indulging in gluttony, boastfulness, improvidence, and aggressiveness. These myths serve as examples to human society, in which animals are metaphors for survival. By analyzing animal behaviour, the Tukano find an order in the physical world within which human activities can be adjusted (Reichel-Dolmatoff 1976).

The Tukano relationship with wildlife is typical of people whose welfare depends on how they manage resources. Like many indigenous peoples, they limit their own harvests, guided by a thorough knowledge of population levels and ecological relationships and restrained by their traditional code of ethics. Such people walk lightly on the landscape, with such success that outsiders often consider their habitats to be a "wilderness," as if no people had ever lived there.

Today, both biological diversity and cultural diversity are being depleted, posing a very real threat to humanity, which can exist in the long term only through a sustainable and interwoven relationship between nature and culture. Unfortunately, western and other civilizations have long viewed nature and culture as distinctly different subjects. Perhaps this separation is one of the root causes of our current environmental problems. An appreciation of traditional knowledge could help bring these two elements back together. Throughout the world, resources historically have been managed by diverse human societies via cultural mechanisms that give social and symbolic value to land and resources beyond their immediate extractive value. These symbolic relationships were based on ecological principles that support a system of social and economic rules that have a highly adaptive value in the ongoing struggle to maintain a viable equilibrium between natural resources and the demands of society. The traditional symbolic values have helped enable societies to avoid overexploitation and to live within the limits imposed by the availability of resources. Today's dominant symbol is money, and it is replacing natural symbols of proven worth to so-called "primitive" peoples.

In his 1992 book, Millennium: Tribal Wisdom and the Modern World, anthropologist David Maybury-Lewis pointed out that as the end of the century draws near, the modern world is marked by unprecedented degrees of confusion, insecurity, and yearning for change. Industrial society is losing self-confidence in the face of the future, and indeed the future itself has been brought into question. Under such conditions, the value of tribal wisdom can be fully appreciated, bringing an opportunity to consider new models for living in balance with our resources. A return to tribal or "primitive" lifestyles is not a realistic answer for the industrialized world or a feasible option for most of the world's 5.5 billion people, or for the projected doubled world population of the next century. Rather, new and sustainable systems of resource use can incorporate the traditional knowledge and wisdom of indigenous peoples. Indeed, the modern world may need traditional wisdom more than tribal peoples need the modern world.

Cultural Diversity:
What is it, how did it originate and why is it important?

Cultural diversity is the measure of the variety of human life. It is reflected in language, material culture. belief, knowledge, myth, and religion. This diversity enables people to adapt to the extremely diverse natural habitats that cover our planet. Indeed, the diversity of cultures may have been stimulated by the need for people to adapt to local environmental conditions, superimposed on historical events. Cultural diversity is now threatened by the new global consumer culture, which is spreading through television, trade, and other means. The loss of cultural diversity means that people are less well adapted to specific local conditions, though they may be able to contribute better to the global economy. But the future is uncertain, and the global consumer culture has not stood the test of time.

The history of the human species is a saga of wave after wave of peoples pursuing or supplanting those who went before them, expropriating their lands and pushing previously settled peoples into areas unwanted or unobtainable by their successors. Thus the global distribution of ethnic groups is a patchwork or overlay of people on people. The term "indigenous" is therefore a rather arbitrary division of a continuum or sequence of transitional human populations. The history of this continuum, however, can be seen as a chronicle of the differentiation of peoples into distinct ethnic or cultural groups. This pattern of differentiation – geographic, behavioral, linguistic, and biological – has created the cultural diversity we know today. Much of this cultural evolution has also been affected by environmental constraints that produced adaptations – behavioral, ethical, and religious – that enabled groups of people to survive in harsh conditions and out-compete their rivals. Cultural evolution in response to environmental pressures has produced a vast body of indigenous knowledge and traditions relating to the natural world, including myriad interpretations – mythological, ethical, religious and philosophical – of the relationship between humans and nature.

The United Nations International Labour Organization's Convention on Indigenous and Tribal Peoples (1989) defines indigenous peoples as "a) tribal peoples in independent countries whose social, cultural and economic conditions distinguish them from other sections of the national community, and whose status is regulated wholly or partially by their own customs or traditions or by special laws or regulations; and b) peoples in independent countries who are regarded as indigenous on account of their descent from the populations which inhabited the country, or a geographical region to which the country belongs, at the time of conquest or colonization or the establishment of present state boundaries and who, irrespective of their legal status, retain some or all of their own social, economic, cultural and political institutions...Self-identification as indigenous or tribal shall be regarded as a fundamental criterion for determining the groups to which the provisions of this convention apply."

According to the United Nations Commission on Human Rights, about 300 million people can be considered to be indigenous under the Convention's definition, spread among 70 countries around the world. China and India together account for almost half of the world's total indigenous population. At least 5,000 indigenous groups can be distinguished based on linguistic and cultural differences and geographic separation. At the request of indigenous organizations, the United Nations General Assembly proclaimed 1993 to be the "International Year for the World's Indigenous People, to strengthen international cooperation for the solution of the problems faced by indigenous communities in areas such as human rights, the environment, development, education and health."

A major effect of economic development has been to tie as many of the world's peoples as possible into the global economy. People in even the most remote areas are expected to produce more for distant markets, and to open up their territories for tourism. Many of them welcome the material goods which result, but the cost is often loss of control of their own resources, and a loss of both biological and cultural diversity.

Traditional relationships between indigenous cultures and the natural world

Being forced to live within the limits of their local ecosystems has encouraged people to develop sophisticated knowledge about resource management. Indigenous people have sometimes over-exploited their resources, leading to the extinction of cultures (such as the Anasazi of Arizona), as well as extinction of species (e.g. moas and mammoths) and large scale ecological degradation (e.g. salinization of irrigated fields in the Tigris/Euphrates watershed under the Mesopotamian empire). In other cases, indigenous people have significantly altered, though not necessarily degraded, the character of ecosystems (e.g. Native American alteration of forest composition, alteration of tropical forests by indigenous peoples, burning of African woodland to create savannas, and alteration of Australian vegetation under Aboriginal fire regimes). This demonstrates that, in many cases, what we think of as "wilderness" owes much of its character to habitation by indigenous peoples. Thus many indigenous peoples have functioned traditionally as an integral part of ecosystems, rather than as separate entities. This indicates that when humans do not out-strip ecological constraints, they can co-exist sustainably with ecosystems. Moreover, humans should never be thought of as somehow living outside of ecosystems, since humans are, in fact, very much a part the environment.

Indigenous peoples have adapted their uses of biological resources to environmental constraints in numerous ways. For example, traditional methods which have helped indigenous groups respond to game depletion include controlling tribal population size; relocating settlements; maintaining small settlements disbursed as widely as possible; trekking to distant hunting areas; increasing the proportion of time spent in undisturbed areas far from the settlement yet near enough to allow travel within a few days; expanding the breadth of game taken (especially the smaller species); and refraining from hunting threatened species (Balee 1985).

The Dai people, an indigenous ethnic group inhabiting Xishuangbanna in the mountainous tropical region of southwest China, have a long tradition of conservation practices. The Dai' traditionally maintain "Holy Hills" and Buddhist temple-yards which are specifically managed for the conservation of biodiversity (species and habitats) through formal or informal norms and rules stemming from their ethical and religious beliefs (Pei Shingji 1991). Holy Hills, a belief derived from an earlier and formerly more dominant polytheistic religious tradition, have helped to preserve areas of diverse vegetation. The Dai people also have had other profound effects on the ecology of their domain. For instance, the introduction and current distribution of many locally cultivated plants in Xishuangbanna is historically related to spread and acceptance of Hinayana Buddhism within the last 1400 years. According to Pei Shingji (1985), "in addition, the

Dai practice of cultivating fuelwood also contributes to the conservation of natural forests and is of economic and ecological significance to human adaptation in humid tropical environments."

The Koyukon Indians of Northern Canada have an elaborate code of respectful behaviour that governs their relationship toward animal species. For example, red squirrel meat should not be cooked on a stick, women must never mention the brown bear's name, beaver bones should be returned to the water, hunters must avoid bragging about prowess, and numerous other such specific rules. They limit their own harvests, guided by a thorough knowledge of population levels and ecological relationships, restrained by their traditional code of ethics (Nelson 1989).

Posey (1982), who spent many years working among the Kayopo Indians of Amazonia, found that while routinely scavenging through the forest, the Indians gathered dozens of plants. carried them back to the forest campsites or trails, and replanted them in natural forest clearings. Such plants included several types of tubers, beans, and other food plants. Such "forest fields" are always located near streams, but even in the savanna, where patches of forest are scattered, areas where collected plants have been replanted form useful food depots for the indians. This age-old pattern has had profound effects on the distribution of plants in the forest and has been an essential contributor to the current biodiversity of Amazonia. Posey found that a Kayopo indian would find it natural to replant, near where he defecated. a portion of the roots, seeds, and cuttings which he had collected. Thus, plant nurturing is very much a part of the Kayopo relationship with nature. In addition, certain game species do not occur in forest unmodified by humans, and important game species of mammals such as deer, tapir, and collared peccary reach much higher densities in modified areas.

Given the human proclivity to deplete natural resources, healthy and energetic societies must develop a set of highly adaptive behavioral rules for survival supported by a coherent belief system with a foundation of deeply motivating values which make endurable the challenges of existence in an unpredictable world. Studies by Reichel-Dolmatoff (1976) found that many primitive aboriginal tribes have a rich body of folklore and myth – often with rituals to match – that provide a social and economic framework which allow tribes to adapt their lifestyles to achieve a balance between their needs and those of the world around them.

The Koyukon Indians of northern Canada, for example, believe that future events will depend on the way people behave today and that the world can be nurtured by prudent use or harmed by unrestrained abuse. But equally important, the natural world will respond to gestures of respect given by those who recognize its sensitivity and awareness, and humble themselves to its power (Nelson 1989). Oren Lyons, a spokesman for the Traditional Elders Circle of the Onondaga Nation in North America, has questioned the values that modern destructive societies are teaching their children. "But from where we come from", he says, "the natural law is simple in this case: we will suffer in exact ratio to our transgressions and the damage done may be permanent to life as we know it today" (Lyons 1990).

Forces driving the loss of cultural diversity

Land use management throughout much of Sub-Saharan Africa has been evolving from a communal land system to more formal and individualistic land title systems. Most traditional communities do not have effective title or control of their land systems, or any effective way to make their views felt at the national policy level. The colonial period was marked by a taking of many of the most desirable lands from long-term resident communities. The post colonial period of nationhood has further served to provide legal vehicles for a taking of land and resources from local communities in the national interest. Added to this are population pressures on the land, contributing to a breakdown of traditional methods of control.

For the Shona of Zimbabwe this scenario of divestiture of land has been all too evident. Traditionally, the Shona managed their lands communally, based on ancestral relationships. Sacred sites and sites of historical importance traditionally were preserved throughout the Shona domain, though outsiders were generally unaware of these areas or of the values attached to them. Consequently, the breakup of Shona lands into small parcels under individualistic ownership schemes failed to maintain traditional land use protection and management systems, and resulted in a loss of cultural heritage and associated sustainable farming practices (IUCN 1993).

The Tuaregs of West Africa are nomadic pastoralists. During the brief West African rainy season, the Tuaregs move their herds of camels and other livestock such as sheep and goats into the desert to take advantage of the ephemeral seasonal grasses. As the dry season returns, the Tuaregs withdraw their herds back to more permanent grazing areas close to water sources. This continuous cycle of movement allows the vegetation to regenerate and replenish itself. Tenuous water sources are also allowed to replenish themselves. The Tuareg rely on their livestock for transport, milk, and occasionally for cash if an animal is sold. Like many pastoralists, the Tuareg also rely on their livestock's manure for cooking and heating fuel (Burger 1990). The French colonization of the region in the early 20th century profoundly changed the Tuareg economy. Raiding, a traditional component of Tuareg culture, was suppressed and the trans-Saharan caravan trade declined in the face of modern transport methods. The imposition of political boundaries, customs duties, and other governmental restrictions caused many Tuareg to abandon their nomadic lifestyle and settle permanently, despite their deeply rooted dislike of agriculture. In their new agricultural lifestyle, the Tuaregs have become more susceptible to drought, such as the major drought of the early 1970s that drove thousands of Tuaregs into Niger and Nigeria (Gaisford 1981).

The Lapps (or Saami) of northern Scandinavia are a distinct ethnic group who migrated to the region from Russia perhaps 10,000 years ago (Gaisford 1981). The majority, around 20,000, live in Norway, with 10,000 in Finland, 3,000 in Sweden, and perhaps 2,000 in Russia. Lapp culture was traditionally decentralized, with families organized into loose associations. This has created tensions with central Scandinavian governments who have sought to establish political control over the Lapps. Lapps live in permanent settlements in the northern tundra, although some live to the south in the coniferous forests, and many live along the coast. Today, only about 10 percent of Lapps are still engaged in the traditional occupation of reindeer herding. For most Lapps, reindeer husbandry is no longer economically viable (Rogers 1993). Many Lapps also continue to practice traditional fishing, trapping and farming. Most Lapps have become thoroughly assimilated within the national Nordic cultures, but the Lapps continue to possess a strong ethnic identity and determination to preserve their culture (Rogers. 1993). Since much of their language and culture is closely linked with their nomadic past, this has proved difficult. Lapps today face the dilemma of trying to find a means of economic survival that will enable them to preserve their culture without forcing them to live on reservations or become tourist attractions.

Even well-meaning efforts can lead to the loss of cultural elements. The Oroqen people once occupied a large area south of the Outer Hinggan Range and north of the Wutsuli River in the northeast of China. A Czarist Russian invasion in the mid-17th century, and later occupation by the Japanese in the 1930s and 40s, drove these nomadic hunters into the northern areas of Heilongjiang Province and the southern forests of the Greater Hinggan Mountains. Disease and poor living conditions reduced Oroqen numbers to only about 1000 individuals. According to He Chongyun (1988), work teams and other assistance were provided to the Oroqen following the founding of the People's Republic of China in 1949. After consultation with Oroqen representatives, a site was chosen for the establishment of new Oroqen community. Today this village is known as "the 18th Station", and is the first "huntsmen's village" in Heilongjinag's Tahe county. In 1985 the community's wooden houses were replaced by brick structures. Other facilities such as schools, medical clinics, a cultural centre and a broadcasting station have also been built for the Oroqen. The Oroqen have increased to around 4,000 individuals and now live in several communities. While the inhabitants of these communities are now predominately farmers, many still maintain pride in their nomadic past and practice traditional hunting skills. Their shamanist religion continues to instill a deep connection with nature and animal symbols, such that ritualistic hunting of certain species (such as bears) remains a central part of their culture. The Chinese consider the Oroqen assistance program to be largely a success, though it is clear that many aspects of the Oroqen culture have been lost as a result of the change from a nomadic lifestyle to a settled, agricultural lifestyle.

Baines (1991) has written about the efforts of indigenous peoples in the South Pacific to nurture economic development while maintaining control over resource management. In the Solomon islands of the South Pacific the last 20 years have witnessed growing conflict between development interests and traditional land/sea tenure systems. Governmental agencies have grown increasingly frustrated with legislative provisions that safeguard the rights of indigenous peoples to maintain control over their lands and coastal areas. Pressure is mounting to introduce legislation to override customary tenure and associated rights. This would give the government access to large areas that could be opened for mining, logging, tourist development, and other forms of development. To a large extent this movement has been promoted by some Pacific islanders who perceive their ancestral systems as impediments to a "progress" they believe only "western" forms of development can provide.

The "Noble Savage": Myth or reality?

Traditional peoples, however, are not instinctive paragons of ecological virtue. Indeed, many traditional societies have been characterized by high levels of aggression toward their neighbours, and there are numerous examples of species hunted to extinction by technologically simple cultures. When the US Congress established "native corporations" to bring Alaskan natives into the economic mainstream in the 1980s, some forests in the rich southeast of the state were stripped bare of their timber, leaving devastation behind. When local people are part of a local ecosystem, their behaviour directly affects their own survival. But cultural mechanisms that have been developed as adaptations to the environment over tens or hundreds of generations are quickly cast aside when trade frees people from traditional ecological constraints, changing them from what the distinguished ecologist Ray Dasmann calls "ecosystem people" into "biosphere people" who can draw from the resources of the entire world (Dasmann 1975).

These had been made a distinction between people who are "leavers" and those who are "takers." The former (like Dasmann's "ecosystem people") are those who live with close "feedback loops" between the way they manage resources and the costs and benefits they receive, leading them to leave resources for future use. The latter (like Dasmann's "biosphere people") are those who consume resources without recognizing the impact of such consumption on local ecosystems; they live within feedback loops so large that individuals do not feel personally responsible for resource use decisions. Indigenous people have small feedback loops, and directly manage the resources upon which they depend.

As Redford (1990) said, "to live and die with the land is to know its rules. When there is no hospital at the other end of the telephone and no grocery store at the end of the street, when there is no bi-weekly paycheck nor microwave oven, when there is nothing to fall back on but nature itself, then a society must discover the secrets of the plants and animals. Thus indigenous peoples process extensive and intensive knowledge of the natural world. In every place where humans have existed, people have received this knowledge from their elders and taught it to their children, along with what has been newly acquired."

The idea of the "noble savage" originated with Jean-Jacques Rousseau's and Thomas More's idealization of "primitive peoples" as innocent of sin and manifestations of goodness and nobility. Anthropologists have shown that indigenous groups often process culturally encoded mores that result in preservation of the resource base. But these documented patterns are sustainable only under conditions of low population density, abundant land, and limited involvement with a market economy. How relevant are such methods and customs to situations where these three conditions no longer exist? Techniques developed to satisfy subsistence needs are unlikely to work when surpluses are needed for cash. To believe that when confronted with market pressures, higher population densities, and increased opportunities, most indigenous peoples will maintain the integrity of their traditional methods is not only to argue against the available evidence, but worse, to fall into the ideological trap that produced the ecologically noble savage (Redford 1990).

Conclusion

Some innovative ways to link culture and conservation are being tested in various parts of the world. The Wasur National Park, in Indonesia's Irian Jaya province near the border with Papua New Guinea, for example, is a savanna habitat which has been managed by people for generations. All areas of the park have strong mythological, spiritual and dietary links to the people. These beliefs will continue to help support the protection of the sanctuary zone as long as cultural protection remains a major consideration and access for certain Marind people continues to be allowed. One area in the sanctuary zone is considered the centre of origin of the Marind tribe. Other areas, called dusun, are traditional gardening, hunting or sacred sites, usually owned by the clans or families to whom they were originally assigned in tribal mythology. A number of dusun are sprinkled throughout the park. As part of the management of the national park, people who traditionally own dusun may have continued access and carry out traditional management practices. The people residing in the 13 villages within the national park may remain there. Traditional hunting (especially of deer) is allowed only for park residents (Craven 1992).

Siberut is the northernmost island in the Mentawai chain, located off the west coast of Sumatra in the Indonesian Archipelago. The Mentawais are home to a rich biological diversity of which 65 percent of the mammals are endemic, including four species of endemic primates. Only on Siberut, however, do expansive stands of tropical rainforest remain, although these too have been heavily logged during the last decade. Sharing the forests are indigenous people who live in ecological harmony with their forests. Only on Siberut does this indigenous Metawaian culture remain largely intact. The indigenous Metawaians are heavily dependent on harvesting primates for food, yet the harvest is conducted sustainably and primates remain abundant. As increasing development (e.g. logging) pressures began to affect Siberut in the 1970s, WWF and IUCN launched a programme to conserve Siberut's biological diversity and indigenous people. This programme has been successful in establishing protected areas (or nature reserves) that incorporate traditional, sustainable uses by indigenous peoples. In addition, the programme provides a system for conserving resources and biodiversity in those areas not officially declared as protected areas. Continuing work to implement the conservation program is being carried out under the auspices of the Asian Development Bank. The island has also been declared a Biosphere Reserve under UNESCO's Man and the Biosphere Programme.

Aboriginal land claims are recognized under Australian law in several states, particularly in the Northern Territory. As a result of this recognition, traditional uses are frequently incorporated into national park management. A number of national parks have been established which subsequently were returned to traditional owners, and in turn leased back for continued use as protected areas for conservation and recreation. Examples of such arrangements in the Northern Territory include Uluru National Park, Kakadu National Park and Nitmiluk National Park (see the chapter by Layton and Titchen in this volume). Leasing arrangements vary, but traditional owners usually receive some form of financial return. Traditional aboriginal owners maintain their rights to hunt, fish and gather plants, though these activities can be restricted if depletion of resources occurs. Aborigines are often employed as park rangers and labourers and (in some states) as consultants on such matters as fire management and cultural interpretation. Aborigines are also often employed in specific management projects such as rare or endangered species recovery. Traditional owners are also consulted as to major policies or decisions involving the park.

The Anangu aborigines of Australia have gained title to Uluru National Park. Since the agreement stipulated that the park would be leased back to the government, in practical terms title only ensured joint management of Uluru by the Anangu and the Australian National Park and Wildlife Service. However, sacred sites were granted full protection and access to the park for ceremonial purposes and aboriginal hunting was guaranteed. The joint management approach was designed to achieve two objectives: the mediation of conflicts over traditional uses of the park and the regulation of tourists. In addition, Anangu knowledge of local ecosystems and animal behaviour have played a central role in coordinating surveys of animal populations and in resource management decisions. However, the joint management plan has been criticized for employing a framework that is completely non-aboriginal in form. While the framework has enabled Anangu to achieve significant gains in controlling their lands, it has not eliminated conflict over aboriginal and non-aboriginal uses of Uluru National Park (IUCN 1993).

In the Pacific, many islanders are growing increasingly resistant to development, and more concerned about traditional values. Debate over a barrage of development proposals (including agriculture, fishing, mineral prospecting, logging and tourism) for the Marovo Lagoon in the Western Solomons led to an alliance between the Marovo village council and the Western Province. Working together, the Marovo Lagoon Resource Management Project was established to provide villagers with greater input into development planning for the area (Baines 1991). Other Solomon Islands communities are taking similar action. Some communities have resisted logging by developing their own conservation organizations, which have been active in managing local, small-scale, silviculturally sound commercialization of forest timber. Villagers on the island of Vella Lavella, concerned about improving the management of their customary natural resources as their population is rapidly growing, have chosen the year 2000 as their deadline for becoming fully involved in resource management decisions (Baines 1991).

In New Zealand, the Resource Management Act of 1991 introduced into law a system for the sustainable management of natural resources. The system also embodied a set of specific safeguards for protecting and enhancing of the interests of the indigenous people of New Zealand, the Maori. While the Treaty of Waitangi signed in 1835 by European settlers and the Maori stipulated that the nation was to be owned, shared, managed and protected by both. cultures, the Maori have been unable to gain political representation or have their concerns incorporated into legal statutes. The Act of 1991, therefore, presents a distinct departure from precedent. Under the new system, a range of consultation mechanisms have been established to involve the Maori in resource management decisions (IUCN 1993).

According to the IUCN (1993), the Dene of Northwestern Canada now co-manage their resources with the Canadian government. The Dene's formal co-management process was developed after negotiations on land claims with the government over several years. However, co-management is viewed by the Dene as only an incremental step in the right direction, with full management control their ultimate goal. The Dene's culture continues to deteriorate, with traditional knowledge and practices rapidly disappearing. This has led to a breakdown in traditional social structures and kinship systems, with a corresponding decrease in self-esteem, one manifestation of which has been an increase in suicide among the young. To help stem the loss of traditional Dene knowledge, a cooperative team was formed including local Dene and non-indigenous social and natural scientists to record traditional knowledge regarding resource management. It is hoped that the codification of traditional knowledge and its transmission to the younger generation will serve the dual purpose of maintaining interest in Dene culture while encouraging sustainable resource management practices.

The Inuit of Nunavik in Northern Quebec have developed a comprehensive information database to record their traditional knowledge of their lands and natural resources. The Inuit have a detailed knowledge of the biological characteristics of many species, as well as a comprehensive understanding of the marine, freshwater and terrestrial ecosystems of Northern Quebec. In a land claims settlement in 1975, the Inuit and Cree Indians of James Bay were granted lands, harvesting rights and participation in resource management and environmental protection regimes in exchange for their surrender of their claim of title to a large area of Quebec. Begun 15 years ago, their information database now provides the foundation for sustainable management of their resources. The Inuit established the data collection system, manage it, and have full control over its uses. However, a joint research program has been set up between Inuit and non-Inuit researchers and resource managers. This program will integrate indigenous knowledge and modern science in a research and management process. The database has been used extensively by the Inuit in resource management and sustainable development decisions, including the development of small-scale commercial fisheries, tourism development, and environmental impact assessment (IUCN 1993).

The conflict between indigenous uses of wildlife and contemporary societal values attached to certain species is vividly illustrated by the current situation facing indigenous Greenlanders. In Greenland, the indigenous peoples have gained self-governance over their land and resources. Hence, the perennial issue of title and control of land is not the problem. Rather, some indigenous Greenlander communities have experienced economic hardships because of the decline in demand in North America and Europe (with the exception of Denmark) for sealskins, one of Greenland's traditional export products. The indigenous Greenlanders argue in favour of increased sealing, based on assurances that seals would be harvested sustainably; sealing is locally regulated, certain protected areas are off limits for sealing, and sealing by non-residents is prohibited. However, while certain indigenous hunting communities may still be dependent on wild harvests, over 90 percent of Greenland's GNP now comes from the commercial fishery sector. Resolution of this issue thus depends largely on the willingness of foreign markets to sanction increased sustainable harvests of seals, or on finding alternative economic solutions (such as within the commercial fishery sector) for indigenous Greenlanders that will nevertheless preserve their cultural heritage (IUCN 1993).

Faced with rapidly diminishing living space as a result of deforestation and occupation of tribal lands by campesinos, some Amerindian groups have organized themselves to fight back. In El Salvador, some Indians have been campaigning, with partial success, for communal lands at the community level, working through the National Agrarian Reform Act (Chapin 1992). In Honduras, several federations have joined forces to work with MOPAW, a development organization, to secure title to tribal lands and forestall colonization of these areas. As part of this program, the Tawahka Sumu have been granted the Tawahka Biosphere Reserve. The Miskito in Nicaragua have formed an organization called Miskito Kupia (or "hear of the Miskito") to advocate an Indian-managed reserve encompassing the entire Miskito Cays area. Similarly, the Kekchi and Mopann Maya of Belize are campaigning for a homeland of some 200,000 hectares. "In Panama, the Kuna, the Embera and the Wounnaan have had some success in establishing tribal homelands as well. However, similar efforts in Panama by other, less politically organized tribes. such as the Guaymi and the Veraguas, have had little success due to conflicts with private and governmental economic interests in these tribal lands" (Chapin 1992).

Two international congresses of indigenous peoples have been held, in 1989 and 1991, to develop strategies for blocking colonization and unsustainable development, and to explore the connections between land rights and natural resource management.

In November 1981, Brazil's President Fernando Color de Melo issued a decree to give the Yanomani, the largest Indian group in the Amazon rainforest, partial control of their traditional lands. The decree came after apparent last-ditch efforts by the Brazilian military to prevent it, because the Yanomani lands, in the north of the Amazon Basin, include the border with Venezuela – a militarily sensitive area. The Yanomani will gain control of their land after the Government has formally surveyed the forest and established the boundaries, at a cost of some US$2 million. Mineral rights will rest with the Government. The decree comes as part of a zoning process which will involve dividing the forest into zones for protected areas, traditional Indian farming and hunting or for rubber tappers and others who use the forest without destroying it, and those areas where logging, roads, mines, dams and other ecologically destructive development can take place.

The tropical developing world holds the lion's share of the world's genetic diversity, as well as a vast body of indigenous knowledge of flora and fauna. The developed world, however, holds the technological capability in biochemistry, genetic engineering and biotechnology needed to develop genetic resources into commercial products. This disparity continues to generate controversy over whether genetic resources and traditional knowledge are part of the "global commons," or whether such resources are the exclusive heritage of their native regions. Under the Convention on Biological Diversity, which entered into force at the end of 1993, most countries now recognize the "sovereign right" of countries to control the utilization of their genetic resources and traditional knowledge. Pharmaceutical, biotechnology and agricultural companies in signatory nations must now reach cooperative agreements with countries from which genetic resources are to be obtained. Under this system, the potential exists for indigenous peoples to market their traditional knowledge. It is to be hoped that this will provide an incentive both for cultural preservation and sustainable utilization of natural resources that will allow biodiversity on tribal lands to be preserved. But the danger of further exploitation of both resources and people is never far from the surface.

References

Baines, G. B. K. (1991). *Asserting traditional rights: community conservation in Solomon Islands*. Cultural Survival **15**: 49-52.
Balee, W. (1985). *Ka'apor ritual hunting*. Human Ecology **13** (4): 485-510.
Burger, J. (1990). *The Gaia Atlas of First Peoples: A Future for the Indigenous World*.
Craven, I. (1992). *Conflicts between Integrating Traditional Peoples into Protected Area Management Systems and Park Zoning: Case examples from Irian Jaya, Indonesia*. Paper from workshop on *People and Protected Areas*, IV World Congress on National Parks and Protected Areas, Caracas.
Dasmann, R. (1975). *National Parks, Nature Conservation, and "future primitive"*. Ecologist **65** (5): 164-167.
Chapin, M. (1992). *The view from the shore: Central America's indians encounter the quincentenary*. Grassroots Development **16**: 2-10.
Gaisford, J. (ed.). (1981). *Atlas of Man*. Marshall Cavendish Books, Ltd., London.
IUCN Inter-Commission Task Force on Indigenous Peoples. (1993). *Indigenous Peoples and Strategies for Sustainability*. Summary of a Workshop on Strategies for Sustainability: March 31 - April 2, 1993. IUCN Conservation Services Division, Social Policy Service. Gland, Switzerland. 23 pp.
Lyons, O. R. (1990). *Traditional native perspectives*. Orion Summer: 31-34.
Maybury-Lewis, D. (1992). *Millennium: Tribal Wisdom and the Modern World*. Viking Penguin, New York.
Nelson, Richard K. (1989). *Hunters and animals in a native land*. Orion, Spring: 49-53.
Newby, J. E. (1992). *Parks for people, a case study from the Air Mountains of Niger*. Oryx **6**: 19-28.

Pei Shingji (1991). *Conservation of biological diversity in temple-yards and holy hills by the Dai ethnic minorities of China*. Ethnobotany **3**: 27-35.
Pei Shingji (1985). *Some effects of the Dai people's cultural beliefs and practices upon the plant environment of Xishuangbanna, Yunnan Province, southeast China*. In Hutterer, K., A.T. Rambo and G. Lovelace (eds.). *Cultural Values and Human Ecology in Southeast Asia*. University of Michigan, Ann Arbor.
Posey, D. A. (1982). *The Keepers of the Forest*. Garden **6**: 18-24.
Posey, D.A. (1990). *The science of the Mebengokre*. Orion Summer: 16-23.
Rogers, A. (ed.). (1993). *The Guinness Guide to Peoples and Cultures*. Guinness Publishing, London.
Redford, K. H. (1990). *The ecologically noble savage*. Orion Summer: 25-29.
Reichel-Dolmatoff, G. (1976). *Cosmology as ecological analysis: A view from the rainforest*. Man **11** (3): 307-318.

Jeffrey A. McNeely and **William S. Keeton** work for IUCN, The World Conservation Union, in Gland, Switzerland.

Chapter 4

Concept, Origin and Meaning of "Landscape"

Wolfgang Haber

The everyday meaning of "landscape" according to the Collins English Dictionary is "an extensive area of scenery as viewed from a single place". This definition connotes essentially an aesthetic impression. In order to understand the meaning of "landscape" as a concept, it is useful to go back to the origin of the term and look into its semantics.

The term "landscape" combines "land" with a word of ancient Germanic origin, the verb "scapjan" which means: to work, to be busy, to do something creative - mostly with a plan or design in mind. During the evolution of the Germanic languages, "scapjan" became "schaffen" in German, thus more or less retaining the original meaning, and "shape" in English, shifting the emphasis to the form ("Gestalt"), the creative design, and to the aesthetic appearance of the land (Müller 1977).

"Schaffen" or "shaping" in or on the land can be done both by natural agents or forces resulting in a "natural landscape" and by humans who create - not always intentionally - a "cultural landscape".

The term culture (or cultural) stems from the Latin word "colere" which has several meanings. It describes the work of farmers ploughing fields, sowing and harvesting wheat, erecting farmsteads and villages - which may grow into large cities losing any agricultural connotations. "Colere" also means careful maintenance, adornment and even veneration.

The verbs mentioned so far - schaffen, shape, colere - generally describe processes, changes, dynamics; or a succession of phenomena, an evolution.

A cultural landscape is the result of a cultural evolution of, or in the land. Land is basically nature, and culture is a basic and unique human peculiarity. If we search for a driving force or an objective of cultural or human evolution, this appears to be emancipation from nature (cf. Häussermann and Siebel 1989). Humans have always wanted to exempt themselves from natural constraints and restrictions, to get as free as possible from nature's harshness and cruelty.

This evolutionary goal has been pursued by exploiting ("scapjan") nature and its resources which were discovered step by step, opening up ever vaster perspectives. The cultural evolution proceeded in different directions, producing great cultural diversity partly on the basis of, and in analogy to natural diversity. "Biodiversity" embraces both. However, one of the directions of cultural evolution has become predominant, leading to the modern "western" style industrial society. Its symbol is the big city, symbol of the urban culture with its heavy imprint on the traditional cultural diversity of the world.

The emancipation, even alienation from nature, as an inevitable result of progressive cultural evolution has surprisingly produced a new and different awareness of the values of nature and of the natural features in our anthropogenic environment. We have begun to "cultivate" islands of genuine nature in our cultural landscape or, where true nature has either disappeared or been "humanized", we cultivate islands or areas of what we feel to be a harmonious, pleasing amalgamation of natural and cultural traits.

Heritage can only be identified by looking from the present at the past and by comparing both. Which pieces of our cultivated land or cultural landscape might be worthy of being raised from a mere productive or economic status to a more protective one? This requires a process of careful selection involving rather diverse value judgements. Out of the variety of meanings of "landscape" mentioned above, we seem to prefer scenery which appears to witness a beautiful and harmonious cultural - essentially rural - design. Likewise we are rather selective regarding the cultural: we disdain the everyday results of human activity (which of course are all cultural), preferring what looks venerable or adorned or beautified by cultural deeds.

Protecting our landscape heritage for future generations does not necessarily mean that the past and present heritage will be the future one too. There is a fundamental problem to overcome: the contradiction between the static character of protection or conservation measures, and the dynamic processes of landscape development or evolution (Willis and Garrod 1992).

Both landscape and culture are dynamic, undergoing changes, sometimes slow, sometimes fast - how can those of their features which bear the heritage properties be maintained? If changes are recognized, they should happen in a certain order and predictability; so the natural heritage experts try to set up guidelines, yardsticks, models. There is an impressive array of institutions from which suggestions or lessons can be drawn: nature reserves, protected sites, national parks, nature parks, nature monuments, areas of outstanding natural beauty, biosphere reserves and so forth. And there is another impressive array of guidelines disguised as catchwords: natural equilibrium, harmony of nature, ecological stability, biological or organic land use, small-scale pattern, sustainable use or development...

What does all this mean and how can it be applied in each special situation? A German regional planner, Gerhard Isbary, declared the German nature parks "model landscapes" ("Vorbildlandschaften", Isbary 1959) - but a model for what? Lately, the same characteristic is being attributed to biosphere reserves. However, it is interesting to note that humans and their activities are increasingly included in these model sites or landscapes from which they tended to be excluded or considered disturbing intruders in earlier conceptions.

In the German tradition, "landscape" (Landschaft) is also a scientific term. The great scholar Alexander von Humboldt, who was both a geographer and biologist, coined the first scientific definition of "landscape" as "total character of a region of the earth" at the beginning of the nineteenth century, and this definition is still considered acceptable. Humboldt was virtually the founder of landscape ecology, though he did not use this term which was first employed as late as 1939 by Carl Troll, another eminent German geographer and botanist. Landscape ecology became a discipline of its own in the German speaking countries, linking physical geography with biological sub-disciplines such as vegetation science (phytosociology) and gave rise to many publications (cf. Troll 1950, Paffen 1973, Hartlieb von Wallthor and Quirin 1977). Troll conceived a mosaic-like composition of the landscape, calling the mosaic pieces "ecotopes". He insisted on the anthropogenic components of the landscape, which tended to be neglected by vegetation scientists or nature conservationists. Ellenberg (1963) and Westhoff (1968) clearly demonstrated the gradient from natural or quasi-natural to human-made or cultural landscape elements, laying the foundations for combining landscape ecology and ecosystem ecology. Elsewhere (Haber 1980, 1990) the author has interpreted Troll's "ecotope" as local representation of an ecosystem. Other authors consider landscape a system of its own, a kind of higher-level ecosystem (cf. Leser 1991). In the 1980s, landscape ecology gained a foothold on the international scene (Naveh and Lieberman 1984, Forman and Godron 1986) and is now well established both in physical geography, general ecology and human ecology.

The development of scientific landscape ecology as sketched out in the preceding paragraph may not concern the identification of the world's heritage landscapes at first sight; but it is important for the management of the landscapes - and perhaps also for the terminology.

In Germany, several landscape planners such as Olschowy (1978) have pleaded for the preservation of valuable cultural landscapes. From the author's point of view as a landscape ecologist, a convincing definition of a highly valued cultural landscape worthy of being elevated to National or even World Heritage status is intricate. The difficulty is partly caused by the rather vague distinction between sites, locations and landscapes; here a landscape ecological approach would be helpful. In addition, most examples of cultural landscapes presently considered for heritage status represent only one main type of culture, namely agri-culture, i.e. rural landscapes. This raises the principal question - if and why such a restriction of the term "cultural" is justifiable.

The author recognizes that his contribution raises more questions than it answers. But in the process of seeking solutions for complex problems, it may be helpful.

References

Ellenberg, H. (1963). *Vegetation Mitteleuropas mit den Alpen*. 1. Auflage. Stuttgart, E. Ulmer (Volume IV/II of Walter H. ed., *Einführung in die Phytologie*.) 5th edition 1995.

Ellenberg, H. (1973). *Versuch einer Klassifikation der Ökosysteme nach funktionalen Gesichtspunkten*. In: Ellenberg, H. ed., *Ökosystemforschung*, pp. 235-265. Berlin/Heidelberg, Springer.

Forman, R. T. T. and Godron, M. (1986). *Landscape Ecology*. Chichester/New York, Wiley.

Haber, W. (1980). *Entwicklung und Probleme der Kulturlandschaft im Spiegel ihrer Ökosysteme*. Forstarchiv **51**: 245-250.

Haber, W. (1990). *Basic concepts of landscape ecology and their application in land management*. Physiology and Ecology Japan 27, 131-146 (Special edition *Ecology for Tomorrow*, Kawanabe, H., Ohgushi, T. and Higashi. M. eds).

Häussermann, H. and Siebel, W. (1989). *Ökologie statt Urbanität?* Universitas **44**: 514-525.

Hartlieb von Wallthor, A. and Quirin, H. (1977). *Landschaft als interdisziplinäres Forschungsproblem*. Münster (Westfalen), Aschendorff.

Isbary, G. (1959). *Der Naturparkgedanke als Ausdruck unserer Zeit*. Naturschutzparke (Mitteilungen des Vereins Naturschutzpark) **15**: 86-90.

Leser, H. (1991). *Landschaftsökologie. Ansatz, Modelle, Methodik, Anwendung* (1st edition 1976). Stuttgart, Ulmer.

Müller, G. (1977). *Zur Geschichte des Wortes Landschaft*. In Hartlieb von Wallthor, A. and Quirin, H. eds., *Landschaft als interdisziplinäres Forschungsproblem*, pp. 4-13. Münster (Westfalen), Aschendorff.

Naveh, Z. and Lieberman, A.S. (1984). *Landscape Ecology. Theory and Application.* New York/Berlin, Springer (2nd edition 1994).

Paffen, K. (ed.) (1973). *Das Wesen der Landschaft.* Darmstadt, Wissenschaftl. Buchgesellschaft.

Troll, C. (1950). *Die geographische Landschaft und ihre Erforschung.* Studium Generale 3 (4/5): 163-181. Reprinted in *Erdkundliches Wissen* (1966) **11**: 14-51.

Westhoff, V. (1968). *Die "ausgeräumte" Landschaft. Biologische Verarmung und Bereicherung der Kulturlandschaften.* In: Buchwald, K. and Engelhardt, W. (eds.), *Handbuch für Landschaftspflege und Naturschutz,* vol. 2, pp. 1–10; *Die Reste der Naturlandschaft und ihre Pflege.* Ibidem vol. 3, pp. 251–265. München, BLV Verlagsgesellschaft.

Willis, K.G. and Garrod, G.D. (1992). *Assessing the value of future landscapes.* Landscape and Urban Planning 23, 17-32.

Wolfgang Haber is Professor Emeritus for Landscape Ecology at the Technical University of Munich, Germany.

Chapter 5

UNESCO and Cultural Landscape Protection[1]

Mechtild Rössler

Introduction

The *Convention Concerning the Protection of the World Cultural and Natural Heritage*, adopted by the General Conference of UNESCO in 1972, established a profoundly unique international instrument recognizing and protecting both the cultural and natural heritage of outstanding universal value. Although the *Convention's* definition of heritage provided an innovative opportunity for the protection of landscapes, recognized by UNESCO in the early 1960s (UNESCO 1962), it was not until the early 1980s that the question of landscape protection again arose at the international level in the work of UNESCO.

Following the 1984 session of the World Heritage Committee discussion focussed on the evaluation of narrowly perceived *rural landscapes* along with the procedure for the evaluation of *mixed properties*. In the early 1990s attempts have been made to specifically define *cultural landscapes*.

Problems in defining cultural landscapes

During the 1984 session of the World Heritage Committee held in Buenos Aires the discussion of the evaluation of *mixed* cultural and natural sites and *rural landscapes* for the inclusion on the World Heritage List arose. The Committee asked that a task force made up of representatives of IUCN, ICOMOS and IFLA be organized to discuss this subject.

The task force met in Paris in 1985[2] and developed a proposal[3] for the modification of the criteria to include cultural landscapes. Unfortunately, the Bureau decided to wait for a nomination of a rural landscape before actually modifying the criteria as proposed. It was considered that to enable the Bureau to more fully evaluate the applicability of the

---

[1] I would like to thank Sarah Titchen for her help in preparing this paper and for sharing her immense knowledge with me (see Titchen 1995).

[2] The Committee requested IUCN to consult with ICOMOS and IFLA to elaborate guidelines for the identification and nomination for inclusion on the List of mixed and natural/cultural properties.

[3] CC-86/CONF.001/003 and the report was presented to the Bureau in 1986.

proposed modifications it would be necessary to test them against a case study nomination.

In 1986 the Bureau welcomed a proposal made by the observer from the UK to present a draft nomination of a rural landscape in the following year. The United Kingdom presented a nomination of the Lake District National Park for inscription on the World Heritage List as a landscape in 1987.[4]

In essence, this narrowed and distorted the debate to one focussed only on the *Lake District rather than a more general discussion concerning the definition of cultural landscapes and criteria for their inclusion in the World Heritage List*. The examination of the nomination was deferred until the Committee clearly defined its position concerning the inscription of cultural landscapes.

The second presentation of the Lake District nomination was made in 1989, deferred by the Bureau in June 1990 and was reexamined by the Committee in 1990. The Committee asked the Secretariat to develop criteria or a criterion specifically for cultural landscapes. The Secretariat's proposal on cultural landscapes was submitted to the Bureau and Committee sessions in 1991.

UNESCO proposal on "cultural landscapes" (1991)[5]

The 1991 UNESCO Secretariat proposal on *cultural landscapes* was based on the discussion of the 1985 task force, the reflections of those within the Secretariat and the advice of the advisory bodies concerned. The proposal was presented to the Fifteenth session of the World Heritage Bureau (Box 1) for consideration. The new draft criterion was more specific to cultural landscapes than the earlier 1985 proposal. Although a new criterion was viewed positively by most Bureau members, IUCN felt that it would lead to

---

Box 1. The 1991 UNESCO proposal on "cultural landscapes"

a, (vi) "be an outstanding example of a cultural landscape resulting from associations of cultural and natural elements significant from the historical, aesthetic, ethnological or anthropological points of view and evidencing a harmonious balance between nature and human activity over a very long period of time which is rare and vulnerable under the impact of irreversible change; or"

b, (ii) in the case of cultural landscapes, have the potential to maintain their integrity (the Committee stresses that there should be a sufficient representation of distinctive landforms, land-uses and patterns of traditional life-style which are necessary for the maintenance of its essential values);

---

[4] ICOMOS was favorable to the inscription, IUCN could not reach a consensus on the question.
[5] Parallel efforts have been made by the Council of Europe for the protection of European landscapes in preparation for special conservation measures. In the Blois conference in fall 1992 the participants recommended among other suggestions to include landscapes in the World Heritage List.

an imbalance between cultural and natural sites on the World Heritage List. Subsequently, a revised version of the criterion was presented to the World Heritage Committee.

The fifteenth session of the World Heritage Committee in Carthage asked for further study concerning the modification of the criteria to include cultural landscapes on the World Heritage List by the Secretariat in coordination with both advisory bodies.

La Petite Pierre proposals (1992)

In May 1992, the World Heritage Centre was established by the Director General of UNESCO. In so doing, he paved the way for a new integrative approach to bring nature and culture (and the work of the different UNESCO divisions) together into one administrative unit. This administrative change founded on a philosophy, itself reflected in the *Convention*, provided an essential precondition for a renewed debate on the question of cultural landscapes.

Another important precondition was the work of the advisory bodies ICOMOS on the one hand and IUCN on the other hand. In particular the work of Bing Lucas from IUCN/CNPPA was very influential. He took a new approach from the IUCN side to accept revised **cultural** criteria to include cultural landscapes.

By invitation of the French Government, who launched a preparatory study on cultural landscapes by an expert from the International Federation of Landscape Architects (IFLA), and in cooperation with ICOMOS and IUCN, an expert meeting was held in La Petite Pierre in France in October 1992. This expert meeting was based on the different reflections already made in the working groups of IUCN (World Congress on National Parks and Protected Areas, Caracas, Venezuela) and ICOMOS (UK landscape working group) as well as considerations made within the Secretariat.

The expert group reviewed the criteria in the Operational Guidelines and redrafted the cultural criteria. They did **not** draft an extra criterion on cultural landscapes neither did they use or rely upon the heavily criticized expressions of beauty and harmony or the concept of landscape aesthetics. Consideration was also given to the need to recognize the associative values of landscapes and landscape features to indigenous people. The expert group's proposal was then submitted to the Sixteenth session of the World Heritage Committee in Santa Fe, New Mexico in the United States (see Box 2).

The Sixteenth session of the World Heritage Committee and the follow-up by the World Heritage Centre in concertation with the different expert groups

At the Santa Fe meeting the UNESCO Secretariat (World Heritage Centre) reported on item 14 of the agenda "Revision of the Operational Guidelines". The representative of ICOMOS commented on the report of the expert meeting and the proposed amendments to the six existing criteria for cultural properties. He also introduced the recommendations for the new interpretative or guiding paragraphs relating to cultural landscapes which would replace the previously existing paragraph 34 of the *Operational Guidelines*. He underlined the broad regional representation of the group of experts as well as their interdisciplinary background and affiliations (ICOMOS, IUCN, IFLA).

Box 2. Revision of the criteria for cultural properties in the Operational Guidelines as adopted by the sixteenth session of the World Heritage Committee in Santa Fe, 13 December 1992

Paragraph 24. (a)

(i) represent a unique artistic achievement, a masterpiece of the creative genius; or

(ii) have exerted great influence, over a span of time or within a cultural area of the world, on developments in architecture, monumental arts, town-planning or **landscape design**; or

(iii) bear a unique or at least exceptional testimony to a civilization or **cultural tradition** which has disappeared; or

(iv) be an outstanding example of a type of building or architectural ensemble **or landscape** which illustrates (a) significant stage(**s**) **in human history**; or

(v) be an outstanding example of traditional human settlement **or land use** which is representative of a culture **(or cultures), especially when** it has become vulnerable under the impact of irreversible change; or

(vi) be directly and tangibly associated with events or **living traditions,** with ideas, or **with beliefs, with artistic and literary works** of outstanding universal significance (the Committee considers that this criterion should justify inclusion on the List only in exceptional circumstance or in conjunction with other criteria);

Paragraph 24. (b)

(i) meet the test of authenticity in design, material, workmanship or setting **and in the case of cultural landscapes their distinctive character and components** (the Committee stressed that reconstruction is only acceptable if it is carried out on the basis of complete and detailed documentation on the original and to no extent on conjecture).

(ii) have adequate legal **and/or traditional** protection and management mechanisms to ensure the conservation of the nominated cultural property or **cultural landscapes**. The existence of protective legislation at the national, provincial or municipal level **or well-established traditional protection** and/ or adequate management mechanisms is therefore essential and must be stated clearly on the nomination form. Assurances of the effective implementation of these laws and/or management mechanisms are also expected. Furthermore, in order to preserve the integrity of cultural sites, particularly those open to large numbers of visitors, the State Party concerned should be able to provide evidence of suitable administrative arrangements to cover the management of the property, its conservation and its accessibility to the public.

Explanatory notes for the revised criteria

(i) For all six criteria the expert group recommended the deletion of the underlining as it serves no particular purpose.

(ii) The expert group preferred to use the term "landscape design". In the French version this is correctly translated as "construction des paysages".

(iii) The phrase "a cultural tradition" was added as this criterion is culturally more neutral. It was considered that a group of people can disappear but that their cultural tradition can be assimilated by the dominant civilization which survives.

(iv) It was considered that this modification would avoid the adoption of a linear view of history.

(v) By adding "or cultures" the expert group emphasized the existence at times of multi-layered landscapes where several cultures are superimposed.

(vi) The group emphasized cultural continuity and the survival of traditions. The concept of associative values was broadened.

The World Heritage Committee examined the report of the La Petite Pierre expert meeting[6] and adopted the revisions to the cultural criteria with the intention of including exceptional outstanding cultural landscapes on the World Heritage List. Only slight changes to the recommendations of the La Petite Pierre meeting were made. These changes included the important recognition of the role of people in the protection of nature and biodiversity and the links between the conservation of landscapes and sustainable land use models. Furthermore, the Committee requested the World Heritage Centre to convene an expert meeting on cultural landscapes, tentative lists and related issues.

As an initial follow up to the Santa Fe meeting, on 10 February 1993 the World Heritage Centre sent a circular letter to all 134 States Parties asking them to submit by 15 August 1993 tentative lists to include cultural landscapes. The submission of such tentative lists would be a precondition for future nominations of cultural landscapes for inclusion on the World Heritage List.

Cultural Landscapes and Tentative Lists

It is important to note that the submission of a tentative list is a requirement and precondition for the nomination of a cultural site for inclusion on the World Heritage List (see Titchen and Rössler in this volume). This has also been a precondition for the nomination of mixed cultural and natural sites. In the past there have been occasions when this requirement, referred to in general terms in the *Convention* (Article II,2) and in specific terms in the *Operational Guidelines*, has not been applied.

When nominating natural sites, according to the *Operational Guidelines*, it is not a requirement for each State Party to prepare a tentative list of natural sites, because IUCN has already prepared a global inventory of the greatest natural areas of the world (IUCN 1982).

The response to the World Heritage Centre's request to the States Parties as of February 1993 has been fair:

13 States Parties have submitted new tentative lists, among them 8 have included cultural landscapes. Several States Parties have communicated that they need to undertake further study on cultural landscapes or to review their national cultural landscape registers (for example, Norway; see Hegard in this volume). For some States Parties the World Heritage Centre had received information that landscape classifications have been undertaken by experts, but no tentative list has been established so far (for example Slovenia; see Habjab and Kolar Planinsic in this volume). 9 States Parties have notified the World Heritage Centre that they are in the process of preparing tentative lists in the light of the recent revisions of the cultural criteria. They envisage that cultural landscapes should appear on these lists. Preparatory assistance from the World Heritage Fund can be provided for this purpose.

---

[6] Document WHC-92/CONF.002/10 Add

The Schorfheide/Templin expert meeting in 1993

An expert meeting held at Schorfheide/Templin, Germany, in October 1993 reviewed the revised criteria in detail and analyzed their application for different parts of the world. The meeting presented an *Action Plan for the Future*, which was adopted by the Committee in December 1993 (see Annex of this volume). The *Action Plan* recommended that regional expert meetings be held to assist with comparative studies of cultural landscapes and that thematic frameworks be assisted for the evaluation of cultural landscapes and to assist the World Heritage Committee in its decsion making concerning cultural landscapes. The expert meeting was a milestone in the implementation of the decisions of the Committee by identifying different methods that States Parties might choose to use when nominating cultural landscapes for inclusion on the World Heritage List. It discussed methodologies for identifying cultural landscapes and gave suggestions towards the classification and evaluation of cultural landscapes. It addressed specific legal, management, socio-economic and conservation issues related to cultural landscapes and gave illustrated examples of outstanding cultural landscapes, which are documented in this volume.

Cultural landscapes as a part of the Global Strategy

In June 1994 the World Heritage Centre and ICOMOS convened an Expert Meeting on the Global Study at UNESCO Headquarters (see von Droste in this volume). The outcome of this meeting was presented as *Global Strategy and thematic studies* for a representative World Heritage List to the eighteenth session of the World Heritage Bureau in July 1994 (see Bureau report, 1994, Annex IV). The need to ensure a representative World Heritage List and to enhance the credibility of World Heritage in general had already been discussed at previous Committee sessions. For example, the two meetings on the World Heritage Strategy in 1992 had come up with Strategic Orientations adopted at the sixteenth session of the World Heritage Committee in December 1992 (see World Heritage Committee report). The Global Strategy meeting, however, identified more clearly the gaps and imbalances of the present World Heritage List: the overrepresentation of Europe as well as historic towns, religious buildings/christian sites, elitist/monumental architecture and historical periods (except prehistory and the 20th century). A linkage between the work to include cultural landscapes on the World Heritage List and the Global Strategy can be seen in the field of living cultures, in particular traditional settlements and sites.

"Even traditional settlements were only included on the list in terms of their "architectural" value, taking no account of their many economic, social, symbolic and philosophical dimensions or of their many continuing interactions with their natural environment in all its diversity (Bureau report, Annex IV, page 4).

Furthermore, among the recommendations of the *Global Strategy report* there are specific ones on human coexistence with the land (movement of people, settlement, modes of subsistence and technological evolution) which relates directly to the outcome work of the cultural landscapes groups, as discussed above, as well as to different thematic studies to be introduced below.

Regional and Thematic Studies

The World Heritage Committee at its seventeenth session followed the recommendations by the Schorfheide/Templin expert meeting and commended different States Parties for their invitations to host regional and thematic expert meetings. In 1994 two States Parties hosted meetings: the expert group on *Heritage Canals* met in Canada in September 1994 and a thematic study meeting on *Routes as cultural heritage* took place in Spain. Both meetings discussed long linear structures and linear landscape features (see Annex of this volume).

In 1995 the first truly regional expert meeting on *Asian Rice Culture and its Terraced Landscapes* was hosted by the Philippines National Commission for UNESCO. It therefore implemented the *Action Plan* by adopting a regional comparative approach. Another meeting was held in Australia discussed the identification and assessment of cultural landscapes with a specific focus on associative cultural landscapes, their definition, identification, and management with a specific focus on boundaries.

The outcome of the regional and thematic meetings was presented both to the World Heritage Committee and its Bureau at the eighteenth and nineteenth sessions. Emphasis was laid on the links between the *Action Plan for the Future (Cultural Landscapes)*, the *Global Strategy*[7], the *Nara Meeting on Authenticity* (see von Droste in this volume) and the overall review and revision of tentative lists presented to the World Heritage Centre to analyze shortcomings of future nominations at an early stage.

Cultural Landscapes on the World Heritage List

The World Heritage Committee at its seventeenth session in December 1993 inscribed - after a lengthy discussion - the first cultural landscape on the World Heritage List, an associative landscape: Tongariro National Park in New Zealand. The site, already included on the List in recognition of its outstanding natural values, had been resubmitted under the revised cultural criteria (see Te Heuheu in this volume). In 1994, another cultural landscape was included on the World Heritage List: Uluru Kata-Tjuta National Park in Australia, which is both, a living and an associative cultural landscape (see Layton and Titchen in this volume).

Conclusion

The purpose of this overview has been to give insight into the recent history of the adoption of the newly revised criteria for the inclusion of cultural landscapes on the World Heritage List. The adoption of the modified criteria is one of the great success stories of the implementation of the *Convention*, because it provides opportunities for the "combined works of nature and of man" as defined in Article 1 of the *Convention*, to be submitted for inclusion on the World Heritage List by States Parties.

---

[7] Since the expert meeting on the Global Study held at UNESCO in Paris in June 1994 the Global Study has been reworked and strengthened, philosophically and practically, to become the Global Strategy.

The Committee, after years of discussion has ensured that the *World Heritage Convention* is the first international legal instrument to recognize and to protect cultural landscapes of outstanding universal value. It is now up to States Parties to identify and to nominate this threatened heritage of humankind to ensure that cultural landscapes receive appropriate recognition and conservation at an international level.

References

Batisse, M. (1992). *The struggle to save our World Heritage*. In: Environment, vol. 34, number 10, December 1992, pp. 12 - 20.

Boardman, R. (1981). *International Organization and the Conservation of Nature*. Bloomington, Indiana University Press.

Brown-Weiss, E. (1989). *In Fairness to Future Generations. International Law, Common Patrimony and Intergenerational Equity*. New York, The United Nations University.

IUCN (1982). *The World's Greatest Natural Areas*. Gland.

Lucas, B. (1992). *Protected Landscapes. A guide for policy-makers and planners*. The World Conservation Union, Chapman and Hall, London.

Masterworks of Man and Nature. Preserving our World Heritage (1992). Harper Mac Rae Publishing PTY Ltd.

Nature and Resources (1992). Different Faces of World Heritage, UNESCO, Parthenon Publishing, vol. 28, number 3.

Our World's Heritage (1987). Published by The National Geographic Society. Washington D.C.

Prott, L. (1992). *A Common heritage: the World Heritage Convention*. In: Lesley Macinnes and C.R. Wickham-Jones (ed.), *All natural things: archeology and the green debate*. Oxford, Oxbow Books (Oxbow Monograph 21). pp. 65-86.

Rössler, M. (1995). *Neue Perspektiven für den Schutz von Kulturlandschaften. Natur und Kultur im Rahmen der Welterbekonvention*. In: Geographische Rundschau **47**, Juni 1995, H. 6, 343-347.

Thorsell, J. and Sawyer, J. (ed.) (1992). *World Heritage Twenty Years Later*, World Conservation Union. IUCN Publication Services, Cambridge.

Titchen, S. (1995). *On the Construction of Outstanding Universal Value. UNESCO's World Heritage Convention and the Identification and Assessment of Cultural Places for inclusion in the World Heritage List*. Doctoral Thesis, Department of Archeology and Anthropology, Canberra.

UNESCO (1962). *Recommendation concerning the Safeguarding of the Beauty and Character of Landscapes and Sites*. 11 December 1962.

"World Heritage Anniversary" (1992). Parks. The international magazine dedicated to the protected areas of the world. Vol 3, No. 3, December 1992.

Mechtild Rössler has an MA in cultural geography and a Ph.D. in natural sciences. She has worked in the UNESCO World Heritage Centre since its creation in 1992 and is responsible for natural sites and cultural landscapes.

Chapter 6

The Evaluation of Cultural Landscapes: The Role of ICOMOS

Henry Cleere

Introduction

ICOMOS and the World Heritage Convention

The International Council on Monuments and Sites (ICOMOS) is one of the three organizations named specifically in the 1972 World Heritage Convention as being invited to attend meetings of the World Heritage Committee "in an advisory capacity" (Article 8.3), in "the implementation of its programmes and projects" (Article 13.7), and in assisting the Director General of UNESCO "to the fullest extent possible" in preparing the Committee's documentation and the agenda of its meetings and the implementation of its decisions (Article 14.2).

This role is amplified in the *Operational Guidelines for the Implementation of the World Heritage Convention* (UNESCO 1995). The two non-governmental organizations (NGOs) responsible for the evaluation of cultural and natural nominations, ICOMOS and IUCN (The World Conservation Union) respectively, are required to undertake "a professional evaluation of each nomination according to the criteria adopted by the Committee" and make recommendations for inscription on the World Heritage List or otherwise (para 66). Each nominated cultural property must be "evaluated relatively, that is, it should be compared with that of other property of the same time type dating from the same period, both inside and outside the State Party's borders" (para 60). The two NGOs "are encouraged to be as strict as possible in their evaluations" (para 62).

The ICOMOS evaluation procedure

Dossiers relating to properties nominated for inscription on the World Heritage List are transmitted to ICOMOS by the UNESCO World Heritage Centre, acting as the Secretariat of the World Heritage Committee, on 1 November of the preceding year[1]). Initial evaluations and recommendations are presented to the meeting of the Bureau of the World Heritage Committee, which normally takes place at the beginning of July each year. Given that these must be delivered to the Secretariat six weeks before the meeting of the Bureau, for distribution in advance to members, the maximum period available for the process of evaluation is no more than six months.

---

[1] A new time table has been adapted for the processing of nominations, which will be effective in 1966. The deadline of receipt of nominations is 1 July each year, and for the transmission of nominations to the advisory bodies 15 September each year.

ICOMOS carries out this work in a series of steps:

1. Initial study of dossiers, identification of experts for (i) scientific evaluation and (ii) field visits to study management and conservation.
2. Obtaining reports from experts on scientific aspects of nominations, including comparative assessments (UNESCO 1995, para 60). These may be requested from ICOMOS International Scientific Committees, individual ICOMOS members, affiliated specialist bodies (eg The International Committee for the Conservation of the Industrial Heritage - TICCIH; the International Federation of Landscape Architects - IFLA) or non-ICOMOS experts nominated by ICOMOS International or National Committees.
3. Preparation of draft evaluations incorporating comments from scientific experts.
4. Despatch of field missions (supplied with relevant documentation from nomination dossiers and draft evaluations).
5. Preparation of evaluations and recommendations for consideration by meeting of ICOMOS Bureau and invited experts.
6. Preparation of final texts of evaluations and recommendations for despatch to the UNESCO World Heritage Centre for transmission to Bureau and Committee members.

At its meeting the Bureau may seek additional information from States Parties and request ICOMOS to carry out further research, to assist the Committee in reaching decisions at its meeting, held annually in December. This information is incorporated into the final evaluations prepared by ICOMOS for that meeting.

ICOMOS and cultural landscapes

As its name implies, ICOMOS, which was founded in 1965, has hitherto been concerned principally with architectural monuments and archaeological sites. This is reflected in the themes of its fourteen International Scientific Committees - for example, Archaeological Heritage Management, Historic Towns and Villages, Rock Art, Vernacular Architecture, etc. The introduction of the concept of the cultural landscape into the work of the World Heritage Convention presents a new challenge to ICOMOS. This paper describes the involvement of ICOMOS with the development of the cultural landscape concept and the accompanying criteria for selection for the World Heritage List, and attempts to lay down some preliminary guidelines for the evaluation of cultural landscapes in the coming years.

The work of only one of the ICOMOS International Committees, that on Historic Gardens and Sites, has hitherto impinged directly upon the field of cultural landscapes. This Committee was established in 1968, only three years after the foundation of ICOMOS. For the past quarter-century it has worked tirelessly in the defence of cultural landscapes.

In 1989, in response to the recognition by the World Heritage Committee of the new dimension that cultural landscapes were assuming in modern society, a Landscape Working Group was created by the Committee. This Group has held a series of meetings around the world (Canada, France, Germany, Italy, Netherlands, Poland, Spain, the UK, the USA), which have resulted in the publication of much important documentation. The Group has also participated in the Cultural Landscapes expert meetings in France (1992) and Germany (1993), where this documentation has played an important role in the development of evaluation criteria for cultural landscapes to be included in the World Heritage List.

The Committee and the Landscape Group are continuing their work on this subject. They were responsible for organizing the meeting on heritage routes in Spain in November 1994, and also made a major contribution to the international conference on authenticity, held in Nara (Japan) in the same month.

Increasing interest has also been shown over the past decade in cultural landscapes by ICOMOS National Committees, especially those in Scandinavia and Australia, looking at organically evolved continuing landscapes and associative landscapes respectively. In the United Kingdom, the invention and evolution of landscape archaeology has been responsible for the identification of significant relict landscapes.

ICOMOS has also been involved in the evaluation of all the fourteen so-called "mixed sites" that are included on the World Heritage List. These include prehistoric rock-art sites such as Kakadu (Australia), sacred mountains such as Huangshan (China - see Yang, in this volume) and exceptional geological features with important religious or secular settlements on them such as Meteora (Greece). Several of these might be deemed to qualify as cultural landscapes under the new criteria. For example, the Kakadu landscape has been shaped by human intervention in the form of "mosaic burning" for some forty millennia whilst the rain-forest of Tikal (Guatemala) reveals substantial evidence of Mayan land management when viewed from satellites.

ICOMOS has in the past had a somewhat ambiguous attitude to what would now be considered, under the revised criteria, to be cultural landscapes. For example, the cultural elements in the "mixed" nominations of Tongariro (see Te Heuheu, in this volume) and Uluru/Ayer's Rock (see Layton and Titchen, in this volume) appear to have been ignored by the World Heritage Secretariat and/or ICOMOS when these were originally submitted. On the other hand, a number of what were in effect category (a) "designed" landscapes were evaluated by ICOMOS taking into account this specific aspect of the nominations, which was given equal weight as the major architectural monuments with which they were associated: the most notable examples are probably the parks at Fontainebleau and Versailles (France), Blenheim Palace and the park at Studley Royal (United Kingdom), the Potsdam palace and park complex (Germany), and the Shalimar Garden in Lahore (Pakistan).

As an advisory body to the World Heritage Committee, ICOMOS was deeply involved in the long, inconclusive discussions on cultural landscapes that began with the creation of a so-called "task force" in 1984. The crucial expert meeting held in the Parc Régional des Vosges in October 1992 was an ICOMOS initiative, organized jointly with the UNESCO World Heritage Centre and sponsored by the French Government, and ICOMOS members from Australia, Canada, Sri Lanka, and the United Kingdom made important contributions to its work. There was also substantial ICOMOS involvement in the international symposium at Schorfheide (Germany), the proceedings of which form the basis for this volume.

Strategies for the evaluation of cultural landscapes

General considerations

The procedures for evaluating nominations to the World Heritage List are clearly laid down in the *Operational Guidelines* (UNESCO 1995) and there is no justification for making any significant changes to these in respect of cultural landscapes. Consideration is being given, however, to the development of a new relationship between the two advisory bodies in preparing evaluations of certain categories of cultural landscape.

In the case of the "mixed sites" already inscribed on the World Heritage List, separate evaluations and recommendations were prepared by both IUCN and ICOMOS, without any consultation between the two bodies, and sites were inscribed under both sets of criteria. Only once has a joint on-site evaluation been carried out of a potential mixed site, in the case of an unsuccessful nomination from Vietnam in 1993. It should be borne in mind, however, that ICOMOS only began to organize site evaluation missions on a systematic basis in 1992.

It has been agreed that, in the case of nominations of cultural landscapes, ICOMOS will be the lead NGO. The general view taken by IUCN is that, since these landscapes are by definition cultural, they are *ipso facto* the primary responsibility of ICOMOS so far as evaluation is concerned. It may be worth mentioning at this point that there is another school of thought that exists within IUCN and its Commission on National Parks and Protected Areas (CNPPA) which holds that there are no truly "natural" landscapes, since every part of the globe has been affected to a lesser or greater extent by human intervention.

In practical terms, however, it is appropriate that a single advisory body should be approached in the first instance to initiate the evaluation procedure. Accordingly, ICOMOS receives nomination dossiers relating to cultural landscapes from the Secretariat on 1 November each year. Copies of the relevant parts of certain of these dossiers will in future be transmitted by ICOMOS to IUCN and a decision will be reached as to whether the site evaluation mission should be joint or whether it can be handled by ICOMOS or IUCN alone. These decisions will be largely dependent upon the category of cultural landscape concerned.

Designed landscapes are wholly creative cultural artefacts and so IUCN will not be involved. In the case of the other categories of landscape, IUCN involvement is likely to be restricted to management aspects, especially where the area concerned forms part or the whole of a national park or protected area. The IUCN CNPPA has defined eight categories of Protected Area, of which Category V (Protected Landscape or Seascape) is of direct relevance to the concept of continuing organically evolved landscape evolved by the World Heritage Committee. Protection here is intended "to maintain harmonious significant landscapes which are characteristic of the harmonious interaction of People and Land, while providing opportunities for public enjoyment through recreation and tourism within the normal lifestyle and economic activity of these areas" (Lucas 1992, 163-5). This objective is directly relevant to the definition of *sites* in Article 1 of the World Heritage Convention, which defines them as "works of man *or the combined works of nature and of man,* and areas including archaeological sites which are of outstanding universal value from the historical, aesthetic, ethnological or anthropological points of view" [author's italics].

ICOMOS procedures: Cultural criteria

ICOMOS is developing procedures for dealing with each of the categories of cultural landscape defined in the *Operational Guidelines*. Its Landscape Working Group is preparing guidelines for their definition and protection which will in due course serve as the doctrinal basis for the practical evaluation work. It is proposed to look at each of these in turn, highlighting the modifications in existing evaluation procedures likely to be required for each. Attention will be directed first to the "cultural" criteria, as laid down in para 24 (a) of the *Operational Guidelines* (UNESCO 1994).

– Designed landscapes

This category presents no problems, since there is already a number of examples on the World Heritage List (see above). The scope of the work of the ICOMOS International Committee on Historic Gardens and Sites is demonstrated in the first issue of the *ICOMOS Scientific Journal*, which is devoted to "Historic Gardens and Sites" (ICOMOS 1993). This contains papers on a wide range of such monuments, along with the ICOMOS-IFLA Charter for Historic Gardens (the Florence Charter) of 1982. The wealth of expertise represented by the Committee and its kindred organization IFLA can be called upon by ICOMOS in preparing its evaluations - and, indeed, has been invoked regularly in the past.

– Organically evolved landscapes: relict landscapes

Relict landscapes are essentially archaeological sites, where a process of organic evolution came to an end at some time in the past and where abundant traces of its former exploitation and development are preserved beneath and within a secondary natural vegetation cover. Examples that might be quoted here are the prehistoric and protohistoric landscapes that survive as earthworks and other features in the moorland landscape of Dartmoor in south-western England or the extensive prehispanic landscapes of irrigation and field systems of the Andes that were abandoned in the Spanish colonial period.

Such landscapes require the specialist advice of archaeologists, either through ICOMOS National Committees or the International Committee on Archaeological Heritage Management. The involvement of archaeologists in the work of ICOMOS has expanded enormously in the past decade and so a worldwide network can be tapped into for this purpose.

There is another important category of relict landscape for which specialist advice will be needed. Industrial activities such as mining, quarrying, and the production of metals, glass, paper, and ceramics, have left profound and ineradicable traces on large tracts of landscape, many of which have not been re-used since industrial operations ceased - the classical silver mines of Lavrion (Greece), for example, or the "Gold Rush" settlements and workings of the Klondyke. There is also the case of "linear" industrial monuments, such as canals, roads, and railways, where the most important examples are often disused. In such cases ICOMOS will consult its affiliated organization, TICCIH, which brings together the expertise of industrial archaeologists and historians from much of the world.

– Organically evolved landscapes: continuing landscapes

ICOMOS recognizes that this is likely to be the most difficult category to evaluate, especially in fulfilling the Committee's injunction that it should "make comparative evaluations of properties belonging to the same type of cultural property" (UNESCO 1995, para 62.c). The problem is fundamentally that of identifying the different types of continuing landscape and the qualities for which they might qualify for inclusion on the World Heritage List.

One approach that is being adopted is the organization of regional expert meetings (see Action Plan Annex 1) at which significant categories of landscape can be identified and criteria drafted. The first of these was held in the Philippines in 1995 and looked at traditional landscapes associated with rice cultivation, with emphasis on high-altitude rice-terraces (see Villalon, in this volume).

Another category of continuing landscape that requires urgent attention is that associated with non-agricultural societies. The landscapes of hunter-gatherer societies such as the Aboriginals of Australia were studied during a mission in 1994 by an ICOMOS mission that visited Kakadu and Uluru; as a result basic evaluation criteria were developed for future application. It is highly likely that in the future there will be nominations of the landscapes associated with pastoralist groups in a number of regions of the world, and it is to be hoped that the work being done by the Nordic working group on the Saami landscapes of northern Scandinavia will provide basic parameters for evaluation.

Agricultural landscapes present the most formidable problems. Studies have already been carried out and designation procedures initiated in certain countries, including Austria (Jeschke, in this volume), Finland, France, Slovenia (Habjan and Kolar Planinsic, in this volume), and Sweden (Riessen, in this volume), whilst Norway (Hegard, in this volume) and UK planning law has provision for various forms of landscape protection (Fowler and Jacques, in this volume). However, extensive consultation and comparative study on a regional basis are essential. It is to be hoped that this will form part of the Global Strategy developed in June 1994 by a working group appointed by the World Heritage Committee. The working group's report was approved by the Bureau in July 1994 and by the Committee at its 18th session in December 1994.

The approach being adopted for the Philippines meeting of focusing on a single staple crop (rice cultivation) is one that might profitably be applied elsewhere. An excellent subject for a study of this kind would be vineyards, which produce spectacular traditional landscapes of high cultural and historical value.

One further aspect of continuing landscapes that needs attention relates to vernacular settlements. The World Heritage List already contains several villages of traditional houses, such as Hollökö (Hungary) and Vlkolínec (Slovakia). The importance of both of these settlements lies in the fact that they are surrounded by land-holding patterns of medieval form that are still in use. The reservations on the part of the Committee in the past towards the inscription of this type of settlement on the basis of architecture and street pattern alone might be mitigated if they were to be presented in the future as the nuclei for extensive landscapes that demonstrate continuity of settlement and use over long periods. The Markim-Orkesta landscape (Riessen, in this volume) is an excellent example of this approach to landscape definition and assessment.

– Associative landscapes

The first property to be inscribed on the World Heritage List as a cultural landscape under the new criteria was Tongariro National Park (New Zealand). This had been nominated under both natural and cultural criteria in 1990, but had only been inscribed on the World Heritage List at the time on the basis of natural criteria, ICOMOS having failed to evaluate it under the cultural criteria. When it was resubmitted under cultural criteria in 1993 ICOMOS sent an expert mission to study the property and to evaluate it against the new criteria for cultural landscapes. As a result, ICOMOS recommended that Tongariro be inscribed on the List on the basis of cultural criterion (vi) in addition to the natural criteria (ii) and (iii).

This recommendation gave rise to a prolonged debate at the meeting of the Committee in Cartagena (Colombia) in December 1993, since the *Operational Guidelines* (UNESCO 1995, para 24) prescribe that "this criterion should justify inclusion in the List only in exceptional circumstances or in conjunction with other criteria." It was in fact only used on eight occasions in isolation, most recently in 1983; since that time the Committee has tended to restrict it to use in conjunction with other criteria. As a mountain range sacred to the Maori people, Tongariro does not qualify under any of the other cultural criteria. The applicability of criterion vi in isolation was challenged in this case, but it was eventually agreed that it was valid when used in conjunction with *natural* criteria. This is an important precedent, since there is a strong presumption that there will be no human intervention of any kind on natural features of this type (Uluru is directly comparable, for example). This is foreseen in the definition in the *Operational Guidelines* (UNESCO 1995, para 39 (iii)):

"The inclusion of such landscapes on the World Heritage List is justifiable by virtue of the powerful religious, artistic or cultural associations of the natural element rather than material cultural evidence, which may be insignificant or even absent."

So far the associative cultural landscapes that have been inscribed on the World Heritage List (which should include such properties as Huangshan and Meteora) are exclusively religious in their associations; it will be generally accepted that most of the world's great religions have universal value. It should be borne in mind, however, that there are smaller-scale religious "landscapes", such as the sacred groves of Ghana (Amoako-Atta, in this volume), where application of the criterion of "outstanding universal value" will require careful evaluation, especially since, though these sites undeniably have natural value, the question of whether they have "outstanding universal qualities" remains an open one.

The evaluation of landscapes with artistic or cultural associations remains to be considered by ICOMOS. The basic criterion must surely be that of the "outstanding universal value" of the artist concerned. The success of a hypothetical nomination of the Montaigne Sainte-Victoire would depend upon the evaluation of the universal significance of Cézanne, who painted it so often. Is there a case for adding criterion vi to the existing inscription of Toledo because of its association with El Greco? Would the significance of Constable justify the inclusion of the landscape round Flatford Mill on the List, or that of Hokusai make a case for Fujiyama? Is Wordsworth's hymning of the beauties of the Lake District of north-western England a strong enough reason for inscribing it, or Catullus's eulogising of Sirmio (now the Lago di Garda)? This is an aspect of the concept of associative cultural landscapes that requires long and deep consideration, and by an organization other than ICOMOS, which is not equipped to pronounce upon matters of non-material culture of this kind.

ICOMOS procedures: non-cultural criteria

Paragraph 24 of the *Operational Guidelines* (UNESCO 1995) specifies, in addition to the six "cultural" criteria, two criteria relating to authenticity and to protection and management mechanisms respectively. It is worthwhile looking at the application of these criteria in the course of ICOMOS evaluations (bearing in mind that authenticity was the subject of a major international meeting in Japan in November 1994, when the criteria for authenticity of cultural landscapes came under careful scrutiny).

– Designed landscapes

As has already been pointed out, these were largely covered by the earlier criteria and a number of examples are already on the World Heritage List. Designed landscapes such as parks and gardens are usually preserved and protected officially, either in isolation or, more frequently, associated with architectural monuments.

Assessment of authenticity creates certain problems of a conceptual nature. The parks laid out by Lancelot "Capability" Brown in England or the gardens of Jacques Le Nôtre in France had a two-dimensional form in their ground layouts which has largely been retained. However, the third dimension has changed over time, as vegetation has grown to maturity and died. The visual qualities of groups of trees as components of the landscape alter as these mature and degenerate. Natural disasters, such as the hurricane which swept southern England in October 1986, can radically change the appearance of a designed landscape. Authenticity in such cases depends essentially upon the degree of respect accorded to the original conception in subsequent replanting and replacement of landscape elements. It is, in effect, a function of management.

– Organically evolved landscapes: relict landscapes

Relict landscapes are generally the result of significant climatic and/or socio-economic changes in the past. An area of intensive settlement becomes transformed into one of vegetational cover - moorland in temperate climates, forest in the tropics.

Generally speaking, authenticity is not a problem in evaluation: the cultural importance of such landscapes resides in surface or buried features from the earlier periods. Of much greater importance is the criterion relating to protection and management.

An area of temperate moorland can be threatened by a variety of factors. Reafforestation can result in the complete removal of the relatively slight traces of past occupation. Regional aid programmes, such as that for "Least Favoured Areas" within the European Union, can lead to the use of heavy subsidies to permit an uneconomic form of agriculture which is equally destructive. Areas of this type are also favoured by governments as military training areas, with consequent destruction of features.

Abandoned ancient irrigation and agricultural landscapes, such as those in the Andean chain, can sometimes be brought back into operation in order to improve the standard of living of the remaining inhabitants. An outstanding example is the Cusichaca project in Perú, where an entire relict landscape has been brought back into cultivation (Kendall 1979, 1983).

In tropical regions, where an ancient landscape may be preserved within areas of rain-forest, uncontrolled logging and mining activities can be equally destructive. Sadly, there are all too many examples of this type of activity all over the world at the present time (see Chalukian, in this volume).

If relict landscapes are to be preserved and protected there must be stringent legislative protection and vigilant management on the part of the governments concerned. The moral problems resulting from potential conflicts between preservation and the future well-being of local communities must be weighed in the balance by States Parties rather than by the advisory bodies. If they accept the cultural importance of such landscapes, their commitment to protection and preservation must be total.

– Organically evolved landscapes: continuing landscapes

This category of cultural landscape contains an implicit contradiction: if it is conceived as "continuing" there can surely be no logical justification for protesting against the insertion of modern elements into it. Thus, if the social and economic trajectory of a given landscape requires the introduction of modern food-processing plant or new communications links, there is not a strong case for opposing these on the basis of cultural significance, since that significance is grounded upon the continuing nature of the landscape. A landscape that is "frozen" in its state at the time when it is inscribed on the World Heritage List paradoxically does not qualify as a continuing landscape. It may be observed here, in parenthesis, that similar considerations apply in the case of historic town centres: these, too, have an organic life of their own which should not be brought to an artificial end by designation or inscription.

In practical terms, however, the problem is one that is capable of rational solution. A continuing landscape in Europe, for example, may contain surviving elements from prehistory up to the present day. It is not unlikely that it may include elements such as railway cuttings that were regarded as unacceptable intrusions when they were built in the 19th century but which now testify to the "continuing" nature of the landscape concerned. A prehistoric earthwork and an 18th century watermill are equally important components of the cultural artefact that is the landscape. The criterion of authenticity here needs liberal interpretation, rejecting only discordant elements from an alien culture (for example, garish billboards advertising western consumer goods in an oriental agricultural landscape).

Management is of great importance in such cases. It would seem to be axiomatic that cultural landscapes of this type that are nominated for the World Heritage List should be protected by effective land-use legislation which controls all forms of intervention.

– Associative landscapes

Authenticity is *ex hypothesi* not a factor in the case of natural features such as holy mountains. Management, on the other hand, is of considerable importance: the erection of unassociated buildings (hotels, sanatoria, sports facilities, etc) or destructive activities such as quarrying cannot be countenanced. States Parties must therefore provide evidence of a will to preserve such landscapes in the form of adequate protective measures and management plans.

Conclusion

The extension of the concept of world cultural heritage to include cultural landscapes is greatly welcomed by ICOMOS, which is actively preparing itself to expand its evaluation work to encompass this non-monumental but equally significant aspect of human creative endeavour.

A good deal of work in developing procedures and criteria remains to be done, especially in the field of continuing evolved landscapes. This will involve a wide range of organizations and individuals, working in close association with the World Heritage Committee, with the UNESCO World Heritage Centre, and with ICOMOS. Much will depend upon the speedy development of the Global Strategy and the outcome of a series of regional expert meetings on specific topics.

Acknowledgments

The author is very grateful to his good friends and colleagues Carmen Añón Feliú (former Chairman, ICOMOS International Committee on Historic Gardens and Sites) and Herb Stovel (former ICOMOS Secretary General) for their helpful comments on this paper.

References

ICOMOS (1993). *Jardins et Sites Historiques*, ICOMOS Journal Scientifique, **1**. - 377 p. Paris, ICOMOS.

Kendall, A. (1979). *The Cusichaca Archaeological Project (Peru): the early stages*. Institute of Archaeology Bulletin [London], 16: 131-157.

Kendall, A. (1983). *The middle stages of the Cusichaca Archaeological Project (Peru)*. Institute of Archaeology Bulletin [London], **20**: 43-71.

Lucas, P.H.C. (1992). *Protected Landscapes: A guide for policy-makers and planners*. - xvi + 297 p.; London, Chapman and Hall.

UNESCO (1995). *Operational Guidelines for the Implementation of the World Heritage Convention* (WHC/2/Revised February 1995). - 47 p. Paris, UNESCO World Heritage Centre.

Henry Cleere is the ICOMOS World Heritage Coordinator.

Chapter 7

Cultural Landscapes and Fauna

Almo Farina

Introduction

The transformation of natural areas in cultural landscapes has generally been a long process dating back thousands of years. A cultural landscape often is an open landscape with scattered trees or sequences of fields bordered by hedgerows, but a great variety of cultural landscapes can be recognized around the world from the Mongolia semi-desert prairies to the upland prairies of the south-Europe mountains, from the olive orchards of the Mediterranean, to the bocage of central Europe, from the monotonous cereal plains of the U.S. midwest to the rice terraces of the Philippine mountains where human presence and its related influence, modification and disturbance have a long history of coevolutionary processes. The feedback between human activity and the response of the natural processes to this disturbance has influenced the composition, abundance and behaviour of many species of animals at the population, community, ecosystem, and landscape level.

For instance, the distribution and abundance of the house sparrow, starling, house martin, and swift, all birds living in strict connection and dependence with human settlements, are related to the land use of an area. Small villages surrounded by agricultural lands are the most suitable parts of the landscape to support large populations of these birds, which find nesting sites in the buildings and food in their surroundings (zooplankton around the livestock manure deposits and seeds in the crop fields). Despite their worldwide distribution, cultural landscapes appear to be poorly studied because they are not considered relevant to the understanding of ecological processes. Most ecological studies emphasize the paradigm that the best approach to investigating ecological processes is to select only ecosystems not disturbed by humans and that humans must be considered intruders in ecosystems.

Cultural landscapes are generally characterized by a relevant sustainable capacity based on the strict feedback couplings that have accompanied many human actions as response to natural processes. Naveh and Liebermann (1993) have characterized the unique nature of the cultural landscape as a tangible meeting point between nature and mind (noosphere). In other words the cultural landscape is the product of the human/nature interactions. In many cases the complexity of nature has been degraded or reduced. In other cases the natural complexity has been magnified by human stewardship, as in the Mediterranean. The human disturbance regimes that have been shifted over a long period by macro-climatic and macro-edaphic changes and historical events such as wars, diseases and famines, represent the main ecological processes driving landscape patterns and dynamics.

In the past, the human-shaping of the landscape was a feedback process eco-oriented toward the sustainability of human populations. Human choices were generally ecologically oriented to modulate the capacity of the system and in many cases the structuring and shaping of the landscapes were strictly related to resource availability and environmental dynamics. A good example is presented by the <u>dehesa</u> of Spain and Portugal where the abiotic and biotic constraints are active. In this fragile system the rotational agro-silvo-pastoral management plays a fundamental role in the maintenance of the oak savanna-like system (Joffre et al. 1988, Joffre and Rambal 1993, Joffre and Lacaze 1993). The importance of <u>dehesa</u> for the conservation of many species of wintering central and north-European birds has been recently stressed by Purroy and Rodero (1986) and Telleria and Santos (1986). This system is a good example of a long-term human and natural interaction that has produced a metastable semi-natural system where both the cultural and natural components are active and strictly integrated (Pinto Correia 1993). As described by Naveh (1991) in detail, cultural landscapes dependant on human disturbance are maintained in a dynamic homeorhetic flow equilibrium by closely interacting natural and cultural processes.

Change of the land use, modernization of agriculture or the climatic changes can produce dramatic collapse of the whole system. The conservation of this agro-silvo-pastoral system like other cultural landscapes, is strategic for the preservation of many species of animals.

The aim of this article is to emphasize the importance of some cultural landscape features and processes for animal distribution, abundance and dynamics. The literature on this subject is not abundant and it is particularly oriented towards the study of recent human transformations of the natural landscape in the rural landscape and their effects on vertebrate fauna. Most investigations focus on vertebrates, birds and mammals but some studies are carried out also on insects.

Spatial pattern in cultural landscapes

The chorological components of the cultural landscape influence the distribution, abundance and behaviour of the animals. Relevant spatial elements are: size, shape, distribution of patches, patch orientation, perimeter/area ratio and boundary form (Wiens et al. 1993) (see Tab. 1).The form of the patches is important in a landscape in terms of vegetation recolonization and animal use of the patches (Forman and Godron 1986). Hardt and Forman (1989) found a direct effect of concave-convex patch forms on the browsing of white-tailed deer (*Odocoileus virginianus*) and eastern cottontail (*Sylvilagus floridanus*). Concave boundaries were browsed more than convex ones. The position of the patches in the landscape is also important for the settlement of breeding sites of migratory birds as stressed by Gutzwiller and Anderson (1992) in the Wyoming riverine landscape.

Structural and functional characters of the cultural landscape relevant for fauna

Although it is difficult to summarize the emergent characters of the cultural landscapes that largely depend on geographical position and human history, some common patterns are important for the fauna. Most of cultural landscapes are characterized by a heterogeneous mosaic of wood and field patches with a sharp contrast at the edges between the

Table 1. The measurable features that can be considered in the analysis of the landscape (from Wiens et al. 1993).

Feature	Description
Size distribution	Frequency distribution of size of patches of a given type
Boundary form	Boundary thickness, continuity, linearity (fractal dimension), length
Perimeter: area ratio	Relates patch area to boundary length; reflects patch size
Patch orientation	Position relative to a directional process of interest (e.g. water flow, passage of migrants)
Context	Immediate mosaic-matrix in which a patch of a given type occurs
Contrast	Magnitude of difference in measures across a given boundary between patches
Connectivity	Degree to which patches of a given type are joined by corridors into a lattice of nodes and links
Richness	Number of different patch types in a given area
Evenness	Equivalence in numbers (or areas) of different patch types in a mosaic (the inverse of the degree of dominance by one or a few patch types)
Dispersion	Distribution pattern of patch types over an area
Predictability	Spatial autocorrelation; the degree to which knowledge about features at a given location reduces uncertainty about variable values at other locations

two land cover types, for example between forests and fields. This is a true mosaic of human modified land (e.g. the fields) and is influenced by remnants of spontaneous vegetation.

Heterogeneity is one of the main characters of the cultural landscape if compared with the homogeneity of natural landscapes on similar scales. In cultural landscapes the shape of the patches is an important factor conditioning movement and preferences of many animals. Edges in cultural landscapes have a lower fractal dimension in comparison with the corresponding natural systems. Due to the heterogeneity of the land mosaic, the microclimate, is strongly affected by the spatial position of some structured elements as scattered trees, hedgerows and wind-fences, and by the size of patches.

Human stewardship influences and modifies the structure and functioning of landscapes and their components. Secondary succession is interrupted by the seasonal disturbance regime of agriculture and the seasonal character of resource availability is enhanced by human activity. Phenology and the impact of the disturbance regime of the human stewardship change over long periods of time due to socio-economic changes but the system appears stable at a meso-scale (few decades).

Hierarchy and scaling in the cultural landscape

Recent theory on the hierarchical organization of ecosystems (Allen and Starr 1982, O'Neill et al. 1986, Allen and Hoekstra 1992) can be successfully used to investigate the

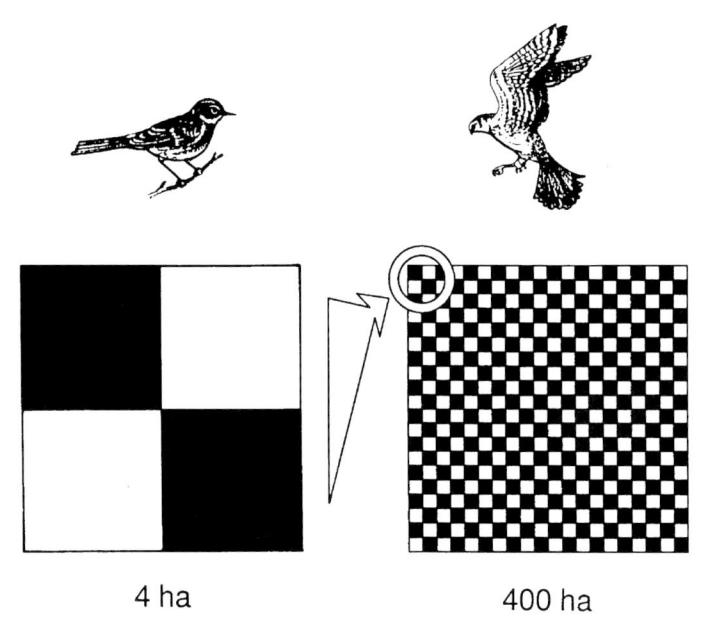

Figure 1. Animals perceive the landscape at different inherent species-specific scales (from Hunter 1990).

patterns and processes of the complex cultural landscape. According to this theory, ecological systems can be divided into sub-systems with different complexities and scalar attributes that are connected to each other by permanent fluxes of energy, materials, organisms and information. The cultural landscape has been structured, changed and shaped by natural processes and human activity, each working at their inherent scales. Complex modelling forces acting on different spatial and temporal dimensions require multi-scalar investigations, so that the observer does not misinterpret the ecological relationships occurring at different scales (Milne et al. 1989). The complexity of the landscape changes according to the area measured. This has important implications in terms of management strategies for fauna that perceives the landscape according an inherent species-specific scale (Fig. 1).

The human disturbance regime and fauna

The disturbance regime is a discrete temporal event that changes the structure of ecosystems, communities and populations and modifies the resource availability, the soil, and the physical environment. When we are dealing with the human disturbance regime we are referring to crop cultivation, forest harvesting, fishing and hunting. In this context I would like to draw special attention to agriculture and forestry. Pruning, tillage, fertilization, grass cutting and livestock grazing are common seasonally-synchronized disturbance actions which allow an extraordinary renewal and mobilization of nutrients, biomass and organisms.

The mostly cyclic human disturbance regime produces a seasonally-changing environment with consequences on the migration movements of many species of animals. The movements of birds have been particularly studied. In southern Europe, a great number of birds spend the winter in cultural landscapes. The species of birds living close to human settlements are chiefly thrushes, finches and crows. In some cases they are considered pests because of the damage they cause to field crop production. In other cases they harvest large amounts of seeds remaining in the field and invading weeds and disperse edible seeds. Olive orchards, the Italian coltura mista and the Spanish-Portuguese oak dehesa are examples of highly attractive cultural landscapes for wintering and transient central-northern European birds (Purroy and Rodero 1986, Telleria and Santos 1986, Farina 1987, 1991, 1992). These landscapes offer a favourable microclimate during the cold season and an abundance of animal and plant resources made available by the traditional agricultural practices all year around.

Landscape fragmentation and animals

The important role of landscape fragmentation for the ecology of animals has been stressed by many authors (e.g. Preston 1962, MacArthur and Wilson 1967, Soulé and Wilcox 1980, Wilcove et al. 1986, Lovejoy et al. 1987, Opdam 1988, 1991, Saunders et al. 1991). Fragmentation of habitats at the landscape level means that favourable areas for foraging, breeding or roosting are patchily dispersed in a non-habitat matrix (*sensu* Forman and Godron 1986). The distance from homogeneous habitats, the time-lag after the fragmentation, the distance between relict patches and their connectivity are important indicators of fragmentation. The environmental factors arising in the surroundings are driving or influencing the fragmented patches (van Dorp and Opdam 1987) although intrinsic factors such as density and resource availability can partially control population dynamics (Bolger et al. 1991) and use (Martin and Karr 1986). Habitat fragmentation has consequences at different functional scales. At the scale of the individual the habitat fragmentation produces alternative behaviour of the individual. At population level the fragmentation produces partial isolation between separate populations that have a reduced rate of interchange.

A fragmented landscape generally has a lower diversity and produces the isolation of populations and genetic drifts (Klein 1989, Leberg 1990). Blake and Karr (1987) have found in fragmented habitats a lower number of breeding migratory tropical birds, that requires interior habitats for breeding. Fragmentation has been studied during the recent destruction both in tropical forests (Lovejoy et al. 1987, Klein 1989) and in the boreal forests of North America and Europe (Harris 1984, Wilcove 1985, Vaisanen et al. 1986). However most of these effects may be different in ancient cultural landscapes in which fragmentation has not been a sudden event but a gradual shift of the landscape mosaic allowing the adaptive coevolution of plants and animals to the new environmental conditions.

Physical and chemical factors operate differently in dense homogeneous habitats than in heterogeneous fragmented landscapes. The fragmentation affects the complex mechanisms regulating the species-specific habitat suitability, the food chains and the prey-predator relationship (Andren et al. 1985, Andren and Angelstam 1988). Animals and plants living at the border of patches in which there is a higher edaphic and

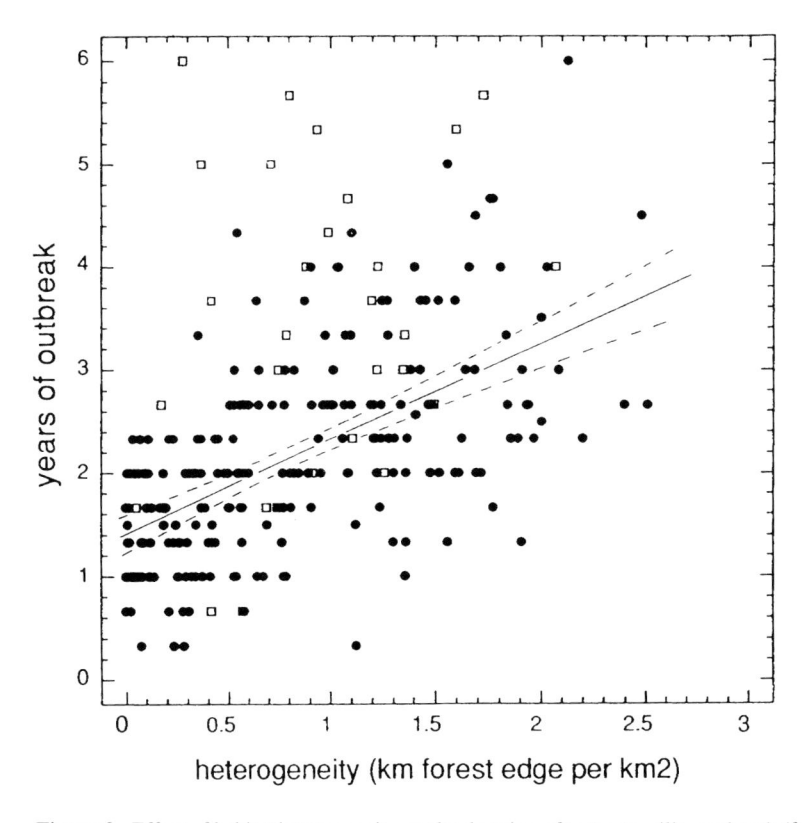

Figure 2. Effect of habitat heterogeneity on the duration of tent caterpillar outbreak (from Roland 1993).

microclimatic constraint are more exposed to sunlight, to wind and aridity. For instance the recent clearing of boreal forests is probably the main cause of the reduced control of parasitoids and pathogens on tent caterpillar (*Malacosoma disstria*) outbreaks in northern Ontario, Canada. Massive outbreaks of this forest defoliator are related to the amount of forest edge per km^2 (Roland 1993) (Fig. 2). The population processes, responsible for the duration of outbreaks, are affected and regulated by the amount of forest edges. This is a good example of predator-prey interactions in a modified landscape. Habitat patchiness affects predator-prey interactions, increasing the irregularity and the extension of outbreaks (Kareiva 1987).

Predation is higher in fragmented landscapes (Whitcomb et al. 1980, Ambuel and Temple 1983, Brittingham and Temple 1983). Evidence of the increase of predation in fragmented landscape on nesting birds has been found by Wilcove (1985) using experimental tests on artificial nest predation (Fig. 3). The effects of fragmentation on animal populations are different according to the biogeographic distribution of the species. The fragmentation may be deleterious for individuals at the border of the geographical range (Hengeveld 1990), altering the temporal and spatial dynamics of native forest birds (Howe 1984). At the other end habitat islands can support a higher number of bird species during migratory period (Martin 1980).

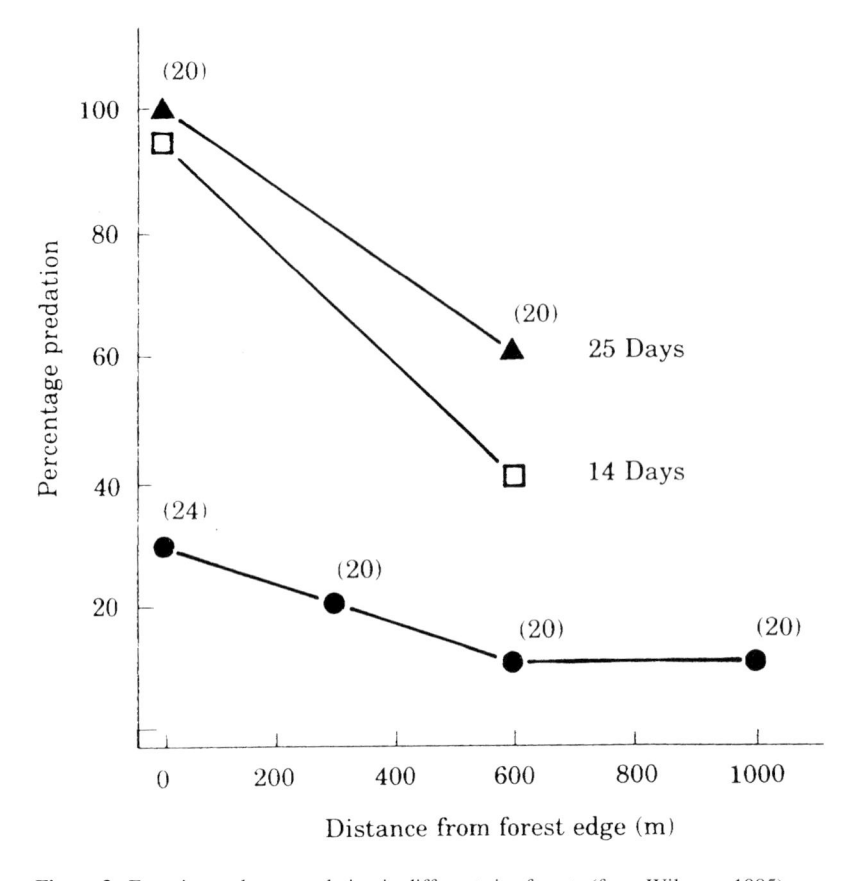

Figure 3. Experimental nest predation in different size forests (from Wilcove, 1985).

Movement of animals across the landscape: corridors and dispersal

Animal dispersal is a well known pattern in population ecology. The dispersal is generally density dependent. In an heterogeneous landscape the dispersal movements are influenced by the distance between suitable habitats and by the presence of corridors. Habitat corridors, narrow strips of suitable habitat, are components of the landscape mosaic frequently used by animals to move from one patch to another. Their role is fundamental in assuring the connectivity between sub-populations of small mammals (e.g. Bennet 1990, Merriam and Lanoue 1990). The quality of the corridors influences the survival rate of sub-populations; high quality corridors (e.g. good vegetation cover to escape predators) allow the connectedness between interdispersed patches assuring the exchange of individuals among patches so that the rate of extinction can be balanced by colonization (f.i. Henein and Merriam 1990). Organisms that move away using corridors are strongly influenced by the spatial position of patches. This effect is smaller for organisms that disperse over long distances (Fahrig and Paloheimo 1988).

To explain the dynamics of sub-populations in a landscape mosaic, Pulliam (1988) has successfully adopted the source-sink model (Lewin 1989). According to this model a population can be considered as sink only when a flux of immigrants can assure survival in a patch. A population is source type when the offspring exceed the emigrants. A constant flux of individuals are moving from the source to the sink patches. The source-sink condition can be inverted seasonally.

Fractal dimension of the cultural landscape

The application of the fractal geometry (Mandelbrot 1977) to the study of the complex geometry of nature (Burrough 1986, Krummel et al. 1987, Milne 1988, 1991,1992, Turner et al. 1989, Wiens and Milne 1989, Baudry 1993) has also gained significance for the study of human-modified cultural landscapes. The geometry of natural landscapes is strictly related to natural disturbance processes, while cultural landscapes show a direct relationship with human activity. The human-modified landscape has a more simplified geometry compared with the natural undisturbed areas (Mladenoff et al. 1993). Krummel et al. (1987) have investigated the behaviour of the ratio perimeter/area in land recently converted from forest to cropland (Mississippi, U.S.) (Fig. 4).

The investigation was carried out on the shape of relict fragmented forest patches. Small patches had a lower fractal dimension compared with larger patches. This result can probably be related to two different processes acting at different scales. The human process of cultivation is operating at small scale while at larger scale are the natural processes such as geo-morphology and climate responsible for patterning the landscape. This hypothesis is important also for understanding the effect of human activity on animal

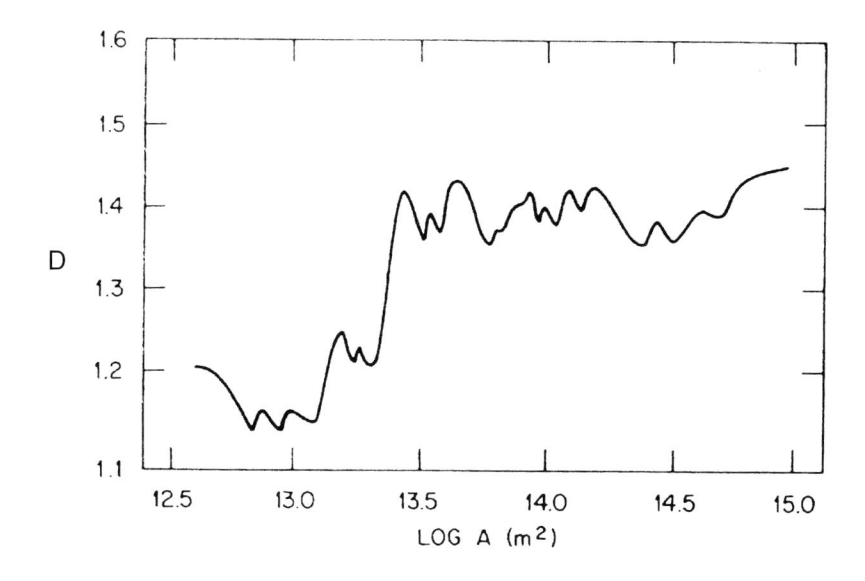

Figure 4. Changing in fractal dimension (D) as the log of area (A) determined by successive regressions of the log of perimeter on log of A. (from Krummel et al. 1987).

populations and for explaining the interactions between human and natural processes across different scales with implications for management strategies to conserve the cultural landscapes and their eco-diversity (Naveh and Lieberman 1993).

Metapopulations: spatial dynamics of the populations in the cultural landscape

In a fragmented landscape composed of patches of different habitats, spatially separate populations of animals are distributed according to species-specific suitability of patches and isolated populations are connected by an exchange of individuals. The whole system has been coined "metapopulation"(Levins, 1970) and can be considered as the demographic unit of the landscape. The concept of metapopulation has been used to describe the behaviour of animal populations in complex-fragmented systems (Gilpin and Hanski 1991, Opdam 1991). Extinction and recolonization are the two driving processes that maintain and assure the genetic fluxes between the sub-populations.

The movements of animals across an heterogeneous landscape are conditioned by the presence of natural and/or human structural and functional barriers, acting in different ways according to the scalar attributes of the species. The sizes of patches are responsible for the extinction and recolonization rate: large patches are longer populated than small ones, isolated patches have a higher risk of extinction and can be vacant of individuals for a longer time than proximate patches (Hansson 1991, Rolstad 1991).

Ecotones and their importance for faunal diversity

Ecotones can be defined as structural and functional discontinuities between two habitats, or the place in which the energy exchange reaches the maximum, or as a tension area between systems at two different maturity levels. They are considered important for many ecological processes (Wiens et al. 1985, Hansen and Di Castri 1992, Wiens 1992). The ecotone is a critical spatial and functional attribute of an heterogeneous landscape and can be utilized by a species as a true barrier or a corridor from an habitat to another. This is especially true in cultural landscapes in which in addition to existing natural ecotones anthropogenic ecotones have also been created. They are essential for the dynamic of the systems functioning as conduit, filter or barrier, source, sink and habitat (Forman and Moore 1992).

Human activity has accelerated the process of fragmentation of the natural vegetational cover, favouring the creation of extended edges, although ecotones can also be produced by animals such as beavers (Johnston and Naiman 1987) or livestock. Across ecotones the energy and material fluxes reach the maximum between two systems. With this view point it is possible to evaluate the effects at individual and population animal levels (Ranney et al. 1981, Noss 1983). The structure of ecotones can be characterized by a) density (number of ecotones per unit distance or area); b) width of adjacent patch; c) contrast, the structural difference between patches; d) ecotone width; e) ecotone shape (Fig. 5). According to the temporal scales we can distinguish permanent (wood/field), seasonal (between two fields) and ephemeral ecotones (snow-bare soil, seasonal grazing) created by natural and/or human induced impacts.

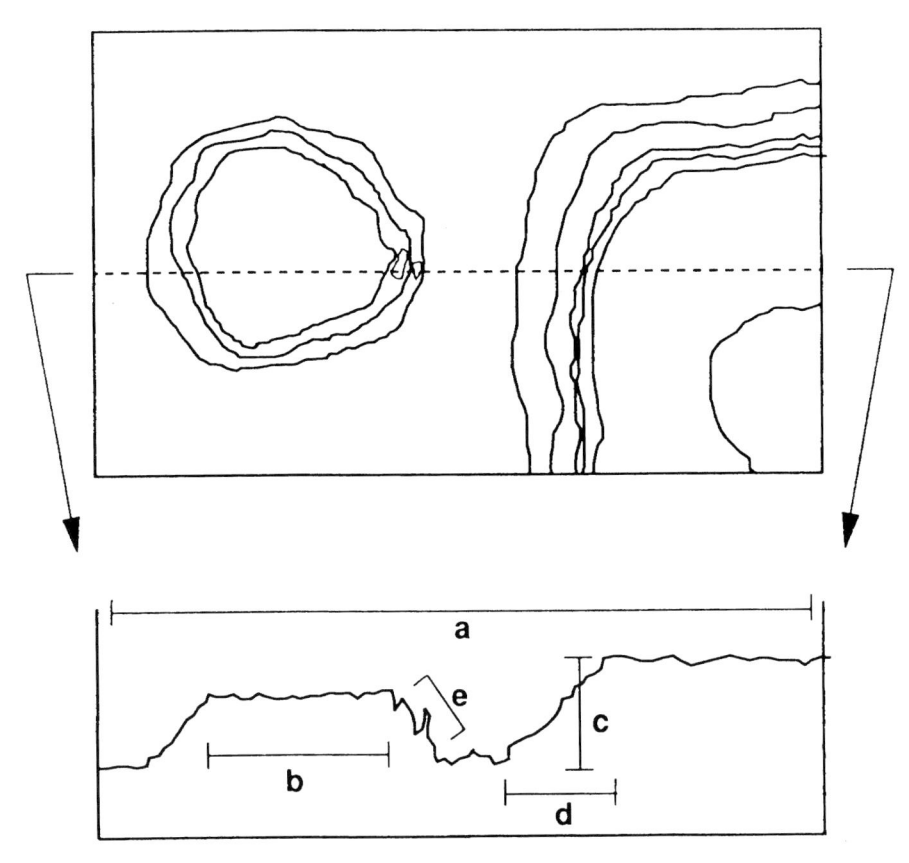

Figure 5. Characters and attributes of the ecotones: (Top) The isopleths represent the discontinuity in the landscape (Bottom). The elements that characterize the ecotones: a) density (number of ecotones per unit distance or area; b) width of adjacent patch; c) contrast; d) width; e) internal heterogeneity (from Hansen et al. 1992).

Generally in cultural landscapes ecotones are narrow, have a linear geometry and are highly contrasted and are less attractive than natural ones, although most of the synanthropic species are living long the ecotones. Percolation theory (Gefen et al. 1983, Orbach 1986, Stauffer 1985, Feder 1988) has been used to describe the behaviour of individuals across ecotones (Gardner et al. 1987, Gardner et al. 1992). Shape, size, and soft and hard contrast of ecotones have a big influence on the behaviour of many animals (Stamps et al. 1987). Fragile species have chance of encountering an ecotone. The probability of crossing the ecotone depends on many species-specific factors . The balance between costs and benefits of changing the patch by crossing the ecotone should be positive and this balance is achieved in different ways according to the type of animal (Fig. 6). For sedentary species, the ecotone is an important barrier to movement. For free moving animals the ecotone can be considered as the limit between a more favourable habitat and an unfavorable one. Ecotones can be attractive for many species of birds that find abundant food or breeding sites and in some cases can be considered ecological traps in which predation is very high.

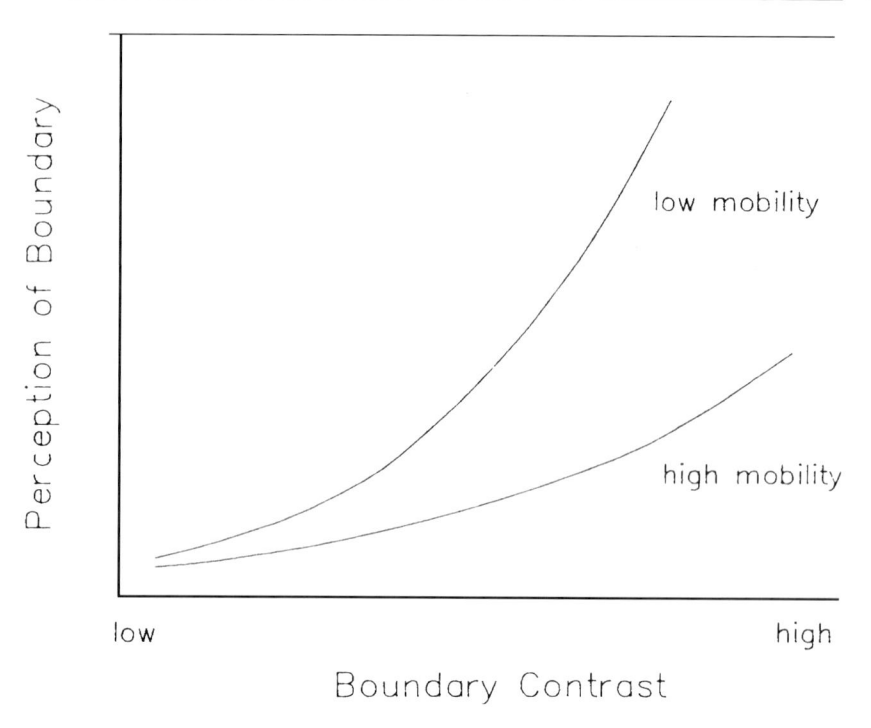

Figure 6. Hypothetical functions of the degree to which an organism perceives an edge as a discontinuity. The response is in relation to the boundary contrast and the fragility of the organism (from Wiens 1992).

Keystone hypothesis and the "human" animal

Recently Holling (1992) has presented an interesting hypothesis on scaling and structuring landscape and the role of animals, man included. According to this hypothesis, all terrestrial ecosystems are to some extent controlled and structured by a small number of organisms (plants, animals, man), these are considered key stone species. In this context, the areas controlled by human activity can be considered cultural landscapes. In his opinion, in the human species an animal and a mind nature can be recognized. These two components of humanity are blended in different ways according to the geographic regions and the "evolution" of the civilization. While in more primitive societies the feed-back between nature and mind was very close and biological conditioned and operating on restricted scales, in modern societies this feed-back has been removed and replaced by socio-economic and technological forces operating from micro to mega-planetary scales.

Disturbance and cultural landscape dynamics

Disturbance is important to maintain the dynamics of a landscape. In the cultural landscape most of the disturbances are produced by agriculture at a seasonal scale with a spatial grain determined by the level of "modernization" of the agricultural practices. The traditional agriculture generally creates a steady state system composed of relatively small fields by a seasonal or annual turnover of crop production. The seasonal disturbance as pruning, seeding, crop harvesting, grazing or the annual or pluri-annual wood clearing, mobilizes energy and matter promptly exploited by many synanthropic species. The long distance migratory birds use the small patches of ploughed fields and the freshly moved grass as foraging stop-over habitats (Farina 1987).

Old and new cultural landscapes

Old cultural landscapes are characterized by a long history of coevolutionary processes between humans and nature. Their conservation is important to maintain cultural heritage and biodiversity, but we do not have sufficient data about the kind and number of animal species lost or gained during these historical periods. The more recent cultural landscapes which are only few centuries old, especially in a way similar to those in America and Australia, have been structured and shaped in similarly structure and shape as the European cultural landscapes but the duration of transformation has been extremely condensed. In some parts of Central and South America, the time lag of these changes is only a few decades. In these "new" cultural landscapes the human impact on animals is quite evident and often dramatic in terms of biological impoverishment. Many studies suggest the possibilities of simulating the complexity of nature to preserve biodiversity (Harris 1984, Mladenoff et al. 1993).

New threats to the cultural landscape and their effects on the fauna diversity

As recently stressed by Naveh and Lieberman (1993) cultural landscapes are facing new threats due to changes of land use, population growth, increase of pollutants in atmosphere, water and soil. Two of the most common causes of cultural landscape degradation are on the one hand the modernization of agriculture by intensification (Green 1989), and on the other hand, land abandonment (Baudry 1991). Both these processes are extremely harmful for the cultural landscape and they are responsible for undesirable changes in animal populations. Modifications due to agricultural intensification and industrialization generally produce sharp changes in the landscape structures, simplifying the land mosaic, decreasing tree cover and causing the disappearance of wood remnants. With the progressive isolation of relict wooded patches the faunal diversity is reduced, and the risks of local extinction are aggravated.

Monocultures discourage animals, which encounter a monotonous landscape where food resources are rare or concentrated only in a short period of the year. This type of landscape, e.g. maize fields after harvesting, can sometimes attract a large number of birds. However, it is just a sink habitat not supporting stable animal populations throughout the year, encouraging synanthropic and cosmopolitan species that contribute only in small part to faunal diversity. The disappearance and isolation of natural refuges make it difficult for animals, especially mammals, to move across the landscape. The decrease is also evident in the invertebrate fauna, especially after the removal of hedgerows, a common practice in the modern agricultural landscape.

Land abandonment is a widespread phenomenon linked to the intensification of agriculture in favourable lands and the emigration of human populations from hilly and mountainous regions. This process has started after the Second World War and is increasing rapidly. It has been studied particularly in southern Europe, around the Mediterranean (Farina 1991, 1992, Ales et al. 1992, Lepart and Debussche 1992, Vos and Stortelder 1992, Gomez-Sal et al. 1993, Pinto Correia 1993, Vos 1993) but is common also in central and north Europe (Bunce 1991, Burel 1991). Land abandonment produces the rapid recover of shrub and woodland and for many species of animals it is a favourable process. In this category we find the medium and large mammals that compete directly with human activity and have long been persecuted with every type of trap and poisoning.

The increase of wood cover long the Apennines chain (Italy) for instance has increased the connectedness of woodland favouring the movement of large mammals such as wild boar, deer and wolves (Farina 1992). But the transformation of cultural landscape into a dense shrubland has disadvantaged most open living animals, such as many bird species. In the Mediterranean land abandonment has caused a real loss of suitable habitats for wintering birds such as thrushes and warblers and also a loss of habitats for long-distance trans-Saharan birds that use open grassy patches or ploughed fields as stop-over foraging sites (Farina 1995).

The management of the cultural landscape for the preservation the faunal diversity

Due to the threats facing cultural landscapes it is urgent to find efficient strategies to conserve, restore and manage these relevant landscapes. The application of landscape ecology, principles and methods can contribute considerably to the solution of the problems that today are distressing land managers and the decision makers (Farina and Naveh 1993).

A large debate is in progress on biodiversity conservation and sustainable development (Naveh 1979, Lubchenco et al. 1991, Norton and Ulanowicz 1992). It is not easy to address many pressing contemporary problems that need urgent replies for the maintenance of the cultural landscape. It seems utopian to believe that the cultural landscape could be maintained in a steady state, stuffed and frozen for future generations. As the landscape is a dynamic homeorhetic system that changes throughout time, the maintenance of fluxes should be the main goal. This requires the restoration and simulation of past management practices that generally were mimicking natural processes (Baker 1989, Kemp and Barrett, 1989, Naveh 1991, Plumb and Dodd 1993, Booth et al. 1993) to reduce the chemical inputs in modern agriculture and assure at the same time an intermediate level of disturbance (Hobbs and Huenneke 1992).

Animals are fragile organisms that need a wide area to live and to breed. The strategy of confining animals in small patches of protected areas surrounded by a desert of technology is not a real strategy. The conservation of animals in cultural landscapes should go along with the conservation of structures as corridors, patterns, processes of the cultural landscape (Harris 1984, Ricklefs et al. 1984, Henderson et al. 1985, Merriam et al. 1989). It is important to maintain fluxes between the metapopulations and to preserve the abundance and also the gene flow. To achieve this result, it is necessary to classify correctly the landscape (Blankson and Green 1991) at a suitable scale and to take in account that a landscape is not an isolated system but that is largely influenced by the surrounding systems (Hansson 1992) of the total human ecosystem.

References

Ales, R. F., Martin, A., Ortega, F. and Ales, E. E. (1992). *Recent changes in landscape structure and function in a Mediterranean region of SW Spain (1950-1984)*. Landscape Ecology **7**: 3-18.

Allen, T. F. H. and Starr, T. B. (1982). *Hierarchy. Perspectives for ecological complexity*. University of Chicago Press, Chicago.

Allen, T. F. H. and Hoekstra, T. W. (1992). *Toward a unified ecology*. Columbia University Press, New York.

Ambuel, B. and Temple, S. A. (1983). *Area-dependent changes in bird communities and vegetation of southern Wisconsin forests*. Ecology **64**: 1057-1068.

Andren, H. and Angelstam, P. (1988). *Elevated predation rates as an edge effect in habitat islands: experimental evidence*. Ecology **69**: 544-547.

Andren, H., Angelstam, P., Lindstrom, E. and Widen, P. (1985). *Differences in predation pressure in relation to habitat fragmentation: an experiment*. Oikos **45**: 273-277.

Baker, W. L. (1989). *Landscape ecology and nature reserve design in the boundary waters canoe area, Minnesota*. Ecology **70**: 23-35.

Baudry, J. (1991). *Ecological consequences of grazing extensification and land abandonment: Role of interactions between environment, society and techniques*. Options Mediterranéennes Serie Seminaires, n. **15**: 13-19.

Baudry, J. (1993). *Landscape dynamics and farming systems: problems of relating patterns and predicting ecological changes*. In: Bunce, R.G.H., Ryszkowski, L. and Paoletti, M.G. (eds.). *Landscape ecology and ecosystems*, Lewis, Boca Raton, Florida. Pp. 21-40.

Bennet, A. F. (1990). *Habitat corridors and the conservation of small mammals in a fragmented forest environment*. Landscape Ecology **4**:109-122

Blake, J. G. and Karr, J. R. (1987). *Breeding birds of isolated woodlots: area and habitat relationships*. Ecology **68**: 1724-1734.

Blankson, E. J. and Green, B. H. (1991). *Use of landscape classification as an essential prerequisite to landscape evaluation*. Landscape and Urban Planning **21**: 149-162.

Bolger, D. T., Albert, A. C. and Soulé, M. E. (1991). *Occurrence patterns of bird species in habitat fragments: sampling, extinction and nested species subsets*. Am. Nat. **137**: 155-166.

Booth, D., Boulter, D., Neave, D., Rotherham, T. and Welsh, D. (1993). *Natural forest landscape management: A strategy for Canada*. Policy edition. Forest Resource Management Edition.

Brittingham, M. C. and Temple, S. A. (1983). *Have cowbirds caused forest songbirds to decline?* BioScience **33**: 31.

Bunce, R. G. H. (1991). *Ecological implications of land abandonment in Britain: some comparison with Europe*. Options Mediterranéennes - Serie Seminaires, n. **15**: 53-59.

Burel, F. (1991). *Ecological consequences of land abandonment on carabid beetles distribution in two contrasted grassland areas*. Options Mediterranéennes - Serie Seminaires, n. **15**: 111-119.

Burrough, P. A. (1986). *Principles of geographical information systems for land resources assessment*. Clarendon Press, Oxford.

Fahrig, L. and Paloheimo, J. (1988). *Effect of spatial arrangement of habitat patches on local population size*. Ecology **69**: 468-475.

Farina, A. (1987). *Autumn-winter structure of bird communities in selected habitats of Tuscany (Italy)*. Boll. Zool. **54**: 243-249.

Farina, A. (1991). *Recent changes of the mosaic patterns in a montane landscape (north Italy) and consequences on vertebrate fauna*. Options Mediterranéennes - Serie Seminaires, n. **15**: 121-134.

Farina, A. (1992). *Appunti sui vertebrati dell'Appennino settentrionale e delle Alpi Apuane in rapporto alle modificazioni del paesaggio rurale.* Memorie Accademia Lunigianese Scienze "Giovanni Capellini". Vol. LX-LXI (1990-1991), 477-486.

Farina, A. (1995). *Distribution and dynamics of birds in a rural sub-Mediterranean landscape.* Agricultural landscape in Europe, Rennes 6-10 June 1993. Landscape and urban planning **31**: 269–280.

Farina, A. and Naveh, Z. (1993). *Landscape approach to regional planning: the future of the Mediterranean landscapes.* Landscape and Urban Planning, special issue, no. 24.

Feder, J. (1988). *Fractals.* Plenum, New York.

Forman, R. T. T. and Godron, M. (1986). *Landscape ecology.* Wiley and Sons, New York.

Forman, R. T. T. and Moore, P. N. (1992). *Theoretical foundations for understanding boundaries in landscape mosaics.* In: A. J. Hansen and F. di Castri (eds.), *Landscape boundaries. Consequences for biotic diversity and ecological flows.* Springer Verlag, New York, pp 236-258.

Gardner, R. H., Milne, B. T., Turner, M. G. and O'Neill, R. V. (1987). *Neutral models for the analysis of broad-scale landscape patterns.* Landscape Ecology **1**: 19-28.

Gardner, R. H., Turner, M. G., Dale, V. H. and O'Neill, R. V. (1992). *A percolation model of ecological flows.* In: A. J. Hansen and F. di Castri (eds.), *Landscape boundaries. Consequences for biotic diversity and ecological flows.* Springer-Verlag, New York, pp. 259-269.

Gefen, Y., Aharony, A. and Alexander, S. (1983). *Anomalus diffusion on percolating clusters.* Physical Rev. Lett. **50**: 77-80.

Gilpin, M. and Hanski, I. (eds.) (1991). *Metapopulation dynamics: empirical and theoretical investigations.* Academic Press, London.

Gomez-Sal, A., Alvarez, J., Munoz-Yanguas, M. A. and Rebollo, S. (1993). *Patterns of change in the agrarian landscape in an area of the Cantabrian Mountains (Spain). Assessment by transition probabilities.* In: Bunce, R. G. H., Ryszkowski, L. and Paoletti, M. G. (eds.), *Landscape Ecology and Agrosystems*, Lewis Publishers, Boca Raton, Florida. pp. 141-152.

Green, B. H. (1989). *Agricultural impacts on the rural environment.* Journal of Applied Ecology **26**: 793-802.

Gutzwiller, K. J. and Anderson, S. H. (1992). *Interception of moving organisms: influence of patch shape, size and orientation on community structure.* Landscape Ecology **6**: 293-303.

Hansen, A. J. and Di Castri, F. (1992). *Landscape boundaries.* Springer-Verlag, New York.

Hansen, A. J., Risser, P. G. and di Castri, F. (1992). *Epilogue: Biodiversity and ecological flows across ecotones.* In: Hansen, A. J. and di Castri, F.(eds.), *Landscape boundaries. Consequences for biotic diversity and ecological flows.* Springer Verlag, New York. pp. 423-438.

Hansson, L. (1991). *Dispersal and connectivity in metapopulations.* Biological Journal of Linnean Society, **42**: 89-103.

Hansson, L. (1992). *Landscape ecology of boreal forests.* Tree **7**: 299-302.

Hardt, R. A. and Forman, R. T. T. (1989). *Boundary form effects on woody colonization of reclaimed surface mines.* Ecology **70**: 1252-1260.

Harris, L. D. (1984). *The fragmented forest, island biogeography theory and the preservation of biotic diversity.* University of Chicago Press, Chicago.

Henderson, M. T., Merriam, G. and Wegner, J. (1985). *Patchy environments and species survival: chipmunks in an agricultural mosaic.* Biological Conservation **31**: 95-105.

Henein, K. and Merriam, G. (1990). *The elements of connectivity where corridor quality is variable.* Landscape Ecology **4**:157-170.

Hengeveld, R. (1990). *Dynamic biogeography.* Cambridge University Press, Cambridge.

Hobbs, R. J. and Huenneke, L. F. (1992). *Disturbance, diversity and invasion: implications for conservation.* Conservation biology **6**: 324–337.

Holling, C. S. (1992). *Cross-scale morphology, geometry and dynamics of ecosystems.* Ecological Monographs **62**: 447-502.

Hornbeck, J. W. and Swank, W. T. (1992). *Watershed ecosystem analysis as a basis for multiple-use management of eastern forests.* Ecological Applications **2**: 238-247.

Howe, R. W. (1984). *Local dynamics of birds assemblages in small forest habitat islands in Australia and North America.* Ecology **65**: 1585-1601.

Hunter, M. L. Jr (1990). *Wildlife, forests and forestry.* Prentice Hall, Engelwood Cliffs, New Jersey.

Joffre, R., Vacher, J., De Los Llanos, C. and Long, G. (1988). *The dehesa: an agrosilvopastoral system of the Mediterranean region with special reference to the Sierra Morena area of Spain.* Agroforestry Systems **6**: 71-96.

Joffre, R. and Lacaze, B. (1993). *Estimating tree density in oak savanna-like 'dehesa' of southern Spain from SPOT data.* Int. J. Remote Sensing, **14**: 685-697.

Joffre, R. and Rambal, S. (1993). *How tree cover influences the water balance of Mediterranean rangelands.* Ecology **74**: 570-582.

Johnston, C. A. and Naiman, R. J. (1987. *Boundary dynamics at the aquatic-terrestrial interface: the influence of beaver and geomorphology.* Landscape Ecology **1**: 47-58.

Kareiva, P. (1987). *Habitat fragmentation and the stability of predator-prey interactions.* Nature **326**: 229-34.

Kemp, J. C. and Barrett, G. W. (1989). *Spatial patterning: impact of uncultivated corridors on arthropod populations within soybean agrosystems.* Ecology **70**: 114-128.

Klein, B. C. (1989). *Effects of forest fragmentation on dung and carrion beetle communities in Central Amazonia.* Ecology **70**:1715-1725.

Krummel, J. R., Gardner, R. H., Sugihara, G., O'Neill, R. V. and Coleman, P. R. (1987). *Landscape patterns in a disturbed environment.* Oikos **48**: 321-324.

Leberg, P. L. (1990). *Influence of fragmentation and bottlenecks on genetic divergence of wild turkey populations.* Conservation Biology **5**: 522-530.

Lepart, J. and Debussche, M. (1992). *Human impact on landscape patterning: Mediterranean examples.* In: Hansen, A. J. and di Castri, F. (eds.), *Landscape Boundaries.* Springer-Verlag, pp. 76-106.

Levins, R. (1970). *Extinction.* In: Gerstenhaubert, M. (ed.), *Some Mathematical questions in biology. Lectures in mathematics in the life sciences.* American Mathematical Society, Providence, Rhode Island, pp. 77-107.

Lewin, R. (1989). *Sources and sinks complicate ecology.* Science **243**: 477-478.

Lovejoy, T. E., Bierregaard, R. O., Rylands, A. B., Malvom, J. R., Quintela, C. E., Harper, L. H., Brown, K. S., Powell, A. H., Powell, G. V. N., Shubart, H. O. R. and Hays, M. B. (1987). *Edge and other effects of isolation on amazon forest fragments.* In: Soulé, M. E. (ed.), *Conservation Biology. The science of scarcity and diversity.* Sinauer Associates, Sunderland, Massachusets. pp. 257-285.

Lubchenco, J., Olson, A. M., Brubaker, L. B., Carpenter, S. R., Holland, M. M., Hubbell, S. P., Levin, S. A., MacMahon, J. A., Matson, P. A., Melillo, M. M., Mooney, H. A., Peterson, C. H., Pulliam, H. R., Real, L. A., Regal, P. J. and Risser, P. G. (1991). *The sustainable biosphere iniziative: an ecological research agenda.* Ecology **72**: 371-412.

MacArthur, R. H. and Wilson, E. O. (1967). *The theory of island biogeography.* Monographs in population biology n. 1. Princeton University Press, Princeton, New Jersey.

Mandelbrot, B. B. (1977). *The fractal geometry of nature.* Freeman, New York.

Martin, T. E. (1980). *Diversity and abundance of spring migratory birds using habitat islands on the great plains.* Condor **82**: 430-439.

Martin, T. E. and Karr, J. R. (1986). *Patch utilization by migrating birds: resource oriented?* Ornis Scandinavica **17**: 165-174.

Merriam, G. and Lanoue, A. (1990). *Corridor use by small mammals: field measurement for three experimental types of Peromyscus leucopus.* Landscape Ecology **4**: 123-132.

Merriam, G., Kozakiewicz, M., Tsuchiya, E. and Hawley, K. (1989). *Barriers as boundaries for meta-populations and demes of Peromyscus leucopus in farm landscape.* Landscape Ecology **2**: 227-235.

Milne, B. T. (1988). *Measuring the fractal geometry of landscapes.* Applied Mathematics and Computation **27**: 67-79.

Milne, B. T. (1991). *Lessons from applying fractal models to landscape patterns*. In: Turner, M.G. and Gardner, R. H. (eds.), *Quantitative methods in landscape ecology*. Springer-Verlag, New York. pp. 199-235.

Milne, B. T. (1992). *Spatial aggregation and neutral models in fractal landscapes*. Am. Nat. **139**: 32-57.

Milne, B. T., Johnston, K. M. and Forman, R. T. T. (1989). *Scale-dependent proximity of wildlife habitat in a spatially-neutral Bayesian model*. Landscape Ecology **2**: 101-110.

Mladenoff, D. J., White, M. A., Pastor, J. and Crow, T. R. (1993). *Comparing spatial pattern in unaltered old-growth and disturbed forest landscapes*. Ecological Applications **3**: 294-306.

Naveh, Z. (1979). *A model of multiple-use management strategies of marginal and untillable Mediterranean upland ecosystems*. In: Cairns, J., Patil, G. P. Jr. and Waters, W.E. (eds.), *Environmental Biomonitoring Assessment, Prediction and managment*. Certain cases studies and related quantitative issues, pp. 269-286.

Naveh, Z. (1991). *Mediterranean uplands as anthropogenic perturbation-dependent systems and their dynamic conservation management*. In: Ravera, O. (ed.), *Terrestrial and aquatic ecosystems: Perturbation and recovery*. Ellis Horwood Ltd., New York, pp. 545-556.

Naveh, Z. and Lieberman, A. S. (1993). *Landscape ecology. Theory and Application*. Second editon. Springer-Verlag, New York.

Norton, B. G. and Ulanowicz, R. E. (1992). *Scale and biodiversity policy: a hierarchical approach*. Ambio **21**: 244-249.

Noss, R. F. (1983). *A regional landscape approach to maintain diversity*. BioScience **33**: 700-706.

Opdam, P. (1988). *Populations in fragmented landscape*. In: K.F. Schreiber (ed.), *Connectivity in landscape ecology*. Proceedings 2nd International seminar of the International Association for Landscape Ecology. Munstersche Geographische Arbeiten 29, Munster, pp. 75-77.

Opdam, P. (1991). *Metapopulation theory and habitat fragmentation: a review of holartic breeding bird studies*. Landscape Ecology **5**: 93-106.

Orbach, R. (1986). *Dynamics of fractal networks*. Science **231**: 814-819.

O'Neill, R. V., DeAngelis, D. L., Waide, J. B. and Allen, T. F. H. (1986). *A hierarchical concept of ecosystems*. Princeton University Press, Princeton.

Pinto Correia, T. (1993). *Threatened landscape in Alentejo, Portugal: the "montado" and other "agro-silvo-pastoral" systems*. In: Farina, A. and Naveh, Z. (eds.). *Landscape Approach to Regional Planning: the Future of the Mediterranean Landscapes*. Landscape and Urban Planning **24**: 43-48.

Plumb, G. E. and Dodd, J. L. (1993). *Foraging ecology of bison and cattle on a mixed prairie: implication for natural area management*. Ecological Applications **3**: 631-643.

Preston, F. W. (1962). *The canonical distribution of commonness and rarity (2 parts)*. Ecology **43**: 185-215; 410-432.

Pulliam, R. (1988). *Sources, sinks ,and population regulation*. Am. Nat. **132**: 652-661.

Purroy, F. J. and Rodero, M. (1986). *Wintering of wood pigeons (Columba palumbus) in the Iberian peninsula*. Proc. First Conf. Birds Wintering in the Mediterranean Region. Suppl. Ric. Biol. Selvaggina, **10**: 275-283.

Ranney, J. W., Bruner, M. C. and Levenson, J. B. (1981). *The importance of edge in the structure and dynamics of forest islands*. In: Burgess, R.L. and Sharpe, D. M. (eds.), *Forest island dynamics in man-dominated landscapes*. Springer-Verlag, New York, pp. 67-95.

Ricklefs, R. E., Naveh, Z. and Turner, R. E. (1984). *Conservation of ecological processes*. Commission on Ecology, Papers number 8, IUCN. pp. 6-16.

Rolstad, J. (1991). *Consequences of forest fragmentation for the dynamics of bird populations: conceptual issues and the evidence*. Biological Journal of Linnean Society **42**: 149-163.

Roland, J. (1993). *Large-scale forest fragmentation increases the duration of tent caterpillar outbreaks*. Oecologia **93**: 25-30.

Saunders, D., Hobbs, R. J. and Margules, C. R. (1991). *Biological consequences of ecosystem fragmentation: a review*. Cons. Biol. **5**: 18-32.

Soulé, M. E. and Wilcox, B. A. (1980). *Conservation Biology: An Evolutionary-ecological approach.* Sinauer Associates, Sunderland, Mass.

Stamp, J. A., Buechner, M. and Krishnan, V. V. (1987). *The effects of edge permeability and habitat geometry on emigration from patches of habitat.* Am. Nat. **129**: 533-552.

Stauffer, D. (1985). *Introduction of percolation theory.* Taylor and Francis, London.

Telleria, J. L. and Santos, T. (1986). *Bird wintering in Spain. A review.* Proc. First Conf. birds Wintering in the Mediterranean region. Suppl. Ric. Biol. Selvaggina, **10**: 319-338.

Turner, M. G., O'Neill, R. V., Gardner, R. H. and Milne, B. T. (1989). *Effects of changing spatial scale on the analysis of landscape pattern.* Landscape Ecology **3**: 153-162.

Vaisanen, R. A., Jarvinen, O. and Rauhala, P. (1986). *How are extensive, human-caused habitat alterations expressed on the scale of local bird populations in boreal forest?* Ornis Scandinavica **17**: 282-292.

Van Dorp, D. and Opdam, P. F. M. (1987). *Effects of patch size, isolation and regional abundance on forest bird communities.* Landscape Ecology **1**: 59-73.

Vos, W. (1993). *Recent landscape transformation in the Tuscan Apennines caused by changing land use.* In: Farina, A. and Naveh, Z. (eds.), *Landscape Approach to Regional Planning: the future of the Mediterranean Landscapes.* Landscape and Urban Planning **24**: 63-68.

Vos, W. and Stortelder A. (1992). *Vanishing Tuscan landscapes.* Pudoc Scientific Publishers, Wageningen.

Whitcomb, R. F., Robbins, C. S., Lynch, J. F., Whitcomb, B. L., Klimkiewicz, M. K., and Bystrak, D. (1980). *Effects of forest fragmentation on avifauna of eastern deciduous forest.* In: Burgess, R. L. and Sharpe, D. M. (eds.), *Forest island dynamics in man-dominated landscapes.* Springer, New York, pp. 125-205.

Wiens, J. A. (1992). *Ecological flows across landscape boundaries: a conceptual overwiev.* In: Hansen, A. J. and di Castri, F. (eds.), *Landscape boundaries. Consequences for biotic diversity and ecological flows.* Springer Verlag, New York, pp. 217-235.

Wiens, J. A. and Milne, B. T. (1989). *Scaling of "landscape" in landscape ecology, or, landscape ecology from a beetle's perspective.* Landscape Ecology **3**:87-96.

Wiens, J. A., Crawford, C. S. and Gosz, R. (1985). *Boundary dynamics: a conceptual framework for studying landscape ecosystems.* Oikos **45**: 421-427.

Wiens, J. A. , Stenseth, N. C., Van Horne, B. and Ims, R. A. (1993). *Ecological mechanisms and landscape ecology.* Oikos **66**: 369-380.

Wilcove, D. S. (1985). *Nest predation in forest tracts and the decline of migratory songbirds.* Ecology **66**: 1211-1214.

Wilcove, D. S., McLellan, C. H. and Dobson, A. P. (1986). *Habitat fragmentation in the temperate zone.* In: Soulé, M. E. (ed.), *Conservation biology. The science of scarcity and diversity.* Sinauer Associates, Sunderland, Mass. Pp. 237-256.

Almo Farina works at the Lunigiana Museum of Natural History in Aulla, Italy

Cultural Landscapes of the World

Africa and Arab States

Sacred Groves in Ghana
Boakye Amoako-Atta

Cultural Landscapes: Maraboutic Sites in Morocco
Dominique Verdugo and Jalila Kadiri Fakir

Chapter 8

Sacred Groves in Ghana

Boakye Amoako-Atta

Introduction

The Republic of Ghana lies on the gulf of Guinea on the West Coast of Africa just a few degrees north of the equator (Figure 1). Land boundaries of 2285 km, with 239 km of coastline, enclose 238,305 km² entirely in the tropics. About half of Ghana is less than 150 m above sea level; the highest elevation (880 m) is reached in a low mountain range along the eastern border.

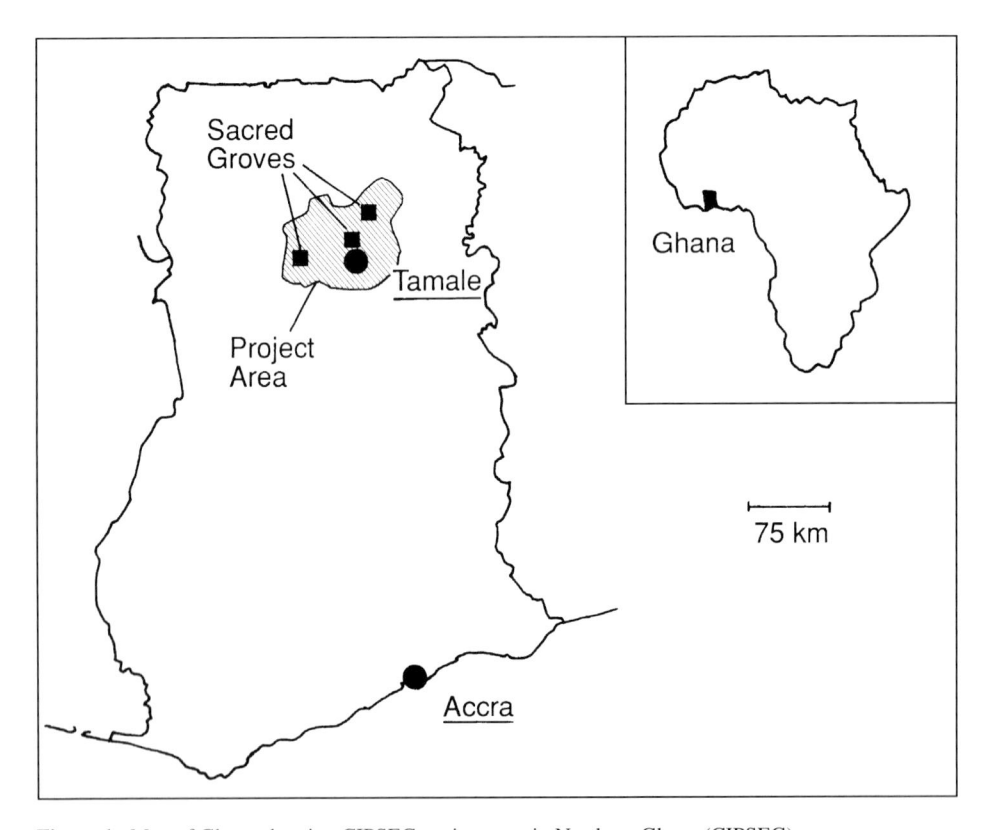

Figure 1. Map of Ghana showing CIPSEG project area in Northern Ghana (CIPSEG)

Ghana's vegetation falls into three biogeographic units (Figure 2): the Guinea-Congolian in the South West, the Sudanian in the North; and the Guinea-Congolian/Sudanian Regional Transition in the centre and South East of the country. A total of about 3600 species occur, of which 43 are thought to be endemic (IUCN 1990). The greatest diversity is found in the forests of the South West. Most of the original vegetation has been considerably modified, degraded or removed. Today only 20 000 - 25 000 km² of closed

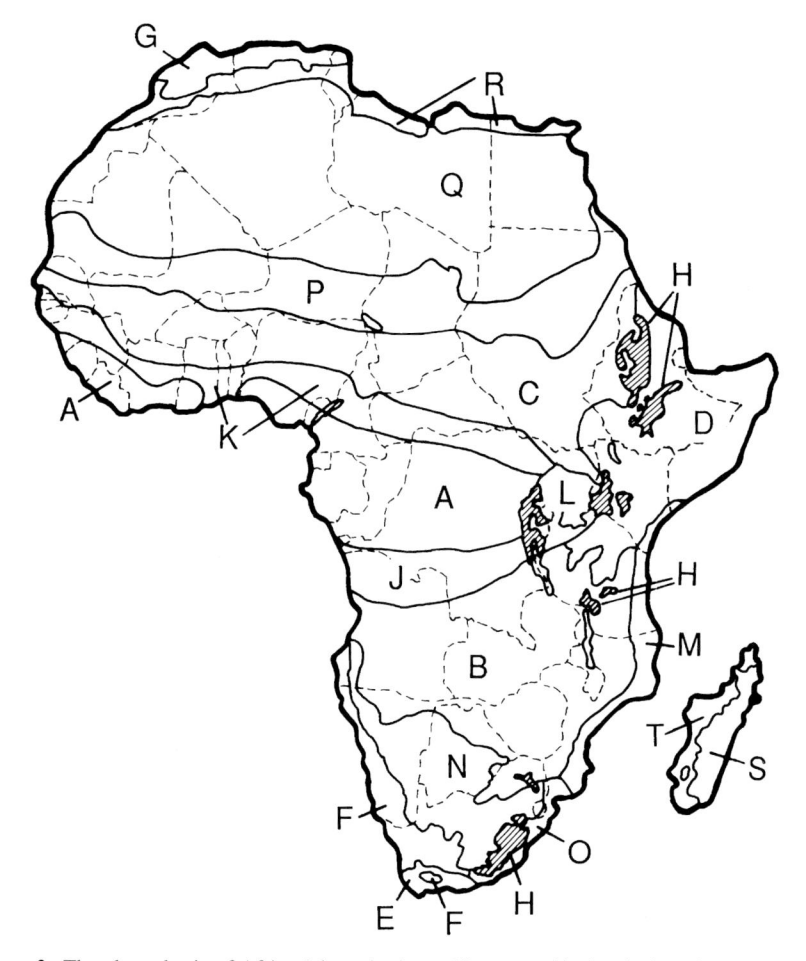

Figure 2. The phytochoria of Africa (phytochoria are biogeographical units based on plant distribution) (Ref. IUCN 1990) Map of biogeographic units of Africa (from White, 1983). A Guinea-Congolian regional centre of endemism, B Zambezian regional centre of endemism, C Sudanian regional centre of endemism, D Somalia-Masai regional centre of endemism, E Capre regional centre of endemism, F Karoo-Namib regional centre of endemism, G Mediterranean regional centre of endemism, H Afromotane archipelago-like region of extreme floristic impoverishment, I Afroalpine archipelago-like regional centre of endemism, J Guinea-Congolial/Zambezian regional transition zone, K Guinea-Congolial/Sudanian regional transition zone, L Lake Victoria regional mosaic, M Zanzibar-Inhambane regional mosaic, N Kalahari-Highveld regional transition zone, O Tongaland-Pondoland regional mosaic, P Sahel regional transition zone, Q Sahara regional transition zone, R Mediterranean/Sahara regional transition zone, S East Malagasi regional centre of endemism, T West Malagasi regional centre of endemism, .

forest representing 24 - 25 percent of the forest zone remain (Government of Ghana 1990). However, small pockets of residual closed-canopy forests near human settlements are scattered throughout Ghana, many of which are classified as "sacred" or fetish groves, preserved for local socio-cultural, and often religious purposes. These groves could play a greater role if accorded definitive legal and universal protection as standing blocks of vegetation, so as to enhance their socio-cultural values and bring out their full ecological potential. Such protection would constitute recognition of the valuable initiatives of local communities and traditional elders in preserving these groves.

Tackling degradation of Ghana's savanna ecosystems

The Co-operative Integrated Project on Savanna Ecosystems in Ghana (CIPSEG) was launched in January 1993 by UNESCO, funded by the Federal Republic of Germany, to tackle degradation and rehabilitation of Ghana's savannas. Environmental and resource degradation in the savannas has had increasingly distressing socio-economic consequences for the local peoples since the early decades of the present century. Loss of surface cover and soil became evident after the 1930s (Lynn 1937, Agyepong 1993). There was considerable effort in the form of land planning and erosion control between the Second World War and 1960 (Biles 1954, Agyepong 1993). An integrated approach to the problem was lacking from the 1960s until the establishment of the Northern Regional Rural Integrated Programme (NORRIP) by the Government of Ghana in the early 1980s. An inter-disciplinary research programme co-ordinated and funded by the USAID did not lead to practical work on the ground. The NORRIP is continuing to work along with other governmental programmes that have been established more recently, including the Smallholder Rehabilitation Project, and the Land Resources Management Project of the Environmental Protection Council. Environmental issues continue to dominate almost all development activities in the northern savanna area of Ghana. It is becoming generally accepted that the biophysical and the socio-economic impact of previous efforts to reverse the degradation of resources and the environment in the savannas has been less than desirable. The devastating effects of drought during 1982-1983 reawaken fears in the minds of people about possible desert encroachment on the savannas. The CIPSEG project was envisaged to demonstrate cohesive values and an intermix of science, education and culture for sustainable development within the northern Ghana Guinea Savanna. It is based on sacred groves - key elements in both the forest and savanna ecosystems in Ghana, which offer reference points for environmental and ecosystem rehabilitation. Shifting cultivation, indiscriminate bush burning and intense overgrazing of domestic animals and livestock have interacted to transform Ghana into an almost man-made environment. However, scattered in the sea of these fast degrading natural forests and vegetation are patches of relict climax vegetation that have survived yearly threats of fire and human disturbance, primarily thanks to the traditional reverence and protection accorded these "fetish" or sacred groves by the local people. The sacred groves, which have been jealously protected and preserved through religious and cultural beliefs and taboos, are under threat from modernisation and urbanisation, with emerging ecological implications for biodiversity. A sites for its programme activities, the CIPSEG has selected three separate groves within a maze of other cluster sacred groves in the Northern Ghana Guinea Savanna ecosystem.

Origins and distribution of sacred groves in Ghana

The origins of sacred groves are rooted in historical conjecture. Most sacred groves take their origin from the towns and villages where they are located. They are usually as old as these towns and villages, and as the custodians or chiefs of these towns and villages recount, the sacred groves are inextricably linked to their ancestors. Successive generations of these villagers have maintained and protected these groves up to the present generation as a moral and traditional duty. Most sacred groves epitomise the soul or symbol of the traditional source of strength and protection of the people and are considered the habitations of the gods or the final resting places of the chiefs, traditional rulers, custodians of the groves, or heroes of the towns and people. Within Ghana's various tribal settings, different generalised names distinguish kinds of grove. Two categories are evident among the Akan. The first is the burial ground or ancestral resting place commonly referred in the Akan language as Nsamanpom. The Nsamanpom is not a burial ground or cemetery in the English sense of the word, but is a burial ground exclusively reserved to the royal family, direct descendants of the royal family, custodians of the groves or local heroes. These Nsamanpom are usually distant from the local cemetery and almost always located in thick virgin forests or completely closed vegetation of unknown history. The Nsamanpom is completely forbidden to all people who do not qualify to be associated with it.

The second category is the fetish grove, or Abosompom in the Akan language, signifying the habitation of the gods. The Abosompom could be a physical object such as a stone, piece of rock, a tree, an animal, a river, lake, waterfall, wooden carving on a mount etc. or thick forest vegetation or closed canopy, which is usually forbidden to intruders or trespassers.

These two categories of groves are common to almost all tribal groupings in modern Ghana: the major tribes such as the Akans (comprising the Ashantis, the Akims, the Akwapims and the Fantis), the Ewes, the Ga/Adangbe people and most other tribes from the rest of the country including the Dagombas, the Mamprusi, the Frafras, Gonjas, Sissala, have groves which fall in line with either one or both of the two broad categories described. Banmuhene, in the Akan language, means the custodian or the person in charge of the Nsamanpom, who is always an indegene and a member of the royal family qualified for the title. A similar title, Tindana, exists in the Dagbani language, and so on. The groves can be distinguished or described with ease by almost all traditional rulers or elders of associated towns and villages.

The existence of local nomenclature and visual interpretation of these groves among different tribes is evidence that sacred groves are inextricably linked with the fabric of almost all Ghanaian societies.

Sacred groves in Ghana are scattered and varied: over 1400 sacred groves have been identified already (Tuffour et al. 1992). Some communities also recognise sea or river gods and others protect coastal lagoons or stream headwaters by restricting water use and activities such as fishing. Others believe certain wildlife species are gods or representatives of gods; the people protect these animals' habitats and do not hunt them. Detailed accounts of the origin of sacred groves have been given for the Malshegu sacred grove in the Northern Savanna region of Ghana (Dorm-Adzobu et al. 1991), and the Boabeng-Fiema grove in the Ashanti region of Ghana (Tuffuor et al. 1991).

Beliefs and attitudes of people to the groves

Most traditionalists explain and believe that sacred groves epitomise the souls and spirits of the communities in which they are located. These communities believe and trust in the origins, myths and legends of the sacred groves. Most people believe that the sacred groves are habitat for the physical and spiritual intermediaries between them, their gods and the creator, and to them they are links between the dead and the living. In the minds of most traditionalists therefore, the sacred groves serve as paths to the gods for society. The grove is looked upon as an oracle to be consulted and as a kind guardian that offers protection, blessings and brings good tidings to society. Accordingly, society makes many gestures of appreciation: depending on the tribe, location or associated local belief, there are rituals, expressions of thanksgiving or sacrifices, or cultural manifestations addressed to the grove by the community. For example, the people of Akwapim celebrate the Odehuro or yam festival and the Odwira festival every year. At such times the fetish priest or priestess visits the groves to perform the appropriate rituals in appreciation of the gods. All descendants and people from those places are expected to come home to join in the festivities which display the culture of the people at its best. Similarly, the Akims celebrate the Ohum festival (yam festival), when the groves are consulted, visited and sacrifices made. The Ga people make similar offerings and sacrifices to their groves during their Homowo festival. The Dagombas have two major festivals - the fire festival and the Damba festival - at which times their groves are also visited and sacrifices made. These festivals are great moments of joy and festivity for which the community puts in a great deal of preparation and cultural display. After all, these festivals are a manifestation of the abundant blessings and prosperities that have come to the community, which the people associate with their kind guardian, the sacred grove.

Beliefs about the powers of the sacred groves

Most people have associated certain miracles, powers and expectations with their respective groves, to the extent that even in modern times most attitudes and behaviour of people are modulated by the powers, miracles or supernatural forces from these sacred groves. For example, in an area about five km west of Tamale is a highly revered and most feared sacred grove which is considered to house the god Kpalevorgu. This grove is at Kumbuyili/Katariga village and is referred to in other writings (Dorm-Adzobu et al. 1990) as the Malshegu Sacred Grove. People from this area, and the Dagbani people in general, believe that famine or war cannot bring the inhabitants to the point of death or destruction because of the absolute protection given by their Kpalevorgu god located in the Malshegu sacred grove. The traditionalists and the community believe that the sacred grove protects them from drought, bad harvest, plagues, and other calamities. Bad people who may otherwise bring discord are silenced by the Kpalevorgu god in the grove.

Explanations given by almost all traditionalists and custodians of these groves suggest that these attributes are common to all groves. However, some groves in particular have been associated with dramatic displays of powers or forces. The Pong Tamale sacred grove, located about 20 km north of Tamale is well known as the god of lightning and thunder, and also a rain god. It is especially famed as the god who exposes evil persons: it is generally believed that if the sacred grove is invoked or consulted to expose a person who may have committed an unsolved crime such as theft, the sacred grove will immediately expose the culprit by striking him down by lightning and concurrently exposing the hidden goods by striking the place where those goods have been kept (a phenomenon that people from the area willingly and easily attest to). Many demonstrations of such oracles have intimidated people in that area to the extent that such crimes are virtually non-existent. The Zinyebo grove at Tanpion in the northern region is associated with fertility and has enabled many barren women to have children. Many stories are told by people in praise of their grove. In the mid 1980s there was an acute shortage of water at Kangbagu where a dam was located and, for the first time, it dried up. The god of the sacred grove in Kangbagu was consulted, sheep and fowls were sacrificed to the god Bugli Chantin so as to give the people water and to the amazement of the people spring water started filling their dam within a few days without any visible rains falling.

Beliefs about the grove as a source of medicine

A basic tenet of belief of most traditionalists is that the role of custodian of a grove is not an automatic right, nor a role that is competed for, but an annointed position directed and chosen by the spirits through revelation to the elders after they consult the grove on the death of the former custodian, who in most cases is a fetish priest or priestess. In other words the spirits and the gods decide who is acceptable as custodian and human intermediary between the groves and the community. The rules and regulations binding the choice of a new custodian are irreversible and not questioned.

These chosen people then also become the custodians of the herbs and plants of medicinal value that remain in abundance in these sacred groves. These groves contain an immense volume of plants of traditional medicinal value because cutting of trees, bush burning and trespassing in the groves are strictly prohibited, as are farming activities and hunting of any sort. Plants of medicinal value that are commonly known to be in most of these groves are used to treat fever of varied origins, gonorrhoea, madness, stroke, diabetes, piles, bone fracture, epilepsy, infertility, impotence, frigidity in women, associated menstrual pains, bleeding, snake bites, lactation in nursing mothers with no milk and other problems. Extremely poisonous plants used to kill also abound in such groves. The potency of some plants is so horrifying that a small portion causes instant death. The herbalists or traditional healers are in close consultation with the custodian or fetish priest or priestess of the groves and often enjoy the full recognition and approbation of the community as special people close to the custodians of the grove.

Traditional conservation strategies

The role played by the sacred groves in the socio-economic and cultural lives of many rural folks in Ghana has been possible because of the collective efforts of people to protect these groves. Over 80 per cent of the sacred groves (Tuffour et al. 1992) in Ghana serve as watersheds or catchment areas that protect drinking sources and provide readily available essential herbs of medicinal importance. Almost all existing sacred groves in Ghana have been, and continue to be protected by taboos, traditional beliefs and some local customs. These traditional regulatory measures or taboos derive their basis from religious beliefs or certain events that occurred in the historical past and have been passed on from generation to generation through oral recollection. Because of the reverence people attach to the sacred groves, free passage through the groves tends to be restricted to the keeper or custodian only as and when necessary. The mystery that people associate with the groves further instils fear into them and even makes people shiver or prevents them from talking freely about these groves for the fear that any derogatory remarks or gestures could invoke punishment from the gods. People's general perception of the groves therefore limits encroachment or unwarranted exploitation of resources within the groves. Investigations into the perception of people in the West Dagomba District of their existing groves clearly suggest that people regard the groves as a source of supernatural forces to the extent that both animate and inanimate objects, trees and all plants in the groves possess spiritual forces which should not be tampered with. This conviction is so absolute in the minds of most traditionalists that they consider it an abomination to harm the trees or living things in the groves, and such unwarranted destruction could result in self-destruction, death or insanity. The unlimited powers vested in the hands of the custodians and elders responsible for the grove make it common knowledge that no individual can enter or move within the groves without the permission of the custodians, and even then, entry must be under proper escort of the custodian or his designated representative. Such rigid regulatory measures are of immense advantage for conserving the perimeter of the groves. Due to the religious implications of the groves, the custodians are customarily obliged to perform some rituals annually to pacify and thank the groves for blessings received by the community.

Complementary community actions are associated with these annual rituals which also tend to protect the groves. During such periods the custodians lead the community to clean the inside perimeter of the groves and also make fire bands (breaks) by weeding a circular

---

Box 1. Regulations related to the Malshegu sacred grove

Actions that are not permitted in and around the groves

- No drumming or whistling on approaching the grove
- No person is allowed entry into the grove on Fridays
- No person is permitted to kill crocodile, alligator or python in and around the grove and no indigene is allowed to eat any of these reptiles
- No entrance to the grove without the prior knowledge or consent of the custodian (in this case the fetish priestess or her designated representative)
- No person is allowed to use ebony as fuelwood for fire
- No cutting of trees from the grove
- Strangers access to and freedom of action in and around the groves is limited and subject to the directives of the custodians
- The fetish priestess as custodian of the grove is not allowed to marry during her reign, neither is she allowed to leave the confines of her room after midnight
- No person is allowed to enter the room of the fetish priestess wearing sandals, shoes, hats of any kind, or without an escort

Actions that are permitted or are mandatory in and around the grove

- Cleaning the inside and immediate surroundings of the grove by the community under the supervision of the custodians is allowed on two occasions per year
- Sacrifices and rituals must be made twice a year
- Meat of animals, apart from crocodiles, alligators, pythons (which are the symbols of the gods), can be eaten by the people from the area

strip of land surrounding the groves. The myth surrounding this annual community-initiated action is that the spirits and gods in the grove must be protected from fire since the gods are not to be seen naked (burning of vegetation would expose the gods). Also cutting of trees, bush burning of any sort close to the outskirts of the groves, hunting of any sort for animals or allowing grazing domestic animals to stray into the groves is strictly forbidden and no person is allowed to farm either inside or close to the sacred groves. People are also forbidden to ease themselves or defile the grove by dumping excreta or garbage on the perimeter of the groves or its immediate surroundings. These environmentally friendly actions are collectively undertaken by the community, and offenders are immediately apprehended and handed to the custodian with often horrible punitive consequences. A more detailed summary of the traditional conservation strategies pursued by the people of Kumbuyili/Katariga towards the protection of the Malshegu sacred grove are summarised in Box 1.

Changing perceptions and management of sacred groves in Ghana

The first step towards any meaningful management of a resource is the recognition and appreciation of its importance and value - the communities which own and depend on them regard the sacred groves as important components of their heritage. An invisible resource cannot be managed; for proper management of such resources on the national level, it is crucial to know their location and for this the comprehensive, although not exhaustive, listing of 1453 sacred groves (Tuffour et al. 1992) is a valuable source of information.

The majority of these sacred groves have been governed by taboos which differ from grove to grove and region to region. These taboos draw their strength from religious beliefs or certain events which took place in the past and which had an impact on the lives of the people in the locality. These taboos range from phenomena that can easily be explained to phenomena that are more difficult to explain. A study of the taboos and practices surrounding sacred groves, however, lends great credit to the conservationist instincts of the rural forefathers. This has been manifested in the siting of certain groves in ecologically sensitive areas and in utilization practices which are based on sustained yield principles. Time and supposed social enlightenment seem to inflict injury on the apparently simple beliefs that have protected the groves, river beds and other ecologically sensitive areas which were hitherto under traditional conservation. The beliefs that were so binding on the people seem to be eroding in the minds of the youth in particular and rural folks in general, due to trial breaking of the taboos with no immediate consequences, and the impact of education and missionary work by Christianity, Islam etc. that continues to make a laughing stock of such taboos. A case in point is the Tafi-Atome sacred grove; it was once an abomination to see women enter the grove but it is now trespassed with impunity by women to the extent that women have established their farms in the best locations of the groves. Similarly, the highly acclaimed Boabeng-Fiema Monkey sanctuary (Tuffuor et al. 1991) rich in monkeys in the late 1960s became a subject of great religious conflict and controversy when in the early 70s, a religious sect emerged which regarded all the monkeys in the sanctuary as source of evil and embarked on an annihilation crusade of the monkeys. The timely intervention of government through a legal Conservation Act eventually preserved the sanctity of the grove, which is now offering ecotourism. Such wanton destruction has immense negative implications for biodiversity conservation and more significantly the socio-cultural beliefs and heritage of communities. The immense values of this biodiversity are as yet untapped, especially so in most African countries where resources are scant and expertise woefully inadequate for such a task.

We need to explore biodiversity in greater depth in order to understand its relationship to ecosystem processes (National Research Council 1980, Solbrig 1991). To assess the role of an organism at the ecosystem level and the significance of biodiversity in the global ecosystem requires a better understanding of its biological features, and the traditional values society places on them. There are many kinds of organisms that grow in unusual, extreme and marginal habitats, whose properties might be of extraordinary interest in relation to efforts to improve the human future. Because of the rapid destruction of most of the relevant biological communities, steps to realise these opportunities must be taken urgently. It is a matter of urgency to record the knowledge of indigenous peoples or other rural peoples living in close contact with these natural communities (particularly traditional elders and custodians). Such knowledge must be viewed as a precious global asset that is rapidly vanishing across Africa, and in Ghana in particular.

Existing legal framework for the protection of locally managed natural resources in Ghana

More than most African and other governments, Ghana has made good progress in understanding the importance of traditional religious practices in natural resource management and in developing national and sub-national policy, legislation, and appropriate actions to facilitate these local efforts. The government's long history of respecting and recognizing traditional socio-cultural aspects and needs recently took a new turn when it outlined specific strategies and laws for promoting cultural traditions that help safeguard the environment, such as sacred groves. Governments of other sub-Saharan African countries and of several Asian nations, as well as the development assistance community should carefully consider Ghana's policies and actions. Early on, the 1948 National Forestry Policy in Ghana (revised in 1989-1990) recognized the socio-cultural and religious importance of sacred groves. Within Forest Reserves, these groves remain accessible to the local people, enabling them to continue practising their traditional religion. Even though no systematic attempt has been made to protect all sacred groves in the forest estate, the approximately 280 Forest Reserves in Ghana constitute one of the most extensive reserve systems in sub-Saharan Africa and encompass numerous sacred groves. The new Forest Policy provides for the same opportunities, recognises the role of trees in land use outside the gazetted permanent forest estates and ensures that forest resources are not used until provision is made for their replacement (Asibey 1989).

In 1963-64, the government expressed concern for the sacred fetishes, shrines, groves, and burial sites in the area slated for flooding by the Volta Dam. To avert local outcry, to enable a peaceful evacuation of the area, and to appease the gods and ancestors, the government ensured in many cases that all necessary libations and sacrifices were performed (often by paying for them). Some fetishes were relocated, usually in government vehicles (including the helicopter of then President Kwame

Nkrumah), and new sanctuaries established. In 1988, the government began developing a National Environmental Action Plan (NEAP) designed to "define a set of policy actions, related investments, and institutional strengthening activities to make Ghana's development strategy more environmentally sustainable" (Government of Ghana 1990). The NEAP preparation included input from the private sector and various local and international NGOs. It also established a process for involving rural resource users in decentralized development planning and implementation. The NEAP reinforces public statements that socio-cultural values and religious practices are indispensable elements of the institutional arrangements for managing the environment, and that environmental planning and projects must recognize the role of such traditional systems and institutions. The plan specifically calls for the promotion of those aspects of indigenous culture that promote conservation and enhancement of the environment, including sacred groves. A law currently under discussion recognizes the environmental, cultural, and scientific role of groves and other sacred sites and, if approved, will authorize traditional authorities to proclaim areas sacred and set the conditions for their protection. The NEAP also proposes a national survey of the unreserved forests in Ghana to examine the number, size, forest cover, and condition of sacred groves in Ghana. Currently, no reliable figures are available for forest cover outside the protected areas in Ghana. Estimates range from 2500 to 7500 km^2. It is known, however, that sacred groves are among the few areas outside Forest Parks and Reserves where primary forest can be found, and most of the remaining forest of the Southern Marginal type in Ghana lies within sacred grove boundaries (Garbrah 1989). In general, the contributions of traditional religious beliefs and practices, especially at the local level, are neither well known nor fully recognized by governments or the development assistance community, and the implications for policy and programming are not well understood or implemented. Few national donor-sponsored Environmental Action Plans, Tropical Forestry Action Plans, Conservation Strategies, or equivalent country-level planning exercises specifically mention sacred groves or develop policy or programme actions for improved protection (Robert Winterbottom, pers. comm. 1990). In sum, Ghana's efforts in recognizing religious practices as a protective force for maintaining natural resources suggest that, with concrete action to back this legal recognition, sacred natural areas may stay intact for a long time to come. Other governments can learn from Ghana's experience.

The role in development of savanna ecosystems and outstanding sacred groves in northern Ghana

Most of my field work and travels are in the company of various specialists. Some are scientists, others engineers, development planners, environmentalists, industrialists and economists. After a days work, we reflect on and discuss our various observations. Sometimes I am not sure that we visited the same place. I may recount the variety and composition of plant and animal species and the mix of ecological features. A timber concessionist however, thinks and observes in terms of the yield in board feet of lumber and, by the end of the day, he possesses a reliable inventory of the area's economic potential for logging. A hydrologist, who is expert at diagnosing the health of the soil, will examine streams and swift cloudy water signalling excess erosion and provide a clue to the misuse of the land and the waters. An engineer will look through the soil and trees as if using x-ray. He wants to build roads and dams. He will need to know the area's geological underpinnings. The geologist will also look downwards searching for evidence of various kinds of hidden treasure. We all see the same environment through different eyes. One landscape can contain dozens of different resources. And we employ experts to help us uncover these natural qualities that we turn to our advantage.

Beyond treasure hunting, we can find wealth in other ways, but it usually takes a person with skill and vision to teach the proverbial "old dog" new tricks, especially when it comes to developing new resources and making more profit from the old ones. To understand the resource base of our sacred groves, we need to see some unexpected dimensions of the word "resources". Although I am not an economist nor an industrialist, I would like to share with you a few exciting insights into resources.

Ghana has some old tricks - gold, cocoa and timber. But nearly all our traditional resources can earn for us in new forms and applications. Ghana has an abundance of untapped, neglected and often unrecognised resources that are being destroyed through misguided actions. An immense number of indigenous plants of medicinal and other values are currently marginalized, and their use restricted locally to the few remaining traditionalists. The pattern for Ghana's economic development was largely made in colonial times. Our economy has suffered much through dependence on one commodity - cocoa. Ghana needs new resource uses and science and technology to help build appropriate economic diversity. For this reason, the proper formulation of wise resource policies has great significance for the future of the nation. For developing countries, especially those with single-commodity economies and a history of careless exploitation, a few straightforward guidelines are recommended. Our first rule-of-thumb for wise resource use is embodied in the phrase "conservation for production". It simply means the need not to destroy the natural patrimony for the sake of temporary gain. Resource diversity - a wise mix of natural and man-made resources, can in itself be a major resource. Diversity signifies stability, particularly when major commodities lose their market value. In a country with meagre resources, an effective conservation policy may mean the difference between down-and-out poverty and the possession of enough resources to provide a foundation for future development. In Ghana, which has a slight head start on its neighbours, wise management of scarce resources can mean maximization of both profits and potential.

The world market for plant essences and extracts, for flavours, perfumes and medicine might be a new source of value for the potential products of species conserved in Ghana's sacred groves. Herein lies an opportunity for the proper recognition and consideration of certain sacred groves, with their tremendous associated traditional knowledge, cultural values and dimensions as ecological reminders of our past heritage, and a stimulus for the development of ethnobotanical expertise that could that could trigger the secret to some life saving tonic.

The sacred groves as relicts of climax vegetation of Ghana's savanna

The UNESCO-CIPSEG project combines the unique attributes of science, education and culture to understand ecosystem functioning in a stressed savanna ecosystem, using the sacred groves as reminders of the climax vegetation of such savannas in a human-centred, culturally sensitive project. Three separate sacred groves have been selected for study and rehabilitation of the surrounding savanna: 1) The Malshegu sacred grove, between Gurugu and Malshegu, about five km west of Tamale (West Dagomba/Tamale district); 2) The Yiworgu grove on the northern outskirts of Yiworgu village about four km from Savelugu (Savelugu/Nanton district); 3) The Tali grove which lies between Tali village and Jaguriyilis about 30 km south-west of Tamale (Tolon/Kumbungu district).

Prevailing climatic conditions provide important parameters for understanding several aspects of existing and proposed resource use within the wider spatial setting of the CIPSEG study area. Northern Ghana as a whole belongs to the Guinea Savanna within the broad Tropical Continental or interior savanna climatic zone of Ghana (Dickson and Benneh 1988). It may be classified as the transition zone between semi-arid and sub-humid zones. Mean monthly temperatures vary from 36°C in March to about 27°C in August. The rainfall is determined by the movement of the Inter-Tropical (ITC) belt and is derived entirely from monsoon air masses. The pattern is characterised by seasonality, inconsistent intra-seasonal distribution and variability from year to year. These characteristics appear to be limiting factors in maintaining plant growth as the annual rainfall is inadequate to support sustained growth. A characteristic feature of the climate is the large variation in the rainfall totals from year to year. Rainfall intensities up to 300 mm an hour occur causing severe erosion of unprotected soils.

The original vegetation in the Northern Region consisted of savanna woodland typical of the forest-savanna transition zone with almost closed canopy attaining a height of about 18 m and varying both in height and density according to site (Rose-Innes 1964). It also had a ground cover of perennial mid or tall grass with forbs. The woody elements are generally fire-resistant, deciduous and broad leaved.

The sacred groves are a rich source of plant biodiversity. The continued availability of such biological resources contributes to the socio-cultural welfare of the people and their development. However, the sacred groves are slowly becoming subjected to environmental stress. Part of the CIPSEG project activities since May/June 1993 has been documenting ethnobotanical data and transcribing Dagbani plant names. Gathering information on the use, distribution and value of plant resources has continued in the three project districts (1993-1994). This is vital to a better understanding of how the local people perceive, use and manage their biological resources which sustain the very fabric of their lives through their dependence on such plant resources to meet needs for medicine, food, energy and many others.

The activities have centred on joint participation by scientists and resource people from CIPSEG, the local communities including the custodians and traditional elders all under the coordinating framework of CIPSEG. The collectors are directly supervised by naturalists and technicians from the Botany Department of the University of Ghana and are assisted by the traditional elders and custodians who provide information about the Dagbani classification and traditional uses of the plants. Close-up photography is made of the plants of potential value and/or scientific interest focussing on distinguishing features and characteristics. The first output has been the compilation and preparation of a plant pictorial key and database consisting of the following:

- An inventory of all plant species within and outside of the sacred groves.
- A discussion of traditional knowledge of the plants including the correspondence of traditional categories to scientific species.

- Definition of traditional conservation practices and suggestions for management guidelines towards the conservation of useful indigenous species inside and outside existing groves.

In depth biological research activity has been progressing in all the project sites since May/June 1993, undertaken by resource scientists from the University of Ghana (Botany Department and Department of Geography and Resource Development), the University of Science and Technology (Institute of Renewable Natural Resources), the Forest Research Institute of Ghana and the National Cultural Centre of the Northern Region under the supervision and coordination of the CIPSEG. A variety of methods has been applied in ethnobotanical, ecological and ecophysiological investigations of woody and non-woody plants, including field surveys, line transects (210 m at 5 m intervals), and marking out eighty-four 1 x 1 m^2 quadrats placed at 5 m intervals above the transect on alternate sides and seven permanent quadrats each measuring 25 x 25 m^2. Permanent sampling plots have been randomly placed in stressed areas adjacent to the targeted sacred groves and different plant species in each plot tagged for growth performance and habit monitoring. Seeds of most of the ethnobotanically important species have been collected for germination and biological studies.

In the biological diversity assessment, a total of 220 species belonging to 69 angiosperm plant families were encountered in the study sites. One hundred and sixty-nine of these species representing 55 families belonged to class Dicotyledonae and the remaining 51 species representing 14 families belonged to the class Monocotyledonae.

The families Caesalpiniaceae, Combretaceae, Malvaceae, Mimosaceae, Papilionaceae, Rubiaceae and Tiliaceae (Dicotyledonae) and families Araceae and Graminae (Monocotyledonae) were highly represented.

The grove at Tali showed the highest species diversity of 183 followed by Malshegu (121) and Yiworgu (108). Therophyte life form was predominant representing over 50 percent of the entire life form spectrum in the sites. Shade-loving herbaceous species such as *Ageratum conysoides*, *Amorphophalus dracontioides*, *Biophytum petersianum*, *Commelina africana*, *Justicia flava*, *Leucas martinicensis*, *Physalis angulata*, *Synedrella nodiflora*, *Triumfetta rhomboidea* and *Wissadula amplissima* were quite prominent within the core of the groves.

The following species were ubiquitous, found both within and outside the core of the groves: *Abutilon mauritianum*, *Allophylus africanus*, *Asparagus africanus*, *Borreria radiata*, *Cassia mimosoides*, *Cassia obtusifolia*, *Curculigo pilosa*, *Desmodium ramosissimum*, *Feretia apadantherea*, *Hyptis suaveolens* and *Hoslundia*.

While *Anogeissus leiocarpus* dominated the core of Malshegu grove, and *Azadirachta indica* dominated the core of Yiworgu grove, no single woody species completely showed dominance within the core of the Tali grove. Outside the core of the groves, no single woody species dominated any of the three sites.

In the ethnobotanical studies, plants from the three groves fall into 14 out of the 18 categories of medicinal uses given in the international classification of Health Problems in Primary Care. The most prominent medicinal categories represented were Digestive, Genito-Urinary, Pregnancy, Childbirth and Peuriperum, and Signs, Symptoms and Ill defined conditions. Eight non-medicinal use categories were also assembled including food for both humans and animals, domestic energy source, crafts, rafters etc. and some unusual usage in weather forecasts or prediction.

The array of plant families so far identified, together with the unfolding ethnobotanical findings, show the Tali and Malshegu sacred groves to be landscapes of immense natural and cultural value, particularly given the rapid degradation of the Sudania regional centre of endemism and the Guinea Congolia/Sudania regional transition zone. These are representatives of continuing cultural landscapes which retain an active social role in contemporary Ghanaian society, inextricably linked with the traditional way of life. The fact that the groves exhibit the biological character of this biogeographic zone which is hard to find anywhere else, and remain a complete contrasting ecosystem in the midst of fast degrading savanna, is a reminder of the continuing interaction of human life with its environment and the cultural bonds that link our present with the past.

Two sacred groves in Ghana as cultural landscapes of outstanding universal value

Of the over 1500 sacred groves scattered over Ghana, two within the northern Ghana savanna zones which have been and are still under critical study stand out as remarkable natural and cultural landscapes, epitomising the cultural values and beliefs of the Dagbani peoples of Ghana. These are (1) the Malshegu Sacred Grove, which houses the traditional "Kpalevorgu" god of the people in the Malshegu enclave (comprising five cluster villages) and (2) the Tali Sacred Grove which houses the god called "Jaagbo" which has the leopard as its symbol.

According to Dorm-Adzobu et al. (1991), the Malshegu sacred grove has been protected and managed by the villagers for nearly three centuries. Entrance into the grove and fetish lands is only permitted during biannual rituals honoring Kpalevorgu god. Only the Kpalna and his aids have regular access to the grove and fetish lands and regularly visit the grove to pay respects to the Kpalevorgu god on the community's behalf. The priest also routinely collects traditional medicinal plants as needed for the community from the grove. Twice each year, the Kpalna, aided by the village chief and other local leaders, organizes a grand durbar and leads the community in prayer and in various rituals in honour of the Kpalevorgu. These religious festivals mark the beginning (May) and the end (September) of the agricultural season and give thanks to the Kpalevorgu god for all the good tidings received by the community during the year. At the conclusion of the ceremonies marking the end of the farming season, a three metre wide firebelt is cleared around the grove and fetish lands by the young people from the participating communities under the direction of the Kpalna to protect the grove from bush fires. These rituals are rigidly obeyed since there is strong belief that failure to comply will result in a bad omen for the community. There are stories of people (including an American) who, despite warnings from the villagers, violated the sanctity of the god and established residency in the fetish lands. They soon fell ill, went insane and eventually lost their lives (Dorm-Adzobu et al. 1991).

The Tali sacred grove which lies south west of Tamale (about 30 km away) is a remarkable piece of climax vegetation that is imposing, a real forest in a savanna setting. The forest has woody trees to the height of over 18 metres, completely closed, with very thick lianas gracefully necklacing the canopy and meandering around the trunks of the trees. The waters of a creek flow through the ribs of the grove. The thickly closed vegetation covers a over 25 km^2 and has survived the test of time without showing any visible beatings or humiliation from the local people. This grove and its surroundings are endowed with a remarkable array of species that are a true representation of the Sudanian regional centre of endemism. A complex of traditional regulatory mechanisms joins five village communities to offer the custodial leadership and guidance of the Jaagbo god and the sacred grove. The Tindana (custodian) position rotates from village to village. This is the only sacred grove of blessed memory in Ghana that has the custodial succession rotating through five different villages. The Tolon Na or the paramount chief of the Tolon people, a dominant group of northerners in the Tolon Kumbungu District, remains the supreme ruler and chief in whose hand the large expanse of the Tali fetish land is held. Although detailed ecological studies are progressing in the Tali grove, base line survey output and focus group interviews affirm the abundance of a complex array of fauna, with visible signs of crocodiles, pythons, many reptiles, monkeys and many wild birds. Abundant evidence of faecal pellets and bird droppings in the centre of the grove, which is so dense as to be a really frightening sight, attest to the ecological complexity of the Tali grove which is a lost drop of thick forest in a vast plain of degraded savanna. The people in the Tali enclave revere their grove and are extremely tight-lipped about even mentioning the name of the grove or the inhabiting Jaagbo god. Though the grove still remains the largest single stretch of climax vegetation to be encountered anywhere in the three districts of Tolon/Kumbungu, Savelegul/Nanton and West Dagomba/Tamale, two factors have reduced its extent. A road has been constructed through the southern edge of the grove, and a reservoir dam has been constructed about two km from the northern edge of the grove.

This is the first time in the history of the grove (which is said to be as old as the Tolon township, traditional capital of the Tolon people dating back to the seventeenth century) that a detailed account of the grove has been presented. The CIPSEG project is conducting field and socio-cultural studies in the wider geographical enclave of Tali.

The Malshegu and Tali sacred groves are cultural landscapes of universal value. They are directly and tangibly associated with recurrent or continuous socio-cultural traditions of the dominant northern tribe of Dagombas whose strong religious traditional beliefs and taboos have resisted change, protecting a phytochoria unit that is devasted by human interference within the northern savanna zone, a zone that transects the whole of West Africa from Senegal to Sudan. These groves are outstanding evidence that traditional values, human settlement and initiative in conservation of a natural landscape through religious beliefs, can resist what is almost irreversible destruction and degradation of a whole biogeographical unit in West Africa.

These cultural landscapes represent the interaction of the forces of nature through natural regeneration of existing biodiversity and the works of man through the jealous and vigilant conservation practices resting on traditional religious beliefs and taboos in the associated communities. Centuries of socio-cultural manifestations have made these sacred groves in the savanna setting landscapes of beauty that should be nominated for inscription on the World Heritage list.

The UNESCO-CIPSEG project has as one of its final goals to document the scientific and cultural basis for the nomination of these two sacred groves among the cultural landscapes of outstanding universal value, representing climax biogeographical vegetation types in Africa, protected up until the present by traditional values and practices which now need to be enhanced to ensure their long-term protection for the benefit of the world.

Acknowledgement

The Co-operative Integrated Project on Savanna Ecosystems in Ghana (CIPSEG) is supported by the BMZ through a funds-in-trust arrangement with UNESCO. We are grateful to the Government and people of the Federal Republic of Germany for their foresight and support.

References

Agyepong, G. T. (1993). *Perspective on Resource Conservation in Ghana.* An Inter-Faculty lecture. University of Ghana.

Asibey, E. O. A. (1989). *Proposals for the Revision of the National Forestry Policy of Ghana.* Accra, Forest Commission.

Biles, D. J. (1954). *The planning of land use and soil and water conservation in the Northern Territories.* In Proceedings of theAfrican Soils Conference, pp. 1143 - 1153. Leopoldville.

Boateng, E. A. (1966). *A Geography of Ghana.* Cambridge,Cambridge University Press.

Dickson, K. B. and Benneh, G. (1988). *A New Geography of Ghana.* 2nd Edition 1988, Longman.

Dorm-Adzobu, C., Ampadu-Agyei, O. and Veit, P. G. (1991). *Religious Beliefs and Environmental Protection: The Malshegu Sacred Grove in Northern Ghana.* World Resources Institute (WRI), ACTS Press.

Garbrah, B. W. (1989). *Environmental Action Plan - an overview.* In *Report on the National Conference on Environmental Action Plan*, edited by Environmental Protection Council (EPC).Accra, EPC.

Government of Ghana (1990). *Environmental Action Plan of Ghana.* Ministry of Local Government and by Environmental Protection Council, Ghana.

IUCN (1990). *Biodiversity in Sub-Saharan Africa and its islands. Conservation, Management and Sustainable Use.* Occasional papers of the IUCN Species Survival Commission No. 6, 242 pp.

Lynn, C. W. (1937). *Agriculture in North Mamprusi.* Department of Agriculture Bulletin No. 34, Department of Agriculture, Gold Coast.

National Research Commission (1980). *Research Priorities in Tropical Biology.* Washington, DC, National Academy of Sciences.

Rose-Innes, R. (1964). *Ecology in Land and Water Survey in Upper Northern Regions*, Ghana. Rome, FAO.

Solbrig, O.T. (1991). *From Genes to Ecosystems: A Research Agenda for Biodiversity.* Report of an IUBS-SCOPE-UNESCO workshop. Paris, International Union of Biological Sciences.

Tuffour, K., Oduro, W., Ghartey, K., Beeko, C., Juam-Musah, A. and Bamfo, R. (1992). *Study of Traditional Conservation of Biodiversity in Ghana.* Forestry Commission Technical Series.

B. Amoako-Atta is the Chief Project Coordinator of the UNESCO-GIPSEG Project in Ghana.

Chapter 9

Cultural Landscapes: Maraboutic sites in Morocco[1]

Dominique Verdugo and Jalila Kadiri Fakir

Maraboutism is one of the expressions of North African Islam. Its sites of worship, maintained by their living traditions, mark spaces of great symbolic value, landscapes charged with meaning by the Moroccans. The marabout, in the shade of a tree, is one of the elements of cultural heritage which lives and is experienced through its exterior. It reverberates on the surrounding space.

The word marabout comes from the name of the dynasty of the Al Mourabitine, the Almoravides, *(mrabet)* and before that from the word *ribat*, meaning a fortified military camp from which the Islamic preachers set out. The words *ribat* and *mourabit*, giving Rabat, marabout and Almoravide, have several meanings: a *ribat* is at once a fortress and a religious centre, while the *mourabitin* are people linked by a spiritual tie, as well as people obliged to defend and to spread by force the doctrines of their Sheikhs.

Maraboutism

At the end of the eighteenth century in the Middle East certain believers reacted against the formalism of Islam and took up an existing mystic movement called Sufism. Al-Junayd said "The Sufi is like the earth; you throw onto it all unwanted waste and only good things come out of it". He also said "The Sufi is like the earth, which is traversed by the innocent and the guilty, like the sky which shades everything, like the rain which waters everything" (Michon 1973).
These Muslims follow special practices decreed by privileged beings who hold benediction. The Sufic doctrine, permitted by the islamic religion, tends to make the human divine, rather than making the divine become human, and it leads to the worship of saints who are but human (an anthropocentric and heterodox practice). These chosen and faithful beings play the role of divine mediators in society. These saints appeal to the heart more than the spirit and they raised a new enthusiasm for Islam.

The worship of nature was the usual practice in North Africa at this time. Maraboutism enabled the transition between Islam and paganism. The marabouts, like the zaouïas and the religious brotherhoods, stand on the margins of Muslim orthodoxy.

The worship of saints is still characteristic of Moroccan Islam. Maraboutism, with the legends, the supernatural and the incredible, is an undeniable traditional force. It is still

---

[1] Translated from the French by Alison Semple.

highly developed and undoubtedly existed well before the introduction of Islam which could but tolerate it. The modest marabouts, sometimes anonymous, and very numerous in Morocco, are undoubtedly ancient mythical figures, already adored in these places before the advent of Islam.

Though Islam in Morocco may have taken on a particular quality, the magical practices and the worship of the saints are not pagan. They do not form another religion, but are integrated into Islam. This adaptation of the Muslim religion to the Moroccan character and traditions gave rise to religious brotherhoods which spread throughout the country. The contradiction between orthodox Islam (no place for the veneration of saints and other intermediaries between God and the believer) and a saint (recognition of the spiritual authority of a patron saint) explains why these people were sometimes persecuted and at other times welcomed as saviours. To try and detach himself from this world below, to detach the spirit from the body, Moulay Abdelslam Ben Mchich isolated himself on the Jbel Alam to give himself up to God. He never found his peace because he had his throat cut some 400 m from his retreat. He did not become the patron saint protector of the Jbala and of all Morocco until three centuries after his death.

These chosen people brought to the rural world a spiritual and poetic message which is still alive today. The *siyyed*, isolated and pious sages who were more or less learned, alternated teaching sessions with prayers and orisons. They held foremost place in intellectual life. Maraboutism had and still has social and political consequences.

The marabouts usually exert their influence over a limited area. Venerated burial places - real or presumed tombs - attract many pilgrims who come to pray, to meditate or to celebrate religious ceremonies. Today, the marabouts are particularly frequented by women, who appeal to the *baraka* (divine emanation) to cure their ills, resolve their domestic difficulties, or even end their sterility. Also, before the marabout, oaths are taken to settle legal disputes when other means of proof are not decisive.

The collective and periodic gatherings of pilgrims around the sanctuary of a saint - the *moussem* - are a social phenomenon deeply rooted in Moroccan society and culture. The Berbers still tend to prefer imploring the marabouts rather than other places of worship.

The devotion to these figures who intercede with Allah, sanctified in their lifetimes or after their deaths, is not restricted to Muslims in Morocco. The Jews also have their saints, relatively as numerous as the Muslim saints. Certain Jewish saints have acquired such a great reputation that even Muslims come to worship their tombs; vice versa, the Moroccan Jews display a particular devotion to certain Muslim saints of the country.

The cultural heritage of the maraboutic site

Expression through the natural element

In the Moroccan plains, the classical picture of these landscapes associated with beliefs almost always represents the sacred tree growing beside the marabouts. The natural completes the cultural. "The tree is the protector of Moulay Abdelslam Ben Mchich, of his son Mohamed and of his servant", said by the Chorfa of Jbel Alam (the tree in question is a *Quercus pireneica*). Many marabouts cover the worship of the tree that shelters them with a thin veil of Islam. According to beliefs, the tree is endowed with a particular *baraka*. The cultural completes the natural. Countless trees have branches covered with scraps of cloth or their lower branches weighed down with stones. Tying a cloth near to a sanctuary or placing a stone on a *kerkour* are rites characterising the expulsion of evil.

Immense dry and bare plains are common in Morocco. In these desolate regions, only a few rare trees appear every now and then to break up the monotony. They carry more scraps of cloth than leaves or thorns and are visited by assiduous pilgrims who believe that evil influences are drawn away through plant life. The jujube of the tagourramt Lalla Oudda among the Nifa, under which people suffering fever sleep, and the oak of the aït Messat, under whose roots they leave their illnesses, are well known (cf. Basset 1920). The marabouts have evidently not replaced the worship of an ancient sacred tree.

In Morocco, certain trees made sacred by their location have a proper name. These holy trees compel love and respect; their branches are not cut and those that fall decompose on the ground. Sacred groves may be abandoned cemeteries and, more often than not, the tombs, invaded by vegetation, can hardly be made out. Groves of windmill palms (*Chamaerops humilis*) may hide a niche of flat stones whitened with lime and full of candles. Plant life, either green or dry, is also sometimes related to the "presence" or "absence" of the saint.

The woody plant species known as outlets for genies and for receiving evil influences are many and varied. The windmill palm is undoubtedly the most commonly venerated sacred bush. Depending on the region, the rural population also asks special favours and pays obeisance to other species. Among the most common are the jujube (*Ziziphus jujuba* or *lotus*), the carob tree (*Ceratonia siliqua*), the olive (*Olea europea*), cactuses, the fig tree (*Ficus carica*), palms, acacias, junipers, the nettle tree (*Celtis australis*), the oleander (*Nerium oleander*), the mastic tree (*Pistacia lenstiscus*), oaks, young elm, the argan tree (*Argania spinosa*), and the tamarisk tree (*Tamarix* sp.). Certain palms are worshipped, but are subject to a particular rite - thin strips of palm leaf are worn as a necklace then placed after a certain number of days at the foot of the tree to request its help.

There are few regions in Morocco where the worship of caves is unknown. Caves are the subject of the same cults as trees, celebrated with the same rites, and pilgrims ask them for the same kinds of help, principally to cure illness. Most often, pilgrims go to the entrance of a cave to get rid of fever. The worship of the caves is in reality worship of the genies (*jnoun*). "The interior of the mountain contains a large city inhabited by more jnouns than there are stars in the sky. Formerly, when humans were better than they are now, the jnoun often came out with their animals; but now, they never leave their city except at night..." Grotte de Lalla Taqandout (cf. Westermarck 1935). Their underground dwellings are known to be caves, trees or springs. The places of worship are not really considered to be the *jnouns*' home, but the entrance to their homes. They do not dwell in the visible cavern, but behind this one, equally or even more important, in the cavern that cannot be seen. The caves symbolise the underground initiatory world of the night. The sacred caves are venerated and feared. They may be deep caverns, simple cavities or rock shelters, or even supposed or imaginary blocked up caves. Sacrifices are celebrated at the entrance to this underground world. The oracle caves or curing caves are the places of *moussems*, (healing genies). There are also some examples of sanctuaries common to two religions - both Muslim and Jewish.

These beliefs in occult forces can all be found in places other than caves. The myth associated with plant life and caves is also found with springs, rocks and stones. For example pilgrimage exists to the tomb of Moulay Abdelslam Ben Mchich, where caves and springs are numerous close to the sanctuary and at the foot of the Jbel Alam. Many beliefs surround these places including that of the "weeping stone": whose water was used for the ablutions of the saint and would flow when women sing a song known to them alone. In North Africa, the cult of water is deeply linked with the that of genies. They are particularly numerous in running water. In popular belief, the worship of *jnoun* is practised, despite the presence of a marabout. Sacred animals, fish or turtles, live in certain springs or pools. Thermal springs are also celebrated. Rites and homage are also addressed to rocks, stood upright temporarily by and for pilgrims, heaped up (*kerkour*), or part of a sanctuary, such as seats, columns or rocks polished by rubbing.

Popular cults often associate different natural elements. A large fig tree hides the entrance to a cave, from a small cave flows a spring, a pool lies in a cave, a sacred tree shades a sacred pool, a large rock from a cliff has fallen close to a carob tree, a pool with tortoises is bordered by a fig tree, two springs emerge into a natural rocky basin, a round stone with a slight hollow lies beneath an olive tree, or a shrub in the middle of a grove of a single species.

Expression through the built element

The built element is a focal point in the Moroccan landscape, a contrast of colour, special volume and original form. Its cubic silhouette, unusual in its isolation, draws the eye and rapidly reveals the mythical character of the site. Pure and sober architectural forms rise under the perpetual movement of a gnarled tree: death and life, the still and the moving, the horizontal and the vertical.

These buildings materialise the places where the saint lived, passed by, or stopped to rest, meditate or pray, and often the saint's burial site. The tomb does not obligatorily or materially contain the body of the saint. Often the cupolas, slightly sloped on the hillsides, indicate *mzaras* or *nzallas*, places of shady rest where the saint stopped on his journeys.

Many tombs were built, more or less luxurious and of variable size and importance depending on the prestige of the saints, their influence and the circumstances. The number of marabouts in Morocco is almost to great to count. Most consist of a small square room with no opening other than the doorway surmounted by a cupola (*qobba*), the whole whitened with lime. They are often the architectural sign of a dominant site. The tombs of the most modest saints can be recognised by a low circular wall surrounding the grave. Deprived of any inheritance, of any resources, they are confided to the piety of the surrounding population.

These places of prayer might also be a small space bordered by stones, a sacred enclosure, an ancient well, a pool, a fragment of column, whitewashed, a small platform of faced stone.... They are often located next to a spring, a cave, a tree or in cemeteries. Women take small amounts of earth from these places and carry it to the sick, if not to cure them, at least to soothe their pain.

The sacred tree or bush, a place of spiritual retreat, is laden with scarves, scraps of cloth (votive ribbons), or blades of cactus attached by women who come on a spiritual visit. These cultural objects are inseparable from their natural environment.

Often dazzlingly white, set against a pure, limpid sky, lost in foliage or melted, colour on colour, earth on earth, the marabouts can bring exaltation, relaxation, affliction or heartbreak. They continually enrich the landscape with their weight of humanity (Figures 1, 2, 3).

1	2
3	4

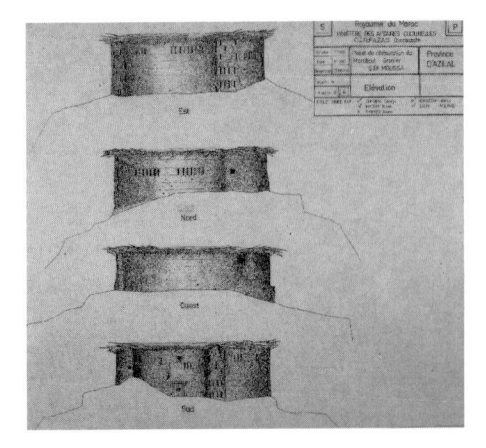

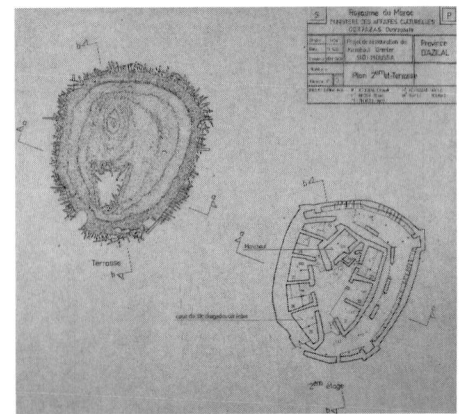

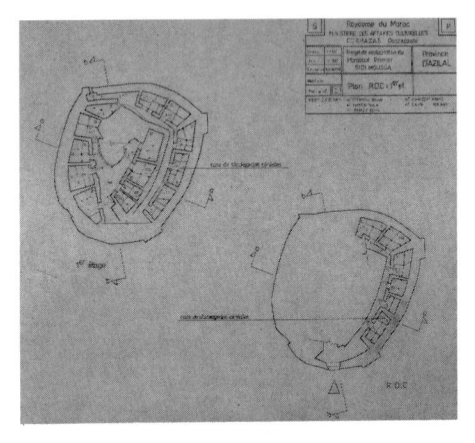

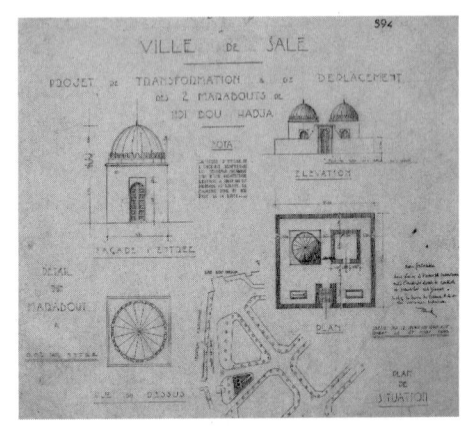

Figures 1–3. Restoration plan (Marabout Grenier).
Figure 4. Ville de Sale.

The land that contains the tomb of the saint is a sacred territory (*horm*) and an inviolable refuge. These lands are the exclusive property of the families who descend or claim to descend from the saint; they escape the direct authority of the State. Usually, once a year, a sort of patronal feast called a *moussem* is held around the tomb; a large gathering of people, who may come from far, crowd in to offer devotions to the *siyyed* and participate in the festivities given in his honour. Each sanctuary, however unimportant, involves some economic management (offerings, maintenance).

The tomb of a saint can include annexes: a prayer room and exceptionally, a true mosque, an oratory, outbuildings, one or more guest rooms to put up travellers or pilgrims who often come from appeal to the *baraka* of a saint, a fountain, abattoirs for cutting the throats of animals (sheep or calves) offered to the saint in accordance with the traditional ritual, even small houses occupied free of charge by the blind.

The site

The sacred character of a site is perpetuated throughout the centuries and successive cults (sometimes even stretching back into prehistory). The popular preacher often chooses such a site as a refuge in order to spread his message from a place already respected and venerated by the local population, capitalising on traditional practice. The site of Moulay Bouselham with its caves, its numerous marabouts and its moussems in a restricted area suggests that it is an ancient sacred place.

In the rural world where the agrarian rite is essential, the holy places are chosen for their remarkable natural character and their aesthetic value: beauty, panorama, woods, isolation, dominating position, freshness and contrast.

The maraboutic site could be a natural element (trees, caves, springs and rocks) or equally a built structure. Often the construction of the sanctuary is superposed on a venerated natural site, increasing its area of influence.

These landscapes associated with beliefs, with religious celebrations and pilgrimages are still today the expression of the interaction between people and the environment, charged with symbolic value, both spiritual and cultural. The maraboutic site is thus one of the expressions and one of the settings of Moroccan culture throughout its history.

The boundaries of a maraboutic site are brought to life by pilgrims in the practice of rites (retreat, prayers, meditation, offerings, sacrifices, *moussems*...) and through certain additions (more recently enclosing walls and doorway, traditionally a rope or piles of stones, plant cover, votive ribbons ground coverings. Slabs of dlem (cork oak) cover the sacred enclosure of the sanctuary of Moulay Abdelslam Ben Mchich, buried on the Jbel Alam, conferring on the site a particular aspect due to the quality and the suppleness of the surrounding ground area.or natural elements, a large rock, shingle, the rising of a spring...). The area of influence of a marabout may cover an entire town, or even a region. (Figure 4.)

Marabout buildings are found in the most diverse places. Most often they are built on high ground, on the summits of hills or mountains, but also on plateaus, or at the foot of a relief, by the sea, on a beach, on a rock that forms an island at high tide (but can be reached at low tide), in a ravine, on a hillside, the bank of a wadi (buildings parallel with the flow of the water), on top of a rock, on an escarpment or crest, at a place of passage, at a mountain pass.

The establishment of these cultural sanctuaries penetrates and rests on the surrounding environment, integrates isolated trees, adapts itself to the plant cover (edges of woods and clearings), profits from and sometimes uses the relief, associates natural sites of worship with the sanctuary. The maraboutic site is not accidental but on the contrary and almost always a specially chosen site.

The marabout, through its establishment and practices becomes a place defined with the elements of landscape that constitute an original site. Even if not materialised, the boundaries of the maraboutic site exist and can be perceived in the space centred on the building, the *horm* (surrounding walls) are respected for the cultural character of the place. Exuberant vegetation often indicates the site before the building is discovered.

Landscape values

In every civilisation there is a place where people and ideas meet, a place which receives their images, their symbols and their myths. The garden is often this space, in which are crystallised the imaginings of the human, artist, poet, dreamer or mystic. The maraboutic site, linked to the idea of the ultimate resting place, corresponds to the concept of the garden, real or imaginary.

At the origin of gardens is the fear felt by primitive man faced with natural phenomena, phenomena strange to everyday experience. This fear transforms itself into admiration then adoration of the genie and spirit of the place. The maraboutic site is a garden, in stone or plant life depending on the physical or climate characteristics of the region.

The art of building (*qobbas*), the art of living (worship, pilgrimages, celebrations) the art of planting (fruit trees), the art of dying (tombs), all exist and are entwined at the same site. The maraboutic sites are gardens liberated of limits, magnified by the surrounding landscape. They respond to the immense desire of the rural population to survive and struggle in a hostile environment that is unpredictable and largely unknown. They are the translation of an idealised conception of the world, the needs of spirituality and pleasure, and more simply the tastes of a community.

The site chosen is allied to the surrounding landscape and integrated into it, while at the same time lifting or transporting saint and pilgrim to a special domain, a more open, vaster space, more wooded, overhanging and dominant, or hidden and isolated. Human intervention is minimal, just slightly disconcerting, to call the attention and confront real with ideal space. Nonetheless, the formal characters of composition and the spatial sequences that constitute the art of gardens can be made out. Indeed, with the sacred grove, the composition becomes like a landscape and the sanctuary becomes a precious reliquary in a consecrated jewel case of plant life. Nature and its disordered vegetation penetrate the tombs of the cemetery sometimes reaching the building of the patron saint itself. The preacher often chose foliage or the celestial vault as the roof of his or her last abode. The volumetry of the trees (many or single) is the principle element of composition and the suppleness of their lines is in tune with the topography. In placing the sanctuary, people chose a site in which the sanctuary would be enhanced by its surroundings. The viewing points and the vistas over the land below are planned and deliberate.

Maraboutic sites are also the secret garden, the oasis that playing on contrast and surprise: oppositions of light and shade, the rigidity of the sanctuary walls and the exuberance of the foliage, limits and immensity, immobility and movement, death and the unexpectedness of life... A clearing of green, of silence, a corner of nature preserved, a strange island, an open parenthesis, elements that give a new landscape value to the maraboutic sites.

The isolated marabout

The isolated marabout, like the oasis that calls to secrecy, to rest, to isolation and renewal becomes an unusual space. From the hillock where the sanctuary stands, the gaze can reach across the plain, watching over cultivated lands, resting on the sea with its jagged coastline to follow the boats of the fishermen. Sheltered in a hollow in the sands, anchored in the clouds, detaching itself in a clearing, the tomb contributes to the poetry of the natural site and makes it easier to read. A peculiar tree, colossal and isolated on a rocky plateau, a cluster of trees or a wood, a monumental rock, a ravine, a cool and humid cave in the desert, catch the eye and create a tale, a myth, a legend. Whether sanctuary, heap of stones, hut, cube surmounted by a cupola, sacred enclosure, the marabout asserts itself and brings the imaginary and the real closer. Sculpture in the landscape, the isolated marabout enhances its environment by its distinctive features (textures, lines, dimensions); it accentuates the polarity of space, provokes and intensifies feelings and perceptions.

The maraboutic complex

The origin of the saltwater lake of Zerga, tucked between two dunes and sheltered from the Atlantic tides, is explained by the miracle of the patron saint of the village. Here, Moulay Bouselham came across, a man who brought in a miraculous catch of fish and challenged him to do the same. Moulay Bouselham made a sign to the ocean with his cloak (*selham*) and marched inland followed by the waves. It took the intercession of a neighbouring woman saint, Lalla Mimouna, to stop the confrontation of the two men and the inrush of the sea. Thus according to popular legend lake Zerga was formed. Today the sanctuary of Moulay Bouselham lies north of the channel, surrounded by its defenders. To the south, the man who challenged him is alone and isolated on a dune, opposite the maraboutic complex of Moulay Bouselham. Each spring, the celebration of Lalla Mimouna, whose tomb is built on the plain a few kilometres away, ends with a pilgrimage to the sanctuary of Moulay Bouselham. The plain joins with the ocean composing a great landscape. Landscape composition combined with cultural practices intensify the legendary value of a site.

The maraboutic site as natural heritage

The right to life of the wild (or planted) plants is respected within the preserved enclosure of these maraboutic sites. The trees guard a natural refuge, the plants regenerate at their rythmn, the insects and birds keep their protected ecosystem. The maraboutic sites are a biological remnant of a local ecosystem, in contrast to the close surrounding land which people have taken in hand, cultivated, exploited and transformed. Charged with meaning by the people, these symbolic spaces have passed through many centuries and are now almost natural conservatories.

The need to safeguard marabout sites as cultural landscapes

Despite their unequal distribution in Morocco, the places of worship represented by the marabouts, maintained by traditional management, still play an active role in contemporary Moroccan society. They are closely associated with the traditional way of life and, over the course of the centuries, they have experienced changing power through the medium of a powerful religion.

At the local or regional scale, these isolated elements, focal points in the Moroccan landscape, are directly linked and associated with beliefs, practices and events recounted at length in many legends and writings, exerting a great influence through a long history up to the present day. Their historical, cultural, aesthetic, ethnological and anthropological value endows them with irreplaceable presence. The marabouts bear witness to an important stage in the history of Morocco.

The visits of pilgrims to marabout sites ensure their upkeep and conservation. On the other hand, the authenticity of these sites is threatened by over-visiting and by changing character of visits. Uncontrolled development of some sites and the extensive construction of shops and guest rooms on the edges of certain sanctuaries are causing progressive irreversible change. The commercialisation and large number of visitors to some sites are causing serious deterioration in the surrounding environment and the quality of the landscape, but also a significant loss of cultural identity. Conversely, the low number of visitors and the abandonment of other marabouts results in the degradation of buildings and the possible disappearance of the mausoleum. Either way, this process is an impoverishment of the vulnerable cultural heritage of Morocco. From an ecological point of view, the marabout sites, respected by the local population and pilgrims, remain an important natural sanctuary for certain plant species and species associations.

References

For the sake of simplicity and clarity in the text, the authors have chosen not to include in the body of the text the references consulted. They ask the authors, or their descendants, to accept their apologies.

Assy, L. (1980). *La vie familiale à travers ses rites chez les Ziayda au Maroc*. Doctoral thesis in ethnosociology 160 pp. Paris, Sorbonne.
Basset, H. and Levi-Provencal, E. (1922). *Chella Nécropole Mérinide*. Hespéris.
Basset, H. (1920). *Le culte des grottes au Maroc*. 120 pp. Algiers, J. Carbonel.
Berriane, M. (1992). *Tourisme national et migrations de loisirs au Maroc*. Série thèses et mémoires 16. Rabat, Publications de la Faculté des Lettres et des Sciences Humaines.
Brunot, L. (n.d.) *Cultes naturalistes à Sefrou*. Archives berbéres, 3.
Colin, G. S. and Levi-Provencal, E. (1932). *Le milieu indigène au Maroc. Les habitants. In Initiation au Maroc*. Rabat, Institut des Hautes Etudes Marocaines, Ecole du Livre.
Brignon, J., Amine A., Boutaleb, B., Martinet, G., Rosenberger, B. and Terrasse, M. (1967). *Histoire du Maroc*. Casablanca, Librairie Nationale/ Paris, Haitier.
Dermengheim, E. (1954). *Le culte des saints dans l'Islam maghrébin*. Paris, Gallimard.
Drague, G. (n.d.) *Esquisse d'histoire religeuse du Maroc*. 332 pp. Paris, Peyronnet & Cie.
Hajji, M. (1976-7). *L'activité intellectuelle au Maroc á l' Epoque Sa'dide*Volumes I and II. Rabat, Publications de Dar el Maghrib.
Hardy, G. and Aures, P. (1921). *Les grandes étapes de l'histoire du Maroc*. Bulletin de l'Enseignement Public du Maroc: 29, March.
Kharchafi, A. (1993). *Les traditions orales au siècle dernier au Maroc*. Doctoral thesis in linguistics, Université d'Aix-en-Provence.
Luccioni, J. (n.d.) *Les fondations pieuses "Habous" au Maroc depuis les origines jusqu'à 1956*. Rabat, Imprimerie Royale.
Marty, P. (1929). *Les Zaouïas marocaines et le Makhzen*. Paris, P. Geuthner.
Mezzine, M. (1988). *Temps des marabouts et des chorfa, essai d'histoire sociale marocaine á travers les écrits de jurisprudence religieuse*. Thesis for Doctorat d'Etat-es-Lettres, Vol.2. Université Paris VII, Jussieu.
Michaux-Bellaire, M. (1919). *Les confréries marocaines*.
Michaux-Bellaire, M. (1923). *Les confréries religieuses au Maroc*. Conférences faites au Cours de Perfectionnement, Direction des Affaires Indigènes et du Service des Renseignements. Rabat, Imprimerie officielle.
Michaux-Bellaire, M. (1925). *L'Islam et le Maroc*. Conférence faite au Cours des Affaires indigènes. Rabat, Imprimerie officielle.
Michon, J.-L. (1973). *Le soufi marocain Ahmad Ibn Ajiba et son miraj, Glossaire de la mystique musulmane*. Paris, CNRS, Librairie Philosophique J. Vrin.
Miege, J.L. (n.d.) *Le Maroc*. B. Arthaud.
Montet, E. (1901). *Les confréries religeuses de l'Islam marocain*. Leur rôle religieux, politique et sociale. Revue de l'histoire des religions, Geneva.
Reysoo, F. (1988). *Des moussems du Maroc, une approche anthropologique de fêtes patronales*. Enschede, Sneldruk.

Saint, Y. (1918). *Les grottes dans les cultes magico-religieux et dans las symbolique primitive*. Paris.
Troin, J. F. (1975). *Les souks marocains: marchés ruraux et organisation de d'espace dans la moitié nord du Maroc*. 2 volumes. Aix-en-Provence, Edisud.
Voinot, L. (1948). *Pélerinages judéo-musulmans du Maroc*. Institut des Hautes Etudes Marocaines.
Voinot, L. (1936). *Confréries et Zaouïas au Maroc*. Bulletin d'Oran: 57.
Voinot, L. (1937). *Confréries et Zaouïas au Maroc*. Bulletin d'Oran: 58.
Westermark, E. (1938). *Survivances païennes dans la civilisation mahométane*.

Dominique Verdugo is a landscape architect, consultant for BCEOM - SECA and is an associate researcher at IAV/DDR, Rabat and is currently working on projects in Morocco.

Jalila Kadiri Fakir is a landscape architect, chief of the "Division des monuments historiques et des sites" at the "Direction du Patrimoine" of the Ministry for Culture, Rabat.

Cultural Landscapes of the World

Asia

The Cultural Lancscape of the Rice Terraces of the Philippine Cordilleras
Augusto F. Villalon

Mt. Huangshan and Mt. Taishan, Outstanding Cultural Landscapes in China
Yang Ying

Changing Cultural Landscapes in Japan
Nakagoshi Nobukazu

Cultural Landscapes of Angkor Region, Cambodia. A Case Study of Planning for a World Heritage Site – The Zoning and Environmental Management Plan for Angkor (ZEMP)
Jonathan Wager

The Cultural Landscape of Sagarmatha National Park in Nepal
Hans Caspary

Chapter 10

The Cultural Landscape of the Rice Terraces of the Philippine Cordilleras

Augusto F. Villalon

Landscape

The terraced landscape of the Cordillera Mountain Range in northern Philippines is regarded by the nation as the primary symbol of its cultural heritage. It is even more noteworthy that a cultural monument of the extent and grandeur of the Cordillera Rice Terraces was totally constructed without the use of slave or enforced labor.

The irregular shapes of the terraces result directly from the need of a rice culture to cultivate its mountainous terrain, by necessity evolving its own traditional environmental and resource management system over the centuries, and orally transferring the traditions and knowledge associated with this system to its succeeding generations. The impressiveness of the site reflects the delicately balanced processes of environmental, social and cultural factors which have intertwined constantly from the time of the original construction to the present to assure the continued maintenance of this remarkable land form. The preservation and maintenance of the site is symbiotic with the continuation of the culture which it nourishes. Terracing was said to have evolved for approximately 2,000 years, as postulated by the region's foremost scholars.

Tradition

Oral tradition indicates that the terraces once fanned out over an area covering most of the central mountain ranges of Luzon Island. Starting from its remaining present location in the northern Cordillera Mountain Range, terraces were likewise found in the adjoining Sierra Mountain Range which, together with the Cordilleras, forms the mountainous central spine of Luzon Island. Terraces were said to have reached as far south as the foothills encircling Laguna de Bay, 20 km south of Manila. The Spanish missionaries of the 16th and 17th Centuries are credited with having convinced the mountain farmers in the Sierra Mountain range to abandon the mountains and their terraces, to descend into the lowlands, and, most importantly, to be Christianized. The southern terraces have since crumbled. However, the northern Cordillera tribes fiercely resisted subjugation by both the Spanish and the American colonizers, preserving their ethnic integrity into the present day.

Today's rice terraces are situated in the mountainous northern end at the centre of Luzon Island, east of the Cordilleran divide, 17 degrees north of the equator, at an elevation varying between 700 and 1,500 meters above sea level. Since at certain times of

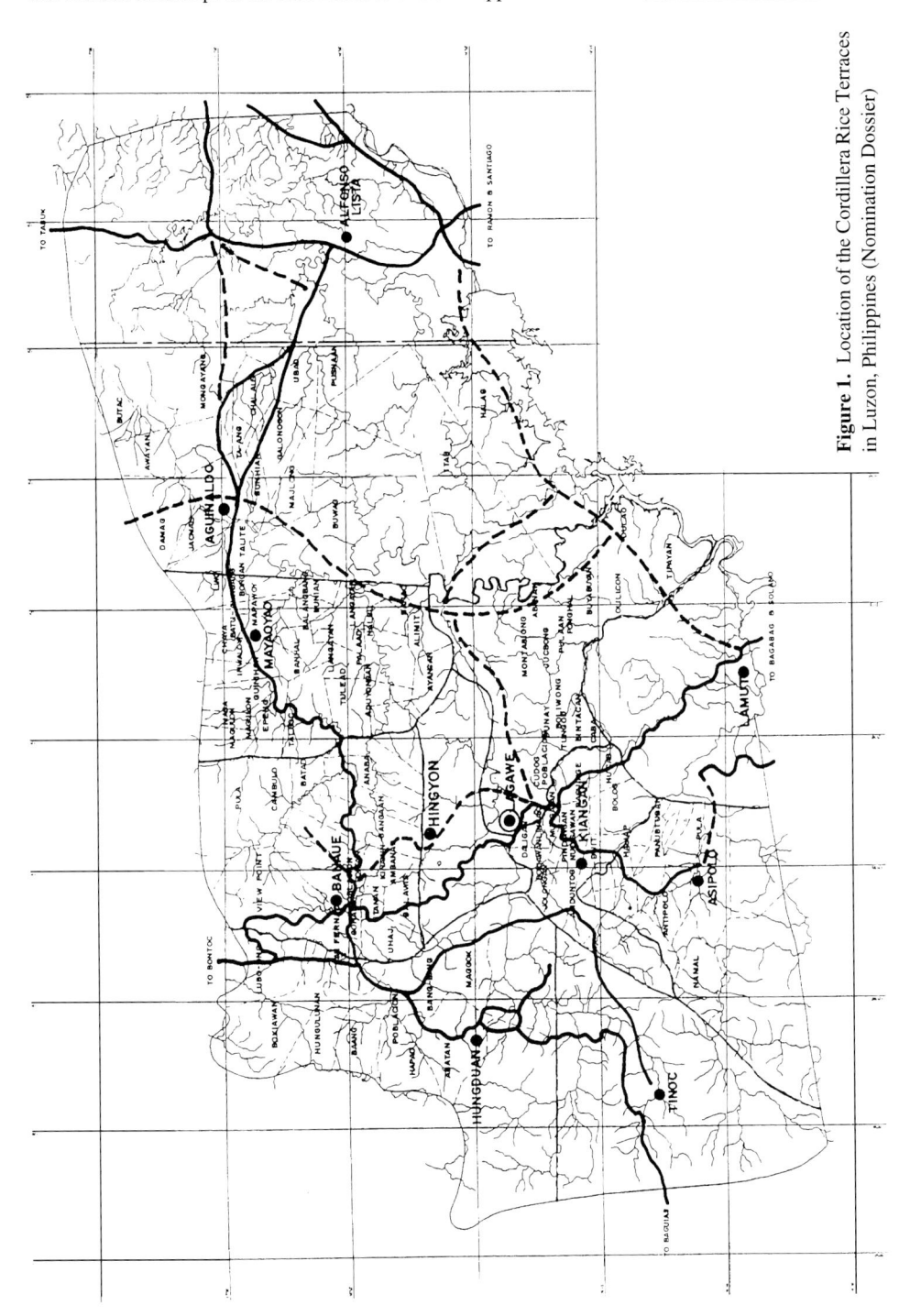

Figure 1. Location of the Cordillera Rice Terraces in Luzon, Philippines (Nomination Dossier)

Figure 2. Rice terrace cluster ringed with privately-owned tribal forests.
Figure 3. Rice terrace cluster showing sacred grove and ritual hut.
Figure 4. Flooded rice terrace cluster J. Emilio Reynoso.
Figure 5. Golden grains of rice ready for harvest. (Photos by Emilio J. Reynoso, The Palawan Sun).

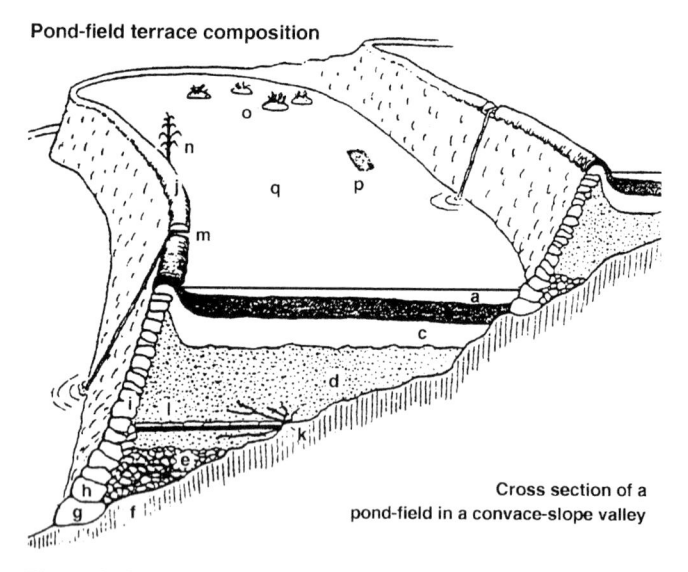

Figure 6. Composition of a pond-field terrace (see: Conklin, Harold C. (1980) *Ethnographic Atlas of Ifugao*. Yale University Press.); a water, b worked pond-field soil, c hard earth fill, d rough gravel fill, e coarse fill, small stones, f bedrock: or luta original valley-floor earth, g foundation stones, markers, h second-course walling stones, i stone retaining wall, j dike. bund. pond-field rim, k submerged water source, l drainage conduit, m spillway, n property marker (site), o vegetable mulch mounds, p fish sump, q enclosed pond-field surface.

the day the peaks of the Cordilleras are covered by clouds, their inhabitants are sometimes referred to as "a people who daily touch the earth and the sky." The inhabitants are placed in eight major ethnoliguistic groups: the Isneg, Kalinga, Bontoc, Ifugao, Kankanay, Ibaloi, Ikalahan and Tingguian. Terraced areas in varying degrees of preservation spread over most of the 20,000 km^2 encompassed by the five present-day provinces of Kalinga-Apayao, Abra, Mountain Province, Ifugao and Benguet. In 1992, these provinces were consolidated into the Cordillera Autonomous Region, providing self-administration in a manner appropriate to preserving its cultural identity and its ethnic solidarity. The approximately 20,000 km^2 land area of the region represents 7% of the total land mass of the Philippines. Population density in the region is from 100 - 250 per km^2.

Terraced rice fields are common throughout Asia. As by its very nature, rice needs to be planted in a flooded pond, even gently rolling terrain is terraced to contain water in ponds for planting rice (Figure 6). The early waves of migration from as far back as 2,000 years ago spread the terrace culture all over Asia. Most terraces found in other countries are monsoon-reliant, which must be ploughed in preparation for planting after having dried out during the summer.

Climate and Topography

The mountainous Cordillera region is the watershed of Luzon Island, where the headwaters of the island's major rivers originate. Annual rainfall exceeds 3,000 mm. In the Cordilleras, due to the abundant rainfall and numerous mountain streams diverted to irrigate the terraces, dryness never occurs. The rice fields are designed as swamps which must be flooded throughout the year for fertilization and for reinforcing their structural integrity to prevent the layers of clay beneath the topsoil and behind the stone walls from cracking. In recent years, two factors have caused a serious drop in the water table. The *El Niño* drought phenomenon was compounded with deforestation to seriously threaten the terraces.

The rice terraces of the Philippines are found at much higher altitudes and are built on steeper slopes than the terraces of its Asian neighbours. Within the topography of the area, the steeper inclines of the mountainous environment are covered with mixed tropical montane forest and dense stands of tall reeds, while irrigated terraces and interspersed wooded ridges dominate the gentler slopes. The lower portions of the high valleys are often completely terraced, with small settlements widely dispersed within them. Cultural and economic activities directly depend on and reinforce the agricultural and ecological balance demanded by the management of the tribal fields and woodland - ponded terraces, dry clearings (swiddens), and private forests (woodlots). Within these swamps thrives a delicately balanced ecosystem. Birds, cartilaginous fish, snails and frogs supply protein and sustenance for the tribes. They are in turn supported by insects, fungi and bacteria, which process decaying vegetation and produce a nutrient balance of organic mulch for abundant rice growth. The same cycle of natural balance has been maintained over the generations.

Culture

The life cycle of the inhabitants is likewise attuned to the stages of work connected with rice cultivation and the four climatic seasons found in the elevated environment. Peak planting season for pond-field rice is from December to March, leaving the dry season from April to June for growth, a harvest season in July, and a low season from August to November. The grain-oriented cycle relates well to the other agricultural activities of the community, swidden farming and timber management. Except during the rice harvest, tree crops and root crop staples are planted and gathered at all times of the year. The main rice crop is planted so that the growing period includes the months of April and May, the time of greatest sunlight and warmth. Harvest comes in July, a month after the onset of the heavy rains. Although one rice cycle can always be completed within a year, the growing season at higher elevations may extend beyond the normal eight months.

Most households require swidden produce, the most common being the sweet potato, to supplement their diet and as insurance against pond-field damage. Therefore, parallel with the rice planting season, swidden produce is planted, harvested during the dry season from April to June. Woodlot trees are tended year-round, with the maximum activity happening during the dry months of April to June.

During the long off-season from August to November, while terraces are kept inundated, the men channel, impound and sluice vast quantities of water. Stone and earth are gathered for the repair and expansion of the pond fields. Labor is manual, tools are rudimentary: sledges, hods, bars, knives, and long-handled paddle spades. Women mulch rice straw, make vegetable mounds of fertile aquatic weeds and mud, clean margins, and begin the year-long process of weeding the swidden-covered and terraced hillsides. Secondary plantings in fields and private forests, catching of pond-field shellfish and repairing of waterworks continue.

During the dry season from April to June, planting of crops other than rice increases on dry terraces and embankments, in woodlots and in old slope fields. Fishing, trapping, and travel for trade happen during this season. In the rice fields, concern with animal and plant pests intensifies. Irrigation and drainage protection against extended dry weather or sudden cloudbursts require constant cleaning, repair and improvement of the water works. Granaries and baskets are either built or repaired. Preparations begin for the rainy season and harvest season. Firewood is split and dried, supplies of rattan, thatching grass and pine root are gathered.

The harvest season in July is the shortest but most intense, agriculturally, ecologically and ritually. Within a few weeks, the crop is cut, bundled, dried and stored, after which all farming activities end. A period of continuous religious celebration commences to include a long series of calendric agricultural rites. Pigs and chickens are sacrificed, home-brewed rice wine drunk, and end-of-harvest rituals celebrated.

The inhabitants are guided through conditions of constant local change by widely held principles of social organization: an abiding concern with the competitive development of land for terracing and rice production; elaborate traditional rituals which always involve interaction with deceased kinsmen; a deep interest in status and rank with its accompanying inherited wealth.

The tribal dwellings likewise reflect the mountain environment from which they derive. A steeply pitched thatched pyramidal roof covers a one-room dwelling for a single family. The wooden dwelling, raised on four posts off the ground, is accessed by a wooden ladder from the space underneath. No matter who joins the family in their daily activities, once the ladder is lifted from the ground at night, only the nuclear family is allowed to remain inside the dwelling. The multi-purpose dwelling, its shape derived from the typical granaries of the region, also serves as a shrine for the family reliquary. Clusters of dwellings form small hamlets of interrelated families which lie within or near a series of irrigated terraces. A hamlet's centrally-located ritual rice field is its focus. This is the first parcel to be planted or harvested. Its owner makes all agricultural decisions, manages the ritual property including a granary housing carved wooden guardians (*bul-ol*) and the basket reliquary in which portions of consecrated sacrifices from all agricultural first rites are kept. The high level of traditional craft production from the area is a reflection of people's fierce protection of their heritage. Related but individual traditions unique to each ethnolinguistic grouping produce woodcarving, weaving and basketry, rooted in culture.

It seems that the great inborn pride in being part of the mountain culture and continuing its unbroken line of 2,000 years of agricultural achievement is not enough to sustain the site and its inhabitants these days. Today's young mountain tribesmen are leaving their homes for the cities in search of an education, many then staying there to find better employment. Only the old remain in their hamlets, carrying on with the manual task of maintaining their agricultural land and its cultural traditions. The recent drought and deforestation has seriously affected the water supply of the terraces. The increased population cannot be maintained by the agriculture of the region. The problem of assuring the maintenance of the site is not only environmental but also economic and cultural as well.

Conclusion

This is a cultural landscape of extreme physical beauty and of high cultural development, an authentic total living system in itself, one that will be severely endangered within this generation. This is an example of an ecological, agricultural and cultural system experiencing difficulty in changing to address the demands of the 21st Century. It is hoped that the Rice Terraces of the Philippine Cordilleras will be included in the World Heritage list by December 1995 to enhance the preservation of such an outstanding cultural landscape.

References

Conklin, Harold C. (1980). *Ethnographic Atlas of Ifugao*. Yale University Press.

Executive Order No.158 (1994). *Creating a Presidential Commission to formulate Short and Long-Term Plans for the Restoration of the Ifugao Rice Terraces in the Municipalities of Banaue, Hungduan, Mayoyao and Kinagan*.

The Rice Terraces of the Philippine Cordilleras (1994). Nomination Dossier. Manila: Philippine National Commission for UNESCO.

The Six Year Masterplan for the Restauration and Preservation of the Igugao Rice Terraces. (1994), Orient Integrated Development Consultants, Manila (2 volumes).

Augusto Villalon is an architect and member of the Philippines National Commission for UNESCO.

Chapter 11

Mt. Huangshan and Mt. Taishan, Outstanding Cultural Landscapes in China

Ying Yang

Introduction

In the Chinese language, landscape is Shan Shui (see Chinese character illustration), literally "Mountains and Water". From very early times, the Chinese have had their Five Mountains: Mt. Taishan (in Shandong Province), Mt. Huashan (in Shannxi Province),

山水

Mt. Hengshan (in Hunan Province), Mt. Hengshan (in Shanxi Province), and Mt. Songshan (in Henan Province). They stand at each corner and in the centre of China and symbolize the ultimate harmony of nature and the universe. In Chinese culture, it is believed that

> "the mountain is the body of the cosmic being, the rocks its bones, the water the blood that gushes through its veins, the trees and grasses its hair, the clouds and mists the vapor of its breath – the cosmic breath which is the visible manifestation of the very essence of life" (Sullivan 1962: 1).

To Chinese people, therefore, the outstanding landscapes are more than spectacular scenes. Their contributions to Chinese culture have extended to Chinese history, philosophy, literature, art, and economy. The outstanding qualities of Mt. Taishan and Mt. Huangshan were recognized by their inscription on the World Heritage List in 1987 and 1990, respectively, under both natural and cultural criteria.

Mt. Huangshan

"One need not go to any other mountains after visiting the Five Mountains; but after visiting Mt. Huangshan, one even need not see the Five".

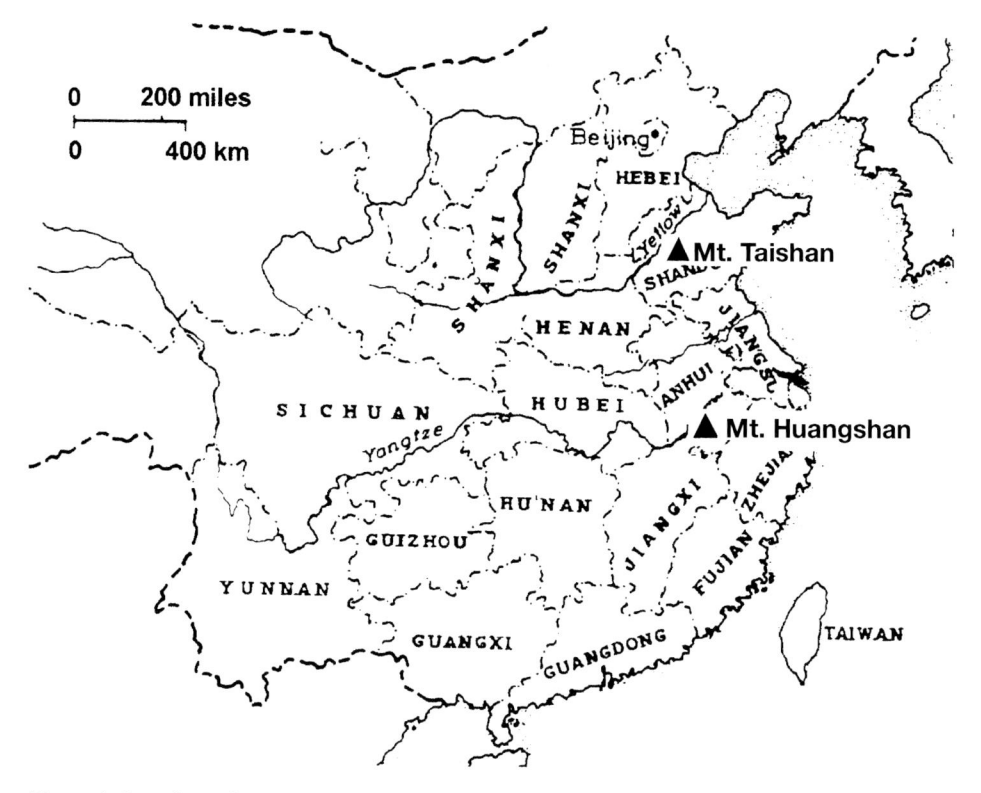

Figure 1. Locations of Mt. Huangshan and Mt. Taishan

This conclusion was drawn by Xu Xia-Ke (1586-1641), the well known geographer and explorer who traveled over half of China and visited most mountains during his lifetime. After he reached the summit of the Lotus Peak of Mt. Huangshan, looking out over the other peaks, he was totally thrilled by the scene:

"It was a most overpowering sight;" said he, "I cried out in ecstasy and could have danced out of sheer joy and admiration" (Li 1974, 82).

Mt. Huangshan stands in the south of Anhui Province, ranging through She, Yi, Taiping, and Huining counties (Figure 1), covering a total area of 1,200 km^2. Huangshan used to be called Yishan in the Qin Dynasty (221-247 B.C.) and was renamed Huangshan in the years of Tian Bao (Emperor) of the Tang Dynasty (747 A.D.).

Mt. Huangshan concentrates all the wonders of mountain scenery which can be only found individually in other mountains, such as the spectacular rocky peaks, the odd-shaped pines, the sea clouds, and the crystal-clear mountain springs. As a real scenic place as well as an aesthetic image, Huangshan is displayed everywhere in China, and climbing the mountain is almost obligatory for Chinese literati and pilgrims.

Huangshan in Legends

The reason for Huangshan being renamed from Yishan is explained by a story about Emperor Huangdi (the Yellow Emperor), the first legendary emperor. According to texts dating from the fourth century A.D., Emperor Huangdi went to Mt. Yishan with his prime ministers Fu Qiugong and Rong Chengzi in search of the pill of immortality (McDermott 1989, 153). They worked day and night refining cinnabar to make this pill. Through long persistent efforts, the pill was finally made and they all became immortals after taking it. Emperor Huangdi then established the 72 peaks as dwelling places for immortals or transcendants. In memory of Huangdi, the name of Mt. Yishan was changed to Mt. Huangshan, and the place where Huangdi made the immortal pill is named "Refining Cinnabar Peak".

Since Mt. Huangshan is the place where immortals live, it has been considered as a sacred mountain. Many Taoist and Buddhist temples were built there throughout history, and many writers and painters visited the mountain in earlier times, expressing their sense of the numinous in the Huangshan peaks.

Huangshan in Literature

Before the Tang Dynasty (618-907), there was almost no poetry about Huangshan (Min 1990: 367). The majority of travel accounts by visitors to Huangshan date from the late Ming Dynasty and after (Cahill 1989, 2). Li Bai (701-762), the most celebrated poet of the Tang Dynasty, once travelled to Huangshan and left a well known poem about its magnificent scenes:

> Huangshan is hundreds of thousands of feet high,
> with numerous soaring peaks lotus-like,
> rock pillars shooting up to kiss empyrean rose like
> so many lilies grown amid a sea of gold. (From: Farewell for Master Wen Back to His Dwelling in Mt. Huangshan)

Ever since the Tang Dynasty, hundreds of poems about Huangshan have been composed by poets from different dynasties. Among them, besides admiration for the magical natural scenery of Huangshan, the most common discovery was the awesome feeling about nature and harmony in Mt. Huangshan. The range of bare, precipitous, pine- and – mist-hung peaks often made people feel that they had transcended into a spiritual world.

Huangshan in Art

Though Huangshan has incredible scenery and natural attractions, it was not recognized until the Tang Dynasty (Tong, Zhang and Bai 1986, 455), and pictures of Huangshan did not become popular until the seventeenth century. It was not until 1606, when the Buddhist monk Pumen established the first temple Ciguang there (DeBevoise and Jang 1981, 44), that Huangshan became a place of pilgrimage. Before that time, travel was not easy and the early visitors could only reach a few places in Huangshan. After 1606, more temples and roads were built, and some villas were constructed in Huangshan by local wealthy families. Along with the increasing number of visitors came scholars, poets, and painters, who began to take Mt. Huangshan as a model for their poems and paintings.

In Chinese history, although Huangshan was visited by many pilgrims and literati, to most ordinary Chinese people it was a remote and inaccessible place. Besides poor transport, this was because of cultural limitations. Chinese people are fond of nature, but they have also been traditionally bound to their land under filial and federal obligations. Leaving home and roaming among Huangshan's peaks and waterfalls, therefore, could only be enjoyed by a small group of wealthy people or literati, while the majority of people were aware of Huangshan mainly through literature and art images. In fact, since images of Huangshan have been illustrated with such sophistication in paintings and the great details of climbing journeys have been vividly described in travel accounts, they have virtually fulfilled Chinese people's dreams of being with the peaks, pines, and sea clouds of Mt. Huangshan.

Huangshan's unique mountain peaks, pine trees, and sea clouds not only attracted poets and painters, but also nurtured a special style of landscape painting in China, identified as the Anhui school. The definition of the Anhui school is based on the traditional *Xin'an pai*, a style designating the school of *Xin'an* or *Huizhou*, which is in Huangshan area, and also includes artists from other parts of Anhui (Cahill 1981: 7).

The artists of the Anhui school were very different from those of the orthodox school who painted ideal landscapes and rarely travelled (DeBevoise and Jang 1981: 43). Anhui artists often visited scenic spots around their area as well as other famous locations. Their most favoured themes were those derived from the local topography, especially from Mt. Huangshan. Among the native Anhui people and patrons, particularly those who lived away from home on business, it was very common to ask artists to translate the scenery of Huangshan into pictures in order to evoke their memories of home. Others wanted to have pictures of Huangshan scenes as souvenirs either in memory of reaching the summit, or for the feeling that they had made the marvellous journey (*ibid*. p. 43). To the artists themselves, Mt. Huangshan served as a medium through which they could feel intimate with nature. Hongren, a famous painter and central figure in the Anhui school (1610-1664), once wrote:

> I have explored deep into the heart of the Mt. Huangshan. Back home at the foot of the fence, chrysanthemums wither and fade. Every day in a pavilion by a stream, I gaze at the forests and ravines. While drinking tea, I dampen my brush and lazily while away the time. (*ibid*. p. 44)

In the early days, besides portraying the scenery, Hongren and other Anhui artists seemed to express a desire for withdrawal from involvement with the human world by painting Huangshan in a dry, linear, and often unpeopled style (Cahill 1981: 10). This was not only determined by the unique features of Mt. Huangshan, its sharply cut and deeply fissured rocks and little vegetation (Figure 2), but also associated with the contemporary political situation as the Ming Dynasty was demolished by the Manchus. Under the control of the Qing Dynasty (1644 - 1911), many Han people, including Hongren, became Buddhist monks or withdrew from public life to avoid involvement with the alien dynasty. So, during the transition between the Ming and the Qing Dynasty, Mt. Huangshan served as a shelter for these unyielding scholars.

Huangshan in Scenery

Mt. Huangshan, the focus of artistic attention, is actually a range of mountains in the southeastern corner of Anhui. Noted for its steep cliffs, unique pine trees, grand sea clouds, and crystal springs, Mt. Huangshan has long been a natural attraction for pilgrims in history and for modern tourists today.

Figure 2. Granite Cliffs and Fractured Faces of Mt. Huangshan

Huangshan is famous for its rocky peaks. The grotesquely shaped peaks and the oddly shaped rocks seem to have been carved by superlative craftsmen. Thousands of peaks in the scenic area cover 154 km^2. Among them are 72 well-known peaks, 36 of them quite high, while the rest are relatively small. The highest is Lotus Flower Peak at 1,800 m, followed by the slightly lower Bright Summit Peak and Heavenly Capital Peak. Nearly every peak has fantastic rocks, such as "a squirrel is jumping to the Heavenly Capital", "a rooster crows to the Heaven Gate", "a monkey watches the sea of clouds", and "a magpie jumps onto the plum tree".

Huangshan is also famous for its pine trees. Pine trees of various shapes are scattered all over the region in all postures. Because of the high mountain wind, cold weather, and heavy snow, the pine trees there are shaped into flat and spreading caps, a few grow upright but many emerge horizontal, upside down, or peculiarly shaped. The steeper the

Figure 3. The Guest-greeting Pine of Mt. Huangshan.

cliffs of Huangshan, the more irregular the shapes of the pines that grow in the crevices. The needle-shaped leaves are short and thick, the boughs and trunks are stout. These pine trees show great vitality against heavy frosts and strong storms. The "cushion pine", "phoenix pine", "chessboard pine", "black tiger pine", and "sleeping pine" are all like living demons. The Guest-greeting Pine (Figure 3) and Farewell Pine in front of Jade Screen Pavilion merit special mention. Growing out of a rocky crevice, Guest-greeting Pine has outstretched boughs like arms welcoming mountain-climbing guests. It has been taken as the model for the huge painting Guest-greeting Pine in the Great People's Hall in Beijing, which has been the backdrop of many photographs taken of Chinese leaders together with foreign guests.

According to those who have visited Mt. Huangshan, the most spectacular sight is the Sea of Clouds:

Early in the morning, particularly after rain, cottony clouds and mist flow into the gullies and ravines, sometimes within human reach. Towering peaks veiled in fog show their heads above the moving cloud mass, to be tinged with rainbow colors as the sun rises. Under the noonday sun, the sea of clouds forms into such cloud sculptures as fairies scattering flowers or dragons roaming the valleys.

About three or four o'clock in the morning in summer, the myriad peaks are the first to show in the morning light, the eastern sky begins to glow, then all becomes light. Dawn over Huangshan brings fanciful cloud formations. Suddenly the big fiery ball of the sun leaps over the eastern horizon, its rays tingling the variously shaped cloud masses and the stately peaks and pines.

(Editorial Board of New World Press and the English Language Service of Radio Peking, 1980: 121).

The hot spring at Huangshan, another famous attraction, never dries up and the water, which is at a constant temperature of 42 °C, is very pure and limpid, fit both for drinking and bathing. The water is carbonated and has extraordinary curative effects on diseases of the digestive system, nervous system, blood system, and the system of consciousness of motion. In Huangshan, there are also many other beautiful scenes, such as the waterfalls, the harping spring, the clear brooks, and various pools like pearls inlaid on the verdant slopes. Emerald Pool near Pine Valley Temple in bright sunshine reflects giant rocks and pines in the crystal clear water. It is indeed one of the most spectacular scenes under heaven.

Huangshan is also blessed as a wonderful natural zoological and botanical garden. In the botanical garden are the well-known Huangshan pine, China fit, gingko tree, Chinese torreya, the ardisia, the leopard-skin camphor, and the mandarin-jacket tree, which dates back 100 million years. In the zoological garden, the Huangshan monkey, David deer, wild deer, lovesick bird, silver pheasant and Huangshan orchestral bird are rare species found only in China (Pu and Wen 1988, 16).

Huangshan in Economy

Like a magician of nature, Mt. Huangshan changes its fascinating view irregularly before people's eyes. It has attracted not only Chinese people but also people from all over the world. Historically, however, Huangshan received very few visitors because of its inaccessible location and poor transport. Before 1949, there were less than a thousand visitors per year. Between 1949 and 1955 the tourism district was virtually a retreat reserved for government officials. Since 1960, the number of visitors has increased. Up to 1965, there were 59,813 arrivals and the peak day reached 716 visitors. During the Cultural Revolution, there were around 20,000 to 30,000 visitors every year (Tong, Zhang, and Bai 1986, 459).

Since 1979, along with economic reform, China has started to open its doors to the West. The first step was to open a series of famous places with outstanding landscapes to the international tourists. Mt. Huangshan was among the first round of selected scenic spots. Since then, the number of visitors in Huangshan has increased 20% per year. Until 1984, the annual visitors in Huangshan numbered 108,000, with the peak day numbering 11,000 (May 1st, 1984) (*ibid.* p. 459).

In terms of construction at Mt. Huangshan, early in 1932 the Agency of Mt. Huangshan was established, organized by a group of Anhui natives and the governor of Anhui Province. Through its organization, survey and mapping of the tourism administration district began in 1935. Interrupted by the Sino-Japanese War, tourism planning was forced to stop in 1937. Later, in 1939, the central government set up a refugee shelter in Huangshan to collect money for restoring Huangshan. Since 1949 when the People's Republic of China was founded, a series of restoration plans were made and many of them were accomplished, such as mountain roads, office buildings, and retreat resorts. During the ten years of the Cultural Revolution, however, many construction works were discontinued.

In 1979, after Deng Xiao-Ping visited Huangshan, the Huangshan tourism district was officially opened to the public. Since then, investment in the infrastructure of the district has been reinforced, and a cable car system was installed in 1984 as a part of the General Plan approved by the central government. Between 1952 and 1984, the government allocated 23.05 million yuan for the construction of Huangshan (*ibid.* p. 460). The total built area increased from 2,000 m^2 in 1952 to 70,000 m^2 in 1984, including 40,788 m of mountain roads, 20 km of highway, 30 bridges, and systems of power, communication, entertainment, and business.

Although a great deal of effort has been put into construction at Huangshan, still two-thirds of the potential tourism area has not been explored. Until 1979, the Huangshan tourism district was often in deficit and generally depended upon government subsidies. The opening of Huangshan to international tourists not only brought about 202,000 yuan in profits right away, but also boosted local business and transportation. In 1991 the arrivals of total tourists numbered 121,364 (Year Book 1992, 382) and the annual rate of increase in income from tourism was 16 per cent (*ibid.* p. 460).

Huangshan in the Future

Tourism has directly benefitted the local economy, and it will continue to become the backbone of Huangshan's economy in the future. Ever since Huangshan opened to the public, however, the main focus of the nation has been on economic development with little attention to the environmental problems caused by increasing human activities. Recently, the situation in Huangshan has caught international attention. In 1991, an international conference on the development and environment of Huangshan was held in Huangshan City. Issues of pollution and invalid management of Huangshan tourism aroused strong reactions among scholars. It was pointed out that the natural beauty of Huangshan could become its own killer if there is no environmental protection installed in its future development. Mt. Huangshan, as an outstanding landscape in China, has a universal value for the whole of humanity. It was inscribed on the World Heritage List in 1990 both under natural criteria (ii) and (iv) and under cultural criterion (ii). The World Heritage Committee recognized Huangshan not only known as the "prettiest mountain of China", but for both its natural values (granite peaks and rocks, plant and animal species) as well as its cultural significance acclaimed through art and literature during a good part of Chinese history. Several workshops on tourism management were held at the site since the date of its inscription. To preserve Mt. Huangshan's natural beauty and environment is, therefore, an obligation not only for the Chinese people but also for the people of the world.

Mt. Taishan

As one of the Five Mountains, Mt. Taishan (or Daizong), has received the highest honor as the Number One Mountain. In fact, among the Five Mountains, Mt. Taishan is not as steep as Mt. Huashan, not as secluded as Mt. Hengshan (in Henan Province); its temples are not as magnificent as Mt. Songshan's, and its sea clouds are not as unique as Mt. Hengshan (in Hunan Province). So why has Mt. Taishan been so respected and even considered to be the symbol of China along with the Yangtze River and the Great Wall?

The Symbolism of Taishan

Among the Five Mountains, Mt. Taishan is situated near the eastern seaboard, in Tai'an County, Shandong Province (Figure 1). In Chinese culture, the East, the place where the sun rises, symbolizes the source of vitality and the beginning of everything. Throughout Chinese history, when emperors were enthroned, they often held grand rituals in Mt. Taishan, called Feng Chan - praying for good fortune. Between the Xia Dynasty (21st - 16th centuries B.C.) and the Zhou Dynasty (ca. 1122 - 221 B.C.) alone, there were 72 emperors who had their ceremonies in Taishan. They built up earthen altars on the top of Taishan to pay homage to the heaven, and dug the dirt at the foot of Taishan to worship the earth.

Mt. Taishan is also a symbol of loftiness and grandeur. Since ancient times, the Chinese have used expressions like as firm as Mt. Taishan and as stable as Mt. Taishan.

The Relics of Taishan

Taishan has attracted not only emperors but also pilgrims and scholars in history. With its temples, steles, and murals built as memorials of Feng Chan and the poems and inscriptions created as eulogies of nature, Taishan is ranked number one in the nation for its collection of cultural relics (Ge 1989, 174). Among numerous relics, the carved stone by the second Emperor of the Qin Dynasty (221 - 206 B.C.), the blank stele of Emperor Wudi of the Han Dynasty (141 - 87 B.C.), the In Memory of Mt. Taishan carved in the rock of Mt. Taishan by Emperor Xuanzong of the Tang Dynasty (712 - 756), and the Tiankuang Hall built in the years of Emperor Zhenzong of the Song Dynasty (1022 -1064) are the best known.

The splendid Tiankuang Hall is one of the most famous of the palace-style buildings of ancient China. It is 48 by 19 meters in size and 22 meters high with a glazed yellow-tile roof and glittering embellishment. Throughout history, most ritual ceremonies were held there, worshipping the God of Mt. Taishan. In 1008, after defeating the invaders of Qidan, a minority from the north, Zhenzong did not try to recover lost territories, but ceded them to Qidan along with 100,000 pieces of silver as indemnity. Instead of strengthening national defense, he was involved in playing games of superstition. In the same year, guided by an instruction from Heaven, Zhenzong held a big ceremony in Taishan and had Tiankuang Hall built in the following year (Wang 1982, 14).

Inside Tiankuang Hall, there is a famous mural, a masterpiece of the Song Dynasty (960-1279), 62 metres long and 3.3 metres wide. It portrays the God of Mt. Taishan with his entourage leaving and returning from an inspection tour. The mural pictures about a thousand figures with various gestures (Fu 1979: 1). As an early art work, it has been highly regarded for its well-considered arrangement and flowing brush strokes (New World Press 1980: 92).

The carved stone by the second Emperor of the Qin Dynasty is one of the most remarkable of the steles found in Taishan. Carved in stone in the style of *Xiaozhuan* (a seal script) in 209 B.C. (Ge 1989, 175) it was originally placed by the pound at the summit of Taishan and was made up of 220 words. Due to thousands of years of weathering, especially the great fire in 1741, there are now only nine and a half words left. Among numerous ancient steles, this masterpiece of Qin is considered the earliest and, therefore, the most remarkable remains of Chinese calligraphy.

Figure 4. The Sutra Stone Valley.

Another unusual calligraphy is found in Sutra Stone Valley (Figure 4). On a large flat rock, an ancient calligrapher has carved the text of the Buddhist Diamond Sutra, each character fifty centimeters high. Although after the ravages of over a thousand years only about 1,067 legible words are left (Wang 1982, 24), it is still the most important cultural relic of Mt. Taishan.

The identity of the author of the stele which bears no word is contested. Some believe it was set up by Qin Shi Huang, the first Emperor of the Qin Dynasty (221-206 B.C.). It was thought that his merits and virtues were too great to be addressed in words, so the memorial stele of Qin Shi Huang was finally designed to be blank. Some other scholars believe that it was built by Wudi of the Han Dynasty (*ibid.* p. 46).

The Charms of Taishan

Rising up from the grand Northern China Plain, Mt. Taishan is like a giant standing between Heaven and Earth. Along the Yellow River, Taishan extends for over 200 km, and its summit is 1,545 meters high. Surrounding Taishan are many other mountains, some of which are fairly famous. Among those mountains, however, none is as high and magnificent as Taishan. Besides its cultural relics, Mt. Taishan is also full of magnificent natural scenery, such as cypress trees, waterfalls, and picturesque rocks. The sunrise and the Buddha Light are the most marvellous sights from Taishan.

To watch the sunrise from the summit of Taishan is always the initiation of a visit to this mountain. It is also the climax of the whole journey:

At about half past four in summer, dawn breaks, the sky glows red, and then
the sun suddenly emerges through the clouds like a great fiery ball from out of
the sea. (New World Press 1980, 95).

Because of the great contrast between the flat plain and high mountain, the sunrise of Taishan seems all the more spectacular and unique. On a clear day, people can see as far as 230 km from the top of Mt. Taishan (Qi, Yu, and Zhang 1984: 158). Since the Taishan sunrise is so famous, everyone is required practically to experience this moment. In order to watch the sunrise, people often wait in the dark for hours. This sentimental moment not only satisfies Chinese people's fantasy about Mt. Taishan, but also fulfills their curiosity about the mighty power often perceived in traditional poems.

The Buddha Light is a unique scene often found in the narrow area from the summit to the South Gate to Heaven. It appears as a giant rainbow-coloured ring with a shadow of Buddha in the middle. Because it only appears a few times in a year, people tend to believe it is how the Buddha of Bixia Yuanjun makes her presence felt (Lu 1982: 77). The Buddha Light is formed by the reflection of sunlight from the clouds and fog, while the shadow of Buddha is actually the shadow of the viewer. Although the Buddha Light is seen in other mountains, such as Mt. Emei, it has always been considered lucky to see the Buddha Light in Taishan, probably because of its privileged status in China.

Eulogy of Taishan

Mencius once said: "When Confucius ascended the summit of Taishan, he realized how small the world is compared with Mt. Taishan." This panoramic view of the world has been shared by Chinese people. With a feeling of great reverence, thousands of poets went to Taishan and left numerous poems behind. Among them, *Looking Up To Taishan*, composed by Du Fu (712 - 770), one of the Three Master Poets in the Tang Dynasty, is the most famous masterpiece about Mt. Taishan:

> What does Taishan look like?
> One cannot see the end of its green from Qi to Lu.
> Concentrated with all the charms of nature,
> The Taishan divides the dark and light.
> Looking up to the hanging clouds,
> Heart is full of joy.
> Following the flying bird returning to the mountain,
> Thinking about climbing to the summit some day,
> When looking down from the top,
> The view of Confucius about the world is totally understood.
> (From: Looking Up to Mt. Taishan, translated by Author)

Besides the joy of climbing to the top of Mt. Taishan, Du Fu implied his ambition of ascending the summit of his career. This poem has influenced Chinese people throughout history and was engraved in a stele displayed at the foot of Mt. Taishan. Mt. Taishan, with its firm and solid structure, frequently appears in Chinese poetry and art to embody loftiness and pride. Poems dedicated to Mt. Taishan number well above a thousand.

The Preservation of Taishan

In 1987 Mt. Taishan was inscribed on the World Heritage List, under both natural (criterion iii) and cultural criteria. However, Taishan is one of the rare examples on the World Heritage list where the World Heritage Committee recognized all six cultural criteria. Mt. Taishan has been the object of an imperial cult for nearly two thousand years and the artistic masterpieces contained within are in perfect harmony with the natural landscape. As an associative landscape, Mt. Taishan has always been a source of inspiration to Chinese artists and scholars and therefore symbolized ancient Chinese civilization and beliefs.

For thousands of years, the Mt. Taishan district has always been densely populated with a highly developed culture, prosperous economy, and sophisticated transportation system. Due to its special status in Chinese culture, it has attracted millions of visitors. Although the facilities of Mt. Taishan have been restored constantly, there are still many ruins from the war.

Taishan Temple (or Dai Miao) suffered in fires several times in its early history. In modern times, it has also been badly damaged. In 1928 when the troops of Jianggaishake were gathered in Mt. Taishan, the front part of Taishan Temple was converted into a market, the back, into a park. Restaurants, public bathrooms, barbers, and even a theatre occupied the temple. The troops not only used the sacred Tiankuang Hall as a stable but also inserted nails and wooden stakes into the famous mural to install mangers. In 1930, the Tiankuang Hall became the target of guns and cannons during the war among warlords (Wang 1982, 6).

The loss of cultural relics is another problem in Taishan. A famous iron tower built in 1533 was originally of twelve levels. There are only five levels left after other pieces were taken away by the Japanese during the Sino-Japanese War (*ibid.* p.15). After 1949, Mt. Taishan was taken over by the communist government. Since then, the government has allocated a certain amount of money to maintain Mt. Taishan each year. However, during the Cultural Revolution from 1966 to 1976, many statues of Buddha were destroyed by the Red Guards in the Movement of Anti-Superstition (*ibid*. p. 12). The total damage from that period of history is of far greater value than money.

Mt. Taishan has faced vicissitudes throughout history, but it has never lost its dignity, charm, and attraction. As a symbol of Chinese culture, Mt. Taishan has always attracted pilgrims and scholars in history and tourists today. Since 1979, Mt. Taishan has been opened to foreign tourists. The development of international tourism has boosted the local economy as well as domestic tourism. In 1991, arrivals of tourists to Mt. Taishan numbered 19,031, about a 50 per cent increase from 1990 (Year Book 1992: 161). In order to attract more tourists, the local tourism offices of Mt. Taishan promoted various attractions in the area. On May Day, 1991, the mountain climbers reached 150,000. On September 9 of the same year, The Fifth Taishan International Mountain Climbing Tournament was held in Mt. Taishan and 765 mountaineers from 37 countries participated. Besides these, exhibitions of art, rocks, Bonsai, and treasures among other things were put on all year around in Mt. Taishan.

Tourism has generated economic profits but also raised new problems in Mt.Taishan. Besides pollution by tourist wastes, the most crucial issue in Taishan is the protection of its cultural landscape. In the past, due to lack of funding for preservation, many buildings were in a shaky condition. However, since tourism has become the main focus in Taishan, the overwhelming investments have become a new threat. Besides the new modern hotels built among traditional buildings, the repainting of historical buildings, as part of routine preservation has often been criticized for its taking away the genuine character of Mt. Taishan.

Conclusions

Mt. Huangshan and Mt. Taishan are the pride of China. Among hundreds of Chinese mountains, they stand out by their impressive landscapes. Although they each have unique physical features and different cultural associations, Mt. Huangshan and Mt. Taishan are both highly regarded as perfect combined works of human and nature. The scenery of both mountains is not only exceptionally beautiful, but also deeply rooted in Chinese culture. In Mt. Huangshan and Mt. Taishan, almost every mountain peak and pine tree is related to vivid fairy tales; and every temple and stele is marked with the vestiges of history. As sites of natural beauty as well as the monuments of Chinese culture, Mt. Huangshan and Mt. Taishan should be shared with the people all over the world.

For a long time in history, Mt. Huangshan and Mt. Taishan were inaccessible to the world. Therefore, they could not be recognized universally and their protection did not keep up with international standards. In China, although there is a nationwide program of protecting historical and cultural relics, it has focused on classified individual relics instead of the whole area. Depending on the age and value of each historical landscape, different relics receive different protection. Due to lack of funds, many lower level relics are often under-protected, while the number of national level relics is very limited. In the past, except for certain buildings and trees marked for national protection, there were few programmes to protect Mt. Huangshan and Mt. Taishan as whole cultural landscapes. Consequently, their conservation was not very effective. In addition, before tourism became the focus of the area, the management of Mt. Huangshan and Mt. Taishan was unsophisticated and handled locally with inadequate funds. For a long time, the maintenance of both mountains was virtually dependent upon government subsidies. The opening of Mt. Huangshan and Mt. Taishan to international tourists at the end of the 1970s brought economic profits to the local areas. The arrival of large numbers of visitors, however, has become a new challenge to both the management and the protection of the relics. The inscription of Mt. Huangshan and Mt. Taishan on the World Heritage list and recognition of their value and identity as cultural landscapes will help preserve their outstanding qualities for the future.

References

The Editorial of Anhui Brief (1984). *Anhui Outline*, Anhui Science and Technology Publishing, Hefei.
Anhui Tourism Administration, (1983). *Anhui Tourism*, Anhui Renmin Publishing, Hefei.
The Editorial Board of The Year Book of China Tourism, (1992). *The Year Book of China Tourism*, The Tourism, Publishing House of China, Beijing, China.
The Editorial Department of New World Press and The English Language Service of Radio Peking (1980). *60 Scenic wonders in China*, New World Press, Beijing, China.
Cahill, J. (1989). *Huangshan Paintings as Pilgrimage Picture,* unpublished paper, University of California, Berkeley.
Cahill, J. ed. (1981). *Shadows of Mt. Huang: Chinese Painting and Printings of the Anhui School*, Berkeley, University Art Museum.
Chen, D. S. and Gao, B. H. (1987). *Economic Geography of Anhui*, Xinhua Publishing, Beijing.
DeBevoise, J. and Jang, S. (1981). *Topography and the Anhui School, Shadows of Mt. Huang: Chinese Painting and Printings of the Anhui School*, Ed. by J. Cahill, Berkeley, University Art Museum.
Fu, X. S. (1979). *The Scenery of Mt. Taishan*, Qilu Book Publishing, Shandong.
Ge, X. Y. (1989). *The Famous Landscape and History of China*. Peking University Press, Beijing, China.
Li, C. (1974). *The Travel Diaries of Hsu Hsia-ko*, Hong Kong, 1974.
Lu, Y. (1982). *The Tourism Guide to Shandong*, Shandong People's Publishing, Jinan.
McDermott, J. (1989). *The Making of a Chinese Mountain, Huangshan: Politics and Wealth in Chinese Art*. Asian Culture; studies, Vol. 17, (Tokyo, International Christian University), March.
Min, L. C. (1628 - 1701) (1990). *Huangshan Zhi Dingben*, Huangshan Publishing, Hefei.
Pu, Z. and Wen, B. (1988). *The Tourist Guide to Anhui*, Huangshan Book Press, Hefei.
Qi, S. T., Yu, D. H. and Zhang, S. B. (1984). *The Tourism Booklet of Shandong*, Shandong Art Publishing, Jinan.
Sullivan, M. (1962). *The Birth of Landscape Painting in China*, University of California Press, Berkeley and Los Angeles.
Tong, B. D., Zhang, S. L. and Bai, M. (1986). *The Situation in Anhui*, Vol. 2 (1949-1984), Anhui People's Government, Hefei.
Wang, X. T. (1982). *The Tourism Guide of Mt. Taishan*. Shandong People's Publishing, Tai'an.

Ying Yang has a Ph.D. in geography and is specializing in Chinese cultural landscapes. She is currently teaching at California State University at Long Beach.

Chapter 12

Changing Cultural Landscapes in Japan

Nobukazu Nakagoshi

Introduction

Japan joined the World Heritage Convention in 1992 and two natural and two cultural sites were inscribed on the World Heritage List in 1993 and another cultural site was added in 1994. No cultural landscapes have been nominated so far.

The Japanese archipelago consists of four major islands, Hokkaido, Honshu, Shikoku and Kyushu. In Honshu, Shikoku and Kyushu islands, paddy cultivation was gradually introduced from fifteen centuries ago, contributing to the country's self-sufficiency in rice production. Most of the area of Hokkaido was untouched and unspoilt until the Meiji Imperial Government introduced western-style development a little over a century ago.

Japan's long agricultural history has created a man-made landscape. A nationwide vegetation survey (Asia Air Survey 1988) revealed that only 19.3% of total land area is covered by natural grasslands and natural forests (Table 1). By contrast, 24.7% was

Table 1. Criteria of degree of vegetation naturalness and its composition in Japan (Asia Air Survey 1988)

Degree	Vegetation type	Composition (km^2 (%))	
		Japan	Japan excluding Hokkaido
10	Climax grasslands	4,038 (1.1)	2,142 (0.8)
9	Climax forests	66,979 (18.2)	27,186 (9.6)
8	Secondary forests (succeeded)	20,046 (5.4)	17,908 (6.3)
7	Secondary forests	70,484 (19.1)	67,648 (23.8)
6	Plantations	91,020 (24.7)	76,889 (27.0)
5	Secondary tall grasslands	5,737 (1.6)	3,406 (1.2)
4	Secondary short grasslands	5,939 (1.6)	4,856 (1.7)
3	Orchards, tree nursery and cultivated woody vegetation	6,798 (1.8)	6,548 (2.3)
2	Paddy and dry fields and inhabited area with green	76,945 (20.9)	59,527 (20.9)
1	Urban area, preparation sites	14,841 (4.0)	13,527 (4.8)
Others	Bare land	1,392 (0.4)	1,121 (0.4)
	Open water	4,170 (1.1)	3,263 (1.1)
	Unidentified	72 (0.1>)	72 (0.1>)
Total		368,470	284,490

established with conifer plantations to reforest broad-leaved forests logged since the 1950s. The concept of the Japanese traditional landscape is characterized by social communities surrounded with paddy fields and rural forests.

Today, almost 21% of Japanese land is farmland with rice paddies. Secondary forests account for nearly a quarter of the total land area and almost all of them are considered as rural forests. Many secondary grasslands used for livestock farming are also located near social communities, however, their total area covers only about 3% of the land. In contrast to European or "Western" agriculture, Japanese agriculture is characterized by the absence of grazing. Historically, cattle were used mainly as animals to work agricultural fields, while cattle breeding and dairy production were not given much importance.

Urban areas have expanded due to rapid population growth flowing into the large cities such as Tokyo and Osaka, as Japan industrialized after the end of World War II. However, these urban areas occupy only 4% of the total national land area.

The major landscape structure, especially in extensive areas in rural and mountainous regions, is formed primarily of arable lands, rural forests and mountain plantations, where man can easily influence vegetation growth and structural development.

This study focuses on the recent changes in three distinct and representative rural cultural landscapes in Hiroshima Prefecture in south western Japan (see Figure 1):

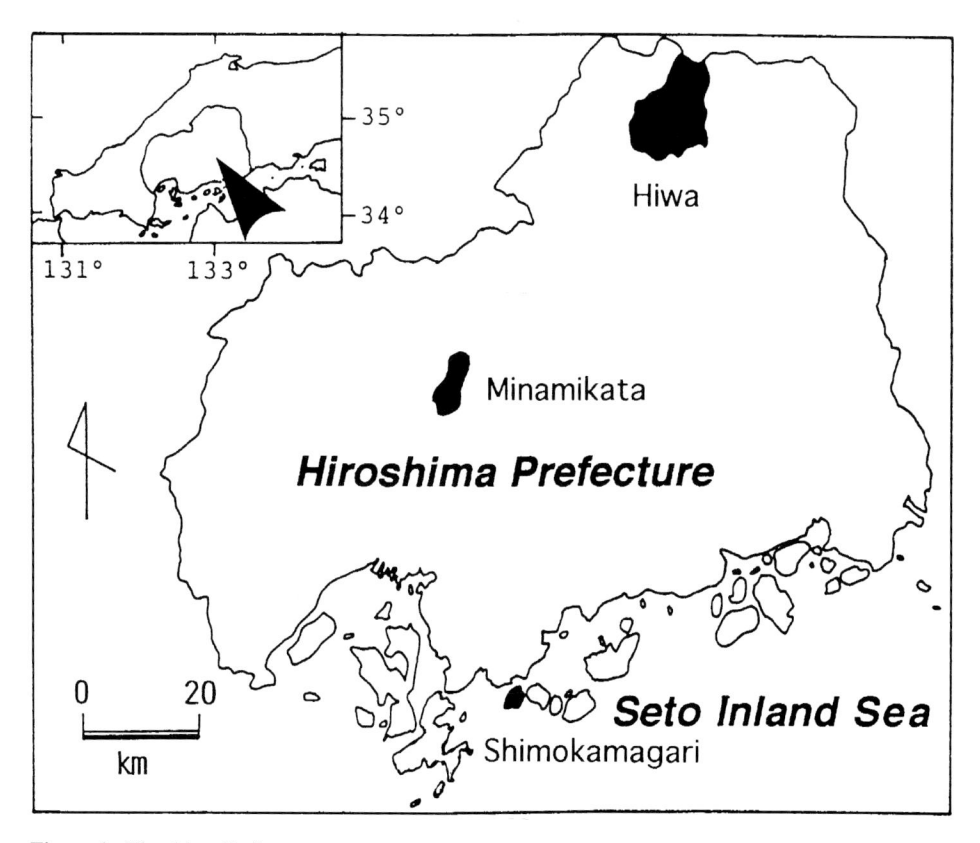

Figure 1. Hiroshima Prefecture.

Minamakita, an agricultural village in Chiyoda-cho (132° 35´ E longitude, 34° 37' N latitude); Shimokamagari, an island farming village (132° 40´ E, 34° 45´ N); Hiwa, a mountain village (132° 00´ E, 35° 00´ N) (Someya et al. 1989; Kamada and Nakagoshi 1990; Nakagoshi and Ohta 1992).

Methods

Vegetation maps (on a scale of 1:25,000) were drawn over the topographical map (Nakagoshi et al. 1989, Kamada and Nakagoshi 1990, Nakagoshi and Ohta 1991). Forest was classified into three types according to height (from 3 m to 8 m) to clearly delineate the developmental condition of forests. Vegetation elements and types were studied quantitatively on these maps. Comparison of the vegetation maps with aerial photographs taken before 1960 indicates the structural changes in landscape. The vegetation was analyzed by units based on physiognomy and not by phytosociological units, because the previous aerial photographs only revealed dominant species, while the small plant species that grew in association were not clearly indicated.

Cultural landscape in Minamakita, a farm village

The principal crop of Japan as an agricultural country was rice. Rice paddies spread nationwide about 1,500 years ago and became an important factor in the formation of the traditional Japanese landscape. Throughout our long history, the complexity of small rice paddies has been maintained. However, individual paddy size has quadrupled due to recent redevelopment. Paddy fields are laid out in series, forming a fairly uniform landscape.

Fertilizer is indispensable for maintaining a paddy field. As cattle breeding did not flourish in Japan, almost all fertilizers were produced from fallen leaf litter collected from rural forests. These forests also provided fodder for cattle and horses, but were most significant as source of fuelwood. Older, larger trees were mainly used for building materials, while younger trees were used for charcoal. The uses and different rural forest vegetation types are shown in Figure 2.

If the forests had been used in the sequence shown, there would have been various types of forest at each time of utilization. The Minamikata vegetation map of 1966, just after the abandonment of the rural forests, shows the traditional structure maintained. Comparison with the 1987 map (Figure 3), 30 years after their abandonment, clearly shows that while a variety of vegetation elements were scattered in 1966, in 1987 tall pine forests have formed as a result of their abandonment. The boundaries of each element have disappeared; as a result, it is forming a dull and unsightly landscape. These abandoned pine forests are aggravating the landscape problem with the incidence of pine wilt disease causing the destruction of pine trees on a large scale. Consequently, succession from pine forests to oak forests is becoming inevitable, as shown by black broken lines (Figure 2 C-F).

The cultural landscape in a farm village is losing its diversity, due to reduction in both the kind and the number of rural forest areas. The unification of once varied vegetation units means loss of flora and fauna appropriate to each stage. As the gene pools of

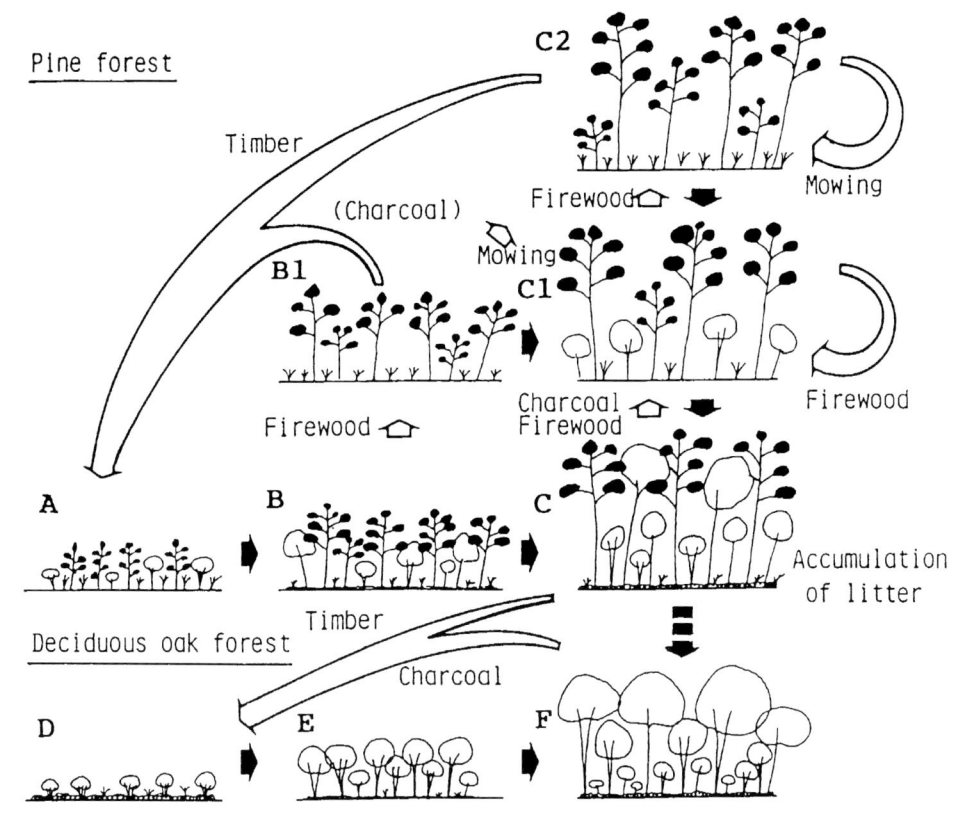

Figure 2. Scheme of traditional cycle of use of rural pine forests and deciduous oak forests in Japan. The white arrows signify the methods of use and the black ones indicate succession of growth after being abandoned. A to C is pine forest series, D to F is oak forest series; A and D is short forest, B and E is mid-height forest and C and F is tall forest.

remaining species are no longer isolated, the independence of faunal and plant communities is also diminished, with loss of genetic variability within populations.

Cultural landscape in Shimokamagari, a citrus producing island

After overcoming the food shortage problem in 1950, the production of mandarin oranges for commerce prospered. The population of Shimokagari Island has decreased since 1965. There are fewer people aged between 15 to 64 years, and the farming population dropped between 1960 and 1965. Table 2 shows the social and economic changes which were connected with orange production.

Orange production reached its peak in 1967. Organic fertilizer was used until the 1950s. Farmers collected litter from pine and oak forests to use directly as organic fertilizer, or they laid the litter on the floor of sheds for livestock fodder and made

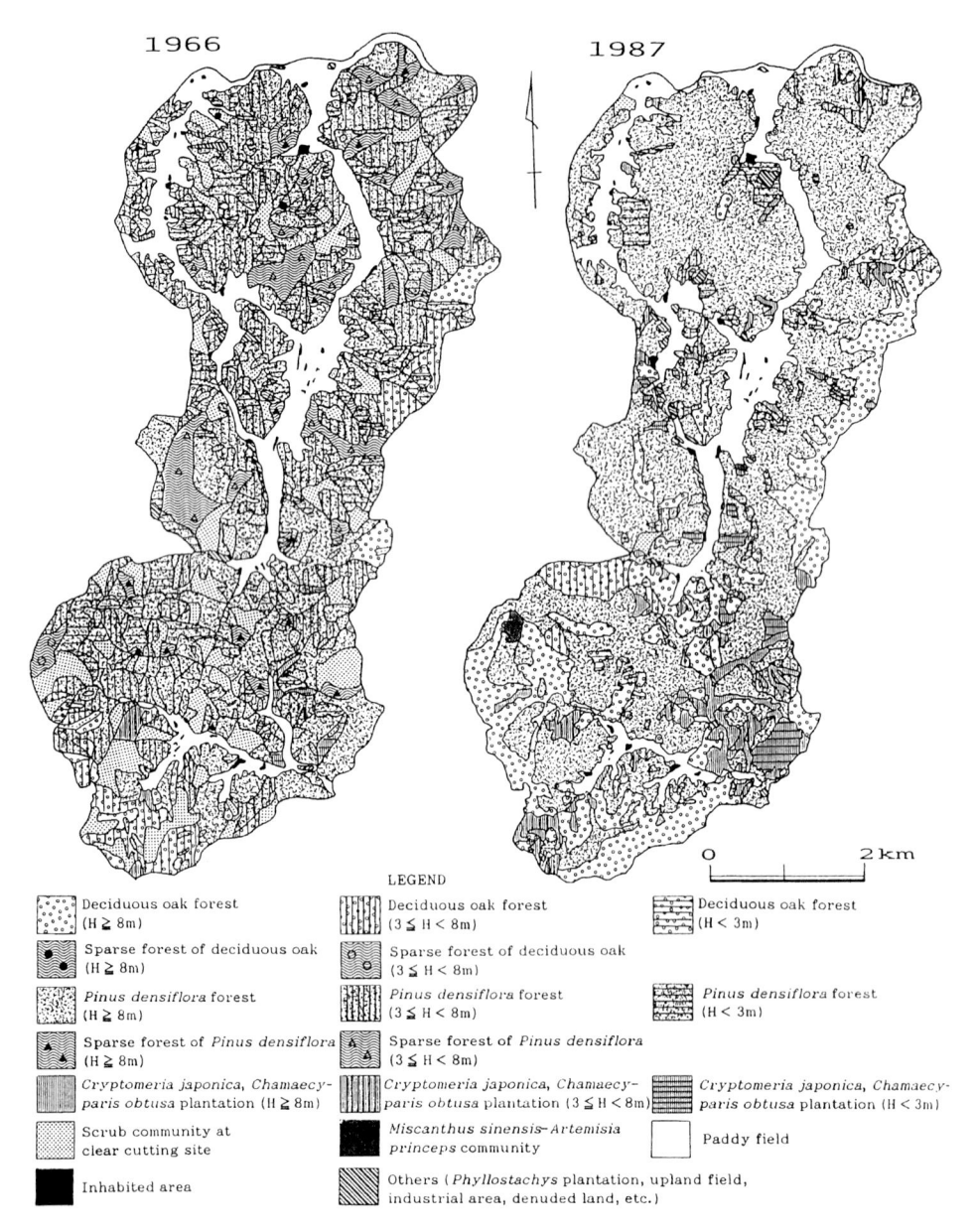

Figure 3. Vegetation maps of Minamikata, a farm village in western Japan in 1966 (left) and 1987 (right). (Kamada and Nakagoshi 1990).

fertilizer out of the dung and litter produced. Human labour was mainly used to transport fertilizers, agricultural products and water for irrigation. Organic fertilizers were replaced by chemical fertilizers in about 1960. The utilization of forests was almost discontinued.

Table 2. social and economic changes in Shimokamagari from 1945 to 1990 (Nakagoshi and Ohta 1992)

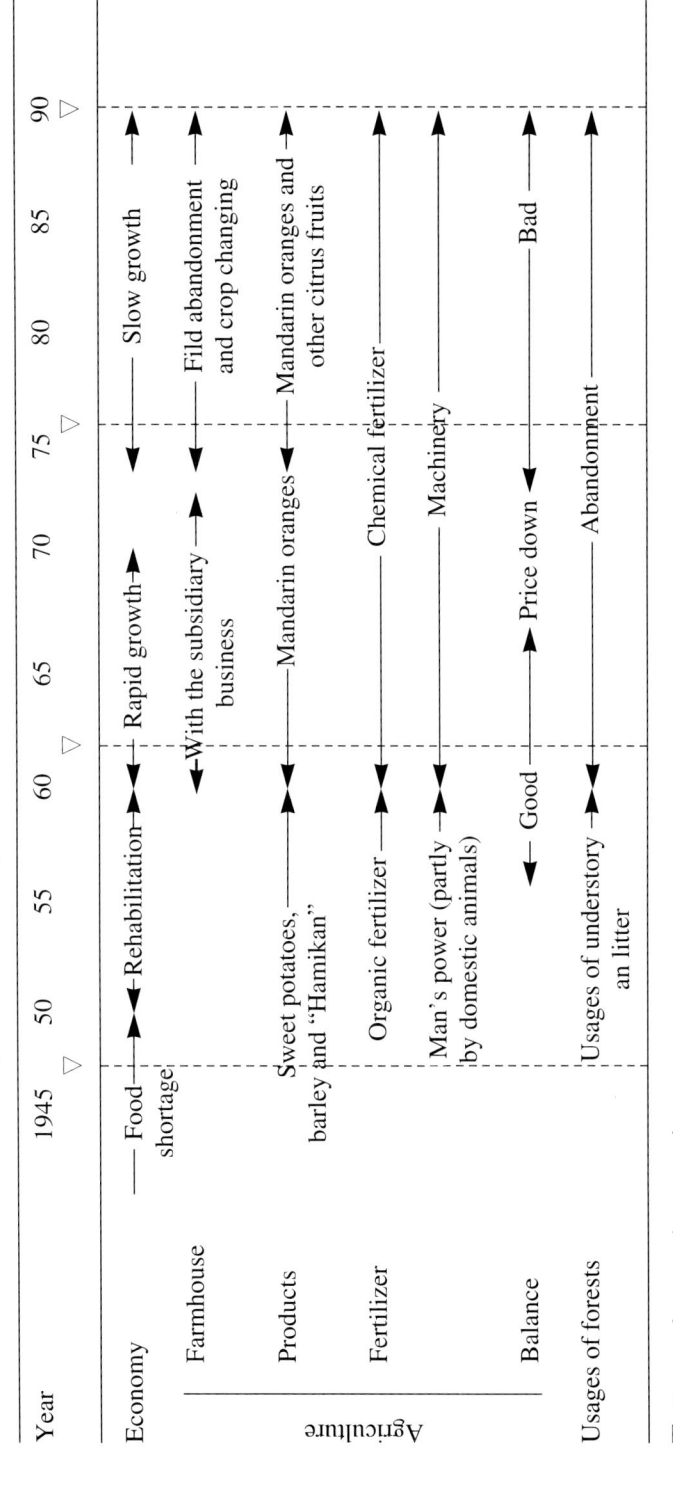

Year		1945	50	55	60	65	70	75	80	85	90
Economy		◁						◁			◁
		——— Food ——— shortage	◀— Rehabilitation —▶			—— Rapid growth —▶		◀—	Slow growth		—▶
Agriculture	Farmhouse					◀— With the subsidiary business		—▶	◀— Fild abandonment and crop changing		—▶
	Products		Sweet potatoes, barley and "Hamikan"		—▶		Mandarin oranges	—▶	◀— Mandarin oranges and other citrus fruits		—▶
	Fertilizer		Organic fertilizer		—▶			Chemical fertilizer			—▶
			Man's power (partly by domestic animals)		—▶			Machinery			—▶
	Balance				◀— Good		Price down —▶		Bad		—▶
Usages of forests			Usages of understory an litter		—▶		Abandonment				—▶

◁ Years of vegetation mapping

Table 3. Change in area of vegetation type, number and area of vegetation elements in Shimokamagari from 1947 to 1990 (Nakagoshi and Ohta 1992)

The items of analysis	Year	Vegetation type*											
		O	Pdt	Pdm	Pds	QQt	PA	Pl	EE	Uf	IH	others	total
Area of vegetation type (%)	1947	38	32	4	2	4	–	–	–	11	3	6	100
	1962	42	32	4	3	5	3	–	–	3	3	5	100
	1976	46	34	2	1	7	–	1	2	1>	3	4	100
	1990	34	33	1	1	13	–	9	3	1	4	1	100
Number of cegetation element	1947	34	106	25	13	28	–	–	–	29	7	47	289
	1962	49	91	43	37	36	14	–	–	19	7	77	373
	1976	31	79	26	15	37	–	10	7	6	11	84	306
	1990	42	67	9	5	42	–	96	32	17	9	80	399
Average area of vegetation element (ha)	1947	8.7	2.3	1.1	1.1	1.2	–	–	–	3.3	2.9	1.2	2.7
	1962	7.1	2.9	0.7	0.6	1.0	1.5	–	–	1.3	3.7	0.6	2.1
	1976	12.6	3.4	0.5	0.6	1.5	–	0.6	1.8	0.4	2.3	0.4	2.6
	1990	6.4	3.7	0.9	0.7	2.3	–	0.7	0.7	0.4	3.0	0.6	2.0

* Vegetation type: O. Citrus orchardt, Pdt. Tall pine forest, Pdm. Medium pine forest, Pds. small pine forest, QQt. Tall oak forest, PA. *Pinus thunbergii-Alnus seiboldiana* plantation, Pl. *Pueraria lobata* community, EE. *Erigeron canadensis-Erigeron sumatrensis* community, UF. Upland field, IH. Inhabited area.

From 1976 to 1990, citrus orchards were largely abandoned. Half of the orchards in 1976 were covered with *Pueraria lobata* communities, and about 30 percent changed through ecological succession to tall pine forests. The primary reason for the abandonment of citrus orchards was lower incomes resulting from high costs of fertilizer and labour. The other major reasons were the aging of farmers, which rendered them incapable of doing the hard farm work, and an increase in other businesses in farmers' families. Forest products such as wood and litter were no longer used as fuel and lost their economic value, and pine and oak forests grew free from human disturbance.

As for landscape structure, from 1947 to 1976 the greatest number of vegetation elements were occupied by tall pine forests, but in 1990 *Pueraria lobata* in abandoned orchards covered the largest number of elements (Table 3). The number of vegetation elements of tall oak forests increased from 1947 to 1990. The number of upland fields had decreased in 1976, and then increased again in 1990.

Looking at average areas of vegetation elements, the area of citrus orchards increased from 1962 to 1976. The average area of tall pine forests increased gradually through time. Though the average area of tall forests was reduced in 1962, it again increased in 1990.

Citrus orchards form a series of steps on a hill slope. Following the abandonment of these orchard terraces, appearance of *Pueraria lobata* communities and also succession to *Pinus densiflora* forests, the structure of terraced fields, considered to be the typical island landscape, is losing its originality, and the beauty of the traditional landscape is on the verge of vanishing. This type of change can be seen in other islands of the Seto Inland Sea and adds greatly to the problem of vanishing traditional landscapes.

Cultural landscape in Hiwa, a mountain village

Japan is a largely mountainous country. Very small areas of farmland are available in every narrow valley of a mountain village. Only a small area of forest around rural settlements was needed to maintain the farmlands. Small vegetation elements were distributed around paddy fields in Hiwa. These areas were originally grasslands resulting from mowing in the past. At present, these grasslands are used in various ways depending on the land owners' individual choices. Landscape diversity has certainly developed in these places.

Landscape diversity on mountain slopes, however, has been minimized by the loss of the mosaic of oak forests which was once a good source of firewood and charcoal (Figure 2, D-F), a process similar to that in the forests of Minamikata. Plantations have often been established after large-scale logging of oak and beech forests.

In the Hiwa area, gently sloping mountain ridges have been used as grasslands for mowing in the past. However, the reduction in mowing has lead to natural succession of this pasture land forming forests or plantation. This succession to forest has accelerated not only around Hiwa, but nationwide. The cultural landscape represented by Hiwa can be characterized as "human - cattle - grassland" landscape, which is distinctly different from the "human - rural forest" interaction found elsewhere. Various rare species of plants are distributed in the secondary grassland, and many of them are in danger of extinction as this type of landscape disappears.

Management of rural forests

Cultural landscape in Japan is undeniably represented by farmlands (Figures 4 and 5). However, these cultural landscapes are on the verge of destruction. If a large quantity of foreign rice flows into Japan nation following the liberalization of rice imports, many paddy fields will be abandoned. When individual farmers stop growing rice, the paddy landscape which is now well distributed in sequences forming a single "carpet", will deteriorate as other vegetation grows in the abandoned fields. This trend is also predicted in the beautiful terraced fields of island citrus orchards. The abandonment of land cultivation will lead to the disappearance of the man-made landscape, which now forms one belt with a beautiful combination of community, arable land and rural forest. Recent socio-economic problems will surely contribute to landscape destruction.

Moreover, rural forest diversity is deteriorating through past agricultural modernization. Dense undergrowth is covering the forest floor, preventing people from entering the forests, and so the forest around the rural settlement is becoming further isolated. This forest was once a common place of relaxation for the Japanese people, a peaceful "home", visited with the object of keeping body and soul together, and this common belief is now being consigned to oblivion from the mind of many Japanese people. We are losing the opportunity to hand over our traditional culture as well as cultural landscape to the coming generation.

Several solutions to these problems are suggested here. Hopefully they are strategic, or at least of help in setting strategic approaches. The list of different methods of rural forest management with potential is shown in Figure 6. Although the high priority is to maintain good productivity, these areas would also be conserved as the habitat for important plant species, and for environmental education as well.

Figure 4. A rural landscape in a farm village in Hiroshima Prefecture (Photo by author).

Figure 5. Citrus terraces on an orange producing island in southern Hiroshima Prefecture (Photo by author)

UTILIZATION OF ABANDONED RURAL FORESTS

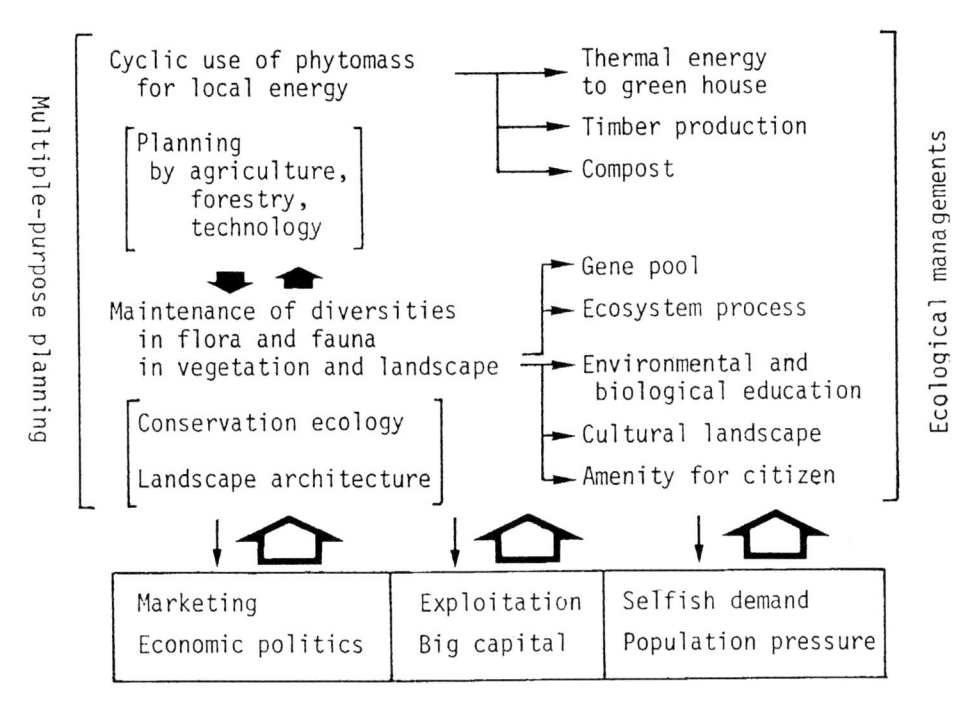

```
┌─ Cyclic use of phytomass ────── Thermal energy
│   for local energy              to green house
│                          ├───── Timber production
│  ┌Planning          ┐    │
│  │ by agriculture,  │    └───── Compost
│  │  forestry,       │
│  │  technology      │
│  └                  ┘
│         ⬇ ⬆                 ┌── Gene pool
│  Maintenance of diversities  ├── Ecosystem process
│  in flora and fauna          │
│  in vegetation and landscape ├── Environmental and
│                              │   biological education
│  ┌Conservation ecology   ┐   ├── Cultural landscape
│  │                       │   │
│  │Landscape architecture ┘   └── Amenity for citizen
└
```

(left bracket label: Multiple-purpose planning; right bracket label: Ecological managements)

| Marketing | Exploitation | Selfish demand |
| Economic politics | Big capital | Population pressure |

Figure 6. Proposed utilisation of rural forests in Japan. It is important for planning for utilization of rural forests to combine demand of production of timber, fuel and fertilizer and its use as an amenity. It must be managed to sustain the gene pool, landscape diversity and cultural landscapes of Japan (Kamada et al. 1991).

The Hiroshima Prefectural Government has undertaken administrative work to conserve these landscapes since 1990. Measures are being taken to deal with landscapes in agricultural villages, island farm villages and mountain villages, by considering future trends. However, economic aspects are a real bottleneck to the implementation of these measures. Depopulation of farm villages and the problems of an aging population are important factors making landscape management a really difficult task.

I write as one of the landscape advisers to Hiroshima Prefecture. From the perspective of landscape ecology, I have made several proposals concerning the conservation of cultural landscape. Conservation of rural forests which have been maintained in their traditional form relies on convincing urban people of the necessity for these cultural landscapes in our lives, and in guiding volunteers to work with them. Restoration of the cultural landscape system is difficult to achieve in a short time, and this is the only action undertaken so far in the present situation in Hiroshima. In other prefectures where no landscape advisers are appointed, it will be no surprise if cultural landscapes rapidly become extinct.

References

Asia Air Survey (1988). *Report of Vegetation Survey (Country Issue) - Third Basic Survey for Conservation of Natural Environment*, 214 p. Tokyo, Asian Air Survey Co. Ltd (in Japanese).

Kamada, M. and Nakagoshi, N. (l990). *Patterns and processes of secondary vegetation at a farm village in southwestern Japan after the 1960s*. Jpn. J. Ecol. **40**: 137-1 (in Japanese).

Kamada, M., Nakagoshi, N., and Nehira, K. (1991). *Pine forest ecology and landscape management: A comparative study in Japan and Korea*. In: *Coniferous forest ecology from an international perspective* (ed. Nakagoshi, N. and Golley, F. B.) pp. 43-62. SPB Academic Publishing, The Hague.

Nakagoshi, N. and Ohta, Y. (1991). *The eco-geography in Shimokamagari-cho*. Furusato Shimokagari Ser. **14**:1-37. Shimokamagari-cho, Shimokanlagari.

Nakagoshi, N. and Ohta, Y. (1992). *Factors affecting the dynamics of vegetation in the landscapes of Shimokamagari Island, southwestern Japan*. Landscape Ecology **7** (2): 119-119

Nakagoshi, N., Someya, T., Kamada, M. and Nehira, K. (1989). *Actual vegetation map of Hiwa-cho, Hiroshima Prefecture*. Mis.Rep. Iliwa Museum. Nat. His. **28**: 1-lO+map.

Nakagoshi, N., Someya, T. and Nehira, K. (1988). *Actual vegetation map of Kure, Hiroshima Prefecture*. Bull. Biol. Soc. Hirosima Univ. **54**: 13-15 + map.

Someya, T., Kamada, M., Nakagoshi, N. and Nehira, K. (1989). *Pattern and process of vegetation landscape in a Mountain farm village*. Geographical Sciences **44**: 53-69.

Nobukazu Nakagoshi is Professor of Landscape Ecology at the University of Hiroshima, Japan.

Chapter 13

Cultural Landscapes of Angkor Region, Cambodia
A Case Study of Planning for a World Heritage Site –
The Zoning and Environmental Management Plan
for Angkor (ZEMP)

Jonathan Wager

Introduction

The site of Angkor was inscribed on the World Heritage list in December 1992 and immediately added to the list of sites *in Danger*. A condition of inscription was that a management plan and legal and administrative structures should be put in place. The Cambodian Authorities requested UNESCO to establish a *Zoning and Environmental Management Planning project*, (ZEMP). An international team of experts started work at the end of 1992 with funding from the UNDP, SIDA, and assistance in kind from other donors. A Discussion Draft of a plan for Angkor (UNESCO 1993d) was presented to the Cambodian Authorities in October 1993. Following discussion with the government, a Final Report will be published by UNESCO in the autumn of 1994. This paper is based on the recommendations contained in the draft plan[1].

What is Angkor?

Angkor is a series of capital cities, on the plain between the Phnom Kulen hills and the Great Lake – Tonle Sap. The ancient metropolitan centres were constructed between the eighth and thirteenth centuries in a region where permanent rivers flow from the forested uplands across the flat alluvial plain to the lake, an area of more than 5000 km^2. In the rainy season, large areas are flooded by the rivers and by a rise in the level of Tonle Sap as flood waters from the Mekong river flow back into the lake. The region incorporates three distinct ecological zones – mountain, plain and lake. The forests and fish-rich wetlands provided an attractive location for prehistoric settlement. The mountains include the watersheds of rivers which were diverted for the creation of the complex network of waterways in Angkor. Archaeological surveys shows that this region was undoubtedly occupied before the establishment of the Angkorian cities. As the wealth of the Khmer kingdoms grew, a succession of "King of the Kings" chose to live in and around Angkor. The most successful extended their Empire over much of Indo-China and what is now northern Thailand and into the Malay Peninsula.

---

[1] Following discussions, the government published a Synthesis Report - Zoning and Environmental Management Plan for the Angkor Region - in March 1994, incorporating many of the ZEMP recommendations.

Khmer architecture was inspired by Indian models both Buddhist and Hindu. However, the ancient Khmer civilisation developed its own art, architecture and spatial organisation as vividly demonstrated in the religious monuments of Angkor and in the design of the cities and the landscapes. The kings built elaborate temples to their gods and decorated them with reliefs. They also developed extensive hydrological systems to manage water for irrigation and to supply the urban and temple complexes. Rivers were straightened into canals and vast storage reservoirs called *barays* were created behind embankments. The largest, 8 km x 2.2 km, has a storage capacity of 70 million m^3. Dykes were built across the flood plain to deflect and retain water to irrigate crops. The annual rise and fall of Tonle Sap was exploited to grow first floating rice on the rising flood and harvested when the water subsides, then receding rice planted as soon as the soils are dry enough after the water has retreated. Massive blocks of sandstone were quarried in the nearby hills and shipped by land and water to the city sites to construct temples.

The outstanding monument of Angkor Wat (mid-twelfth century) has a wall and moat 5.5 km long. The central temple rises to over 55 m in height. Angkor Thom, the largest and last of the cities, is formed in a square and surrounded by a wall 8 m high and has a moat 12 km long. At its height Angkor Thom may have held over one million inhabitants who would have depended on a large suburban hinterland. However, no archaeological remains of the domestic buildings have been recovered as these were constructed of timber and have rotted in the humid tropical conditions.

For the past 100 years, archaeological research has concentrated on the architecture and the historic, symbolic and religious aspects of the period. Archaeologists however, anticipate that a wealth of information lies buried underground. Although new evidence has been discovered of the extent and density of the Angkor archaeological remains, many details of the pre-Angkorian and Angkorian civilisations have still to be discovered.

Preservation Efforts to Date

Stimulated by the nineteenth century "re-discovery" of Angkor by Europeans, the Ecole Française d'Extrême-Orient (EFEO) began work in the area in the early 1900s. For the next 70 years, EFEO conducted comprehensive documentation and restoration projects on most of the principal monuments and vastly expanded international knowledge of Cambodia's rich cultural heritage. Such activities continued through the 1960s until brought to an abrupt halt in the early 1970s by the civil war.

On-site maintenance and restoration work was conducted by the "Conservation d'Angkor" (referred to as the Angkor Conservation Office) between 1908 and 1975. As part of the general effort to preserve and restore the Angkor sites, a policy for forest protection and management was also adopted in 1911. These pioneering efforts combined site maintenance and afforestation with opening access roads and clearing around each monument. In 1925 a small, but clearly delimited area was officially declared as the Angkor Archaeological Park and managed, with some expansion and modifications of the boundaries for the next 50 years. Although the Angkor Conservation Office has re-opened, efforts to take up the work of preserving Angkor are severely hampered by lack of funds, manpower, and technical expertise.

The successful efforts over recent years to achieve political stability, have led to a more peaceful, constructive period for Cambodians and have provided opportunities for a renewed international interest in conserving Angkor. In 1989, the Supreme National Council in Cambodia requested UNESCO to coordinate international assistance to protect the Angkor monuments. Since that time a number of countries, through both bilateral and multilateral channels, have responded to the Appeal of Director-General of UNESCO to provide assistance. With the renewed global awareness and concern for Angkor, a new set of challenges lies ahead. These are how to manage and balance tourist interests, archaeological research and restoration requirements and the socio-economic needs of the population who live in the area.

World Heritage Status

In 1991 Cambodia ratified the World Heritage Convention and in December 1992 the sites of Angkor were submitted and accepted for inscription on the World Heritage List (UNESCO 1992b; UNESCO 1993c) on the basis of the following criteria:

(i) it represents a unique artistic achievement, a masterpiece of creative genius;
(ii) it has exerted great influence over a span of time, within a cultural area of the world, on developments in architecture, monumental arts, and landscaping;
(iii) it bears a unique exceptional testimony to a civilisation which has disappeared; and
(iv) it is an outstanding example of an architectural ensemble which illustrates a significant stage in history.

The World Heritage Committee at its sixteenth session in 1992 agreed to the inscription although not all the usual requirements for listing were met. They therefore made the listing conditional upon: (a) the promulgation of adequate protective legislation, (b) the establishment of a national protection agency to coordinate site administration, (c) the demarcation of permanent boundaries and (d) buffer zones, and (e) international monitoring and coordination. In the Convention on the Protection of the World Cultural and Natural Heritage (UNESCO 1972) Article 3 imposes obligations on State Parties to have adequate instruments of protection and development for a site. To achieve this, overall integrated land use planning strategies are necessary. There must also be management plans for the sites themselves which must be implemented in practice to achieve the desired effects on the ground (UNESCO 1992a).

Preparation of a comprehensive management plan should provide the means for appropriate development of the site. The tools include: a site plan, financial support, a marketing strategy, a legal framework and regulations, a system of effective administration, a programme for staff training and arrangements for public participation. The management plan should contain direct undertakings concerning long-term commitments to implementation, especially mechanisms to provide the necessary financial resources. Control of tourism should be orientated to the tourist capacity of the site and acceptable types of tourism should be specified, for instance sustainable forms of cultural tourism and 'ecotourism'. There should be information on how to prevent adverse impacts on the culture of the inhabitants from tourists. Management plans should include permanent arrangements for monitoring impacts. Everything should be done to maintain and recreate the unity of history, culture and nature of the site. This would not be in the sense of going back but looking ahead to the future.

To meet the requirements of inscription, the Cambodian authorities requested UNESCO, in cooperation with the then Supreme National Council of Cambodia and the Ministries of Culture, Agriculture (for environment), Public Works and Tourism and the Siem Reap provincial authorities, to initiate and execute a zoning and environmental management plan for Angkor. The purpose of the plan was to delimit appropriate boundaries and zones for protection of the Angkor World Heritage Site and to recommend options for an integrated management framework which would include:

(a) long-term, sustainable and environmentally sound management strategies for the protection of the area's archaeological, cultural and natural resource;
(b) a framework for integrating the area into the development strategy of Siem Reap Province, taking into account the impact of tourism and opportunities for employment creation, and including land-use zoning and management plans which incorporate environmental, cultural and historic and tourism/development aspects;
(c) a legal framework and implementation guidelines;
(d) design of an information and decision making system for future spatial and environmental management of the site;
and in a second phase;
(e) professional training for present and future national park administrators in order that they may be able to deal effectively with the complexity of managing the Angkor World Heritage Site, including the special areas of archaeological concern and ecologically sensitive zones within and outside the delimitations of the formally protected zones.

The ZEMP Process

The ZEMP project is part of a process to study the cultural and natural resources of the Angkor region and to identify areas and sites in need of protection. It also attempts to integrate considerations of heritage conservation with those of socio-economic development in the region. The aim was to propose guidelines for policies and zones which will support sustainable use (for tourism, agriculture, etc.) while at the same time assure the protection of archaeological sites and monuments. ZEMP also explored the kind of legal and management frameworks required to ensure protection of the archaeology and tourist attraction of the area.

The ZEMP team was a multi-disciplinary group of more than 25 experts both international and Cambodian. Participants came from the fields of resource mapping, GIS and data management, prehistoric and Khmer history and archaeology, architectural conservation, hydrology, ecology and wildlife conservation, agronomy, forestry and rural development, social anthropology, tourism development, urban and transport planning, park planning, administration and legal affairs.

Recognizing the need for analysis of a large amount of raw data which would be generated from the ZEMP sectoral studies, the project was designed using a Geographic Information System (GIS). The Angkor-GIS is a computerized data base of all types of environmental, archaeological and socio-economic data that can be analyzed and mapped for land-use planning. The GIS allowed the ZEMP experts to cross reference all parts of the data bank in order to model different strategic options and to present the information in various formats: as text, as statistics and charts, or spatially as maps. Photographs, remote-sensing and video images, plans and drawings are also part of the GIS and can be retrieved together with text, statistics and maps.

The ZEMP study was carried out in a transitional period in Cambodia. Since the main ZEMP studies were completed, a new Constitution has been promulgated and a new Royal Government is in place. The process to which ZEMP contributes is evolving and government policy is being defined. Each contribution sharpens the focus and provides new detail in the development of a management strategy and organisation for the protection of the sites at Angkor.

The first step in the planning process was to compile all previously available information from EFEO and elsewhere, such as maps, site reports, plans of the monuments, census data etc. and enter this data into the GIS system. New information was added from satellite and recent aerial photography, which both corrected and substantially extended the previous data. From this process a *study area* was established, which covered approximately 5000 km^2. This area has the highest known density of important archaeological sites. It also features substantial areas of critical ecological habitats and a variety of human uses of the land.

The ZEMP planning process was built on the corpus of known information about Angkor and previous zoning studies (Ministry of Education, Culture and Public Works 1970, State of Cambodia 1991 and 1992) to incorporate the latest thinking on the planning and management of national parks and protected areas (IUCN 1986, WTO and UNEP 1992, FNNPE 1993, Lucas 1993) and international guidelines on the planning and management of World Heritage Sites (Jokilehto and Fielding 1993). The objective was to produce a comprehensive zoning plan for the Angkor area.

During the five month period from December 1992 to April 1993 most ZEMP experts made two visits to the site. The first was to survey the existing data, interpret aerial photo cover and report on the status and potential of the area, providing data in a suitable form for digitising into the GIS. The second visit was to participate in a three week workshop to review and analyse the data in individual expert reports, previous regulations (State of Cambodia 1992, Supreme National Council 1993 a,b). The resulting policies, zones and guidelines are a synthesis of this analysis. The plan made recommendations for geographical zones to protect important archaeological sites, to manage ecological areas and to identify areas for urban conservation and new development particularly for tourism, and to delimit permanent boundaries for the Angkor World Heritage Sites. The system of zones will be given a sound legal and regulatory basis and the impacts of development monitored using the Angkor-GIS established by ZEMP.

Angkor as a Cultural Landscape

The extensive complex of archaeological sites found at Angkor needs protection as an integral unit. Conserving a cluster of monuments or a small group of sites not adequate as it would not recognise the multiple and interdependent functions of the metropolitan cities and their hinterlands. The aim should be therefore, to preserve the above and below ground archaeological remains, together with the distinctive natural surroundings, in their entirety where this is possible.

Although Angkorian monuments are spread across a large part of Northern Cambodia and found in Northern Thailand, the two most significant areas are the Roluos group and the Angkor group of monuments near the modern town of Siem Reap. Here the location of present day villages on ancient dykes provides the continuity with Angkorian and pre-Angkorian settlement which transformed the territory. The landscape contains numerous relict features which include ancient habitation sites, the skeletons of temples, canals, reservoirs, dykes and roads, some of which are still in use to day. These elements give rise to both a relict cultural landscape and a continuing landscape of outstanding cultural significance.

The outstanding archaeological significance of Angkor is recognised by the upstanding monuments listed in the dossier accompanying the inscription of Angkor as a World Heritage Site. It is however, the whole assemblage of features across the region that makes Angkor an outstanding cultural landscape. The protection of this landscape and the features in it will enable further archaeological research to understand the significance of the Khmer civilisation and will give pleasure to visitors and provide a focus for the national identity of the modern Cambodian nation state.

Among the archaeological treasures found at Angkor, inscriptions describe in formal terms a royal view of Angkor; works of art depict life in images in base-relief; and a Chinese visitor in the thirteenth century described his impressions of a great capital city at its height. The cultural history of the Khmer has largely been examined in epigraphic and iconographic terms and the main knowledge of the site is derived from the study of its architecture. However, the significance of Angkor is also as an urban complex.

Although not much is known of the cities because they were built of wood and nothing remains above ground, further study of aerial photographs and careful excavation in the future will almost certainly yield a great deal of evidence of the urban landscape and the relationship between the different functions of water management, agricultural production and form of settlement. There is a need to interpret the process by which this cultural landscape came about, notably the sequence of canalised rivers, dykes, *barays* (reservoirs) and rice growing areas.

Angkor as a Cultural Landscape on the World Heritage List

The World Heritage Committee has recently revised the criteria of the Operational Guidelines for inclusion of cultural sites in the World Heritage List (UNESCO 1993b,1994) to include the concept of *outstanding cultural landscapes*. The Angkor area meets the criteria for World Heritage Cultural Landscapes. This would enable the authorities to delimit the boundaries of the Angkor World Heritage site to cover an extensive area including both the monuments and their surrounding landscape.

As an outstanding site, Angkor represents the "combined works of nature and of man" designated in Article 1 of the Convention. To quote from paragraph 36 of the revised Operational Guidelines, Angkor is "illustrative of the evolution of human society and settlement over time, under the influence of the physical constraints and/or opportunities presented by their natural environment and of successive social, economic and cultural forces, both external and internal" (UNESCO, 1994). The site of Angkor is unique in the region, placed as it is between the rivers rising in the Phnom Kulen and flowing into the Tonle Sap. In this area between the mountains and the lake the classic urban sites of

Angkor are found, a habitation zone which both responds to the opportunities of the environment and overcomes the constraints. The common re-structuring of the terrain aimed at recreating the universe in microcosm, the two main elements of which were the monuments and water features. These conformed to a set of requirements which demanded much of the inhabitants. The materials to build the monuments had not only to be carved but quarried and transported to the site. The cosmological demand for rectilinear water features was elaborated by the Khmer to a far greater degree than in India, and could only have emerged from a sophisticated tradition of water management.

The Angkor zone may be justified as an outstanding cultural landscape on a number of counts. It has 'evolved organically' (revised Operational Guidelines paragraph 39) from the pattern of ancient rice fields, elevated habitation mounds exploiting river systems, and the redefinition of the terrain within the city sites. Morphological changes to the natural environment reflected the religious imperatives of the Khmer from the eighth to fourteenth centuries.

Much of the ZEMP study area is valued as a 'continuing landscape .. one which retains an active social (and economic) role in contemporary society' (paragraph 39) with many significant material features remaining such as dykes, canals, dams, sluices and bridges. Furthermore, prehistoric sites exhibit both the ethnographic evidence of a disappearing 'traditional' way of life, and a long term habitation zone.

The core areas of Roluos and Angkor groups of monuments are also relic landscapes (paragraph 39) and contain the largely intact structures of the state temples and their associated moats, causeways and access roads, representing 500 years of development.

Cultural landscapes often reflect specific techniques of sustainable land use, considering the characteristics and limits of natural environment they are established in, and a specific spiritual relationship to nature (paragraph 38). The techniques of water management at Angkor are an example of the sophisticated management of natural resources. They were designed to irrigate rice, supply a large population and to provide for religious ceremonies. The Angkor water management system differed from those of earlier periods. Research may lead to an understanding of the evolutionary "flow" of man's relationship with the environment which lead to the extraordinary achievements of the Khmer at Angkor and then to their decline. A full description of the cultures(s) remains for the future, however the distribution of elevated mounds adjacent to water courses has yielded pottery and lithic artifacts (ZEMP expert reports) and future survey will undoubtedly enlarge this knowledge to include metal working sites. Exploration of how early man modified his environment may explain the origins of the achievements reached in the historical period.

The area to be delimited as the Angkor World Heritage Site should relate to the functions of the cities in Khmer times. It should also represent the different ecological and hydrological zones which illustrate the essential and distinctive cultural elements of the Angkor landscape.

At the time of inscription the World Heritage Committee recommended the delimitation of zones within the Angkor area of at least two levels of protection:

(a) restricted zones around the monumental areas, areas of archaeological interest, ecologically sensitive areas, and areas of mixed cultural and natural interest; and
(b) a support zone (buffer zone) which would include the entire cultural heritage landscape of the Kulen hills, the Angkor Plain and the Tonle Sap wetland area.

The general criteria for conservation and management laid down in the Operational Guidelines (paragraph 24 (b)(ii) for cultural sites apply equally to cultural landscapes. Assurances of the effective implementation of "adequate legal and/or traditional protection and management mechanisms to ensure the conservation of the .. cultural landscape" are required. Furthermore, in order to preserve the integrity of cultural sites, particularly those open to large numbers of visitors, evidence of suitable administrative arrangements to cover the management of the property, its conservation and its accessibility to the public must be provided.

The Zoning Plan

The ZEMP team identified the areas and possible boundaries for zones of protection and proposed regulatory guidelines for each zone. The team proposed zones based on the principles of protected area management and site development planning. Administrative options designed to implement the zoning regulations were recommended. The zones were kept simple as Cambodia lacks the institutional capacity to enforce regulations and is short of professional and technical skills to manage complex zones.

The areas with the greatest density of archaeological sites and which constitute the core of the cultural landscape were proposed as the *Angkor Parks*. These zones require maximum protection and intensive management. They consist of:

(a) *The Angkor Archaeological Park*[2] an area of 380 km^2 around the core monuments in the Angkor and Roluos groups which are of greatest historic and tourist interest.
(b) *The Phnom Kulen Park* an area of 370 km^2 in the mountains containing numerous archaeological sites. As the catchment area of the rivers and covered by high forest, it has hydrological and ecological interest and also recreational value.

ZEMP recommended the establishment of an *Angkor Parks Agency* to manage the components of the Angkor Parks. This could be done by amendment of the decision of the Supreme National Council for the Protection of Cultural Property (February 10 1993) under the Ministry of Culture and supported by a decree on the Creation and Designation of Protected Areas (November 1 1993) by the Ministry of Environment (Royal Government of Cambodia 1993). The appropriate institutional structure would be developed by the government as responsibilities of Ministries and of central and local government are clarified. The proposed role of the Angkor Parks Agency is to plan, develop, maintain and administer the zones comprising the Angkor Parks. The agency would absorb and extend the functions of the present Angkor Conservation Office.

---

[2] Since this paper was prepared, the new government has adopted a *national system of protected cultural sites* based on ZEMP recommendations and other considerations. The system comprises four categories of site: Protected Archaeological Reserves, Monumental Sites, Sites of Archaeological, Anthropological or Historic Interest and Protected Cultural Landscapes. The area recommended by ZEMP as the Angkor Archaeological Park includes; three Protected Archaeological Reserves for Angkor, Roluos and Banteay Srei. These Archaeological Reserves have within them Monumental Sites and are also linked by Protected Cultural Landscapes which follow the historic rivers and causeways.

While the Angkor Parks require the most intensive management because of their high tourist interest, they are only part of the wider cultural landscape which contains a wealth of archaeological sites. ZEMP therefore proposed that the entire Angkor region, embracing the whole Siem Reap Province, should be accorded a level of protection. This region has a large population of 500,000 people and will come under increasing pressure for rural development. Managing development will require a high level of awareness and concern for the heritage. Therefore specific zones were identified to give special protection to important ecological areas and to stimulate urban development in appropriate locations. The zones are:

(i) *Sites of Archaeological, Anthropological or Historic Interest* where archaeological sites lying outside the boundaries of the Angkor Parks, will be listed and protected.
(ii) *Ecologically Sensitive Zones* comprising Tonle Sap wetlands, primary forest areas and water corridors to ensure the sustainability of critical local land and water resources.
(iii) *Sustainable Development Areas* for rural development, urban conservation and new urban development and tourism where historic human environments are preserved and planned new development accommodated.

The proposed zones are accompanied by guidelines which attempt to balance the needs for protection of archaeological heritage and sustainable use of natural resources with those of economic development and new construction.

ZEMP recommended that development in the Angkor region should require approval from a high level authority consisting of representatives of concerned ministries, government agencies and local government authorities. The authority would assess the impacts of all development on the cultural and natural resources and should apply guidelines and require mitigation measures to conserve the cultural heritage.

To concentrate and facilitate the development of tourism, special *Tourist Development Zones* were proposed in which the modern tourist facilities would be encouraged. ZEMP further proposed the establishment of a *Tourist Development Corporation* for Siem Reap which would acquire land within the tourist development zone and prepare and service sites for sale or lease to investors under terms which would require the highest standards of quality development and operation. These zones are shown on Figures 1 and 2.

Principles for Guiding Development in the Angkor Cultural Landscape

As one of the world's pre-eminent cultural achievements, the monuments of Angkor hold great attraction for tourists. Explosive tourist development has both positive and negative aspects. On the one hand, it can provide new socio-economic opportunities over a considerable range of skills. On the other hand, if not properly planned for, a massive influx of tourists could quickly degrade the fragile archaeological monuments, deplete the natural resources and shatter the cultural fabric of the local communities. Unsustainable types of speculative tourist development would only serve to enrich a small number of foreign investors who may take the profits out of the country, thus excluding the majority of the Cambodian people from receiving the full economic benefits from the tourist boom.

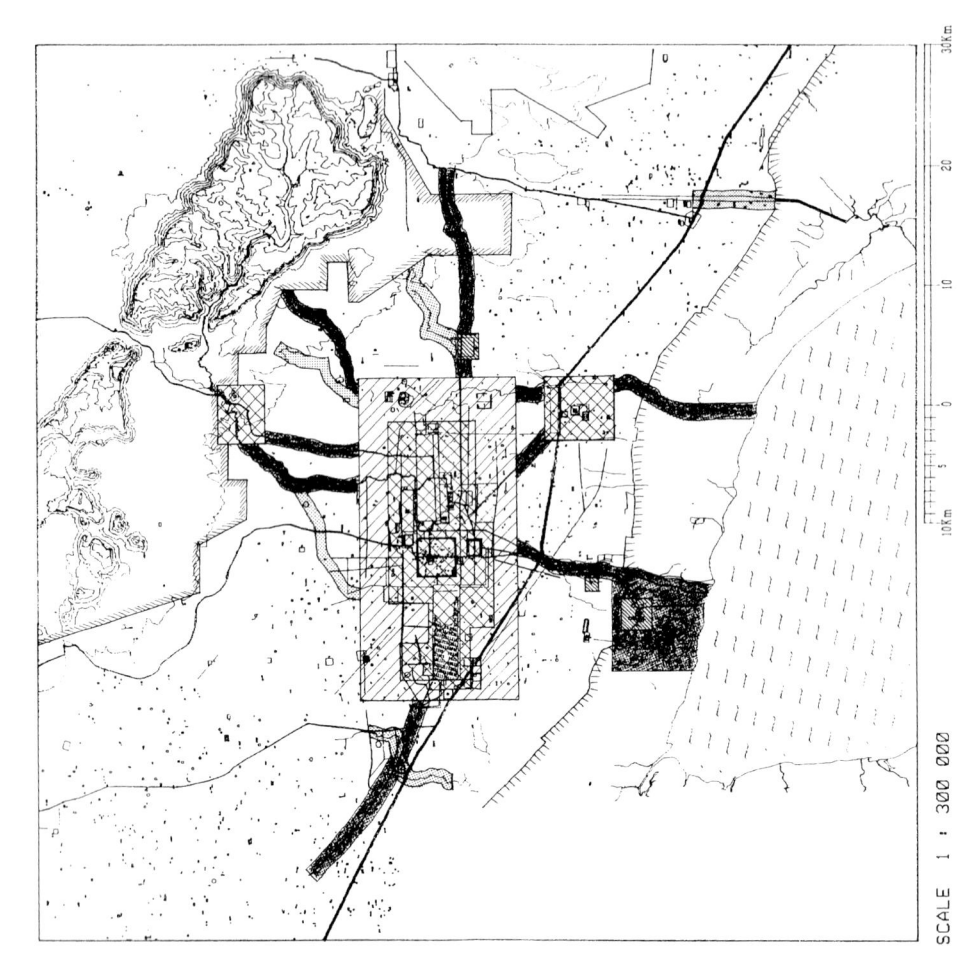

Figures 1 and 2. Proposed Zones in the Siem Reap-Angkor Region (Ministry of Culture-UNESCO, Angkor Gis. 1994)

Cultural Landscapes of Angkor Region, Cambodia _____ 149

PROPOSED ZONES IN THE SIEM REAP-ANGKOR REGION

ZONING AND ENVIRONMENTAL MANAGEMENT PLAN FOR THE ANGKOR REGION

LEGEND

Protected Cultural Sites
Protected Archaeological Reserves
Monumental Sites
Sites of Archaeological, Anthropological or Historic Interest

Urban Development Zones
Urban Conservation zones
Urban Expansion Zones
Tourist Development Zones
Proposed Road Corridors

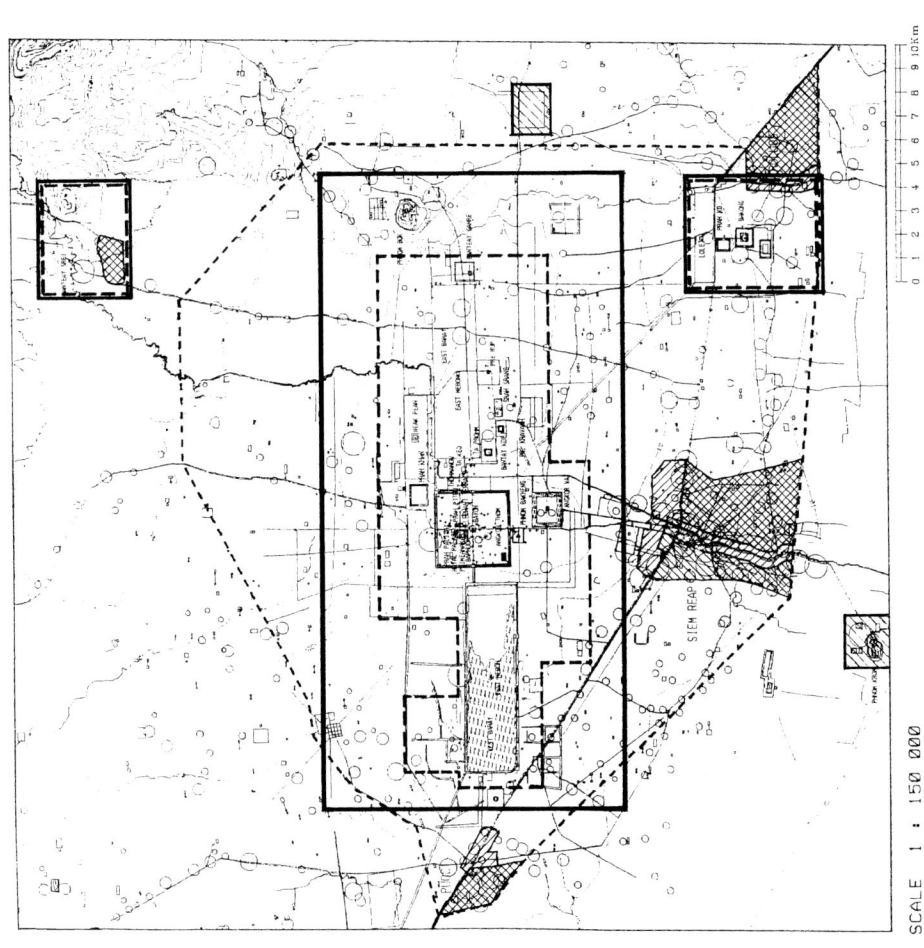

SCALE 1 : 150 000

Therefore, development of the area must be directed by an approach to strategic zoning and phasing that supports sustainable tourism. This could lead to an equitable distribution of wealth and preservation of Angkor's cultural and natural resources.

The following principles should guide development in the Angkor region and reflect the principles for sustainable development (IUCN, UNEP, WWF 1991; Tourism Concern 1992; IIED 1993):

(a) Development should not degrade the resource base upon which it depends.
(b) Cultural, ecological and economic diversity should be maximised.
(c) Archaeological and environmental conservation can be tools to stimulate economic development.
(d) Development activities should be based on local value systems.
(e) Short-term benefits should not take precedence over long-term costs.
(f) Economic benefits should be equitably distributed among the local population.
(g) Development should be undertaken within a legal regulatory framework.
(h) Developers should pay for all costs of negative impacts.
(i) Zoning is a tool to achieve resource compatibility.
(j) Sustainable development is a process; so plan as you proceed within a strategic framework and vision.

With proper controls, considerable economic development around the Angkor area can take place without endangering the monuments or underground archaeological sites and should therefore be encouraged. For the foreseeable future, it is anticipated that tourism will form the principle economic base of the Siem Reap town economy. Elsewhere exploitation of forests, minerals and other natural resources will provide another source of income, but these resources risk depletion. Culture tourism should assume a larger role as a basis for provincial and national economic growth.

Planned development reduces risks and increases the benefits from investment actions. Planned development in the rural sector requires an integrated strategy for agriculture, forestry, aquaculture and community development. Planned development in the urban sector requires a strategy for development and adoption of a regulatory system to control land use and uphold environmental standards.

Protecting the Wider Region

The northern shores of Tonle Sap, the Angkor plain and the Kulen hills form a region of outstanding biodiversity. The unique freshwater wetland system of Tonle Sap is currently being studied as a potential World Heritage (natural) area. The ZEMP team recommended that the proposed Phnom Kulen Park should form an extension of the Angkor World Heritage Site or be inscribed as a separate mixed (cultural and natural) Site following further study once security in the area is improved. Therefore, in addition to the initial sites at Angkor, other areas in the Angkor region may be suitable for inscription on the World Heritage List.

Given the present lack of government structures for conservation, it is not advisable to attempt to nominate for World Heritage listing very extensive areas of either Tonle Sap as a natural site or the Angkor Plain as a cultural landscape. The workshop on the World Heritage Convention, held during the 4th World Congress on National Parks and Protected Areas, recommended that State Parties, in developing management plans for World

Heritage sites, should define a *World Heritage Site Management Area* that transcends the site/s boundaries, and to use the biosphere approach to manage the overall area.

A support zone which includes the entire Angkor region could be appropriate as a eco-cultural *biosphere reserve* to be managed in harmony with the guidelines set forth in the ZEMP report and by the World Heritage Committee and UNESCO's Man and the Biosphere Programme. This area would link biodiversity conservation and socio-economic development and could provide for the management of the Angkor World Heritage (cultural) Site, the proposed Phnom Kulen Park and a possible Tonle Sap World Heritage (natural) Site.

Delimiting the Angkor World Heritage Site

One objective of ZEMP was to recommend boundaries for the Angkor World Heritage Site. In delimiting boundaries it is recognised that the monuments are part of a "continuing " cultural landscape. The following factors were considered:

(a) the inclusion of areas with outstanding qualities that relate to scenic values, historical content and the need to maintain biodiversity;
(b) the survival of the socio-economic systems that created the contemporary form of the area;
(c) recognition by the authorities of the values in the landscape and;
(d) the existence of adequate measures for management and future planning.

It is important to involve the community as far as possible in deciding the area to be protected. The residents need to be committed to the conservation and management of the World Heritage Site to ensure successful, long-term protection. Effective planning and management of the area is a two-way process between the people and the planners, to establish a mutual understanding and an agreed programme of action. Inscription may create opportunities as well as constraints for socio-economic development. Designation is not enough; mechanisms to manage change need to be established to achieve economic development while respecting the qualities for which the site or landscape is inscribed. At Angkor, conservation concerns should be a central component of all tourism development in the area.

ZEMP originally considered recommending the entire Angkor region as the area of the World Heritage Site. However, there is an urgent need for development in this area which could conflict with the conservation of a World Heritage property. The region in fact, acts as the support zone in which sustainable agriculture and harvesting of fish and forest products are encouraged, while recognising the need to conserve the cultural heritage. The alternative option was to recommend as the World Heritage Site only the area of the Angkor Parks. This is the area of maximum protection in which management resources should be concentrated. It is therefore recommended that, in the first instance, the Ankgor World Heritage Site should be the area of the Angkor Archaeological Park[3]. It includes the original Angkor Archaeological Park together with additional areas to protect

---

[3] This area comprises the Angkor, Roluos and Banteay Srei Protected Archaeological Reserves and associated Protected Cultural Landscapes.

archaeological sites and a buffer zone, particularly to protect the area between the town of Siem Reap and monument of Angkor Wat which is only 2-3 km wide. The core area of the site is already in public ownership which makes the strict application of regulations easier. This area is the focus of visitor attraction and will require intensive management of visitor facilities to meet the needs of increasing numbers of tourists.

Classifying the Angkor World Heritage Site as a Cultural Landscape

The area of the Angkor World Heritage Site meets the criteria for listing as a *cultural landscape*. By giving the Site the status of a cultural landscape, the importance of the contribution of rivers, forest, land uses and the local population to the heritage (in addition to the monuments) would be recognised. Each component of the landscape such as canalised waterways and hydraulic structures, ancient cities and their hinterlands and the irrigated areas and settlement, makes a significant contribution to the cultural heritage, and the whole complex should be preserved.

The activities of a number of ministries impact on Angkor and all need to be involved in the management of the area. The Minister of Culture has responsibility for management of cultural sites, the Minister of Environment for the future of protected natural areas. The activities of the Ministries of Finance and Economy, Agriculture and Forestry, Public Works and Tourism will also impact on, and these ministries should be made responsible for, the protection of the heritage. The classification of Angkor as a Cultural Landscape on the World Heritage List would require these interests to work together for the preservation of the site.

The Zoning and Environmental Management Plan for Angkor provide guidelines for the socio-economic development of the area along sustainable directions while safeguarding the cultural landscape and archaeological features. The Government of Cambodia has taken up the challenge to preserve this outstanding site and to maintain a cultural landscape of immeasurable value.

References

Federation of Nature and National Parks of Europe (FNNPE) (1993). *Loving them to death? -Sustainable tourism in Europe's Nature and National Parks.* Grafenau, FNNPE.

IIED (1993). *Earth Summit 1992 – United Nations Conference on Environment and Development Rio de Janeiro 1992.* Regency Press, London.

IUCN (1986). *Managing Protected Areas in the Tropics*, compiled by John and Kathy MacKinnon, Graham Child and Jim Thorsell. IUCN, Gland.

IUCN – the World Conservation Union, *UNEP – United Nations Environment Programme, WWF – World Wide Fund for Nature (1991). Caring for the Earth, a Strategy for Sustainable Living.* IUCN, UNEP, WWF, Gland.

Jokilehto, J. and Fielding, B. (eds) (1993). *Guidelines for the Management of World Cultural Heritage Sites.* ICCROM, Rome.

Lucas, P.H.C. (1993). *Protected Landscapes, a Guide for Policy-makers and Planners.* Chapman and Hall, London.

Ministry of Education, Culture and Public Works (1970). *Plan directeur pour la protection du patrimoine culturel d'Angkor.* VannMolyvan/Arte-Charpentier, Phnom Penh.

Royal Government of Cambodia (1993). *Decree on Creation and Designation of Protected Areas*, Phnom Penh.
State of Cambodia (1991). *Parcs Archeologiques d'Angkor*. Phnom Penh, Vann Molyvan/Arte-Charpentier.
State of Cambodia (1992). Council of Ministers, *Resolution No.84*, Phnom Penh.
Supreme National Committee (1993a). *Decision on the National Heritage Protection* Authority of Cambodia, Phnom Penh.
Supreme National Committee (1993b). *Decision on the Protection of the Cultural Heritage*, Phnom Penh.
Tourism Concern (1992). *Beyond the Green Horizon – Principles for Sustainable Tourism*, edited by Shirley Eber, WWF (UK).
UNESCO (1972). *Convention Concerning the Protection of the World Cultural and Natural Heritage.* UNESCO, Paris.
UNESCO (1992a). *Intergovernmental Committee for the Protection of the World Cultural and Natural Heritage, Operational Guidelines for the Implementation of the World Heritage Convention.* UNESCO, Paris.
UNESCO (1992b). *Proposition d'inscription du Parc Archaeologique d'Angkor et des sites associés de Roluos et Banteay Srei sur la liste du Patrimoine Mondial*, Phnom Penh.
UNESCO (1993a). *Safeguarding and Development of Angkor*, prepared for the Inter-governmental Conference, Tokyo 12-13 October 1993, Paris.
UNESCO (1993b). *World Heritage Centre Circular Letter No. 4, Revision of the criteria for cultural properties in the Operational Guidelines.* UNESCO, Paris.
UNESCO (1993c). *World Heritage Committee, Report of Sixteenth Session, Santa Fe, USA.* UNESCO, Paris.
UNESCO (1993d). *Zoning and Environmental Management Plan for Angkor*, prepared by the ZEMP Expert Team, Phnom Penh. Selected ZEMP Expert Reports: Angkor and the Khmer History; Ancient Habitation on the Angkor Plain; Angkor Monument Conservation; Surveys among the Population; Urban Development for Siem Reap and the Angkor site; Water Management; Tourism; Vegetation Ecology; Recommended system of Administration for the Angkor Park Agency; Tasks to be Addressed by Legislation.
UNESCO (1994a). *Final Report of the Zoning and Environmental Management Plan for Angkor* (ZEMP). UNESCO, Paris.
UNESCO (1994b). *Operational Guidelines for the Implementation of the World Heritage Convention.*
WTO – World Tourism Organisation and UNEP (1992). *Guidelines: Development of National Parks and Protected Areas for Tourism.* Technical report Series No.13. IE/PAL, Madrid.

Jonathan Wager is an Environmental Planning Consultant and the ZEMP Team Leader.

Chapter 14

The Cultural Landscape of Sagarmatha National Park in Nepal

Hans Caspary

Introduction

In 1979, the World Heritage Committee, following the nomination by the Government of Nepal, inscribed Sagarmatha National Park on the World Heritage List, as an area of exceptional natural beauty, containing superlative natural phenomena. According to the justification given by the representative of IUCN, the site is characterized as the central piece of the highest and youngest mountain chain of the world, containing not less than four peaks of more than 8000 m altitude. It is the product of one of the great events of the evolution of the Earth and an open window on ongoing geological processes. But it was mentioned too, that the park is not only a natural site. It is the home country of the famous Sherpa people, a member of which, Tensing Norgay, was the first man to stand, in 1953, with Sir Edmund Hillary on the highest point of the world.

Geography of Sagarmatha National Park

The area covered by Sagarmatha National Park is of 1244 sq km. The park's northern boundary is the main divide of the Great Himalayan Range extending along the international border between Nepal and the People's Republic of China (Tibet Autonomous Region) from a point south of Dingjung Ri (6249 m) in the south-west to Pethangse (6710 m) in the east and including the highest point on the earth's surface, Sagarmatha (Mount Everest) at 8848 m. From the Great Himalayan Range, the border follows the mountain ridges until it reaches the lowest altitude at the park entrance station at Monjo (2845 m) in the Dudh Kosi valley. It thus forms a discrete physical entity in the Khumbu region.

The park is a dramatic area of geological young high mountains and glaciers with and often deeply-incised valley system cut through sedimentary rocks and underlying granites and draining to the south through the Dudh Kosi and its tributaries.

It contains a cross-section of mountain ecosystems with its altitudinal range of 6000 m and valley as well as alpine habitats. It has a varied but low density population of mammals including the musk deer and has a rich and diverse bird life with 118 species recorded.

There is significant tourism, mostly on foot, by trekking parties supported by porters. Mountaineering expeditions have a marked impact, especially along the major access route from the park entrance, through Namche Basar, past Thyangboche and to the Everest Base Camp.

History and Identity of the Sherpas

Until 400 years ago, the Sherpas lived in Tibet. In the 16th century, they crossed the Nangpa-La pass eastside of Cho-Oyu and settled in villages up to 4200 m altitude, some of them being among the highest in the world. During centuries, Sherpas have mostly been tradesmen. They brought salt and wool from Tibet to Nepal, and iron, wheat and barley from Nepal to Tibet. In 1953, when the chinese army occupied Tibet and the frontier was closed, the traditional economy of the Sherpas broke down. The same year, Hillary reached the top of Mount Everest. More and more mountaineers and tourists then followed him, and more and more Sherpas were engaged as porters and guides.

In Upper Khumbu, the Sherpa country, the main village is Namche Basar, situated near the junction of two valleys leading, one to Nangpa-La and the other to Mount Everest base camp. Still today, Namche Basar is a trading center. On Saturday mornings, hundreds of men and women meet on the road near the lower entrance to the village and display what they have brought from more or less distant places.

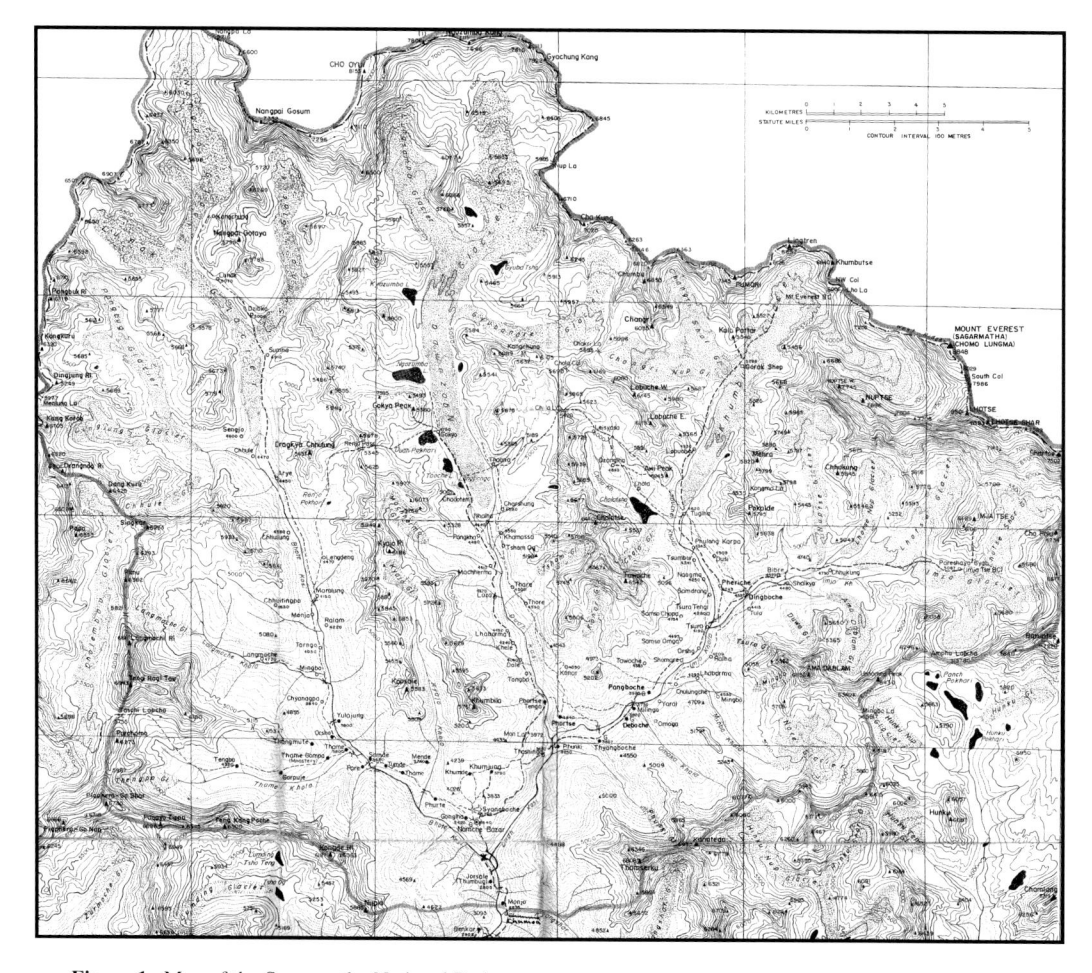

Figure 1. Map of the Sagarmatha National Park.

2

3

4

The Cultural Landscape of Sagarmatha National Park in Nepal   157

Figure 2. Stupa at the monastery Tengpoche (photo by author).
Figure 3. Women selecting potatoes for planting (photo by author).
Figure 4. Potato planting at Namche Bazar in March (photo by author).
Figure 5. Tengpoche (reconstruction of destroyed monastery) (photo by author).
Figure 6. Mural painting at rock above Namche Bazar (photo by author).

Namche Basar is a growing village: a lot of lodges and campsites have been built in the last twenty years. But at the same time, it has lost nearly all the forests once surrounding the village. They have been cut down to serve as firewood and for the construction of lodges and new houses. Visitors coming to Namche Basar may be surprised when discovering the new situation. The forests once growing on the hillside behind the village have disappeared. But new trees are growing inside the stone walls, protecting them against goats, dry winds and avalanches.

Interaction between Man and Nature in Sagarmatha National Park

No inventory of Sagarmatha National Park would be complete without comment on the role of human settlement and its social and cultural significance as well as its modifying influence on the natural environment. On the positive side, there is no doubt that the presence of a predominantly Sherpa population living and farming within enclaves inside the overall park boundaries but excluded from its jurisdiction does much to enhance the natural splendour and interest of the park. On the negative side, there is no doubt that the presence of a sizeable resident population, dependent on the grazing and forest resources of the park, creates problems aggravated by the changing economic patterns and demands on resources, resulting from the rise in tourism to the park and from large-scale mountaineering expeditions.

Sherpa houses, using natural stone, wood and slate, are unobtrusively sited along the contours of the land and blend harmoniously with the landscape. The people developed a pattern of agriculture practised in fields enclosed by stone walls based on buckwheat and barley and, following their introduction, dominated by potatoes. Some families engaged in pastoralism with herds of domestic yaks and cattle cross-breeds moving to high alpine pastures where seasonal settlements with houses occupied for limited periods were established.

The villages are surrounded by terraced fields where barley, wheat and potatoes grow. The ground floors of the farm houses are used as stables for yaks and sheep. Boys and girls carry baskets full of dung on their backs and distribute it on the fields. In springtime, six to eight members of a neighborhood meet each day on a different field and plant potatoes together. English soldiers brought the first potatoes to the Kumbhu region in the middle of the 19th century. They soon replaced the famous tsampa made out of the flour of roasted barley, which has been up to today the every-day food of the Sherpas, and is still made by the Tibetans.

The Sherpas had their own systems of local government with village meetings to determine such issues as dates and limits for the removal of yak and cattle herds from the villages away from growing crops to the high alpine pastures. A traditional office was that of "Shing-i nawa", the protectors of the village forests who had the right to regulate the cutting of wood and to fine offenders. They were very successful at forest preservation before the influx of visitors and before the government gave this charge to people coming from outside the Khumbu region who are less respected by the locals.

Reforestation is one of the main items of the development programme established for Sagarmatha National Park by the government in Kathmandu, in collaboration with the Sir Edmund Hillary Foundation of Canada, one of the four Foundations created by Hillary and his friends in New Zealand, Great Britain, USA and Canada. Other items include the improvement of education and medical services as well as the construction of sturdy bridges crossing the torrents.

In the forest nursery situated on the trekking way westside of Namche Basar, young trees - mostly firs and juniper trees - are grown for the first three or four years. Sherpa women take care of them. When they are big enough to be planted on the hills, the young trees are taken out of the nursery the first rainy days of the Monsoon season and planted in their final place. From then on, instead of human women, Padmasambhava, the most popular Buddhist saint will take care of them. His colorful figure is painted on a rock in the very centre of the protected area.

Associative Values of the Park

The Sherpas' religion is Buddhism. They belong to the "Nyingmapa" sect of Tibetan Buddhism, which was founded by the revered Guru Rimpoche who was legendarily born of a lotus in the middle of a lake. It is to him that the ever-present prayers and mani wall inscriptions are addressed: "Om mani padme hum" - "hail to the jewel of the lotus".

Religious buildings such as "tshorten","mani" walls and water-driven prayer wheels may often be found in and around the villages. Figures of popular deities are painted on the rocks to protect houses, trees (as mentioned earlier) or travellers crossing a risky bridge. Bigger villages have a gompa (Buddhist church), where pujas (holy services) are held by monks of a nearby monastery.

The main monasteries are those of Thame and Tengpoche. Thame, situated on the way to Tibet, has lost much of its former importance since the frontier has been closed. At the same time, Tengpoche has been rising to become a centre of Buddhist culture, despite its destruction by an earthquake in 1934 and by a fire in 1988. The twice reconstructed and enlarged monastery dominates a plateau crossed by the path leading up to Mount Everest and is surrounded by spectacular peaks such as Kantega and Ama Dablam.

Conclusion

There is no better place in the Himalayas to contemplate the highest mountains of the world and to reflect about their spiritual values. Sagarmatha National Park has been enlisted as a natural site, but the material and religious culture of the Sherpas is closely linked to their natural surroundings, they are an inseparable part of this landscape.

Acknowledgement

I would like to thank Lisa Lundby and Mechtild Rössler for their advice and comments on earlier versions of this article.

References

Brower, B.A. (1987). *Livestock and Landscape: The Pastoral System of Sherpas in Sagarmatha (Mt. Everest) National Park, Nepal*. PhD Dissertation, University of California, Berkely.

Byers, A.C. (1986). *A Geomorphic Study of Man-induced Soil Erosion in the Sagarmatha (Mt Everest) National Park, Khumbu, Nepal.* East-West-Center.

Garratt, K.J. (1981). *Sagarmatha National Park Management Plan,* HMG/New Zealand Co-operation Project.

Nomination of Sagarmatha National Park for the World Heritage List (1979). Government of Nepal.

Sherpa, L.N. (1979). *Considerations for Management Planning of Sagarmatha National Park.* Diploma Dissertation, Parks and Recreation, Lincoln College, University of Canterbury.

Sherpa, L.N. (1987). *Conservation and Management of Biological Resources in Protected Areas with Indigenous People. A proposal for Forest Research and Management in Sagarmatha (Mt. Everest) National Park, Nepal.* College of Forest Resources, University of Washington, Seattle.

Speechly, H.T. (1976). *Proposal for Forest Management in Sagarmantha National Park.* Report. Department of National Parks and Wildlife Conservation, Nepal.

Warth, H. (1987). *Nationalpark der Achttausender.* Berge, das internationale Magazin der Bergwelt, Nr. 28.

Hans Caspary has a Ph.D. in art history and works at the Landesamt für Denkmalpflege of Rheinland-Pfalz, Mainz, Germany.

Cultural Landscapes of the World

Australia and the Pacific

Outstanding Cultural Landscapes in Australia, New Zealand and the Pacific: the Footprint of Man in the Wilderness
Peter Bridgewater and Theo Hooy

A Sacred Gift: Tongariro National Park, New Zealand
Tumu Te Heuheu

Uluru: An Outstanding Australian Aboriginal Cultural Landscape
Robert Layton and Sarah Titchen

Australian Colonial Landscapes
Ken Taylor

Chapter 15

Outstanding Cultural Landscapes in Australia, New Zealand and the Pacific: the Footprint of Man in the Wilderness

Peter Bridgewater and Theo Hooy

European derived cultural landscapes currently dominate much of present day Australia and New Zealand, and to some extent the Pacific. As in most parts of the world, in the Australian/Pacific region the 'natural' or pre-European environment was in large part an artefact of the original human inhabitants. Despite popular misconception all the landscapes of terrestrial Australia are, to some degree, anthropogenic (Taylor, 1990; Bridgewater et al., 1992 a,b). The vegetation cover of Australia in 1788 was, with very few exceptions, an artefact of Aboriginal burning practices. New Zealand was greatly changed by the Polynesian colonization, especially the extinction of the Moa, and consequent vegetational changes.

'Naturalness', therefore, is effectively indivisible from cultural influences. Natural phenomena and natural resources find definition in culture and we should understand the scientific and political constructs which underlie our perceptions (Machlis, 1992). We cannot understand and manage the 'natural' environment unless we understand the human culture that shaped it. Our management itself becomes thus part of the culture. We must of course understand the environment to understand what helped to shape that culture.

The determinates of a cultural landscape are a combination of management process, artistic and linguistic linkages and spiritual beliefs. In the context of the Australian/Pacific region these are intertwined, and there are few rules that can be applied. The issue is further complicated by the sacred and secret nature of many of the spiritual beliefs, which indigenous peoples are reluctant to speak about except on conditions of great trust. Although the term 'cultural landscape' has typically referred solely to land, the nature of Aboriginal and Polynesian linkages with the sea mean these principles can be applied to seascapes, including reefal systems and associated cays.

What then is the essence of a cultural landscape in this region?

Human activity has shaped the land physically, humankind has left monuments great and small scattered through the landscape, and especially has woven a spiritual net over the land. As Teilhard de Chardin (1966) has said, there is a noosphere created by humankind. Cultural landscapes are thus those where noosphere and biosphere meet. Natural landscapes are thus those where this process does not occur. But how does a spiritual net manifest itself, and what judgements are able to be made concerning where these are "significant"?

We need to understand a little of the history and pre-history of this region, before tackling this question. Although there is a general similarity between Polynesians and Maori, the size and variety of New Zealand has produced a different focus from that of the Polynesians. Morton and Morton Johnston (1988) note that the physical and cultural uniformity of the Polynesians suggest some common centre early on, probably Samoa, in the millennium after 1000 BC, while the Celts were invading Britain. The expansionism of the Polynesians (in the Polynesian triangle 1) meant new lands, and new landscapes to conquer, although all within a broad cultural experience. Cox and Elmqvist (1993) discuss the case of the Polynesians, where the insular ecological templates in which their cultures developed imposed harsh and rigorous selection against environmental degradation.

New Zealand offered a different experience, to the obvious relief of the early voyagers, who must have experienced longer than typical voyages, into colder waters and certainly colder lands.

Morton and Morton Johnston (1988) relate this as follows:

Maori traditions tell us their ancestors left the homeland, Hawaiki, for New Zealand. Some writers believe this to be Ra'iatea, near Tahiti, as its old name was Havai'i. It is possible the name became more generalized, meaning just East Polynesia, or even simply an island paradise, like the Arthurian Avalon.

"The crew ....found a land beyond their wildest dreams.....Neither tradition nor memory could have prepared them for it.....The snow-capped uninhabitable mountains in the distance looked good for gods, and the huge forests which loomed everywhere were bound to contain many spirits...."

Thus began in New Zealand the development of cultural landscapes with a strong spiritual emphasis. Couple that with the ferrying in of the Polynesian dog and rat, and the introduction of Kumara, Pukeko (swamp hen) and Karaka (a plant with edible berries, picked up en route in the Kermadec Islands) and the stage is set for dramatic changes and the establishment of substantially modified landscapes.

The situation in Australia was, of course, different - in that there was at least a 5-fold longer time for human-landscape interaction, during which period the climate also changed significantly. Two major cultural influences have impacted upon Australian landscapes: Aboriginal culture for at least 50,000 years and European culture for little more than 200 years (Bridgewater, 1987; Jones, 1990). Cultural landscapes derived from a European perspective dominate much of the settled areas of present day Australia; Aboriginal cultural landscapes, seen by the earliest European settlers, only now are beginning to be understood (see Walsh, 1990). This understanding has come about in conjunction with the developing science of landscape ecology.

While the extent of modification to the Australian environment by Aborigines and Islanders is still the subject of debate (Hobbs, 1990), it is clear that the impacts of Aboriginal and Islander cultures have been important in shaping the Australian environment both on the land, and in the coastal region, including our tropical reefal systems.

The myth of the Aborigine as a purely nomadic person is being replaced by a view that in many areas there were permanent and complex settlements - including the World Heritage listed site of Willandra Lakes. The complexity of indigenous methods of environmental management have often been understated: to quote Lines (1991) on the habits of Aborigines people in Victoria:

"Aborigines also practiced river control and on northern rivers built dams to enlarge the area of lagoons for fish, plant and bird life. In south-western Victoria, Aborigines built dykes, races, canals, traps and stone walls to create marshlands for fish, eels and birds. Aborigines planted yams ... And reintroduced young animals into areas after droughts to replenish stocks."

Hardly farming European Community style, over 50 000 years such impacts produce distinct change to the landscape.

Turning to the World Heritage Convention, it focuses on both cultural and natural heritage. The Convention, considers the following as 'cultural heritage':
"monuments", "groups of buildings" and "sites: works of man or the combined works of nature and of man and areas including archaeological sites which are of outstanding universal value from the historical, aesthetic, ethnological or anthropological points of view" (Article 1).

The following are considered as 'natural heritage': "natural features", "geological and physiographical formations" and "habitats of threatened species of animals and plants of outstanding universal value from the point of view of science or conservation" and "Natural sites or...areas of outstanding universal value from the point of view of science, conservation or natural beauty" (Article 2).

In terms of the Convention definitions, maintaining a difference between cultural and natural heritage is clearly somewhat artificial, and there are an increasing number of sites which are listed for both values. The fathers of the Convention (adopted in 1972 by the UNESCO General Conference as the Convention Concerning the Protection of the World Cultural and Natural Heritage or what is now known as the World Heritage Convention) appeared to see it as a "golden list" of the world's treasures. In that sense we must clearly ensure that we treat carefully and fairly all potential properties, and that means clearly understanding the place of **cultural landscapes**.

Australia has inscribed some stunning places on the World Heritage List - from the temperate forests of Tasmania, to the richly textured seascape of the Great Barrier Reef, from the arid splendor of Uluru to the lands and seas of Shark Bay, the arid remnants of a once flourishing settlement at Willandra Lakes to the still flourishing complex cultural/natural mixture of Kakadu, from Lord Howe and Fraser Islands to the unique rainforests of New South Wales and far north Queensland. These areas represent a great diversity of natural and, or, cultural landscapes.

All the Australian sites are listed for natural values, and three - Kakadu National Park, the Willandra Lakes Region and the Tasmanian Wilderness - have also been inscribed on the basis of their cultural values. To these we should add Uluru-Kata Tjuta National Park, which was inscribed on the World Heritage List under cultural criteria (v) and (vi) at the eighteenth session of the World Heritage Committee in 1994. It was nominated and inscribed for its natural values already in 1987 but has important cultural values in the ongoing traditional life of local Aboriginal communities (see chapter by Layton/Titchen in this volume).

All four places are cultural landscapes or incorporate cultural landscapes of the past. They represent important aspects of the interaction between human culture and the natural environment. It is significant that for both Kakadu and Uluru there is cultural continuity in this interaction. The cultural landscapes of the Willandra Lakes and South West Tasmania may be categorized as 'relict cultural landscapes'. However, these also hold symbolic values for modern Aborigines. They are symbols of cultural continuity over many millennia (McBryde, 1992).

Figure 1. Uluru-Kata Tjuta National Park, Australia (Photo Jim Thorsell (IUCN)).

Naturalness is one of the essential requirements for inscription of outstanding 'natural' properties on the World Heritage List. But what is this naturalness?

Of the ten Australian World Heritage Areas all but the Lord Howe Island Group exhibit evidence of Aboriginal occupation. Most of these areas have been affected significantly by Aborigines. Uluru National Park, for example, was inscribed on the World Heritage List in 1987 only on the basis of its 'natural' values. But these are very much the product of, and absolutely depend on, traditional management practices by the Aboriginal owners of the land. Maintenance of traditional cultural practices is essential to protect the cultural landscape that the World Heritage Committee has determined is of World Heritage significance because of its natural values!

We must confess that we find the terms natural or cultural landscape somewhat tautological. The global biodiversity strategy defines a landscape as "...A land and water territory whose limits are defined not by political boundaries, but by the geographical limits of human communities and ecological systems" (Global Biodiversity Strategy, 1992). This is, in essence, the 'combined works of nature and man' designated in Article 1 of the World Heritage Convention.

The artificial distinction between natural and cultural landscapes is well illustrated in the case of "wilderness": a cultural concept seemingly increasingly embraced by non-indigenous settlers in Australia and North America. Nevertheless, it was accepted by the Commission on National Parks and Protected Areas (CNPPA) of the IUCN in their draft 'Guidelines for Protected Area Management Categories' (IUCN/CNPPA, 1993).

The draft guidelines establish six categories of protected areas. Category IB, Areas managed mainly for wilderness protection, is defined as:

Large areas of unmodified or slightly modified land, and/or sea, retaining their natural character and influence, without permanent or significant habitation, which are protected and managed so as to preserve their natural condition.

The term natural is used here as it is defined in "Caring For The Earth":

"Ecosystems where since the industrial revolution (1750) human impact (a) has been no greater than that of any other native species, and (b) has not affected the ecosystem's structure. Climate change is excluded from this definition" (IUCN, 1991).

This recognizes the role that, for example, Aborigines had in creating Australian landscapes.

On the other hand Category V, Protected landscape/seascape: areas managed mainly for landscape/seascape conservation and recreation, is defined as:

"Areas of land, with coast and sea as appropriate, where the interaction of people and nature over time has produced an area of distinct character with significant aesthetic, cultural and/or ecological value, and often with high biological diversity. Safeguarding the integrity of this traditional interaction is vital to the protection, maintenance and evolution of such an area".

From a eurocentric (in terms of peoples origins) viewpoint the two definitions would appear to be poles apart, and, in fact, they are seen as being at the opposite ends of the spectrum by the CNPPA. In the Australian context, however, there is no way of determining in many instances whether a property should be placed in Category IB or Category V!

The situation is further complicated by Category IV and Category VI. Category IV, Nature conservation reserve / Managed nature reserve / Wildlife sanctuary, areas managed mainly for conservation through management intervention, is defined as:

"Areas of land and/or sea subject to active intervention for management purposes so as to ensure the maintenance of habitats and/or to meet the requirements of specific species".

In many parts of Australia nature conservation managers deliberately intervene and manipulate the environment by use of fire to replicate traditional Aboriginal burning practices.

Category VI, Managed Resource Protected areas, protected areas managed mainly for the sustainable use of natural ecosystems, is defined as

"Areas containing predominantly unmodified natural systems, managed to ensure long term protection and maintenance of biological diversity, while providing at the same time a sustainable flow of natural products and services to meet community needs".

Kakadu and Uluru-Kata Tjuta National Parks provide for traditional use by their traditional owners and would seem to fit in this category as well as national park and equivalent areas. Therefore, when considering an Australian cultural landscape we may be looking at a property falling into any or all of four different IUCN categories!

The Kakadu National Park Board of Management, which has a majority of Aboriginal people, sees no difference between wilderness and land used traditionally by Aboriginal people. Accordingly the board of management defined wilderness as: 'an area of land substantially unmodified by balanda (non-Aborigines), or capable of restoration to such a state, where perceptions of solitude, space and wildness are readily achieved and sustained' (ANPWS, 1991).

In the context of Kakadu National Park 'substantially unmodified' alludes in the main to modifications which qualitatively change the landscape such as roads, tracks and other earthworks, constructions such as buildings, mines and towers, and equipment both fixed and mobile such as vehicles, aircraft and plant. But this is best expressed as 'one person's wilderness is another's living room'.

As Elizabeth Dowdeswell the United Nations Under-Secretary-General of UNEP and the UN Centre for Human Settlements has said (1993):

"We know, for instance, that the traditional notion of preserving 'virgin' jungle and forest is in error; as many observers have now noted, there are really very few if any 'virgin' forests in the world. Most have been managed to a greater or lesser extent by aboriginal peoples over time to maximize hunting, foraging, or medicinal uses in a sustainable fashion. Habitat preservation and restoration efforts without this understanding have been counterproductive of our efforts to safeguard indigenous cultures.

To avoid this kind of error in the future, we welcome your suggestions about the feasibility of perhaps identifying traditional 'wisdom keepers' from indigenous communities, who could help guide our policies for species management, diversity auditing, and habitat restoration."

The Australian Nature Conservation Agency (ANCA) has, since, its earliest involvement with the World Heritage areas of Kakadu and Uluru-Kata Tjuta National Parks engaged the traditional owners of these areas as 'wisdom keepers' or as we call them cultural advisers. The traditional owners of the parks advise on and in some cases carry out surveys and maintenance of art sites and wildlife monitoring and management programs to ensure these 'natural' World Heritage areas remain in a 'pristine' condition.

In addition to considering the physical landscape we must also consider the spiritual landscape, which in many indigenous cultures, including those of Australia's indigenous inhabitants, is essentially interrelated with physical landscapes. In Polynesia the people acted as stewards of the land and sea, with chiefs largely fulfilling the roles of resource managers not only for their current extended families, but also for their dead ancestors as well as for future unborn generations. The religious system of 'tapu' was used to protect resources considered particularly vulnerable (Cox and Elmqvist 1993). In Australia, similarly, the most profound and important aspect which links Aborigines with one another and, in turn, unites them with the land is the 'law' or 'tjukurpa' as it is referred to by the Pitjantjatjara people of central Australia.

According to Aboriginal lore the land was created in the 'Dreamtime' by beings who gave shape to the land and life and provided the 'law' governing human behaviour and obligations to the land. As a consequence many unmodified natural features have important cultural values. They constitute sacred places, or sites that embody the social and spiritual relationships and obligations between Aboriginal people and their land (McBryde, 1992).

The spiritual and physical in these instances are indivisible. Maintaining the landscape of group territories and places within them was a traditional duty enjoined by the Dreamtime beings. It is an important social obligation to care for the resources of the landscape, such as stone quarries, important trees or yamfields. Spiritual and economic obligations are therefore indivisible and directed management practices that maintained a particular landscape. (McBryde, 1992).

For example, in parts of Australia areas must be burnt on entering or leaving in accordance with the 'law' or established religious rules of behaviour. This has an economic impact in that burning the country in this way controls the availability of game and other food resources. In Australia at least, a landscape can be natural, domestic/economic or spiritual!

Most Australian landscapes meet the definition of 'organically evolved landscapes' as 'continuing landscapes' and also meet the definition of 'associative cultural landscape' (World Heritage Committee, 1992; and Operational Guidelines 1995). Setting boundaries on 'associative' landscapes can be particularly difficult. Occupation sites and spiritual sites are often discrete areas separated by large distances interconnected by trading routes or the paths of ancestral 'Dreamtime' beings, *i.e.* the 'Songlines'. How, therefore, do we identify, map and maintain these outstanding linear landscapes that link sites often over vast distances?

The issue of serial or linked sites is becoming more and more important from the point of view of identification of World Heritage sites. There are already a number of examples of natural serial sites on the World Heritage List. The East Coast Temperate and Subtropical Rainforest World Heritage Area in New South Wales, Australia is an example. We must also recognize the importance of serial sites for cultural landscapes. Many Aboriginal sites and themes only make sense if they are recognized as serial sites. Each component of this network in itself may not display outstanding features, but the totality of sites in the network does ...(McBryde, 1992).

The Australian-Pacific region also has some outstanding cultural landscapes which persist from the activities of the colonial peoples from Europe. These vary from the "convict scapes" of Norfolk Island and Tasmania to colonial settlements in Polynesia.

Australian places nominated to date on cultural criteria are all aboriginal or prehistoric cultural sites. We must recognize that Australia has a number of eighteenth and nineteenth century sites of World Heritage significance that relate to global historic themes. For example:

– the Victorian gold mining landscapes relate to the world wide gold rushes of the mid nineteenth century;
– colonial frontier settlement and expansion landscapes demonstrate historical processes of world significance;
– Norfolk Island and Port Arthur are representative of the eighteenth and nineteenth century convict systems;
– communication systems such as the long distance telegraph systems spanning the continent, demonstrating emerging communications technology and minimisation of the 'tyranny of distance' (McBryde, 1992).

The presence of culturally significant natural features, indigenous art, artefacts, and, all importantly, stories and legends about the landscape and its creatures all combine to create a powerful cultural landscape. Such a landscape is capable of being listed, and managed, as World Heritage property justifies the values that make it significant. And just as nettles (*Urtica* spp.) typify cultural aspects of landscape in Europe, so we must grasp the metaphorical nettle in our region where we have some the world's truly significant cultural landscapes.

References

Australian National Parks and Wildlife Service (1991). *Kakadu National Park Plan of Management Commonwealth of Australia*, Canberra.

Bridgewater, P.B. (1987). *The Present Australian Environment - Terrestrial and Freshwater*. In: Dyne, G.R. and Walton, D.W. (eds), *Fauna of Australia*, Vol. 1A, pp. 69-100. General Articles Canberra: Australian Government Publishing Service.

Bridgewater, P., Bennett, A.F., Landsberg, J., McMichael, D.F., Mott, J.J., Noble, I.R., Quilty, P.G. and Walton, D.W. (1992a). *Biodiversity: Its Maintenance and Management*. In: Scientific Aspects of Major Environmental Issues: Biodiversity Papers prepared by two independent working groups for consideration by the Prime Minister's Science Council at its sixth meeting, 18 May 1992. Canberra : Australian Government Publishing Service, pp. 8-19.

Bridgewater, P.B., Walton, D.W., Busby, J.R. and Reville, B.J. (1992b). *Theory and practice in framing a national system for conservation in Australia*. In: Biodiversity - Broadening the Debate Canberra : Australian National Parks and Wildlife Service, pp. 3-16.

Cox, P.A. and Elmqvist, T. (1993). *Ecocolonialism and Indigenous Knowledge Systems: Village Controlled Rainforesat Preserves in Samoa*, Pacific Conservation Biology Vol. 1, No. 1 pp. 6 - 13.

Chardin, T. de (1966). *Man's place in nature*. Collins, 124pp.

Dowdeswell, E. (1993). *Walking in Two Worlds, Statement to the InterAmerican Indigenous People's Conference*, Vancouver, BC, Canada.

Hobbs, R.J. and Hopkins, A.J.M. (1990). *From frontier to fragments: European impact on Australia's vegetation*. In: Saunders, D.A., Hopkins, A.J.M. and How, R.A. (eds.) *Australian Ecosystems: 200 years of Utilization, Degradation and Reconstruction*. Proceedings of the Ecological Society of Australia 16: i-viii 1-602, pp. 93-114.

IUCN/CNPPA (1993). *Guidelines for Protected Area Management Categories*, IUCN, Gland.

IUCN (1991). *Caring for the Earth: a Strategy for Sustainable Living*, IUCN, Gland.

Jones, R. Roberts, B. G. and Smith, M.A. (1990). *Thermoluminescence Dating of a 50,000 Year Old Human Occupation Site in Northern Australia*, Nature Vol 345, No 6271, pp 153 - 156.

Lines, W. J. (1991). *Taming the Great South Land: a History of the Conquest of Nature in Australia*. Allen and Unwin, North Sydney.

McBryde, I. (1992). *Australia's World heritage Sites: Implications for Listing of Australian Cultural Landscape*, Presentation to expert meeting on cultural landscapes held at La Petite Pierre near Strasburg, 23 - 26 October 1992.

Morton, H. and Morton Johnston, C. (1988). *The Farthest Corner: New Zealand, a Twice Discovered Land*, University of Hawaii Press, Honolulu.

Taylor, S.G. (1990). *Naturalness: the concept and its application to Australian ecosystems*. in: Saunders, D.A., Hopkins, A.J.M. and How, R.A. (eds.) *Australian Ecosystems: 200 years of Utilization, Degradation and Reconstruction*. Proceedings of the Ecological Society of Australia 16: i-viii 1-602, pp. 411-418.

UNESCO (1992). *Convention Concerning the Protection of the World Cultural and Natural Heritage*, Paris

Walsh, F.J. (1990). *An ecological study of traditional Aboriginal use of "country": Martu in the Great and Little Sandy Deserts*, Western Australia. In: Saunders, D.A., Hopkins, A.J.M. and How, R.A. (eds.) *Australian Ecosystems: 200 years of Utilization, Degradation and Reconstruction*. Proceedings of the Ecological Society of Australia 16: i-viii 1-602, pp. 23-37.

World Heritage Committee (1992). *Revision of the Criteria for Cultural Properties in the Operational Guidelines* as Adopted by the Sixteenth Session of the World Heritage Committee in Santa Fe, 13 December 1992. World Heritage Centre, Paris.

World Resources Institute (1992). *Global Biodiversity Strategy*, IUCN, UNEP Gland.

Peter Bridgewater and **Theo Hooy** are working at the Australian Nature Conservation Agency in Canberra.

Chapter 16

A Sacred Gift: Tongariro National Park, New Zealand

Tumu Te Heuheu

Opening Waiata (Song)

Kati au ka hoki ki taku whenua tapu,	But now I return to my native land,
Ki te wai koropupu i heria mai nei	To the boiling pools there, which were brought
I Hawaiki ra ano e Ngatoroirangi,	From distant Hawaiki by Ngatoroirangi
E ona tuahine Te Hoatu-u-Te-Pupu;	And his sisters Te Hoata and Te Tupu;
E hu ra ki Tongariro,	To fume up there on Tongariro,
ka mahana i taku kiri,	giving warmth to my body
Na Rangi mai ano nana i marena	It was Rangi who did join him in wedlock
Ko Pihanga te wahine, ai ua, ai hau,	With Pihanga as the bride, hence the rain, wind
Ai marangai ki te muri-e, kokiri!	And storms in the west; Leap forth (my love)!

Introduction

I greet you in my native tongue, not to flout the instruction that English was to be the language of this book, nor to test the abilities of the translation services. My use of the language is to emphasise the point that for Maori people, and I suspect for all other indigenous peoples, culture and language are synonymous.

I greet you all, your ancestors, and all those others dear to you who are now deceased. They have been acknowledged and mourned. We of the world of the living, greetings to us all. The lament that you have just listened to is an invocation by one of my ancestors calling for warmth as he scaled the slopes of a mountain not yet named, in Aotearoa. In this way, language moulds the landscape to fit our culture.

The Cultural Context

Presumably, everyone knows where New Zealand is? Once you have found New Zealand it is then much easier to find Australia. We Maori are a Polynesian people whose ancestors travelled across the Pacific Ocean many generations ago making various landings along the coastline upon arrival. Navigation skills over seas and oceans were converted and used for exploration purposes on land. To Ngatoroirangi (navigator of the Arawa canoe and conqueror of Mt. Tongariro) this conversion allowed him to venture into the central region of the North Island, and on seeing a cluster of mountains in the distance, was determined to climb the highest peak and thereby claim sovereignty over the neighbouring land. Coming from a tropical climate, he was not used to the robust and sudden climatic changes of this new country and the cold threatened to defeat him before he accomplished his quest. He summoned aid from his sisters, seeking then to send fire to warm his body before he was borne away in the cold south wind:

"Ka riro au ki te tonga, haria mai he ahi moku!"
(I am borne away in the cold south wind. Send fire to warm me!).

Hence the naming of the mountain as Tongariro, the name of the National Park. My tribe has sound reason to believe that Ngatotoirangi also exercised some knowledge of volcanology in drawing similarities between the natural processes and formations in this land with other islands in the South Pacific region.

It was not an uncommon practice in those very easily days to give natural features human and superhuman characteristics, and to bond geography to humanity. Some features had such prestige bestowed upon them that passers-by averted their eyes in trepidation that some catastrophe may befall them. Tongariro was in this category. This factor features highly in the Maori holistic and spiritualistic approach to the natural world.

The Gift of the Park

We advance the clock to the 1800s, the period of colonisation and the arrival and importation of new cultures to New Zealand. We see cultures with different habits, needs and demands. The greatest need and demand was for land. It was not an easy task to hold at bay, the machinery of advancement where control of the executive and legislature was in one set of hands with the appetite for land almost insatiable.

Such pressures were brought to bear on my ancestors and the need to learn the ways of the colonising force became a matter of urgency. Long sittings in magisterial courts became the order of the day. The paramount chief of the Ngati Tuwharetoa (Maori tribe who have traditionally occupied the Tongariro-Taupo area) at that time, Te Heuheu Tukino, agonized after one court hearing where he said to his son-in-law:

"If our mountains of Tongariro are included in the blocks passed through the court in the ordinary way, what will become of them? They will be cut up and perhaps sold, a piece going to one pakeha (white person) and a piece to another. They will become of no account for the tapu (sacredness) will be gone. Tongariro is my ancestor, my tupuna; it is my head; my mana (prestige) centres around Tongariro. My father's bones lie there today. After I am dead, what will be their fate?"

The son-in-law replied:

"Why not make them a tapu place of the Crown, a sacred place under the mana of the Queen? That is the only possible way in which to preserve them forever as places out of which no person shall make money."

Paramount chief:

"Yes, that is the best course, the right thing to do! They will be a sacred place of the Crown, a gift forever from me and my people..."

On 23 September 1887, Tongariro became New Zealand's first National Park.

Figure 1. Tongariro National Park (Photo: C. Rudge).

Figure 2. National Park Centenary 1987: The Prime Minister and Governor General being welcomed (Photo: Department of Conservation).

A Century Later

On the dawn of 23 September 1987, centenary celebrations began with prayers on the slopes of Mount Ruapehu. This was a time where Ngati Tuwharetoa publicly reaffirmed the cultural values associated with the mountain tops. Sir Hepi Te Heuheu, the present paramount chief of the tribe said:

"...His gift says these sacred mountains are to be owned by no-one and yet are for everyone. My Tuwharetoa people wish his gift to be remembered for all time. The mountains of the south wind have spoken to us for centuries. Now we wish them to speak to all who come in peace and in respect of their tapu. This land of Tongariro National Park is our mutual heritage..."

The centennial provided an opportunity for the whole nation to reflect on the deeper significance of the gift and the philosophies of protecting natural, spiritual and cultural values without change and development. While the concept of sacredness may have different shades of meaning in modern multi-cultural New Zealand, within the Maori culture there is no such diminution of change.

Conclusion

I presented to you the cultural landscape of Tongariro National Park. I am mindful that the inclusion of Tongariro National Park on the World Heritage List under the cultural criterion (vi) as an associative cultural landscape of outstanding value, has added to and enhanced the status of this place to a wider international audience. This is a factor Ngati Tuwharetoa is comfortable with.

In closing I note that this book is for those with expertise in the area of cultural values. I do not necessarily claim to be an expert but my credentials are by right of birth. I am a fourth generation direct descendant of Tukino Te Heuheu, and I write here with the blessing of my father, the paramount chief of Ngati Tuwharetoa. It is that physical, cultural and spiritual connection which brings me to share with you the reasons why this landscape is so special to the tribe. And if this be reason or not for a World Heritage classification so be it, for my affection for Tongariro will not be affected in any way.

"*Te ha o taku maunga, ko taku manawa*" (The breath of my mountain is my heart).
"*No rira, tena kouto, tena koutou, tena koutou katoa.*"

Closing Waiata (song)

Ka u ki Matanuku	I arrive where unknown earth is under my feet,
Ka u ki Matarangi,	I arrive where a new sky is above me;
Ka u ki tenei whenua,	I arrive at this land, a resting place for me;
Hei whenua,	O spirit of earth! This stranger humbly
Mau e kai te namawa o tauhou	offers his heart as food for you.

References

Nomination of Tongariro National Park by the Government of New Zealand for inclusion in the World Heritage List. May (1993). New Zealand, 24 pp.

Evaluation of Tongariro National Park, New Zealand as an Associative cultural Landscape of Outstanding Universal Value. A report to ICOMOS, prepared by Sarah M. Titchen, Australia, November 1993.

Rößler, M. (1994). *Tongariro: first cultural landscape on the World Heritage List.* The World Heritage Newsletter No. **4**: 15.

Tumu Te Heuheu is working at the Department of Conservation (Te Papa Atawhai), Wellington, New Zealand. He is member of the Tongariro Conservation Board, the National Maori Congress and is, as deputy for his father, Sir Hepi Te Heuheu KBE, Paramount Chief of Ngati Tuwharetoa.

Chapter 17

Uluru:
An Outstanding Australian Aboriginal Cultural Landscape

Robert Layton and Sarah Titchen

The Setting

Uluru stands in the Western Desert of Central Australia, far from the main centres of European settlement in the Australian continent. A vast sandstone monolith, Uluru is visible for many miles across the desert. Recent archaeological and palaeoenvironmental investigation and interpretation indicates that Central Australia has been inhabited for 30,000 years (Smith personal communication; Smith 1987; Smith 1989). Evidence suggests that the contemporary social adaptations of the Anangu people of Central Australia were achieved during a period of change spanning the last five thousand years which included the introduction of new tools, a broader diet and more complex patterns of

Figure 1. Living and associative cultural landscape: Uluru Kata Tjuta National Park, Australia (Photo: Jim Thorsell (IUCN)).

social organisation (Smith 1986; Layton 1993: 236-7). Beneath the sheltering slopes of Uluru are two semi-permanent waterholes (Mutitjulu and Kanju), and numerous food-bearing plants. Uluru is a traditional base camp for members of the Anangu community. Many of its striking rock features are the transformed bodies or implements of the creative heroes of Anangu religion. Since the 1930s there have been substantial changes in diet and settlement patterns, in response to European colonisation.

Uluru has been known to non-Aboriginal Australians only since the late nineteenth century (Gosse 1874; Giles 1879) and was included as part of the South West Aboriginal Reserve in 1920. In 1958 Uluru was excised from the Aboriginal Reserve and, since that time, as one of Australia's most well known national parks has become a popular destination for tourists. The conservation and economic values of Uluru (Ayers Rock-Mount Olga) National Park are well recognized. For the last thirty years, mainly as a result of the publications of Harney and Mountford (Mountford 1950; Harney 1963; Mountford 1965; Harney 1968), Uluru has exerted considerable influence over other peoples' understanding of indigenous Australian culture. Since the Australian Government returned ownership of the Uluru National Park to its traditional Anangu owners in 1985, their knowledge and role as custodians of Uluru have been properly recognized (ANPWS 1991). Consequently Uluru has become known not only as a nationally and internationally recognizable natural heritage symbol of the "Dead Heart", "Outback" or "Red Centre" of Australia, but also as a symbol of and forum for cooperative management and intercultural communication.

Definition of cultural and natural heritage

At the time of its initial nomination for inclusion on the World Heritage List Uluru was considered by the Australian Government to be an example of cultural and natural heritage of "outstanding universal value". Indeed in November 1986 Uluru (Ayers Rock-Mount Olga) National Park was nominated for inclusion on the World Heritage List as both a cultural and a natural property (ANPWS 1986: 12).

According to the definitions of cultural and natural heritage given in Articles 1 and 2 of the Convention Concerning the Protection of the World Cultural and Natural Heritage Uluru may be most appropriately considered part of the Anangu people's cultural heritage as an expression of the "... combined works of nature and of man ... which are of outstanding universal value from the historical, aesthetic ... [and] ... anthropological points of view" (UNESCO 1972: Article 1). Furthermore Uluru is a natural heritage property of outstanding universal value - it was specified as such at the time of nomination in 1986. All three elements of the definition of natural heritage, as extracted from the Convention and presented below, are applicable and appropriate in describing Uluru:

– natural features consisting of physical and biological formations or groups of such formations, which are of outstanding universal value from the aesthetic or scientific point of view;
– geological and physiographical formations and precisely delineated areas which constitute the habitat of threatened species of animals and plants of outstanding universal value from the point of view of science or conservation;
– natural sites or precisely delineated natural areas of outstanding universal value from the point of view of science, conservation or natural beauty (UNESCO 1972: Article 2).

Both the beautiful natural scenic grandeur of the unique geological and landform features and the continuing social and religious importance of the place to Anangu, and symbolic value to Aboriginal and non-Aboriginal people, nationally and internationally, were used to justify the nomination of Uluru. However, the nomination did not include reference to specific natural heritage criteria or cultural heritage criteria. The World Conservation Union (IUCN) evaluation of Uluru recommended its inclusion on the World Heritage List on the basis of natural heritage criteria ii and iii. The IUCN noted the importance of the place for its demonstration of "on-going geological processes" (natural heritage criterion ii), referred to Uluru's "exceptional natural beauty and exceptional combination of natural and cultural elements" (natural heritage criterion iii) and recognized the "overlay of ... aboriginal occupation" at Uluru (IUCN 1987). The cultural values of Uluru were not evaluated by ICOMOS (International Council on Monuments and Sites) at the time of the initial nomination.

In December 1987, at the eleventh session of the World Heritage Committee, Uluru was inscribed on the World Heritage List on the basis of natural heritage criteria ii and iii (UNESCO 1987). The disappointing fact that Uluru was not inscribed on the World Heritage List in recognition of its outstanding cultural values in 1987 has been previously noted (McBryde 1990; Titchen 1992). Furthermore, with the removal of the references to "man's interaction with his natural environment" and "exceptional combinations of natural and cultural elements" from the text of natural criteria ii and iii respectively in December 1992 (UNESCO 1992b: 54-55; UNESCO 1993), the continuing relationship between Anangu and their land at Uluru is even less well recognized than at the time of Uluru's original inclusion on the World Heritage List. Consequently international recognition of the traditional significance of Uluru to the Anangu people has effectively been denied in the context of Uluru as World Heritage until the Uluru National Park was re-inscribed on the World Heritage List, as a cultural landscape of outstanding universal value, in December 1994.

Recent revisions to the cultural heritage criteria to better accommodate cultural landscapes on the World Heritage List (UNESCO 1992b: 55) revived the debate in Australia concerning the international recognition of the cultural values of Uluru. The revised cultural heritage criteria are supported by new interpretive paragraphs included in the Operational Guidelines for the Implementation of the World Heritage Convention (UNESCO 1994). The new paragraphs provide guidance concerning the definition of three categories of cultural landscapes of outstanding universal value. The three categories of cultural landscapes are:

(i) the clearly defined landscape designed and created intentionally by humans;
(ii) the organically evolved landscape, whether it be a relict or fossil landscape or a continuing landscape; and,
(iii) the associative landscape (UNESCO 1994).

According to the Operational Guidelines the inclusion of associative cultural landscapes on the World Heritage List "is justifiable by virtue of the powerful religious, artistic or cultural associations of the natural element rather than material cultural evidence, which may be insignificant or even absent" (UNESCO 1994). The criteria insist, however, that the associative qualities of a cultural landscape will only carry weight if that landscape also satisfies one or other of the first two criteria. This posed an important problem of cultural translation because, in the traditional owners' worldview, Uluru is created by the ancestral heroes and is as much a cultural artefact, imbued with spiritual power, as is a European cathedral. European ontology reduces this vision to one of cultural associations adhering to a natural environment. Fortunately, the surrounding landscape is the product of a continuing regime of traditional fire management, rendering the National Park an intentionally-created landscape even in European terms. The revised cultural heritage criteria and the new interpretive or guiding paragraphs have provided the opportunity and incentive for the Australian Government to review the inclusion of Uluru on the World Heritage List as a cultural landscape of outstanding universal value.

Unique and universal?

The cultural and natural heritage criteria used to justify the inclusion of properties on the World Heritage List are included in the Operational Guidelines (UNESCO 1994). These criteria provide definition of the expression "outstanding universal value" as a subtle but intentional combination of the notions of the unique (with reference made to the "outstanding", "superlative" and "exceptional") and the universal (with reference made to "examples" and the "representative") (UNESCO 1972; UNESCO 1994). As a cluster of sacred sites, the form of Uluru incorporates the actions, artefacts and bodies of ancestral heroes celebrated in Anangu religion. Cultural traditions in which the landscape functions as a mnemonic for historic events are certainly widespread, if not universal. Among hunter-gatherers, the Inuit offer another example; among peasants, the Paez of Colombia and the Portuguese region of Alto Minho (see contributors to Layton 1989).

In detail, however, the indigenous Australian philosophy of the *tjukur* is unique. Its importance was, as we have noted, recognized in the Australian Government's 1986 nomination of the Uluru National Park on the World Heritage List (ANPWS 1986: 4-5). Popularly known in European languages as "The Dreamtime", the *tjukurpa* is better understood as the Time of Law or Epic Time. During this time heroic beings travelled, singly or in groups, shaping the landscape as they foraged, camped and fought with one another. At the same time, the heroes performed prototypical ceremonies and laid down the laws of social conduct. The most important places are those where beings of the *tjukurpa* went into the ground. Here their fecundity is concentrated, and can be released to propagate the associated natural species. Each living individual incarnates an ancestral being. The association is determined by the place at which the stub of the newborn baby's umbilical cord falls off. Their *kurunpa* (spirit, self or will) is expected to follow that of the hero they embody. As well as a distinct period of the past, the *tjukur* is also a mode of being which can be attained today during ceremony, when living people "become" ancestors. Several heroic beings entered the ground at Uluru.

Uluru is a clear example of an "associative cultural landscape" of outstanding universal value as recently defined by UNESCO (UNESCO 1994). Inclusion of Uluru on the World Heritage List can be justified by virtue of the powerful religious and cultural associations the traditional lands hold for the Anangu. Uluru Kata Tjuta National Park was renominated by the Australian Government in 1994 (Government of Australia 1994) and reviewed by the World Heritage Committee at its eighteenth session in December 1994. The cultural landscape was inscribed on the World Heritage List under cultural criteria (v) and (vi), thus adding to its 1987 inclusion natural values.

Delimiting the landscape/representing the totality

The Operational Guideline's guiding paragraphs relating to cultural landscapes include the following statement concerning the delimitation of the boundaries of cultural landscapes of outstanding universal value. "The extent of a cultural landscape for inclusion on the World Heritage List is relative to its functionality and intelligibility. In any case, the sample selected must be substantial enough to adequately represent the totality of the cultural landscape that it illustrates. The possibility of designating long linear areas which represent culturally significant transport and communication networks should not be excluded" (UNESCO 1994: 11-12).

In the West we are given to thinking of buildings and landscapes in terms of central and peripheral sites. No doubt this is a function of our embeddedness in centralised political systems. Anangu, whose political system is egalitarian and uncentralised, visualise places in the landscape as nodes in a network of ancestral tracks. The Anangu cultural landscape is thus not susceptible to division into discrete areas. Overlapping spheres of influence extend out from the base camps traditionally occupied by local groups during drought. Uluru and Kata Tjuta are the two base camps within the National Park. Others are located on adjacent Aboriginal land or pastoral leases. The surrounding bush consists of alternating patches of two principal ecological zones: mulga flat and sandhill. The National Park includes part of the foraging range of people based at Uluru and Kata Tjuta. This range extends into the same zones on surrounding Aboriginal land. Atila is another, structurally similar traditional base camp, now located on a pastoral lease outside the park.

This cultural landscape is made intelligible to those who visit Uluru through interpretive park leaflets and a video prepared by the Anangu community. *An Aboriginal History of Uluru* (Layton 1986) is on sale in the Park. The area inscribed on the World Heritage List in 1987 represents only the area now known as the Uluru (Ayers Rock-Mount Olga) National Park - that is, only a portion of the intelligible spiritual and functional landscape described above. As previously discussed, "functionality and intelligibility" are preconditions for the inclusion of cultural landscapes on the World Heritage List (UNESCO 1994: 11-12). A more coherent totality of the Uluru cultural landscape might be gained by including the area granted to the Anangu community as a result of the Uluru land claim (Toohey 1980). This, however, would have taken the area beyond the confines of the National Park.

Human interaction with the environment

Hunting and gathering in central Australia is part of a fragile, unpredictable ecosystem. Rain is scarce and falls patchily; wild foods are vulnerable to over exploitation. By following the *tjukur*, Anangu ensure the even spacing of people across the land, and guarantee reciprocal access to the resources of neighbouring groups. People hold a country such as Uluru by protecting places created by the ancestors from trespass, by performing increase rites at such places and by re-enacting the heroes' travels in ceremony. The term *walytja* means both a kinsperson and someone one cares for. Ultimately, a person becomes kin to the country they care for (*ngura walytjaringanyi*). Since this can only be done by making that country the locus of one's life movement, the law of the *tjukur* has the effect of spacing groups evenly across the landscape. Reciprocal access to neighbouring countries during times of local plenty or drought is underwritten by the premise that the countries themselves are siblings or cousins created by the same ancestral heroes and that, if food is abundant in one's own country one year, it may be scarce the next. Travel across the desert toward waterholes hidden in hollows among the dunes was, and is, facilitated by the knowledge that each lies on the line of travel taken by particular heroes between visible hills (Lewis 1976).

The importance of these ancestral pathways was recognized in the original nomination of Uluru for inclusion on the World Heritage List - "The most important items of cultural property are those networks of tracks ... which comprise the threads of the vital social and religious fabric of Anangu life" (ANPWS 1986: 12). In recognizing interactions that exist between the cultural and natural heritage the World Heritage Convention established a system of "collective" protection of the cultural and natural heritage of outstanding universal value (UNESCO 1972: Preamble). Furthermore, Article 1 of the Convention includes in its definition of the cultural heritage reference to the place of groups of buildings "in the landscape" and to "the combined works of nature and of man" (UNESCO 1972: Article 1). Consistent with this definition, recent revision to the cultural heritage criteria to better accommodate cultural landscapes on the World Heritage List were made after first acknowledging that the term cultural landscape "embraces a diversity of manifestations of the interaction between humankind and its natural environment" (UNESCO 1993). Despite better accommodating the inclusion of cultural landscapes on the World Heritage List the relationship between people and their environment is not well articulated in the newly revised cultural heritage criteria. Up until December 1992 natural heritage criteria ii and iii made reference to "man's interaction with his natural environment" and "exceptional combinations of natural and cultural elements" (UNESCO 1992a). These references were deleted from the natural heritage criteria in December 1992 (see UNESCO 1992a; UNESCO 1992b; UNESCO 1993).

Returning to the newly revised cultural heritage criteria, the cultural landscape of Uluru exemplifies the distinctive features of Australian Aboriginal hunter-gatherer culture and its management of a fragile and unpredictable environment. This is not a "stage" in history as expressed in cultural heritage criterion iv (this reveals an outmoded notion of evolution as progress), rather it is a unique adaptation. Uluru is not "a unique or at least exceptional testimony to a ... cultural tradition which has disappeared" (cultural heritage criterion iii) rather it is representative of an outstanding and continuing cultural tradition. The cultural landscape of Uluru is directly associated with a living tradition which has been maintained despite the pressure of colonial settlement. Uluru is an "outstanding example of a traditional ... land-use" which is representative of Anangu culture and is directly and tangibly associated with events, living traditions, ideas and beliefs of outstanding universal significance (cultural heritage criterion vi).

Uluru should also be recognized internationally through the process of World Heritage listing as an outstanding cultural landscape representing "man's interaction with his natural environment" and an "exceptional combination of natural and cultural elements". As already noted both these references were formerly included, and recently deleted from, natural heritage criteria ii and iii respectively. We deplore the deletion of references to human agency from the natural heritage criteria. The deletions appear to revive the outmoded concept of wilderness areas purified of human action precisely at a time when "many are now coming to see that the human presence ... has always been part of the wilderness experience" (U.S. Department of the Interior 1993: 1). We fear that in promoting the idea of wholly natural landscapes, UNESCO may inadvertantly deny the continuing traditional use of the natural resources contained within World Heritage properties by indigenous peoples and unwittingly collude in the displacement of indigenous peoples from areas included in the World Heritage List.

Uluru amply satisfies UNESCO's criteria for an associative cultural landscape of outstanding universal value. Furthermore an evaluation of Uluru as a cultural landscape provides substantial reason for further revision of the cultural heritage criteria. Further revision of the cultural heritage criteria must build on the recent revisions to the cultural heritage criteria and counteract the impact of the deletions made to natural heritage criteria ii and iii. Such revisions are needed to ensure recognition of the interactions and combinations that exist between people and the natural environment and the continuing living traditions of indigenous societies such as are represented in Aboriginal Australia[1].

References

ANPWS (1986). *Nomination of Uluru (Ayers Rock-Mount Olga) National Park for inclusion on the World Heritage List*. Canberra: Australian National Parks and Wildlife Service.

ANPWS (1991). *Uluru (Ayers Rock-Mount Olga) National Park Plan of Management*. Canberra: Uluru-Kata Tjuta Board of Management, Australian National Parks and Wildlife Service.

Giles, W. E. P. (1879). *Australia Twice Traversed*. Sydney: Doubleday.

Gosse, W. C. (1874). *Report and diary of Mr W.C. Gosse's central and western exploring expedition, 1873*. Adelaide: South Australian Government Printer.

Gould, R. A. (1971). The archaeologist as ethnographer: a case from the Western Desert of Australia. *World Archaeology*, **3**: 143-177.

Government of Australia (1994). *Renomination of Uluru - Kata Tjuta National Park by the Government of Australia for inscription on the World Heritage List*. Canberra, Department of the Environment, Sports and Territories.

Harney, W. E. (1963). *To Ayers Rock and beyond*. Adelaide: Rigby.

Harney, W. E. (1968). *The significance of Ayers Rock for Aborigines*. Alice Springs: Northern Territory Reserves Board.

IUCN (1987). *World Heritage Nomination — IUCN Technical Evaluation 447 Uluru National Park (Australia)*. Gland, IUCN.

Layton, R. H. (1986). *Uluru: an Aboriginal history of Ayers Rock*. Canberra: Aboriginal Studies Press.

Layton, R. H. (ed) (1989). *Who Needs the Past? Indigenous values and archaeology*. London: Unwin.

Layton, R. H. (1992). *Australian rock art, a new synthesis*. Cambridge: Cambridge University Press.

Lewis, D. (1976). Observations on route-finding and spatial orientation ... (in) central Australia. *Oceania*, 46: 249-282.

McBryde, I. (1990). 'Those truly outstanding examples ...': Kakadu in the Context of Australia's World Heritage Properties - A Response. In: Domicelj, J. and S. (eds) *A Sense of Place? A Conversation in three cultures*, pp. 15-(19. Proceedings of an Australian expert workshop held in Canberra on 24 April 1989 with the support of the Australian Heritage Commission and with reference to parallel workshops in India and Argentina. Australian Heritage Commission Technical Publications Series Number 1. Canberra: Australian Government Publishing Service.

---

[1] Revisions to the cultural heritage criteria which address some of the criticisms of the criteria contained in this paper were discussed and rectified by the World Heritage Committee at its eighteenth session in December 1994.

Mountford, C. P. (1950). *Brown men and red sand*. Sydney: Angus and Robertson.

Mountford, C. P. (1977). *Ayers Rock: its people, their beliefs and their art*. Adelaide: Rigby.

Smith, M. A. (1986). *The antiquity of seed grinding in arid Australia*. Archaeology in Oceania, **21**: 29-39.

Smith, M. A. (1987). *Pleistocene occupation in arid Australia*. Nature, 328: 710-711.

Smith, M. A. (1989). *The case for a resident human population in the Central Australian Ranges during full glacial aridity*. Archaeology in Oceania, **24** (3): 93-105.

Titchen, S. M. (1992). *The assessment of World Heritage cultural values*. In: Scougall, B. (ed.) *Cultural Heritage of the Australian Alps*, pp. 37-53. Proceedings of the symposium on cultural heritage of the Australian Alps, (1991), Jindabyne. Canberra: Australian Alps Liaison Committee.

Toohey, J. (1980). *Uluru (Ayers Rock) National Park and Lake Amadeus/Luritja land claim: report by the Aboriginal Land Commissioner*. Canberra: Australian Government Printing Service.

UNESCO (1972). *Convention Concerning the Protection of the World Cultural and Natural Heritage*. Paris: UNESCO.

UNESCO (1987). *Convention Concerning the Protection of the World Cultural and Natural Heritage*. Report of the World Heritage Committee Eleventh Session. Unesco Headquarters, 7-11 December 1987. SC-87/CONF.005/9. Paris: UNESCO.

UNESCO (1992a). *Operational Guidelines for the Implementation of the World Heritage Convention*. WHC/2/Revised 27 March 1992. Paris: UNESCO

UNESCO (1992b). *Convention Concerning the Protection of the World Cultural and Natural Heritage*. World Heritage Committee. Sixteenth Session, Santa Fe, United States of America. 7-14 December 1992. *Report*. WHC-92/CONF.002/12–14 December 1992. Original: English/French. Paris: UNESCO.

UNESCO (1993). *Bureau of the World Heritage Committee, Seventeenth Session, 21-26 July 1993. Item 4 of the Provisional Agenda: Examination of the revised version of the Guidelines for the Implementation of the Convention*. WHC-93/CONF.001/2. Paris: UNESCO.

UNESCO (1994). *Operational Guidelines for the Implementation of the World Heritage Convention*. WHC/2/Revised February 1994. Paris: UNESCO

U.S. Department of the Interior (1993). *Archeology in the Wilderness*. Federal Archeology Report 6 (3), Fall (1993). Washington D.C.: National Park Service, Departmental Consulting Archeologist/Archeological Assistance Program.

Robert H. Layton is Professor at the Department of Anthropology, University of Durham, England.

Sarah M. Titchen has recently completed her doctoral thesis on World Heritage in the Department of Archaeology and Anthropology, The Australian National University, Canberra.

Chapter 18

Australian Colonial Landscapes

Ken Taylor

Theme

Images and visions of landscape have been central to the forging of a European Australian identity from the landing of the first fleet in 1788. Landscape as a cultural construct quickly became, and has remained, crucial to the development of attitudes of Australians to their country. (Taylor 1992). Perceptions of the landscape have been, and still are, at the very heart of what it means to be Australian. Ann-Marie Willis (1993, p61), for example, suggests that 'landscape is the most pervasive theme in Australian high culture.'

Landscape assumed a dominant role in nineteenth century cultural life, particularly in writing and painting, underscoring the way Australian identity became intimately bound up with the land. References to the picturesque qualities and grazing potential of the landscape constantly appeared in surveyors' journals, in travel diaries and settlers' letters. In painting, the fascination with landscape continues to the present day to the extent that it is a dominant tradition. A bond with the landscape has been part of a particular Australian legend and preoccupation with national identity for well over a century.

The beginnings of a national identity through landscape can be seen in nineteenth century colonial Australia. The culmination came in the late nineteenth century paintings of the Heidelberg School and the ballads, poetry, and writings of various Australian authors exemplified in A. J. 'Banjo' Paterson's "vision splendid of the sunlit plains extended" in Clancy of the Overflow (1889). In painting, representation of landscape moved from an early nineteenth rural colonial Arcadia genre to the later emblematic national vision of the Heidelberg School with its images of a fruitful and optimistic pastoral landscape. From mid-century the social focus for the movement was bush-life and honest rural toil. The term 'bush' increasingly became synonymous with the pastoral landscape. The uniquely Australian character, the bushman, emerged as the national type. Here was portrayed the phlegmatic nature and humour of the pioneers, the ordinary, everyday Australians who worked the land. By their honest toil they were seen to be transforming a harsh, and often lonely, environment - subject to drought and fire - into a productive land. Most importantly this was achieved by ordinary people with that particularly Australian trait of mateship binding them together. This stock image of the ordinariness of Australians persists and has become part of the Australian legend. Most recently it was portrayed in the film Crocodile Dundee. It was important to Australians in the latter part of the last century. It confirmed the superiority of a different social grouping over the class system of England. It also supported the superiority of the ideal of rural bush life over the city, not just the sweat shops of industrial England, but in contrast to city life in Australia, where Banjo Paterson (1889) declared that "the hurrying people daunt me, and their pallid faces haunt me."

The classic Australian pastoral image of the nineteenth century still informs the way many Australians see the landscape. It is part of their intellectual and cultural background, a cultural construct, a way of seeing. It is an emblematic national symbol of a way of life that has deep meaning in the Australian consciousness.

This essay abstracts these nineteenth century images and relates them to the current interest in Australian history and the cultural heritage conservation movement. It shows how much of the current pastoral landscape settled in the nineteenth century is a valuable historical document, a cultural landscape which, as a remarkable window into the past, informs a sense of history and creates resonant links with the past, "the sense of the stream of time" so eloquently expressed by Kevin Lynch (1972). It has previously been proposed that significant examples of this type of Australian cultural landscape deserve conservation protection (Taylor 1984 and 1988). As an example, reference is made at the end of the paper to a particular case study where conservation measures have been instigated by a local planning authority following an historic cultural landscape analysis.

The picturesque ideal transported

The colonial pastoral landscape ideal and its perpetuation as part of a national identity are directly attributable to the way in which early settlers and explorers, with their Anglo-Celtic background, saw the landscape. "As soon as white people landed on Australia's shores they began to construct the landscape according to European preconceptions and conventions." (Topliss 1992, p5). These preconceptions were a direct line from English eighteenth century tastes, particularly the sublime and the picturesque. They were part of the essential cultural baggage which the settlers brought. It would have been surprising indeed if they had not brought this baggage with them. The preconceptions emphasize that landscape as an entity is essentially a cultural construct, not a physical construct. It is developed around a way of seeing based on experience, where what we see has meaning for us, either privately or as part of our collective memory. For the purposes of this paper it is the picturesque ideal with its connections to the pastoral image that is important.

When the first explorers and then settlers arrived, a common reaction to the landscape was one of a limitless Arcadia. They saw a vast land of grazing potential where the eighteenth century notions of landscape beauty and pastoral utility combined readily into the ideal picturesque landscape image. The reaction was not, therefore, one based simply on visual notions of a pleasing prospect. It was a way of seeing the landscape informed by the concept of the picturesque. It was that where the picturesque, as proposed by Dixon Hunt and Willis (1975, p342) referring to the writings of eighteenth century scholar Richard Payne Knight, was "a theory of association, a function of the imagination."

In response to these associations, the ideal picturesque Arcadia in the antipodes appeared as a natural abundance waiting to be occupied. In keeping with the eighteenth century picturesque vision of scenery, as in the idealized scenes of Claude Lorrain or in the everyday country scenes of the Dutch landscape painters, to the settlers the savannah landscapes of Australia reflected Richard Payne Knight's (1794) "true ingredients of the painters grace" where "in the picture all delusions fly, and nature's genuine charms we there descry." The picturesque was focally involved with the roughness and "intricacies of nature" (Jellicoe 1987). It was exactly this sort of scene which confronted the settlers, but without visible signs of settled occupation. Here was the picturesque as nature intended. It was relatively open timbered country - sclerophyll eucalypt forest or woodland - with about 15 to 25 eucalypt trees per hectare and a grassy understorey. Shrubs were notably absent. Eucalypt trees, of which over 600 species grow in Australia, were the dominant tree and themselves have become regarded as a distinctively Australian symbol. This grassy, timbered country occurred extensively in southeastern Australia - New South Wales and Victoria - in parts of South Australia and parts of Western Australia.

The assumption that what the settlers saw was a natural landscape was universally accepted as a self evident truth. Michael Williams (1974), in his introductory discussion of historical attitudes to the landscape of South Australia, refers to a mid-nineteenth century traveller in the open savannah woodlands east of the Barossa Valley, South Australia, who described the district as "almost fresh from the Maker's hands, man has scarcely interfered with it" (p16). The traveller could not think of anywhere in England that rivalled its natural beauty except the eighteenth century park at Chatsworth. This is an interesting simile in that Chatsworth was an artificial creation, an idealized, but utilitarian, pastoral landscape. Similar commentaries abound. Farquar McKenzie, who travelled and described the scenery in the vicinity of what is now Canberra, referred in 1837 to a property, Lanyon[1], which still exists, as "Wright's place .... one of the most picturesque places I have seen in the colony and all natural beauty. Art having as yet contributed almost nothing toward its improvement ..." (Ray 1981, p22). What of course is now known is that, what confronted the settlers was not a natural landscape, an Urlandschaft, but an Aboriginal cultural landscape which was the product of thousands of years of management by burning.

The Australian legend portrayed in the colonial landscape image with its associated rural life in the bush - the bush and bush life being a particularly Australian construct (Taylor 1992) - has had, it must be acknowledged, its recent critics. Ross (1988) comments, however, that the critical revision "sometimes overlook[s] the fact that whatever the inadequacies of its stock type and images, the fundamental reason for its importance is that it embodies the earliest attempts to adapt a culture derived in Europe to the Australian environment." Also the semiotic landscape images in colonial writing and painting are part of a known body of Australian work relevant to the history of ideas and cultural identity. As Frank McDonald points out in the Forward to Helen Topliss's recent book (1992, pvii) on the Heidelberg era,"the majority of the paintings considered notable in their day are still known now .... we are dealing with a known body of work." He suggests that they are still the most popular works in Australian state galleries. They are prolifically reproduced in countless prints and greeting cards.

---

[1] Lanyon is some 35 kilometres south of Canberra. It consists of about 1500 hectares of grazing land from the nineteenth century property of 4000 hectares originally settled in 1834. At its hub is a an 1849 homestead with some 1830s buildings. The homestead is now an 1860s style museum but the land is still grazed as a working property. The 1500 hectares of cultural landscape with the homestead were gazetted in 1985 by the Australian Heritage Commission in the Register of the National estate (see Taylor 1990).

A colonial Arcadia

From the landing of the first fleet of transported convicts in 1788 the seemingly endless park-like appearance of the countryside interspersed with open grassy plains was a source of intense approbation. Many of the early reactions were linked to the hope of people of means establishing themselves in a manner comparable with the landed estates of England. At the same time there was intense scientific interest in the new country with its hitherto unknown flora and fauna. As the colonial period moved into the 1830s the possibilities of settling people from Britain became increasingly popular. Emigration was encouraged as a means of relieving working class poverty; simultaneously large landholders wanted to attract labour. Australia was, therefore, depicted as a rural utopia, a pastoral Arcadia; this was even supported by the tales of some released convicts who indicated that "a poor man might make good in the Antipodes" where "as one ballad put it, there was 'a lot of jolly good living over there.' " (White 1981, p30). England also needed to enlarge its outlets for manufactured goods and to import wool for one of its major manufacturing industries. Emigration schemes were, therefore, set up with the rural utopia images as the attraction. 150,000 people emigrated between 1832 and 1850 (White 1981).

Once started the image of the Arcadian paradise persisted and grew with landscape as its leit motif. As the century progressed the colonial landscape image "moved from background to symbolism" and became increasingly "important because of the desire for a distinctive national identity." (Bourke 1993, p18).

Early landscape responses

The admiration for the landscape of the colony of New South Wales was a recurrent early theme. It consistently focussed on comparison with the eighteenth century estates of Britain, frequently mentioned the park-like appearance, and often commented on the grazing potential of the land. The landscape of the site of Sydney received considerable praise as the following descriptions show.

Sydney Parkinson (cited in Smith 1985, p179), artist on Cook's ship Endeavour, recorded in 1773 that :

the trees, quite free from underwood, appeared like plantations in a gentleman's park ...

Arthur Bowes, Assistant Surgeon on the convict ship Lady Penhryn, 1788, (ibid) saw what he thought were:

the finest terra's, lawns, and grottos, with distinct plantations of the tallest and most stately trees I ever saw in any nobleman's grounds.

Elizabeth Macarthur (cited in Seddon 1976, p10), who lived at Parramatta House, Sydney, declared that:

The greater part of the country is like an English park, and the trees give it the appearance of a wilderness or shrubbery, commonly attached to the habitations of people of fortune, filled with a variety of native plants, placed in a wild, irregular manner.

Surgeon Peter Cunningham (1827, reprinted 1966, Macmillan ed, p11) liked the country some thirty kilometres inland from Sydney, even though he was botanically incorrect on the comment that the trees never shed their leaves (eucalypts shed leaves all year round):

> *the trees also being slightly clothed and all evergreens, consequently never shedding their leaves, afford both a cool retreat for the cattle in the summer heats and a tolerable protection for the sward of native grasses which everywhere abounds. Hence all kinds of stock may be kept here at the very outset.*

In 1836 Thomas Shepherd was much impressed by the same locality as Cunningham:

> *Here scattered are to be seen the most stately and majestic trees of eucalypts, such tablelands appearing more like a park - the trees standing singly or in clumps, as if planted by the hands of a landscape gardener.*

Four thousand kilometres away across the continent in Western Australia to the south of the initial Swan River Settlement (Perth) John Bussell (cited in Shann 1926 p53) who was looking for land to occupy in 1832 found:

> *The country here was so clear that a farmer could hardly grudge to the fine spreading trees ... the small portions of ground that they occupied only to ornament.*

His daughter, Fanny Bussell, was equally charmed by the country (ibid. p66):

> *pretty cheerful pasture land, ornamented with some magnificent trees, but not heavily timbered ... with the country in its unredeemed state, which is so completely park-like that you would scarcely believe that a year and ten months only have elapsed since the improving hand of the Europeans was first extended over its glades.*

Early nineteenth century landscape paintings complemented the contemporary written descriptions of the genteel park-like nature of the country and its pastoral potential. The artists were intent on showing what Bonyhady (1991) calls "A Pastoral Arcadia". They painted actual scenes which, according to Bonyhady (p40),

> *demonstrated the recent achievements of individual squatters and the frequently ostentatious houses they built. Their paintings were Arcadian, however, in their sense of ease and plenitude and their concealment of the hardships faced by the early settlers. They were pastoral in the way that they showed Australia as a land of sheep and cattle ...*

Joseph Lycett, transported for forgery in 1813-14, had been a portrait painter in England. He turned to painting pastoral views in Australia. These were intended for the English market as well as for his own aesthetic sensibilities and those of his patrons, the landed squatters[2]. Lycett's views depicted rural scenes reminiscent of England and demonstrated Australia's potential for immigration and investment. Notably, though, his scenes concentrated on the houses built by the pastoralists and their surrounds, rather than showing the sheep and cattle which brought the wealth (Bonyhady 1991). Typical is his 1825 aquatint of Elizabeth Farm[3], The Residence of John Macarthur Esq., near Parramatta, New

---

[2] 'Squatter' was the term used for the people who had the means to buy and lease large tracts of land to set up pastoral stations. Later the word was substituted by the term 'pastoralist'.

[3] The buildings which were Elizabeth Farm survive as a museum in Sydney.

South Wales. Here we see the kind of scene genteelly described by Elizabeth Macarthur, John Macarthur's wife, and the application of Dixon-Hunt's "theory of association' (see above). The aquatint shows the elegant Georgian house in a gently sloping river valley landscape dotted with trees. The overall effect is a picturesque scene with hints of a Repton style improvement and even hints of the gardenesque style of additional planting. Bonyhady (1991, p44) records that "The text accompanying the view noted the land surrounding the house was 'mown in the hay season, as in England', while the grounds and gardens ... contained 'the choicest fruits and productions of Europe and of tropical climates'. Although Elizabeth Farm was said to afford 'excellent pasturage for Sheep, Cattle, and Horses', Lycett showed no animals in his view. The scene is one of elegance and refinement undisturbed by work. A lady and gentleman promenade in the foreground.".

Other early artists who painted the park-like pastoral settings included John Glover, Augustus Earle, George Angus; they were succeeded by Eugen Von Guérard and Louis Buvelot. "Earle considered that his watercolour, June Park, Van Diemen's Land (Tasmania), ... about 80 kilometres from Hobart, revealed 'the grand appearance of the country in its natural state, Perfect Park Scenery.' " (ibid, p46).

John Glover came from the English Lake District to Tasmania in 1831 at the age of sixty-three. In England Glover had painted rural scenes in a Romantic picturesque style with the "subdued melancholy of Claude Lorraine and Poussin whom he admired." (Lynn 1977, p10) and "was known as one of the 'English Claudes.' " (Bonyhady 1991, p47). In Australia, Glover continued to paint in the eighteenth century manner. Nevertheless his style adapted to Australian conditions, albeit still influenced by Claude whose landscapes remained the model for the "pastoral arcadia he perceived in Tasmania." (ibid). Glover's paintings suggest idyllic pastoral scenes for squatter and worker as in Patterdale Landscape with Cattle, a c1835 view of his own property in Tasmania. The stockman sits on a log quietly watching the contented cattle; his hut nestles amongst the majestic eucalypts in the picturesque park-like setting. The tranquil scene reflects the beginnings of the bush myth and associated ideals of honest, but not degrading, rural labour. In reality conditions for assigned convict labour and immigrant rural workers were neither easy nor idyllic. The same image is extended by Glover in other paintings such as Patterdale, Van Diemen's Land (c1835) where a shepherd and his dog, watching over a flock of sheep, suggest a rural life of ease and contentment. What is particularly significant about Glover's work is that it has a distinctively Australian flavour. Of note also is the fact that these scenes are still identifiable in today's Tasmanian landscape. Glover's paintings are then a doubly important historical record. They express nineteenth century attitudes to a new country and show how today's landscape still reflects the historic patterns captured by Glover.

The colonial vision of Australia gathered impetus, therefore, in the 1820s and 1830s with set images of productive flocks of sheep and herds of cattle. It was encouraged by poets such as W.C. Wentworth, Charles Harpur, and Henry Parkes who used landscape imagery as "the indispensable vehicle of colonial poetry" (Elliott 1967, p63). Wentworth in his poem Australasia (1823) was confident of the new Arcadia's role with sentiments such as:

> *Theirs too in flow'ry mead, or thymy steep*
> *To tend with watchful dog the timid sheep;*
> *And, as their fleecy charge are lying round,*
> *To wake the woodlands with their pipe's soft sound.*

Henry Parkes eulogized Australia as a land of opportunity in contrast to industrialized England in the poem "Our Coming Countrymen":

Though no workhouse mandate now
May your suffering spirits bow;
Though you feel, and justly may,
Ye have won your daily bread each day.

Complementing the poetry were Romantic images portrayed in the picturesque paintings of Conrad Martens who arrived from England in Sydney in 1835. He had painted country houses in England and found a market for his talents in Sydney and surrounding rural areas. His luminous and opalescent style (Lynn 1977) was very much influenced by that of William Turner and his rural paintings always included sublime aspects in them. He "subjected what he viewed to a filter of cultivated aesthetic taste" which "would have influenced what [his clients] would have come to regard as the most pleasing aspects of their own environment." (Willis 1993, p69). Such is his painting, View of Throsby Park, c1836 (Figure 1), commissioned by Charles Throsby when he had built the house 'Throsby Park" on his uncle's extensive land grant of 1820. Here a shepherd in the foreground watches over a flock of sheep looking onto a rolling, pastoral Arcadia with the sublime wilderness - waiting to be tamed into pasture - occupying the background and framing the elegant Georgian house.

Lachlan Macquarie, Governor of the Colony of New South Wales (1810-1822), travelled extensively through the Colonies of New South Wales and Van Diemen's Land.

Figure 1. Conrad Martens 1801-1878, Australia. View of Throsby Park, c1836. Watercolour 46.2 x 67.4. Private collection.

During these travels he kept a journal in which he recorded impressions of the landscape. These impressions consistently combined educated tastes on landscape beauty with the potential of pastoral utility. In 1820 he visited the southern part of New South Wales and went to see the explorer Charles Throsby, to whom he had made a land grant of 1000 acres. Describing the view before Throsby Park house was built, but the same view that Martens painted some sixteen years later, Macquarie recorded in his journal (p145-146):

> We met a numerous herd of about 400 head of cattle belonging to Mr Throsby feeding in a fine rich meadow ... The grounds adjoining Mr Throsby's hut are extremely pretty, gentle hills and dales with an extensive rich valley in his front, the whole surrounding grounds having a very park-like appearance, being very thinly wooded.

Conrad Martens and other colonial artists including Nicholas Chevalier, William Charles Piguenit, and Eugen Von Guérard also painted sublime wilderness scenes. Here was a parallel picturesque rendition of landscape, but one "that registered the strange, the exotic ... nature as wild and spectacular, fit to be gazed on in awe..." (Willis 1993, p70). Often these paintings included small human figures in the foreground or hints of the civilizing influence of settlement and improvement. This pleased the critics because "the sense of overpowering nature was reduced by some form of European presence" (Bonyhady 1991, p77). These wonders of nature - the untrammelled forests and cliffs - were also probably seen as portraying something which no longer existed in Europe and therefore substituted for Europe's antiquities. Roderick Nash (1973) in Wilderness and the American Mind describes the same phenomenon in the nature paintings of nineteenth century America.

The bush image

The ideal of the bush myth, building on the earlier images in poetry and painting, gathered momentum through the 1850s. The associated idea of mateship took root amongst the rural workers and a legend was created whereby the bush-workers were seen to be better than their city counterpart. They were "rugged and independent, anti-authoritarian but loyal to [their] fellows ... as good as [their] master." (Ritchie 1975, p62). The mateship image no doubt has some basis in the fact that people needed to help each other, to be strong willed and able to cope with isolation in the new country. The work was hard and conditions not easy as the remarkable collection of archival photographs from the last century in Country Life in Old Australia (Dutton ed.1987) shows. This collection concentrates on ordinary people, the bush-workers, to reveal something of the harshness of bush life, but also its camaraderie. It shows the role played by men and women in forging a national consciousness. Dutton in the Introduction points to the way these photographs show a country in the making and how life went on in the face of droughts, fires, strikes, and hard economic times. The photographs point to the endless labour of the men and to the primary role of women struggling to raise a family, to cook, sew, mend, garden, wash, and above all provide a family life in the bush. In Jan Carter's sensitive portrayals of women with their evocative accounts of bush life from nearly a century of Australian history, Nothing to Spare, Recollections of Australian Pioneering Women, the timbergetter's daughter hints at her fortitude (pp 66-67):

> *It was very hard in those years ... I looked after the garden too ... Water was a dreadful problem. You had to cart water from a soak, cart it to the tank. I used to do the washing under a tree in two kerosene tins; a fire in the open, a line between two trees. The house was just a room with walls of canvas. Our furniture was packing cases.*

The beginnings of mateship in the bush are likely to have been on the early pastoral properties where assigned convict labour and itinerant rural workers formed small isolated, and virtually self-sufficient, communities attached to the properties. In 1828, for example, Throsby Park had some thirty employees, mostly assigned, working as labourers, stockmen, shepherds, watchmen, hutkeepers, an overseer, a ploughman, a gardener, a fencer, and a shoemaker (Roxburgh 1989).

National identity and colonial landscape

An increasing sense of national identity from the middle of the nineteenth century onwards "is possibly best observed in the contemporary songs and ballads, and also in the contributions of Australia's poets, writers and painters" (Powell 1977, p74). It was part of a movement to create an Australian culture and a sense of place with a landscape focus. It was encouraged by a group of writers and artists predominantly born in Australia in the 1860s, or who emigrated as young people, whose work led to "a new vitality in the development of art and literature from the mid-1880s." (White 1981, p86). As the national movement gained impetus, the term bush became increasingly associated with the pastoral landscape. It was an emblematic image that became, and has remained, part of an Australian iconography.

A favourite vehicle for broadcasting the bush ethos was ballad poetry, ballads being the popular poetry of the time. "Landscape, environment, spirit of place always remained primary" with the balladists (Elliott 1967, p150). The ballads were clichés but they made a deep and lasting impression. Henry Lawson, A.B. (Banjo) Paterson, and Adam Lindsay Gordon were the most celebrated balladists. Lawson, for example, hauntingly captured the allure of the bush in On the Night Train with words like:

> *Have you seen the Bush by moonlight, from the train go running by,*
> *Here a patch of glassy water, there a glance of mystic sky?*
> *Have you heard the still voice calling, yet so warm and yet so cold,*
> *I'm the Mother-Bush that bore you! Come to me when you are old.*

In romantic, but nationalistic prose, Lawson eulogized the Australianness of the bush and its special qualities in The Bush Undertaker with the words, "the grand Australian bush - the nurse and tutor of eccentric minds, the home of the weird, and much that is different from things in other lands." Australia was not an England in another hemisphere. Lawson, as he unfortunately became more affected by alcohol, was increasingly maudlin about the bush and the miseries it could invoke through such experiences as loneliness, hardship, drought, and fire. Later his ballads were criticized for not upholding the courage and cheerfulness of the men and women of the bush (White 1981).

In contrast 'Banjo' Paterson was consistently more cheerful and adventurous. He portrayed the toughness of the bush-workers with creations like Clancy of the Overflow in The Man from Snowy River:

As the stock are slowly stringing, Clancy rides behind them singing,
For the drover's life has pleasures that the townsfolk never know.

And the bush has friends to meet him, and their kindly voices greet him
In the murmur of the breezes and the river on its bars,
And he sees the vision splendid of the sunlit plains extended,
And at night the wondrous glory of the everlasting stars.

Paterson's words were utter cliché, but he concentrated a vision of the Australian rural landscape which became what Bolton (1981) refers to as "typically Australian" and which today still represents a vision of continuity. The significance of Paterson's prose lies in "the quality of the vision - the capacity of the eye to see, the senses to feel" (Elliott 1967, p128).

Adam Lindsay Gordon also struck a nationalistic note in his ballads. It was Gordon who imparted to wattle[4] blossom "the first poetical image to acquire emblematic status of a definite kind." (ibid p133). He raised it to a national symbol with such lines as "... when the wattle gold trembles / Twixt shadow and shine" or "... the bells on distant cattle waft across the range, through the golden tufted wattle, Music low and sweet ..."

During the 1860s and 1870s pastoral landscape paintings maintained their popularity, not least amongst the pastoralists who wanted their substantial homesteads and properties recording. Louis Buvelot was one of the artists and was particularly influential. He painted picturesque rural scenes in a Romantic style, sometimes reminiscent of Constable's compositions. More importantly was his recognition "in the Australian landscape of the prevailing and insistent azure and range of golds from bleached grass to brazen sunsets" which influenced the next major phase of landscape painting, the Heidelberg School (Lynn 1977 p14). Buvelot pioneered the plein air style of painting in Australia which became a hallmark of the Heidelberg School. Frederick McCubbin, a member of this School of painting, thought that Buvelot's pastorals lifted 'the scene from the dreariness of the commonplace to the charm of the picturesque ... in a sense he was a forerunner." (McCubbin 1916, pp85-86).

The Heidelberg School

The highwater mark of nineteenth Australian landscape painting and national identity through landscape images occurred in the 1880s and 1890s with the group of painters known as the Heidelberg School. It was the most celebrated period in Australian art

---

[4] Wattle is the common name for *Acacia* spp. (mimosa) which are indigenous shrubs and small trees found throughout Australia. They create a spectacular flower display in late winter and spring with their profusion of yellow and golden yellow flowers. The yellow of the flower is one of Australia's national colours, the other being green.

history. Heidelberg is an area to the northeast of Melbourne where the artists had a painting camp. The period when they were most prolific, c1885 to 1891, is known as the Golden Summers. The best known painters were Tom Roberts, Arthur Streeton, Frederick McCubbin, and Charles Conder. Their mission was to paint Australian themes that fulfilled the visual evocation of Paterson's "vision splendid of the sunlit plains extended." Significantly they produced "for a first time, a naturalistic interpretation of the Australian landscape ... They depicted the colour and luminosity of the pale shadows of midsummer - blue, turquoise, pink, and rose violet; the atmospheric effects of dust, heat-haze, and afterglow. But they loved most the warm coloured stillness of summer evenings ... They brought a new sense of optimism, joy and love of the sun" (Smith 1971, p82).

These artists painted everyday scenes around Melbourne and in New South Wales, including beach scenes. They immortalized the sunlit rural landscape dotted with lofty gum trees and sheep, peopled by pioneers, drovers, and shearers or just ordinary folk in the country. Their scenes were of the commonplace, although heavily romanticized. The paintings suited the nationalistic mood in Australia and indeed guided it. They proudly showed a fruitful and optimistic landscape being shaped by a hardworking nation. The landscapes in the paintings tell us about the ideals and aspirations of late colonial Australia (Topliss 1992). They represented an association of ideas, not necessarily reality, and thereby fixed a national vision centred on the landscape. We can still recognize the message in the paintings, recognize the localities and feel part of the cultural landscape making process. Willis (1993 p88)) suggests that the landscapes of the Golden Summers act "as a reference point in the national culture" of Australia. Australians still look at these landscape images with nostalgia and sense of belonging.

The Heidelberg artists painted en plein air, using naturalism and realism as their preferred styles. They were influenced by European art ideas, in particular those of the Barbizon School, aestheticism, and impressionism.

Tom Roberts was instrumental in inspiring the new painting movement on his return from Europe in 1885. He painted the ordinary and commonplace, the life of the drover, shepherd, pioneer and bushranger (outlaw). In Robert's Shearing the Rams (1890) can be seen the idealization of honest toil and the symbol of Australia's staple industry, wool. Robert's suggested that he had painted what delighted and fascinated him about the great pastoral life (Clark and Whitelaw 1985).

In A Break away! (1891) (Figure 2) Roberts captures the intense heat, dust, and glare of summer in a golden tawny and blue landscape as "a lone Australian stockman heroically gallop[s] to head off the stampede to water of thirst crazed sheep" (Radford 1991). Radford, in the celebration of the centenary of the painting in 1991, suggests that A Break away!, is a masterpiece, Robert's tour de force, and one of Australia's best-known and best-loved paintings. "The parched outback landscape subject was deliberately chosen to capture the sympathy and imagination of all Australians" with the galloping horseman reflecting the independent Australian colonies gallop towards Federation in 1901 (ibid).

Arthur Streeton showed a remarkable affinity to the bush. He captured all its moods, its remoteness, its brittle midday light, and the haunting evanescence of its evening light. He "persuaded Australians that theirs was a vast, golden, tawny landscape, its leisurely rivers and equally leisurely vistas, blessed with an eternally blue sky ... 'I fancy' he wrote 'canvases all glowing and moving in the happy light and others expressive of the hot, drying winds and slow immense heat' " (Lynn 1977, p68).

Figure 2. Tom Roberts 1851-1931, Australian. A Break away!, 1891. Oil on canvas 137.2 x 168.1 cm. Reproduced by permission of the Art Gallery of South Australia, Adelaide, Elder Bequest Fund 1889.

Streeton's love of the Australian landscape is seen in his The Purple Noon's Transparent Might (1896), one of a series on the Hawkesbury River near Sydney. McCubbin (1916 p89) thought this painting could be taken as "a National Symbol and that

> *One cannot imagine anything more typically Australian than this poem of heat and light. It brings home to us so forcibly such a sense of boundless regions of pastures flecked with sheep and cattle, of the long rolling plains of the Never-Never, the bush crowned hills, the purple seas of our continent.*

Streeton's Near Heidelberg (1890) captures the very ordinariness of many of the landscapes and the brilliant blue and gold palette which Streeton perfected to portray the happy light and slow summer heat that he loved. The slender silhouetted gum tree is unmistakably Australian and appears as a symbol in the image.

Frederick McCubbin had a "relationship with the Australian bush that was quieter and more intimate than Streeton's or Robert's ... he reveals a delicacy and tender grace in the Australian landscape" (Clark and Whitelow 1985, p142). His paintings show human interest revolving around the pioneer theme and the dignity of ordinary toil in poetic local

Australian settings, reflecting what Willis (1993 p73) nicely calls "provincial nationalism". McCubbin's paintings are closer to Lawson's reflective and sometimes melancholic view of the bush as in The Pioneer (1904) and On the Wallaby Track (1894). McCubbin also painted charming bush scenes enveloped in soft light as in Winter Evening, Hawthorn (1886) and Bush Idyll (1893). All his paintings celebrated the place of the ordinary pioneer in settling Australia.

The lasting significance of the Golden Summers is their projection of continuity of a quintessential Australian landscape image. "While landscape in the Heidelberg School style is no longer the dominant image of 'the real Australia', it has not disappeared - instead it has passed into art history and nostalgia, taking on a life as a reference point in the national culture." (Willis 1993, p88).

Current Australian sense of place in cultural landscapes

Australians have increasingly discovered over the past twenty years that the two-hundred years since European settlement started have left a meaningful historical pattern and document reflecting cultural associations with the Australian landscape as human setting. A wave of interest in the past has swept the country, somewhat encouraged by the 1988 bicentennial of the landing of the first fleet. The role of landscapes in this community interest in history is inextricably associated with the history of events and the people involved.

Community interest in history has assisted the role of Australian cultural heritage conservation practice, not least because community interaction inevitably has come to the notice of politicians. Also of note is that much of the historical interest now focuses on the achievements of ordinary people and what may be seen as ordinary places, cultural landscapes. This is hardly surprising given the background to the nineteenth century with its images of bush-life and the emergence of the symbolic colonial pastoral landscape as a powerful historical theme. The emphasis on place rather than individual sites in Australian heritage conservation encourages community awareness of the connections in history and associated heritage values. For example, one is now likely to find community support for protecting an area of land around an historic building or site because of the connections perceived between people, events, and places. The interconnectedness of places and things is widely appreciated. The Australian Heritage Commission Act (1975) in defining the National Estate refers to "those places ... that have aesthetic, historic, scientific or social significance ...". The Australia ICOMOS Charter for the Conservation of Places of Cultural Significance (The Burra Charter), which provides a process model for conservation studies linking cultural significance to the assessment of cultural values, adopts the term 'place'.

Paralleling the places approach is an emphasis in Australian cultural heritage practice on themes through history where the themes embrace the totality of places, people, and events through time. Examples of post -1788 themes which summarize human development of an area or region with associated social values will, inter alia, include:

Exploration and Pioneering
Convictism
Pastoralism
Rural Technology

Transport (including circulation routes and corridors)
Communication Systems
Forestry
Mining

Some of these will embrace national themes of identity including, for example, First Settlement, Gold Mining, or Pastoralism, and some have international connections as with Gold Mining. Pastoralism with its classic Australian landscape image based on nineteenth century colonial connections is a recurrent theme. The pastoral landscape image is a national symbol of a way of life that has meaning in the Australian consciousness. A formative period in the history of the nation is encapsulated in the pastoral landscapes. Reading them presents a social history, a history of the achievements of people, enriches our understanding of the making of the who, what, why, when, and where of this type of cultural landscape and adds to the heritage values that people attach to them, as in the following case study. They are a demonstration of Hoskins' (1955) maxim that "the ... landscape itself to those who know how to read it aright is the richest historical record we possess" (p14).

Wingecarribee Shire historic landscape study

Wingecarribee Shire is part of the Tablelands region in New South Wales which is mid-way between Sydney and Canberra. The area generally is known as the Southern Highlands. It has an undulating hill and valley topography with an altitude of about 500 metres under sea level. The area, explored in the early 1800s, was first settled in the 1820s when extensive land grants were given and people moved in with cattle and sheep. During the 1840s the Southern Highlands area was known as one of the finest wheat growing districts in the colony of New South Wales. However, its main fame was as excellent grazing country, a reputation which survives today. There is also a number of historically significant country towns distributed through the area.

In 1990/91 an Historic Cultural Landscape Assessment Study (Landscan Pty Ltd & Taylor 1992) was undertaken as part of a wider cultural heritage study for the New South Wales Department of Planning and Wingecarribee Shire Council Planning Department. The call for a study came partly from sections of the community and from the planning agencies as rural residential and suburban development pressures threaten the rural landscape. Freeway construction has linked the area with Sydney thereby adding to development pressure. The Southern Highlands region is also a tourist destination and attracts retirees.

In the landscape study a series of settlement themes is identified to provide a framework for understanding the present landscape, its making, its meaning, and its cultural values. Evidence of past activity in today's landscape from the following themes was investigated:

Early Exploration and Settlement 1800-1840s

The region is important as an early route for explorers followed by settlement. This period saw the establishment of large pastoral holdings like Throsby's where the homestead "Throsby Park", shown in Figure 1, was built in 1836. In addition a number of small grants were made to free settlers, many of which were later amalgamated or bought out. It was this period which saw the establishment of grazing as a major land-use.

Consolidation of Major pastoral holdings 1840-1860

This was a period of establishment and consolidation of the large pastoral holdings and the introduction of crops including wheat.

Post 1860 Rural Extensions

The 1860s saw rural extension as selectors took up small land parcels following the passing of the 1861 Robertson Land Act. Land hitherto thought to be too densely timbered was occupied and cleared for dairying and crops such as potatoes. This period also saw the subdivision into smaller rural blocks for dairying of limited parts of some of the large grants. Dairying subdivision continued in the present century.

Community Development post-1860

The rural economy of the area encouraged the development of a number of country towns and villages which remain part of the landscape character.

Tourism and Recreation 1868

Present The area became popular as a tourist destination after the opening of the railway from Sydney in 1867. Its scenic attractions and summer weather cooler than Sydney proved a magnet. Boarding houses were built from 1871, to be followed by the building of country residences for wealthy Sydney people. Figure 3 shows "Hillview" bought in 1882 for the use of the Governor of New South Wales.

Figure 3. Wingecarribee Shire Historic Landscape Assessment Study: View towards Throsby Park from the direction of Conrad Marten's c1836 painting (see figure 1). (Photograph: K. Taylor.)

The study area readily subdivided into ten rural cultural landscape units on the basis of land-use and landscape patterns. These were assessed and analyzed using archival data and field observation. As a result five Key Historic Cultural Landscape Units were identified. These are the landscape units which are particularly crucial in the development of the historic landscape setting of the Shire. They are regarded as displaying high level Interpretative Value and Associative Value, i.e. they are particularly able to inform and enlighten us on the history of the landscape, promote a sense of place, and relate this to the people involved in the landscape making. The key units also display a high level of integrity or intactness where past historic landscape patterns are still visible in spite of later layers of settlement.

The key units include examples of landscape types from the early major holdings and from the post-1860 dairying era. Figure 10 is a present-day view over the landscape at Throsby Park painted by Martens in 1836 and described by Governor Lachlan Macquarie some sixteen years earlier. The fact that there is clear historical evidence to authenticate the continuity of the nineteenth century landscape heightens its sense of place and value to the present generation. We experience contact with the past. From the post-1860s settlement a smaller scale dairying landscape emerged, a yeoman landscape which still retains its nineteenth century character as seen in Figure 11.

As a result of the study, Wingecarribee Shire Council has created through the Environmental Planning and Assessment Act of 1979 a Draft Local Environment Plan. This outlines a Landscape Protection Zone covering the key historic units. The action recognizes the cultural significance of these landscapes to the present generation and future generations and restricts land-use to rural. There have been no major public objections. Rather the zoning is welcomed as a way of protecting the historic landscape integrity.

Conclusion

The importance of the colonial pastoral landscapes in an Australian sense of place and heritage consciousness is clearly established. They are part of an attachment to what is a tangible, resonant past with which all people seem to need contact, what Henry James called "the palpable, imaginable, visitable past". Such places and experiences allow us to reach back in an effort to find identity with past events, people, and places that are part of our collective memory. The essence of this is aptly argued by David Lowenthal (1985 pxxv) in The Past is a Foreign Country:

> *We have partly domesticated that past, where we do things differently, and brought it into the present as a marketable commodity ... But we must not repudiate it, for it is a proof that we have really lived ... To be is to have been, and to project our messy, malleable past into our unknown future.*

References

Bolton, G. (1981). *Spoils and Spoilers*. Allen & Unwin, Sydney.

Bonyhady, T. (1991). *Images in Opposition: Australian Landscape Painting 1801-1890*. Oxford University Press, Melbourne.

Bourke, L. (1993). *A Place in History: The Ash Range, Landscape and Identity*, Westerly No 1 Autumn 1993; 17-24. (University of Western Australia).

Carter, J. (1981). *Nothing to Spare. Recollections of Australian Pioneering Women*, Penguin Books, Ringwood, Australia.

Clarke, J. and Whitelaw, B. (1985). *Golden Summers; Heidelberg and Beyond*, National Gallery of Victoria

Dixon Hunt, J. and Willis, P. eds. (1975). *The Genius of the Place. The English Landscape Garden 1620-1820*. Paul Elek, London.

Dutton, G. ed. (1984). *Country life in Old Australia*, Penguin Books, Ringwood.

Elliott, B. (1967). *The Landscape of Australian Poetry*. F. W. Cheshire, Melbourne.

Hoskins, W. G. (1955). *The Making of the English Landscape*. Hodder and Stoughton, London.

Jellicoe G. and S. (1987). *The Landscape of Man. Shaping the Environment from Prehistory to the Present Day*. Thames and Hudson, London.

Lachlan Ma., (1836). *Journals of his Tours in New South Wales and Van Diemen's Land 1810-1822*. Reprinted 1956 by the Trustees of the Public Library of New South Wales, Sydney.

Landscan and Taylor, K. (1992). *Historic Cultural Landscape Assessment for Wingecarribee Shire*, New South Wales; Wingecarribee Shire council, Moss Vale, NSW and Department of Planning, Sydney.

Lowenthal, D. (1985). *The Past is a Foreign Country*. Cambridge University Press, Cambridge.

Lynch, K. (1972). *What Time Is This Place*, MIT Press.

Lynn, E. (1977). *The Australian Landscape and its Artists*. Bay Books, Sydney.

McCubbin, F. (1916). *Some Remarks on the History of Australian Art*. In: McDonald, R. and McCubbin, F. *The Art of Frederick McCubbin*. Reprinted 1986 by Boolarong Publications, Brisbane.

Macmillan, D. S. ed (1966). *Reprint of Peter Cunningham, Surgeon R. N. (1827). Two Years in New South Wales*. Angus and Robertson in association with the Royal Australian Historical Society.

Nash, R. (1973). *Wilderness and the American Mind*, New Haven.

Paterson, A. B. (Banjo). (1889). *Clancy of the Overflow in The Man From Snowy River*.

Powell, J. M. (1977). *Mirrors of the New World: Images and Image-Makers in the Settlement Process*. Wm. Dawson and Son, Folkestone, Australia.

Radford, R. (1991). *A National Picture for a National Gallery*. In: *Tom Roberts A Break away!* Art Gallery Catalogue, Art Gallery of South Australia, Adelaide.

Ray, P. (1981). *Lanyon*. Lanyon Restoration and Acquisitions Committee, Museums Unit, ACT Administration, Canberra.

Ritchie, J. (1975). *Australia: as once we were*. Heinemann, Melbourne.

Ross, B. C. (1988). *Australian Literature and Australian Culture*, 3-26 in Hergenham, L. ed. New Literary History of Australia. Penguin Books, Australia.

Roxburgh, R. (1989). *Throsby Park. An Account of the Throsby Family in Australia 1802-1940*. NSW National Parks and Wildlife Service, Sydney.

Seddon, G. (1975). *The Evolution of Perceptual Attitudes*, 9-17, In Seddon, G. and Davis, M. (eds). *Man and Landscape in Australia*. Towards an Ecological Vision, Australian Government Publishing Service, Canberra.

Shann, E. O. G. (1926). *Cattle Chosen. The story of the First Group Settlement in Western Australia 1829-1841*. Facsimile edition published 1978 by University of Western Australia, Perth.

Shepherd, T., (1836). *Lectures on Landscape Gardening in Australia*, Wm. McGarvie, Sydney.

Smith, B. (1971). *Australian Painting*, Oxford University Press, Melbourne.

Taylor, K. (1984). *Rural Landscape Protection; The Need for a Broader Conservation Base*, Heritage Australia 3:2, 3-8.

Taylor, K. (1988). *Rural Cultural Landscapes: A Case for Heritage Interpretation, Conservation and Management; Lanyon A.C.T. A Role Model,* Landscape Australia 1/89, 28-34.

Taylor, K. (1990). *Historic Cultural Landscapes and Emerging Heritage Values: An Australian Perspective.* Landscape Research **15**: 2, 12-18.

Taylor, K. (1992). *A Symbolic Australian Landscape. Images in Writing and Painting,* Landscape Journal **11**: 2, 127-144.

Topliss, H. (1992). *The Artist's Camps: 'Plein Air Painting in Australia*, Hedley, Melbourne.

White, R. (1981). *Inventing Australia. Images and Identity 1688-1980*, Allen and Unwin, Sydney.

Willis, A.-M., (1993). *Illusions of Identity. The Art of Nation*, Hale and Iremonger, Sydney.

Ken Taylor is Professor of Landscape Architecture and Co-Director of the Cultural Heritage Research Centre at the University of Canberra, Australia.

Cultural Landscapes of the World

The Americas

Cultural Landscapes in Honduras: the Mosquitia
Silvia C. Chalukian and Jeffery W. Bentley

Cultural Landscapes in North America: an Overview of Status in the United States and Canada
Patricia M. O'Donnell

Cultural Landscapes in the United States
Nora J. Mitchell

Cultural Landscapes in Canada
Susan Buggey

Chapter 19

Cultural Landscapes in Honduras: the Mosquitia

Silvia C. Chalukian and Jeffery W. Bentley

Honduras is the second largest country in Central America, with an area of about 112.088 km^2. It is also one of the poorest countries in Latin America, with 60% of the population living in rural areas.

The country has a great variety of landscapes and biota, particularly in the lowland rain forests of the northern area. Cultural landscapes, defined as habitats modified by humans, cover most of the Honduran territory. Natural habitats are scarce and rapidly dissapearing to give place to pastures, farms, monocultures (e.g. banana, pineapple, coffee, sugar cane, rice, shrimp) and degraded forests. Cultural landscapes, resulting from an equilibrium between natural resources and human traditional activities still exist, but are in danger.

The tropical forests of Central America are relatively new. About 11,000 years ago the climate turned warm and wet and tropical vegetation expanded. By 8,000 BC almost all the isthmus was covered by forests, and though it is not clear when it became inhabited, groups of Paleoindian hunters and gatherers must have been living in the area by 9,000 BC. This however caused little impact on the forests.

Ancient settlements are preserved at the Copán Maya Site and the Río Plátano Biosphere Reserve, both listed as World Cultural and Natural Heritage sites. Nowadays, minority ethnic groups struggle between their traditional way of life, aculturation and colonization. Poverty, capitalism and indifference are driving their cultural heritage and natural habitats towards extinction.

Rio Platano Reserve

The Río Plátano Reserve was created in 1969 as an archaeological site, to protect many cultural resources including the legendary "White City", beleived to exist near the Río Plátano headwaters. The Río Plátano was established as a Biosphere Reserve in 1980 because of its importance as a unique center of biocultural diversity.

Placed in a tropical lowland forested region called The Mosquitia (Figure 1), the reserve has an area of about 525,100 ha and a population of about 25,000. This reserve contains the largest and most remote intact natural vegetation that is still left in Central America. Broad-leafed forests, swamps, savannas and pine forests contain a high diversity of native fauna, many of them classified as threatened or vulnerable (Cruz 1991). Tapirs, peccaries, jaguars, guans, deers, parrots, harpy eagles, manatees, anteaters, turtles, crocodiles, iguanas, many fish species (cuyamel is one of the most important) shared rivers and forests with people for centuries.

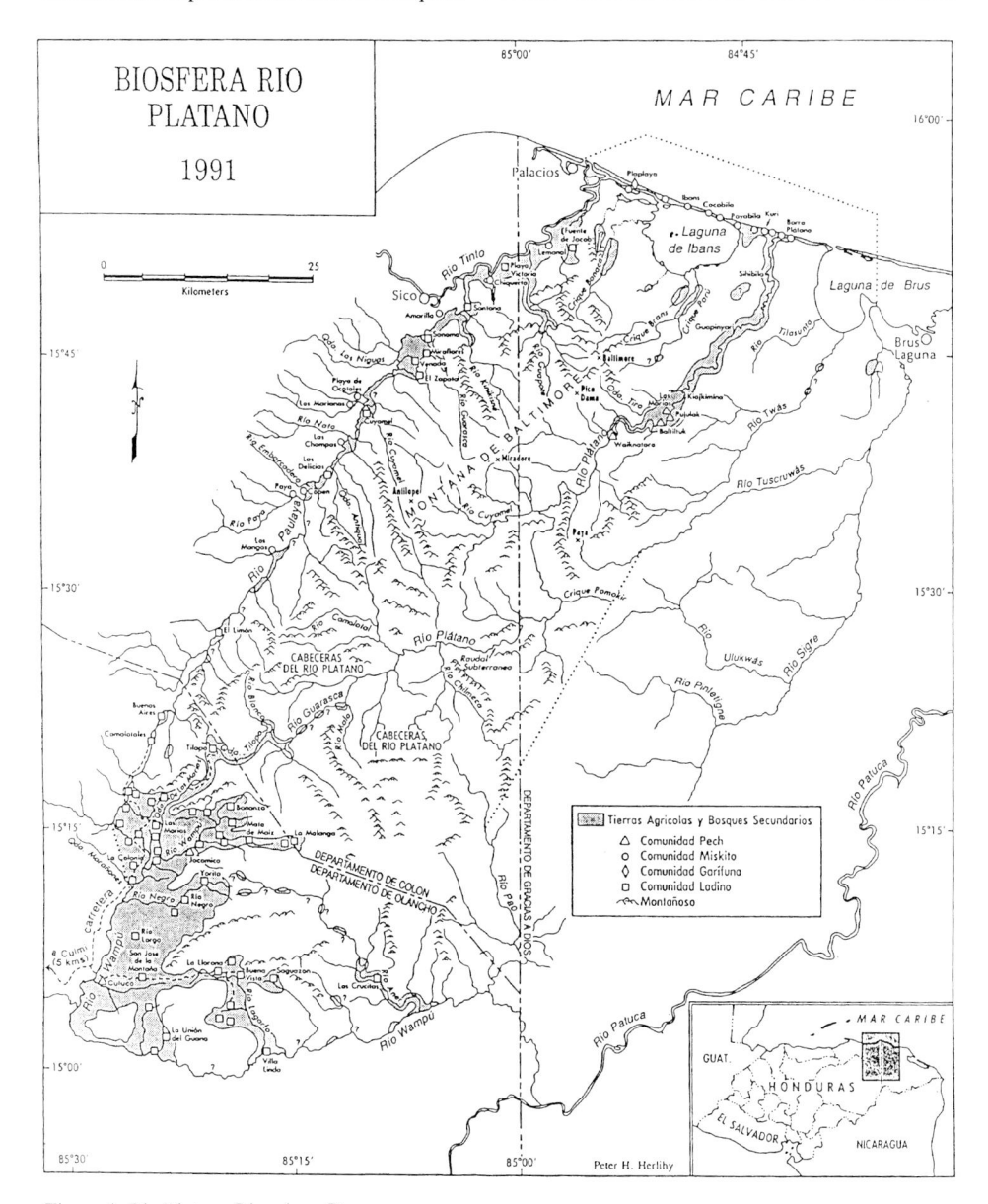

Figure 1. Rio Platano Biosphere Reserve.

The key to the Mosquitia geomorphology is a jumble of mountains (Sierra Río Tinto, Sierra Punta Piedra, Montaña de Colón, Cordillera Entre Ríos). Some peaks are as jagged as the Alps and over 1600 meters high. The rivers that drain them run north to the Caribbean, over a forested apron. Pines form patches on the grassy savanna of the sandy, north-eastern, coastal plain. Near the coast the rivers meander, leaving ox-bow lakes and arcs of rich land and serpentine forests. Over geological time the streams meander up and down the coast dumping sediments into the sea, building up a sea wall. Shallow water lagoons form behind the beaches. Some are filled with fresh water and fish, turtles and manatees. The Miskito coast is a white sand beach, hundreds of kilometers long and a few yards wide, with the Caribbean sea on one side and lagoons on the other. Tourists are just starting to discover it.

The Culture

Since early historic times there have been reports of a great city, "La Ciudad Blanca" (the White City), inland, in the Mosquitia. The site was never found. Topographic maps of the area show ruins covering a square kilometer. The site of Marañones is an example of the remains of a high civilization which once occupied the Mosquitia. Marañones was situated in the rain forest at the edge of the Mosquitia. A few years ago cattle ranchers started cutting the forest for pasture. Mounds, ballcourts and ridges were then identified. The clearing of the trees at least makes the ruins more visible.

In another un-named site in Mata de Maíz there is a colonist's house of sticks and mud on a pre-Columbian housemound. On the site there is a strange jaguar head about a meter long made of fine, black basalt (Bentley, pers. obs.). The sculpture represents a creature's head, twice normal size, half human and half jaguar. It is a work of art that could be compared to Michelangelo's.

In 1985, a British expedition detected about 80 archaeological sites in the Reserve. Unfortunately, maps could not be drawn. Nevertheless enough information was gathered to prove the cultural importance of the ancient civilization that inhabited the area (Pinto and Hasemann 1991).

We have no name for the culture that carved the jaguar-man and built the pyramids. The prehistoric Maya are well-known to archaeologists. The prehistoric culture of the nearby Mosquitia is undocumented. It may be of Caribbean and Amazonian affinity. No doubt the ancient people of the Mosquitia knew and trafficked with the Maya.

The Mosquitia is one of the least known pockets of native people in Latin America. Four ethnic groups live in the Reserve (Table 1) and conserve traditional management of landscape.

Table 1. Ethnic groups living in the Mosquitia. Source: Herlihy & Herlihy 1991; Herlihy & Leake 1991.

Ethnia	Communities	Population	Area
Miskito	19	4,500	Coast
Pech	4	250	Rio Platano
	2		Rio Wampu
Garifuna	1	370	Coast
Tawahka	5	750	Rio Patuca
Ladinos	8	450	Paulaya
	46	6,500	Rio Wampu
	1	50	Rio Patuca

The dominant group is the Miskito, native Americans of the coast. They joined in with British pirates to fight the Spanish until the 19th century. The Miskito language is still spoken. It has many words borrowed from English, but few from Spanish. The area is culturally distinct from the Latin-American interior of the country. Their capital was on the coast in a village called Palacios (palaces). The Miskito "kings" lived there and ruled for the British. On the beach at Palacios you can still sweep the sand off 18th century Spanish canyons stolen by buccaneers and manned by the Miskitos.

Many Miskitos live on the coast during winter (rainy season) and on their small farms along the rivers during the dry season. But their traditional life style is changing. Lobster industry is an attractive activity that offers high salaries, but also illness and death because of the lack of training. Miskito divers are paid by the pound of lobster. The boat captains encourage them to stay underwater for as many as nine tanks of air a day. Coming up fast when a tank is exhausted leads to death or paralysis from decompression sickness. Lobster collection is also causing the dissociation of the Miskito family. Men spend much of the time sailing, drinking and smoking. Women have to take care of the family and the farming (Herlihy and Herlihy 1991, Bentley, pers. obs.).

The Pech (also known as Paya) are now a remnant population of the original inhabitants of much of the central highlands of Honduras. Nowadays they live along the medium part of the Río Plátano. Most of the Pech people are mixed with Miskitos, and are facing cultural changes. They depend on their crops (mostly cassava and corn) and subsistence hunting and fishing.

The Garífuna (formerly known as the Black Carib) also live on the coast, and although of Afro-Caribbean origin, have lived in Honduras since the 1700s. Though they cultivate the land, they are traditionally fishermen. They have worked for wages for decades. While men are sailing or hunting, women take care of the crops (mostly cassava) and the children. The status of women in the community is relatively high.

The Ladinos (Hispanic people) have lived in Honduras for 450 years, but are relative new-comers to the Río Plátano area. A few Ladinos have lived along the coast since the early twentieth century, but by far the majority of the Ladinos in the Río Plátano Reserve are recent migrants flooding in from the southern highlands, causing the displacement of the Pech people.

Tawahka Indians also live further up the river, deeper in the forest, along the Patuca river and its tributaries. This group used to forage in a large area, but nowadays they have been displaced by the Miskitos and the Ladinos to the headwaters of the Mosquitia. Tawahka people farm along the river beds, raise some livestock and collect products from the forest: firewood, medicines, meat, fruits, building materials. In the past they earned money with forest products; nowadays they build and sell carved out canoes, cattle, meat or crops to each other and they also pan gold (Herlihy and Herlihy 1991, Herlihy and Leake 1991).

A Glimpse at the Lanscape: Paradise and Hell

Transportation in most of the Mosquitia is by plane and small boat. There are roads in some areas, especially the south of the Mosquitia, where ecological refugees from southern Honduras are turning the rainforest into a mudscape. There are Native communities deeper in the forest. The Mosquitia is roadless. There are airstrips for light aircraft in a few places, including Brus Laguna, Palacios, Puerto Lempira, Awás and Wampusirpe. The rivers and lagoons are travelled in carved out canoes, often made out of a single log of red mahogany. A few of these people are wealthy enough to afford outboard motors for their canoes.

Remnant forest patches, between clearings for Indian rice fields, can be seen from the river. The Miskitos often stand up to pole their canoes. They plant the poles on the river bottom and bend down to the water like gymnasts in slow motion.

There are no trails along the Patuca River between Wampusirpe and Krausirpe. The river is the road. People leave their villages in the morning and pole their canoes to their fields. The villages are clusters of one-room wooden plank houses, built on stilts to keep out the wet. The roofs are tight weavings of palm leaves. Sometimes the Indian hunters shoot monkeys or birds. Eating monkey brains gives children the wisdom never to get lost in the forest. Monkey is a rare treat. Most meals are made of boiled rice, boiled beans and boiled bananas. At night the family sleeps on the bare wooden floor. When they sweep the floor they can stick all their possessions (a knife, a bowl, some twine) into cracks in the wall.

The Montaña de Colón is a wild mountain across the river from the Tawahka village of Krausirpe. There is a narrow path through the mountain. Some Indians hunt there. The mountains are mesozoic limestone karst, riddled with caves. In Mayan folklore, mountain caves were entrances to the underworld, guarded by demons. The Tawahka say the mountains are dangerous. It's too easy to fall into a cave.

Miskito and Tawahka farms are patches along the river. No one farms very far inland. It would be too hard to get the products out. Bananas and rice can be hauled from riverside farms into the canoes. People cut down the secondary forest, let it lie there in the dry season and then torch it. They plant rice and sometimes beans, cassava, and a little maize. Until a few years ago people planted a handful of cacao trees to make chocolate for breakfast. Development agencies are encouraging the Indians to grow commercial cocoa. The trees do well in the clearings, under the shade of banana plants. Now most people have a cocoa grove. Cocoa has a high-value and is easy to sell, it is one of the few sources of cash. Sometimes the Tawahka build a raft and load it with rice or bananas and float it for 10 or 14 days down to the coast. There brokers buy food to take to the Bay Islands and the North Coast.

Landscapes in Danger

The Mosquitia is the least known area of Honduras. Its natural, cultural and archaeological richness is almost unknown even to Hondurans.

The northern part of the Río Plátano Reserve, is inhabited by Miskitos, Garífunas and Pech that still maintain much of their traditional way of natural resources use, so it is not heavily degraded. In the central area, there are few human communities and the largest populations of wildlife are found there. The southern part, historically inhabited by Pech people, has been heavily disturbed by colonization.

In 1980 the Río Plátano Biosphere Reserve was still nearly all forested. Agricultural activities of indigenous people, mostly subsistence, did not seem to degrade the ecosystem. But by the early 1990s there was a colonization front all along the southern border of the Biosphere, rapidly invading the nucleus zone. There were paths, ribbons of mud, where the mules passed carrying the coffee. Farmers cut down the forest and burned the vegetation ("slash and burn"). As coffee grows in the shade, the only trees the colonists leave standing are the ones to shade the coffee plants. The colonists level the rest of the forest to plant corn but will let the land become overgrown after a year or two. A family that could live on a hectare or two takes up twenty because each one claims the land they clear. The more they clear, the more they own. The hills are green with grass, not trees. The colonists may also sell the land after clearing the forest for pastures. Deforestation is sometimes financially supported by cattle ranchers who later buy the "improved" land from the peasants who have cleared the forest (Salaverry 1991).

Forests are cut down for timber, farming and cattle ranching. Loggers roads open the way for the colonists that come from the most populated areas of the country. Extensive cattle ranching is one of the most important and destructive activities. A strong competition between small farmers and rich cattle breeders, and a complete lack of control, policy or land planification causes chaos. This process is not only degrading the land but forcing traditional communities to move to the poorest lands, where survival is more and more difficult.

Granting concessions to foreign firms for timber exploitation and oil exploration is another threat to the area. Mahogany, a native tree, almost commercially extinct in Central America, is the main product obtained from these forests. Its exploitation is carried out without any control or planning. This valuable wood is even split for rough roof shingles where colonists live. The common use of dynamite for fishing is depleting an important resource for indigenous people, and eliminating the rivers' biota.

Many of the invaders are cattle ranchers that come from Olancho. Olancho is an arid valley twisted between pine covered mountains. The peasants plow with oxen, wear cowboy hats, and carry pistols in their belts. Many families in Olancho are involved in blood feuds with their neighbors. Funeral processions for murdered victims are common sights in the villages.

The Rights of the Land

All the movements of people into the Reserve during the last twenty years have not been organized or supervised by governmental entities (GFA 1991). Most of the existing land market is not legal. Neither the people who have worked the land for over ten years, nor indigenous communities within the Reserve, own the land.

The Mosquitia is attracting NGOs. A Honduran village with several dozen houses usually has few public buildings: a school, maybe a church, a store or two. In 1994, the village of Krausirpe had all of these as well as a government health center (with a nurse but no medicine), and an office of MOPAWI (Mosquitia Pawisa, Development of the Mosquitia), and one for FITH (Federación Indígena Tawahka de Honduras). There has also been a UN "cultural rescue" project in the village and CCD (Comisión Cristiana del Desarrollo) has built an office-hotel there.

MOPAWI and FITH are local organizations, run by the Indians. The cultural survival project has hired the best people. In spite of the efforts of these organizations, people from the Honduran interior still invade the Mosquitia. The government is doing little to police the decreed protected areas.

Nevertheless, indigenous peoples of the Mosquitia fight for their rights, for the ownership of their ancestral lands and their traditional way of using the natural resources.

On September 1992, the First Congress on Indigenous Lands of the Mosquitia was held in Tegucigalpa. A reaffirmation of their cultural heritage and a social land use map was presented to the Honduran people and the world. Many people just learned that the area is inhabited and not "for sale".

Epilog

Olancho borders the Mosquitia. The ranchers have cleared the trees on the Wampú river, that Paul Theroux describes as deep forest in his novel, *The Mosquito Coast*. They have gutted the forest down to where the Wampú drains into the Patuca River. The Tawahka lived there until many of them died during the influenza epidemic of 1918. Their grandparents are buried there. The land is sacred to them, but the ranchers have logged out the heart of Tawahka country to raise beef.

During his tenure as president of Honduras, Rafael Leonardo Callejas declared the Tawahka country, including the Wampú, as part of a Tawahka Reserve that borders the Río Platano Biosphere Reserve. Many good intentions still remain on paper.

Mountains and ruined cities covered in rainforest, Indian rice fields strung along the river bank, canoes ("pipantes" or "cayucos"), fishing nets and harpoons along the clear rivers, armed ranchers and refugee peasants, NGOs and international agencies. That is the cultural landscape of the Honduran Mosquitia today.

What was the role of this area and cultures in the past? Geographic isolation kept this refuge almost untouched by modern society. But this is coming to an end. Poverty, hunger and ambition is opening the difficult road through the forest, the rivers and the Natives. Cultural and natural landscapes of Hondurans and all Mesoamericans are in danger. A heritage that must not be lost. Native people are aware, they have started the fight against extinction. But it is not enough.

References

Cruz, G. A. (1991). *La Biodiversidad de la Reserva*. In: Murphy, V. (Ed.) *Herencia de nuestro pasado: La Reserva de la Biósfera Río Plátano*. Tegucigalpa, ROCAP (USAID), WWF, COHDEFOR/AID. Pp 20-26.

Gesellschaft Für Agrarprojekte (GFA). (1991). *Proyecto Manejo y Protección de la Reserva de la Biosfera del Río Plátano*. COHDEFOR, Honduras.

Herlihy, P. H. and Herlihy, L. H. (1991). *La herencia cultural de la Reserva de la Biósfera del Río Plátano: Un área de confluencias étnicas en La Mosquitia*. In: Murphy, V. (Ed.) *Herencia de nuestro pasado: La Reserva de la Biósfera Río Plátano*. Tegucigalpa, ROCAP (USAID)/WWF/COHDEFOR/AID. Pp 9-15.

Herlihy, P. H. and Leake, A. P. (1991). *Propuesta Reserva Forestal Tawahka Sumu*. Folleto. Tegucigalpa, Honduras: Mosquitia Pawisa (MOPAWI), Federación Indígena Tawahka de Honduras (FITH), Instituto Hondureño de Antropología e Historia (IHAH).

Pinto, G. L. and Hasemann, G. (1991). *Leyendas y Arqueología: ¿Cuántas Ciudades Blancas hay en la Mosquitia?*. In: Murphy, V. (Ed.) *Herencia de nuestro pasado: La Reserva de la Biósfera Río Plátano*. Tegucigalpa, ROCAP (USAID), WWF, COHDEFOR/AID. Pp 16-19.

Salaverry, J. (1991). *La Situación Actual de la Reserva.* In: Murphy, V. (Ed.) *Herencia de nuestro pasado: La Reserva de la Biósfera Río Plátano.* Tegucigalpa, ROCAP (USAID), WWF, COHDEFOR/AID.Pp. 20-26.

Silvia C. Chalukian is an Ecologist, she teaches Wildlife Management and Conservation Biology at the Panamerican Agriculture School (Zamorano), Department of Natural Resources and Conservation Biology.

Jeffery W. Bentley is an Anthropologist. He is an independent consultor in Bolivia.

Chapter 20

Cultural Landscapes of North America: An Overview of Status in the United States and Canada

Patricia M. O'Donnell

Introduction

The diversity of landscape types throughout the United States and Canada, the portions of North America addressed in this paper, is a function of vast size, varied geography and broad climatic range. Cultural landscapes of many categories and scales can be found within North America to include urban, rural, suburban and exurban landscapes that may be categorized as: residential properties or communities; gardens; public building sites; institutional properties; estates; botanical gardens; public squares, commons, public monument grounds; streetscapes; parks, parkways, park systems; burial grounds and cemeteries; battlefields, fortifications; farms and agricultural areas; cities; towns; subdivisions; ceremonial places, commemorative locations; and large scale linear landscapes such as settlement trails, distinctive highways, river valleys, mountain ranges and the like. This diversity of type and scale presents considerable challenges for the identification and safeguarding of valuable cultural landscapes in North America.

Both the United States and Canada have preservation mechanisms to address historically significant cultural resources at the local, state or provincial and national levels. Our cultural landscapes are valuable at the local, regional, national and potentially international levels, but the lack of understanding of cultural landscapes, in the form of comprehensive surveys and theme studies in both the United States and Canada, is hindering our ability to put forward indicative lists of cultural landscapes that may be of outstanding and universal value. Due to this lack of overall context and indicative lists, this paper addresses cultural landscape preservation issues, the state of the art and diverse examples from both nations, providing an overview of the field. Companion papers by Buggey and Mitchell address each nation in more detail and provide examples of significant cultural landscapes in the United States and Canada.

Cultural Landscapes in the United States

United States Legal Basis and Designation System

The legal basis for historic preservation in the United States stems from the 1906 Antiquities Act, the 1935 Historic Sites Act and the 1966 National Historic Preservation Act. These key pieces of legislation address the preservation of cultural resources for the benefit of present and future generations. The historic preservation programs resulting from these laws are administered by the National Park Service in cooperation with the State Historic Preservation Offices, certified local governments and municipalities. The 1966 National Historic Preservation Act as amended in 1981 addresses the need to preserve "the historical and cultural foundations of the Nation. . . as a living part of our community life and development in order to give a sense of orientation to the American people. . . the increased knowledge of our historic resources, the establishment of better means of identifying and administering them, and the encouragement of their preservation will improve the planning and execution of Federal and federally assisted project and will assist economic growth and development." (Advisory Council 1981)

The National Park Service, within the United States Department of the Interior, establishes national policy and sets standards for all aspects of historic preservation. Through the National Historic Landmarks and National Register Programs, the National Park Service administers the inventory, evaluation, and listing of historically significant cultural properties in the United States nominations for designation through either of these programs is generally initiated at the local or state level.

In the United States the accepted definition of a *cultural landscape*, published and circulated by the National Park Service, is:

a geographic area, including both cultural and natural resources, and the wildlife and domestic animals therein, associated with a historic event, activity or person, or exhibiting other cultural or aesthetic values. (NPS 28)

Four types of cultural landscapes are described in National Park Service guidance. They are relevant to the cultural properties within the National Park system and also apply to the breadth of cultural landscapes in public and private ownership nationwide. They are:

Historic Site: the location of a significant event or activity, or a building or structure, whether standing, ruined or vanished, where the location itself possesses historic, cultural, or archaeological value regardless or the value of any existing structure.

Historic Designed Landscape: a landscape having historic significance as a design or work of art because it was consciously designed and laid out by a landscape architect, master gardener, architect or horticulturist according to design principles, or by an owner or other amateur using a recognized style or tradition in response or reaction to a recognized style or tradition; has a historic association with a significant person or persons, trend, or event in landscape gardening or landscape architecture; or a significant relationship to the theory and practice of landscape architecture.

Historic Vernacular Landscape: a landscape whose use, construction, or physical layout reflects endemic traditions, customs, beliefs of values; in which the expression of cultural values, social behavior, and individual actions over time is manifested in the physical features and materials and their interrelationships, including patterns of spatial organization, land use, circulation, vegetation, structures and objects; in which the physical, biological, and cultural features reflect the customs and everyday lives of people.

Ethnographic Landscape: a landscape traditionally associated with a contemporary ethnic group, typically used for such activities as subsistence hunting and gathering, religious or sacred ceremonies, and traditional meetings.

Although they are not directly transferable, these four types achieve some parallels with the recently adopted World Heritage types: The historic designed landscape is directly comparable to the defined or designed category; the historic vernacular landscape and the ethnographic landscape parallel the continuing evolved landscape but do not explicitly imply the relict landscape; the historic site and the ethnographic landscape are both encompassed in the associative landscape category, although aspects of poetry and painting, which are included in the World Heritage language, are missing from both these definitions.

In cultural landscapes the aggregation of features and processes that characterized the property during its period of significance collectively comprise its historic character. These character-defining features and processes include: topography, vegetation, circulation, landscape structures, water features, site furnishings, objects, spatial relationships and views, surroundings and setting and related natural systems. (Guidelines, NPS, May 1992) In current professional practice historic character is analyzed using these components as evidence of the survival of physical characteristics. They guide comparison of the historic and current conditions to determine to authenticity of the cultural landscapes' historic identity as evidenced by intact historic character – the integrity of the historic landscape.

United States Registration System

The National Register of Historic Places is the official list of nationally recognized properties which are significant in American history, architecture, engineering and culture. The National Historic Landmarks Survey was established by the Historic Sites Act of 1935 and a small collection of historic properties were designated in the following decades. The National Register of Historic Places, authorized in 1966, superseded this listing to expand Federal recognition to historic properties of local and state significance as well as national import. The process of designation begins at the locality with a nomination to the state or territory through the state historic preservation office or through Federal agencies. The documentation then follows a review process, a determination of eligibility and is forwarded to the National Register program within the National Park Service, Cultural Resource Division for eventual listing if accepted. Properties listed on the National Register must possess historic significance and integrity in relationship to major trends and within an overall historic context that can be shown to demonstrate the property's significance. Four aspects of significance in American history are recognized: (NR Bulletin 16A)

- Association with historic events, activities or patterns;
- Association with important persons;
- Distinctive physical characteristics of design, construction or form as a type or method of construction, the work of a master, or possessing high artistic values; or
- Potential to provide important information about prehistory or history at the local, state or national level.

Since 1966 a large number of properties have been identified, researched and listed on the National Register of Historic Places, generally focusing on cultural resources that are at least fifty years old to give a perspective on their value, but including some more contemporary properties. In past decades recognition of historic value has focused predominantly on historic architecture – first as buildings associated with important historic events, such as the World Heritage listed Independence Hall in Philadelphia, then as important examples of high style architecture, moving to clusters of buildings in historic districts and more recently to thematic and multiple resource nominations that have include landscape components and finally to landscapes as primary cultural resources. Although direct comparisons are difficult, because structures and landscapes can both be included in district, thematic and multiple resource nominations, in general the registration of cultural landscapes has lagged behind that of architecture with only a small fraction of landscapes listed in comparison to the vast number of buildings.

Efforts have been made in recent years to provide guidance for listing landscapes on the National Register. Four National Register Bulletins *18: How to Evaluate and Nominate Designed Historic Landscapes*; *30: Guidelines for Evaluating and Documenting Rural Historic Landscapes*; *38: Guidelines for Evaluating and Documenting Traditional Cultural Properties*, *40: Guidelines for Identifying, Evaluating and Registering America's Historic Battlefields*; *41: How to Evaluate and Nominate Cemeteries and Burial Places*, have been published by the Interagency Resources Division to provide needed guidance for State Historic Preservation Offices and preservation professionals. Additional tools for technical guidance include the NPS Preservation Assistance Division's recently completed revisions to the existing *Secretary of the Interior's Standards for Historic Preservation Projects*, which uses terminology that is inclusive of cultural landscapes. This division has also widely distributed a draft *Guidelines for the Treatment of Historic Landscapes* for testing on projects, review and eventual refinement.

Listing on the National Register provides public recognition of importance in American history, consideration in planning Federal projects, eligibility for architectural rehabilitation tax credits and qualification to compete for Federal grants when available. (NR Bulletin 16A) It does not ensure preservation. In projects where Federal monies are to be spent, Section 106 of the National Historic Preservation Act provides for an advisory review of anticipated impacts to cultural resources in an effort to seek the least damaging alternatives. Historic designation at the state and local level is often a stronger preservation tool than National Register listing. For example, in Connecticut, enabling legislation provides for a local historic commission to oversee designated properties or districts with a procedure for carefully reviewing changes and providing a certificate of appropriateness. At the local level some aspects of the cultural landscape, such as spatial organization, building setbacks and massing, fencing, driveways and parking areas, are included in the review process.

Demonstrated national significance raises the cultural property to National Landmark level. Only from this eminence can a cultural resource can be considered for international significance and World Heritage listing.

State of Understanding in the United States

Cultural landscapes are experiencing a surge of interest nationwide. Thanks to intensive efforts beginning in the late 1970s, we now have over fifteen years of work that has formed a foundation for current practice. A series of events in the late 1970s and early 1980s laid a foundation for the current breadth and depth of activities. In 1978 the founding of the Alliance for Historic Landscape Preservation, a multi-disciplinary group from the US and Canada, brought together a small band of interested professionals. In 1980 the Alliance hosted an intensive training session in Williamsburg which was the first of its kind. By 1981-2 the American Society of Landscape Architects Historic

Preservation Open Committee was reaching out within the profession and to like-minded groups. National legislation commemorating Frederick Law Olmsted, Sr. and other early practitioners and calling for nation-wide inventory of historic designed landscapes was first introduced in the US Congress in November 1983. A coalition of interested groups participated in four rounds of this legislative drive, without success in passage, but with greatly increased awareness.

In May 1984, the ASLA Historic Preservation Open Committee, with the author as chairperson, initiated a <u>National Historic Landscapes Survey</u> with the broad distribution of a four-page survey form which also raised awareness nation-wide in addition to generating a group of completed forms. Subsequent inventories have been undertaken on a site-specific, regional and state basis, with many referencing this early ASLA format.

This increasing level of activity brought about a meeting in February 1985 between the National Park Service, Cultural Resources Division, ASLA Historic Preservation Open Committee, National Association for Olmsted Parks (NAOP), the Frederick Law Olmsted Papers and other involved individuals. At that meeting the National Park Service set forth the first listing of elements of what would become the Historic Landscapes Initiative, which is making significant progress today. The tasks outlined at that time included development of a definition of historic landscape architect, a historic landscapes bibliography, model National Register and Landmark nominations, model cultural landscape reports, HABS/HAER documentation standards for landscapes, technical publications, and a theme study of historic landscapes. While many of these directions have been fruitfully pursued over the past nine years, others, such as the theme study, await broader progress. In order to make these advances, National Park Service professional staff, with credentials in landscape preservation, have been added to Washington and regional offices. In addition a National Parks Cultural Landscape Inventory underway and cultural landscape reports on specific parks and historic sites are in progress or anticipated in the near future.

In 1986 the Congressional Office of Technology Assessment undertook a study of *Technologies for Historic and Prehistoric Preservation* which included a workshop on *Technologies for the Preservation of Planned Landscapes and Other Outdoor Sites*. The report of this session and others on the technologies of underwater archaeology and maritime preservation, archaeological sites and historic structures, called for the creation of a national center that would be a consortium of federal, states and local government agencies, academe and the corporate sector focused on preservation technology transfer. The banner was carried forward with the formation of the National Coalition for Applied Preservation Technology (CAPT) and in 1987 the University Consortium for Preservation Science and Technology (USAT). In October 1990 legislation that would provide for this center was introduced each year until it achieved passage as the *National Historic Preservation Act Amendments* in the 1992-93 Congressional year. One component of this bill is the establishment of a National Center for Preservation Technology and Training in Natchitoches, Louisiana. An important conference on cultural landscapes as linear corridors was hosted at the new center in December 1992. This new Center should play an important role in the advancement of the field in the coming years.

Another important aspect of the cultural landscape preservation movement is the Catalog of Landscape Records in the United States. Established in 1987, it gathers information about design professionals and the location and content of collections relevant to landscape history. Biographical information, drawings, surveys, design plans, postcards, plant lists, photographs, or seed catalogs, and other records contribute to this expanding database. For access within accepted systems all information is organized using the Archival and Manuscripts Control (AMC) format, while the Library of Congress Name Authority and Subject Authority files and the *Art and Architecture Thesaurus* (AAT) are the sources of the descriptive language. This type of effort for compatibility and broad access is an excellent model for other nations. The availability of this type of information has recently been augmented by research about historic landscape architects, gardeners, engineers, superintendents, etc. nationwide that has been compiled as the first phase of an annotated bibliography entitled *Pioneers of American Landscape Design*. (Birnbaum 1993) This project will continue to work with interested professionals from all parts of the United States to enlarge this database on persons who have made important contributions to the historic designed landscape of the United States.

In recent years there has been an increasing breadth of historic landscape project work including research, inventory, analysis, treatment, management and interpretation. These projects have addressed properties of local, state and national ownership. Increasingly, historic and cultural aspects of these resources are being recognized as critical components of future stewardship and management, and cultural landscape architects and landscape historians are leading or being included in project teams. To date state-wide survey projects in Rhode Island, Maine and Georgia have proceeded with the identification and documentation of some types of cultural landscapes. In Maine the project focuses on designed landscapes. It began with public landscapes, is continuing with residential landscapes and will proceed with city and regional plans, subdivisions, suburban communities and institutional grounds (ICOMOS Landscapes Working Group Newsletter 1993).

In urban areas public parks and open spaces are often historic. These resources are subject to intense use and management pressures that can alter their historic character. In the past decade, throughout the United States park departments and private park conservancy groups have worked with landscape preservation consultants to develop comprehensive plans for these historic designed landscapes that respect historic character and preserve historic components. These parks are precious community resources often deteriorated from deferred maintenance and unfunded capital projects. One example is the authors' current work with talented colleagues for the Olmsted Parks and Parkways of Louisville, Kentucky, where the planning issues include: infrastructure deterioration; community concerns for public safety; conflict resolution among passive, active and group uses; bolstering and retraining maintenance crews; financing needed capital projects; and recapturing the ecological health and sustainability; all while respecting the historic character of these public cultural landscape resources. (Sauer and O'Donnell, et al 1994)

Access to focused educational opportunities has increased as well. A decade ago students in landscape architecture, planning, historic preservation or art and architectural history were offered limited access to a cultural landscape preservation specialization. There have been numerous advances in availability of specialized courses at several universities, with some offering degree programs. Accredited landscape architecture programs offering specializations today include the Universities of Pennsylvania, Georgia, Wisconsin-Madison, Ball State (Indiana) and SUNY at Syracuse. Continuing education workshops, seminars and certificate programs have also become more widely available.

A series of recent publications, many developed through the National Park Service's Historic Landscape Initiative, attest to the growing interest and expertise in cultural landscape preservation in the United States. These include the National Register Bulletins noted above and several additional information sources. A general awareness-raising brochure, *America's Landscape Legacy*, was developed by the NPS Preservation Assistance Division in cooperation with the American Society of Landscape Architects. Widely distributed recent publications include thematic issues of the National Trust's *Preservation Forum* (May/June 1993), and *Cultural Resource Management Bulletin, CRM: "A Reality Check for Our Nation's Parks"* (April 1993), both edited by Charles A. Birnbaum, coordinator of the NPS Historic Landscape Preservation Initiative. The *Workbook Series*, a group of short research and practice reports, has been published by the National Association for Olmsted Parks with four volumes to date. *The Historic Landscape Directory* is an annotated information compendium with listing on training, technical assistance, educational programs, research facilities, and other resources. Two useful annotated bibliographies, *Preserving Historic Landscapes* and *Making Educated Decisions*, have also been published and disseminated.

Technical assistance and training in historic landscape preservation has increased notably over the last several years. To address the unique skills and approach required to care for cultural landscapes, the National Park Service has been upgrading park staff skills in annual historic landscape planning and maintenance training sessions in several regions over the past three years. Since 1987 annual ASLA/NPS Historic Landscape Preservation Symposia have explored the state-of-the-art. Educational sessions sponsored by the Alliance for Historic Landscape Preservation, the National Trust, the National Association for Olmsted Parks and the National Park Service among others, have all been useful in providing learning opportunities and professional exchanges about the state-of-the-art.

All of these activities express a vitality and rich dialogue in the field of cultural landscape preservation in the United States. This dialogue is reaching a broad audience of preservation professionals and cultural landscape advocates of all types as recognition of cultural landscape values becomes more widespread and preservation activities expand.

United States Theme Studies and Indicative Lists

In order to consider cultural landscapes more thoroughly for listing as National Landmarks, a nation-wide theme study of cultural landscapes is required to develop a comprehensive context that would provide a basis for assessing national significance. Congressional funding for the needed theme study has been advocated over the past several years without success. Two useful, but limited, components of a broad theme study are currently underway within the National Park Service. A service-wide Cultural Landscape Inventory that seeks to identify cultural landscapes within National Park Service properties is in early stages nationwide. Research and assessment of cultural landscapes developed by National Parks staff since the inception of the service in 1915 through 1945 is also underway. This project will address the design overlays that have provided public access and visitor services to many of the nation's most treasured natural resources, like Yellowstone, Grand Canyon, Redwood and Yosemite National Parks. Interestingly, these parks are World Heritage Sites listed under natural criteria.

A basis providing the historic context for all types of cultural landscapes would be an extremely valuable tool since each isolated preservation effort could then be understood as a part of the larger universe of resources. The need for a comprehensive theme study, perhaps most suitably as a series of focused studies on specific topics, is evident in all aspects of cultural landscape preservation. A few historic designed landscapes have been elevated to landmark status. Lacking a theme study, there is reasonable hesitation to bring a number of cultural landscapes to the National Landmark level because landmark status, predicated on clear national significance and a high level of integrity, implies that the particular cultural landscape is exemplary of its type valued above numerous other examples. The lack of a well-researched basis, the product of a theme study, makes it extremely difficult to make assertions about the national level of significance for a group of exemplary cultural landscapes.

In the United States, both the National Register and the National Historic Landmarks Programs use a thematic approach to evaluate a property's historic significance which is periodically revised to reflect changes in the understanding of United States history and culture (U.S Department of the Interior, National Park Service 1987a). The National Historic Landmarks Program is closely linked to nominations of United States sites to the World Heritage List. According to the current United States regulations for the implementation of the World Heritage Convention, a property must be determined to be nationally significant before being nominated to the World Heritage List (Policies and Procedures for United States Participation in the World Heritage Convention, 36 Code of Federal Regulations, Part 73.7). These regulations specify that a property can be determined nationally significant by designation as a National Historic Landmark or a National Natural Landmark, or as an area established by Congress or by Presidential Proclamation, providing that a property has national significance prior to consideration for international designation.

The existing framework consists of thirty-four prehistoric and historic contexts which include topics directly relevant to cultural landscapes such as landscape architecture, agriculture, conservation of natural resources, and transportation. To identify historic properties of national import, the National Historic Landmarks Program undertakes theme studies which are generally comparative analyses of properties which provide a broad historic context. Evaluation criteria used in this program are similar to those for cultural properties in the World Heritage Committee's Operational Guidelines. All National Historic Landmark nominations are reviewed by the National Park Service and the National Park Service Advisory Board, whose members are professionals outside the National Park Service. As of 1990, there were over 2,000 National Historic Landmarks (United States Department of the Interior and Advisory Council on Historic Preservation 1990). Some landmarks are owned and managed by the United States as units of the National Park System, but many in state or municipal government or private ownership.

Although most existing landmarks were designated prior to the definition of cultural landscapes as a type of cultural property, some are cultural landscapes. A review of the Catalog of National Historic Landmarks identified forty properties, listed under a variety of historic themes, which could be classified as cultural landscapes (United States Department of the Interior 1987b). Only ten properties are listed under the theme of landscape architecture, including the Boston Common, the Boston Public Garden and the Frederick Law Olmsted National Historic Site in Massachusetts; Central Park in New York; the Lawrenceville School in New Jersey; the National Capital Parks in Washington DC and Maryland; Middleton Place in South Carolina; the Missouri Botanical Garden in Missouri; Green Springs Historic District in Virginia; and the Riverside Historic District in Illinois. The lack of a theme study for landscape architecture accounts for this small number of entries. Recent efforts to provide a Congressional appropriation for the needed study have been unsuccessful to date.

Theme studies in areas other than landscape architecture have also identified important cultural landscapes. For example, a theme study on the Conservation of Natural Resources was completed in 1963 and identified a number of important landscapes including Fairsted, the home and office of Frederick Law Olmsted (now administered by the National Park Service as the Frederick Law Olmsted National Historic Site); Central Park, New York City; Adirondack Forest Preserve; Yosemite and Yellowstone National Parks; and the Gifford Pinchot Home, Grey Towers, Pennsylvania (United States Department of the Interior 1963). All of these sites, except the two national parks, have been designated as National Historic Landmarks. Future theme studies in areas such as agriculture, transportation, and military history will undoubtedly identify important landscapes within those contexts.

The thematic framework developed by National Historic Landmarks Program has provided an effective tool for using comparative analyses to identify and evaluate properties of historical significance. A similar thematic approach has recently been advocated for evaluation of World Heritage nominations. The World Heritage Committee has initiated a Global Strategy which would establish a contextual framework worldwide (see World Heritage Committee Report, Eighteenth Session, Pukhet, Thailand 12-18 December 1994).

Lacking a theme study and therefore a body of cultural landscapes that are National Landmarks, no cultural landscapes have been listed for potential inclusion on the World Heritage List. The National Park Service, International Division, is responsible for putting forward World Heritage nominations. The policy followed to date has been to advance only those properties that are Federally owned for potential inclusion because of the stewardship commitment required for World Heritage listing. (Cooke to O'Donnell 1993) While reconsideration of these issues is underway, the restriction to federal ownership, plus the lack of a strong basis in historic research and context, limits the ability of the United States to put forward an indicative list that would include cultural landscapes of outstanding and universal value in the near future.

Cultural Landscapes in Canada

Canadian Legal Basis and Designation System

At the federal level operational policy addressing cultural resources in Canada is readily applicable to cultural landscapes. (Canadian Heritage 1994) The framework used may be of interest to other nations. It focuses on five sets of principles which are excerpted, in part, as follows:
- Principles of Value - In Parks Canada, resources that have historic value are called cultural resources. It is for this value that cultural resources will be safeguarded and presented for public benefit. Parks Canada will value most highly those cultural resources of national historic significance. Parks Canada will value cultural resources in their context and will consider resources as a whole as well as discrete parts. A cultural resource whose historic value derives from its witness to many periods in history will be respected for that evolution, not just for its existence at a single moment in time. A

cultural resource that derives its historic value from the interaction of nature and human activities will be valued for both its cultural and natural qualities.
- Principles of Public Benefit - Cultural resources are dedicated and held in trust so that present and future generations may enjoy and benefit from them. To understand and appreciate cultural resources and the sometimes complex themes they illustrate, the public will be provided with information and services that effectively communicate the importance and value of those resources and their themes. Appropriate uses of cultural resources will be those uses and activities that respect the historic value and physical integrity of the resources, and promote public understanding and appreciation. In the interest of long-term public benefit, new uses that threaten cultural resources of national historic significance will not be considered, and existing uses which threaten them will be discontinued or modified to remove the threat.
- Principles of Understanding - The care and presentation of cultural resources require knowledge and understanding of those resources of the history they represent, and of the most effective means to communicate that history to the public for whom the resources are held in trust. Cultural resources management activities will be based on knowledge and professional and technical skills and expertise. Parks Canada will integrate the contributions of relevant disciplines in planning and implementing cultural resource management, and will place a particular importance on interdisciplinary teamwork. Adequate research, recording and investigation will precede any action that might affect cultural resources and their presentation. Parks Canada will identify the nature and various interests of the public to develop effective means of communication.
- Principles of Respect - Those who hold our heritage in trust are responsible for passing on that heritage in ways that maintain its potential for future understanding, appreciation and study. As an irreplaceable part of this heritage, cultural resources will be managed with continuous care and with respect for their historic character; that is, for the qualities for which they are valued.
- Principles of Integrity - Parks Canada will present the past in a manner that accurately reflects the range and complexity of the human history commemorated at or represented in a national historic site, historic canal or national park. Evidence that is specific to a resource or site will always be preferred to general evidence of a type or period. The use of indirect or comparative evidence will be acknowledged. Depictions of the past without basis in knowledge will not be considered. Cultural resources should be distinguishable from, and not overwhelmed by, efforts to conserve, enhance and present them. New work of all kinds will be distinguished from the work of the past.

In the past two years cooperation between the Parks Canada and the National Capital Commission (NCC) has led to increased awareness and a shared working definition and typology for cultural landscapes. A February 1993 cultural landscapes workshop included participants from the NCC, Parks Canada, federal departments, heritage agencies and universities. This important gathering provided a forum for productive discussion of terminology, level of awareness and potential strategies to address cultural landscapes through a collaborative effort. (ICOMOS Landscapes Working Group Newsletter, September 1993)

Following the workshop, the NCC drafted a broader definition of cultural landscapes based on the characterization of each element:

Cultural Landscapes are geographical terrains identifiable in topographical or morphological terms, which, as a result of an authentic and tangible or intangible human interaction with the natural environment, exhibit characteristics of the way of life, the types of land management and of government or organization of, or which represent the moral, social, or aesthetic values of, an identifiable society.

Those attending this meeting supported the use of the broad cultural landscape categories set forward in the World Heritage operational guidelines. These are: 1. the <u>defined landscape</u> designed and created intentionally; 2. the <u>organically evolved landscape</u> resulting from social, economic, administrative, and/or religious imperatives, developed in response to its natural environment in two subcategories as a <u>relict (or fossil) landscape</u> where evolutionary process have ended or a <u>continuing landscape</u> which retains an active social role in contemporary society; 3. the <u>associative cultural landscape</u> with powerful religious, artistic or cultural associations of the natural elements rather than material cultural evidence. (UNESCO, World Heritage Committee, December 1992.) Parks Canada, the National Capital Commission and others concerned with cultural landscapes intend to use this vocabulary and adapt it as necessary to the cultural landscape resources in Canada as preservation efforts proceed.

Canadian Registration System

National legislation, framed in the Historic Sites and Monuments Act, enables preservation action rather than requiring it. Heritage legislation and policy is developed more completely at the ten provinces and two territories. Each province and territory has its own system with heritage protection and management activities focusing at this level of government supplemented by municipal level functions in local heritage protection. Cultural landscapes have not been identified in legislation and policy guidance in the past although in some cases existing heritage and planning acts apply to landscape. New heritage legislation coming forward in British Columbia, New Brunswick and Ontario have included cultural landscapes in background documents for public discussion.

Evaluation to determine national significance is undertaken by the federal Historic Sites and Monuments Board of Canada. Proposals for World Heritage Listing address resources of international significance. Responsibility for World Heritage in Canada is assigned to the Minister of Canadian Heritage, responsible for Parks Canada.

The purpose of evaluating cultural landscapes is to enhance understanding by defining their distinguishing qualities from different perspectives, by identifying significance through intrinsic and comparative values, and by articulating these aspects so that they may be considered, respected, and protected in the context of change. Identification and evaluation are, however, merely the first steps in the recognition of cultural landscapes, and they must be recognized as a means to this end, not the end in itself.

The critical mechanisms for the long term stewardship of cultural landscapes are protection, planning, and conservation. Canada has currently no legislation, either federal or provincial, that addresses cultural landscapes directly. However, increasing awareness of their heritage significance has led to their explicit inclusion in background documents, discussion papers and consultations working towards new legislation in at least three provinces (British Columbia, Ontario, and New Brunswick). Cultural landscapes may also be eligible for designation and protection under some existing legislation, particularly heritage and planning acts, and they are included in some policies which, while not providing legal protection, may afford processes, incentives, or straightforward moral persuasion to gain understanding, respect, and public support.

Planning processes, which increasingly involve community consultation, or community-based projects, such as Heritage Canada's Heritage Regions program, currently appear to provide the greatest opportunities for recognition of cultural landscapes. Such tools as by-laws, zoning, local heritage advisory committees, advocacy, and strategic plans can facilitate stewardship of cultural landscapes. Long-term conservation requires such practical strategies as guiding principles, technical advice, education, and community commitment. While strong planning processes may play roles of protection for heritage places in Europe, elsewhere such mechanisms may not be as successful in gaining community acceptance or may not be in place. Traditional management systems, legal protection and active community involvement are all specified by the World Heritage Committee guidelines, but how they actually operate for World Heritage Sites that are broad cultural landscapes remains to be seen.

State of Understanding in Canada

The Canadian heritage community is expressing considerable interest in cultural landscapes. Although the level of expert knowledge is building, it is generally low and this category of cultural resources is vaguely understood. However, cultural landscapes are appearing as a topic on an increasing number of conference programs and training sessions. Issues of cultural values are also coming forward in the context of environmental considerations. As the dialogue increases about ecosystem management at the regional scale, issues of cultural heritage and the human imprint on the cultural landscape are a component of that dialogue.

An expanded awareness of cultural landscapes is one of the components of this trend to a broader, community-based heritage. Canadians recognize that their country has many different landscapes. The interrelationship of culture and nature and the related social dimensions of a community and a society are emerging factors in the definition of cultural landscapes. Socio-economic roles and values as well as environmental factors are seen as an integral part of cultural landscapes.

In general, research to identify and inventory cultural landscapes is in the early stages in Canada. There is no nationwide approach but there are regional and provincial efforts that are making a start on this large undertaking. Canada's experience with heritage has largely focussed in the past on buildings and archaeological sites and on object and archaeological collections. All these fields have developed systems for establishing and recording the nature and extent of the resources. Particularly for buildings, systems for evaluating intrinsic and associated values as well as groups of resources have been developed, refined and extensively applied. The Canadian Inventory of Historic Building provides a computerized database of systematically recorded information on more than 200,000 buildings across Canada. This extensive database facilitates comparison of styles, types, construction technologies, distribution, and authenticity of buildings in various provinces and over time.

National federal programs for implementing Canada's Federal Heritage Buildings Policy and the Heritage Railways Stations Protection Act have developed now well-established criteria for evaluation of these building types, which include consideration of site, setting, and landmark value. In the face of current stringent economic constraints, the priority-setting role of a systematic approach for identification and assessment established by past practice may be expected to apply also to cultural landscapes which are to be preserved. Widespread application of inventory and evaluation mechanisms to cultural landscapes has, however, yet to be achieved. Some approaches to inventory have been described in Heritage Landscapes in British Columbia (Paterson and Colby 1989) and "Heritage Advocacy" (Pollock-Ellwand 1992). A provincial study of cultural landscapes has been initiated in Alberta. Some specific projects on designed historic landscapes have resulted in heritage designations for individual landscapes. In a thesis for the University of York, England, one Canadian landscape architect has adapted the Federal Heritage Buildings' evaluation criteria to assess one type of cultural landscape, historic parks and gardens (Fardin). In addition, Alberta's Historic Sites Service has initiated a study to advise how that province will address cultural landscapes, while a number of site specific studies are underway in Ontario for the Oak Ridge Moraine, the Grand River, the Niagara Escarpment, and the Rideau Canal. In Quebec, an aerial inventory and a computerized data system provide an extensive resource on landscapes associated with buildings

The National Capital Commission prepared a draft list of cultural landscapes in the NCC and within the federal real asset portfolio. This list includes symbolic landscapes such as the Parliamentary Precinct, urban corridors, portage sites and a number of viewpoints along the Ottawa, Rideau and Gatineau rivers. Research and consultation are underway to confirm the identification of such sites as cultural landscapes. Future steps include: the listing of cultural landscapes within the National Capital Region; the development of evaluative criteria for cultural landscapes; and the official recognition by the NCC of the most important federal cultural landscapes in the NCR, and their use as yet one more tool for the sensible development of the Canadian capital. Eventually consultations are expected to take place with all the municipalities and both provincial governments represented in the NCR to extend the protection of cultural landscapes to non-federal sites.

Studies addressing Native peoples in the Canadian north have identified cultural landscapes as a component of native heritage. One example of an evolved relict landscape, Head-Smashed-In Bison Jump in southern Alberta, is important for a highly developed method of communal hunting and as a personal vision questing spiritual site. Some cultural landscapes have been addressed through the concept of "écomusée" as a part of a multiple resource complex. The university community has been instrumental in providing scholarly debate and courses of study and in directing thesis projects to cultural landscapes. Community-based efforts to preserve cultural landscapes are also evident, as in the inventory and conservation project of the Puslinch Township's historic roadside trees by the citizens' Puslinch Roadside Heritage Tree Society. (Pollock-Ellwand 1992)

All these efforts are the initial building blocks of a large task. Overall the body of research and inventory amassed to date is limited and considerable effort over a period of years will be required to reach a comprehensive level of knowledge regarding the Canadian cultural landscape heritage. The recent *APT Bulletin* special issue on conserving historic landscapes, edited by Susan Buggey, added a series of useful articles from both Canada and the United States to the literature as have previous special historic landscape issues. Although publications such as landscape focused issues of the *APT Bulletin* have contributed to the widely available body of information, a series of Canadian models and case studies in cultural landscape preservation has not yet been developed.

Canadian Indicative Lists

Due to the state of knowledge nationwide there is no indicative list of cultural landscapes available for Canada at this time. The lack of a comprehensive basis leaves Canada unprepared to advance such a list in the near future. No cultural landscapes are currently included on the Canadian indicative list. One example of an important linear landscape that may eventually achieve international recognition is the Rideau Canal. This 200 kilometer canal is a continuing, evolved landscape of national import developed originally as a defensive waterway, which shifted to commercial and then recreational uses. As in other nations, some properties considered for World Heritage listing may be cultural landscapes as well as being defined as internationally important cultural resources in other categories. Such is the case with Head-Smashed-In Bison Jump, an evolved landscape in relict form that records native cultural development over a period of at least 5,700 years.

Diverse North American Cultural Landscapes

North American Designed Landscapes

The legacy of designed landscapes in North America includes many types and scales ranging from small, private gardens to large public parks, extensive corridors and city plans. These designed landscape also vary in significance, design intent and style, and their current level of authenticity. For example, the plan for Washington, DC, evolved as a designed landscape over two distinct periods. Beginning in 1791 the work of Frenchman Pierre L'Enfant laid out the radial pattern of the nation's capitol under the direction of first president George Washington. This plan created over 220 green spaces at intersections and other square and circles that comprise 55% of the city land area. In 1902 the McMillan Commission overlaid the earlier plan, formalizing the city's core and altering portions of the L'Enfant vision. The historic and existing conditions of the L'Enfant-McMillan Plan have been documented over the past three years by the Historic American Building Survey. Figure 1 shows the overall plan of the city in 1791. The historic designed landscape of the Canadian capitol, Ottawa-Hull, developed under a plan by Jacques Gréber, is another urban example at a large scale. Gréber was commissioned to develop an urban plan for the Canadian capital in Ottawa where he planned the broad structure shaped by parks, parkways, monuments, broad and controlled views and public open spaces.

Important estate properties are found, in various states of preservation, throughout the more populated areas of both nations. In many cases these properties have been significantly altered by historical compression—the reduction of overall land area over time. A notable example with good integrity is the Vanderbilt Mansion National Historic Site, Hyde Park, New York, initially designed by Belgian landscape gardener André Parmentier with owner and horticultural enthusiast, Dr. David Hosack, in the years from 1828 to 1831. Subsequent owners the Langdons and the Vanderbilts, retained the circulation and spatial organization of that earlier design with modest additions to the 211-acre property. An exhaustive cultural landscape report has been developed over the past four years to include a detailed history, documentation of existing conditions, analysis and assessment of integrity and significance, exploration of preservation treatment and recommendation of a restoration treatment that will recapture the late Vanderbilt

Figure 1. Plan of Washington DC 1791, showing L'Enfant axial organization of the capitol city. Courtesy Historic American Building Survey.

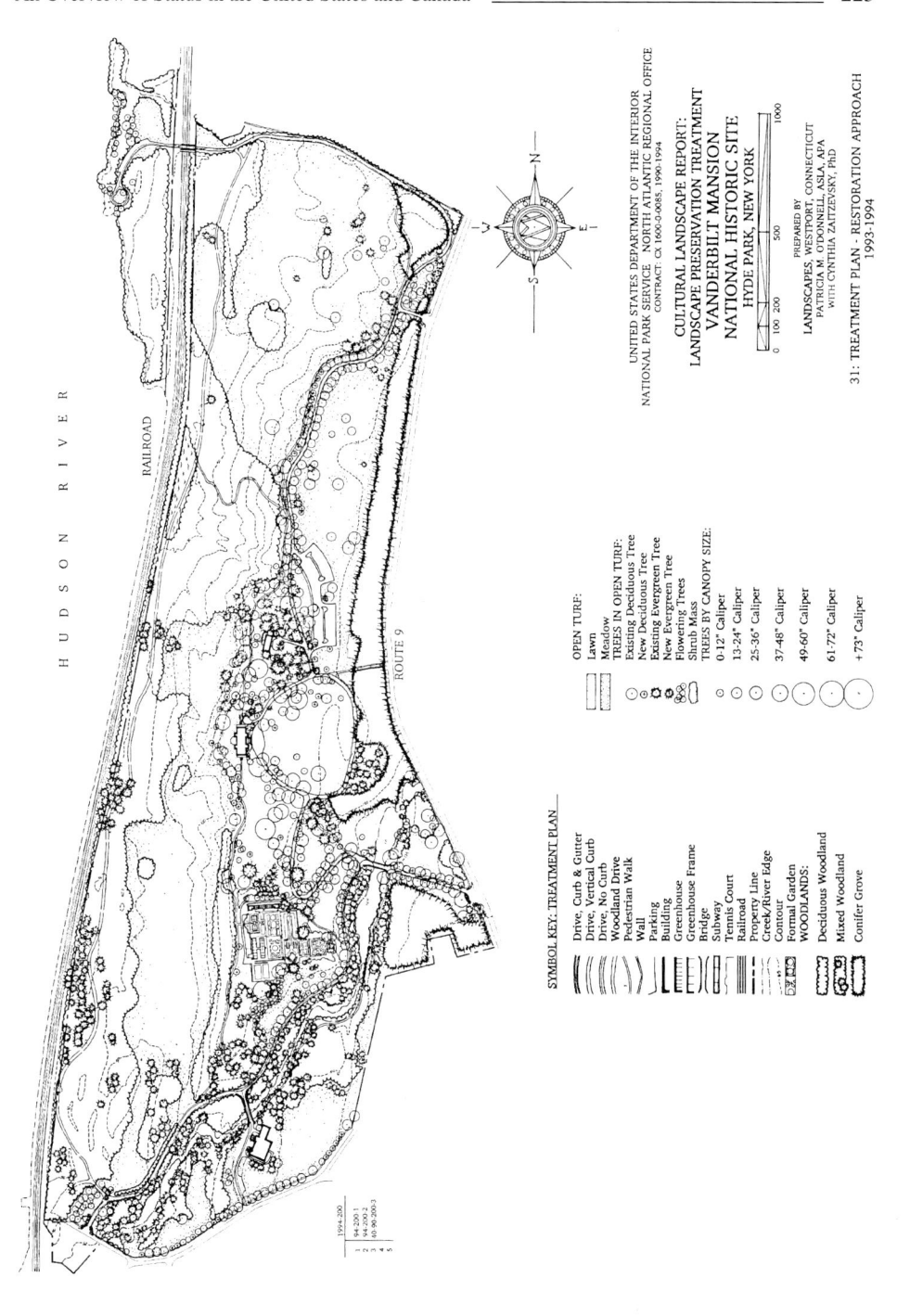

An Overview of Status in the United States and Canada   225

Figure 2. Treatment plan showing restoration approach for the 211 acre Vanderbilt property at Hyde Park, NY. Courtesy LANDSCAPES Landscape Architecture, Planning, Historic Preservation.

condition of the property to the greatest possible extent. (O'Donnell et al 1992 and draft 1994) The recommended Treatment Plan - Restoration Approach is shown in Figure 2.

The agrarian landscape of the W.R. Motherwell Homestead, near Abernethy, Saskatchewan, is a good example of a designed historic landscape, in part because it is not a high style garden, park or estate. A Canadian National Historic Site, it represents the Anglo-Canadian settlement of the western prairies as an adaptation of the Ontarian farmstead to prairie conditions. The plan, developed in quadrants, includes 1) dugout zone and shelter belt that collected precipitation, 2) barn quadrant in which grain was stored, animals cared for and farm hands housed, 3) ornamental gardens and fashionable recreation activities in the house quadrant in proximity to the principal dwelling, and 4) food production for in the vegetable garden quadrant.

North American Evolved Landscapes

When considering evolved relict landscapes in North America, one most often thinks of the remnant places where early inhabitants dwelled or worshipped. Native peoples in both the United States and Canada have left significant evidence of their interaction with the land that formed early cultural landscapes. Such a property is the World Heritage site Cahokia Mounds State Historic Park in Illinois, located at a bend in the Mississippi River. Many other villages, burial mounds, rock art sites, and sacred places provide evidence of long ago inhabited places in relict form. The National Park Service conserves several southwestern American Indian communities in relict form within the World Heritage-

Figure 3. A view of the Hawaiian petroglyphs at Puuloa with holes and images carved into lava flows. Courtesy O'Donnell.

listed Chaco Canyon National Historical Park. These sites, such as the Bandeliero National Monument, contain visible and below grade remains of a former village of ground and cliff dwellings within a small stream valley. Other imprints of early inhabitants are found throughout the southwest in the form of rock art and cave art carving and paintings. On the island of Hawaii a large collection of petroglyphs are found on a lava flow at Puuloa in a place known as the "Hill of Long Life". A small section showing the markings chipped into the lava surface is seen in Figure 3. This area, customarily used as a marking place to witness the birth of a child, contains as many as 15,000 individual markings. (Cox and Stasack 1970)

Evolved continuing landscapes are most often represented as large scale settlements, agrarian landscapes and corridor landscapes that remain inhabited and in continual use. Examples might include the Amish farm communities of Lancaster County, Pennsylvania and the Mennonite communities of southern Ontario. Historic landscape systems, such as canals, riverways, trails and highways that continue in use would come under this heading.

Ebey's Landing, an area on Whidbey Island in the northwestern United States, is a fine example of an evolved, continuing landscape, seen in Figure 4. This area of 17,400 acres, extending from the south at Keystone Spit to the north of Penn Cove on the west side of the island is the nation's first National Historical Reserve, established in 1978. The purpose of the Ebey's Landing National Historical Reserve is the preservation and protection of "a rural community which provides an unbroken historical record from the nineteenth century exploration and settlement of Puget Sound to the present time." (Gilbert and Luxenburg 1990)

Figure 4. View of Ebey's Landing agricultural landscape with interpretive panels in foreground. Courtesy O'Donnell.

Figure 5. Spangler Farm fences at Gettysburg National Military Park showing variations in fence types for different uses. Courtesy O'Donnell.

Built by the British Corps of Royal Engineers from 1826 to 1832, the Rideau Canal is an excellent example of an engineering feat. As a series of artifacts built under a plan, it is a designed landscape, and as a landscape altered in use and in character-defining components over a century and a half, it is also a continuing, evolved landscape. In recent years the canal has become a recreational waterway for all its abutting communities for both summer and winter sports uses. With its waterways under the jurisdiction of Parks Canada and abutting properties in multiple jurisdictions, this unique canal system is a living cultural landscape connected to contemporary life in adjacent communities along its course.

North American Associative Landscapes

Associative landscapes are most often recognized as significant for an important historical person or event. A large group of historic sites, many including both structures and landscapes, are recognized in both nations. Battlefields represent another important associative property that is a landscape. Less frequently landscapes recognized as spiritually or artistically important have been given recognition but with the new World Heritage guidelines consideration of these landscapes is more likely. The associative category has the potential to include a diverse group of resources. For example, the northern Quebec landscape is a huge area with associative value. Traditional nomadic peoples have used this vast expanse of land for generations with minimal impact on the natural landscape. However, they have assigned spiritual values to specific natural features and used them with limited traces of human imprint.

Several armed conflicts, most notably the American Revolution and the Civil Wars, are marked on the lands of the United States. The Civil War battlefield and memorial landscape of Gettysburg, Pennsylvania, dating to July 1-3 1863, is an important historic site and the subject of considerable preservation planning and implementation in recent years. Today the Gettysburg National Military Park contains some 15,360 acres and includes farms, fields, orchards, hills, ridges, creeks, woodlands, defense works, archaeological sites, fences, memorial avenues, tablets, markers and monuments. Recent projects have reconstructed battle era fences and orchards, reinstating the historic spatial organization so that the cultural landscape is able to be understood more fully by visitors. Figure 5 shows a current view of the historically documented and reconstructed fences at the Gettysburg Spangler farm.

North American Corridor Landscapes

In recent years an increasing focus has been turned on corridor landscapes that have prehistoric or historic significance as routes of migration, settlement, travel and recreation. The Chilkoot Trail, an aboriginal trade route overlaid by a mining exploration trail, is a corridor example that is managed by both Parks Canada and the National Park Service (Cameron 1993). Railroad routes criss-crossed the North American continent in the second half of the nineteenth century revolutionizing the movement of goods and people. As this system is dismantled in the late twentieth century preservation questions abound (Cameron 1993). In 1939 John Steinbeck immortalized U.S. Highway 66 as the "Mother Road" in his book The Grapes of Wrath. With origins as an aboriginal route, the surge of automobile use in the 1920s led to the improvement and designation of a continuous highway from Chicago to Los Angeles. A 35 mile segment of this route in Arizona has been inventoried in abandoned, rural and urban segments as a preparation for nomination to the National Register and development of management strategies (Cleeland 1993). In Louisiana a comprehensive approach to the states' transportation history has resulted in the delineation of three principal eras, the steamboat years from 1812 to the early 1860s, the railroad boom from the 1860s to the early twentieth century and the early automobile age from 1909 through the 1940s (Fricker 1993). This is attempting to identify and preserve the cultural resources of diverse transportation corridors before the continuing surge of change obliterates them. Associative corridors have been identified as well. For example, the Selma to Montgomery National Trail in Alabama is the route travelled by African-American voting rights activists in 1965, is being studied for commemoration of that famous protest march. Recent efforts to preserve portions of the Hudson River Valley as an historic river and greenway corridor address continuing evolved, relict, designed and associative values which exemplify the diverse properties that line the river banks. Within North America lengthy corridor landscapes represent the history of mobile cultures and present especially complex identification, preservation and management issues.

North American Landscapes at the Interface of Culture and Nature

Landscapes, because of their biotic nature, embrace both natural and cultural components. This convergence of natural and cultural resources in the cultural landscape is becoming more widely understood and more adequately addressed. The former division between ecology and natural resource conservation and cultural resource preservation and management is false and counter-productive in the field of cultural landscape preservation.

Increasingly, work in North American cultural landscapes is approached with multidisciplinary teams that include the appropriate skills in resource preservation, conservation and sustainability so that preservation and conservation issues are simultaneously addressed. Projects for historic urban parks provide numerous examples of such resource management coordination. Throughout the United States and Canada there were over 5000 public and private properties designed by the Frederick Law Olmsted, Sr., John Charles Olmsted and Frederick L. Olmsted, Jr. between 1857 and 1949, to include nearly 650 municipal parks in cities throughout the nation. Seneca Park, Rochester, New York is one such public landscape that has recently been the subject of comprehensive preservation planning and implementation with rehabilitation treatment projects (Beck et al. 1990). This park along the Genesee River gorge is a blend of notable scenery, river and gorge side natural resources and heavily used historic park lands. A current project focuses on the Trout Pond area addressing natural and cultural resources in the rehabilitation of a wetland area, pond, meadow and open woodland while reinstating components of the historic character. This balancing of cultural and natural factors is an increasingly important issue in achieving a sustainable preservation treatment of the biotic components of cultural landscapes

The participants of the Cultural Landscape Expert Meeting in Schorfiede-Chorin brought this same diversity of expertise to the discussion and a consensus that both cultural and natural resources can and should be addressed in the cultural landscape field.

This movement toward integration of cultural and natural resource preservation, conservation and sustainability is an exciting and challenging breakthrough for the field. As cultural landscape architects and allied professionals undertake the vast work ahead, only the integrated collaboration of disciplines will bring the needed skills to the work.

Future tasks to identify and nominate North American cultural landscapes of outstanding, universal value

In order to elevate internationally important cultural landscapes to World Heritage level in both the United States and Canada several initiatives need to be pursued. The first among these is the identification process, to address the breadth of our heritage of cultural landscapes acknowledging locally, regionally and nationally significant landscapes. Until a greater level of knowledge of these cultural landscape is achieved, both nations will be stymied in their efforts to provide a broad context for cultural landscapes that will provide a context for the selection and nomination of those few that are of outstanding, universal value. Current private and public sector work in both nations is beginning to put in place small portions of the needed inventory, but broader efforts are needed. Due to this lack of identification and evaluation in both countries, indicative lists published to date do not include potential World Heritage cultural landscapes as such.

As professional practice proceeds, the processes for preservation are becoming clearer, case study guidance is more readily available and skill development opportunities are increasing. (O'Donnell, pending 1994) This growing body of knowledge and expertise must be shared and exchanged among an international group of colleagues so that a global effort to identify, protect and honor cultural landscapes of outstanding and universal value proceeds expeditiously. The threats to our shared heritage within the cultural landscape are numerous and serious. Recognition and protection must be pursued in a timely manner so that more of these precious resources are not degraded or lost. Meetings such as the gathering at Shorfiede-Chorin forge important links in our international network and extend our individual abilities through shared experience and the process of learning from each other. It is hoped that the diverse North American legacy of cultural landscapes and the efforts to protect this legacy can proceed aggressively. Our work in North America, shared with our international colleagues, will be a part of the global recognition of cultural landscapes, the places in which we live, learn, work and recreate. As we proceed with these efforts we must all strive to integrate the shared heritage of land and culture, the fruits of the interaction of humanity and nature, and achieve the needed balance of sustainability so that our cherished cultural landscapes are preserved for generations.

Acknowledgement

The author wishes to acknowledge the contributions of her colleagues, Susan Buggey and Nora Mitchell, who provided information for some sections of this paper and gave useful comments on the draft version.

References

Advisory Council on Historic Preservation. (1981). *National Historic Preservation Act of 1966, as amended. Washington, D.C.: Advisory Council on Historic Preservation.*

Andrus, P. W. (1992). *National Register Bulletin 40: Guidelines for Identifying, Evaluating, and Registering America's Historic Battlefields*. Washington, D.C.: U.S. Department of the Interior, National Park Service, Interagency Resources Division.

ASLA Historic Preservation Open Committee. May (1984). *"National Historic Landscape Survey"*. Washington, D.C.: American Society of Landscape Architects.

Association for Preservation Technology. (1983). *APT Bulletin, The Journal of Preservation Technology: Landscape Preservation*. vol. XV, no. 4. Fredericksburg, Virginia: Association for Preservation Technology International.

Association for Preservation Technology. (1992). *APT Bulletin, The Journal of Preservation Technology*, Special Issue, Conserving Historic Landscapes. vol. XXIV, no. 3-4. Fredericksburg, Virginia: Association for Preservation Technology International.

Beck, J., O'Donnell, P. and Beveridge C. (1990). *Seneca Park Master Plan: Including Seneca Park, Lower Falls Park, and Maplewood Rose Garden*. Rochester, New York: County of Monroe.

Birnbaum, C. A. and Crowder, L. E. eds. (1993). *Pioneers of American Landscape Design, An Annotated Bibliography*. Washington, D.C.: U.S. Department of the Interior, National Park Service, Cultural Resources, Preservation Assistance Division.

Birnbaum, C. and Jandl, W. (1993). *"America's Landscape Legacy" Brochure*. Washington, D.C.: National Park Service, Preservation Assistance Division.

Birnbaum, C. A., ed. (1993). *Cultural Resource Management Bulletin*, Thematic Issue, *"A Reality Check for Our Nation's Parks,"* vol. 16, no. 4. Washington, D.C.: U.S. Department of the Interior, National Park Service, Cultural Resources.

Birnbaum, C. A., and Wagner, C. eds. (1994). *Making Educated Decisions: A Landscape Preservation Bibliography*, Washington, D.C.: U.S. Department of the Interior, National Park Service, Cultural Resources, Preservation Assistance Division, Historic Landscape Initiative.

Canadian Heritage, Parks Canada. (1994). *Guiding Principles and Operational Policies*. Canada: Minister of Supply and Services.

Cliver, E. B., ed. (1993). *Cultural Resource Management Bulletin*, Thematic Issue, *"Historic Transportation Corridors,"* vol. 16, no. 11, Washington, D.C.: U.S. Department of the Interior, National Park Service, Cultural Resources.

Cooke, R., (1993). *Correspondence to Patricia M. O'Donnell.*

Cox, J. H. and Stasack, E. (1970). *Hawaiian Petroglyphs*. Honolulu, Hawaii: Bishop Museum Press.

Gilbert, C., Luxenburg, G. and Comp T. A. (1990). *The Land, the People, the Place: An Introduction to the Inventory, Ebey's Landing National Historical Reserve*. Seattle: Pacific Northwest Region, National Park Service, Cultural Resources Division

Keller, J. T., and Keller, G. P. (1987). *National Register Bulletin 18: How to Evaluate and Nominate Designed Historic Landscapes*. Washington, D.C.: U.S. Department of the Interior, National Parks Service, Interagency Division.

McClelland, Flint, L., Keller, J. T., Keller, G. P. and Melnick, R. Z. (1990). *National Register Bulletin 30: Guidelines for Evaluating and Documenting Rural Historic Landscapes*. Washington, D.C.: U.S. Department of the Interior, National Park Service, Interagency Resources Division.

Meier, L. G., ed. (1991). *Historic Landscape Directory*. Washington, D.C.: U.S. Department of the Interior, National Park Service, Cultural Resources, Preservation Assistance Division.

Morton, W. Brown, and Hume, G. L. (1985). *The Secretary of the Interior's Standards for Historic Preservation Projects with Guidelines for Applying the Standards*. Washington, D.C.: U.S. Department of the Interior, National Park Service.

National Park Service (1992). *National Register Bulletin 38: Guidelines for Evaluating and Documenting Traditional Cultural Properties*. Washington, D.C.: U.S. Department of the Interior, National Park Service, Interagency Resources Division.

National Park Service. *"Puukohola Heiau National Historic Site"*, Brochure. Hawaii: U.S. Department of the Interior, National Park Service.

National Association for Olmsted Parks. *Workbook Series*, Volumes 1-4. Bethesda, Maryland: National Association for Olmsted Parks.

National Capital Commission. (1991). *A Capital in the Making: Reflections of the Past Vision of the Future*. Canada: National Capital Commission, Planning Branch. pgs. 20-31

National Trust for Historic Preservation. May/June (1993). *Historic Preservation Forum: Focus on Landscape Preservation*. vol. 7, no. 3. Washington, D.C.: National Trust for Historic Preservation.

O'Donnell, P., Birnbaum, C. and Zaitzevsky, C. (1992). *Cultural Landscape Report for Vanderbilt Mansion National Historic Site, Volume 1: Site History, Existing Conditions, and Analysis*. Boston: National Park Service, North Atlantic Region, Division of Cultural Resources Management.

O'Donnell, P., ed. (September 1993). *ICOMOS Landscapes Working Group Newsletter*, No. 6, North American Issue.

O'Donnell, P., Wilson, B. Viteretto, P. and Zaitzevsky, C. (1994). *Cultural Landscape Report for Vanderbilt Mansion National Historic Site, Volume 2: Landscape Preservation Treatment Recommendations*. Boston: National Park Service, North Atlantic Region, Division of Cultural Resources Management.

O'Donnell, P., forthcoming (1995). *Cultural Landscape Case Studies in the United States*. Washington, D.C.: U.S. Department of the Interior, National Park Service, Preservation Assistance Division and the Alliance for Historic Landscape Preservation.

Paterson, D. D. and Colby L. J. (1989). *Heritage Landscapes in British Columbia: A Guide to their Identification, Documentation and Preservation*. Vancouver, Canada: University of British Columbia, Landscape Architecture Program.

Pollock-Ellwand, N. (1992). *"Heritage Advocacy in the Cultural Landscape"* from *APT Bulletin, The Journal of Preservation Technology, Special Issue, Conserving Historic Landscapes*. vol. XXIV, no. 3-4, pp. 71-77.

Potter, E. W., and Boland, B. (1992). *National Register Bulletin 41: Guidelines for Evaluating and Registering Cemeteries and Burial Places*. Washington, D.C.: U.S. Department of the Interior, National Park Service, Interagency Resources Division.

Sauer, R. and O'Donnell, P. (1994). *Master Plan for Louisville's Olmsted Parks and Parkways: A Guide to Management and Renewal*. Louisville, Kentucky: Louisville Olmsted Parks and Conservancy, Inc.

Schreiber, L. R. (1993). *Unexplained Places Exploring Mysteries Around the World*. New York: BDD Illustrated Books.

U.S. Congress, Office of Technology Assessment. (1986). *Technologies for the Preservation of Planned Landscapes and Other Outdoor Sites*. Washington, D.C.: U.S. Government Printing Office.

U.S. Department of the Interior. (1991). *National Register Bulletin 16A: How to Complete the National Register Registration Form*. Washington, D.C.: U.S. Department of the Interior, National Park Service, Interagency Resources Division.

U.S. Department of the Interior. (1992). *Guidelines for the Treatment of Historic Landscapes (Draft)*. Washington, D.C.: National Park Service, Preservation Assistance Division.

U.S. Department of the Interior. (1990). *Preserving Historic Landscapes*. Washington, D.C.: U.S. Department of the Interior, National Park Service, Preservation Assistance Division.

U.S. Department of the Interior. (1987a). *History and Prehistory in the National Park System and the National Landmarks Program*. Washington, D.C.: National Park Service, History Division.

U.S. Department of the Interior. (1987b). *Catalog of National Historic Landmarks*. Washington, D.C.: National Park Service, History Division.

UNESCO, World Heritage Committee. December (1992). *Convention Concerning the Protection of the World Cultural and Natural Heritage Report*. Santa Fe, New Mexico: United Nations Educational, Scientific and Cultural Organization.

Patricia M. O'Donnell is an Historic Landscape Architect and Preservation Planner and is principal of LANDSCAPES, a consulting firm specializing in Landscape Architecture, Planning and Historic Preservation in Westport, Connecticut and Charlotte, Vermont, USA

Chapter 21

Cultural Landscapes in the United States

Nora J. Mitchell

Introduction

The last decade has witnessed an increasing level of interest in cultural landscapes in the U.S. and an impressive number of conservation successes (Tishler 1989, Conzen 1990, Page 1990, Meier 1991a, Birnbaum 1993a). A diversity of cultural landscapes ranging from important historic gardens of less than an acre to rural vernacular historic districts of several thousand acres have been conserved. Recently, a proposal for a system of nationally recognized heritage areas has focussed attention on larger scale landscapes where an array of cultural and natural values shape regional character and identity (Greenberg 1993, Bray 1994).

During this decade, the U.S. National Park Service has provided leadership in landscape preservation through philosophical and technical guidance for professional practitioners and for the general public (Morton and Hume 1985, U.S. Department of the Interior 1992 a,b). In addition, the role of the U.S. National Park Service has expanded from manager of the units of the National Park System to partner and facilitator in preservation efforts. This shift in the role of the federal government is partly in response to the increasingly important and influential role played by a wide variety of public and private organizations and local communities in promoting and accomplishing landscape preservation (Stokes et al. 1989, Meier 1991b, Birnbaum 1993a,b, Greenberg 1993, Sanchis 1993). In addition, the continuity of ownership and management of many cultural landscapes is now recognized as integral to the value and protection of those places.

Many countries around the world have also recognized the diversity and value of cultural landscapes concurrent with this trend in the U.S. This burgeoning world-wide interest created the momentum for revising the criteria for World Heritage Sites to include cultural landscapes (see Rossler in this volume).

This paper reviews the current status of cultural landscape preservation in the U.S. in relation to the World Heritage Convention. Examples of U.S. landscapes are used to illustrate the categories described in the recently revised World Heritage Committee's guidelines. These examples are not intended to be comprehensive nor prescriptive but rather are meant to stimulate interest in development of a more systematic review of U.S. landscapes as potential World Heritage Sites. The final section of the paper discusses the principle issues raised by considering designation of certain significant landscapes as World Heritage Sites. In particular, this paper examines the concept of authenticity and definition of effective protection for diverse and complex landscapes.

Selected U.S. Landscapes which illustrate the World Heritage Convention's typology of cultural landscapes

The recent revision to the World Heritage criteria established three categories of cultural landscapes. A high degree of consistency and comparability exists between the U.S. National Park Service definition and categories for cultural landscapes and those of the revised Operational Guidelines of the World Heritage Convention (UNESCO 1994). The Operational Guidelines define cultural landscapes as: "illustrative of the evolution of human society and settlement over time, under the influence of the physical constraints and/or opportunities presented by their natural environment and of successive social, economic and cultural forces, both external and internal" (UNESCO 1994).

In the U.S., the National Park Service also defines a cultural landscape very broadly as "a geographic area including both natural and cultural resources...associated with a historic event, activity or person or exhibiting other cultural or aesthetic values" (National Park Service 1994). Recently, the National Park Service has defined four types of cultural landscapes: historic designed landscapes, historic vernacular landscapes, historic sites, and ethnographic landscapes. These categories have close parallels in the World Heritage landscape definitions. The four U.S. cultural landscape categories are, like those in the World Heritage Convention Operational Guidelines, not intended to be mutually exclusive.

Reexamination of Existing U.S. World Heritage Sites as Cultural Landscapes

Of the 18 current U.S. World Heritage Sites (including one joint Canadian-U.S. property), 10 are listed under natural criteria and 8 under cultural criteria. Although not originally listed as cultural landscapes, some of the existing U.S. sites clearly meet the definitions established in the revised World Heritage Committee Operational Guidelines. For example, the landscape of Chaco Culture National Historical Park has monumental ruins and outlying settlements connected by a road system which are all integral to the significance of the property and thus the site could be listed as a cultural landscape. Similarly, Thomas Jefferson's designs for Monticello and the University of Virginia in Charlottesville, Virginia, encompass both the structures and the landscape, although the recent nomination form did not evaluate the landscape at either site.

Certain existing U.S. World Heritage Sites listed for their natural value may also be considered cultural landscapes. For example, Yellowstone National Park, designated for its natural resources, also has cultural value due to its important role in the history of the conservation of natural resources, as the world's first national park in 1872. In the Conservation of Natural Resources theme study, both Yellowstone and Yosemite National Parks were identified as potential National Historic Landmarks (U.S. Department of the Interior 1963). Given the international impact of the "national park idea" first implemented in the U.S., Yellowstone National Park appears to possess both natural and cultural significance. The nomination form for Yellowstone National Park does, in fact, refer to this cultural value, however, the site was listed only under the natural resource criteria. The World Heritage Convention Operational Guidelines allow recognition of dual value through the designation of a "mixed" natural and cultural site. To qualify as a mixed site, a property must meet both the natural and cultural criteria in the Operational Guidelines.

This cursory review of U.S. existing World Heritage Sites indicates that certain landscape resources which contribute to the sites' significance may have been overlooked in the initial nomination process. It is therefore important to undertake a reevaluation of existing sites, to ensure that, where necessary, current boundaries and management strategies are modified in order to provide appropriate protection for previously unrecognized landscape resources.

Identifying Cultural Landscapes as Potential World Heritage Sites

In the U.S., World Heritage nominations are drawn from a "tentative list" of future World Heritage Site nominations (the nomination process is reviewed in O'Donnell in this volume). Early in 1993, as a follow-up to the revised Operational Guidelines, all State Parties to the World Heritage Convention were asked to prepare new tentative lists that include cultural landscapes (UNESCO World Heritage Centre. Letter to State Parties of the World Heritage Convention. 10 February 1993). This request provides an incentive to review and update the U.S. tentative list.

The following selected U.S. landscapes illustrate the three cultural landscape categories described in the Operational Guidelines. These examples are not intended to be comprehensive nor necessarily recommended as U.S. nominations to the World Heritage List, although certain of these examples may ultimately prove to be eligible. These landscapes are chosen to illustrate the diversity of resources and potential international significance. Ideally, these examples will stimulate interest in development of a more systematic review of U.S. landscapes as World Heritage sites. For a more comprehensive review of North American landscapes, readers should refer to the papers by Patricia O'Donnell and Susan Buggey in this volume.

Category 1: Designed Landscapes

The first of three categories of cultural landscapes described in the World Heritage Convention's Operational Guidelines is a "clearly *defined landscape* designed and created intentionally by man. This embraces garden and parkland landscapes constructed for aesthetic reasons which are often (but not always) associated with religious or other monumental buildings and ensembles." There are historic designed landscapes already on the World Heritage list (such as the Palace and Park of Versailles in France and Studley Royal Park including the Ruins of Fountains Abbey in the U.K., see also Cleere and Rossler in this volume).

The U.S. has not yet nominated any landscapes in this category, although, as noted previously, Monticello and the University of Virginia may qualify. Despite the relatively recent history of landscape design in the U.S., there are several types of designed landscapes which have potential international significance. For example, private estates (such as Frederick W. Vanderbilt Estate in Hyde Park, New York or Biltmore, the George W. Vanderbilt Estate in Asheville, North Carolina), suburbs (such as Llewellyn Park in

New Jersey ca. 1860s and Riverside in Illinois ca. 1869); utopian communities (such as New Harmony, Indiana ca. 1825); and designed cities (such as New Orleans, Louisiana ca. 1718, Savannah, Georgia ca. 1730s, Philadelphia, Pennsylvania ca. 1682 and L'Enfant's 1791 plan for Washington, D.C.) (Newton 1971, Conzen 1990). Savannah Historic District and New Harmony Historic District are currently on the U.S. tentative list of World Heritage Sites and the Biltmore Estate and Riverside Historic District are National Historic Landmarks. Although historic towns can be considered a type of cultural landscape, the World Heritage Convention's Operational Guidelines have distinct criteria for evaluation of historic towns (UNESCO 1994).

The U.S. also has a rich legacy associated with the development of public parks. Mount Auburn Cemetery, Central Park, and the Blue Ridge Parkway are three designed landscapes that represent important aspects of the history of park design. **Mount Auburn Cemetery** (Cambridge, Massachusetts), established in 1831, was the first rural cemetery in the U.S. It was created under the auspices of the Massachusetts Horticultural Society at the urging of Dr. Jacob Bigelow, a Boston physician and botanist who was convinced that the traditional churchyard burying ground was a menace to public health (Linden-Ward 1989a, Berg 1992, 1993). The founders of Mount Auburn Cemetery created a naturalistic landscape with mature trees, winding roads, carefully created vistas, and isolated classical monuments (Berg 1992). The rural cemetery has been called "a completely American invention" (Newton 1971). Mount Auburn Cemetery and others based on this prototype became immensely popular "pleasure grounds" and tourist attractions that were "all the rage" in the nineteenth century (Linden-Ward 1989b). Guidebooks were written to direct visitors, including international guests, to the important features of the cemetery. The design of Mount Auburn was subsequently used as a model for cemeteries across the country such as Laurel Hill in Philadelphia (1835), Green-Wood Cemetery in the City of Brooklyn (1838), and Chicago's Graceland (1860). The naturalistic design was also an important precedent for the nineteenth century public parks movement (Schuyler 1986, Berg 1993). In 1975, Mount Auburn was determined to be nationally significant and listed on the National Register of Historic Places.

Frederick Law Olmsted, Sr. (1822-1903) and Calvert Vaux's (1824-1895) "Greensward" plan, the winning entry in New York's **Central Park** design competition in 1858, created a rural landscape retreat for a rapidly expanding city. Their plan, designed in the naturalistic style, used a richly-varied palette of pastoral scenery with undulating meadows and scattered trees, tranquil lakes, and brooks tumbling through woodlands (Figure 1). The park was created on the northern fringe of New York City on a barren rectangle of 843 acres that was completely reshaped between 1857 and 1876, a monumental feat of engineering that cost $14 million, approximately $118 million in 1984 dollars (Rogers 1987).

Following the success of Central Park, Olmsted became a leading practitioner in the field of landscape architecture, which his work had defined. With his partners and staff, Olmsted worked on over 600 projects, including Prospect Park (1865-73) in Brooklyn, the residential community of Riverside, Illinois (1868-1870), Mount Royal Park (1874-81) in Montreal, the United States Capitol grounds (1874-91), the campus of Stanford University (1886-91), municipal park systems in Boston (1878), Rochester, New York (1888), and Louisville, Kentucky (1891), and George W. Vanderbilt's Biltmore Estate (1888-95) in Asheville, North Carolina. Due to this prodigious volume of influential work, Olmsted is now recognized as one of the world's leading landscape architects of the late nineteenth

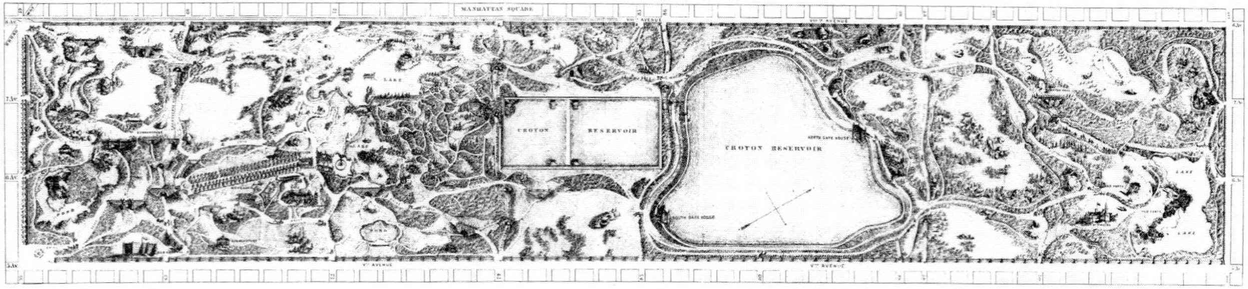

Figure 1. Plan of Central Park, New York, 1870 (National Park Service, US Dept. of the Interior, Frederick Law Olmsted National Historic Site).

Figure 2. Blue Ridge Parkway (National Park Service, US Dept. of the Interior, Blue Ridge Parkway).

century (Beveridge 1989, Mosser and Teyssot 1991). In 1963, Central Park's historical significance was recognized through designation as a National Historic Landmark.

Parkways were a significant achievement in landscape architecture and engineering in the United States, influencing the evolution of the modern highway as well as the development of city, regional, and national parks. As the first rural national parkway, the **Blue Ridge Parkway** (Virginia and North Carolina) represents the peak of development of the linear park and epitomizes the vision of its era (Howett 1991). The idea of parkways was developed in America in the 1860s by Frederick Law Olmsted and Calvert Vaux in their proposals for Prospect Park in Brooklyn and for parks and suburban developments in Buffalo and Chicago. These three proposals defined the parkway idea which was then adopted by other designers for other cities (Firth 1992). The Blue Ridge Parkway follows the crest of the Blue Ridge of the Southern Appalachian Mountains between Shenandoah National Park and the Great Smoky Mountains National Park (Figure 2). This 470-mile parkway was constructed between 1935 and 1987 to link two national parks and to provide opportunities for recreational automobile touring (Firth 1992). Designed and constructed by the National Park Service and the Bureau of Public Roads, this parkway had features characteristic of earlier parkways, but also illustrated important innovations.

Category 2: Evolved Landscapes

The second category, the organically *evolved landscape* which "results from an initial social, economic, administrative and/or religious imperative and has developed its present form by association with and in response to its natural environment." This is a broad category, and so two subcategories have been defined. The first subcategory is called the *relict (or fossil) landscape*. This type of landscape "is one in which an evolutionary process came to an end at some time in the past, either abruptly or over a period."

This type of landscape is currently represented on the World Heritage List by three U.S. sites: **Chaco Culture National Historical Park (New Mexico)**, **Mesa Verde National Park (Colorado)**, and **Cahokia Mounds State Historic Site (Illinois)**. Several additional sites are on the U.S. World Heritage tentative list including Hopewell Indian archeological sites at **Mound City Group National Monument (Ohio)** and the **Hohokam Pima National Monument (in Arizona)** which preserves the archeological remains of the Hohokam culture. Another site of potential significance is **Canyon de Chelly National Monument** (Arizona). Two 1000-foot deep canyons contain important Anasazi archeological sites dating from 350 through 1300 (Ferguson and Rohn 1987). From the mid-seventeenth century until today, Navajo Indians have lived and farmed Canyon de Chelly (Travis 1994).

It is important to point out that many sites qualify as relict landscapes since at some point in the past the populations dramatically declined or abandoned the area. In some cases, such as Canyon de Chelly, a relict landscape may have been re-settled by cultural group and thus may be a continuing landscape as well (see description below). In addition, terms such as "abandoned", "relict", and "fossil" may represent a cultural perspective foreign to the descendants of cultural groups or others with a current association with these sites.

The second subcategory of evolved landscapes is the *continuing landscape*. This type of landscape retains "an active social role in contemporary society closely associated with the traditional way of life, and in which the evolutionary process is still in progress. At the same time it exhibits significant material evidence of its evolution over time."

In the U.S., this is a particularly challenging category since there has been very limited work on historic contexts for relevant themes such as settlement history, agriculture, industrial development, or transportation. Thus, there is a minimal inventory and comparative analysis for this type of landscape. The best overview, to date, is Michael Conzen's book The Making of the American Landscape, a set of essays on the major historical forces that have shaped the American landscape (Conzen 1990). For the purposes of this paper, a few landscapes were selected to illustrate the diversity within this category — an example of the Indian landscape legacy at Taos and at Canyon de Chelly, ethnic landscapes from European settlement, agricultural landscapes of western settlement, and cultural landscapes of river corridors.

An outstanding example of a *continuing landscape*, **Pueblo de Taos in New Mexico**, was added to the World Heritage List in 1992. The Taos Pueblo has been continuously occupied since 1450. Today, over 1,500 Taos Indians reside here and continue many of their cultural traditions (Wood 1989, Gordon-McCutchan 1991). The Rio de Taos, which originates in the mountains at their Sacred Blue Lake, still provides the primary source of water. The two large multi-storied, adobe structures are excellent examples of pueblo architecture. This landscape, in particular the Sacred Blue Lake has associative value as well (see discussion under the third landscape category below).

The Navajo cultural landscape of **Canyon de Chelly National Monument (Arizona)** is another example of a continuing landscape where over the last 300 years a pastoral economy has been sustained (Figure 3). There is remarkable continuity of traditions such

Figure 3. Canyon de Chelly (National Park Service, US Dept. of the Interior, Canyon de Chelly National Monument, Photographer: Fred E. Mang, Jr.).

as retention of the hogan as the primary habitational unit, the maintenance of trail systems, and the retention of Navajo place names. These traditions have been combined with adaptation and innovation in agricultural practices and equipment and introduction of new construction techniques (Jett and Spencer 1981). Although the components of the landscape have changed over time, their relationship to each other and the cultural traditions have continued (Travis 1994).

European settlement of the North American continent created an imprint of ethnic landscapes (Harris 1990, Hilliard 1990, Hornbeck 1990, Lewis 1990). The Spanish, French, and the British were dominant colonizing influences and their contributions to today's regional landscapes are still apparent. This European influence is illustrated in certain cities such as Savannah and New Orleans (as mentioned previously in the section on designed landscapes). In addition, many major cities of the southwest, such as Santa Fe, were built upon Spanish foundations.

Settlement patterns on the regional landscape also illustrate ethnic traditions transposed onto a new continent. The missions of the southwest, are visible remanents of Spain's colonization strategy in the new world (Hornbeck 1990). **San Antonio Missions now a National Historical Park (Texas)** are on the U.S. World Heritage indicative list. French agricultural settlement in North America employed a system of "long lots" which can still

Figure 4. Aerial view of the Upper St. John Valley. The pattern of fields is suggestive of the original long lot land grants (American Folklife Center, Photographer: David A. Whitman).

be seen in certain regions such as along the St. Lawrence and southern Mississippi Rivers and in the St. John River Valley on the U.S.-Canadian border (Figure 4).

The settlement of the prairie is intertwined with the history of agriculture in the U.S. and the advent of railroads in the 1850s. Family farms and railroad towns developed on the rectangular land survey grid. Today, the wheat farms in Kansas, the corn belt in Illinois and cattle ranching for beef or dairy represent a remarkable continuity with the region's agricultural history (Hudson 1990). **Grant-Kohrs National Historic Site (Montana)** was the home ranch of one of the largest 19th century range ranches and is representative of the frontier cattle industry of the 1860s to 1930s.

River corridors were the first major transportation networks and consequently played a critical role in regional landscape development. The **Hudson River Valley (New York)**, a 150-mile corridor from Albany to New York City, is a significant landscape with multiple resource values reflecting many layers and many themes of history. This valley landscape retains early 17th and 18th century settlement patterns as well as an impressive 19th century legacy in architecture and landscape design (Newton 1971, Noble 1984, Creese 1985). The Hudson River played a critical role in the American Revolution and subsequently continued to serve as an important transportation corridor (Diamant 1989). The valley was inspirational in the early 19th century Romantic movement in the United States with historical associations in both art history and the American park movement (O'Brien 1981). There are numerous National Register properties and National Historic Landmarks within the Hudson Valley reflecting its rich layers of history. In addition, the

Hudson River, an estuarine ecosystem with high biological diversity, has natural resource value. The protection of this important landscape today is achieved through an impressive web of federal, state and local legislation and private initiatives.

Category 3: Associative Landscapes

The third category is *associative cultural landscapes*, which have "powerful religious, artistic, or cultural associations of the natural element rather than the material cultural evidence, which may be insignificant or even absent."

Similar to *continuing landscapes*, this category of landscapes in the U.S. has not been fully explored, so the examples given here are illustrative. With the increasing active participation of many cultural groups in preservation of their heritage and a growing interest in ethnography, additional associative landscapes will be recognized.

Many natural areas have associative cultural value to Native American tribes. For example, Hopi Indians claim the Grand Canyon (a natural World Heritage Site) as the place ("sipap") where their ancestors emerged from the underworld (Ferguson and Rohn 1987). Other natural areas have associative value in relation to the history of conservation. Yellowstone National Park is the world's first national park and Yosemite National Park is closely associated with John Muir, 19th century writer and conservationist, and is a symbol of the wilderness preservation movement. Both of these sites are on the World Heritage List for their natural resource value.

In the U.S., many places are valued for their association with historical events or people. Battlefields of the Revolutionary and Civil Wars, for example, are places of memory with evocative power. In Edward Linenthal's recent book, battlefields are referred to as "sacred ground" (Linenthal 1993). One of his case studies discusses **Minute Man National Historical Park (Massachusetts)** which commemorates the beginning of the American Revolution and the birth of the nation on April 19, 1775. Establishment of a national park on this site in 1959 was a continuation of memorial efforts beginning in 1776 when Lexington's minister began annual memorial sermons. The national park includes the North Bridge as well as a 4-mile section of the battle road, along which the minutemen chased the retreating British towards Boston (Gross 1976).

Designation of U.S. cultural landscapes: principle issues

The current U.S. process of evaluating World Heritage Sites is challenged by the complexity, scale, and dynamic quality of cultural landscapes. The following principle issues are discussed briefly here:
(1) evaluating the multiple resource values of cultural landscapes,
(2) evaluating authenticity, and
(3) defining protection and management mechanisms.

Evaluating the Multiple Resource Values of Cultural Landscapes

Cultural landscapes are an integrated complex of cultural and natural resources whose value derives from the physical qualities of their resources as well as from associated human endeavors and traditions. It is therefore critical that the system used to identify and evaluate cultural landscapes be able to assess multiple values.

The current U.S. framework for evaluating historically significant cultural properties (reviewed in O'Donnell in this volume) has proven to be very successful. Even so, this system was designed to assess a property's historic value, consequently the other potential values of landscapes are not usually considered in the evaluation of a site as a National Historic Landmark. There are, however, other evaluation systems which have been developed for assessing both cultural and natural resource values of landscapes. To date, these other systems have not been integrated with the National Historic Landmarks Program evaluation process.

The National Historic Preservation Act provides a broad definition of cultural heritage including "the historical and cultural foundations of the Nation as living parts of community life" (Parker 1993). In practice, however, the identification and evaluation of properties with significance to cultural groups has lagged behind that of properties with historic value. To encourage additional recognition of cultural significance of properties, the National Register Program published a bulletin providing guidance on evaluation of traditional cultural properties (Parker and King 1990, Parker 1993).

This National Register bulletin defines culture as "the traditions, beliefs, practices, lifeways, arts, crafts, and social institutions of any community, be it an Indian tribe, a local ethnic group, or the people of the nation as a whole." In other words, traditional cultural significance is derived from the role of a property in a community's historically rooted beliefs, customs, and practices (Parker and King 1990). These properties are often central to a community's identity. Clearly, many landscapes will have this type of associative cultural value and, in those cases, an ethnographic evaluation will be critical in the assessment of significance.

Many landscapes also possess significant natural resource value. At present, there is a similar but distinctly separate evaluation process for natural resource significance in the U.S. (National Natural Landmarks Program, 36 Code of Federal Regulations, Part 62). Although it is widely recognized that natural resources may be an important component of cultural landscapes, in practice, it is still unusual for a natural resource evaluation to be conducted as part of the analysis of a cultural property.

A recent trend in natural resource conservation may be of assistance in bridging this gap. In both U.S. and in the work of IUCN (International Union for the Conservation of Nature and Natural Resources now World Conservation Union), there has been an increasing interest in the role of culture in the conservation of natural resources. The Nature Conservancy in the U.S. has initiated a new program of bioreserves where human activity is integrated into the conservation strategy for biologically diverse landscape regions (Stevens 1992, Dillon 1993). As of 1992, there were twelve of these bioreserves in the U.S. and Latin America (Stevens 1992). This inclusiveness of human settlement is a distinct break from the U.S. traditional natural resource conservation approach which generally attempts to exclude people from the protected area.

At the Commission of Parks and Protected Area's (CNPPA/IUCN) most recent World Congress on National Parks and Protected Areas in Caracas, Venezuela in 1992, the role of people in protected areas was a consistent theme (IUCN 1993). Many presentations at the Congress recognized that human communities often have long-standing relationships with protected areas and that cultural traditions can, in fact, play a role in sustaining biological diversity. Presentations described several examples of past conservation efforts which overlooked the relationship with cultural traditions to the detriment of both the natural and cultural diversity. In its recommendations, the Congress called for new conservation approaches which integrally involve local communities in landscape protection. This direction is consistent with IUCN's interest in landscape conservation through the designation of "Protected Landscapes," one of the categories of protected areas (Poore and Poore 1987, Foster 1988, Lucas 1992, Aitchison and Beresford 1993). Representatives of IUCN/CNPPA have recently agreed to participate in the evaluation of the natural resource value of cultural landscapes for the World Heritage Committee. There is, however, still much work to be done to effectively integrate the identification and evaluation of natural resource value in evaluations of cultural landscapes.

The potential for multiple values is greatest in large-scale regional landscapes which would usually be considered under the World Heritage continuing landscape category. The difficulties of evaluating regional landscapes has been the subject of recent debate in the U.S. related to the proposed National Heritage Area legislation (Oldham 1991, Liebs 1993). It is clear from this debate that the existing evaluation systems are not readily able to provide an appraisal of the overall significance of these large-scale landscapes. It is now necessary to reexamine the various existing methodologies and synthesize a more comprehensive approach to ensure that the multiple values of cultural landscapes are adequately considered in evaluating significance and, eventually, in management.

Evaluating Authenticity

To be nominated to the World Heritage List, a property must, in addition to meeting one or more of the cultural properties criteria, also meet "the test of authenticity". The World Heritage Convention's Operational Guidelines define authenticity in terms of "design, material, workmanship or setting and in the case of cultural landscapes their distinctive character and components" (UNESCO 1994).

In the U.S., the term integrity is used in place of authenticity. Integrity is defined as "the ability of a property to convey its significance" (U.S. Department of the Interior 1991). Seven qualities - location, design, setting, materials, workmanship, feeling, and association - define integrity, these qualities are generally consistent with the World Heritage Convention's Guidelines on authenticity. In the U.S., a property must have integrity in order to have significance. The evaluation of integrity is a professional judgement, but it is based on knowledge of the distinguishing characteristics of a property, how they relate to its significance, and how change over time has affected those characteristics. In the U.S., the characteristics of a property can include physical features, processes such as land use, and associated cultural values. Ultimately, integrity is judged by the degree to which the characteristics that define its significance are retained.

Landscapes, more than other types of cultural resources, change over time, resulting in the need for special considerations in the evaluation of integrity. Vegetation and land use, in particular, are dynamic components of landscapes (National Park Service 1994, Mitchell and Page 1993). Vegetation grows and eventually dies, resulting in modifications in scale, vistas, and spatial relationships (National Park Service 1994, Meier and Mitchell 1990). Land use may change in response to alterations in economic conditions, to evolving technology, and to socio-cultural factors and demographic change (Gilbert et al. 1984, Webb 1987, Liles 1991, Orlando and Luxenberg 1992, Brabec 1993).

In assessing the integrity of **designed landscapes**, the property today is compared to the landscape during its period of significance, usually at the time the design was implemented (Keller and Keller 1987). The impact of any alterations made since that time are judged in the integrity analysis. If the level of change has been such that the landscape no longer conveys the historic design, then authenticity would be substantially diminished and the property would not be significant. There are properties, however, where alterations made at later time have significance themselves. For example, at Mount Auburn Cemetery the multiple layers of design history represented on the landscape contribute to its significance. Analyses therefore need to consider all significant layers of history in the assessment of integrity.

Alterations may also be necessary in order to perpetuate historic use. For example, in historically designed urban parks, such as Central Park, modifications to the historic design and to individual features may be needed to respond to changing patterns of urban recreation (Rogers 1987). In other cases, such as the Blue Ridge Parkway, alterations to the historic design may become necessary to meet modern safety standards (Firth 1992). Although these alterations have the potential to detract from the site's integrity, if modifications are carefully planned with adequate consideration to the historic design, the landscape's significance can be protected and the historic use successfully continued.

Assessing the impact of change over time on a landscape's integrity is particularly challenging for the World Heritage landscape category of *continuing landscapes* and for certain *associative landscapes* (Cameron 1993). These types of landscapes are, by definition, the expression of many layers of history and the shaping of these landscapes through traditional land use often continues today. In many *continuing landscapes*, it is generally the cultural systems and traditional activities such as agriculture, mining or fishing which have created the pattern of land use that is characteristic of the landscape. These traditional activities are often interwoven with the economic and social systems and may, together with continuity of use, be the most important characteristics in an integrity evaluation. In many *continuing landscapes*, particularly those which have extensive acreage, loss of individual features is less important than the overall structure and character of the landscape (McClelland et al. 1990; National Park Service 1994; Greenberg 1993).

In the evaluation of certain *associative landscapes*, such as traditional cultural properties in the U.S., the most important parameter of integrity is whether the property retains the relationship to the traditional cultural practice or beliefs (Parker and King 1990). In some cases, properties can retain their cultural significance in spite of substantial modifications.

The diversity of values and the dynamic nature of cultural landscapes test the established approach to the evaluation of integrity. Combining evaluation of the landscape's important characteristics with a recognition that change is often integral to the resource will allow full consideration of the authenticity of cultural landscapes.

Defining Protection and Management Mechanisms

It is clearly the intent of the World Heritage Convention to ensure protection of all properties on the World Heritage List. Thus, the Operational Guidelines require that all nominations demonstrate "adequate legal and/or traditional protection and management mechanisms to ensure the conservation of the nominated cultural property or cultural landscapes" (UNESCO 1994). In order to define appropriate protection strategies, it is critical that an understanding of the characteristics of the resource which make it significant is used to guide management. Given the diversity of cultural landscapes, a wide range of protection strategies are necessary.

In some types of landscapes, such as the World Heritage category of *designed landscapes* or *relict landscapes*, it may be appropriate to retain the landscape as it is today or to approximate the condition at a particular point in time through restoration. This approach is consistent with the traditional preservation of historic structures.

This traditional preservation approach, however, can not readily be applied to *continuing landscapes* where change is often an important characteristic integral to the property's significance. In *continuing landscapes*, an alternate preservation strategy is required - one which recognizes cultural traditions and accommodates on-going change. Thus, the protection of *continuing landscapes* has much in common with conservation of historic towns and of vernacular architecture (see ICOMOS Charter for the Conservation of Historic Towns and Urban Areas 1987, Stovel 1990). In all these resources, there is continuing use associated with cultural patterns and traditions and consequent alteration of physical resources. To develop a conservation strategy for vernacular architecture, for example, Herb Stovel, has written about developing principles for "effective management of dynamic change" and the importance of maintaining "the process which has given birth to vernacular forms", in addition to protecting the historic structures themselves (Stovel 1990).

In addition to integrating change, protection strategies also need to recognize that in many places, private ownership and stewardship are important characteristics of a cultural landscape. Land use, systems of land tenure, and local economic activities are sustained by social systems and communities which are integral to the landscape's significance. In this environment, the traditional role of the national government in the U.S. - purchasing property in order to protect it - does not work. Instead, the government or alternatively, private conservation organizations, can provide support and technical assistance to other organizations, local government, and/or private citizens who are directly responsible for landscape management. As noted in the introduction, the U.S. National Park Service has, over the last few years, increasingly played a technical assistance and facilitator role in many local conservation efforts.

Landscape protection strategies generally involve some type of intervention designed to "level the playing field" for conservation. For example, certain market forces, often those outside the community itself, can erode the traditions and lifeways that created and sustain the cultural landscape. Economic forces, if carefully directed, can create new market opportunities that serve heritage objectives. Some initiatives can be taken at the local level; others may require the support of federal government policies and programs (Countryside Stewardship: Report of the 1991 International Exchange 1992). The community and private landowners are the decision-makers on whether or not to intervene and on the type and direction of intervention for heritage protection.

In the development of landscape-specific protection strategies, there are a variety of conservation methods and techniques. The challenge is to find the most effective means for a particular situation. As noted by Robert Z. Melnick, based on his work on U.S. vernacular landscapes, "there are no single answers which can be applied everywhere...Specific solutions must be developed for a specific landscape, with an explicit recognition of its political, social, cultural, economic, and physical contexts...To suggest there is an answer, just one answer, denies the individual qualities of these places and of the players involved" (Melnick 1988).

The U.S. has only recently begun to meet the challenges of developing innovative, effective, local conservation strategies (Diamant 1991, Liles 1991, Oldham 1991, Brabec

1993, Sampson 1993). The development of locally-based protection strategies for cultural landscapes is currently one of the most challenging types of conservation. This approach to conservation is, according to U.S. National Park Service Superintendent Rolf Diamant, "like democracy itself, ... not valued so much for its efficiency as for its eventual success in achieving consensus and a long-term commitment to the future" (Diamant 1991).

Conclusion

It is critical to undertake a more comprehensive, systematic evaluation of national and internationally significant landscapes in order to enhance the recognition and preservation of this part of our cultural legacy - a legacy which has been overlooked in the past. The diversity, complexity, and dynamic nature of cultural landscapes will test established approaches to evaluation and management of cultural properties. It is therefore important to re-examine existing methodologies for inventory and evaluation to ensure that the multiple values are considered. In particular, change is characteristic of many significant landscapes and must be considered in any integrity (or authenticity) discussion.

Clearly, the protection of cultural landscapes, as with all other cultural properties, needs to be ensured as part of the World Heritage nomination process. Given new and innovative strategies involved in the conservation of U.S. cultural landscapes, previously accepted ways of evaluating the adequacy of management mechanisms need to be re-considered and broadened. The World Heritage Committee in its recent deliberations on revisions to the Operational Guidelines, did broaden one of its interpretations of protection by specifically recognizing "traditional protection" of cultural landscapes as a legitimate management technique. In the U.S. where the primary strategy for protection of World Heritage Sites has been government ownership, the current laws and regulations need to be revised to ensure that new and effective means of conservation such as those described above, are accepted. This re-evaluation is critical for future inclusion of diverse and complex cultural landscapes as World Heritage Sites.

Acknowledgements

I thank Patricia O'Donnell and Susan Buggey for their insights and for their collaboration on this article. I also gratefully acknowledge critical reviews by Rolf Diamant, Heidi Hohmann, Robert R. Page, Ethan Carr, Lauren Meier, Tara Travis, and Rebecca Joseph. Ethan Carr, Ian Firth, Bill Clendaniel, and Tara Travis generously offered comments on the landscape examples. I was also given assistance with locating and obtaining illustrations from Lucy Lawliss, Joyce Connolly, and Tara Travis.

References

Aitchison, J., and Beresford, M. (1993). *Protected Landscapes: One Way Forward*. The George Wright Forum, vol. **10**, no. 1, pp. 48-54.

Berg, S. P. (1992). *Approaches to Landscape Preservation Treatment At Mount Auburn Cemetery*. APT Bulletin, The Journal of Preservation Technology, vol. **XXIV**, no. 3-4, pp. 52-58.

Berg, S. P. (1993). *The Nation's Oldest Rural Cemetery: Mount Auburn, Cambridge.* Cultural Resources Management, vol. **16**, no. 4, pp. 17-19.

Beveridge, C. E. (1989). *Frederick Law Olmsted.* In: Tishler, W. H. (ed.) *American Landscape Architecture: Designers and Places.* Washington, D.C.: The Preservation Press, pp. 38-43.

Birnbaum, C. A. (1993a). *Landscape Preservation Today: From the Back Room to the Ballroom.* Historic Preservation Forum, vol. **7**, no. 3, pp. 6-15.

Birnbaum, C. A., ed. (1993b). *Cultural Resources Management*, Thematic Issue, vol. 16, no. 4.

Brabec, E.. (1993). *Tomorrow's Parks and Open Spaces: Preservation Strategy for Waterford Village.* Cultural Resources Management, vol. **16**, no. 4, pp. 20-22.

Bray, P. M. (1994). *The Heritage Area Phenomenon, Where it is Coming From.* Cultural Resources Management, vol. **17**, no. 8, pp. 3-4.

Cameron, Ch. (1993). *The Challenges of Historic Corridors.* Cultural Resources Management, Thematic Issue, vol. **16**, no. 11, pp. 5-7, 60.

Conzen, M. P., ed. (1990). *The Making of the American Landscape.* Boston: Unwin Hyman.

Countryside Stewardship: Report of the 1991 International Exchange. 1992. Barnard, VT: The Countryside Institute.

Creese, W. L. (1985). *The Crowning of the American Landscape, Eight Great Spaces and Their Buildings..* Princeton: Princeton University Press.

Diamant, L. (1989). *Chaining the Hudson, The Fight for the River in the American Revolution.* New York: Carol Publishing Group.

Diamant, R. (1991). *National Heritage Corridors: Redefining the Conservation Agenda of the '90s.* The George Wright Forum, vol. **8**, no. 2, pp. 13-16.

Dillon, D. (1993). *Deep in the Heart: How Does a Rural Region of Texas Preserve its Character While Accommodating Change? The LBJ Heartland Council Blazes New Trails.* Historic Preservation, vol. **45**, no. 5, pp. 28-37,91.

Ferguson, W. M. and A. H. Rohn. (1987). *Anasazi Ruins of the Southwest in Color.* Albuquerque: The University of New Mexico Press.

Firth, I. J. W. (1992). *The Blue Ridge Parkway Historic Resources Study.* Unpublished draft.

Foster, J. (1988). *Protected Landscapes: Summary Proceedings of an International Symposium*, Lake District, United Kingdom, 5-10 October 1987. Gland, Switzerland: IUCN (International Union for the Conservation of Nature and Natural Resources).

Gilbert, C., Luxenberg, G. and Comp, A. (1984). *The Land, The People, The Place: An Introduction to the Inventory of Ebey's Landing National Historical Reserve.* Seattle: National Park Service, Pacific Northwest Region, pp. 5-7.

Gordon-McCutchan, R. C. (1991). *The Taos Indians and the Battle for Blue Lake.* Santa Fe: Red Crane Books.

Greenberg, R. M., ed. (1993). *Cultural Resources Management*, Thematic Issue on Historic Transportation Corridors, vol. **16**, no.11.

Gross, R. A. (1976). *The Minutemen and Their World.* New York: Hill and Wang.

Harris, C. (1990). *French landscapes in North America.* In: Conzen, M. P. (ed.) *The Making of the American Landscape.* Boston: Unwin Hyman, pp. 63-79.

Hilliard, S. B. (1990). *Plantations and the moulding of the Southern landscape.* In: Conzen, M. P. (ed.) *The Making of the American Landscape.* Boston: Unwin Hyman, pp. 104-126.

Hornbeck, D. (1990). *Spanish legacy in the Borderlands.* In: Conzen, M. P. (ed.) *The Making of the American Landscape.* Boston: Unwin Hyman, pp. 51-62.

Howett, C. (1991). *Recreation Facilities in the United States (1930-1940).* In: Mosser, M. and Teyssot, G. (ed.) *The Architecture of Western Gardens: A Design History from the Renaissance to the Present Day.* Cambridge, MA: The MIT Press, pp. 510-512.

Hudson, J. C. (1990). *Settlement of the American grassland.* In: Conzen, M. P. (ed.) *The Making of the American Landscape.* Boston: Unwin Hyman, pp. 169-185.

IUCN (International Union for the Conservation of Nature and Natural Resources). (1993). *Parks for Life: Report of the IVth World Congress on National Parks and Protected Areas.* Gland, Switzerland: IUCN.

Jett, S. C. and Spencer, V. (1981). *Navajo Architecture.* Tuscon: University of Arizona Press.

Keller, J. T., and Keller, G. P. (1987). *National Register Bulletin 18: How to Evaluate and Nominate Designed Historic Landscapes.* Washington, D.C.: U.S. Department of the Interior, National Park Service, Interagency Division.

Lewis, P. F. (1990). The Northeast and the making of American geographical habits. In: Conzen, M. P. (ed.) *The Making of the American Landscape.* Boston: Unwin Hyman, pp. 80-103.

Liebs, C. H. (1993). Reconnecting People with Place: The Potential of Heritage Transportation Corridors. Cultural Resources Management, Thematic Issue, vol. **16**, no. 11, pp. 9-11.

Liles, J. (1991). The Boxley Valley of Buffalo National River: A U.S. National Park Service Historic District in Private Hands. The George Wright Forum vol. **7**, no. 3, pp. 2-5.

Linden-Ward, B. (1989a). *Silent City on a Hill: Landscapes of Memory and Boston's Mount Auburn Cemetery.* Columbus: Ohio State University Press.

Linden-Ward, B. (1989b). *Cemeteries.* In: Tishler, W. H. (ed.) *American Landscape Architecture: Designers and Places.* Washington, D.C.: The Preservation Press, pp. 120-125.

Linenthal, E. T. (1993). *Sacred Ground, Americans and Their Battlefields.* 2nd ed. Chicago: University of Illinois Press.

Lucas, P. H. C. (1992). *Protected Landscapes - A Guide for Policy Makers and Planners.* London: Chapman & Hall.

McClelland, L. F., Keller, J. T., Keller, G. P. and Melnick, R. Z. (1990). *National Register Bulletin 30: Guidelines for Evaluating and Documenting Rural Historic Landscapes.* Washington, D.C.: U.S. Department of the Interior, National Park Service, Interagency Resources Division.

Meier, L. (1991a). *National Programs in Historic Landscape Preservation.* In: *Prairie in the City: Naturalism in Chicago's Parks, 1870-1940.* Chicago: Chicago Historical Society, pp. 42-46.

Meier, L., ed. (1991b). *Historic Landscapes Directory: A Sourcebook of Agencies, Organizations, and Institutions Providing Information on Historic Landscape Preservation.* Washington, D.C.: U.S. Department of the Interior, National Park Service, Preservation Assistance Division.

Meier, L., and Mitchell, N. (1990). *Principles for Preserving Historic Plant Material.* Cultural Resources Management, vol. **13**, no. 6, pp. 17-24.

Mitchell, N. J., and Page, R. R. (1993). *Managing the Past for the Future: The Stewardship of America's Landscape Legacy.* Historic Preservation Forum, vol. **7**, no. 3, pp. 46-61.

Melnick, R. Z. (1988). Where Am I Now? Regionalism and Rural Landscape Protection. In: Proceedings of the Landscape Preservation Seminar, University of Massachusetts, University of Massachusetts, March 25-26, 1988. Amherst, MA: University of Massachusetts, Division of Continuing Education, p. 69.

Morton, W. Brown, and Hume, G. L. (1985). *The Secretary of the Interior's Standards for Historic Preservation Projects with Guidelines for Applying the Standards.* Washington, D.C.: U.S. Department of the Interior, National Park Service.

Mosser, M., and Teyssot, G. (ed.) (1991). *The Architecture of Western Gardens: A Design History from the Renaissance to the Present Day.* Cambridge, MA: The MIT Press.

National Park Service. (1994). *Management Guideline for Cultural Resources*, NPS-28. Washington, D.C.: U.S. Department of the Interior, National Park Service.

Newton, N. T. (1971). *Design on the Land: The Development of Landscape Architecture.* Cambridge, MA: The Belknap Press of Harvard University Press.

Noble, A. G. (1984). *Wood, Brick, and Stone, The North American Settlement Landscape.* Volume 1: Houses. Amherst, Massachusetts: University of Massachusetts Press.

O'Brien, R. J. (1981). *American Sublime, Landscape and Scenery of the Lower Hudson Valley.* New York: Columbia University Press.

Oldham, S. G. (1991). *Heritage Areas: A Policy Perspective.* The George Wright Forum, vol. **8**, no. 2, pp. 17-25.

Orlando, C., and Luxenberg, G. (1992). *Ebey's Landing National Historical Reserve: Nontraditional Management of a Nationally Significant Resource.* In: Greenberg, R. (ed.) *Partnerships in Parks & Preservation,* Proceedings and Bibliography, Albany, New York, September 9-12, 1991, Washington, D.C.: National Park Service, 1992, pp. 95-97.

Page, R. R., ed. (1990). *Cultural Resources Management*, vol. **14**, no. 6.

Parker, P. L., ed. (1993). *Traditional Cultural Properties.* Cultural Resources Management, vol. **16**, Special Issue.

Parker, P. L., and King, T. F. (1990). *National Register Bulletin 38: Guidelines for Evaluating and Documenting Traditional Cultural Properties.* Washington, D.C.: U.S. Department of the Interior, National Park Service, Interagency Resources Division.

Poore, D., and Poore, J. (1987). *Protected Landscapes: The United Kingdom Experience.* Gland, Switzerland: IUCN (International Union for the Conservation of Nature and Natural Resources).

Rogers, E. B. (1987). *Rebuilding Central Park: A Management and Restoration Plan.* Cambridge, MA: The MIT Press.

Sampson, D. S. (1993). *Hudson River Valley Greenway.* Cultural Resources Management, vol. **16**, no. 11, pp. 45-46.

Sanchis, F., (1993). *Landscape Initiatives of the National Trust.* Historic Preservation Forum vol. **7**, no. 3, pp. 62-65.

Schuyler, D. (1968). *The New Urban Landscape: The Redefinition of City Form in Nineteenth-Century America.* Baltimore, MD: The Johns Hopkins University Press.

Stevens, W. K. (1992). *Novel Strategy Puts People at Heart of Texas Preserve.* The New York Times, 31 March, 1992, Science Times, pp. C1,C8.

Stokes, S. N., Watson, A. E., Keller, G. P. and Keller, J. T. (1989). *Saving America's Countryside-A Guide to Rural Conservation.* Baltimore, MD: The Johns Hopkins University Press.

Stovel, H. (1990). *Guiding Conservation Principles for Vernacular Architecture: The Need to Focus on Process.* Paper Presented at the ICOMOS General Assembly, Lausanne, Switzerland.

Tishler, W. H., ed. (1989). *American Landscape Architecture: Designers and Places.* Washington, D.C.: The Preservation Press.

Travis, T. (1994). *Canyon de Chelly National Monument, Interpreting a Dynamic Cultural System.* Cultural Resources Management, vol. **17**, no. 7, pp. 19-22.

UNESCO. (1994). *Operational Guidelines for the Implementation of the World Heritage Convention* (February 1994).

U.S. Department of the Interior. (1963). *The National Survey of Historic Sites and Buildings*, Theme XXX - Conservation of Natural Resources. Washington, D.C.: National Park Service, History Division.

U.S. Department of the Interior. (1991). *National Register Bulletin 15: How to Apply National Register Criteria for Evaluation.* Washington, D.C.: U.S. Department of the Interior, National Park Service, Interagency Resources Division.

U.S. Department of the Interior. (1992a). *The Secretary of the Interior's Standards for Rehabilitation.* Washington, D.C.: National Park Service, Preservation Assistance Division.

U.S. Department of the Interior. (1992b). *Guidelines for the Treatment of Historic Landscapes* (Draft). Washington, D.C.: National Park Service, Preservation Assistance Division.

Webb, M. (1987). *Cultural Landscapes in the National Park Service.* The Public Historian, vol. **9**, no. 2, pp. 77-89.

Wood, N. (1989). *Taos Pueblo.* New York: Alfred A. Knopf.

Nora Mitchell is Director of the Olmsted Center for Landscape Preservation of the National Park Service in Boston, Massachusetts.

Chapter 22

Cultural Landscapes in Canada

Susan Buggey

Canada is a country where culture and nature are inextricably intertwined. From Anne Marriott's poem "The Wind, Our Enemy" to Gilles Vigneault's song "Mon pays, c'est l'hiver", nature is personified and symbolized in the experience of the Canadian people. The Group of Seven's paintings of the rugged beauty of the Canadian Shield and Canada's big wilderness national parks are among the best known images of Canadian identity. Our motto, "From Sea to Sea to Sea", ties us to land and water and geography. For many years the interpretation of Canadian history was dominated by the thesis of geographical determinism (Berger, 1976, 101-103). As Gaile McGregor explains, "... nature, like other aspects of reality, is not simply perceived but socially constructed. By mythicizing our environment we convert it into a body of symbols, a kind of code which - like all language - reveals the ability both to reflect and to coerce our experience of the world" (McGregor 1985, vii; cf. Atwood 1972, 49). Cultural landscapes are the physical expression of this interrelationship of culture and nature, "geographical terrains which exhibit characteristics of or which represent the values of a society as a result of human interaction with the environment" (Parks Canada 1991).

This paper addresses the Canadian context for the identification, designation and preservation of cultural landscapes.[1] By examination of examples from across the country, it demonstrates the application of the World Heritage Committee's criteria for cultural landscapes to Canada and in doing so, raises some questions regarding interpretation of the World Heritage Convention's Operational Guidelines. It concludes with some discussion of the meaning of authenticity when applied to cultural landscapes.

The term "cultural landscape" is used in a broad sense in Canada. Parks Canada's *Guiding Principles and Operating Policies* (1994, 119) defines it as "any geographical area that has been modified, influenced, or given special cultural meaning by people". This breadth has been widely applied by different jurisdictions to refer to such diverse landscapes as multi-structure sites, historic districts, agricultural communities, rural villages, urban planned environments, and natural areas with cultural associations. The term has been used increasingly over the past few years to focus a move away from heritage units as individual structures, whether monumental, high style, or vernacular, to a recognition of the grouping of structures and spaces as heritage areas and to give

---

[1] The legal basis and the designation and registration systems for cultural landscapes in Canada are outlined in Patricia M. O'Donnell, "Cultural Landscapes in North America: an Overview of Status in the United States and Canada" in this volume.

emphasis to the social, not solely the physical, characteristics of these areas. A national conference on heritage in 1990 brought together about 400 representatives, people speaking for music, dance and folklore as much as for natural resource protection, architectural conservation, and museology. What the conference made clear was the broad range of heritage as a cultural phenomenon linking past and present, and its ownership by people and communities rather than by institutions and organizations (Heritage 1990).

An expanded awareness of cultural landscapes is one of the components of this trend to a broader, community-based heritage. Canadians recognize that their country has many different landscapes. The interrelationship of culture and nature and the related social dimensions of a community and a society are emerging factors in the definition of cultural landscapes. Socio-economic roles and values as well as environmental factors are seen as an integral part of cultural landscapes. As Michael Hough, among others, has recently made clear (Hough 1993, 1990), it is no longer acceptable to inventory only the physical resources of a cultural landscape; it is essential to establish the social value that the community attaches to the landscape, whether as landmark, as economic resource, as social centre, or as self-expression. It is important to remember that cultural landscapes are not dead places. They live in our time as well as embody important aspects of life in the past. They are not places frozen in time as depictions of past values, technologies or ecologies. If they are to survive into the future, they must have meaning in our time as well as in the past. They belong to the people who live there now. Change is an inherent part of cultural landscapes. What remains in those that retain value as cultural landscapes is the character of their past significance. As John Lehr has observed with regard to ethnic landscapes, they can only be preserved by "the establishment of entire districts within which the local population cooperates with heritage agencies to nurture a growing, evolving, living landscape" (Lehr 1990).

The World Heritage Convention's framework for the identification of cultural landscapes can be readily applied to Canada. Examples of designed, evolved, and associative landscapes in accordance with the Convention's typology for cultural landscapes illustrate this application and give evidence of distinctiveness that reflects Canadian geography, history and society. The argument is not advanced that any of the examples given are potential World Heritage Sites, nor is the nomination of any, upon strong candidacy deriving from further assessment, necessarily excluded. The World Heritage Committee assesses historic towns, or historically important areas thereof, under separate criteria from those for cultural landscapes (UNESCO 1994, 26-34; Dorion and Blanche 1991); the Old Historic Quarter of Québec, a World Heritage Site in accordance with these criteria, is currently the headquarters for the secretariat of World Heritage Towns. This paper does not, therefore, address significant examples of townscape and urban form which, in Canada, would be considered cultural landscapes.

The World Heritage Committee has recognized cultural landscapes as representing the "combined works of nature and of man" within the intention of Article 1 of the World Heritage Convention. Their particular distinguishing characteristics are (UNESCO 1994, 35-38):[2]

---

[2] UNESCO, 1994, Operational Guidelines, para. 35-38 provide the basis for this section, including verbatim wording where useful for clarity.

- that they illustrate the evolution of human society and settlement over time. They do not, thus, derive their primary importance from a single moment in time, nor do they invite a management approach that presents a moment frozen in time.
- that such evolution has taken place under the influence of the physical constraints and/or opportunities presented by the natural environment. Think of such constraints and opportunities as climate, topography, geology, water, soils, vegetation in shaping human society and settlement.
- that such evolution has also taken place under the influence of successive social, economic and cultural forces, both internal to the society and external to it. Think of such forces as conquest, political amalgamation, or, less catastrophically, fashion and taste that create architectural forms, changes in land use, religious dicta.
- that the best examples are representative of a clearly defined geo-cultural region and are capable of illustrating the essential and distinct cultural elements of such regions.
- that cultural landscapes often reflect specific techniques of sustainable land use and can contribute to modern techniques of sustainable land use.
- that cultural landscapes often reflect a specific spiritual relation to nature.
- that protection of traditional cultural landscapes is helpful in maintaining biological diversity.

It is the product of this conjuncture of the natural and cultural influences over time that distinguishes the cultural landscape. It is the interaction between humans and their natural environment that is the essence of the cultural landscape.

Designed landscapes

The most readily identifiable category of cultural landscapes under the Operational Guidelines is the group of landscapes designed and created intentionally by man, particularly garden and parkland landscapes constructed for aesthetic reasons (UNESCO, 1994, 39(i)). Despite its long and frigid winters, Canada has a tradition of gardening and landscape design that goes back to centuries-old Aboriginal occupation of fertile areas and early European settlement. From AD500 Aboriginal cultures around the Great Lakes and along the St Lawrence River gradually evolved agricultural settlements. With European colonization in the 17th century, substantial conventual gardens associated with religious institutions in Quebec mark the translation of the medieval monastic garden to the North American frontier; for example, the walled Sulpician Seminary Garden (Rue Notre-Dame, Montréal), partially enclosed by its seminary and Notre-Dame Basilica (1825), still retains its formal geometric form of parterres and quiet walks, now sheltered by mature trees. It continues to illustrate both the practical role of sustenance and the spiritual role of contemplative solitude that has set it apart from its surrounding, and evolving, urban environment. Authentic picturesque villa estates inspired by the English landscape tradition, like Mount Uniacke in Nova Scotia and Dundurn in Ontario, are now rare survivors of the designed grounds of the colonial social and political elite. The gardenesque tradition, equally favoured, is now best represented by the municipally-owned Halifax Public Gardens, a popular public park which retains much of its 1870s design by Richard Power, a protégé of Joseph Paxton of Crystal Palace fame. With increasing population in eastern Canada and the expansion of Euro-Canadian settlement to

Figure 1. Halifax Public Gardens, Halifax, Nova Scotia (Photo by author).

the arid western prairies in the late 19th century, a federal system of experimental farms gradually laid out practical and ornamental testing grounds across the country, which continue to contribute to scientific improvements in agriculture and horticulture. Limited inventories, established criteria, and individual site studies have enabled the Historic Sites and Monuments Board of Canada, advisers to the federal minister responsible for Canadian Heritage, to recommmend designation of national historic sites in all these types of designed landscapes.

Large public urban parks are also notable Canadian examples of designed landscapes. Established amid the rapid demographic and industrial expansion of the late 19th and early 20th centuries, they remain important features of contemporary cities. Born of the park movement that cried out for "lungs of the city" and civic beautification in the face of increasing industrialization, they matured amid the growing emphasis on recreation as the base of a healthy citizenry. The environmental movement of the 1980s has given them new public focus. Unlike New York's famed Central Park, Canada's largest urban parks have rarely involved re-engineering; rather, they have built upon the existing natural environment. From the "mountain" of Mount Royal (Montréal) to the "primeval forest" of Stanley Park (Vancouver) to the Waterford River running through Bowring Park (St John's), siting, topography, water, and native vegetation have been fundamental character-defining features of park design. Characteristically inspired by the English landscape tradition, they typically comprise from 50 to 1000 acres in area, located at the time of establishment on the suburban edges of civic development. Whether designed by renowned landscape architects like Frederick Law Olmsted (Mount Royal) or local park superintendents like George Champion (St. Vital Park, Winnipeg), they reflect the civic boosterism, moral reform, and local improvement of their age. Scenic drives welcome the automobile and the bicycle through open spaces recalling meadows, through natural and planted wooded areas, and along sea- and riverfront edges. Conservatories, ornamental gardens, and woodland walks transport urbanites to nature modified, but celebrated. Water bodies like Stanley Park's Beaver Lake and High Park (Toronto)'s duck pond are havens for birds and waterfowl while zoos and more natural habitats have been show places for native and exotic fauna. Pavilions, tea houses and club buildings provide both visual focal points in the landscape and facilities for park users. Cricket, soccer, and tennis are among the sports popular on playing fields and courts. Statues and memorials recognize the moral and spiritual value of parks, while plantings like the wild heather bank in Point Pleasant Park (Halifax) and the English Garden in Assiniboine Park (Winnipeg) evoke associations of homelands far away. Some, like Mount Royal, have recently been the subject of major planning exercises to protect and enhance their heritage, recreational, ecological and tourism qualities, while others, like Stanley Park, have been the object of debate between animal rights and cultural heritage advocates. While not necessarily under threat, large urban parks are currently challenged by decreasing municipal budgets, changing social mores, and alternative political priorities which impact on their heritage character (von Baeyer 1984; Markham 1988, Wright 1984; Ville de Montréal 1990).

Organically evolved landscapes

The World Heritage Convention's second category of cultural landscapes, the organically evolved landscape, "results from an initial social, economic, administrative and/or religious imperative and has developed its present form by association with and in response to its natural environment. Such landscapes reflect that process of evolution in their form and component features." Two subcategories divide the organically evolved landscape into relict landscapes where "an evolutionary process came to an end at some time in the past, either abruptly or over a period" and continuing landscapes where the evolutionary process continues. In both cases, the landscape exhibits significant evidence of its distinguishing characteristics in material form (UNESCO 1994, 39(ii)).

Relict Landscapes

Some of the best known and most readily identifiable landscapes in Canada which appear to be relict are designated historic sites of either provincial/territorial or national significance. Such sites have often been identified because of their association with historically important people or with historic events which clearly ended in the past. In order to provide a focal point for educational or interpretive programming designed to fulfill the site's commemorative role and to offer visitors an experience of the past, such sites have often been "frozen in time" at their point of historical importance. Site management approaches have preserved them, that is, intervened to prevent further evolution, either natural or cultural, and in some cases, more interventionist approaches, such as restoration and reconstruction, have been undertaken to return the cultural resources of the site to the perceived appearance of the historically significant era. Later buildings may have been removed, alterations reversed, and landscape features reintroduced through regrading, vegetative clearing, replanting, and architectural re-creation. Extensive historical research may have ensured accurate reproductions and historically appropriate species and materials, and photographic evidence may have illustrated not only details such as finishes and placement but also a sense of place for directing the re-creation. The resulting site may re-establish the appearance of an earlier era and thus suggest a relict cultural landscape. Despite such first indications, the substantial changes to achieve this character, and the on-going interventions required to perform its commemorative role as a historic site, challenge the categorization of such cultural landscapes as relict. Equally, however, such sites sit uncomfortably in the category of continuing landscape for they are not normally closely associated with the traditional way of life (Parks Canada 1993).

Rather than restoration and reconstruction, current conservation philosophy for historic sites encourages respect for the past evolution of the site. Other interpretive means, such as exhibits, films, publications, interactive electronic equipment, and cultural activities may be used to achieve the site's commemorative intent. The Chilkoot Trail National Historic Site, the 53 km route from Skagway, Alaska over the Coastal Mountains to Bennett, British Columbia, illustrates this management approach. The trail originated with indigenous peoples' use of the corridor as a trading route over centuries. With the onset of the Klondike Gold Rush of 1896-99, it carried thousands of trekkers to the rich goldfields of the Yukon. Famed photographs of adventurers hauling their worldly goods up the wild snow-covered mountain terrain embody the challenge of nature. Trappers' cabins, graveyards, an abandoned church, and objects ranging from folding boats to discarded containers still remain along today's recreational trail. Inventory of the in situ historic resources along the corridor, trail management to enhance visitor safety and awareness,

Figure 2. Boatmen's Encampment, Chilkoot Trail, Yukon (Photo: Parks Canada)

and minimal intervention approaches to resource protection treat this relict landscape. Acceptance of the commanding regeneration of vegetation, which had been stripped from the land during the Gold Rush era, as a character-defining feature of the trail rather than an encroachment marks the growing understanding of the interaction of cultural and natural heritage (Parks Canada 1988). Elsewhere, ghost towns, both of abandoned mining settlements and prairie agricultural centres, represent a substantial area of relict cultural landscapes worth exploring in the context of cultural landscape values in addition to their more conventional technological and economic contexts.

Relict cultural landscapes also include places of natural and cultural significance to Aboriginal peoples. Atlantic Canada, recognized by Mi'kmaq people as their place of creation, has a long history of Native cultural presence. Within Kejimkujik National Park in central Nova Scotia, protected for its glaciated landscape and Acadian forest ecosystem, lies one of the most intensive areas of Mi'kmaq occupation in the province. A 4000 year history of traditional land use, from the Late Archaic period to the 20th century, is evident in three major settlement sites, numerous small camps and farms, a cemetery, and one of the largest concentrations of petroglyphs in eastern North America. Land use has also included both a spiritual relationship with the natural environment and harvesting its wealth of river resources and diverse wildlife. The petroglyphs, engraved on slate outcrops along the principal transportation route of the region, are significant cultural expressions of the Mi'kmaq mainly dating from the 19th century; they are remarkable for the quantity, diversity and detail of their images and as a direct record of changing Mi'kmaq society (Christmas et al. 1994).

Head-Smashed-In Bison Jump, situated in the Porcupine Hills of southwestern Alberta, is both a Provincial Historic Resource and a World Heritage Site designated before the World Heritage Committee adopted criteria for assessment of cultural landscapes. It is nonetheless an excellent example of a relict evolved cultural landscape. Reported as "the oldest, largest and best-preserved bison jump in North America," it "represents a unique and unsurpassed communal way of hunting used for thousands of years by native peoples of the Great Plains." Taking advantage of favourable prevailing winds and of the natural topography, which offered a 40 km^2 gathering basin where bison regularly grazed and an 18 metre high cliff over which they could be driven, Aboriginal peoples herded the animals into drive lines marked by stone cairns and over the precipice to slaughter and butchering below. The adjacent Oldman River valley bottom served as their campsite for the hunt and their winter camps, while Chief Mountain, an important spiritual site, stands in the distance. The buffalo itself was a rich resource for the Plains Indian, providing meat, hides for clothing and shelter, and bone for tools. Skeletal remains and cultural objects as well as a significantly undisturbed site attest to their sophisticated harvesting technique dependent on manipulation of the natural environment and complex social organization (Parks Canada 1992). A sensitively sited modern interpretive centre presents this cultural history.

Continuing Landscapes

Long recorded occupations by Aboriginal peoples, continuous habitation in old European settled areas, and sustained traditional land uses have made continuing evolved landscapes the most commonly perceived type of cultural landscapes in Canada. Many "retain an active social role in contemporary society closely associated with the traditional way of life, and in which the evolutionary process is still in progress" (UNESCO 1994, 39(ii)). Continuing landscapes pose particular challenges of both identification and authenticity. Given the continuing evolution of these landscapes, how are boundaries defined that recognize the interaction of older established settlement areas with more recent growth? How are the values that reflect the historic past - as expressed in form and component features - integrated with on-going socio-cultural and economic demands without unacceptable loss of character? How much change as well as what nature of change is acceptable before the "distinctive character and component features" of a cultural landscape are too diminished to speak to the initial imperative and its process of evolution? What management approaches and practical economic, social and cultural strategies can achieve effective cooperative action among the many jurisdictions which cross these complex and evolving cultural landscapes?

Six thousand years of successive occupations of the Tipperary Creek Valley and adjacent uplands north of Saskatoon, Saskatchewan have created one of the most widely known cultural landscapes in Canada, now protected under the Saskatchewan Heritage Act. Archaeological investigations led by Ernest G. Walker beginning in 1982 identified more than 20 sites associated with Northern Plains or Plains Transition peoples representing material evidences of at least a dozen cultural groupings from the Historic to the Oxbow and Pelican Lake Complexes dating from about the 1870s to 5400 years before present. Multidisciplinary analysis examined the subsistence/settlement pattern of the largely undisturbed natural landscape which attracted nomadic hunters by affording shelter, along with reliable food and water resources, especially during the excruciatingly

Figure 3. Tipperary Creek Valley, Wanuskewin, Saskatchewan (Photo by author).

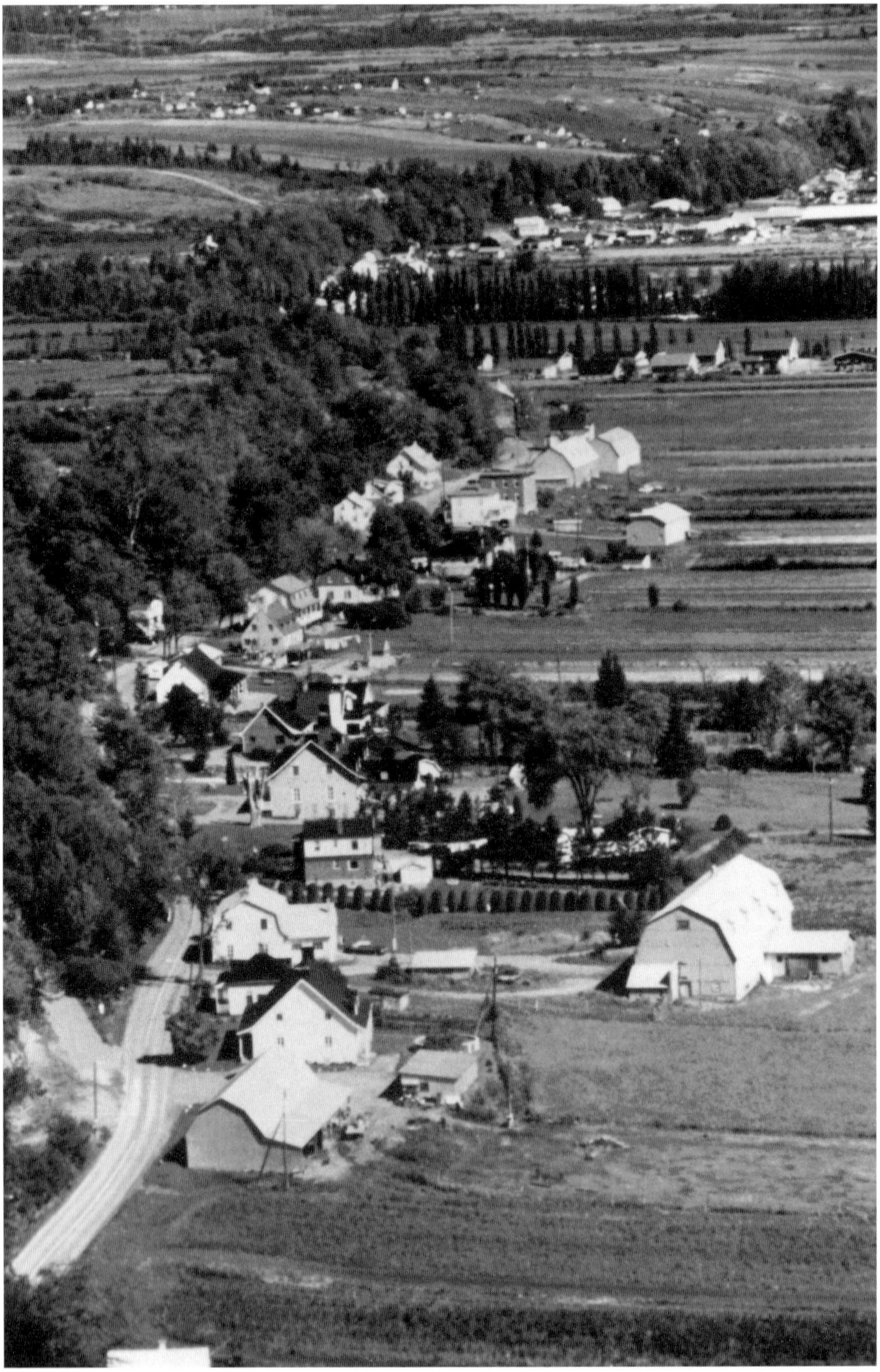

long and severe Canadian winter. As well, the area contains bison jump sites, bison pound sites, drive lanes, and processing sites where animals were slaughtered and processed. Tipi rings, a medicine wheel, stone cairns, campsite areas, and other culturally diagnostic materials further reflect the interaction of cultural and natural forces in Aboriginal cultures in the plains-boreal transition zone. Initially included in Raymond Moriyama's *100 Year Conceptual Master Plan for the Meewasin Valley* (Saskatoon, ca. 1980), the site has been developed with multi-jurisdictional involvement and the active and continuing participation of the First Nations' people of the province. Historically a place of spiritual significance, it has a similar role as well as contemporary cultural and educational values today. A symbolically designed visitor centre and trail opened in 1992, offering interpretive experiences and traditional cultural activities which now complement the site as Wanuskewin Heritage Park.

One of the most distinctive continuing cultural landscapes in Canada occurs in old settled areas of the province of Quebec. The Côte-de-Beaupré, running northeast from Quebec City, is a remarkable example of traditional settlement in the St Lawrence Valley. A dozen villages, such as L'Ange-Gardien, Château-Richer, Sainte-Anne-de-Beaupré, and Saint-Joachim, were among the first established by the French when they settled North America beginning in the early 17th century. These clusters and the continuous band of agricultural implantations connecting them continue to reflect the land pattern of this early settlement era. Until the mid-19th century, an institutional system of land tenure gave seigneurs and tenant farmers long rectangular lots, each with narrow river frontage and, typically, access to several soil and vegetation types, including woodlot, as well as to transportation and to neighbours. Fieldstone farmhouses, symmetrical in design, set low to the ground, and topped with steep bellcast roofs, were built, of which significant examples survive. Some owners benefitted from sheltered coves, others from terraced overhangs that were vestiges of the glacial Champlain Sea. The land was fertile, a mixed agricultural economy was installed, and today numerous market gardens prosper there, still situated on ancestral lands. An interpretation centre in the Petit-Pré mill in Château-Richer portraying the development of the area through models, exhibits and audio-visual programs reflects community pride in the area. This harmonious agricultural landscape also encompasses some exceptional sites. Montmorency Falls, the 84 m. cataract falling to the St. Lawrence River, was first popular for tobogganing when its ice cone froze and then became an important centre for industrial activity. The pilgrimage centre (basilica, chapels, Way of the Cross) of Sainte-Anne-de-Beaupré has both played an important role in the historic development of the region and now attracts over a million visitors a year. More recently, the National Wildlife Reserve at Cap-Tourmente and the internationally renowned ski centre at Mont-Sainte-Anne have added to the tourism attractions of the region. Under the pressure of encroaching urbanization, the rural landscape is disappearing, but this very threat has led both citizens and organizations to work for the protection of the distinctive traditional architecture which no longer disappears but is often re-affirmed in spectacular

Figure 4. Château-Richer, Côte-de-Beaupré, Quebec (Photo par P. Lahoud, Quebec).

fashion (Michaud 1990, 323-341).[3] On Ile d'Orléans nearby, in contrast, a much more traditional Québécois rural landscape remains.

The transformation of the great midwestern plains from open lands occupied by nomadic Native peoples to grid-dominated agricultural settlement made them, like the Russian steppes and the Argentinian pampas, one of the great breadbaskets of the world. The rural agricultural settlement pattern of the prairies derives from the Dominion Lands Act of 1872, which provided for the survey of western land into a grid of square mile sectioning organized into townships of 36 sections. In most areas, even-numbered sections were disposed as quarter-section homesteads to settlers who were required to break and crop their lands, build residences, and live on their lands. Towns situated rhythmically along the transcontinental railway lines emerged as the service centres for these dispersed homesteads. The transformation of the great plains represents permanent change — the prairie grasses were superseded by wheat and other economic crops. Many small agricultural communities of this culture remain today although the expansion of agribusiness and recent low grain prices are threatening.

The community of Gardenton, Manitoba is a continuing evolved landscape that represents the continuity of cultural tradition from first settlement to today. Founded as an early example of Canada's national immigration policy of 1896 to encourage experienced European farmers to settle on the western prairies, Gardenton and its associated agricultural community epitomize the first generation movement of Ukrainian families, primarily from Bukovyna and Galicia, to the Canadian West. They comprised one of the largest immigrant groups to the region - an estimated 170,000 between 1896 and 1914 - and one of the strongest in replicating and retaining their cultural traditions after settlement in Canada. By preference they formed cultural communities on the woodland margins rather than on the open prairie, on lands most resembling their homelands in the western Ukraine. Thwarted from re-establishing their traditional village settlements by the Canadian government regulations that required residency on individual homesteads, they created grouped settlements by choosing contiguous land and building their farmsteads at the intersection of four quarter-section homesteads. This "four corner" settlement pattern represented efforts by various settlement groups, including Ukrainians, to retain community ties. It is represented with particular authenticity in the Gardenton area.

Located at one such corner and now owned by the Ukrainian Museum and Village Society, the Korol farmstead is an excellent example of Bukovynian folk tradition translated to the Canadian prairies. A rare surviving combined house and stable, complemented by a "new" detached house built within a few years, recall the traditional architecture of the western Ukraine. The orientation and placement of supplementary structures, gardens and shelter belts round out the characteristic central yard. The Denyshchuk farmstead, on an adjacent corner, represents the familiar pattern of resettlement of early Ukrainian pioneers to lands of better quality within the community once they had met the homestead requirements and accumulated sufficient equity to

---

[3] I am indebted to Claude Michaud, architect, of Quebec, for providing me with much of this section on Côte-de-Beaupré; see also his "De Québec à Baie Sainte-Catherine" in *Les Chemins de la Mémoire. Monuments et sites historiques du Québec* (Québec: Les publications du Québec, 1990), tome 1, pp.323-341.

relocate. Family-occupied for 70 years, it resisted the frequent mid-20th-century abandonment of traditional farmsteads. St Demetrius Ukrainian Greek Orthodox Church, with an associated bell tower and cemetery, sits on a third corner property, while the fourth property remains characteristic aspen parkland (Dick 1987; Dick and Harris 1989). Traditional religious affiliations, separating Greek Orthodox and Greek Catholic adherents, were reflected in the early consecration of separate cemeteries and separate churches in the Gardenton area. St Michael's Greek Orthodox Church and its freestanding bell tower embody the Byzantine/Baroque traditions of ecclesiastical architecture in the Ukraine, including the distinctive onion-shaped domes, but simplify them to the craftsmanship, materials and technologies of the pioneer community. It is a fine example of these skills (Hunter 1987). Its associated cemetery, where concrete gravemarkers of Orthodox Christian cross design replaced the original wooden markers in the 1930s, denotes the continuity of the cultural tradition. Religious ceremonies, festivals and language remain integral and distinguished aspects of community life.

Continuing evolved landscapes are by no means solely agricultural settlements. Fishing villages on Canada's East Coast are equally distinctive expressions of their particular interaction of cultural and natural forces. People in the Maritime Provinces and Newfoundland rarely live far from the sea, although fishing populations are common on some coasts and sparse on others. Spatial organization of communities varies from long linear configurations such as Bottle Cove, Newfoundland to irregular groupings like Hall's Harbour, Nova Scotia. Structures asssociated with seafaring activity huddle close to the harbour, where increasingly rare finger wharves stretch out from the shoreline to dock local fishing vessels. Typically, gable-ended rectangular structures of one or one-and-a-half storeys are built of wood, often painted white, red or sometimes ochre. Symmetrical aperture patterns have often been distorted over time, as has the simple massing by variously scaled additions. Complementing these commercial and industrial waterfront structures, residences are frequently sited, for example on rises of land, for visibility out to sea. Rooftop viewing spots enclosed by ornamental iron railings, known as "widow's walks", enhance some of the more elaborate hipped roof buildings. The recent dramatic decline of the East Coast cod stocks and the associated fishing industry threaten the livelihood of many of these picturesque hamlets.

The transformation of natural watercourses, shaped by human ingenuity and ambition, to canal systems - for example, the streets of Venice, the waterways of Britain, or the defensive canals of eastern Canada - constitutes a third significant type of continuing landscape in Canada. The Rideau Canal, running 120 miles between Ottawa and Kingston, Ontario, epitomizes this transformation in North America. Built by British Royal Engineers between 1826 and 1832, it was constructed as an inland route for the transport of troops and goods in case of invasion of Canada and control of the principal water route, the St Lawrence River. Using natural lakes and rivers as a base, the builders controlled, redirected and reshaped them through a series of dams, locks, and lock stations. The canal was an extraordinary engineering feat in its time, and exceptional craftsmanship applied to local construction materials, primarily stone, has resulted in many of the original locks, dams, and defensible lockmaster's houses being still in place today. Community development at numerous points along the canal has seen economic and social transformation from military to commercial to, more recently, recreational activity. The corridor today is characterized by a combination of canal buildings and engineering works, urban and rural landscapes, wetlands, woodlands, scenic areas and shorelands which, in their totality, create a diverse and distinctive cultural landscape (Parks Canada 1994b).[4]

Industrial activity sustains and shapes other continuing cultural landscapes. Successive waves of miners and mining activity have created a distinct sense of place in the Klondike Gold Fields in Canada's northern Yukon Territory. The discovery of gold on Bonanza Creek in 1896 launched the last of the great 19th century gold rushes. The 30,000 people drawn to the region by the Klondike Gold Rush panned the creeks on 250 foot wide claims. Their simple hydraulic techniques to thaw the frozen ground were soon replaced by huge placer mining dredges which dug to bedrock and spewed out massive tailing piles as they wrenched their way along the river valleys. The individual miner society, famed in the poetry of Robert Service, was soon replaced by corporate mining camps headquartered at Bear Creek - a pattern that lasted until the 1950s. While the 800 ounce a day extraction of the 1940s is unlikely to be seen again, mining continues on the creeks today, largely through small mining operations, rising and falling in investment and volume with the fluctuating price of gold. Vegetative regeneration, as well as new mining activity and tourism, is changing the visual and social face of the Gold Fields.

Associative landscapes

The World Heritage Convention's final category of cultural landscapes, the associative landscape, is characterized by the "powerful religious, artistic or cultural associations of the natural element rather than material cultural evidence, which may be insignificant or even absent" (UNESCO 1994, 39 (iii)). Cultural landscapes known primarily for their literary or artistic associations of natural elements are found across Canada (Simpson-Housley and Norcliffe 1992). The Annapolis Valley of Ernest Buckler's *The Mountain and the Valley*, the rural Quebec landscape of Louis Hémon's *Maria Chapdelaine* and Anne Hébert's *Kamouraska*, the Canadian Shield of E.J. Pratt's *Towards the Last Spike*, the prairies of W.O. Mitchell's *Who Has Seen the Wind?*, the British Columbia mountains of Earle Birney's *David*, and the Yukon of Robert Service's *Songs of a Sourdough* are all examples of nature assigned a personified role in the narrative evolution that gives an intense sense of place through dramatic description and associated events. Each has achieved literary renown that has become an integral part of the culture of the actual places from which the literary inspiration sprang, and each has become a part of the Canadian psyche in relating cultural experience to the land.

The Canadian Shield is less renowned as a literary landscape than as an artistic one. In such areas as Algonquin Park, Georgian Bay and Algoma, it proferred the experience of nature that inspired the Group of Seven, an influential Toronto-based group of artists for over 20 years (1911-1933). They dramatically translated the Precambrian rock, secluded lakes and rivers, broad skies, dark conifers and brilliant reds and golds of the deciduous vegetation of the Ontario Northland in autumn into a stylized, spiritual symbol of Canada

---

[4] Parks Canada currently has underway a study of the Rideau Canal as a cultural landscape which will develop a framework for examination of the canal as a cultural landscape and identify the canal's values in this context.

Figure 5. A.Y. Jackson, The Red Maple (CourtesyNational Gallery of Canada, Ottawa).

that also sprang from the late 19th century concept of nationalism which rooted a nation's identity in the land. Allen Sapp's depictions of rural prairie/parkland settings and Emily Carr's perceptions of British Columbia's coastal rainforests present other Canadian symbols.

The most widespread tradition of associative cultural landscapes in Canada occurs in Aboriginal cultures, where the natural landscape is full of spiritual meaning. Long and continuous relationships of native peoples with the land can be "mapped" through the places they identify with their cultural history. Creation legends explain the topography of their territories, while mnemonic devices such as place names reinforce these legendary maps that have led generations through lands traversed in seasonal movements in search of sustenance. Brian Craik of the Grand Council of the Crees of Quebec explains the relationship this way: "The natural environment has a great significance. The trees, the flowers, the birds, the animals all have significance because they are permanent parts of Cree culture ... It is easy to see the symbolic significance that the landscape and the natural environment carry for the Cree people... The Cree words for the geography are poetic maps of the landscape." Aboriginal place names epitomize the cultural associations of the physical landscape. The east coast of James Bay, for example, embodies the mythic chase of two brothers, the younger transformed into a beaver, between the Rupert River and the Great Whale River. Sites along their route such as "The Great Beaver's Sitting Place, The

Great Beaver's House, and The Place Where the Older Brother Made His Conjuring Tent" all mark the regional topography associated with this traditional Cree story (Namagoose and Craik 1992).

Among the Dene of the Mackenzie River Basin of the western subarctic, the physical landscape likewise embodies important cultural traditions. Narratives carried from generation to generation by oral recounting are reflected in the local toponymy of the area; in such stories, actions of legendary figures and events "when the world was new" and traditional knowledge of the mores and environment of the culture are closely interrelated with the landscape. The mythic chase of harmful giant beaver by the legendary figure known as Yampa Deja from the South Nahanni and as Yamoria from Great Bear Lake, and their slaying and permanent exposure on Bear Rock Mountain near Fort Norman, are variant forms of a creation tale common among the Dene. As told by Fort Franklin elder George Blondin, Yamoria, "the most powerful medicine man of ancient times", chased threatening giant beaver from Great Bear Lake to the Mackenzie River. The site of the dam the fleeing beaver built on the Bear River to obstruct Yamoria, the outline of the pelts of the slain beaver on Bear Rock Mountain, two poles signifying arrows he shot into the river, and the perennial fire of his campsite are all landscape features linked to his presence as guardian, lawgiver, and adventurer among the Dene (Blondin 1990). Archaeological investigations have documented Aboriginal use of the base and slopes of Bear Rock Mountain over time. Other sites are sacred places associated with the quest for spiritual power and spiritual experiences, which relate landscape to the spiritual life of Aboriginal peoples.

Conclusion

While the World Heritage Convention's typology for cultural landscapes can be readily applied to landscapes in Canada, many issues surrounding their identification, assessment, and management remain. One of the fundamental issues in addressing cultural landscapes - and it is one in which Canadians take an active interest (Stovel 1993, 1994) - is the application and interpretation of the term "authenticity". The organic and evolved/evolving nature of cultural landscapes makes the measure of authenticity problematic. Nonetheless, the minutes of the sixteenth session of the World Heritage Committee in Santa Fe, which adopted guidelines for cultural landscapes, are explicit in stating that "it is essential to ensure that cultural landscapes nominated for the World Heritage List meet the highest standards of universal significance and integrity that characterize sites inscribed previously under natural and cultural criteria".

The World Heritage Convention criteria for cultural sites require that a listed site "meet the test of authenticity in design, material, workmanship or setting and in the case of cultural landscapes their distinctive character and components ...." (UNESCO 1994, 24 (b)(i); Feilden and Jokilehto 1993, ch. 8). The fourth measure of authenticity, setting, broadens the scope somewhat by asking whether the nominated site has retained a context that complements its heritage values or, in contrast, whether it has lost authenticity of setting by becoming isolated, an island, in a substantially changed environment. For cultural landscapes, while the preceding four measures are not dismissed, the principal measures are understood to be "their distinctive character and components". How are such factors to be identified and described?

The *American Heritage Dictionary* defines the word "authenticity" as "the condition or quality of being authentic, trustworthy, or genuine", more specifically the term "authentic" implying "acceptance of historical or attributable reliability rather than visible proof". In many jurisdictions, in determining the principal measure of acceptability for designation as a cultural site of heritage value, this "historical reliability" has been interpreted as the physical integrity of the place. This "state of being unimpaired", as the *American Heritage Dictionary* describes it, has underlain the assessment of designated places in various jurisdictions. The World Heritage Committee's traditional interpretation of authenticity, as Léon Pressouyre has so clearly set out (1993, 11-15), has been based in a European concept that emphasizes the value of the original, rather than the evolved, resource and places the highest value on the continuity of historic fabric. Current discussions led by ICOMOS on the interpretation of the concept of authenticity are re-assessing this focus. For example, David Lowenthal's exploration of different kinds of authenticity notes the non-monumental and the non-material aspects of heritage and their role in defining authenticity; as he observes, "fidelity of spirit ... takes precedence over substance where little was built to endure" (Lowenthal 1994, 36). Such broader interpretation of authenticity is more compatible with the evolving organic nature of landscapes.

The process of identifying cultural landscapes in Canada that may be of international significance is just beginning. The fundamental criterion for their identification is that they embody the cultural and natural heritage of the Canadian experience in an exceptional manner. What are the societal values, it may be asked, that they embody, and how well do they illustrate this aspect of Canadian heritage that they represent? What is the appropriate inventory of comparisons against which such landscapes should be measured? How well do they reflect representativeness, socio-cultural significance, complexity, and completeness? To ensure that cultural landscapes are "illustrative of the evolution of human society and settlement over time" and not primarily of importance related to a single moment in time, authenticity would appear to be most effectively measured by the continuity of land uses, processes, traditions, and overall character. Land use is probably the most fundamental determinant of the cultural landscape; it reflects the psychological and socio-economic processes of the society. Use of the natural environment, patterns of spatial organization, circulation networks, choice of building forms, materials and technologies may be significant indicators. Cultural traditions such as spiritual associations, role assignments, skills and knowledge are likewise factors in assessing cultural landscapes.

Another critical aspect of authenticity is extent: is there enough of the landscape surviving to illustrate clearly the character that gives it distinction? The World Heritage Committee has tied the issue of extent to the "functionality" and "intelligibility" of the landscape and has defined this scope as "enough to adequately represent the totality of the cultural landscape that it illustrates" (UNESCO 1994, 40). While it may not yet be clear what "enough" will mean across the variety of types of landscapes, it does indicate the need to identify not only scale and boundaries but also distinguishing features in light of understanding the particular cultural landscape - an approach similar to the ecosystem concept.

The role of adaptation needs to be examined in the context of these several factors. Authenticity is influenced by changes that have taken place in the landscape. The organic nature of landscapes makes physical change fundamental. Changes may be part of the significant evolution of the landscape or they may reduce its integrity by undermining its fundamental character. What are the acceptable limits of change? Parks Canada's principles of cultural resource management derived from international charters of conservation - value, public benefit, understanding, respect, and integrity - may provide a framework for such assessment (Parks Canada 1994a).

Acknowledgements

Thank you to Nora Mitchell, Patricia O'Donnell and Mechtild Rössler for their perspectives in developing this paper and to many colleagues, particularly in Parks Canada, who offered comments on draft segments.

References

Atwood, M. (1972). *Survival. A Thematic Guide to Canadian Literature* (Toronto: House of Anansi).
Berger, C. (1976). *The Writing of Canadian History. Aspects of English-Canadian Historical Writing: 1900-1970* (Toronto: Oxford University Press).
Blondin, G. (1990). *When the World was New. Stories of the Sahtú Dene* (Yellowknife, NWT: Outcrop, The Northern Publishers).
Cameron, C. (1993). *The Challenges of Historic Corridors,* CRM, special issue on Historic Transportation Corridors, **16**:11, pp.5-7, 60.
Christmas, P., et al. (1994). *Mi'kmaq Culture History, Kejimkujik National Park, Nova Scotia* (Parks Canada, unpublished report).
Dick, L. (1987). *A History of Prairie Settlement Patterns, 1870-1930* (Parks Canada, unpublished report).
Dick, L. and Harris, J. (1989). *Prairie Settlement Patterns: Resource Analysis* (Parks Canada, unpublished report).
Dorion, H., dir, et Blanche, J. (1991). *Cités souvenir Cités d'avenir. Villes du patrimoine mondial* (Québec: Musée de la civilisation).
Feilden, B. M. and Jokilehto, J. (1993). *Management Guidelines for World Heritage Sites* (Rome: ICCROM).
Hanks, C. C. and Pokotylo, D. L. (1989). *The Mackenzie Basin: An Alternative Approach to Dene and Metis Archaeology* Arctic, **42**:2, 139-47.
Heritage in the 1990s - Towards a Government of Canada Strategy. Summary Report, 1990 (Edmonton).
Hough, M. (1993). *Keynote address*, Association for Preservation Technology conference, Ottawa, APT Communique, XXII:4.
Hough, M. (1990). *Out of Place. Restoring Identity to the Regional Landscape* (New Haven: Yale University Press).
Hunter, R. (1987). *St Michael's Ukrainian Greek Orthodox Church, Gardenton, Manitoba* (Parks Canada, unpublished report, 1987-35).
Lehr, J. C. (1990). *Preservation of the Ethnic Landscape in Western Canada*, Prairie Forum, special issue on Heritage Conservation, eds. Alan F.J. Artibise and Jean Friesen, 15:2.
Lehr, J. C. (1982). *The Landscape of Ukrainian Settlement in the Canadian West,* Great Plains Quarterly, 2:2, pp.94-105.
Lowenthal, D. (1994). *Criteria of Authenticity*, Conference on Authenticity in Relation to the World Heritage Convention, Preparatory Workshop Proceedings (Bergen, Norway), eds. Knut Einar Larsen and Nils Marstein, pp. 35-64.

Markham, S. E. (1988). *The Development of Parks and Playgrounds in Selected Canadian Prairie Cities 1880-1930* (PhD thesis, University of Alberta).

McGregor, G. (1985). *The Wacousta Syndrome*. Explorations in the Canadian Langscape (Toronto: University of Toronto Press).

Michaud, C. (1990). *De Québec à Baie Sainte-Catherine*, in: *Les Chemins de la Mémoire*. Monuments et sites historiques du Québec (Québec: Les publications du Québec), tome 1.

Namagoose, B. and Craik, B. (1992). *Environment and Heritage. The Point-of-View of the Crees of Quebec*, ICOMOS CANADA Bulletin, **1**:1, pp. 17-22.

Parks Canada (1988). *Proposed Chilkoot Trail National Historic Park: Management Plan* (Winnipeg).

Parks Canada (1991). *Cultural Landscape Indicators*, Architectural History Branch.

Parks Canada (1992). *World Heritage* (Ottawa).

Parks Canada (1993). *Proceedings of the Canadian Parks Service Reconstruction Workshop* (Ottawa).

Parks Canada (1994a). *Guiding Principles and Operational Policies* (Ottawa: Supply and Services Canada).

Parks Canada (1994b). *Working Towards a Shared Future, Rideau Canal Management Plan* (Ontario Region)

Parks Canada. *Miscellaneous Files*.

Pressouyre, L. (1993). *La Convention du patrimoine mondial, vingt ans après* (Paris: Editions UNESCO).

Simpson-Housley, P. and Norcliffe, G. (eds). (1992). *A Few Acres of Snow. Literary and Artistic Images of Canada* (Toronto: Dundurn Press).

Stovel, H. (1993). *Authenticity: an introduction to the issues*, unpublished paper for ICOMOS/UNESCO.

Stovel, H. (1994). *Notes on Authenticity*, Conference on Authenticity in Relation to the World Heritage Convention, Preparatory Workshop Proceedings (Bergen, Norway), eds. Knut Einar Larsen and Nils Marstein, pp. 101-116.

UNESCO (1994). *World Heritage Convention, Operational Guidelines for the Implementation of the World Heritage Convention* (February 1994).

Ville de Montréal (1990). *Plan préliminaire de mise en valeur du mont Royal* (Montréal).

von Baeyer, E. (1984). *Rhetoric and Roses A History of Canadian Gardening 1900-1930* (Markham, Ontario: Fitzhenry & Whiteside).

Wright, J. (1984). *Urban Parks in Ontario*, 2 vols. (Toronto).

Susan Buggey is an historian by training (MA, Dalhousie University), and is currently Director of Historical Services, National Historic Sites Directorate, Parks Canada in Ottawa.

Cultural Landscapes of the World

Europe

Cultural Landscapes in Europe: A Geographical Perspective
John Aitchison

On the Traces of the Mediterranean Landscape
Yves Luginbühl

Aranjuez: Nature, Agriculture and the Art of the Landscape
Carmen Añon Feliu

Cultural Landscapes in France
Alain Megret and Gérard Collin

Slovenian Cultural Landscapes and Triglav National Park
Jelka Habjan and Vesna Kolar-Planinšič

*Austrian Cultural Landscapes:
Methodological Aspects for an Inventory*
Hans Peter Jeschke

*The Schorfheide-Chorin Biosphere Reserve, Germany:
Unique Species Diversity in a Centuries Old Cultivated Landscape*
Eberhard Henne

Cultural Landscapes in Britain
Peter Fowler and David Jacques

The Cultural Landscapes of Markim/Orkesta
Kerstin Riessen

*Nature and Culture – Two Aspects of the Same Story.
Norwegian Landscape Management in the 1990s*
Tonte Hegard

Chapter 23

Cultural Landscapes in Europe: A Geographical Perspective

John Aitchison

"Cultural Landscape - a concrete and characteristic product of the complicated interplay between a given human community, embodying certain cultural preferences and potentials, and a particular set of natural circumstances. It is a heritage of many eras of natural evolution and of many generations of human effort" (Wagner and Mikesell, 1962).

Introduction

If the terms 'landscape' and 'culture' are profoundly difficult to elucidate, as critical social theorists in particular would argue - largely because of their ideological and ontological rootedness (to use their lexicon) - then the concept of a 'cultural landscape' must be equally so. Certainly, the fact that culture and landscape are so intimately and reciprocally associated (suffused) - each one feeding and animating the other - confounds matters considerably. For landscapes and cultures are both moulds and mirrors, subjects and objects, forms and processes. Cultural landscapes are in a state of 'being' and 'becoming'; they are reflexive and contribute to the determination of their own futures. Furthermore, as "ways of seeing", they demand both "idealist and materialist explanation" (Cosgrove, 1984). The task of disentangling this nexus of contradictions and duplicities is challenging in the extreme. So much so, in fact, that to expect to reach consensus on definitions, meanings and methodologies is to expect too much; for cultural landscapes will always remain elusive expressions of "a persistent desire to make the earth over in the image of some heaven" (Jackson, 1952). This applies to the readers of such landscapes, as much as it does to their authors (Figure 1).

Such theoretical musings could be regarded as scholastically incidental to the more substantive task facing the World Heritage Committee and its advisors - that of identifying cultural landscapes of universal value on the ground - but it cannot be gainsaid that at some stage or other agreement has to be reached on the interpretation and application of basic principles and operational guidelines - on the "ways of seeing". This has to be so, since the differentiation and rating of cultural landscapes is a collective endeavor that requires as rigorous and standardized an approach as possible.

Subjectivity will always intrude, but cultural and intellectual relativism should be minimized. This has to be the case if "universality" is a fundamental criterion - as indeed it is. Fortunately, preparatory meetings have already clarified many key issues in this regard, and the need now is hopefully mainly one of fine tuning. More theoretical debates will doubtlessly continue (as they should); but the more immediate concern is to translate

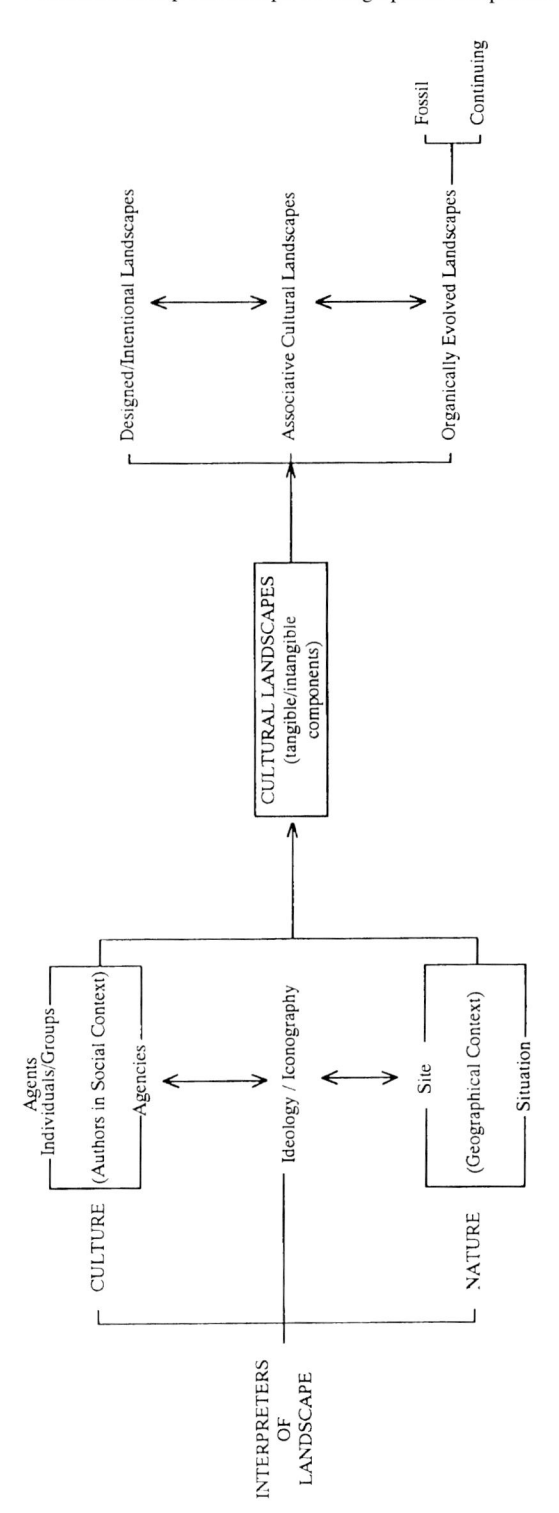

Figure 1. Cultural Landscapes - Conceptual Framework

ideas that recognize the importance of cultural landscapes into actions that seek to ensure their protection for posterity.

With such practical matters in mind, the limited aim of this paper is to provide an introductory overview to a series of more focussed and detailed presentations that will deal with cultural landscapes in various regions of Europe. That this meeting has chosen to structure much of the debate around regional contributions is noteworthy, for it underlines the fact that there is a geography to cultural landscapes; such landscapes express themselves in space, and gain their identity from the natural and human endowments of the localities in which they are set. Cultural landscapes do not only occupy sites, however, they are also "situated". When it comes to explaining the character and evolutionary development of particular landscapes, it is often their situation in relation to flows and movements of people, ideas and technologies that is a major determining influence. This applies generally of course, but is especially true of the European context.

Having broached the issue of geography, it would seem appropriate at the outset to draw attention to the contribution that practitioners of the discipline have made towards a clarification of basic concepts and ideas. Before so doing, however, it perhaps worth observing at the outset that the revision of the criteria that constitute the Operational Guidelines of the World Heritage Convention was concluded in Santa Fe. The significance of this - and no doubt it was in the minds of those who organized the proceedings - is that Santa Fe happens to be the home-base of one of the most highly regarded thinkers and writers on cultural landscape issues - John Brinkerhoff Jackson. Although not trained as such, he was a self-professed human geographer, and his celebrated journal 'Landscape' (first published in 1951) was sub-titled accordingly. His view was that it required a special "geographical" literacy "to read landscapes". In his opening editorial he proclaimed, with celebratory enthusiasm, that: "Wherever we go, whatever the nature of our work, we adorn the face of the earth with a living design which changes and is eventually replaced by that of a future generation. How can one tire of looking at this variety, or of marveling (sic) at the forces within man (sic) and nature that brought it about" (Jackson, 1951).

Jackson was thinking of the American Southwest when he crafted these lines; but they apply of course to landscapes worldwide. Deeply humanistic, even radical, Jackson was also concerned that landscapes (he used the term to represent the integration of community and environment) should not just be viewed or preserved for purely aesthetic reasons. To him it was essential to understand, experience and appreciate landscapes in living terms - in the terms of their inhabitants, whether they be of the past, the present or the future.

As it happens, in his thinking on cultural landscapes, Jackson gained much of his inspiration from the work of early European geographers. Since many of the concepts and ideas that are relevant to an appreciation of cultural landscapes have a long heritage in geographical literature, it is worth a brief digression here to recall some of the main arguments that have stimulated debate over the years. To assure a degree cohesion to the discussion these same arguments are deployed below (implicitly or explicitly) in describing the broad geography of cultural landscapes in Europe.

Cultural Landscapes in Geographical Discourse

As with Santa Fe, it is again fitting that this particular meeting should be held here in Germany, for as is well known the German tradition in landscape studies has contributed very significantly to the development of ideas and methodologies. The work of Alfred Hettner (1859-1941) was seminal in this regard, for it drew attention to the intimate relationships that bind humankind to their local environments; relationships that frequently express themselves in the emergence of highly distinctive regional landscapes. Thus, he emphasized the centrality of Länderkunde to geographical study. In so doing, however, he tended to look more towards the natural environment for explanation of regional patterns than he did to human agency. It was in reaction to this "deterministic" position that Otto Schlüter (1872-1959) sought to redress the balance by emphasizing the formative influence of human activity in shaping the use of natural resources. For Schlüter "the essential object of geographical inquiry was landscape morphology as a cultural product" (Livingstone, 1992, 264) - Landschaftskunde. This he demonstrated through studies such as that in the Unstrut valley where variations in settlement patterns within the same physical setting were attributed to the different cultural values of German and Slav settlers. Kulturlandschaft was distinguished from Naturlandschaft. Interestingly, Schlüter was of the opinion that the cultural focus should be on that which is visible in the landscape, rather on the non-material components of culture (eg religion and language, and associated values, customs and traditions). There was an inevitable reaction to this thinning of perspective, and subsequently there were many studies that traced the impact of such forces as language and religion on the form and character of landscapes.

Although dismissed by many as a non-issue, as two variations on the same theme, the distinction between Länderkunde (regional synthesis) and Landschaftskunde (landscape morphology) is still recognized as being of some pertinence, as a recent diagrammatic representation of systematic fields within geography illustrates (Figure 2). It draws attention to the integrating function of landscapes - surfaces where the natural and social worlds meet (and sometimes collide).

The emphasis that Schlüter placed on the material traits of culture as manifest in the landscape also characterized the highly influential work - Carl Sauer (1889-1975) and the Berkeley School of Geography. Sauer was strongly influenced by the German tradition in the historical and cultural sciences (Geisteswissenschaften) and was deeply concerned to understand morphological change - the linkages that bind form to process. In his formative paper The Morphology of Landscape (1926) Sauer stated: "The cultural landscape is fashioned from a natural landscape by a culture group. Culture is the agent, the natural area the medium, the cultural landscape the result".

Sauer's reification of culture as a super-organic entity, with its own internal logic and momentum, has since been heavily criticized by social theorists. The point at issue is whether or not culture has an independent existence, above and beyond the individuals and groups that "flesh it out" (Zelinsky, 1973), and whether or not causative powers can be attached to culture per se. Again, these may appear rather abstruse matters, but they do impinge on the question as to what actually constitutes a cultural landscape of distinctiveness or outstanding universal merit. It certainly raises doubts concerning the definition of cultural landscapes purely on the basis of material components or ensembles.

In this context it is apposite to note that Jackson of Santa Fe recognized the contribution made by Sauer and his disciples, and indeed many of the latter contributed to his journal Landscape. But Jackson was much more of a humanist in his approach and drew heavily on French rather German traditions in landscape studies. In particular he identified with the work of Paul Vidal de la Blache and his regional syntheses in which 'homme, milieu et genre de vie' determine 'la physionomie des paysages' and can lead to the emergence

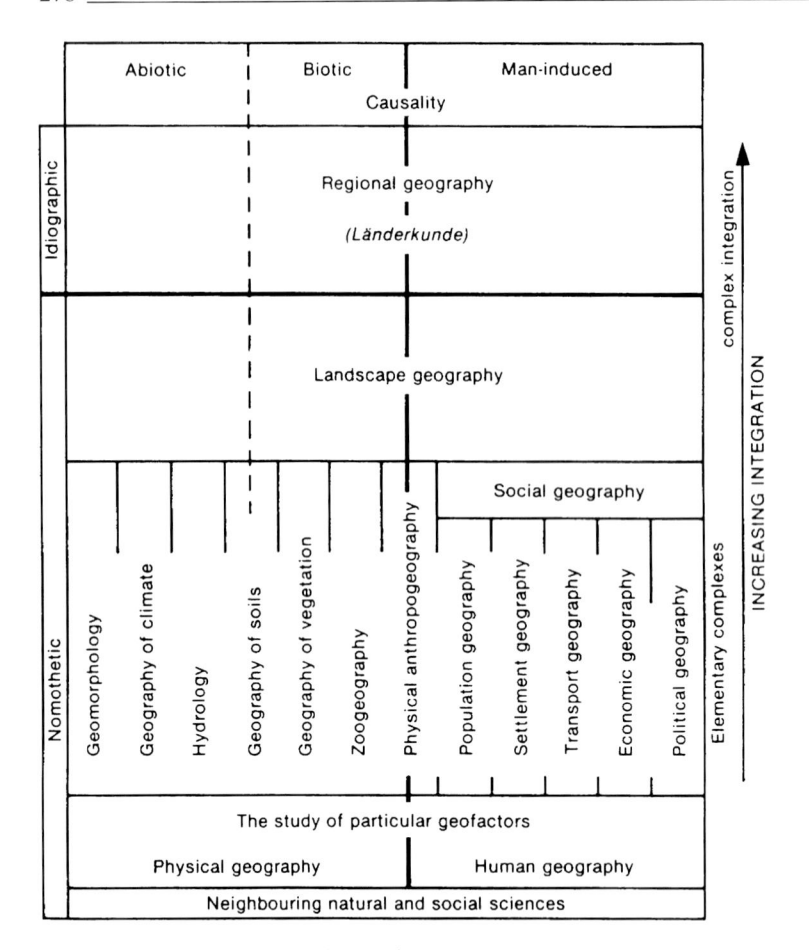

Figure 2. The Organization of Geography

of 'pays' with their own unique characteristics and their own personalities. 'Pays' are very special cultural landscapes, set in physical environments that place limits on human activity, but at the same time offer opportunities for creative developments. Here, "man (sic) and nature are moulded together like a snail and its shell" (Wrigley, 1965).

In his Tableau de la Géographie de la France (1903), Vidal asserts that: "One must start from the notion that a land is a reservoir containing dormant energies, of which nature has planted the seed, but whose use depends on man (sic). It is he who, by moulding them to his purpose, demonstrates his individuality. Man establishes the connection between disparate elements by substituting a purposeful organization of forces for the incoherent effects of local circumstances. In this manner a region acquires identity and differentiates itself from others, becoming in the course of time like a medal struck in the image of a people".

The issue of regional consciousness and sense of place figured prominently in the 'école vidalienne'. People frequently attach deep symbolic and affective meaning to landscapes; furthermore, they do not just make cultural landscapes, they are in them and of them. France, especially rural France, was a mosaic of small, named regions (pays) with which local residents strongly identified (eg Beauce and Brie in the Paris Basin).

As his ideas evolved Jackson came to recognize the importance of landscapes as settings for a whole variety human activities and not just as scenes or backdrops to be admired for their beauty. Thus he argued that in judging and evaluating such areas we should "abandon the spectator stance", and an excessive focussing on the aesthetic, and ask ourselves : "What chances does the landscape offer for making a living? What chances does it offer for freedom of choice of action? What chances for meaningful relationships with other men and with the landscape itself? What chances for individual fulfillment and for social change?"

Inevitably, given this ideological position, Jackson was concerned that due recognition should be accorded to the vernacular in landscapes, and not just of the past (eg romanticized traditional rural landscapes), but also of the present. This means that interest should encompass not just élite landscapes (landscapes designed or espoused by élite groups), but ordinary landscapes that reflect contemporary social and economic processes. Such landscapes may not necessarily be beautiful, but they often matter to the people who live in them. This modernist view contrasts with that of others, such as W.G. Hoskins who, in his much referenced The Making of the English Landscape (Hoskins, 1955) considered that since the later years of the nineteenth century, and especially since 1914 "every change in the English landscape has either uglified it or destroyed its meaning or both.... It is a distasteful subject...". Interestingly, despite their differences, Michael Conzen in The Making of the American Landscape states that "This book has its roots in the fertile bicontinental traditions of landscape study nurtured by William G. Hoskins and John Brinckerhoff Jackson" (Conzen, 1990).

In reviewing geographical perspectives on cultural landscapes it is necessary to refer to the development of humanistic approaches which look for insights into the depiction and interpretation of regional landscapes through the works of writers, artists and musicians, and through biographical reconstructions of the landscapes concerned. Such reconstructions require reference to the meanings and messages of the authors who created them.

"... the created landscapes of man (sic) are much like any other product of human creativity. They have much in common with the manifold forms of human art and artifice. That is they are constrained by need and context, but they are also expressions of authorship"(Samuels,1979).

Finally, over more recent times geographers of more radical persuasion have called for a critical analytic approach to the study of cultural landscapes. The main arguments developed here rest on the belief that in the past insufficient attention has been paid to the "way cultures are produced and reproduced through actual social practices that take place in historically contingent and geographically specific contexts" (Jackson, 1989). As it happens, this paradigmatic stance has been applied with force by Denis Cosgrove in his analysis of landscape change in Europe for the critical period 1400-1900. In his exegesis Social Formation and the Symbolic Landscape (1984) he explores the impacts of feudalism and the capitalist transition on modes of production and social organization, and on associated forms and conceptualizations of landscapes. While it would clearly be possible to present an introduction to European cultural landscapes through this particular "way of seeing", the intention below is to adopt a more traditional and descriptive approach; one that simply seeks to highlight broad regional contrasts in the physical and human geography of Europe, and to trace the impact of human agency on the ever-changing form and function of resultant landscapes. An attempt is also made to tie this description to the types of landscapes identified by the World Heritage Committee.

Cultural Landscapes in Europe - A Descriptive Overview

To suggest that Europe is rich and diverse in its natural and cultural endowment is commonplace, but nonetheless the true for all that. It certainly impressed itself on the Greek geographer Strabo, for in the first century BC he noted that "this part of the world is the most varied".

Although long subject to scholarly dispute, it is generally accepted that, in a strictly physical and morphological sense, Europe is a "promontory of Asia", lying to the west of the Urals, the Ural River and the crest of the Caucasus range. But it is a promontory that covers nearly 10 million km^2 (7% of the total land surface of the globe) and takes its configuration from a complex of peninsulas, mountains, lowland and upland basins, and a multitude of rivers, inland seas, lakes and islands. This fretted and variegated scene is based on a complex solid geology, laterally and vertically shifted over time by major crustal movements and continuously shaped by geomorphological processes of deposition and erosion (Figure 3a); processes which in their turn have been heavily determined by ever-changing climatic regimes. Geology, geomorphology and climate have combined to fashion topographies and to create an array of bio-geographical environments of immense diversity and richness.

Although set within the extensive palaearctic province in terms of its biogeography, it is possible to discern within the region a series of biomes that have been variously exploited by differing cultural and ethnic groups (Figure 3b). In the far north a skirt of tundra environments fringe the Arctic Sea; to south of these lies an extensive swathe of boreal coniferous forests (the Taiga) based on infertile podzol soils and a harsh continental climate. This latter zone encompasses much of Scandinavia and dominates throughout northern Russia. To south of this is the Great European Plain, a sweep of essentially lowland and heavily glaciated country where the natural vegetation is one of temperate broadleaf forests and woodlands. Early settlers quickly removed the forest cover in this area, and most particularly where wind-blown loess deposits offered opportunities for cultivation. In south-eastern parts of Russia, in the Ukraine, and in the central Hungarian depression drier conditions and the impress of man have resulted in the development of steppe environments. In parts these soils are intensively cultivated, in others they are extensively grazed by livestock. The zones described thus far define, broad, fairly homogeneous and laterally-defined bands in northern and eastern sections of the continent.

Figure 3a. The structure of Europe: 1. Ancient crystalline masses; 2. Alpine ranges and folds; 3. Sedimentary areas not much affected by folding; 4. The great plain of Europe, largely glaciated; 5. General directions of alpine folds; 6. General orientation of ancient folds; 7. Main groupings of morainic hills; 8. Limit of the maximum extension of the great northern icecap. Volcanic areas are indicated by black patches.

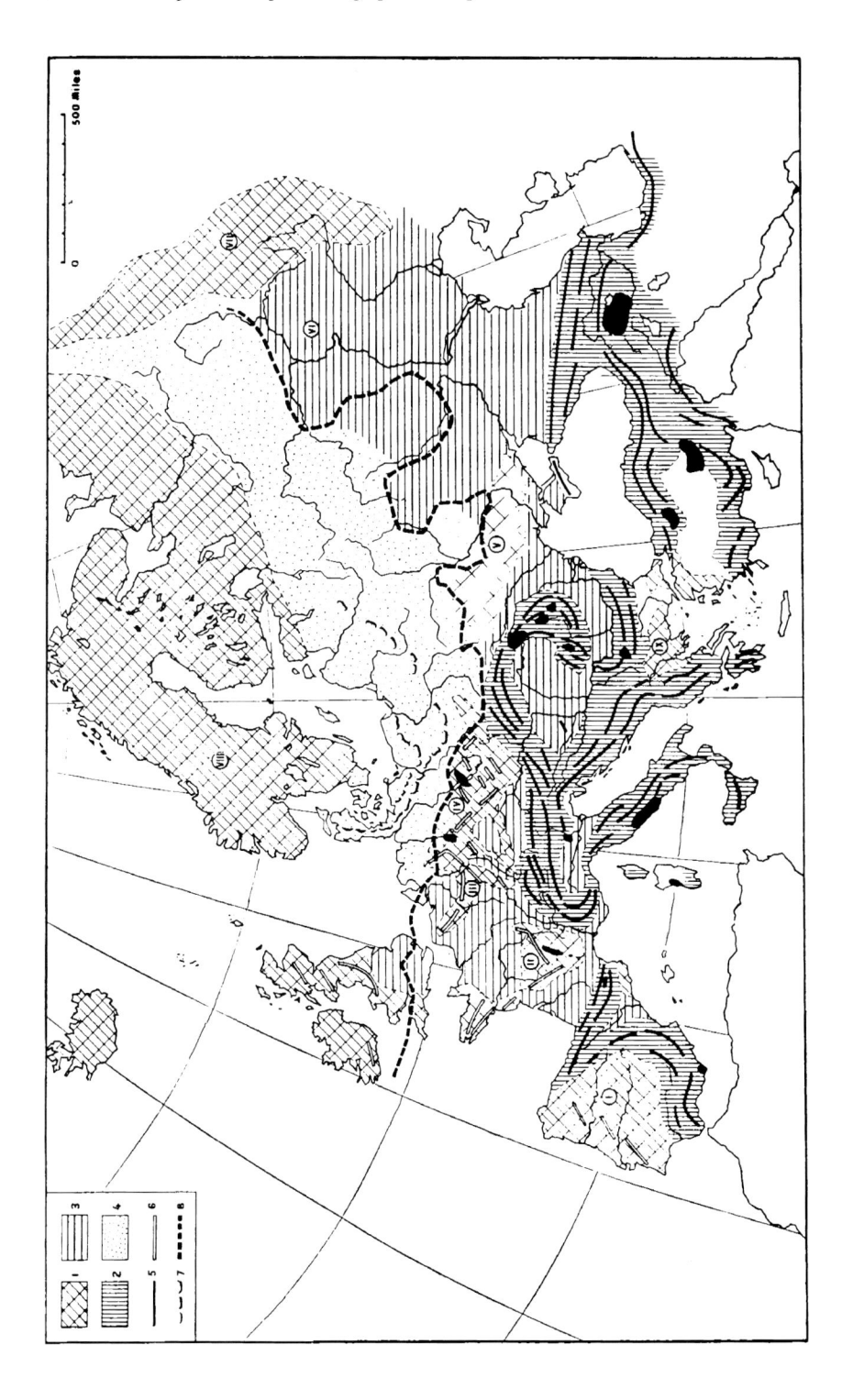

Cultural Landscapes in Europe: A Geographical Perspective —————— 279

The picture becomes much more intricate in Atlantic, Alpine and Mediterranean regions to the west and south. Here, micro and meso-scale variations become more prominent, and render summary description and generalization that much more difficult. Suffice it to say that physical landscapes in many parts of Western Europe are delineated by sharp geological and bio-climatic gradients (both lateral and vertical). In this more densely populated realm, the natural landscapes have been heavily modified by human activity. Thus, in many Alpine mountain areas the evergreen hardwood cover has been cleared, giving way to scrub vegetation - maquis and garrigues. Away from the main mountain ranges, on the Iberian Peninsula and along coastal regions of the Mediterranean sclerophyllous forest and scrub were the natural cover, but as elsewhere the scene has been heavily transformed by generations of farmers and pastoralists. Finally, in terms of its physical geography reference should be made to the complex of land/sea interfaces that have figured so prominently in the settlement and development of the continent. They add a further dimension to a highly diverse scene.

This, in very broad terms, is the differentially-endowed stage on which the many cultural and ethnic groups that have established themselves in the region have acted out their lives. The recently published Atlas of World Cultures (Price, 1989) identifies nearly a hundred extant cultural groupings in Europe. Many of these now hold only minority status, and their integrity - if not their very survival - has long been threatened. Of the latter, many are to be found in the remoter out-reaches of the Arctic north and in the western Celtic periphery; significant numbers have also established homelands in the fractured mountain (and now highly troubled) realms of the Balkans and the Caucasus. While Paul Valery may have argued that the idea of Europe is "Greece, plus Rome, plus Christianity", these groups with their different heritages confirm that it is much more than that. There are over fifty different languages, and many hundreds of dialects. The four main linguistic families customarily recognized - Germanic, Romance, Slavic and Celtic - by no means embrace this immense variety. Language, together with religion (predominantly Catholic, Protestant, Eastern Orthodox and Moslem), shape the way people conceive of their worlds and frequently express themselves in tangible landscape features. They are formative and important in determining the distinctiveness of many cultural landscapes in Europe. Landscapes are not just ways of seeing, they are also ways of speaking. Landscapes are conceived and perceived through language. In the end landscapes themselves are both texts and languages.

Figure 3b. Vegetation and land use in Europe. In most of Europe, man has reshaped the natural landscape so thoroughly that vegetation cannot be studied aside from land use. This map endeavors to describe in a schematic way the predominant types of land use in Europe through the dominant features of the vegation as it appears in the present landscape. Explanation of legend (at upper left): 1, tundra and poorer northern windswept moors; 2, northern forest (predominantly conifers with some birch trees); 3, mixed forest (coniferous and deciduous); 4, zone of cleared forests where tilled areas alternate with woodlands; 5, forest and meadows of alpine mountains (higher zone of poor pastures and glaciers is left in blank); 6, zone of mixed Hercynien woodlands with clearings; 7, zone of intensive cultivation, with predominance of grains; 8, zone of intense cultivation oriented towards a cattle economy; 9, zone of Mediterranean agriculture affected by altitude or backwardness; 10, zone of intense Mediterranean polyculture, oriented towards vines, orchards truck farming, and the like.

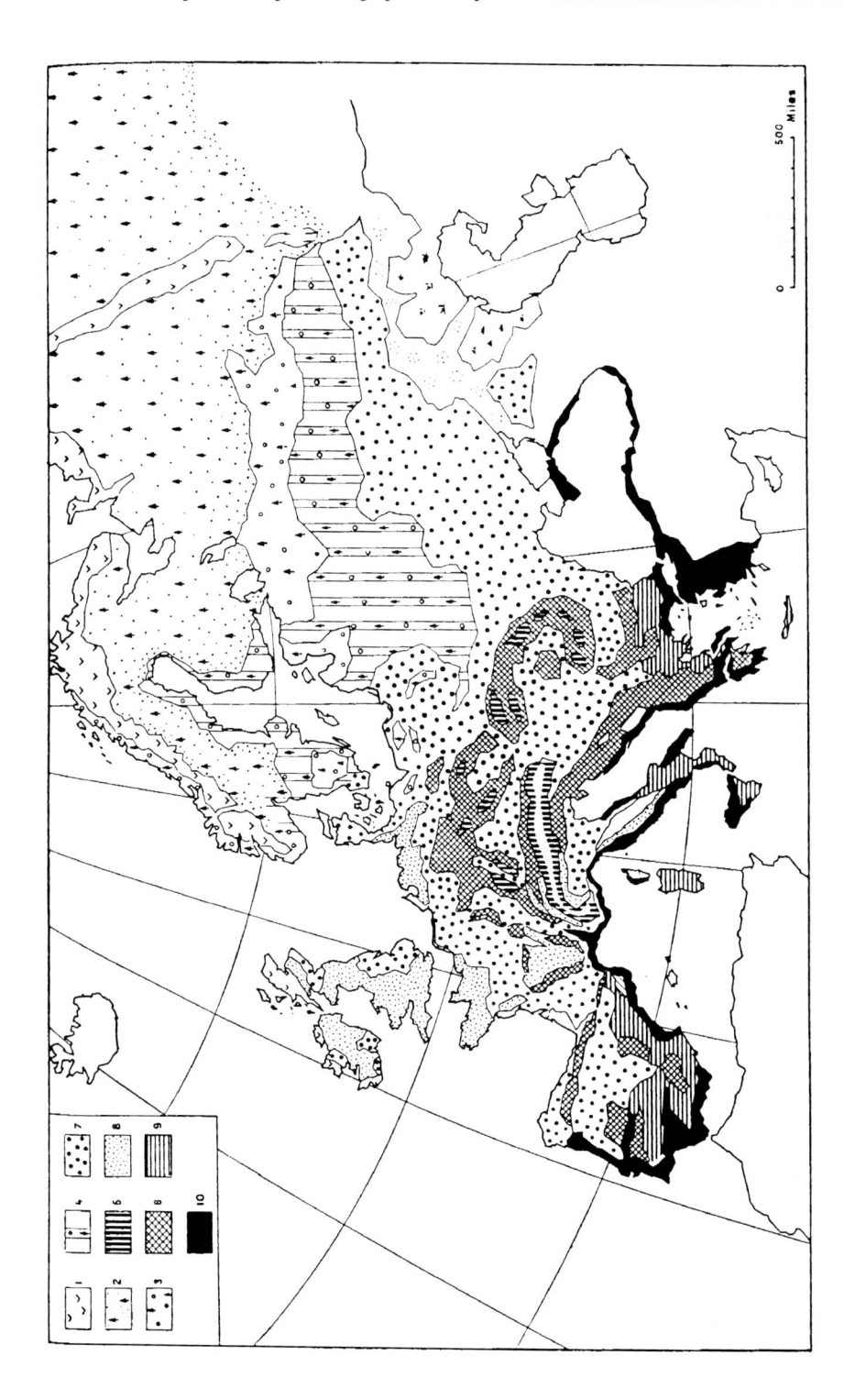

Cultural Landscapes in Europe: A Geographical Perspective 281

The cultural diversity that exits in Europe derives not only from the variety of different ethnic groupings that are to be found in the region, it stems also from the ebb, flow and mixing of these groupings over a long period of time. The physical geography of Europe has greatly facilitated the extensive diffusion of peoples, together with their associated cultures. The dense network of river systems, the east-west alignment of the topography, and the opportunities for movement across inland seas and along coastal waters have brought differing cultures into contact. This contact has sometimes resulted in a harmonious co-existence and/or miscegenation of cultures, giving rise to multi-form landscapes (eg along many frontier zones); conversely, of course, cultural contact can lead (as it has, and still does) to the destruction and replacement of indigenous cultural landscapes by those of alien groups. Europe is a palimpsest of cultural landscapes - like the physical terrain in which they are set and from which they emerge, these landscapes have been subject to processes of accumulation, erosion and continual re-working.

Reflecting on this cultural profusion the geographer Jean Gottmann has observed that the differentiation in regional and landscape types "occurs with a greater frequency and perhaps a greater intensity in Europe than in any other country" (Gottmann, 1962). The peoples of Europe have profoundly transformed the natural order, and re-shaped their worlds to satisfy physical and spiritual needs. As has been noted, the main initial transformation involved the clearing of forest covers in both lowlands and uplands. In the west and north-west bocage field systems developed, creating hedge-rowed, banked and walled landscapes, associated in the main with polycultural systems. Typical examples are to be found in central England, parts of Scandinavia, Brittany, and north-western Spain. Elsewhere collectively-farmed, open-field cultivation came to characterize large stretches of the continent - the Paris Basin, the Spanish Meseta, the Mezzogiorno, much of central Europe and the steppe lands of Russia and the Ukraine. Of course, these differing landscape types are associated with very special but differing systems of land tenure and modes of production. In their origins and subsequent evolutions they capture feudal, capitalist and socialist transitions.

A leitmotif of considerable consequence for the cultural landscapes of Europe has been that of water control. In drier regions of the south ancient and modern systems of irrigation have given form and function to deltas, alluvial lowlands and valley bottoms. The infrastructures on which they are based (barrages, pumps, aqueducts, tunnels, networks of canals and channels) are important features of these landscape, as are the settlement patterns and very varied forms of agricultural production to which they have given rise (from extensively grazed water meadows to intensively managed huertas). Elsewhere, the problem has been more one of controlling water levels and of large-scale drainage and reclamation. Throughout Europe, but most especially along coastal margins, marshlands and wetlands in variety have over the centuries been drained and reclaimed for cultivation and grazing (eg the fen lands of East Anglia, the Po Valley). Of all the areas of this type perhaps the most notable are the polder lands of the Netherlands - "a masterpiece of masonry". Similar reclamations typify coastal flats in northern Germany (Niedersachsen) and south-west Denmark. In other parts traditional systems of extensive grazing have been based on carefully regulated water-tables (eg the Marais Poitevin and Briere regions of western France, the Halvergate Marshlands in the Broads of eastern England, the Somerset levels). In alluding to these water-based landscapes, with their distinctive geometries, it is pertinent to note that many of them are of ancient origin, but have subsequently been reconstructed and extended (eg the irrigated lowlands of Fium'Orbo in eastern Corsica that were first drained and irrigated by Greek and Roman settlers).

Equally distinct in the landscapes of Europe are the efforts to wrest and protect land on mountain and hill slopes through terracing. Like the polders these contoured features bear testimony to the immense physical labours of rural communities over the ages. Although in many places still "living" landscapes (eg the vineyard terraces of the middle Rhine, the fruit-tree terraces of the Rhone), in others they are degraded, relict forms (eg former olive, chestnut, and cereal growing terraces in Mediterranean mountain regions).

It is clearly not possible here to do justice to the variety of cultural landscapes that exist in Europe. The above discussion is partial, highly selective, and very broad-brush. Inevitably, it has tended to emphasize landscapes where the imprint of humankind has been (is) most obvious in material/physical terms. There are however many rural communities, often associated with the most difficult terrains, that may not have built extensive, heavy or permanent structures but that have nonetheless developed "landscapes of living" that are closely integrated with their natural environments. The communities of the Taiga and Tundra, and of remote islands and open moorlands are cases in point. Their impress may not be writ large, but for all that it is a significant and abiding part of the European heritage.

In regard to cultural landscapes that might be worthy of being included in the World Heritage List it is evident that State Parties in Europe are likely to be able to propose many suitable candidates. As has been demonstrated this follows from the long, and complex history of the continent, and from the immensely varied geography (both natural and cultural) that is packed into such a limited space. Circumspectly, Jim Thorsell of IUCN recently opined that "the greatest number of sites that might qualify as World Heritage cultural landscapes are located in Europe" (Thorsell, 1992).

In terms of the types of cultural landscapes recognized in the operational guidelines it is evident that Europe contains exemplars for each of the four categories identified (Figure 1). There are living landscapes that carry vestiges of past uses but are organically evolving in a sensitive and quasi-sustainable manner (eg many of the areas now formally designated as protected landscapes); others are fossilized landscapes that display traces of previous resource management systems, but which have since fallen into desuetude (eg social fallows in terraced mountain regions, vernacular buildings in abandoned rural areas); many more are small finely-etched landscapes that have been designed to make manifest particular visions or ideals (eg parks and gardens). Some bear witness to designed or planned transformations of natural habitats for utilitarian ends (eg reclaimed polders). Inevitably, many of these various landscapes types have inspired outstanding artistic expression in all genres, adding further meaning and resonance to the localities concerned. In places, they and others might be seen as associative landscapes that are held in high spiritual or symbolic regard by local or national communities. While it is possible to assign particular landscapes to each of the four typal categories, it is clear that some could be multiply represented, and furthermore that several types could be found within a single area - forming a mosaic of landscapes.

As yet there is no single study of the "making" of the European cultural landscape comparable to the integrated set of essays edited by Michael Conzen for America (1990). That said, there is clearly a wealth of material that could be called upon should such an undertaking ever be contemplated. In the meantime it is important that multi-disciplinary studies of the type recently completed for the Ystrad region of southern Sweden be encouraged in other parts of Europe (Berglund, 1992). To date much of the information available is piecemeal and based on particular systematic interests.

That Europe is rich in cultural landscapes is evident to all. Rather belatedly, the realization has come that this very special heritage is under threat, either through neglect and abandonment, or through the impact of modern developments. The various dimensions of the problem are well known and need not be elaborated upon. Suffice it to say that they include problems arising from the non-viability of many traditional farming systems, intensification of agricultural practices (especially in the European Community areas), major urban, industrial and infrastructural projects, insensitive and inadequately regulated tourism developments, disregard for traditional building styles (designs and materials), and pollution of soils and watercourses.

Cultural Landscapes and Protected Landscapes

As it happens, over the years national governments and regional authorities in many parts of Europe have structured policies and management systems that seek to conserve the special attributes of particular landscapes. Although reference to cultural attributes may not be explicit (often tending to be overshadowed by concerns for the condition of natural environments), such matters are frequently implicit. In this regard it is of interest to note the significance in Europe of those designated areas that qualify as "protected landscapes" within the IUCN typology of protected areas. These category V landscapes by definition constitute very special cultural landscapes. Using the terminology of the WHC guidelines they are organically evolving and display close symbiotic associations between local cultures and their natural environments. In a recently re-drafted set of guidelines, Category V Protected Landscapes are defined thus :

"Areas of land, with coast and sea as appropriate, where the interaction of people and nature over time has produced an area of distinct character with significant aesthetic, cultural and/or ecological value, and often with high biological diversity. Safeguarding the integrity of this traditional interaction is vital to the protection, maintenance and evolution of such an area".

Apart from its focus on people-nature linkages, this descriptive statement also alludes to the importance of managing such landscapes to assure their long-term viability. Concern for the future well-being of cultural landscapes also figures in the WHC guidelines, for it is recognized that according a very special status label to landscapes of universal significance must carry with it an obligation on the part of the stakeholders concerned to have management and control systems in place that will safeguard their integrity. It is an obligation that is owed both to the nameable and nameless "authors" who fashioned the landscapes concerned, and to present and future generations who have (will have) "a eye to perceive and a heart to enjoy" their very special qualities. The IUCN guidelines concerning management state that the main objectives are:

- to maintain the harmonious interaction of nature and culture through the protection of landscape and/or seascape and the continuation of traditional land uses, building practices and social and cultural manifestations;
- to support lifestyles and economic activities which are in harmony with nature and the preservation of the social and cultural fabric of the communities;
- to maintain the diversity of landscape and habitat, and of associated species and ecosystems;

- to eliminate where necessary, and thereafter prevent, land uses and activities which are inappropriate in scale and/or character;
- to provide opportunities for public enjoyment through recreation and tourism appropriate in type and scale to the essential qualities of the areas;
- to encourage scientific and educational activities which will contribute to the long term well-being of resident populations and to the development of public support for the environmental protection of such areas; and
- to bring benefits to, and to contribute to the welfare of, the local community through the provision of natural products (such as forest and fisheries products) and services (such as clean water or income derived from sustainable forms of tourism).

To achieve these objectives, management regimes should be instituted which endeavor to integrate the needs of owners and other interest groups. Furthermore, "these regimes should be subject to a degree of planning or other control and supported, where appropriate, by public funding and other incentives, to ensure that the quality of the landscape/seascape and the relevant local customs and beliefs are maintained in the long term.

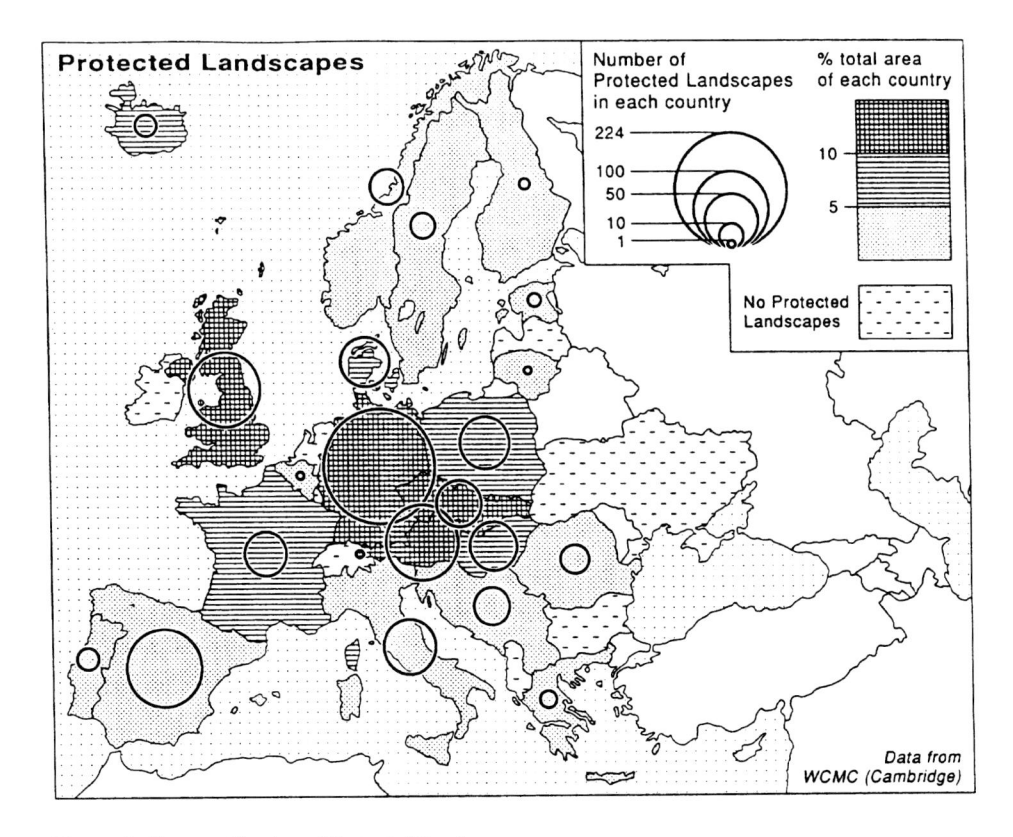

Figure 4. Europe : Number of Protected Landscapes

Here, the centrality of cultural considerations is again strongly in evidence. It is too in the guidelines that have been proposed for an area to qualify for the designation. Thus, "the area should possess a landscape and/or coastal and island seascape of high scenic quality, with diverse associated habitats, flora and fauna along with manifestations of unique or traditional land use patterns and social organizations as evidenced in human settlements and local customs, livelihoods and beliefs".

It is of interest to note that in Europe (excluding Russia) there are currently nearly 900 protected landscapes, covering some 240,000 km^2 (approximately 5% of the total land area). Together these areas account for 54% of all such areas in the world[1]. This statistic alone serves to underline the importance of the continent in regard to its cultural landscape heritage. However, as is evident from Figures 4 and 5, there are considerable regional variations in the distribution of protected landscapes at state level. Significant expanses of countryside are seen to have been designated in Germany, the United Kingdom and France (over 40,000 km^2 in each case). Other states with over 10,000 km^2 are Poland, the former Czechoslovakia, Austria and Spain. Protected landscapes cover over 10% of

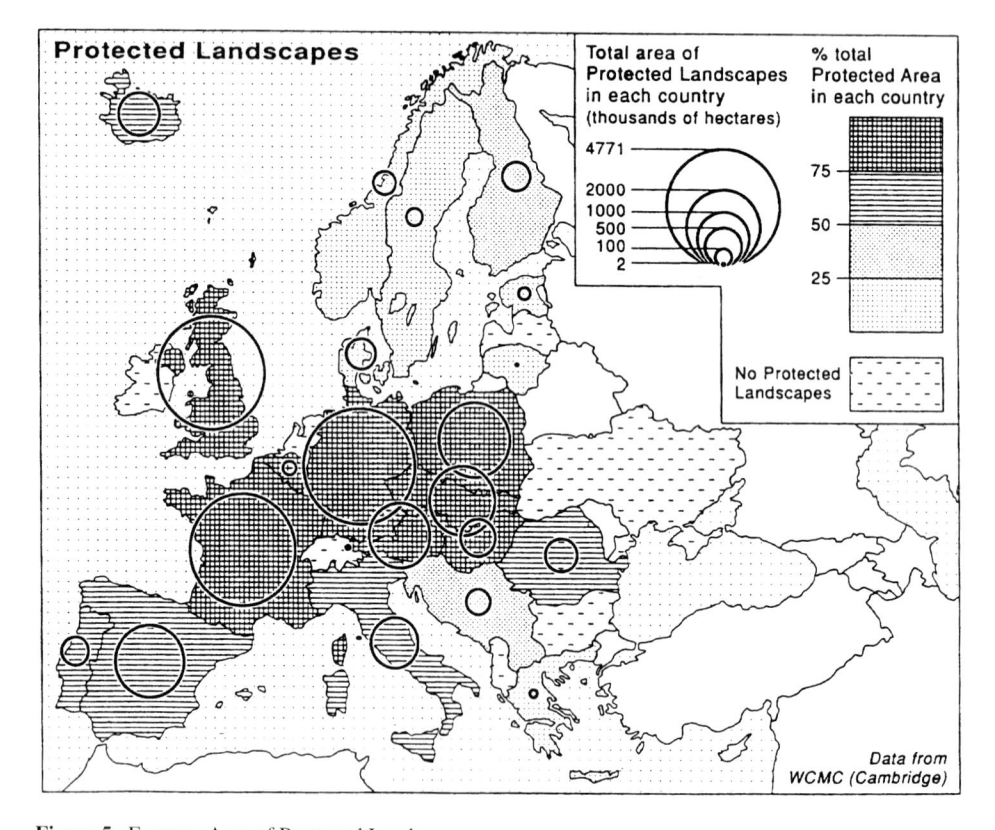

Figure 5. Europe : Area of Protected Landscapes.

---

[1] The data on which these maps are based were drawn from the United Nations List of National Parks and Protected areas.

national territories in Austria, the former Czechoslovakia, Germany, the United Kingdom and Liechtenstein. The scope for an expansion of the protected landscape system is clearly considerable, and is to be further encouraged. It would serve as a much-needed complement to the very special and select types of areas that are likely to be included on the World Heritage List in the years to come.

The same can be said in regard to a recent call from Adrian Phillips concerning the need for a Convention on the Conservation of the Rural Landscapes of Europe (Phillips, 1992). His argument was (is) that Europe is blessed with a profusion of landscapes that manifests an intimate association between rural communities and their working, natural environments. The problem is that many of these areas are under threat and could be lost or irreparably damaged, unless development is guided to take account of landscape heritage. The intent is not to halt or hinder change, but to monitor and, where necessary, take control of it in the long-term interests of the landscapes and communities concerned. In proposing a Convention Phillips had in mind the Berne (1979) and Granada (1985) treaties that seek respectively, to conserve and protect wildlife and natural habitats, and the architectural heritage of Europe. His ideas and recommendations have much to commend them, and should certainly be pursued further.

Conclusion

The main aim of this paper has been to highlight a number of themes emphasized by geographers in their evaluation and appreciation of cultural landscapes, and then to use these in a very general description of associated patterns and processes within Europe.

The discussion has demonstrated that the continent displays an extraordinary diversity of physical environments within a very small compass, and that these environments have been variously moulded by communities over a very long period of time to create a miscellany of cultural landscapes. Attention has been drawn to the fact that cultural landscapes everywhere are under pressure from neglect and damaging (even destructive) developments. Some efforts have been made to safeguard the cultural landscape heritage (eg through systems of protected landscapes), but in general these have been insufficiently developed. The recognition of cultural landscapes within the World Heritage Convention will certainly help give significant momentum to the wider movement concerned with the protection of such landscapes world-wide.

References

Beglund, B. E. (1991). *The Cultural landscape during 6000 years in southern Sweden*, Ecological Bulletins, 41.
Conzen, M., ed. (1990). *The making of the American Landscape*, Unwin Hyman.
Cosgrove, D. (1984). *Social Formation and Symbolic Landscape*, Croom Helm.
Gottmann, J. (1962). *A Geography of Europe*, Holt, Rhinehart and Winston.
Holt-Jensen, A. (1988). *Geography : History and Concepts*, PCP.
Hoskins, W. G. (1955). *The Making of the English Landscape*, Hodder and Stoughton.
Jackson, J. B. (1951). *The need of being versed in country things*, Landscape, **1**, 4-5.
Jackson, J. B. (1952). *Human, All Too Human Geography*, Landscape, **2**, 5-7.
Jackson, P. (1989). *Maps of Meaning*, Unwin Hyman.

Livingstone, D. N. (1992). *The Geographical Tradition. Episodes in the History of a Contested Enterprise*, Blackwell.

Phillips, A. (1993). *Proposal for a Convention on the Conservation of the Rural Landscapes of Europe*, Paysages et Aménagement.

Price, D. H. (1989). *Atlas of World Cultures*, Sage Publications.

Samuels, M. (1979). *The Biography of Landscape*. In Meinig, D. (ed.), *The Interpretation of Ordinary Landscapes*, Oxford.

Sauer, C. O. (1929). *The morphology of landscape*. University of California Publications in Geography.

Thorsell, J. (1992). *From strength to strength : World Heritage in its 20th year.* In *IUCN World Heritage 20 Years Later.*

Wagner, P. L. and Mikesell, M. W., eds. (1962). *Readings in Cultural Geography*, University of Chicago Press.

Wrigley, E. A. (1965). *Changes in the Philosophy of Geography*. In Chorley, R.J. and Haggett, P. *Frontiers in Geographical Teaching*, Methuen.

Zelinsky, W. (1973). *The Cultural Geography of the United States*, Englewood Cliffs.

John Aitchison is Director of the International Centre for Protected Landscapes at the Institute of Earth Studies, University of Wales Aberystwyth. He also holds the Gregynog Chair of Human Geography at Aberystwyth.

Chapter 24

On the Traces of the Mediterranean Landscape[1]

Yves Luginbühl

Many specialists seem to accept that the idea of landscape was born on the shores of the North Sea, in that flat Flemish countryside where, from waves of mist, hazy steeples emerge, mirrored by their reflections in pools and canals. This was the Renaissance, when agronomic science, inspired by the principles of the Ancient scholars, reinvented the draining of marshland, allowing the eye to glimpse through the window a countryside beautiful like the *Landskap* of the canvases of Van Eyck or Breugel.

If it is true that this *Landskap* ushered in a new era for landscape, which spread across Europe through the brushes of the masters as *Landschaft, landscape, paysage, paesaggio* and *paisaje*, its origin remains uncertain: the painters certainly helped to see the light of day, but where are its roots? Do they lie in the gaze of the Northern European peoples who discovered their ability to master a way of organizing nature in their living space, thanks to hydraulics and drainage, making marshlands productive and inventing polders? It is not so obvious. There are many signs scattered in gardens and in paintings - many of the trails which open in the landscapes of Europe lead southwards and open the question of the origins of "landscape".

Facets of landscape borrowed from the South

First, there is light: golden in the first and last hours of the day, symbolising the agreement between Apollo, god of beauty, and Dionysos, god of festivity, gaeity and popular forces. At midday, Apollo is too powerful and with his light he crushes peoples who, in the Mediterranean, shelter behind thick walls that conserve the accumulated coolness of the night and open to the outside through narrow windows (Luginbühl, 1992). It is this light, falling obliquely in sunbeams, that pervades the landscapes of Renaissance Northern Europe in the canvases of the Masters, artists who saw the journey to Rome as obligatory and found the study of the classical forms and canons of beauty an indispensable source of inspiration.

At first sight, this discovery of Mediterranean light is a phenomenon which only touches the world of art. But on careful reflection, the intrusion of Mediterranean light into the pictorial landscape overflows the purely plastic dimension because it places the landscape directly in the balance sought between Apollo and Dionysos, like a collective

---

[1] translated from French by Alison Semple.

work of the peoples which the light helps us to recognise as spectacular and an object of contemplation. The transfer to Northern Europe of that element of the landscape idea contained in Mediterranean light is one of the first examples of the aesthetic drift of a meaning initially derived from popular sensibilities, but which the European Bourgeoisie was later to divert for its own benefit.

With poetic justice, the arrival of light was to reach its climax *en route* for the Mediterranean, in the work of the Impressionists, who took landscape painting to its apogee on the shores of the Côte d'Azur and the *baous* of Provence.

After light, comes Virgil's *Bucolics*, in which he expresses with poetic finesse his precise observation of the knowledge and practices of the countryside, steeped in Latin mythology. Clearly the Roman poet served not only as a continual reference for the agronomists, particularly those of the Renaissance, but also for the creators of gardens. This idea of the bucolic, or pastoral, enduringly permeated European models of landscape, and English gardens in particular.

The pastoral model, essential in English gardens, in which the countryside is recomposed and structured by its enclosures (hedges), is evidently an aesthetic reference borrowed from Latin culture in which pastoral farming is a foundation of the agricultural system. Whether considering the open spaces of the mountains and hills of the Mediterranean where shepherds drive their herds, as certain painters fixed them on their canvases or as they appear on Ancient frescoes[2], or looking at the forests of evergreen oak of the Spanish *dehesa* which still exist in Andalusia or in Extremadura, one has before one's eyes that pastoral model which the masters of the English landscape, such as Constable or Gainsborough, adapted to the damp, oceanic English climate. The *dehesa* is an agro-sylvo-pastoral system associating a forest of evergreen and/or cork oaks with extensive pig, sheep or cattle raising and annual crops.

Equally, this pastoral model inspired the creators of gardens, such as Capability Brown or Repton, who conjured up the "English pastoral" from which all traces of agricultural activity disappeared, leaving an idea of the verdant landscape dotted with groves of trees, but without hedges or fences, suitable for the horseback hunting practised by large landowners of the eighteenth century. In fact, this free space, marked here and there with shady groves of pine, derived from those under which the Arcardian shepherds came to rest or play the Pan pipes, is also sometimes found in the olive groves of the Mediterranean, and was transposed by the imagination of the English social elite into different social and ecological conditions. The art critic Gilpin, in his famous seventeenth century essay on the beautiful and the picturesque, insisted on the necessity of removing all traces of agricultural activity to compose a beautiful landscape, though sheep were allowed because of the way in which they evoke the pastoral scene.

Then comes the art of scenery, drawn from the precepts of tragedy and Greek theatre, then imparted to opera, in which the Italians excelled. A stage set is transposed into the elements of nature, particularly in the first great gardens of the Renaissance, such as those found in in Guisto Uten's famous images conserved in the Florence Topographical Museum. The villas Petraïa, Ambrogiana, Castello etc., reveal this art of scenography in gardens organised like theatres for the masters of the land, from the terraces reflecting the

---

[1] Of course, the Ancient frescoes do not represent landscapes properly speaking. But it is the idea of the pastoral which is present, especially in the representation of the shepherd and his Pan pipe.

tiers of seats, to the villa watching the display of nature organised. This is theatre with a double meaning: one for the master and another for the people he dominates; to see and to be seen. The landscaping effects, the stairways that lead from the garden to the principal terrace of the villa, act as a set designed to heighten the splendour of the spectacle, the woods drawn back from the garden, a transition to the surrounding countryside evoking the wings where one invents another face or personality.

The garden is primarily Mediterranean, and not Flemish like the *Landskap*. *Paraidiza* of the Iranians, *paradeisos* of the Greeks, it became a corner of Eden recomposed according to a myth of dreamt of harmony between man and nature. To those who see only landscape thinking in societies where the term to designate landscapes exists side by side with pictorial representations and an art of gardens, one might point out that this art of gardens is fundamentally Mediterranean, developed from the Roman period on and sophisticated in the Arabic societies, and it is absent from the societies of Northern Europe.

The Arabic garden firstly symbolises Paradise in its organisation, as in the first gardens built by the Moors in Andalusia, Seville or Grenada - before the Italians founded their symmetrical model which so strongly inspired French style. The Arabic garden shows the meeting of the four rivers of Paradise, bordered by paths that cross at right angles to the flower beds, which lie on a lower level so that the master can pick his oranges or grenadines without effort. This geometrical structure, often portrayed in the pattern of carpets, perhaps derived from the Roman garden, is evidently at the origin of the organisation of the Italian gardens of the Renaissance, and it was to mark the art of the garden in Western Europe until the seventeenth century when the "English" or landscape style came to dominate. The subsequent southward diffusion of the English model is in fact a return to its origins, after decomposition and recomposition by the social elite of Northern Europe.

Interestingly, in his description of Paradise lost written in 1667, John Milton, an English poet, translates this image of the Mediterranean garden landscape, where the four rivers of Paradise come together before disappearing underground, offering the coolness of their waters to the first two members of man and watering a vegetation borrowed largely from the Mediterranean flora: palms, vines, pines etc. One finds characteristics of the Mediterranean even in the vegetation that protects the refuge of happiness: hirsute vegetation, capricious and wild like that which grows on the slopes of the southern mountains, such as *maquis* and *garrigue*.

The Mediterranean garden exploits the human sensibility for nature, but nature cultivated for the pleasure of the senses which Arab poetry often expressed: the pleasure of sight, certainly, but not solely; it is not only the continuity of the senses that holds the attention to the perfumes of plants, the taste of their fruits, the sound of fountains or the song of the birds, and the touch of the plants and stones, but also the continuity of spatial scales, from the sight of the perfumed flower to the wider vision of the countryside seen from the window; indispensable principle of the art of the garden, on which Gilpin theorised in his essay. This continuity of the senses is also noted by Milton:

"Out of the fertile ground He caused to grow all trees of noblest kind for sight, smell, taste."

In reality, this art of shaping nature in space was not invented at a stroke by the creators of gardens. The art of mastering the use and organisation of water, the soil and the plant realm, y has always been practised by agricultural societies in their individual and collective projects. We need only to look at the forms of the Mediterranean agricultural landscape to recognise in it the essential precepts of the art of gardens. Terraces, fountains, and irrigation canals in the Middle East or in the plains of the southern Mediterranean that trace strange networks to save a scarce resource, cisterns and impluvia demonstrate understanding of a climate that does not offer its abundant water when the plants most need it. These are also sources of inspiration of the creators of landscape, borrowed from people of the Mediterranean.

The return to southern shores

The preceding examples are only the most obvious. Following other leads, we would certainly discover many others. Perhaps the hydraulic engineering with which the Flemish created their polders was inspired by Roman techniques for sanitising marshland. This is only a hypothesis which would have to be verified. But it is certain that all the agronomists of Europe, in seeking to invent a new agronomic science, have always reread their Latin predecessors: the works on learned agronomy that appeared in France or in Italy at the begin of Renaissance, almost without exception, by immersing the reader in the knowledge of Varon, Columel or Virgil.

Although the art of designing nature that appeared in the Latin or Arab gardens was extended to the countryside of Northern Europe, it rapidly manifested a sense of the exotic, of an elsewhere dream of better that the great travellers, with their tales of newly discovered landscapes, only served to strengthen. It is also clear that the Flemish *Landskap* inaugurated a new era, in which the eyes of the European social elite turned little by little towards the South, to the shores of the Mediterranean and its islands, to landscapes cradled by the movement of palms, bathed in sunlight, where perpetually flourishes that multiform and complex culture, developed exchange by exchange through the bloody confrontations, collisions and encounters of countless peoples.

Certainly, the strategic value of this vast basin of exchange and communication between the Orient and Europe was of fundamental importance in the economic ambitions of people in Northern Europe. It was undoubtedly the first goal of their campaigns; also important were religious interests in the region, symbolized by the crusades to the Holy Land. But as the gaze of Northern and Western Europe turned to the south, this fascination with the sources of artistic inspiration offered by Ancient culture set in train a movement that went beyond the primary economic, religious and strategic aims.

The idea of the journey itself, inaugurated by Ulysses and his Greek companions in Mediterranean culture, is the first sign of this movement to which people of Northern Europe were to contribute. We customarily credit the English with the new practice of travelling, no longer warlike or mercantile but contemplative, which they established in the second half of the eighteenth century and which developed massively in the nineteenth. There were many means and objectives of the journeys in which the English embarked the Mediterranean, but they have one thing in common: they almost always tended to decompose and recompose the Mediterranean landscape, and they became the route of a slow appropriation of the landscape, at first symbolic, then more material, by the bourgeois elite and finally by the popular masses of Northern Europe.

The diverse representations of the Mediterranean landscape from the end of the seventeenth century show its slow and subtle decomposition/recomposition, which tended to reconstruct it as an "exotic" object. Research has revealed this process of remodelling the landscape through the practices of tourism in Provence, on the Côte d'Azur or in other regions of the Mediterranean (Luginbühl, 1989). This recomposition is manifested in pictures: towards the end of the nineteenth century, the palm was introduced on the Promenade des Anglais, establishing almost conclusively the "exotic" status of the Mediterranean coast, which the bourgeois elite of Northern Europe had made its summer resort. This introduction provoked a local conflict between the partisans of the palm and those of the olive, who defended the "local" tree in accordance with the aspirations of the regionalist movement of the time (Chamboredon and Mejean, 1985; Marié and Viard, 1977).

The multitude of advertising posters that appeared in Europe from the second half of the nineteenth century onward, and their continuity over time, are a fine illustration of this process, as images of the local vegetation are progressively replaced with plants from more southern shores, such as the palm, always represented as the emblem of the Mediterranean, or the banana, the aloe, the bougainvillier or others brought from far flung countries. The appropriation of the landscape by tourism can also be seen in the appearance in these landscape representations of the villas which progressively colonise the space, presented on the posters, like signs of bourgeois practices that catch the attention, drawing it to the spectacle of the beaches, rocks and blue waves of the sea.

The return of the landscape to the Mediterranean manifested itself even before the launch and development of the vast tourist movement, first through painting, then with the invention of photography. This new way of fixing landscapes, and so of appropriating them, was at the origin of an enormous campaign of photographers, sent to this mythic space by the aristocratic elites or the great European bourgeoisie to engrave the most famous sites first on plates then on paper. The aim was to collect the landscapes and historic monuments that hold an essential place in Western Europe: the Acropolis, the pyramids of Egypt, Baalbeck, the Dead Sea, Toledo, the windmills of La Mancha, Seville, Venice, Palermo etc., were immortalised on paper during the "Grand Tour" of the Mediterranean, made by photographers known for their mastery of this revolutionary technique that was to play an intense part in the socialisation of landscapes. These were photographers such as J. Ortiz-Echague, A. Beato, Bonfils, C. Naya, Girault de Prangey, J. Laurent, to mention only a few, who set off, armed with their equipment, to discover Mediterranean landscapes to satisfy both their own thirst to perfect their techniques and the aspirations of their financiers, such as the Grand Duke Constantin of Russia or the publishers in vogue such as Gabriel de Rumine, director of the Gazette du Nord (Zannier, 1992).

The pictorial Impressionist Movement took this photographic movement to perfection and its appearance can be considered a determining moment in this return to the South. The great impressionists began by painting the landscapes of the outskirts of the Paris region, such as Argenteuil or Bougival, and Normandy, that the train enabled them to reach more rapidly than the old stagecoaches. In fact, through their mastery of light, they retrace the social movement of the city population, first the petite bourgeoisie, then the popular classes who contributed to the construction of mass tourism in the canvases of the Impressionists; one can see the Paris train stations, from where the city dwellers set out for the country, to the banks of the Marne or the Seine, to find entertainment in the joys of fishing or *guingettes* (places of refreshment with music and dancing). Then came the discovery of the pleasures of bathing on the shores of the Channel, the cliffs at Etretat or the port of Honfleur, or simply the sea; then savouring the blazing sun of the Mediterranean, following the path traced by Cézanne, Monet, Renoir and many others. A journey suggestive of the socialisation of popular tourism that lead people of Northern Europe, particularly the working class, to the Mediterranean beaches, thanks to paid leave.

This journey through the Mediterranean landscape, reconstructed step by step at the will of make-believe and new social, technological and political conditions, reveals the progressive elaboration of a culture that spread right across Europe, a culture made up by a multitude of elements borrowed from elsewhere. While the Mediterranean landscape seems to provide this culture with many of its references, it is evident that the Mediterranean today receives in return a way of thinking that was structured in a different social environment. The privileged place given to Northern European ideas of landscape is challenged by this return to the South, where people evidently do not think of the environment in which they live in the same way like people around the North Sea. Thinking through the Mediterranean landscape perhaps means inventing another way of seeing, according to the social, political and cultural context of the Mediterranean, rather than simply applying Anglo-Saxon techniques to territories and populations that cannot understand them. In other words, it means trying to bring the light of day, from popular sensibilities of the Mediterranean, to models that structure Mediterranean representations of landscape.

References

Chamboredon, J. C. and Mejean, A. (1985). *Récits de voyage et perception du territoire: La Provence (XVIIIème siècle et XXème siècle)*. Territoires, 2. Paris, Ecole Normale Supérieure.

Luginbühl, Y. (1989). *Paysages, représentations du paysage du Siècle des Lumières à nos jours*. Paris, La Manufacture.

Luginbühl, Y. (1992). *Apollinien et dionysiaque*. In Luginbühl, Y. (ed.), *Paysage méditerranéen, catalogue to the exhibition Mediterranean Landscape,* Seville, June-October 1992. Milan, Electa.

Marié, M. and Viard, J. (1977). *La campagne réinventée,* Maussenet-les-Alpilles, Actes-Sud.

Zannier, I. (1992): *Le paysage photographié au cours du Grand Tour méditerranéan.* In Luginbühl, Y. (ed.), *Paysage méditerranéen, catalogue to the exhibition Mediterranean Landscape,* Seville, June-October 1992. Milan, Electa.

Yves Luginbühl is a geographer and works at the STRATES (Stratégies Territoriales et Dynamiques des Espaces) of the CNRS in Paris.

Chapter 25

Aranjuez: Nature, Agriculture and the Art of Landscape

Carmen Añon Feliu

Aranjuez remains one of the few places in Europe where the relentless action of man on nature over centuries has not brought about its destruction. On the contrary, human intervention has helped to preserve and enrich the environment, improving the original diversity and abundance of the place with the finest products, created with ingenuity and artistic imagination by successive generations.

This process has eventually resulted in a complex mixture of landmarks, situations and works, integrated into a natural environment of outstanding features, thus producing a very original and harmonious landscape. Virtually unchanged spots coexist with examples of first-rate cosmopolitan culture, both close to a bustling and enterprising small town.

These few pages just aim at going on a journey – which will be basically visual – through the history and landscape of Aranjuez, making some brief comments as we go along. First, however, it will be necessary to provide you with some facts about the geography and history of Aranjuez.

Geographical introduction

Aranjuez, which was officially granted the status of «Real Sitio y Villa» (Royal Site and Town), is 50 kilometres south of Madrid, on the very spot where the Tagus – the longest river in the Iberian Peninsula – and the Jarama – its main tributary – come together. The whole of the Castilian plateau has a Mediterranean-continental climate and only dry farming is possible, but Aranjuez stands out as a green island of luxuriant vegetation in the middle. This is due to the abundant waters and fertile sedimentary soils that the valley possesses, in contrast to the barren, chalky soils of surrounding lands.

An extensive irrigation network was installed on this exuberant verdure, so that vegetable gardens, orchards and landscape gardens were able to grow, greatly enhancing the vegetational environment. After the roads, ways and bridges were built, the area became easily accessible.

Having always had good communications with the economic and political centres of the nation, Aranjuez has gone through a peculiar historical process (summarized below) that eventually resulted in the present-day situation.

Today, Aranjuez is a town with a large municipal district where an intensive agricultural cultivation is carried out. Some of its 40,000 inhabitants live in the historical old part of the town and some in the new areas of expansion. They are engaged mainly in industry, commerce and, to a lesser extent, tourism.

Historical introduction

Although inhabited since ancient times by Carpetans (Iberians inhabiting the Toledo region), Romans, Visigoths and Muslims, the real history of Aranjuez started in medieval times, when the military order of Saint James came into possession of the town by royal grant. The knights built a palace in the middle of the woods, which were then replete with game.

The status of Aranjuez as a Royal Site begins with the Catholic Kings (15th century), who annexed it as a Crown holding. Their grandson, the emperor Charles V, liked the place and continued to give it his support. But it was Philip II (16th century) who fostered a first period of splendour by building a new palace and large ornamental and vegetable gardens laid out according to geometric principles. The monarch wished to symbolise in these works his ruling of vast domains in the world and also have at his disposal a quiet and cosy country retreat halfway between the royal sites surrounding Madrid and Toledo. Thus Aranjuez became a kind of personal, private residence for the king, as opposed to El Escorial, which was burdened with state and dynastic duties. At the same time, the Aranjuez of Philip II became a centre for botanic experimentation, a place for acclimatizing plant species from all over the world. Hydraulic practices were also carried out, aimed at trying out the advanced waterway traffic systems of Central Europe and Italy.

But it is the reputation of its gardens that lasted during the 17th century. At this time Aranjuez was the scene of magnificent theatrical performances of a courtly atmosphere. The magic of the place was also a source of inspiration for some of the greatest Spanish poets of the Golden Age. From then on Aranjuez became the usual abode of royalty and courtiers for long sojourns every year, during which merriment and hunting prevailed.

A new splendour appeared in the 18th century, which eventually culminated in the building of a new town close to the palace. Half baroque, half enlightened, it was the appropriate setting for the extravagant and festive everyday life led by Ferdinand VI and his wife María Bárbara. However, his brother Charles III encouraged a physiocratic experience. The Royal Site was scattered with agronomical and livestock operations which were to have important effects on the landscape. The king also improved the town with valuable installations and works worthy of the Age of Enlightenment.

During the 19th century the population continued to increase. The early construction of a railway line between Madrid and Aranjuez brought about vigorous agricultural and industrial activities, making Aranjuez one of the most dynamic centres in New Castile. At the same time, the leading role of the Royal Family diminished, and by the turn of the century their stays were brief and sporadic.

When in the early 1960s Spain began to join industrial Europe with firm steps, and the urban area of Madrid reached great proportions (a population of 5.000.000 inhabitants), Aranjuez was practically left out of this huge metropolitan area. This circumstance allowed the town to keep its demographic and economic balance as well as preserve its landscape and artistic wealth.

In recent years considerable works of infrastructure have been undertaken, which have given its original beauty back to the town as a whole. Moreover, a series of conservation measures and ambitious restoration projects have been planned and accomplished, some results of which are beginning to be seen in the landscape of the Royal Site.

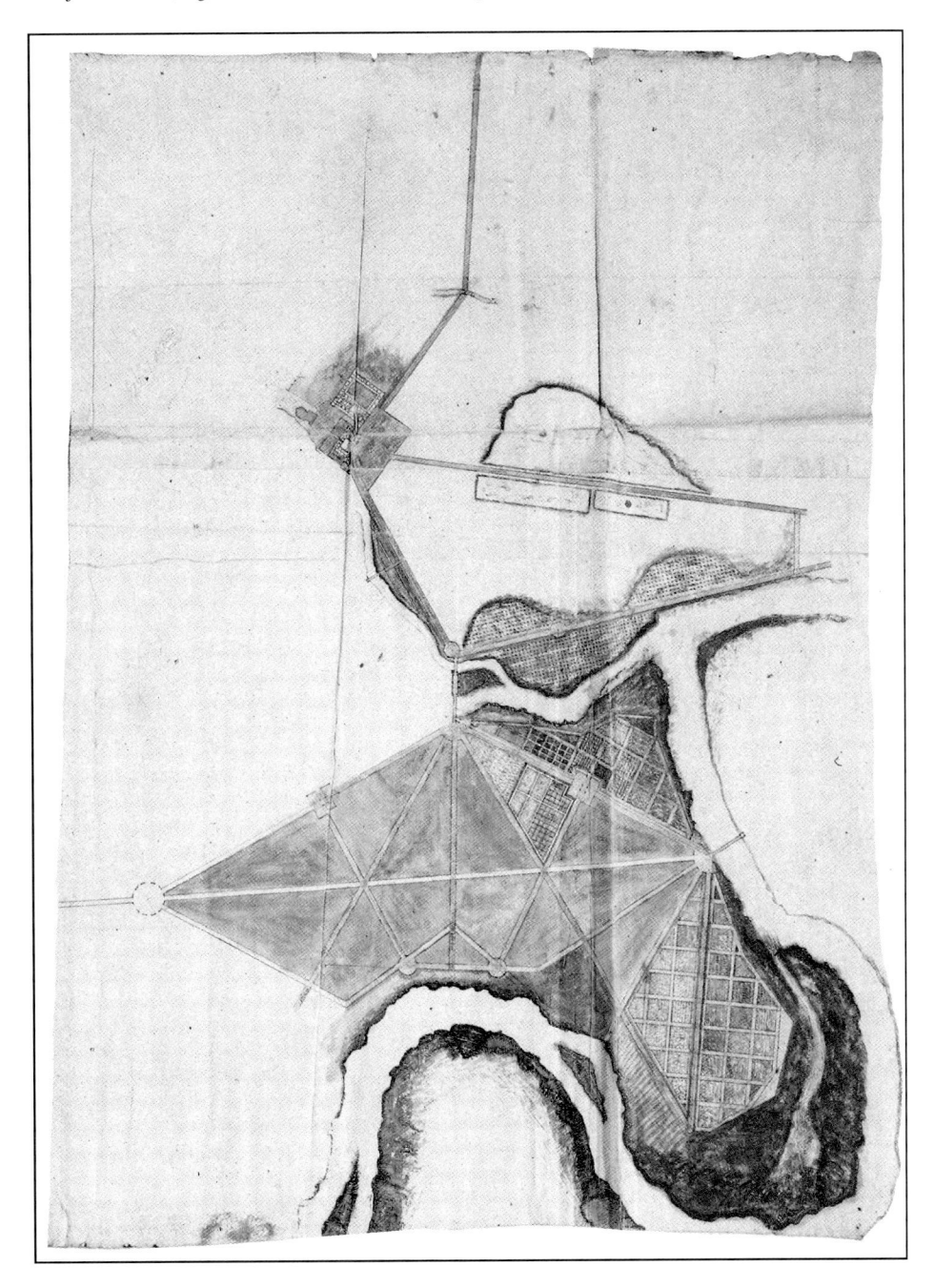

Figure 1. Anonymous, attributed to Juan de Herrera. "Maps of the palace, Casa de Oficios, Toledo and Madrid roads and Picotaja vegetable gardens". 1581. Biblioteca del Palacio Real de Madrid, dib. IX-M-242, fasc- 2 (3-4).

Figure 2. Martinez de Mazo: "The gardens of Aranguez". Madrid. prado Museum.

Aranjuez, a cultural landscape

The most striking feature of present-day Aranjuez is the occurrence of symbiotic actions between man and nature, something that has been going on for centuries. In the surrounding lands, due to local characteristics or the unrelenting action of farmers and woodcutters, the vegetation (always being in a rich and precarious balance) virtually disappeared, whereas in Aranjuez biological abundance increased to a great extent over time, due to the addition of a wide range of patterns and relationships.

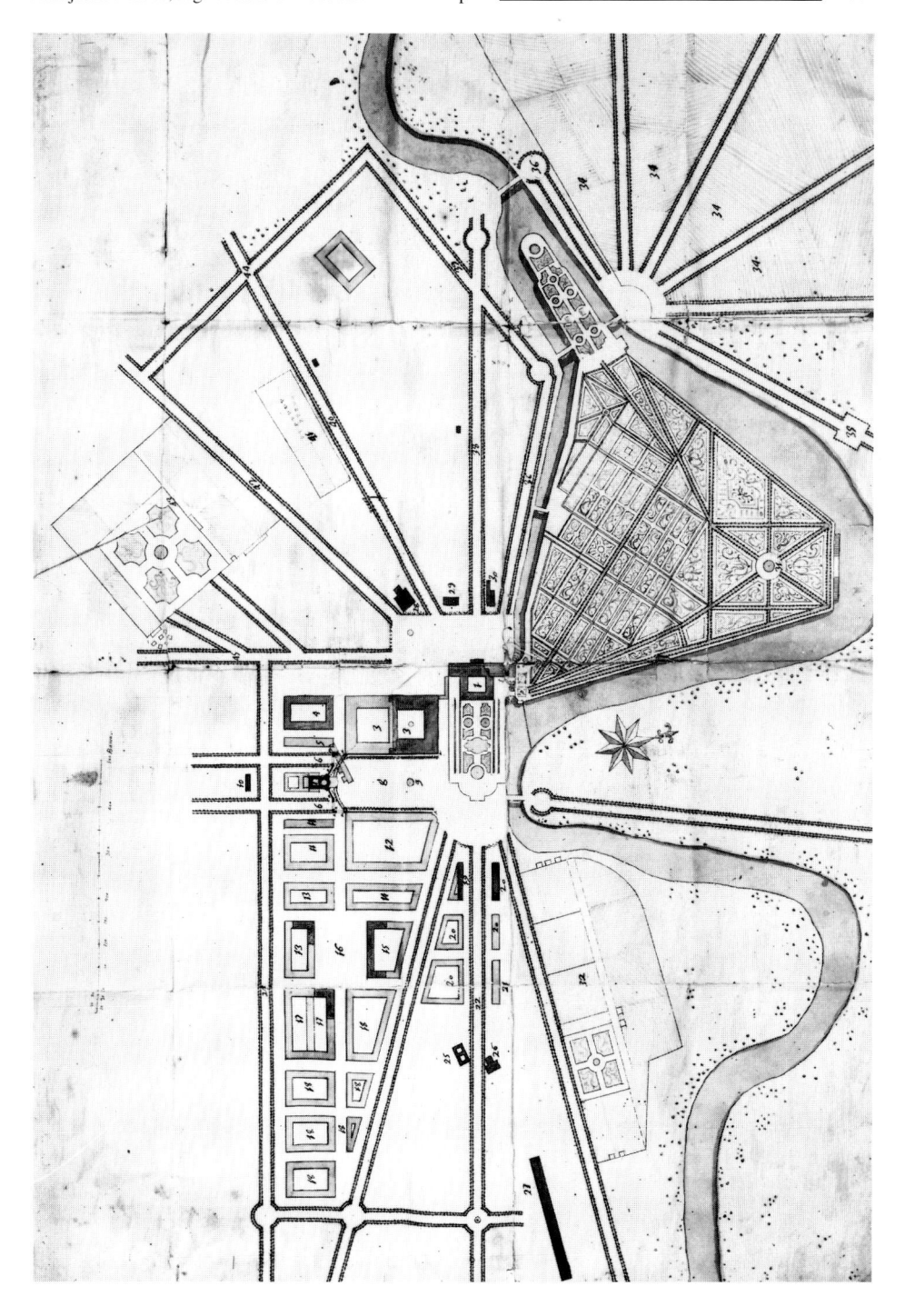

Figure 3. Santiago Bonavia: "General map of the Place, gardens and the new town". Museum.

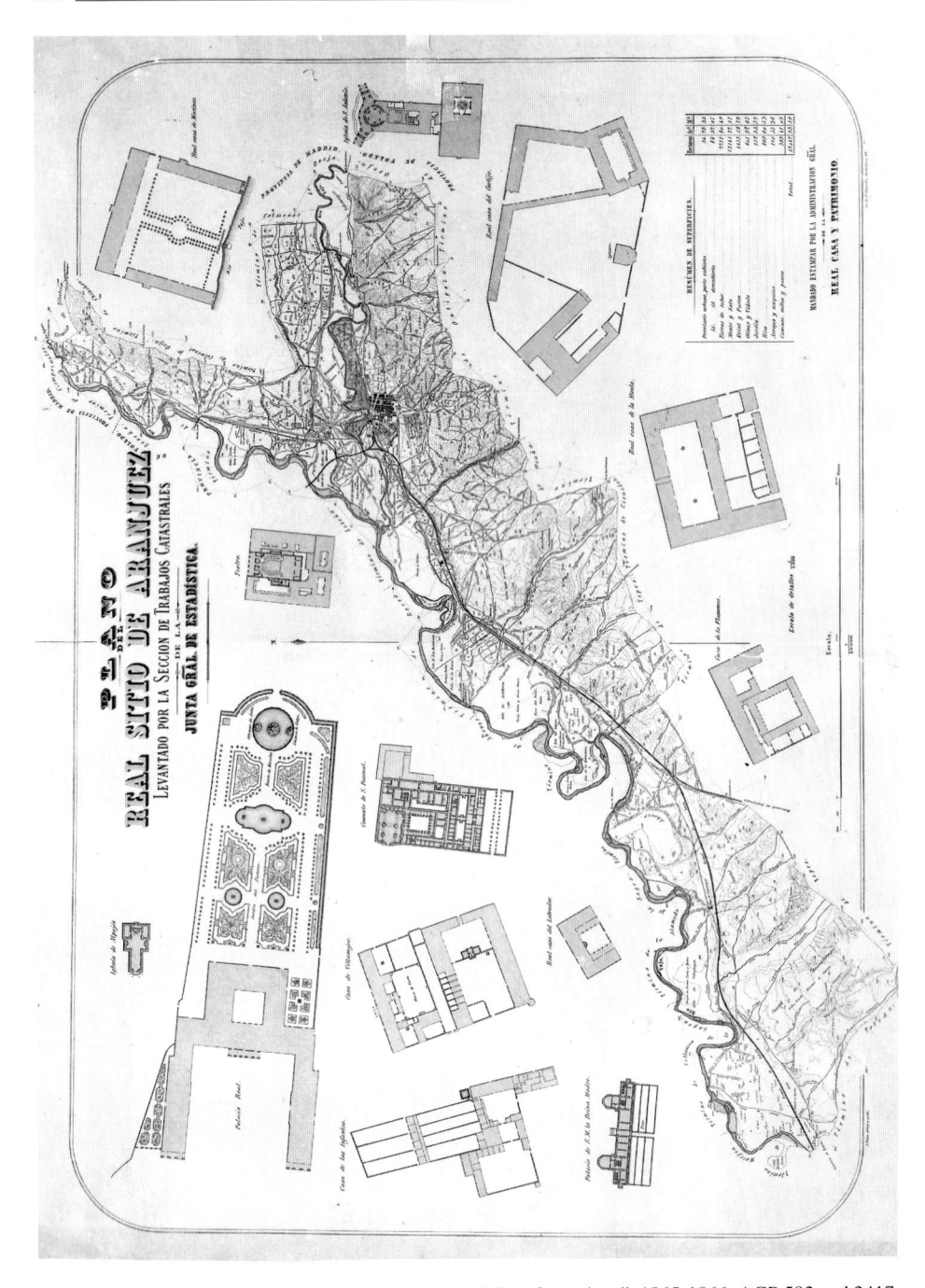

Figure 4. Junta general estadística; "Maps of the royal site of Aranjuez". 1865-1866. AGP 592 and 2417.

But this happened not only because Aranjuez was a holding under the patronage of the Crown or because the court wanted to keep a first-rate hunting ground unchanged. Above all, this has been due to a sustained and conscious effort to create a place of enjoyment and well-being, an earthly paradise where its dwellers may live in happiness.

The landscape of Aranjuez combines some of the most adequate conditions for the habitation of man and development of nature, harmoniously united in an aggregate comprising a town, gardens, farms, groves by the rivers, small lakes and barren lands. The joint action of several physical and historic factors has given the place its definitive aspect.

The great landscape-shaping factors

The water landscape: rivers, channels, dams, fountains

Tagus and Jarama: up until the middle of the present century the riverbeds in Aranjuez were unsteady, on certain occasions they changed their course. Active meanders, periodic floods and changing courses caused the valley to be filled with marshy places, oozes, «madres viejas» (old strangulated meanders), woods and damp grounds. The early history of Aranjuez is the history of an effort to tame and take advantage of the rivers: by keeping them in check, crossing them, containing them, sailing across them. The riverbeds were filled with dams, dikes, «embocadores» (sluiced mouth of streams), bridges, all of them setting an unprecedented and pioneering example of hydraulic engineering.

The rivers regulated life in Aranjuez along a winding course of luxuriant vegetation.

Irrigation: the rivers led to the development of a complex irrigation system, which had obvious Arab and medieval influences, later improved by Renaissance engineers. This system consisted of a thick network of irrigation canals and ditches, impelled by Philip II's European dream: transplanting a stretch of land from Flanders or Italy to Castile in order to irrigate the fertile lands of the valley.

The main channels skirt the boundaries of the valley: outside, steep hills and barren land; inside, orchards and vegetable gardens.

The channels give the true limits of the Aranjuez landscape, showing the clear-cut difference between dry and irrigation farming.

Water as recreation and ornament: the symbolic value of water – a source of life and happiness – also reigns over the whole environment of Aranjuez. The river is an ideal setting for festivities and celebrations. The water draining from the hills into reservoirs – locally nicknamed «seas» – is used to feed the ornamental lakes and fountains in the gardens.

In the past there were shipyards, fleets and sailors in Aranjuez. Statues representing rivers, Hercules columns, Narcissus and Neptune fountains... everything celebrating water as being the mythical and physical origin of landscape.

A green landscape: modification and conservation of a biological wealth

The region and its soil: the Aranjuez valley (the so-called «vega») is an extensive, flat tract of land hemmed in by hills made of Tertiary detritus. The hills, descending in steep slopes constitute a landscape of thyme and esparto fields covering loamy and chalky soils. Some remains of Mediterranean vegetation can still be found, such as holm oaks, kermes oaks, broom, etc. In certain parts, the abundant salt favours the growing of halophyte plants of great ecological value.

Figure 5. The Prince Garden: "Apollo Fountain".

In the valley itself, the soil has plenty of organic matter: thick woods can be found along the rivers. Intensive farming can be carried out, thanks to fertile soils and abundance of water.

The agricultural landscape, vegetable gardens: the market-gardening tradition shapes the flat horizons of the fertile valley. The nearby influence of Mediterranean irrigation farming maps the parallel furrowed plots and patches of fruit trees.

Irrigation farming in Aranjuez dates back to Roman and Visigothic times, as shown by important archaeological remains and numerous records from the late Middle Ages, before the Crown took an interest in the place.

The Kings discarded «common vegetables» and promoted the growth of «worthy and royal» crops. The whole irrigated plain was scattered with exemplary farms in which experiments on agricultural and livestock products, inspired by distant Flemish, Swiss, Valencian models, took place. Remarkable arable lands and farms spread across the landscape, organizing and classifying the lands.

Aranjuez gave its name to exquisite fruits: strawberries, asparagus, plums, juicy pears. There existed a bird-breeding farm, a cow-raising farm and, above all, a Royal Herd of Horses, of paramount importance for the raising of the Spanish horse race.

The gardens, a delectable landscape: under the shelter of the river Tagus arose a complex and harmonious summary of the history of Spanish landscape: Renaissance gardens, with a cosy Arab flavour; baroque, classicist in the French style; «Anglo-Chinese», with a slight English influence; nineteenth-century, urban and bourgeois gardens...

Gardens that spread out into orchards and groves, vegetable gardens that once were landscape gardens. The traces of every century, of every king and queen strolling around have remained in them. Trees and shrubs transplanted from all four corners of the old Spanish empire, acclimated, crossbred, have at times returned to their former wild condition.

Aranjuez, is a place always felt and lived in as having a happy and quiet atmosphere, opposed to bustling and official Madrid, to solemn and transcendent El Escorial, to military and ecclesiastical Toledo.

Survival of the natural environment: the gardens contrast with the groves grown by the rivers; the vegetable gardens contrast with the higher barren lands and chalky soils with a few kermes oak groves. Aranjuez has preserved, in a rather miraculous way, untouched areas with indigenous flora and fauna. Longitudinal gallery-forming woods on inaccessible banks of the Tagus; steep ravines where important endemisms grow, such as the "pítano" *(Vella pseudocytisus)* or the thyme native to Aranjuez. One of the best hunting grounds for lepidoptera in Europe: the «Regajal» may also be found here. At times even human ingenuity can be replaced by nature in the course of time: old plantations of holm oaks turn into wild pastures; reservoirs that were built with ashlar stones revert to marshy grounds and reedbeds in which migratory birds spend the night.

In Aranjuez the bounds between the hand of man and the hand of time become blurred.

The constructed landscape: roads, architecture, town

The capital cities and the great communications axes: Aranjuez has always been at crossroads. Toledo, as the head of the first Spanish kingdom, and later Madrid, as the capital city of modern Spain, were centres from which roadways, highways, railway lines started. Halfway between both of them, Aranjuez is astride the great transversal axis, the river Tagus, astride the transhumant routes of cattle tracks, the main road going across from south and east to the centre of the nation and the earliest railway lines. Roads and railways helped to develop agriculture and industry, but also to impair landscape and historical heritage. Today again they are both essential factors for a future likely to be based on tourism and cultural activities.

Present-day Aranjuez arises from the crossing of rivers and roads. The efforts for its conservation must take into account its most valuable asset: its nearness to both national and international communications and decision-making centres.

The town against the landscape: the eighteenth-century «New Town» was built opposite the river and the palace, surrounded by tree-lined avenues, as a constructed garden in which the buildings would serve as parterres. Houses stood on the sides of wide streets and spacious squares, with architectural façades serving as frames to decorate the large vegetational volumes.

Radial and reticulate patterns, perpendicular axes, cupolas and arcades appear to be superimposed against a background of woods and gardens. The blocks of houses stand severe and discreet, identical to themselves and aware of their modesty compared with the greeness of the nearby vegetal kingdom.

Today the town, free from the former traffic which burdened its daily life, is regaining its spacious, tidy and calm areas, and along with them its welcoming and peaceful mood.

Landscape and geometry

The layouts of wooded areas as integrating elements of the territory: the rectilinear tree-lined streets, arranged in complex geometric patterns, superimposed on whimsical river courses and on the irregular imprint of the ways, constitute the true law in force in the «cultural landscape» of Aranjuez; the tools of successive generations of kings and queens, architects, gardeners, farmers, who created the wonder of present-day Aranjuez.

Vegetable and landscape gardens, palaces and bridges were the reason for creating a juxtaposed series of streets characterized by their respective tree species of great variety. They combined the practical need for communication with the purely aesthetic satisfaction and also with deeply symbolic, political, even magic meanings.

The town incorporated its new streets into the rural layouts; tree-lined avenues of gardens went through the urban areas, and town streets extended into roads, bridges and fan-shaped wooded places.

The new farms created, in turn, their own geometrically patterned areas, with layouts that finally were integrated into a single whole.

For five hundred years the logic of the layouts was enriched until attaining completion, until characterizing by itself a singular, unmatched landscape in the middle of the Castilian tableland.

This ability to integrate, by means of the universal gesture afforded by the tree-lined street, natural elements with artificial ones, water and vegetation with architecture, is perhaps the best lesson that the Aranjuez landscape may offer to our modern inexperienced eyes.

Laws applicable to natural areas in Aranjuez

General Laws

1. Decreto 3 de Noviembre 78. Vías pecuarias. (Aplicable a Colada del Regajal)
2. Convento de Berna C.E.E. 1979. Aplicable a la protección de avutardas y otras aves de nuestro término.

3. Ley 13/1985 de 25 de Junio del Patrimonio Histórico Español: aplicable a entorno jardines, sotos y huertas históricas.
4. Ley 4/1989 de 27 de Marzo de Conservación de los Espacios Naturales y de la Fauna y Flora silvestres. Protege especies y hábitats a nivel nacional.
5. Ley 2/1991 para la Protección y Regulación de la Fauna y Flora silvestres en la C.A.M. Protege especies y hábitats.
6. Ley 10/1991 de 4 de Abril para la Protección del Medio Ambiente de la Conserjería y Presidencia de la C.A.M. Aplicable a cualquier actividad en zonas naturales.
7. Decreto 18/92 de 26 de Marzo por el que se aprueba el Catálogo Regional de especies amenazadas de fauna y flora silvestres y se crea la categoría de árboles singulares (Incluye en su anexo lepidópteros presentes en el Regajal, aves y flora presentes en nuestro término: sapina, pítano, martinete, etc.

Specific Laws

1. Zonas de Especial Protección para las Aves/(ZEPAS) Directiva (79/409/CEE) 1.979. Red de ZEPAS Comunitaria: Carrizales y Sotos de Aranjuez.
2. Plan General de Ordenación Urbana de Aranjuez. 1981. Define suelo no urbanizable protegido y cataloga elementos de importancia histórica y artística.
3. Plan Especial del Casco Antigüo. 1981.
4. Declaración de Conjunto Histórico-Artístico. 1983.
5. Ley 16/85 de 25 de Junio de Patrimonio Histórico Español R.D. 111/86 de 10 de Enero de Desarrollo Parcial de la Ley de Patrimonio Histórico, y Resolución de la D.G. de Patrimonio Cultural para la incoación de expediente de Declaración de Bienes de Interés Cultural a favor de la Zona de Protección Arqueológica de Aranjuez (Madrid) zonas de protección I, II y III inscrito con el código A-R-I-55_241.
6. Carta municipal de Medio Ambiente de Aranjuez. Mayo 1987.
7. Ley 7/1990 de 28 de Junio de Protección de Embalses y Zonas húmedas de la CAM (BOCM 17-7-90). Humedales de Aranjuez.
8. Decreto 72/90 de 19 de Julio de la Conserjería de la Presidencia por el que se establece un régimen de protección preventiva para el espacio natural El Regajal-Mar de Ontígola en término municipal de Aranjuez (BOCAM n° 174 de 24-7-90) en base a la Ley 4/89 de 27 de Marzo de Conservación de los Espacios Naturales y de la Flora y Fauna Silvestres (BOCM 5-3-91). Actualmente se encuentra en tramitación la aprobación del Plan de Ordenación de los Recursos Naturales de la Reserva Natural El Regajal-Mar de Ontígola.
9. Propuesta de creación de un Parque Regional en torno a los ejes de los ríos Manzanares y Jarama. A.M.A. Julio 1990. (Pendiente de aprobación, incluirá parte del término de Aranjuez).
10. Decreto 21/91 de 21 de Marzo por el que se declara reserva natural El Carrizal de Villamejor en término municipal de Aranjuez (BOCM n° 78 de 3 de Abril de 1.991).
11. Decreto 18/92 de 26 de Marzo (BOCAM n° 85 de 6 de Abril) por el que se aprueba el Catálogo Regional de especies amenazadas de fauna y flora silvestres y se crea la categoría de árboles singulares. (20 ud en término de Aranjuez), en base a la Ley 2/91 de 14 de Febrero para la protección y regulación de la fauna y flora silvestre (BOCM 5-3-91).

12. Decreto 55/93 de 20 de Mayo por el que se aprueba el Plan de Ordenación de los Recursos Naturales de la Reserva Natural El Carrizal de Villamejor (BOCM nº 135 de 9 de Junio 1.993).

References

AAVV. *Plaza de San Antonio*. Arte, Historia, Ciudad.
Album-Guía del Real Sitio de Aranjuez. Edición facsímil de 1902.
Alvarez de Quindós, Juan Antonio. *Descripción histórica del Real Bosque y Casa de Aranjuez*. Edición Facsímil de 1804.
Arroniz, C. (1945). *El cultivo de la fresa en Aranjuez. El cultivo del espárrago en Aranjuez*. Ministerio de Agricultura, hojas divulgadoras, Madrid.
Blanco Castro, E. (1989). *«Areas y enclaves de interés botánico en España (flora silvestre y vegetación)»*. Ecología. Nº 3, pp. 7-21
Carmena y Ruiz, F. (1912). *Los espárragos. Su cultivo y explotación. Sistemas de Aranjuez y de Gressent*. Málaga, 1912.
Carrera, S. Mª C. (1980). *Estudio geográfico de Aranjuez y su área de influencia*. Tesis doctoral, Universidad Complutense, Madrid.
Chaves, T. y Pedraza, F. *La gloria de Niquea. Una invención en la corte de Felipe IV*.
COPLACO (1992). *Aranjuez, Plan especial de reforma del interior del casco*. Ministerio de Obras Públicas y Urbanismo. Madrid. Tomo I: 144 pp. Tomo II: 7 planos.
COPLACO (1982). *Aranjuez: Plan general de ordenación, revisión y adaptación*. MOPU Madrid. Tomo I: 195 pp. Tomo II: 11 planos.
Cámara Oficial de Comercio e Industria (1985). *Aranjuez: Análisis socioeconómico*. Madrid.
Díaz Gallegos, C. (1986). *«El Real Sitio de Aranjuez, ejemplo de urbanismo barroco en España: sus calles y plazas»*, en Reales Sitios. Nº 87, XXIII pp. 29-36.
Fundación Puente Barcas. *Claves de la realidad socioeconómica de Aranjuez*.
Gómez Campo, C. y al. (1987). *El libro rojo de las especies vegetales amenazadas de España. Península e Islas Baleares*. ICONTA. Madrid.
López y Malta, C. (1868). *Historia descriptiva del Real Sitio de Aranjuez, escrita en 1868 por ....., sobre lo que escribió en 1804 D. Juan Alvarez de Quindós*.
Martí Gilabert, F. (1972). *El motín de Aranjuez*. Universidad de Navarra CSIC, Pamplona.
Menéndez-Amor, J. *«Un endemismo español»*. El monitor de la farmacia y de la terapeútica. Nº 1.327, 20 de Septiembre de 1943.
Ordenanzas para el gobierno del Real Sitio de Aranjuez. Edición facsímil de 1795.
Ortiz Córdoba, A. *Aldea, Sitio, Pueblo: Aranjuez 1750-1841*.
Romero Aguirre, M. y Escario Ubarri, J. L. (1955). *Análisis de Aranjuez*. Instituto de Estudios de Administración Local. Seminario de Urbanismo Gráf. Uguina, Madrid. 62 pp + lams. I-XXIII.
Sancho Gaspar, J. L. y Martínez-Atienza Rodrigo, J. *Cartografía histórica de Aranjuez: cinco siglos de ordenación del territorio*.
Terán, M. de (1949): *«Huertas y jardines de Aranjuez»*, en Revista de la Biblioteca, Archivo y Museo Municipales, XVIII, nº 58, págs. 261-296.
Viñas, S. (1890). *Aranjuez*.

Carmen Añon Feliu is a Garden Historian and works for the Royal Gardens in Madrid.

Chapter 26

Cultural Landscapes in France

Alain Megret and Gérard Collin

Introduction

When today's traveller or tourist visits a country it is surely to discover the richness of its history, its monuments and its palaces or for the quality and the renown of its wide open natural spaces, but in fact the images that he will retain and that he will try to memorize will not necessarily be those sites of a strict cultural or natural nature, but something more diffuse, wider, more subjective: in fact to travel through Tuscany, Bourgogne, or the English countryside, is to find oneself in universally known and renowned landscapes. One comes "to see" these landscapes, to penetrate them, without having the feeling that they were man-made, or else accepting that man "built" them, but with the intuitive idea that they have to be alive for the pleasure of all those who pass through. That's the paradox of man-made cultural landscapes: one would wish them to be unchanged whereas for the most part they evolve with time, changing economies, the new tastes of contemporary mankind.

Awareness of the intrinsic value of landscapes has become more sensitive due to the upheavals caused by modern economic society. This is particularly the case for landscape structures that live along side the activity of the agricultural world.

It has now become necessary to accept on an international level the obligation to preserve the landscape structures of exceptional universal value.

Due to remarkable progress made by UNESCO and the World Heritage Convention, the notion of cultural heritage has been widened to include the concept of cultural landscapes (see Chapters 1-3 in this volume).

The diversity of French landscapes (Mediterranean, Atlantic, mountains, wide plains, vineyards, etc...) necessitates a choice in the tentative list of cultural landscapes of properties to be proposed for consideration to the organs of the Convention.

Of course, in the light of the Operational Guidelines and the types of cultural landscapes outlined in the framework of the Convention, it is most easy to identify clearly defined landscapes, internationally created by man (e.g. grand castle gardens). But the most interesting and most difficult will be to define the so-called organically evolved landscape.

In fact, in the case of other cultural properties such as historical cities, there is an interaction between the cultural landscape and contemporary human economic activities, but the links are even more marked in the case of cultural landscapes: a historical city can "live" alongside the modern city, but in the case of cultural landscapes, man lives and cultivates within the landscape and he works, consciously or not, for the maintenance and preservation of the cultural landscape.

Consequently, it is the kind of management as a tool for preservation that should be valued more than the material and aesthetic criteria as outlined in the Operational Guidelines:
- man always works on cultural landscapes to ensure the authenticity (perpetuity) of their character or distinctive components;
- this does not imply juridical protection for historical monuments or national parks inscribed on the World Heritage List, but a type of management, traditional or revised (touristic activity) which lives alongside the landscape shaped by man over the centuries.

The continuation of human activity is one of the conditions of perpetuity of the principal types of cultural landscapes: but how can the designation and protection of sites be ensured?

The Protection of Organically Evolved Landscapes

The contractual aspect should be emphasized and sought in order to afford protection to evolved landscapes, e.g.:
- establishment of a contract, protocol, or practice to maintain economic activity such as vineyards, breeding, salt works, navigation activities;
- the economic contract will becomes a moral one (that is, the obligation to ensure the preservation of landscapes) as soon as the property is inscribed on the World Heritage List.

But as with all human activity, it is only a temporary contract, renewable, evolving, with a follow-up of objectives, a contract to be reconciled with the principle of a everlasting designation in the framework of World Heritage. Hence, the difficulty to find elements enabling the appreciation at the national level as well as at the level of the Convention itself.

The decisions of the World Heritage Committee are going to lead, much more than with cultural or natural properties, to the definition of a new approach to the protection of properties, the contractual approach, already developed in France in the past few years with regard to natural areas and landscapes.

In order to ensure the designation of landscapes, support from the population is needed. Designation cannot be achieved without the total adhesion of the economic actors who are "responsible" in a certain manner for the perpetuity of the landscapes.

Public awareness must taken into account: the landscape "is enjoyed on a daily basis", and consequently the almost daily appreciation of the landscape by the populations is a motivating factor in the concern for the conservation and protection of these landscapes.

Therefore, the establishment of a tentative list of cultural properties including cultural landscapes, should not be a nonsensical and clandestine action: it necessitates a concerted effort.

Apart from the cultural and natural properties already declared as World Heritage, France disposes of a rich and wide diversity in terms of landscapes. So, how to go about making a choice in accordance with the Operational Guidelines of the Convention with a view to an inscription on the tentative list of French cultural landscapes? First of all, the following elements must be considered:

- the exceptional universal value;
- the degree of perreniality (authenticity) more difficult to identify in the case of living landscapes (see von Droste, in this volume);
- the spiritual and aesthetic value of which the appreciation can differ according to individuals;
- the economic value (see Fowler and Jacques, in this volume).

With regard to choice, it is necessary to question the representativity of the types of landscape in terms of geocultural regions: in Germany there are also noteworthy vineyard landscapes, and equivalence or complementarity will have to be identified with the French vineyards which might be some day inscribed in the World Heritage List.

In certain cases, the capacity to maintain the economic activities effecting the perenniality of the cultural landscape will also have to be considered.

Finally, if citizens or foreign tourists are questioned in a sort of "referendum on the choice of sites", it is almost certain that preference will be given to living cultural landscapes (it is the first lived-in impression that gives value to the cultural landscapes) or to more specific sites, not always in line with the idea of World Heritage, that tourists return to visit each year.

According to the above criteria, we believe that the choice of significant French landscapes should be made in such a way that they may be managed globally. World Heritage designation provides just such an opportunity: thus, if the Midi Canal is proposed, its length, diversity (and at the same time the fact that being a canal gives it unity) countryside covered, necessitates an overall management of the site between the Atlantic and the Mediterranean, a challenge, taking into account all the administrations and economic actors susceptible "to intervene" on the canal. And it is exactly the aspect of "challenge" that will partly guide the choice.

Examples for a tentative list of cultural landscapes

First of all there will be an initial list of indisputable sites:
- the *Cevennes and the Larzac National Park*
- the *Camargue and Crau, associated with the Town of Arles*, already designated cultural heritage. It is unnecessary to further develop the interest this very well known site holds on an international level. A natural area of high biological richness (natural reserve with lakes) a landscape in which the economic development takes into account the conservation of the area and the natural surroundings (the natural regional Park of the Camargue) cultural areas of great importance (Arles, Aigues Mortes) and finally the Crau, the last stony Mediterranean steppe, an area also rich in biological resources and a superb landscape marvelously modelled by traditional human activities such as sheep farming and hay production. The preparation of this dossier constitutes an absorbing exercise (more than 100,000 ha) especially from the perspective of the management of the landscape.
- the *Forest of the Fontainbleau Massif*
- the *Salt Marshes of Guerande* where, around the fortified town of Guerande is one of the last examples of the traditional exploitation of salt, at least in western Europe.

The French vineyards have shaped our countryside and it is a universally renowned image of France: but taking into account the number of potential sites, the choice is first and foremost as follows:

– the *Champagne*
– a *vineyard of Bordelais de Saint-Emilion*

But further investigations will be required for two other sites:

– *Bourgogne* (Cotes de Beaune, for example)
– *Alsatian vineyards*

The next sites to be considered are more complex but edifying at the level of exemplary overall management:

– the *Loire Valley* between Tours and Saumur (Royal river and cradle of civilization);
– the *Canal du Midi*, an excellent example of an important lineal area associated with significant transport and communication networks.

Finally, the choice could lie in the overseas departments and territories in agreement with the populations (for example "Gaugin Island" in the Pacific).

To better comprehend these choices, the characteristics of two of these landscape sites are cited below highlighting their originality in particular from the perspective of their structure and their conservation problems once they are inscribed on the World Heritage List.

The descriptions of two cultural landscapes are given further on: the *Cevennes*, and the *Canal du Midi*. The compilation of these descriptions was based on elements provided by the regional environmental offices and the departmental offices of architecture.

The Cevennes and Larzac: Landscapes shaped by man and nature

At the very southernmost part of the French Massif Central, overlooking the Languedoc plains, the Cevennes harbour treasures of space, landscapes and natural sites. Three types of rock (granite, schism and chalk) have in turn formed the panoramas, grandiose and intimate, where generation after generation, the very diversified local cultures have created a living environment and formed their identity.

The Cevennes National Park (created in 1970) and its Biosphere Reserve (recognized by UNESCO in 1985) have undertaken important conservation actions to protect their heritage, be it through the management of the countryside with agriculture, protection of wildlife, scientific research or control of hunting activities.

In this area, strongly influenced by man but with a wide biological diversity, the laws and action of the National Park and the Biosphere Reserve help to reinforce the maintenance and the dialogue between man and nature dating back several thousands of years.

For those who wish to analyze the evolution of the Cevenol landscape, the "scenery" with its internal dynamism has first to be described, then these two points should be combined to an analysis of the socio-economic activity of the Cevennes. The history of the Cevenol landscape is rendered particularly interesting by a very slow evolutive process where the hand of mankind is blurred with that of nature. The chestnut plantation is certainly a most striking example of this ambiguity, but other examples can be found in the history of the Cevenol landscape.

First and foremost, the Cevenol countryside is of a steeply-sloped nature forming the southern part of the Massif Central. The area is deeply marked by numerous rapidly flowing rivers and torrents. These rivers flow in parallel directions and are separated by long straight ridges. The rivers which flow through the principal valleys (Long Valley, French Valley, Borgne Valley) receive many torrents cutting across the ravine-like slopes (deep valleys). However, these are only sloping rockfaces and loose broken stones because the Cevennes are essentially composed of schist which splits easily.

The Cevennes form part of the Mediterranean climate but whilst constituting one of the northern points, they integrate other more temperate climatic elements. Despite the altitude, the mountain can experience summers almost as hot as those of the Languedoc plains and mild winters (very few days of frost). Rainfall is characterized by an important summer drought often followed by torrential rains at the beginning of autumn. The irregularity of the rainfall matches their violence. These characteristics have of course fundamental effects on the evolution of the relief, the volume of the rivers, the vegetation and the socio-economic development.

The great difference in altitude (150 to 1,700 m) and the various exposures (the slopes always more "Mediterranean") have led to a great variety of vegetation. At the altitude of 150-500 m, evergreen and holly oaks grow in the form of low-level brushwood, dominated by white heather growth. It is at this level that the Cevenole people have chosen to cultivate olives, mulberries and grapevines. The chestnut tree level (400-800 m) is marked by an abundance of breadfruit trees, occasionally with the common oak, the chestnut oak and the durmast oak that man has little by little eliminated in favour of a more economically rewarding species (chestnut). The beech tree level (800-1500 m) comprises, other than beech, Norway pine, birch and silver fir. Its surface has been reduced on the inner borders by the encroachment of chestnuts, favoured by man, and on its higher limits by the extension of grazing land and commonage. The subalpine level (1500-1700 m) only concerns the summits of the high mountain masses in the Cevennes (Aigoual, Mont Lozere) and is mostly heathland of a diversified nature and or grassland. The heath landscapes have a tendency to become less accessible due to an important decrease in pastoral life. Encroachment by various tree species is already noticeable (birch, mountain ash, pine).

In a country with a difficult relief and climate, complex because of its exposed slopes and different vegetation levels, it is not simple to manage the arable lands. Only a very small fraction of the Cevennes is cultivable, and only in a very fragmented form (this dispersal is the cause of an equally scattered habitation pattern). In order to create fields, terraces had to be created. These terraces which retain the earth and mankind, were constructed on all the slopes of the mountains and carefully maintained for centuries. Here nature appears to have bowed down to man's will. It is no longer the schist rock that constitutes the mountain but the dry stone wall of schist. It is no longer the vertiginous path of the river which attracts the attention but the horizontal and undulating lines of irrigation channels.

Another consequence for the landscape as well as for daily life: these intense and expansive cultivation works require frequent and diverse moving about. The landscape is therefore marked by an extraordinary local transportation network (steps, culverts, mule tracks...) to which history (Camisards War) and the economic evolution has superimposed or added interregional means of communication.

The Cevennes only appears to have been inhabited by Palaeolithic man episodically (hunting and fruit gathering). Although a formal statement cannot be made with regard to how the land was occupied during Neolithic times, it can be confirmed that this was the first real use of the Cevennes region as a whole. This movement was emphasized during the Chalcolithic period with the first clearing of the forests.

After an important new phase of reclaiming land around the 3rd century AD, it was not until the year 1,000 that a new phase of landscape modification took place. The monastic orders, here the same as elsewhere, but mostly Benedictines (Cendras Abbey), contributed towards a major colonization of the Cevennes. The chestnut, already present in a small way in the region of the Cevennes, was be encouraged (plantations, grafting) at the expense of other species present (especially holly oaks, oak groves). This increase encouraged by successive hot climatic conditions between the 8th and 13th centuries, met with a cold climatic spell during the 14th century which resulted in eliminating the chestnut groves on the higher grounds (where the chestnut had been pushed to its ecological limit) and destroyed the more Mediterranean cultures on the lower levels (vine, olives, figs). This episode displays how the image of a chestnut landscape has been constant throughout the history of the Cevennes, as well as in this geographical region, but over the years, the chestnut space has fluctuated/changed.

The cold episode and the 1348 bubonic plague led to an important depopulation which corresponds to a pause in the progression of the chestnut. Natural cycles then regained the upper hand with the extension of the betel-nut and the pine forests in altitude and of the oak and holly-oak groves on lower slopes. By the end of the 15th Century, with the increase of the population, the chestnut will start spreading again with the conquest of

Figure 1. Saint Emilion (Région Aquitaine) (Photo: J. G. SDA).

forests and the planting of new trees in the existing chestnut plantations. It will also take over ploughed land and vineyards, which shows the importance of the chestnut for the Cevenols. In parallel to the extension of the chestnut, the extension of terraces continues.

A second tree, also the symbol of the Cevenol landscape, will widely develop from the end of the 17th century or the beginning of the 18th century: the mulberry-tree. Present in the mountains for a long time already (perhaps since the 13th century), this tree will benefit from two things: during the winter of 1709 the olive trees froze leaving more space for other species and the royal administration will help during the 18th century by allocating subsidies. By the end of the 18th century, the "classical" Cevennes landscape is in place, the area is completely mapped out, down to the smallest fragments, offering visitors of those days the impression of a "built" mountain where chestnuts, mulberries and terraces predominate.

The maximum extension of the bread-tree and the gold-tree was reached between 1760 and 1820 and so was the maximum increase in population. The balance of the landscape corresponding to a socio-economic equilibrium will be short-lived. The Cevenols will from then on have to search elsewhere in order to complement their income (seasonal migrations) and finally will have to leave the country permanently. From 1845 onwards, the disease of the silk-worm will trigger a decrease in production which will lead to a first partial and momentary withdrawal from the mulberry plantations. The origins of the disease and the way to combat it were discovered around the 1870s and led to a halt in the decrease of the mulberry. This remission will not last for long because of the competition with oriental silks from 1880 onwards. The mulberry-tree will then gradually leave the foreground of the Cevenol countryside.

The surface of the chestnut forest diminished in a way it had not done for quite a few centuries due to the conjugation of many factors. It seems that the land, after a constant use for the same specie, was impoverished. The ink disease spread quickly over the whole of the chestnut forest (1870), leading the owners to cut down and sell the trees for the tannin. The decline in population also contributed to that of the chestnut forest: the tree that man had developed to such an extent required too much up-keep and care in order to be maintained in an area too vast for him.

Nevertheless, at the end of the 19th century, new landscapes were created locally. On the Aigoual, the forest coverage had been ruined by the opening of spaces for grazing and the cutting of trees in order to supply foundries and glass-works. The reforestation undertaken by Fabre led to a change in the aspect of the massif with the introduction of new species adapted to difficult conditions (laricio from Corsica, picea, larch, hook pine-trees) and with the regeneration of the beech-groves. On the abandoned plots closest to the mining basin, the mining companies planted maritime pines to supply wood for the supporting of the mine galleries.

The Cevenol countryside that we see today is directly linked to the one that we have inherited from the end of the 19th century. The degradation of the chestnut forest continues slowly due to a new disease (endothia) and the lack of the up-keeping of the plantations. The growth of pine trees has also continued, naturally or by plantation. Is nature going to take back its rights and make this landscape, marked by the silhouette of mulberries and chestnuts, buttressing on their ancient terraces, disappear? Man nevertheless still plays a part in this landscape, and he can intervene. The catastrophic forest fires show how an abandoned mediterranean landscape is fragile, but that there are ways of making a better use of land which is unoccupied. Experience now shows that with the help of farmers and forest-rangers there could be a new cooperation and implementation of projects in the Cevenol mountain landscape which could lead to a new configuration of the Cevenol countryside. The Cevennes national park, in charge of the conservation, has undertaken a research on possibilities of evolution of the Cevenole chestnut forest, taking into account ecological as well as socio-economical factors.

The story of the Cevennes landscape has not ended as yet. It seems that once again, man and nature are getting ready to write a new episode together.

The Canal du Midi

The "Canal du Midi" was built by Pierre Paul Riquet. It is an example of how the occupation of a vulnerable traditional landscape was to change it irreversibly, but maintaining at the same time an authentic character. King Louis XIV's October 1666 Edict, explains the reasons for building the Canal du Midi : "To join the Ocean Sea and the Mediterranean through a navigation canal, to make commerce flourish, to give the provinces of Languedoc and Guyenne more advantages". All along its itinerary the Canal du Midi has transformed landscapes. It is itself a constituent of the countryside. It was conceived, originally, in a global and precise way, including in its concepts the landscape and the plantations.

The alignment of trees with varied essences has lasted throughout the centuries. There are still more than 100 000 trees from Toulouse to the Thau pond. The nurseries belonging

Figure 2. Canal du Midi (Photo: Ministry for the Environment, Paris).

to the Canal covered 17 hectares. Dispersed on both sides of the canal, the trees produce varied optical effects, either like a road bordered by trees, or like a tunnel, a roof, a vault of greenery. Sometimes the countryside and the sky disappear, are isolated or meet in continuity.

When looking through this greenery, one can set eyes on isolated farms or picturesque villages languishing in the sun, of which some of the have been in direct contact with the Canal. The interruption of the rows of trees suddenly leads to discover the whole of the countryside, medieval cities, towns with a prestigious name and past.

The Canal du Midi has often been compared to a garden. De Lalande wrote in 1778: "It is a continuous garden where you can admire the rows of trees and the hydraulic architecture. Some of areas remind us of the "Grand Canal" at Versailles: water running down, rows of trees, foot-bridges, stairs, bridges over locks, ornamental lakes and ponds in steps ; these arrangements remind us those of the classical French gardens."

The Canal is an example of the occupation of a traditional territory, a remarkable economic tool. The initial vocation of the Canal du Midi was the transport of merchandise, at first cereals. The second vocation of the Canal has been and still is the irrigation of agricultural land. The Canal's newest vocation is touristic activity, which has been in constant development for the last ten years and requires a good maintenance of the Canal.

The Canal represents culture in two ways. The first is through workmanship such as bridges, aqueducts, locks and other everyday constructions for eating, resting and working. The second is through the family; the Canal du Midi brings together a big family, the "people of the water", a closed world attached to secular traditions.

Conclusion

France is a country with a rich diversity of cultural landscapes.

The project of the revision of the tentative list by France including cultural landscapes is quite advanced. The example of the Canal du Midi was presented to the expert meeting on Heritage Canals in September 1994 in Canada and the nomination of the Canal is under preparation. Other cultural landscapes in France mentioned in this contribution have to be carefully considered, both at the national level and in comparison with other sites to meet the criteria of outstanding universal values. As indicated, most important is the management of these complex sites and the involvement of the local population.

References

UNESCO (1995). *Operational Guidelines for the Implementation of the World Heritage Convention.* Paris.

Gramont, A., *Managing rural landscapes; from a free by-product to a paid commodity*, Paysage et Aménagement, No 21, octobre 1992.

Numero spécial *"Droit et paysage"*, Paysage et Aménagement, No 24, juillet 1993.

Loi No 93-24 du 8 janvier 1993 sur la protection et la mise en valeur des paysages, Journal officiel de la République Francaise, 9 janvier 1993, pp. 503-505.

Alain Megret and **Gérard Collin** are working in the Landscape and Nature Division of the French Ministry for the Environment, Paris.

Chapter 27

Slovenian Cultural Landscapes and the Triglav National Park

Jelka Habjan and Vesna Kolar-Planinšič

Characteristics of Slovenian landscapes

Slovenia is a small country with the area of 20,256 km² and a population of about two million. Yet it has, for the most part, a mosaic-like structure of small-scale landscape patterns, which have been formed over the centuries as a result of a number of natural and human factors.

The diversity of nature and landscape may be attributed primarily to the inextricable link between the four major biogeographic systems, the Alps, the Dinarides, the Mediterranean, and the Pannonian plain, and particularly to the tectonic and lithologic stratum (Strategija 1994) and to the relief, which descends from the 2864 m-high-peak of Triglav in the Alps down to the plains of Prekmurje and the Adriatic coast.

Geographical surface and relief

As 53 % of the area is composed of carbonate rocks, which are dissolved by carbon dioxide and water, approximately half of the country has strong karstic features. On account of the percentage of the karst, and the character which karstic features give to the area, and to its inhabitants Slovenia may also be called a karst country. Kras (the Karst) - a rugged area in the surroundings of Trst (Trieste) - aroused interest of researchers long ago, and they started describing its karstic features. Until now, as many as 6,287 caves have been registered in Slovenia (Strategija varstva narave v Sloveniji 1994). In 1986, the Škocjan Caves were included in the UNESCO World Heritage List under natural criteria (ii) and (iii). Karst formations occur not only underground but a number of them are also found above the ground like grooves, karrens, doline, valleys and dry valleys, and polja with periodic lakes, all of which helped to create a typical cultural landscape over the centuries.

Waterways

The major part of Slovenia is a catchment area with mountain streams and torrents, most of which have remained, to a large extent, intact. Diverse vegetation along these waterways makes the landscape most attractive and has a large ecological value. The picturesque scenery is often complemented by watermills and sawmills, due to the former use of water power, which is nowadays replaced with small hydroelectric power plants. Of the bigger rivers in Slovenia at least two have to be mentioned: the Soca and the Mura. The Soca River is one of the five best preserved Alpine rivers in Europe. It is a symbol of the nation and of the country due to its natural features, unique cultural landscape and significant cultural heritage that is of importance for national history. It is part of the Triglav National Park, which is described in the proposal for landscapes of outstanding value in Slovenia. The Mura is a lowland river with wide flood plains as it has been channelized only partly. It thus represents a type of landscape which is rare in Slovenia.

Vegetation

Slovenia may be regarded as a wooded county as over half of its area (51%) is covered by forests (Kmecl 1990). Agricultural land (39%), urbanized areas and infertile land above the forest line constitute the rest of the country land cover. The percentage of forest area is increasing since agricultural land that is not easily accessible tends to become overgrown with shrubs and trees. Of 74 typical forest communities, seven cover more than 50 % of the whole forest area (Kmecl 1990).

The diversity of vegetation is also reflected in the number of plant species in Slovenia, where as many as 3,000 species of higher plants can be found, and the density is of 0.15 species/km^2. Of the 3,000 species, 60 are endemic, compared, for example, to 1,400 species that occur in Denmark, of which only one species is endemic, and the density is of 0.033 species/km^2. The flora of Greece consists of 5,500 species, of which 763 are endemic, and the density is of 0.042 species/km^2 (Strategija varstva narave v Sloveniji 1994).

Development of cultural landscapes: agricultural, forest and urban landscapes

The territory of the present-day Slovenia was settled as early as during the Hallstatt Age. In the latter half of the 6th and 7th centuries the Slavs settled an already cultivated land, which was most appropriate for agriculture already in Roman times. This shows continuity of settlement in the Slovene cultural landscape (Gospodarska in druzbena zgodovina Slovencev, Zgodovina agrarnih panog 1970). Later, settlement was orientated towards higher, mountainous and forested regions, which were deforested so that new arable land was obtained.

The landscape heterogeneity in Slovenia is characterized by forests and agriculture. Agriculture has had an important influence on spatial development since ancient times. The diversity of ecological conditions has made a wide range of produce possible, from Mediterranean fruits and vegetables to vines, cereals, hops and other crops. Grassland and forest play a major role in the appearance of the Slovene landscape. Different species composition of the forest and seasonal dynamic of deciduous trees give the area a very distinctive character. Forest as a symbol of nature and grassland as a symbol of civilization constitute the foundation of the landscape structure (Ogrin 1989), which is complemented by the patchwork pattern of fields, vineyards and orchards. As industrialization started later in Slovenia than elsewhere in Western Europe and the transition from agriculture was not all that forcible, traditional agriculture and small scale farm structure have been preserved until today (Habjan 1992). However, small scale agriculture has largely changed or lost its function, changing into multiple-functional landscapes for recreation, tourism and nature conservation.

As many as some 6,000 urban communities, villages and hamlets, and similar number of isolated farms, castles and churches also characterize the Slovene landscape. The relationship between natural landscapes and urbanized areas ranges from a complete fusion of built-up areas and their natural surroundings to a distinct separation, which is especially true of churches and castles in exposed positions (Ogrin 1989). A study of architectural landscapes, in which Slovenia is divided into 14 regions with 70 architectural landscapes, has been carried out (Fister 1993).

Landscape conservation in Slovene legislation

At present, the planning of natural and cultural heritage protection is based on the 1981 Natural and Cultural Heritage Act, which will be changed shortly. According to this law, the Ministry of Culture is responsible for heritage protection through its administrative institutions like the state and regional institutes for the conservation of natural and cultural heritage. They have responsibilities regarding evaluation of heritage, preparation of conservation and protection laws, coordination with other departments, and professional supervision.

The 1981 Act does not define the terms "cultural landscape" and "heritage landscape". A landscape can be protected within the framework of a regional or landscape park, where its preservation and adequate use are governed by protection regulations. In September 1993, 8% of the whole territory of Slovenia was protected comprising one national park, 29 landscape parks, 34 natural reserves, 720 natural monuments, 77 historic parks and gardens, and 10 cultural and natural monuments (Skoberne 1994).

To preserve the main characteristics of Slovene cultural landscapes, legal protection must be connected with adequate management techniques and an up-to-date approach at national level. Some of the current projects, sponsored by the government, are aimed at establishing a scientific basis for further actions. Examples of such studies are: Landscape Assessment as the Base for Conservation Planning (Kolar-Planinšič 1993), Architectural Landscapes and Regions of Slovenia (Fister 1993) and an overall study of landscape typology in the whole Slovene territory (Ogrin and Marusic 1992 b). The Nature Conservation Unit at the Slovene Institute for the Conservation of Natural and Cultural Heritage has recently designed a nature conservation strategy, which will serve as a base for future policy of nature conservation. One of the main objectives of the strategy is to preserve the logical development of cultural landscapes (Skoberne 1994).

Regionalization of landscape types in Slovenia

The Department of Landscape Architecture of the Ljubljana University has recently conducted a project entitled "Regionalization of landscape types in Slovenia" (Ogrin and Marusic 1992b), which was sponsored by the Ministry of Environment and Physical Planning.

The aims of a typological division of landscapes are twofold:
(1) to identify potential attractions of a landscape for visitors, that is, for recreational activities in an open landscape, and
(2) to identify objects in a cultural landscape that are part of Slovenia's national heritage, and to take steps accordingly in order to set in motion the mechanism for preservation of a landscape, or of individual, most important constituent parts of heritage.

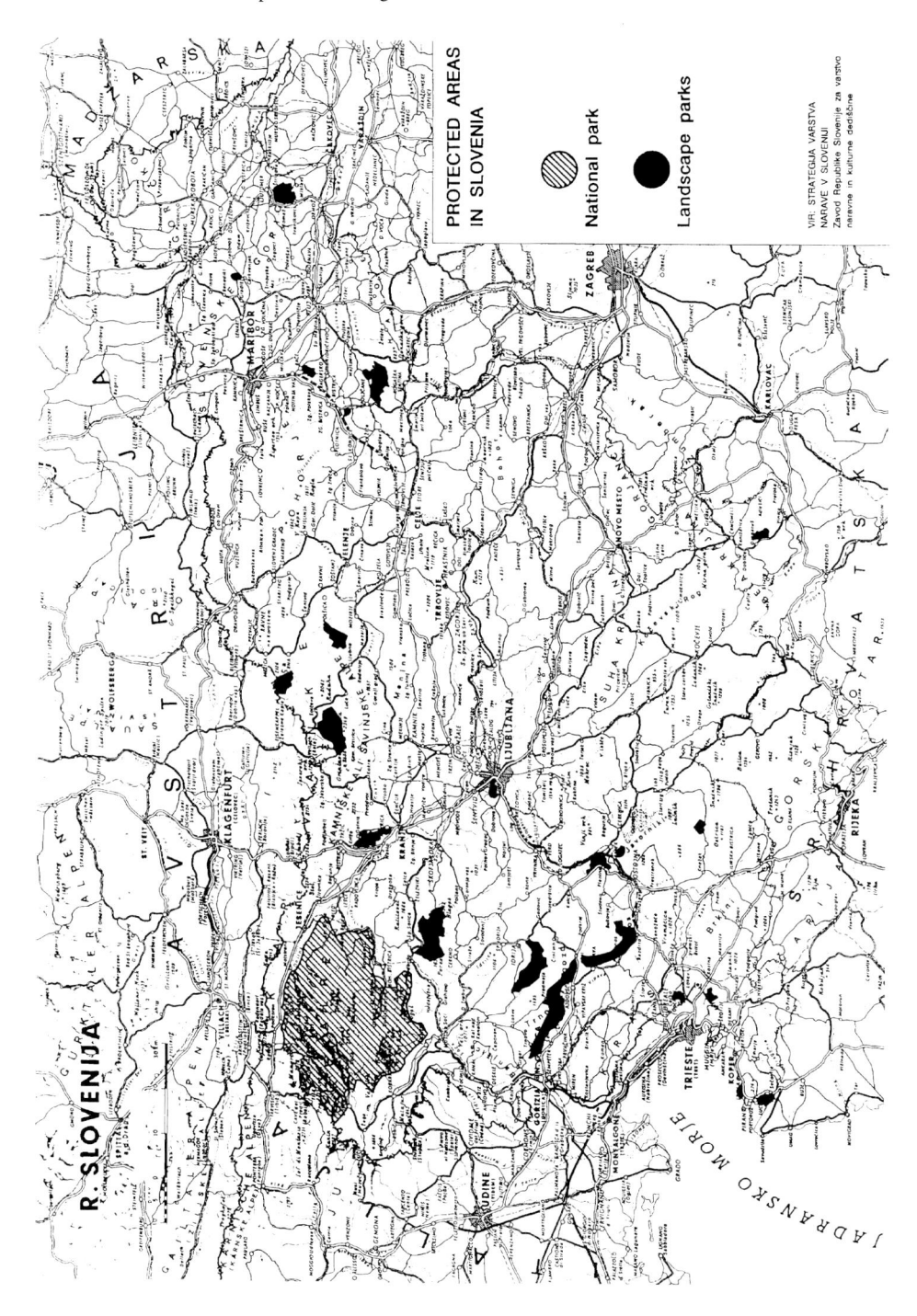

Figure 1: Protected areas in Slovenia.

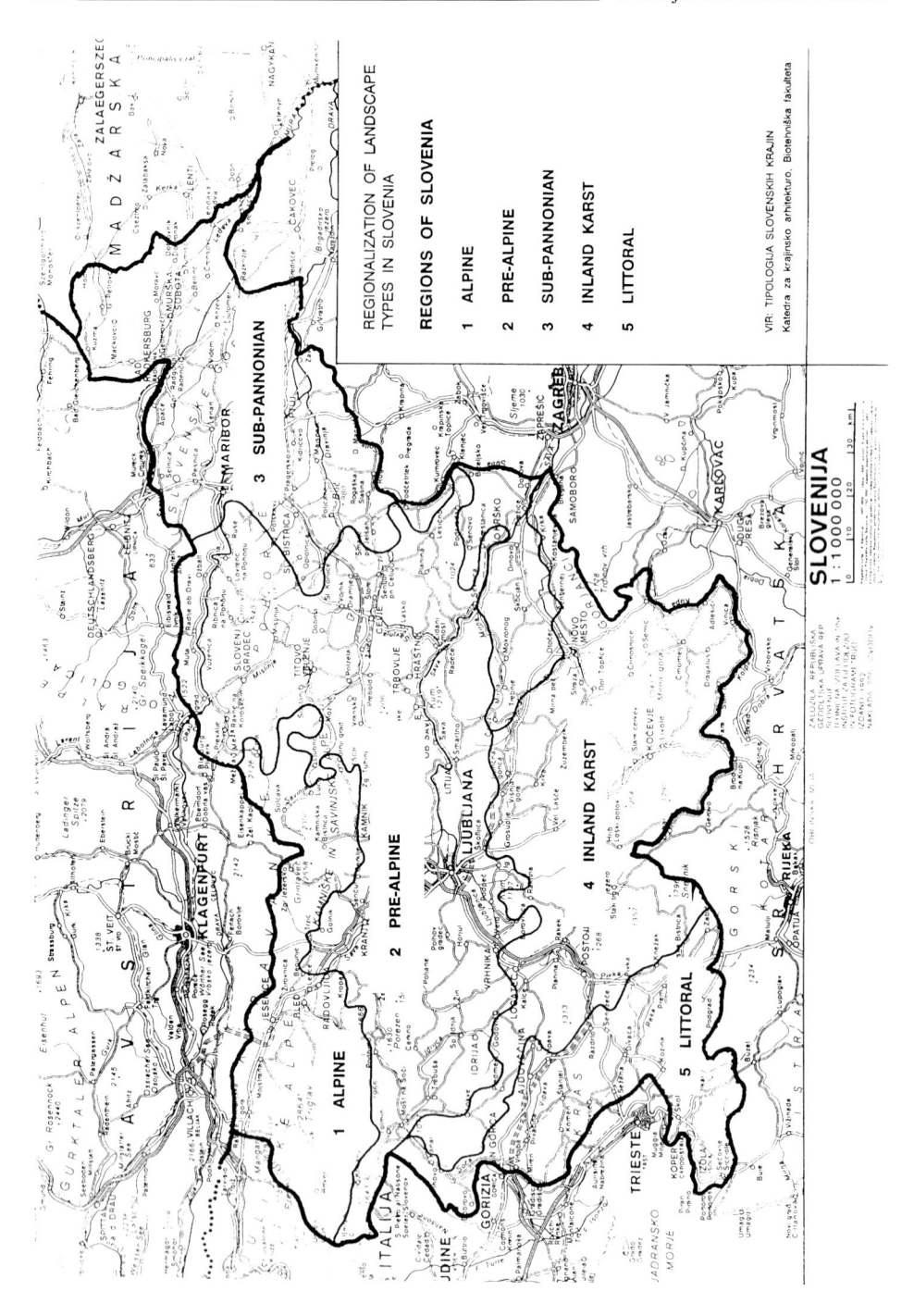

Figure 2: Regionalization of landscape types in Slovenia

These aims form the basis for the following objectives which are:

(1) to determine outstanding landscapes to be protected,
(2) to provide guidelines for recreational activities and for subsidies for the promotion of countryside tourism, and
(3) to determine landscapes in which farming would be modernized according to market forces, as well as landscapes in which traditional farming would be retained with the aid of government subsidies.

Studies on similar issues carried out in other countries were examined. As distinct differences in the relevant source material were established, the authors decided on their own approach to a classification of landscapes, which was supported by expert opinion. Regionalization is based on natural features of Slovenia and climatic conditions. Macro-relief and the character of a landscape are also taken into account. The latter is represented by a landscape pattern which is either typical of a certain spatial unit or gives it its own identity.

The proposal for regionalization of landscape types which uses the scale of 1 : 400,000, comprises 253 landscape units, belonging to the following regions of Slovenia: (1) Alpine, (2) pre-Alpine, (3) sub-Pannonian, (4) inland Karst, (5) littoral.

The following data is given for each landscape unit:
– numerical code and name of the unit,
– name of the region to which it belongs,
– name of the town district to which it belongs,
– selection of patterns representing the landscape unit; the number of patterns is specified in advance but a short description of a pattern should include one or more of the following characteristics:
    (a) typical patterns of the area, or patterns that give the area its own identity,
    (b) prevalent patterns in the area,
    (c) exceptional patterns in the area,
    (d) patterns unique to the area (by a broader comparison),
    (e) patterns which are typologically similar to patterns in other areas,
    (f) patterns with symbolic meaning,
    (g) patterns indicative of changes in the character of a landscape,
    (h) patterns indicative of phenomena or processes of decline,
    (i) patterns indicative of endangerment or vulnerability of a landscape,
    (j) other characteristics.

Description of the unit comprises:
– short description of geographical, natural and man-made features,
– the target-state of the unit,
– a photograph or photographs of patterns.

In the study Slovenia is divided into 253 landscape units, of which the unit of Planinsko polje (Encl. No. 1: Typology of Slovene Landscapes) was selected as an example. The authors of the project described above have suggested further studies. One of them would be aimed at completing the inventory and at defining possibilities for the application of typology in physical planning while the intent of the other would be to select landscapes of outstanding value in Slovenia, map their sites, and evaluate them.

The study of the landscape assessment
for the conservation of the Triglav National Park

Triglav National Park, situated in the middle of the Eastern Julian Alps, takes up 5% of the Slovene territory. It can be divided into two zones: the central zone, which falls into IUCN category 2, and the buffer zone, where cultural landscapes with pastures and forests, mountain huts and sheds are of greater importance. The main features of the park are:
- the Alpine karst with typical karstic features above and below the ground (three caves at a depth of over 1,000 m),
- the U-shaped Upper Soca Valley, which is one of the best preserved riverside landscapes in Europe,
- the Alpine lake Bohinj, surrounded by cultural landscape on glacial deposits,
- a system of pastures on mountain sides with hay huts and cottages,
- villages incorporated in natural surroundings, for example the village of Studor with its interesting hayracks,
- a cultural landscape associated with the First World War, when some battles were fought on the Soca (Isonzo) front in the mountains at over 2000 m. After the war, Ernest Hemingway wrote a story about it with the title "A Farewell to Arms".
- many military cemeteries in the Soca Valley because over 300,000 soldiers died there.

The main aim of the study was to contribute to the development of methodology for the assessment and conservation of landscapes. The methodology of landscape assessment, criteria, techniques and integration into the planning systems on national, regional and local level have been studied in Denmark, Great Britain and USA. After analyzing Slovenian open landscape characteristics, a new method of landscape assessment has been proposed for use in Slovenia (Kolar-Planinšič 1992).

The methodology has been tested on the area of north-western part of the country - the area of Triglav National Park. The method is based on homogeneous landscape units definition, evaluation and conservation interest ranking for each landscape unit. The homogeneous landscape units according to geology, pedological surface, relief, vegetation and habitats have been established, combined into landscape types and each of them evaluated. Next six landscape types have been defined: high mountain plateau, alpine valleys and flat land, lake landscape, slopes with canyons or narrow valleys, high mountain slopes.

Landscape assessment criteria have been studied according to theory and practice and then organized in seven groups as follows:
1. criteria of natural science: geology, geomorphology, biology, zoology, hydrology, entomology, ecology;
2. criteria of cultural history: history, archaeology, art history;
3. criteria of aesthetics: visual, shape, scale, harmony, color, texture, view points, contribution to the surrounding landscape, etc.;
4. association criteria: history, archaeology, culture(presentation in literature, music, painting);
5. relation to other areas: national rarity, typical landscape;
6. scientific potential: nature and culture preserved areas;
7. recreational potential: degree of access, natural purity, visual quality.

A landscape evaluation project was carried out using 18 overlay maps with the scale of 1:50,000. This evaluation will now be used as an assessment for landscape conservation, planning, development proposals and environmental impact assessment.

The areas with the highest values represent cultural landscapes of national importance, in particular lake landscapes and high mountain areas with a great variety of natural and cultural heritage. These landscapes meet the World Heritage Committee criteria for cultural landscapes of outstanding value and could be proposed for the Slovenian tentative List.

Conclusion

The paper deals briefly with characteristics and development of Slovene cultural landscapes and discusses a project on landscape types outlining its concept and a case study for Triglav National Park. Slovenia has in response to the 1993 expert meeting on outstanding cultural landscape prepared a tentative list for the inscription of sites on the World Heritage List. This list includes two cultural landscapes: "The classic Karsts" and the "Fuzina Hills in Bohinj". Slovenia is small country, and therefore its cultural landscapes are comparatively small in scale. However, it is difficult to find such a diversity of landscape types in a small area elsewhere in Europe.

References

Fister, P. (1993). *Arhitekturne krajine in regije Slovenije - Arhitekturna identiteta.*- 245 p; Ljubljana: Ministrstvo za okolje in prostor - Zavod RS za prostorsko planiranje.

Gospodarska in druzbena zgodovina Slovencev, Zgodovina agrarnih panog - 1. zvezek (1970).- 650 p; Ljubljana: Drzavna zalozba Slovenije.

Habjan, J. (1992). *Cultural Landscapes or Heritage Landscapes in Slovenia.* Papers on the agricultural landscapes in Europe.- International colloquium. Council of Europe. Stockholm.- 51-55.

Kmecl, M. (1990). *Slovenija brez gozda? Obup!.*- 73 p; Ljubljana: Institut za gozdno in lesno gospodarstvo.

Kolar-Planinšič, V. (1993). *Landscape Assessment as the Base for the Conservation Planning. A case study of Triglav National Park area.*- 235 p; Ljubljana: University of Ljubljana, Faculty of architecture, civil ingineering and geodesy, IPSPUP, M.Sc. Thesis.

Marusic, I. and Ogrin, D. (1992a). *Regionalna razdelitev krajinskih tipov v Sloveniji - Porocilo o raziskovalni nalogi.*- 34 p; Ljubljana: Katedra za krajinsko arhitekturo - Univerza v Ljubljani.

Marusic, I. and Ogrin, D. (1992b). *Tipologija slovenskih krajin - Raziskovalna naloga.*- 458 p; Ljubljana: Katedra za krajinsko arhitekturo - Univerza v Ljubljani.

Ogrin, D. (1989). *Slovenske krajine.*- 239 p; Ljubljana: Drzavna zalozba Slovenije.

Skoberne, P. and Peterlin, S. (eds.) (1991). *Inventar najpomembnejse naravne dediscine Slovenije* - 2. del: osrednja Slovenija.- 606 p; Ljubljana: Zavod Republike Slovenije za varstvo naravne in kulturne dediscine.

Strategija varstva narave v Sloveniji - Inacica 2.0 (1994).- 35 p; Ljubljana: Zavod Republike Slovenije za varstvo naravne in kulturne dediscine.

Jelka Habjan is a landscape architect at the Ministry of Environment and Physical Planning, Nature Protection Administration, Plecnikov trg 2, Ljubljana, Slovenija.

Vesna Kolar-Planinšič is a landscape architect at the Regional Institute for the Conservation of Natural and Cultural Heritage, Tomšičeva 44, 64000 Kranj, Slovenia.

Chapter 28

Austrian Cultural Landscapes: Methodological Aspects for an Inventory

Hans Peter Jeschke

Introduction

Lately, cultural and ecological factors have been gaining significance and becoming central in designing, developing and planning our environment. But, it is only when we realize that every culture represents an expression of generally accepted values that a dialogue between international, national and regional cultures can be initiated. The dialogue must be founded on mutual acceptance, appreciation, and will then hopefully lead to a better coordination in the preservation of our heritage and its future development.

Even though Austria signed the World Heritage Convention in 1992 only, it played an important part in drafting the text of the Convention. Austria also has a long history in the protection of cultural and natural heritage on both the national and European level.

Geographical overview

Located in the heart of Europe, Austria lies 500m above sea level. The country is subdivided into three major landscape divisions: (a) the Alps, (b) the granite and gneiss highlands, (c) the forelands and basins. 60 percent of the country is alpine and ten percent consists of the granite and gneissic division, a landscape of hills and moderate slopes. The eastern forelands and basins consist of primarily sedimentary rock. The southwestern area is dominated by the Alps, with peaks as high as 3600 m. An oceanic climate prevails in the Alps with a total average annual precipitation of up to 3000 mm. The annual rainfall in the east amounts to only 880 mm. The south is subject to a humid continental climate. Rivers cover a total length of 90'000 km and there are over 9,000 lakes and ponds in Austria. The major rivers include the Danube, which divides the north-east of the country and the March which runs along the Czech Republic and Slovakian borders.

Legislation, preservation and current initiatives concerning cultural heritage and cultural landscapes in Austria

National and regional legislation

In Austria, all matters concerning the preservation of nature are placed under the jurisdiction of each of the nine Länder (provincial governments). The protection and the conservation of monuments and sites (ensembles) comes under federal legislation, but this protection applies only to individual monuments, so the governments of the Länder and of several cities have developed additional legal, financial and planning measures in order to promote the preservation of rural sites and town centres.

International legal framework

Austria is a member of the Council of Europe. As of 1990, eighteen biogenic reserves in Austria have been declared by the Council. In the Land of Salzburg, one of the sites received the European Diploma of the Council of Europe in 1967. Austria has signed and ratified the Berne Convention on the Conservation of European Wildlife and Natural Habitats. It is a party to the Convention on Wetlands, the Ramsar Convention on Waterfowl Habitat (ratified in 1982) and five wetland sites have been registered up to today. Five sites have also been approved as biosphere reserves under the UNESCO Man and Biosphere Programme, which acknowledges the importance of these biogeographical regions. Austria signed the World Heritage Convention in 1992, after paying voluntary contributions into the World Heritage Fund for a number of years.

Environmental Protection, Cultural Landscape Maintenance
and Cultural Heritage Preservation in Austria

In addition to the intensive regional activities carried out by the Länder, the Federal office for the Environment has been assisting the Ministry for Environment, Youth and Family, among other things, in mapping and developing support programmes for the protection of Austria's cultural landscape. Within the framework of a federal programme entitled "Concept for the Preservation of Federal Interest in protecting the Environment", the Ministry for Environment, Youth, and Family is pursuing the following trans-regional activities : creation of national parks, securing and protecting valuable cultural landscapes, translation of international agreements on nature conservation, landscape planning, protection of endangered species and biotopes. It is also important to mention that two provinces (Salzburg and Upper Austria) have already introduced landscape inventories. In addition, concerning cultural heritage, a federal and two provincial monument registries have been created, including in them, a comprehensive cultural heritage register by Upper Austria and an art inventory by Tyrol.

Cultural Landscape Research Programme

The Federal Ministry for Science and Research has initiated a comprehensive cultural landscape research programme entitled "Sustainable Development of Austrian Cultural Landscapes". This research puts an emphasis on standardizing cross-frontier cultural landscape classification employing internationally accepted methods, establishing a set of instruments for defining cultural landscape development models, elaborating methods and sets of measures for model-oriented cultural landscape development, developing integrated monitoring of systems with ecological, economic, social, technological, and political parameters as a precondition for comprehensively controlling changes in the landscape entity under consideration and establishing a European network of cultural landscape research.

The programme aims at harmonizing evaluation systems and developing scientific projects and case studies. Currently, a case study is being carried out on the Upper Austria landscape and its vernacular architecture.

326 — H. P. Jeschke

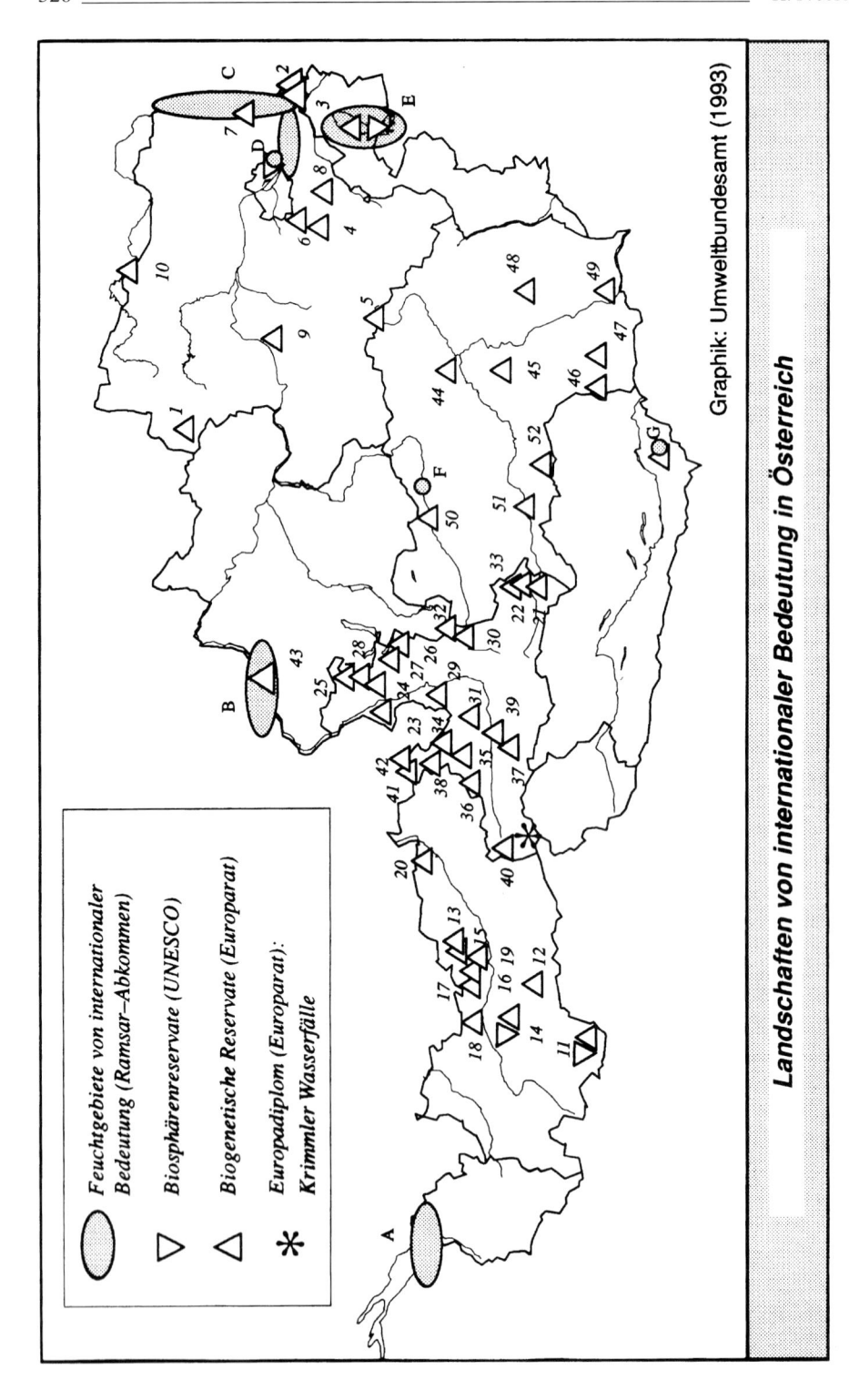

Figure 1. Landscapes of international significance in Austria (Umweltbundesamt 1993).

The Austrian tentative list for Cultural Heritage

Austria submitted in August 1994 a tentative list for cultural sites to be nominated in the future for the World Heritage List[1]. This list includes the following six cultural landscapes:

1) *Semmering Railway* in Lower Austria and Styria: a steep railway over a length of 40 km which is a first-class technological achievement and a innovative work of civil engineering.
2) *Wachau* in Lower Austria: the Wachau valley is a picturesque part of the Danube landscape featuring well-preserved urban and rural ensembles.
3) *Salzkammergut* in Salzburg, Upper Austria and Styria: it is an example of interplay between nature and man-made environment, industrial activities and salt mining are dating back to early times, harmoniously integrated between mountains and lakes.
4) Cultural landscape of *Neusiedler lake and surroundings* in the Burgenland: the Neusiedler lake is a unique formation in central Europe as a flat steppe lake.
5) *Styrian Erzberg and Iron Road* in Styria: the Erzberg region in Styria has been coined in terms of architecture and landscape by its iron mining, smelting and trading activities since the middle-ages.
6) *Bregenz forest* in Vorarlberg: the Bregenz Forest has maintained its traditional farming structure and characteristic wooden buildings.

Results of a Study on the Mapping of Upper Austria's Cultural Landscape

Methodological objectives for the Upper Austrian case study

- *Cultural heritage and regional planning*: In relation to regional planning, landscape planning, and other instruments for maintaining and preserving cultural landscapes, the following aspects have to be considered :
  - A site-oriented planning policy
  - Recognition of the importance of cultural landscapes in both urban and rural areas (see figure 3 and 4)
  - A scale-sensitive framework for planning policies especially for the regional and local levels.
- *Type of inventory categories of the cultural heritage for the local level.*
- *The World Heritage Convention defines three categories of cultural property* : monuments, groups of buildings, and sites (Article 1). These types of cultural properties cannot be seen as isolated, but in many cases within a landscape and as an integral part of it. For maintaining the historical, cultural, art-historical expression of buildings and their environment it is necessary to introduce surrounding zones as an additional category. This has been explained in paragraph 17 of the operational guidelines: "Whenever necessary for the proper conservation of a cultural or natural property nominated an adequate "buffer zone" around a property should be afforded the

---

[2] See tentative list, World Heritage Documentation Centre.

necessary protection." Three zones should be an integral part of areas under preservation and consist of either bob-developed areas such as open spaces, farm land, vineyards or areas with building structures belonging to the original environment.

- *Definition and methods*: In reference on the World Heritage Convention the definition "geo-cultural region" and their "essential distinct elements" was used as a basic point. Out of these definitions, specific method had been developed to identify "cultural landscape units" as "geo-cultural regions" (Fig. 2). These definitions of the comprehensive landscape units were to complete with the description of their specific "identity" (cultural landscape types, cultural landscape elements and the cultural heritage). Results of mapping selected "part resources of the natural environment" ("Naturraumpotentialkartierung") qualified the interaction "mail and nature" in these "geo-cultural regions" of Upper Austria. The cultural landscape-orientated mapping of

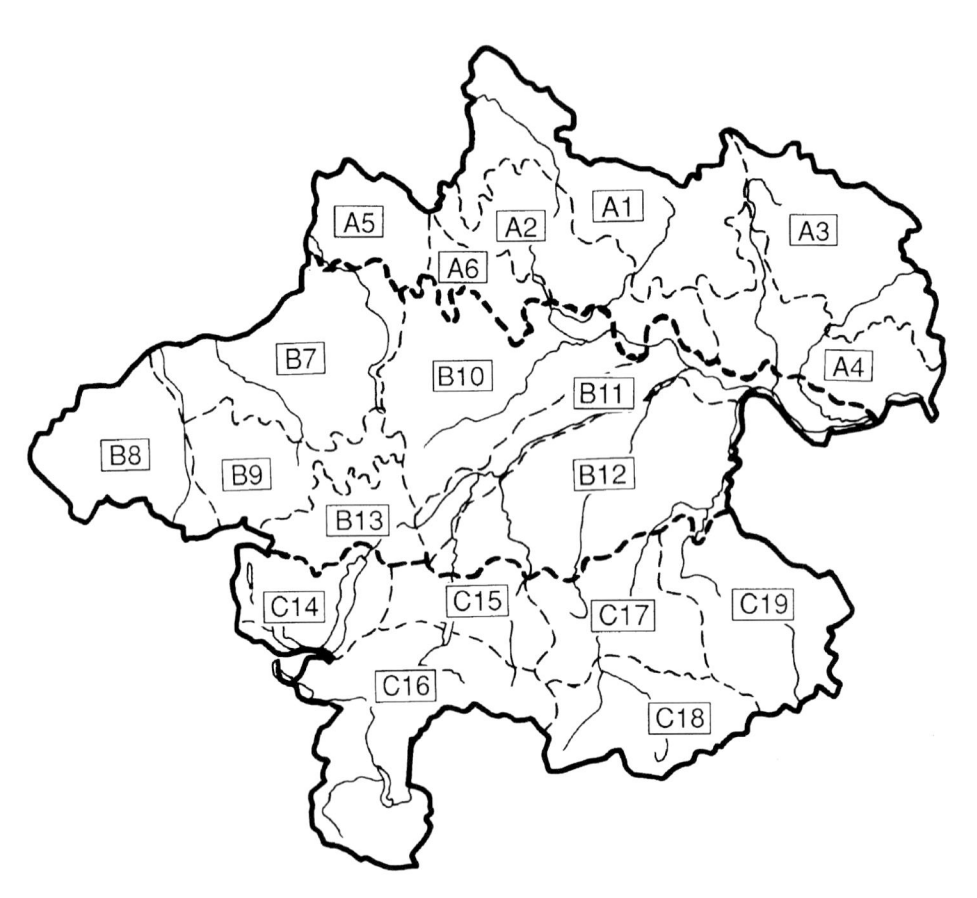

Figure 2. Cultural landscape units in Upper Austria (Maurer 1993): This map covers the geo-cultural landscape units in the context of the cultural landscape regions:
A - Bohemian massif (six cultural landscape units A1-A6)
B - Alpine Forelands (seven landscape units B1-B7)
C - northern Alpine area (six cultural landscape units C1-C6)

rural used as a descriptive element and a criteria of categorizing cultural landscape units on the other hand. The need for a scale - sensitive framework led up to a method for spatial (cultural landscape - oriented) inventorying of the cultural heritage on the local level according international criteria and a comprehensive evaluation system with different criteria (spatial merit, architectural and historical merits, significance) and range of cultural heritage.

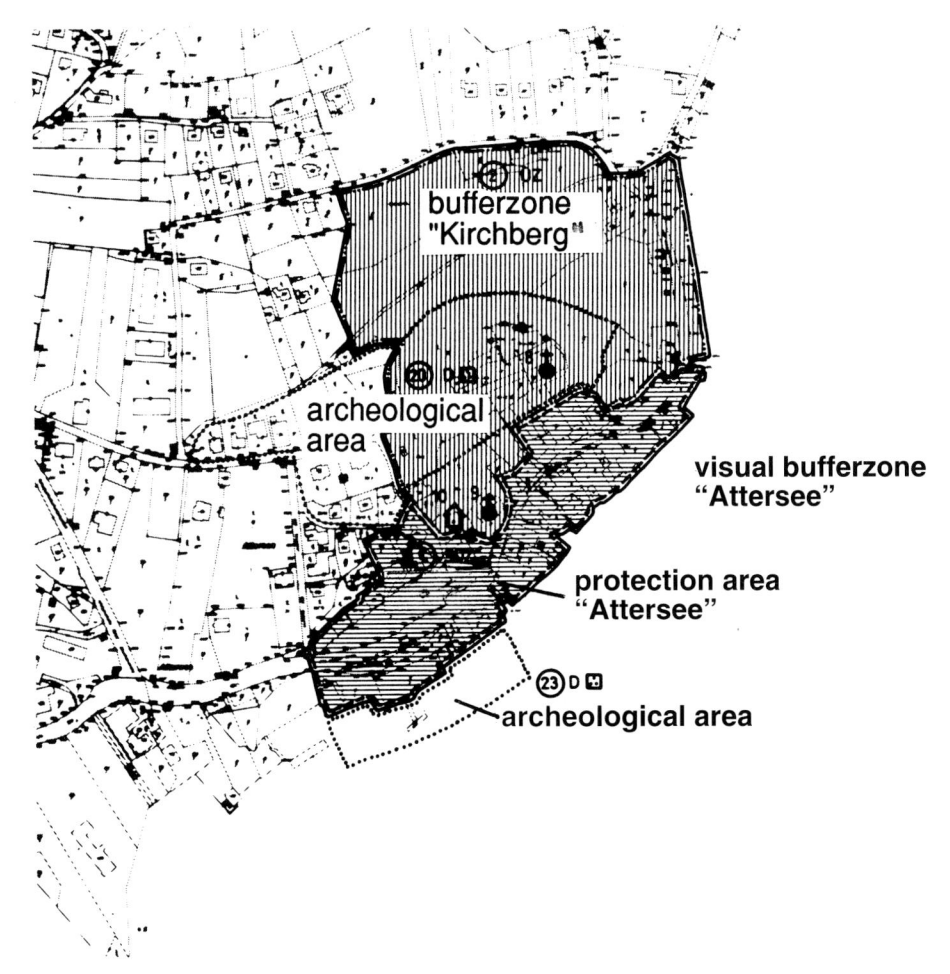

Figure 3. Evaluation of areas under protection at the Attersee on cultural heritage map (part 1, detail) and picture 2 (zoning map).

The method used in Upper Austria described below is based on a survey of the various constituents of a built-on site which can be perceived, demarcated and described as units in the present state of the town or village in question. Demarcation is based on three criteria :

- Units deriving from historical periods of growth or from characteristics peculiar to the region;

○ Units with morphological or spatial features in common;
○ Units requiring identical protection;

It is not always easy to recognize the three criteria of history, geography and protection when defining areas, ensembles and surroundings. The area represented on a plan frequently results from priority having been given to one of the three criteria and in some instances a balancing of the three factors could lead the boundaries, being shifted slightly (Heusser Keller 1982).

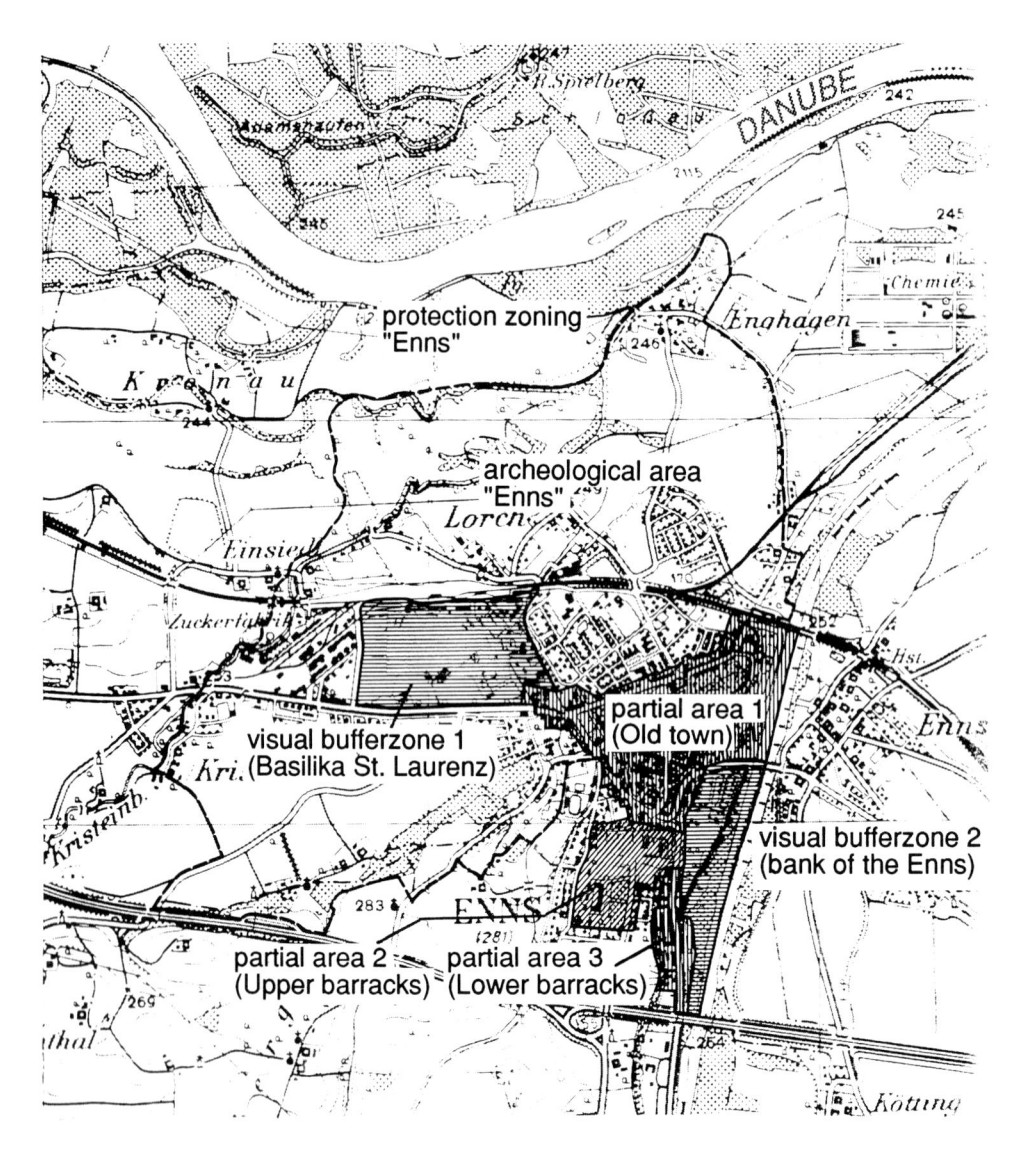

Figure 4. Subcategorization in protection zone using cultural heritage at Enns (picture 1, detail). The map (picture 2) shows the protection area, and picture 3 the river bank of Enns.

General References to the Contents of the Study on Mapping Upper Austrian Cultural Landscape

At the regional level, 19 comprehensive cultural units have been developed for Upper Austria, according to nationally executable criteria to the geo-cultural model. These units are primarily belong to the Bohemian massif - the granite and gneissic highlands (units no. A1-A6), the Alpine forelands (units no. B7-B13) and the northern Alpine area (units no. C14-C19) (see Figure 2). The description of these units was proceeded to according to following criteria: ecological landscape classification (cultural landscape types together with botanic and zoological aspects structural elements close to nature (cultural landscape elements such as biotops, rural orchards, etc.). To qualify the interaction between "man and landscape", the results of the Upper Austrian study concerning the mapping of the "resources of the natural environment" were used for e.g. landscape dependant recreation potential, fertility potential of soil and forestry, watersystem potential and raw materials potential. Besides an analysis of these cultural landscape units, future aspects and objectives of agricultural and landscape planning as well as spatial planning (NUT - regions and Convention for Alpine Preservation) are included to reinforce and to promote a comprehensive cultural landscape policy by these planning and preservation instruments. Rural settlements and vernicular architecture transcend to historical descriptive elements of the regional study. A socio-economic regional classification of local government units and depiction of population development offers indications of endogenous development potential in the different cultural landscape units. Inventorying the cultural heritage on local level was verified by rural (Figure 4) and urban (Figure 5) studies based on the landscape-oriented mapping and evaluation method. The systematic compilation and information provided is shown in the comprehensive Cultural Heritage Information System (Kulturgüterinformationssystem Oberösterreich) and the Upper Austrian Mapping of Resources of the Natural Environment.

Summary

Although Austria joined the World Heritage Convention late, Austrian experts were involved in the origins of the Convention of 1972, which became in 1992 the first international legal instrument to protect cultural landscapes. Austria has a broad experience in the legislation of the conservation of both, cultural and natural heritage and landscape protection. The Federal Ministry for Science and Research has started a comprehensive research programme entitled "Sustainable Development of Austrian Cultural Landscapes". In some regions extensive inventories and mapping out cultural landscapes have been carried out, in particular in Upper Austria with a comprehensive methodological approach. Specific methods have been developed to identify cultural landscapes and cultural heritage at regional and local levels. For mapping the different types of cultural properties, an extensive system for cataloging and evaluation was used at the local level. The different activities and the 1994 tentative list provide a basis for a future landscape nomination for inclusion in the World Heritage List.

Acknowlegement

I wish to thank Mechtild Rössler and Lisa Lundby for their cooperation in editing this article.

References

Council of Europe (1993). *Architectural Heritage Documentation Centres in Europe*, Directory, Strasbourg.

Fink, M., Gruenweis, F., Wrbka, T., et al. (1989). *Kartierung ausgewählter Kulturlandschaftstypen in Österreich*, Monographien, Bd. 11, Wien.

Heusser-Keller (1979). *Ortsbildinventarisierung - Grundlage der Ortsbildgestaltuung*. Vortrag Linz, Landesbaudirektion. Linz.

Jeschke, P.(1989). *Village renovation and rural district development: co-operation between the public, planners and local authorities*. Strasbourg, Council of Europe.

Jeschke, H.P. (1992). *Das Oberösterreichisch Ortsbildgesetz und der "Umfassende Kulturgüter- und Ortsbildkataster" in Oberösterreich, - Instrumente der Gestaltung und des Schutzes des Ortsbildes in Oberösterreich*. In *Stadterhaltung - Ensembleschutz im internationalen Vergleich, Stadtplanung Wien* - Band 38 der Beiträge zur Stadtforschung, Stadtentwicklung und Stadtgestaltung, Wien, pp. 50-62.

Jeschke, H.P., und Jeschke, C., (eds.) (1994). *Die Kulturlandschaft Oberösterreichs und ihre bäuerlichen Siedlungsformen*, Wien.

Maurer, H. (1994). *Die Kulturlandschaftseinheiten Oberöstereichs*. In Jeschke, H. P. und Jeschke, C. (1994).

Österreichische Raumordnungskonferenz (1988). *Epfehlungen zur Erstellung von Naturraumpotentialkarten*. Wien.

Smoliner, C. (1992). *Sustainable Development of Austrian Cultural Landscapes*. Federal Ministry for Science and Research. Wien.

Umweltbundesamt (1993). *Landschaften von internationaler Bedeutung in Österreich*, Maschinenschrift, Wien.

UNESCO (1972). *Convention Concerning the Protection of the World Cultural and Natural Heritage*, Paris.

UNESCO (1995). *Operational Guidelines for the Implementation of the World Heritage Convention*, Paris.

Hans Peter Jeschke is the head of the Upper Austrian Cultural Heritage Information System of the Upper Austrian Spatial Planning Office in Linz and a member of ICOMOS Austria.

Chapter 29

The Schorfheide-Chorin Biosphere Reserve, Germany: Unique Species Diversity in a Centuries-Old Cultivated Landscape

Eberhard Henne

Introduction

In the Schorfheide-Chorin Biosphere Reserve, is a protected area of 129 161 ha north of Berlin, a cultivated landscape created by humanity over the course of centuries managed in an integrated way, which contains a wealth of species that is unique in Europe. The area manifests the entire glacial series of a landscape shaped by the Pommeranian Stage of the Vistula Glaciation of 15 000 years ago. The extensive, multifaceted forests and cultivated lands of the glacial spillways and outwash areas, the ground and end moraine chains of the region, with the lakes embedded in them, the streams and countless bogs provide ideal habitats for numerous species. The variegated soil structures, the continentally-influenced climate and the natural limitations on utilisation by humans have provided the basis for a multifaceted vegetation cover in the Biosphere Reserve, which in turn permits a wealth of fauna species. The areas with the greatest species diversity have been secured in extensive natural protected areas. The majority of human settlements in the Schorfheide-Chorin Biosphere Reserve were founded in the thirteenth century. Villages on the good soil of the round-topped ground moraines grew, and in order to obtain farmland for their growing populations, they extended their clearance areas into the Central European Forest, which was at that time still a contiguous area. Other villages, particularly those which had been founded on the rockier soils of the flat end moraine chains, were abandoned and their clearances were reclaimed by the forest. Such abandoned settlements can often be found today.

Agriculture reshaped the landscape continuously, with wars, famines and plagues playing their part. Not until the nineteenth century did the division between farmland and woodland become established.

A richly structured farming landscape emerged, a landscape with a great wealth of species. Animal and plant species from the unforested eastern European grasslands followed humanity into farmed grassland. In this way, the hare, the black-bellied hamster, the great bustard, the white stork, the changeable toad, the meadow pasque-flower and many other species found new habitats in Central Europe.

With the development of new technologies and the introduction of inorganic fertilisers, a countervailing trend set in at the end of the nineteenth century. The field sizes changed, obstacles in the landscapes were removed, the landscape was impoverished. Habitats for animal and plant species were destroyed, at the same time species diversity was reduced in the farmland itself. During the early decades, this phenomenon was hardly noticeable, but it grew with the increasing intensification of agricultural production.

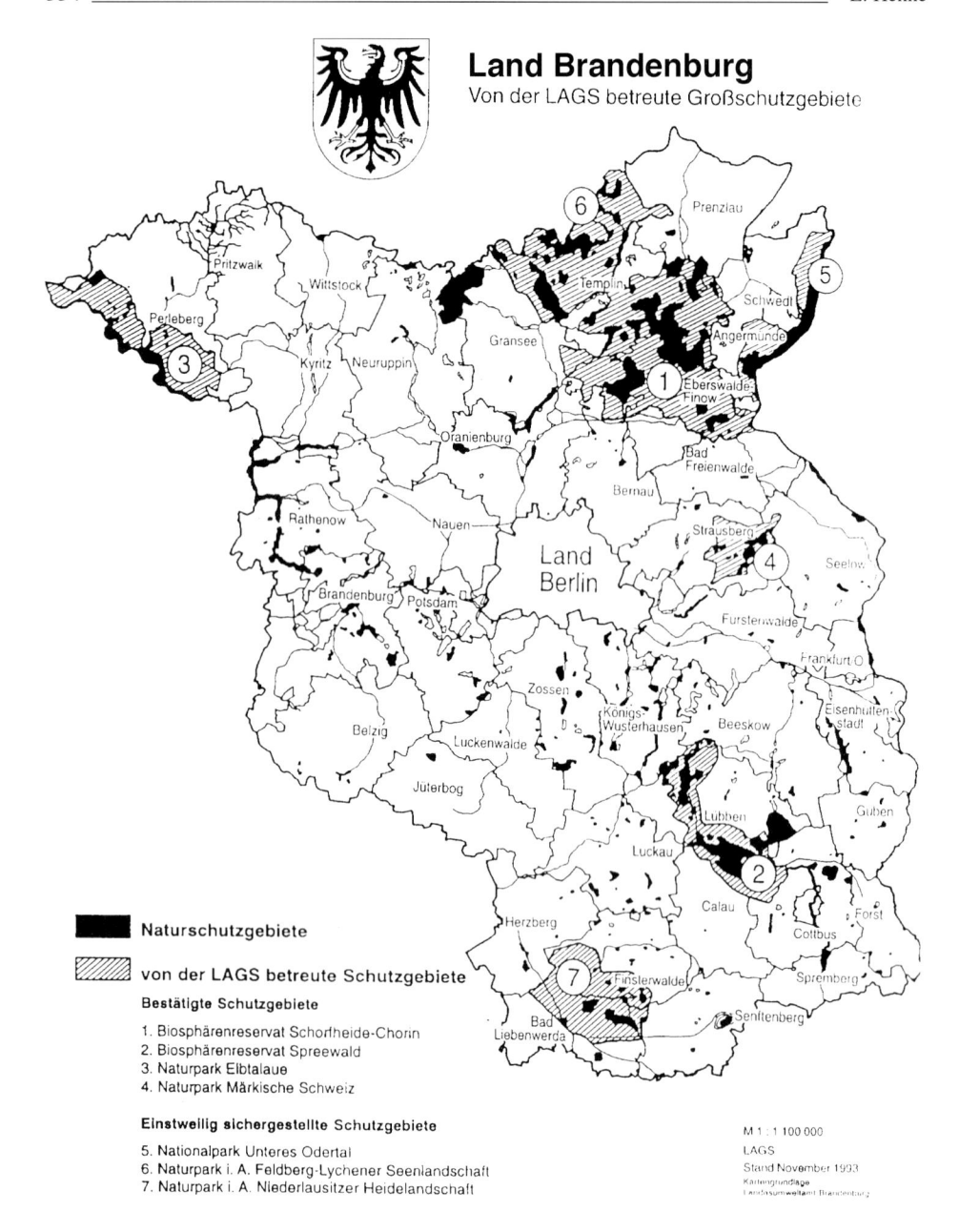

Land Brandenburg
Von der LAGS betreute Großschutzgebiete

Naturschutzgebiete

von der LAGS betreute Schutzgebiete

Bestätigte Schutzgebiete
1. Biosphärenreservat Schorfheide-Chorin
2. Biosphärenreservat Spreewald
3. Naturpark Elbtalaue
4. Naturpark Märkische Schweiz

Einstweilig sichergestellte Schutzgebiete
5. Nationalpark Unteres Odertal
6. Naturpark i. A. Feldberg-Lychener Seenlandschaft
7. Naturpark i. A. Niederlausitzer Heidelandschaft

M 1 : 1 100 000
LAGS
Stand November 1993
Kartengrundlage
Landesumweltamt Brandenburg

Figure 1. Nature protected areas and larger protected areas in the Land Brandenburg (LAG).

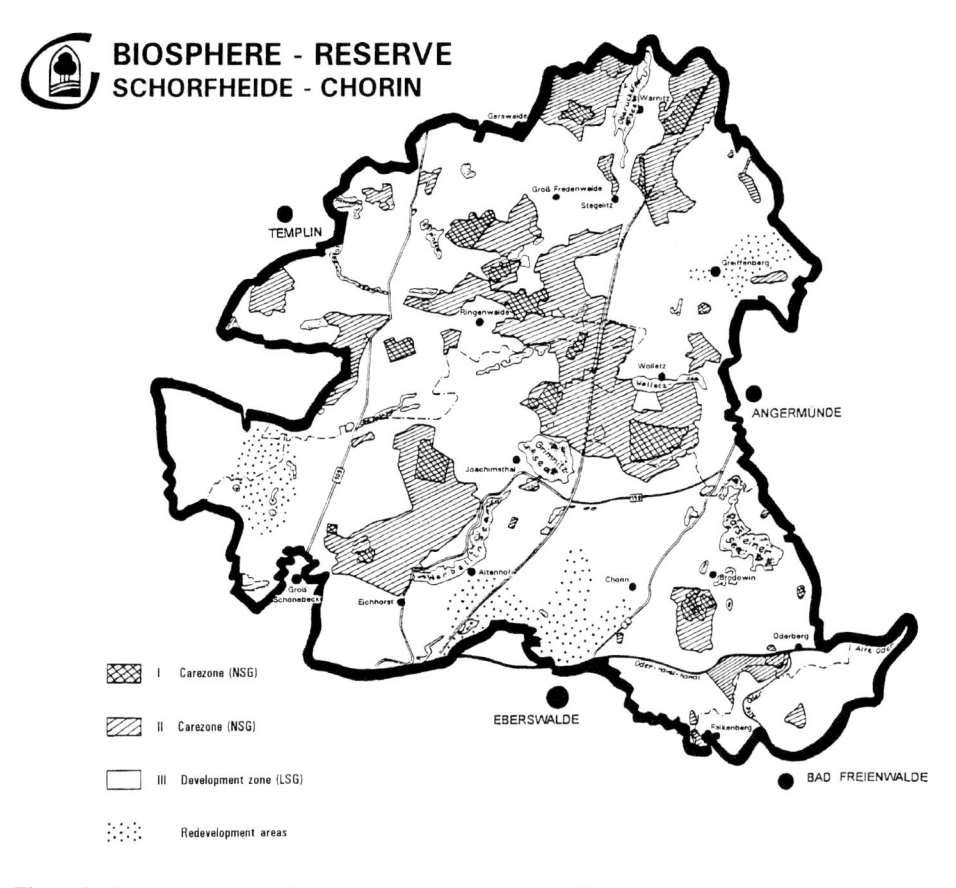

Figure 2. The zonation of the Biosphere Reserve "Schorfheide-Chorin".

During the last few decades, such processes have become undeniably evident. More and more hedgerows have been cleared, and kettle holes in the fields reclaimed, embankments have been flattened and field fringes removed, thus creating field sizes of more than 100 ha with no landscape features of any significance. Together with intensive production methods involving large-scale use of inorganic fertilisers and agricultural chemicals, this has spelt the end for many animal and plant species. Rapid species disappearance and the extinction of many species have resulted. This process was most extreme in those areas where massive amounts of liquid manure and drainage improvement measures were applied.

However, the multifaceted landscape profile of the Uckermark region did not permit high-intensity agriculture everywhere. Many kettle holes and basin bogs, dry-meadow hillocks and cliffsides, groves and hedgerows survived the massive assault of industrially-organised agricultural production methods. Thus, areas with a multifaceted agricultural landscape predominate, even today, alongside the cleared-out large-scale farmlands of the north-eastern part of the Biosphere Reserve, and the soils in the south which have been damaged by liquid-manure fertilisation. Numerous kettle holes and small lakes are embedded in the hilly ground moraines. Hedgerows, culverts lined with stands of willow, small groves and field-paths lined with fruit trees enrich the scenery. Hills and cliffsides covered with dry-meadow associations have been preserved in all areas. Ditches and field-fringes interconnect the remaining large-scale areas. Abandoned sand and clay quarries, as well as the numerous piles of stones gathered from the fields during reclamation constitute new habitats. In the cleared-out farmland, new hedgerows are being planted for habitat-interconnection, and the surviving groves are being enlarged. As old stands of willow are cared for, cuttings are taken in order to replace old fallen trees. In some areas, new orchard meadows have been planted, and existing stands have been extended. So called "Benjes" hedges, new tree-lined roadways, and many newly-planted individual trees in the villages complete the picture of the activities being undertaken to reform the damaged areas of the open countryside.

In the past, low-lying bogland was transformed into intensively planted grassland. Mineralisation of the peat in the low-lying bogs and mullification of the soil was the result. However, some remote low-lying bogs were spared this fate. Because of their low yields, especially as orchard meadows, they were gradually abandoned. Increased mechanisation meant that the heavier vehicles could no longer operate in such areas. Thus, the Sernitz meadows near Greiffenberg were removed from use as early as 1960-65. Rushes and willow shrubs grew, and today they cover the several hundred ha of former meadowland entirely. Extensive agricultural utilisation of all grassland areas is the goal of the Biosphere Reserve; some enterprises have been practising this for the past two years out of economic necessity. The first successful results can be seen in the successful breeding of meadow-nesters, and in the use of grasslands as a feeding habitat by other bird species. Improved water level retention and dismantling of drainage facilities have supported this process.

Extensive forest associations:
a typical element of the Schorfheide-Chorin Biosphere Reserve

Oak forest associations are a distinct characteristic of this Biosphere Reserve. While the forests English oak depend on ground water influenced sandy sites, the durmast oak forests grow on dry soils. Oak forests are long-lived with very high value wood, but with weak capacity for natural regeneration. In this landscape with its long-term human impact, natural oak associations have survived in a near natural state at very few sites. Under the pressure of intensive animal pasturing, and later, of excessively high wildlife populations and over-utilisation during the reign of King Frederick II (1740- 1783), oaks were hardly able to regenerate in the Schorfheide. Gradually, particularly during the eighteenth century, the so called Rümden - small groves - which thus emerged were transformed into monocultural pine forests.

The residual occurrence of natural pine forest gives the Biosphere Reserve a special value. For the pine is a species characteristic of the boreal coniferous forest zone, and the state of Brandenburg is at the western edge of its range. Outside its contiguous growth area, it flourishes only at special sites. Here in the Schorfheide, the transition from the maritime-influenced climatic zone to the subcontinental zone permitted the pine to spread beyond the dune sands more rapidly than usual.

By contrast to its natural range in the taiga zone of the Eurasian land mass, which has relatively high levels of water reserves in its soils and a long winter resting period for vegetation, the mild winters which have become ever more frequent in our area deny the evergreens a resting period for their metabolic processes. The resulting metabolic stress is reinforced by increasing water deficits, an excess of nitrate nutrients and air pollution, as well as secondary pests. For this reason, the pine which, more than any other tree species, was spread throughout the North German Plain by humans and has even become the symbolic tree of Brandenburg, is particularly threatened in this the area which is the border of its natural range.

While the pine forests at the better sites might be transformed into deciduous forests appropriate to these sites by means of various forest-management measures, the valuable pine forests in the few areas which are not so strongly eutrophied should be preserved as long as possible.

The beech forests of the Biosphere Reserve are located at the south-eastern range border of the great South Baltic beech forest area. Due to the climate change, it is to be expected that the expansion of beech growth, which has been clearly evident in recent times, will be reversed. The beech forests at the borders of its range will be the first to be affected. The climate-induced transformation of our forest ecology systems will be an important subject of research for the Biosphere Reserve. It is to be expected that drought resistant deciduous forests will dominate the forest picture in the future.

Restructuring of the forests - the work of generations

Forestry is the economic activity which covers the greatest area in the Biosphere Reserve. The forest area is assigned to four Forestry Agencies (subordinate forest authorities), with 13 Superior Forestry Operations and 64 Ranges.

Approximately 40% of the stands show damage from pollution, insects, climatic stress or overgrazing by wildlife. The health of the forest can be rated medium, with local fluctuations. In addition to wildlife, nitrate input contributes to visible damage to trees and to changes in ground vegetation.

The 200 year old pine monoculture forest on sites formerly occupied by deciduous trees is now experiencing considerable ecological problems affecting its productivity and stability. Pollution and climatic anomalies have worsened the situation still more. The pine is the tree least able to cope with such stress factors. In the course of a whole year, it uses much more water than a deciduous tree does during its vegetative period, which lasts a maximum of six months. But pollution threatens not only the pines, but also the preferred trees for such locations, the oaks and beeches.

The primary goal of forestry in the Biosphere Reserve is the restructuring of such forests to become species-variegated and structurally multifaceted mixed forests with a full age range, and the avoidance of clear-cutting. In addition to this goal of near-natural forestry, it will also be necessary to continue existing species-protection programmes, as well as those yet to be developed under the direction of the Biosphere Reserve. Selected areas should be left to develop naturally (Zone 1). Here, long-term scientific observation is to be carried out. In the forests of Protective Zone 2, near-natural forestry is planned. Potential natural forest associations are an important indicator for tree selection. The proportion of naturally-occurring deciduous tree and shrub species (beech, English and durmast oak, linden and hornbeam) is to be increased at all appropriate sites. Near-natural forestry can only be achieved if the excessive game populations of are reduced to a level appropriate to the ecosystem. The "intensive wildlife maintenance" system in the Biosphere Reserve during the Honnecker era led to extremely high game populations. This had a severe effect on the plant associations at the herbaceous and shrub levels. There are hardly any herbaceous or shrub plants left other than wavy hairgrass and beech grass, which is increasing, and there is very little natural innovation. Even pine plantings have to be fenced off for their own protection.

Thus, hunting is an important form of land use and habitat care. The game population density must be reduced to the level consistent with the protective goals set for Zones 1 and 2. In other areas, too, the desired level of natural innovation must be made possible without fencing. The guidelines call for springtime-populations of approximately two red deer or five fallow deer, and five roe deer and one wild boar on 100 ha of forest land.

The forestry methods in the Biosphere Reserve serve as a model for the creation of a future-oriented forest economy for the entire State of Brandenburg. The naturally-oriented forest economy is one of the examples for the unity of ecology and economy, as demonstrated by numerous forest operations in the western states. However, the possibilities offered by such a future-oriented forest economy depend on the extent to which forestry services which have been provided free of charge, such as the preservation of recreational, educational and protective functions of the forest and the reconstitution of drinking-water reserves, can in the future be compensated by society. This issue is all the more important in this area, which is only fifty km from Berlin, a city with 3.4 million people.

Boglands: rare diversity

All the bog types characteristic of the North German Plain occur here: swamp-forming bogs, alluviation bogs, fontinal bogs, through-flow bogs and basin bogs. Some are nutrient-rich formations with paludal alder forests, bullrush thickets and great sedge reeds, some are nutrient-poor, acidic formations with open peat-moss and cotton-grass reed vegetation, the latter sometimes with a light cover of pubescent birch and pine. There are still scattered surviving nutrient-poor but alkaline and limestone-rich bogs, often with sedge-reed and saw-grass thickets. As the result of a few individual investigations, we now have our first exact geobotanical/phytosociological and also stratigraphic/ historical development information. Initial counts have shown that there are approximately 1150 bogs with areas of more than one ha in the Biosphere Reserve, and an additional 2000 - 3000 of less than one ha. The total surface area of the bogs is approximately 13 800 ha, or more than 10% of the total surface area of the Biosphere Reserve.

Most characteristic of the Biosphere Reserve are the countless very small basin bogs. They are found mostly in the end moraines, the hilly ground moraines and at the beginnings of the outwashes. Their creation can for the most part be traced back to the meltdown of blocks of fossil ice buried during the Ice Age. Their stratigraphic structure is uniform. On a base of a peat-bog formation several tens of metres thick, and consisting of brown moss peat and, in some cases, sedge and twig peat from late glaciation, there is a mud layer of greatly varying thickness, indicating the formation of a body of water due to deep-thawing fossil ice following a weak phase of swamp formation. Alluviation by way of mud formation began more than 11 000 years ago, as is indicated by a time-marker that is found frequently in the basin bogs. A one cm thick whitish-yellow tuff band embedded in the lowest mud layer points to the strong volcanic eruptions in the Eifel mountains 11 000 years ago, which covered our area with a rain of ash. Only in these small bogs has it been preserved undisturbed. The pond stage is concluded by the complete filling of the pond with brown mosses. These are virtually undecomposed, so that the species composition can be ascertained very precisely. Once the fossil ice had melted away some 9000-10 000 years ago, and a relatively dry climate developed, the ponds dried out quickly, and the alluviation process was concluded with the formation of a quaking-bog cover, generally characterised by brown-moss/sedge-peat layers. That was followed by a period of interruption of bog development - approximately 6000 - 8000 years ago for the smaller basins, although the larger ones took longer to alluviate. Some 2000 to 4000 years ago, peat began to grow up to a height of eight m. Such peat growth after alluviation can only occur as the result of precipitation and through surface-level inflow of soil water. Thus, smaller bogs usually manifest mesotrophic- acid site conditions, while larger bogs have extensive areas with oligotrophic-acidic conditions at their centres. Since basin bogs are maintained by tiny drainage areas, they are strongly dependant on weather conditions. Periods of several wet years in a row cause rapid peat growth, followed, in dry periods, by renewed shrinkage, during which time the central area is fed largely by rainwater. Relative dryness of the upper layer of peat permits tree growth, largely pine and birch, which dies off again during wet periods. The vegetation cover of the undrained basin bogs manifests a concentric zoning which is found repeatedly. At the border with the larger inorganic environment, there is a fringe swamp, a so-called "Lagg", several metres in width, which is like a watery ring, at least in spring. It is overgrown with sedge, rushes, marsh fern and swamp calla. Towards the centre of the basin bog there is a zone with tussocks, often more than 50 cm in height, built up of sturdy haircap moss, with individual plants of up to 15 cm. These mounds of moss are intertwined with cranberries. The centres of these basin bogs are usually characterised by copse-like growths of cotton-grass, which, during its seeding period - late May and early June - covers the bog with a white veil, which contrasts strongly with the dark green covering of peat moss.

Characteristic species in these peat moss/ cotton grass meadows are bog rosemary and marsh tea, and also roundleafed sundew. Some basin bogs in the Uckermark also have a so called "Kolk" (lit.; "pothole") in their centres, a pool that rises with the growth of the peat. Almost vertical underwater peat edges several metres in length tell the story of the creation of these pools. The old natural reserves Hechtdiebel and Plötzendiebel in the centre of the Biosphere Reserve, which are today in a total-protection area, are typical examples of such basin bogs with a central pool. The prominent German bog researcher and conservationist Kurt Hueck wrote his dissertation about these bogs during the 1920s. Another separate type of bog, especially found in the moraine areas, are the swamp-forming bogs which occur here in large numbers. If the water budget is undisturbed, they maintain paludal alder forests which flourish on centuries-old moss tussocks 1-2 m high, while water-filled hollows spread between them, often do not drying out until fall. In these hollows grow yellow-flag iris, feather foil and water dropwood.

By contrast to the bog formations of five, ten and even 15 m in thickness in the quickly-forming basin bogs, the bog-covers of the swamp-forming bogs are 1-2 m thick; moreover, these peats are very rich in minerals and strongly decomposed as a result of water-level fluctuations and their natural dry phases. An additional bog type is the fontinal bog, a characteristic feature of end-moraine areas. These too, are very small in area, and develop at points or along lines where water rises from the ground (fontinal points).

Probably the most important fontinal-bog complex in Germany lies in the northern portion of the Biosphere Reserve, in the old natural reserve Fauler Ort. Here, there are hundreds of springs emerging from the moraines, forming arcs of springs, and repeatedly building up new fontinal domes, in the middle of an extensive beech forests on the edge of cliffs. In the greatest of these fontinal domes are fontinal bogs more than eight m thick which grew up in the post-Ice Age. They are formed of fontinal limestone generated by the high calcium content of the spring water, interspersed with highly-decomposed organic material. It is hardly possible to walk on these bogs, which are home to a specific form of paludal alder forest, the bittercress/ paludal alder swamp. Between the alders swaying on soft, water-logged soil grows the bittercress, which blooms in May. At the end of April, the yellow blossoms of the marsh marigold shine in these dark reaches, and in summer, the common valerian with its pink blossoms decorates the dark forest. A similar, but smaller fontinal bog is located at Haus Lake near Suckow.

Many of the usually extensive stream bogs in the Biosphere Reserve have been severely drained during the past decades, for instance in the Finow valley and in the Sernitz-Welse valley. In the area of moraine water gaps and root outwashes in the forests, a few have managed to survive with their original vegetation. These include the new natural reserves of Lieper Posse and Fett Lake, both of which are located in the area of the Chorin end-moraine arc. They owe their existence to a water flow which passes through a hollow and is building up a peat body. Often, the stream bogs have grown up on old, long-since alluviated lakes. The typical sedge and brown moss peats, several metres thick and hardly decomposed, are evidence of a high degree of water saturation and a rapid growth process.

By contrast to the nutrient-poor acidic basin bogs with almost stagnant surface water, the flow-through bogs are alkaline and often calcium-rich, due to flow of soil water. The high calcium content of the young-moraine landscape is the cause of the alkalinity of its groundwater. Brown moss, sedge reeds, interspersed with shallow hollows with Scotch asphodel and bladderwort associations dominate the vegetation here. A few calciphilous orchid species have adapted themselves to such sites, including the epipactis, the twayblade and the loose-flowered orchid. But there are also many other bog plants, which are very rare today, which give this type of bog a very high conservation value.

Two hundred and thirty lakes in the Biosphere Reserve

Lakes, likes bogs, are present in this young moraine landscape in great variety. The largest of the approximately 230 lakes is the Parstein Lake, with more than 1100 ha of water. All five of the basic hydrological types which exist in the North German Plain are present in the Biosphere Reserve. Largely restricted to the outwash land formation are the so-called "sky lakes" (Himmelseen). These are small roundish lakes in the middle of the dune landscape which emerged in the post-Ice Age, with no connection to any body of ground water, let alone to any stream; they are fed entirely by precipitation. They are nutrient-poor, weakly acidic lakes (pH values between 4.8 and 6.5), often surrounded by peat-moss and sedge-based quaking bogs. Of the seven lakes of this type in the Biosphere Reserve, two have been largely spared from damage. Their water is still clear, and they still have their characteristic biotic communities. On the lake floors, various mosses form a thick carpet. In the quaking bogs, rare plants such as sun dew, *Scheuchzeria*, mud sedge, bog rosemary and break rush flourish.

The basin lakes, a second type of lake, are likewise small, but very deep. They are to be found chiefly in the moraine areas, and probably trace their origins to melted buried fossil ice blocks. Since they are fed by precipitation and by streams from the surrounding area, their natural inflow of nutrients has been low. These are mesotrophic/weakly acidic or mesotrophic/alkaline clear-water lakes with rich underwater vegetation consisting of charophyta. TheTiefer See near *Bölkendorf,* located in a deep moraine hollow east of the Parstein Lake, is a typical basin lake. It is 34 m deep, its intense blue water colour is due to its high purity.

Another type of lake is the so-called fontinal lake, fed principally by spring water which emerges from the ground at the lake_s edge or at the lake floor. These are mostly nutrient-poor, calcium-rich waters, with thick sediments of limestone deposits. The only lake of this type is Aalgast Lake, which is fed by the fontinal bogs of the Fauler Ort natural reserve area.

The majority of our lakes in the landscapes late Pleistocene landscapes are flow-through lakes, i.e., lakes which receive a significant share of their water from directional groundwater flows from the surrounding area. The numerous lakes in the outwashes and in the transverse outwashes belong to this category of lake. They are often connected to one another by streams, and include such bodies as Dölln Lakes, the Stadtsee chain north of Eberswalde, the lake chain near Templin, Krinert Lake and the Prässnick Lakes. These were once characterised by very great visibility depths of five m or more, and by richly-developed underwater vegetation caused by the transparency of the water. charophyta, rooted and assimilated in the lake floor, formed characteristic "underwater meadows".

In the assimilation process, the limestone dissolved in the water precipitates on the living plants. When the plants die in the fall, the limestone forms a sediment on the lake floor. This explains the massive limestone deposits of up to 20 m thickness on the lake floors. The meadows of charophyta settle in the translucent lakes down to a depth of ten meters. These lake- floor meadows produce oxygen, are habitats for food-plants for aquatic fauna, and produce sediments of lake chalk or, with somewhat higher organic components, limestone mud. Such chalk-rich sediments have the characteristic of binding the freely- available phosphorus in the water, so that this nutrient is available in the lake ecosystem only to a limited degree. In this way, our lakes were able to sustain themselves as clear-water lakes filled with a rich variety of life.

A characteristic fish species of these lakes, which are rich in oxygen all the way to their floors, is the marena, a highly-prized game fish. However, in these lakes with their high water transparency, ospreys, terns, goosanders and cormorants could also spot the fish in the water. Today, due to anthropogenic changes, most of the lakes are no longer in their natural condition. Among the larger lakes, only Parstein Lake comes anywhere near its former quality.

The last lake type in the Biosphere Reserve which should be mentioned is the stream lake. This type of lake, tied to river floodplains and valley sand deposits - in this case, glacial spillways - is characterised by high water through-flow. Oderberg Lake in the lower Oder Marsh is a typical stream lake. Most of these naturally nutrient-rich and therefore highly-productive lakes are currently in general overburdened by nutrients and pollutants, due to the heavy contamination of our rivers. Thus, Oderberg Lake today also has a highly polytrophic status. The lake is literally drowning in its own decomposing sediments. The once varied water plant life has died out, except for stands of water and cow lilies. Once, the lake was rich in wels, eel, pike-perch, eel-pout and pike; now, it is no longer worthwhile to fish there.

Once, the lake was one of our most important water-fowl habitats; now, water-fowl only come to the lake to rest or sleep. Six species of duck, three species of grebe, gray-leg geese, kingfishers, common and black terns, great and small bitterns, and three species of moor hen were all still present here 30 years ago. Then, the surface of the lake was covered with floating heart, a plant of the gentian family with floating leaves, whose frayed yellow blossoms decorated the lake in late June. This interesting plant species has today died out altogether, followed by many others. A clean-up of the lake by an expensive mud-removing process is urgently needed.

Species diversity - characteristic of a healthy landscape

According to a preliminary list, 904 species of vascular plants are recorded for the Biosphere Reserve, of which 119 can be considered endangered in Germany generally. For 1992, 31 beaver habitats are listed, and the otter was present in virtually the entire Reserve. To date, 14 species of bat have been observed. A total of 148 bird species nest in the area. The significant presence of rare and endangered large bird species, which underscores the importance of this Reserve for the maintenance of species diversity, is under special supervision. The Biosphere Reserve harbours nesting areas of all three eagle species of the North German Plain. In addition to the 15 breeding pairs of white-tailed eagle, numerous young eagles can be observed, for whom particular regions of the Biosphere Reserve provide favourable feeding conditions.

The osprey population, currently including 18 breeding pairs, indicated a significant upwards trend during recent years. The favourable reproduction rates - 3.1 young per nesting pair in 1992 - show that ideal conditions exist for this species in this area. For the spotted eagle, a significant reduction in population is evident, accompanied by a shift of the population from the larger forest areas toward extensive grassland areas. There are currently six breeding pairs in the Biosphere Reserve, and there are five pairs in the Randow-Welse Marsh, a large grassland area at the edge of the Biosphere Reserve. This population is also under the care of the Species Protection Section of the Biosphere Reserve. During the past five years, a pronounced population increase could be ascertained here. This area also is important for non-breeding spotted eagles, who enter it as feeding guests during the mowing season. In June 1992, up to 51 were counted on a number of occasions.

Of the other rare species of bird of prey, there are three suspected breeding pairs of Montague's harrier. In 1992, two broods of hen harrier could be substantiated with certainty. An interesting phenomenon is the increase in breeding pairs of short-eared owl. The extensively-utilised meadows and the fringes of the wet meadows provide an ecological niche for this species.

In 1993, the first eagle-owl brood was substantiated in the Reserve. The golden eagle, observed in 1992 and 1993, is probably a coincidental guest. The other species of bird of prey are present in the area with good, sustainable populations. In the bogs and the alluviation zones of the lakes, 150 to 180 pairs of crane are breeding. The increasing breeding density is causing many of the potential woodland wet habitats to be occupied, so that usable breeding spaces in open country are being settled. However, the high populations of wild boar and fox and the low water levels in many bogs has been reflected in recent years by a reduction in reproduction rates.

The great bustard occurs in the north-eastern part of the Biosphere Reserve, with a residual population in the bordering Randow-Welse Marsh. The population is under the care of a special working group under the direction of the Biosphere Reserve. The population consists of approximately 10-15 animals. Young have been substantiated in every year. In 1992, two young great bustards were certainly raised. For 1993, two broods have been substantiated.

Ten pairs of black stork have found breeding possibilities in these forests interspersed with wetlands. This species, too, shows a clear increase in recent years. A specific phenomenon is the appearance of a concentration of black stork in late summer, at migration time. Thus, 36 black storks were present for 14 days in the proximity of resting cranes in the north-eastern part of the Biosphere Reserve.

The white stork still breeds with good populations in the Biosphere Reserve. In the richly structured bog and lake areas, there are also other rare bird species. Thus, the great and the small bittern, the rednecked and the blacknecked grebe, the goosander, the common and the black tern, the feruginous and the golden-eye duck and the green sandpiper can still be observed at many locations.

In a few wet meadows, the corn crake, the blue-throat and the great curlew still occur. The hoopoe, the corn bunting and the great gray shrike profit from the broad, extensively-used fields, the grasslands and the fallow lands.

Of the reptiles, threatened species which occur here include the European pond turtle, the fire-bellied toad, the tree-frog, the changeable toad, the viper, the smooth adder and the warty newt. A mapping of fish has so far substantiated 41 species, of which seven are carried on the Federal list of endangered animal species. These include the brook lamprey, the spined and the bearded loach, the bull-head, the bitterling, the minnow, the great and the small marena, the brook trout, and the eel-pout.

Harmonising regional development and conservation

The southern Uckermark and the Schorfheide are characterised by sparse settlement and employment oriented towards agriculture and forestry. The political changes and the current economic development have, here as elsewhere, led to serious collapse in the labour market and in the structure of the remaining enterprises. Many therefore see conservation as a luxury, or even as antagonistic to economic development.

It is therefore the task of the Biosphere Reserve to harmonise the interests of the people living in the region with the preservation of nature. That means preserving agriculture in the region, by finding new concepts to support the production of ecologically pure food, and to compensate farmers for their contribution toward the preservation of the farming landscape. The village communities must remain viable. Toward this end, it is necessary to repair the village structures, restore the valuable building stock, and to demonstrate possibilities for the maintenance of infrastructure in the villages and for their interconnection through the expansion of public transportation. New housing construction should take into account the existing appearance of the village and its historically developed structure. From a planning standpoint, designation as a village or mixed area in the Biosphere Reserve opens the possibility of retaining agricultural enterprises in the village, and providing small production and service enterprises with the chance of establishing themselves in the rural area.

The development of environmentally benign tourism should be recognised and supported as a further major feature of the region. For this purpose, the construction of vacation homes, bed and breakfasts accomodation and small hotels should be given clear priority over large-scale tourism projects. Lodging and provisions for one-day- visitors and recreation-seekers should become a pillar of the economic development of the Biosphere Reserve.

In accordance with the zoning regulations of the State of Brandenburg, new commercial areas are planned near the nearby county seats and Eberswalde, Angermünde, Prenzlau and Templin in the newly-formed Regional Commercial Centres, or in the townships. Priority is to be given to commercial enterprises whose production methods do not disturb the adjoining settlement areas and the natural environment. In this regard, the communities could be supported by the administration of the Biosphere Reserve, e.g. with a model plan for appropriate commercial areas. Available old sites of industrial and commercial production should be cleaned up and reused for environmentally-appropriate production. The Biosphere Reserve supports the preservation of production methods and enterprises typical of the region, such a charcoal production.

The legislature should require approval by the Biosphere Reserve administration for the drafting of zoning and construction plans, and for projects and development plans, as well as for statutes for construction in built-up areas. This is not meant to hamper economic development and construction activity; rather, the idea is to direct them in a direction that preserves our unique landscape rather than destroying it. For this purpose, multifaceted consultation processes are required, and the conflicts between utilisation interests must be discussed until resolved. In most cases, however, there are alternatives and solutions for construction projects in the region. Here, too, the Biosphere Reserve does not see itself as an antagonist, but rather as a partner of the communities, since the goal is to reconcile our further development with our natural environment, and not to leave the moulding of our landscape to the real estate speculators.

Agriculture as an example

Our principle in the Biosphere Reserve is: preservation and development of the cultivated landscape - and for that, we need the farmer. Agriculture should continue production on the available area extensively, or in accordance with the criteria of organic farming. In this way, the requirement for environmentally appropriate land use, which UNESCO prescribes for Biosphere Reserve recognition, is fulfilled, and the farmers are given the possibility of working their entire land area.

The Biosphere Reserve regulations for the most part formulate requirements for naturally appropriate agriculture; only a small area in the care zone is exempted, where the strict protective status "Natural Reserve" imposes conditions on the farmers for which they have to be compensated.

This contrasts with a land-use pattern which requires ever greater quantities of inorganic fertilisers and pesticides in order to try to keep up with the ever dropping market price for agricultural produce, and which in addition is dependant upon EC subsidies paid out as fallow-land premiums (set aside). The results of ever higher- intensity agriculture are mass-produced farm products with residue contamination, damaged soils, contaminated ground water and sinking prices. This path is hopeless in the long-term. This type of intensive production puts food contaminated with residues, food-preservers and taste-correctors onto the market - food to which humans should really not be subjected. Consequently, this form of production is not only uneconomical in the long term, but also immoral.

It is just as senseless to lay land fallow if, as is the case for land subjected to high liquid-manure use, the fields are severely contaminated with nitrates, in some cases up to a depth of 50 m so that there is danger to the drinking water. For these lands, uses need to be found which provide for further extensive farming that harvests biomass, but which does not inject any more pesticides or fertilisers into the soil. Extensive land use is, in our view, a good alternative for farming the land in the future. In addition to unburdening the market, it contributes optimally to the regeneration of the soil by having animals graze off the biomass. In such cases, fertilisation is possible with organic solid fertiliser up to 1.4 large-animal units per hectare. This would greatly benefit the soil, and in addition, the farmer would be making a considerable contribution to society as a whole. Relief for the soil from chemical contamination contributes to the formation of clean ground water and thus guarantees good quality drinking water. And although this means a sacrifice for the farmer, society does not currently compensate him for it in any way. For this purpose, new regulations and parameters are necessary.

Other possibilities for additional income also hold promise for the farmer - in the area of landscape care and rural tourism. In this regard, we must recognise that rural tourism needs extensive agricultural production methods, since it will be difficult to combine it with intensive agriculture. For the environmental consciousness of those who are to visit here is growing, and if the farmer heads for the fields with tanks of poison, he will not be able to tell the tourists much of a story about healthy country food. Landscape care is necessary as a source of income, if we are to maintain the cultivated landscape. Who is supposed to do that, if not the farmer? But for that, the farmer wants compensation. We will see the farmer pulling back increasingly from marginal sites, for reasons of economic necessity, since, they simply no longer pay their way, due to dropping produce prices. However, if these areas are no longer kept open and cared for through extensive agriculture, the natural sequence will, in the long run, reclaim them for the forest. That would not benefit the harmonious development of the landscape; it would have a detrimental effect on the historically developed cultivated landscape.

The natural conditions - soil quality and heterogeneity - are insurmountable barriers for high-intensity production in large areas of Brandenburg. Moreover, in eastern Brandenburg, with annual precipitation of 450-550 mm, climatic conditions are such that farmers have to worry about drought. All these conditions are very unfavourable in the context of the European Community market, so that subsidies for landscape care and extensive farming are necessary. The administration of the Biosphere Reserve only funds and supports such utilisation methods, not intensive agriculture. For this purpose, the following funding scales are used: for landscape care with sheep and cattle 300 000 DM were paid in 1993, for other landscape care measures e.g. orchard- meadow care and establishment, willow-grove care or the mowing of fields, the level was 400 000 DM. Since 1992 funding has been allocated to the transformation of farmland into extensively-utilised grassland, the establishment and care of protective strips along the shorelines of bodies of water, and the integration of such areas. Finally, we support extensive grassland farming. All of this will not show results from one day to the next, but we do have good co-operation with the farmers. A total of 880 000 DM was paid for these measures in 1993. All in all, of our 2 million DM budget in 1993, 1.6 million was spent on special support programs for extensive agriculture. This has helped the Biosphere Reserve considerably to raise the level of acceptance among the local population. Since 1992, more than 7000 ha of farmland have been converted to extensive farming. And the farmers are showing a greater interest in this, to the extent that we are not currently able to provide support to all the farmers who would like it.

An important step towards the acceptance of these measures was the formation of the landscape care associations, and of the Uckermark-Schorfheide Landscape Care Network (Landschaftspflegeverband) as an umbrella organisation for these associations. For an example, the Landscape Care Network has implemented individual projects within its member associations to the tune of 700 000 DM, money which has nothing to do with the budget of the Biosphere Reserve, and which was, in some cases, invested beyond its borders. One that deserves mention is a special-machine club, established so that farmers who cannot and will not acquire needed machinery themselves, at least for the time being, can nonetheless carry out landscape care measures. The machines are provided free of charge, and experience has shown, are fairly fully utilised. The Biosphere Reserve is represented on the Supervisory Board of the Landscape Care Network, which operates entirely independently.

This has proven to be a decision-making body where everyone gets his or her say. Currently, the challenge is to strengthen the consultative activity of the network. What we want, however, is not consultants who want a money from subsidy programmes, but rather consultants who will remain tied to the enterprises during the phase of extensive land use all the way to the marketing and sale of the products. The first approaches have been realised both in the eco-village of Brodowin, on the Hohenwalde eco-farm and in the Stegelitz producer collective. Some 15 enterprises keep cows on an extensive basis, the largest with a herd of approximately 500 cows.

Shepherding operations are a problem. Subsidy funds are needed to maintain and expand the sheep flocks. A few special operations such as keeping milk-goats for the production of organic goats' milk cheese, etc. are developing; these are certainly niche-type production operations, but have a significant for the market in Berlin. The agriculture of tomorrow - the way we will need it - can be seen today in the Schorfheide-Chorin Biosphere Reserve.

Under the umbrella of research

Ecological research has, until now, largely been concerned with questions of the construction of natural systems and the interconnection between individual, highly specialised modules. The development over time of such natural systems - be they entire landscapes or mini-habitats - and the reasons for that development have hardly been examined, or else such research has been limited to specific scientific fields. To remedy this situation, the research concepts of the individual protected areas are co-ordinated with one another in such a way that the results are comparable with one another and worldwide. In the course of the international networking of all protected areas in the world, a working group is developing a geographic information system (GIS) for the Schorfheide-Chorin Biosphere Reserve. For this purpose the German MAB National Committee has provided high-performance hardware and software. This information system is capable of interfacing basic geographic data (maps) with other data such as soil composition, plant associations or animal species, and of processing data in accordance with specific requirements. Planning, administrative or research factors may be taken into account.

In addition, the construction of a network of Biosphere Reserve databanks is being undertaken. This will in the future provide a toolkit of great significance for the state administration, the counties and the Biosphere Reserve, as well as for ecosystem researchers. In the current phase, methodological considerations and many data-collection operations are necessary. For this purpose, the many years of experience of the Berchtesgaden National Park are useful. Hardly any German landscape other than the Schorfheide-Chorin Biosphere Reserve can look back on such an intensive tradition of research, going back more than a century. The surrounding research centres in Eberswalde (forestry, agriculture, meteorology) and Berlin (various universities, colleges and institutes) have a wealth of scientific potential and a unique store of knowledge about this landscape. Realising this potential in order to formulate land use plans in the Biosphere Reserve in an environmentally and socially appropriate manner is one of the goals of our research strategy (Box 1).

Box 1. Research projects at the Schorfheide-Chorin Biosphere Reserve.

Research projects include:

- Landscape planning and formation in the area of the Brodowin Eco-Village (Berlin University of Technology)
- Forest protection in Protected Zone 1; Limnological and hydrological investigations of the lakes (Humboldt University of Berlin)
- Definition of forest ecology systems (Eberswalde College of Forestry, University of Göttingen)
- Ecological field-utilisation systems (Müncheberg Central Institute for Farmland and Land-Use Research - ZALF)
- Extensive grassland farming (Brandenburg Ecological Professional
- Support, Educational and Research Project, Paulinenaue
- Job Creation Measures (ABM-BBB)
  Research on bioindicators as an environmental early-warning system (German Entomological Institute);
- Report on game (Staab & Marx Co., Saarbrücken);
  Network project on environmental and conservation research in theSchorfheide-Chorin Biosphere Reserve (BMFT, Bonn);
- Ecological land-use systems (DBU);
  Development of a geographic information system for integrative processing (State Institute for Major Protected Areas, Eberswalde);
- Ascertainment, evaluation and protection of bogs in the Schorfheide-Chorin Biosphere Reserve (Berlin University of Technology)

One example is a major research project which addresses conservation management in open, agriculturally-utilised farm country. Development in recent years and decades has shown that sustainable water, soil and air resource protection, as well as the permanent preservation of natural diversity of wild plant and animal species and of their biotopes cannot be achieved through the spatial separation of nature protection from agricultural operation. Solutions are needed that combine the interests of environmental and natural protection with those of agriculture in the same region. For this, however, it is necessary to know which ecological goals are envisioned for specific areas of the agricultural landscape which can then serve as a basis for action recommendations for landscape operation. The creation of such landscape models, and of concrete environmental, conservation and landscape goals derived from them, has, certainly, been called for some time, but has been possible until now due to methodological inadequacies. It is an interdisciplinary task, for which data on the various components of the natural budget (e.g. soil water, air, organisms) and on real and potential utilisation, including socio-economic parameters, need to be collated. The task of the network project, which is funded with 13.1 million DM by the Federal Ministry for Research and Technology (BMFT) and the German Federal Foundation for the Environment (DBU), is the development of comprehensive guideline models and concrete environmental, landscape and conservation goals for the future development of a complex landscape section of the northern German agricultural landscape. On the basis of these goals, land-use forms and production procedures can be developed which enable the farmer to produce competitively. The processing, treatment and marketing of quality produce from environmentally and naturally appropriate farming is designed to improve profitably in rural areas, and thus to reduce dependence of agriculture on public funds. Within the framework of the Network project, additional proposals for the further development of instruments, funding measures and parameters are to be submitted at the state, federal and EC levels, in order to enable the farmer, by means primarily of economic incentives, to incorporate environmental and conservation needs into economic decision-making.

With this close connection between the development of the scientific foundations and the transfer of the results to practice, the project is intended to create solutions ready to be applied to minimise conflict in the agricultural policy/agriculture/conservation problem complex.

In 1990, UNESCO selected the Schorfheide-Chorin Biosphere Reserve as the research and testing area, since it constituted a representative cross-section of the North German Plain. Here, the goals of the large-scale integration of conservation into the human-utilised landscape, which were decisive for the BMFT-DBU networking project, can be implemented in an exemplary fashion, for here the idea of the cohabitation of "Man and the Biosphere" (MAB) has top priority.

The development of the natural and anthropogenic landscape over the centuries, and the resulting utilisation forms, have led to the emergence of a great site-specific variety of flora, fauna, and biotopes. Many animal and plant species which are considered extremely rare or were thought to be extinct nation-wide are still present here today. In order to preserve this natural potential, which is largely dependant on human land utilisation, it will be necessary to take new conservation directions which involve the people living in the area. Due to the changing agricultural policy parameters, there is an immediate need - but also a great opportunity - for action, especially with regard to the farmland of the Biosphere Reserve which is in agricultural use.

The results of the BMFT-DBU Network Project are being incorporated into a new EU-funded project, whose goal is the optimisation of EU agricultural policy measures with the aim of formulating an environmentally and site-appropriate pattern of land-use and rural-development.

References

Haensel, J. (1994). *Artenschutzprogramm Fledermäuse für das Biosphärenreservat Schorfheide-Chorin.* Unpublished study.

Kray, E. (1992). *Tourismus in einem Biosphärenreservat: Möglichkeiten einer umwelt- und sozialverträglichen Entwicklung im Biosphärenreservat Schorfheide-Chorin.* Diplomarbeit.

LAGS (ed.) (1994). *Naturschutz in der offenen agrar genutzten Kulturlandschaft am Beispiel des Biosphärenreservates Schorfheide-Chorin.* Rahmenkonzept zum BMFT-DBU Verbundprojekt.

Schulzke, D. (1991). *Leitlinien der Analyse, Pflege und Entwicklung des Biosphärenreservates Schorfheide-Chorin.* Unpublished study.

Eberhard Henne is Director of the Schorfheide-Chorin Biosphere Reserve.

Chapter 30

Cultural Landscapes in Britain

Peter Fowler and David Jacques

Introduction

Britain is a single archaeological site, fragmented into lots of islands. It is therefore one cultural landscape. This concept is intellectually sustainable, for Britain, Europe's offshore islands, has been extensively busy with people for a long time. They have occupied, hunted over, felled and burnt trees on, farmed in, communicated across and extracted resources from virtually every hectare of the islands' extremely varied terrain since the late stages of the last glaciation 12,000 years and more ago. The result of this activity is the present landscape.

'Archaeology' is used here in the sense that the discipline is to do with anything and everything which is hand-made or man-influenced, whether the artefact be a small object or a landscape. The subject is also very much concerned with the processes which have produced the artefact, and the processes, of social change or landscape development, for example, which can be inferred from the object. The discipline is not merely concerned with a few archaeological sites existing in isolation; nor is it in any way confined by an excavation methodology. An 'archaeological landscape' is, then, almost tantamount to a 'cultural landscape', but not quite; for an associative cultural landscape could theoretically be quite natural, with no artefacts upon or in it. Nevertheless, in most cases it would be foolish to ignore the archaeological dimension in identifying cultural landscapes; without it, few cultural landscapes could be understood.

Of course solid, and to some extent drift, geology provide basics for cultural landscapes; but even they can be affected by what people do. Geology provides exploitable resources which people have been quick to find and use, altering in minor ways the shapes of the basics in the landscape and, much more significantly, turning inert materials into powerful agents of landscape change in the right hands. Thus flint, for example, variously used for implements from the Upper Palaeolithic onwards, was mined and widely used to chop down trees from the 4th millennium BC onwards, iron ore was increasingly converted into strong and more and more common tools from the mid-lst millennium BC onwards, impacting on soils as ard-tips and spades, on rocks as quarry tools and on vegetation as axe-heads. Whether felled by stone, bronze or iron, timber's uses included massive trackways which converted uninhabited fens into wet cultural landscapes from the 4th millennium BC. Timber was also used to build, for ceremony and religion, organic structures of which the embanked and ditched elements survive as henge monuments and the like from the 3rd millennium BC. And all this and more was happening **before** improving Roman and medieval technology, and growing populations, contributed yet more to the anthropogenically-driven evolution of landscape as a developing phenomenon.

To discuss 'cultural landscapes', in the plural, immediately requires, therefore, a willingness to make subdivisions within a concept. Landscapes have to be deconstructed from landscape; identifiers have to be defined and criteria established. Or, as we propose to do, one can simply name names, not intuitively but - indeed the exact opposite, - on the basis of our knowledge of the British landscape. In fact, there are too many individual cultural landscapes of quality within the single British one to mention them all, so the following examples are but a selection, consciously representative across a range of time and situation.

Islands

Given Britain's insular situation and geographical nature, it seems reasonable to begin with marine and coastal contexts. In the far south west, out in the Atlantic Ocean, the Isles of Scilly embrace a superb cultural landscape, partly submarine and partly tidal as a result of long-term change in the land-sea relationship. Much of that change, with former agrarian landscapes sinking below the sea, is of the last few hundred years, though some of the landscape elements now beneath the waves are of c 2000 BC. That the whole still constitutes a landscape, however, is demonstrated by the physical links, of field walls for example, from present islands down on to tidal flats, and by dramatic sections in the cliffs showing long sequences of deposition intermingled with evidence of human activity.

Similar sequences, almost of 'vertical landscapes' if the concept be allowed, exist in many other exposures around the British isles: on the west coast of Lindisfarne (or Holy Island) off the Northumbrian coast, for example, a stratified cliff-face looks landwards across the tidal mudflats where once what is now the island was joined to the mainland. Lindisfarne itself is typical of many a small island around the coasts of Britain with a visible archaeology and a long history from Mesolithic microlith-users to the present clutter of the tourist economy. With thousands of islands just off-shore, Britain is particularly rich in insular cultural landscapes: St. Kilda, well west of the Outer Hebrides, is already a World Heritage Site and possesses a marvellous, now unfortunately 'relict', cultural landscape as well as a significant wildlife interest. Many islands off the west coast of Scotland could make equally strong claims to bear outstanding cultural landscapes: examples would include the whole of Iona, mostly rocky and uninhabited but throughout its confines imbued with the spirit of St. Columba and a place of fundamental importance in the transmission of Early Christian culture to western Europe; and the Machrie area of Arran, in the Firth of Clyde, with its 'megalithic landscape'. Well to its south, Anglesey just off the north Welsh coast, is another single island with a profound, but totally different, cultural landscape.

Off the north Scottish coast, Orkney, like Scilly, is not a single island but a group of islands and, also like the Isles of Scilly, exemplifies an isolated and fragmented land surface bearing an outstanding archaeological assemblage. Orkney's spans c 3500BC - 1200 AD in particular, bringing in a rich vein of varied cultures from those of the first farmers to that of the Norsemen, yet the monumental archaeology exists still within a 'working' agrarian landscape. This cultural landscape reflects a traditional way of life based in large part on the harvest of the sea and the joint capacity of land and long hours

Figure 1. Orkney Mainland, Scotland: Stones of Stenness in a cultural landscape of prehistoric burial mounds and other ritual sites of the 4th and 3rd millennia BC, preserved in a working landscape still exploiting the natural resources available to neolithic farmers (Crown Copyright: Historic Scotland).

of daylight to produce two grass crops each year. Both landscape and life-way are now modified of course, not least by economics and tourism, but, conditioned by the basics of climate, geology and sea, they continue to represent a distinct culture resulting from the long-term interaction of people and that particular combination of environmental factors in that particular place. Orkney in particular must warrant serious consideration if the 'cultural landscape' concept is to be developed within the World Heritage remit.

Coastland

Britain also contains some outstanding coastal cultural landscapes. Some are high along the cliffs; others involve estuaries, mudflats and tidal reaches. The extreme south western end of England, West Penwith in West Cornwall, is an outstanding example of the former. Surrounded on three sides by sea, its granite cliffs edge an interior which witnesses not just many phases of different uses and lots of archaeological sites from the 3rd millennium BC onwards; they also bound a landscape which both perpetuates in current use many old features, such as massive Cornish 'hedges' - actually large, built, linear dykes, - and yet at the same time is not in general despoiled by the visual crassness of the 20th century. Furthermore, the more enquiry is made of this landscape, the more fulfilling appears to be its capacity to respond; whether the objective be serious scientific fieldwork on the ancient agrarian landscape, the settlement patterns of Early Christian times or the now defunct landscapes of tin-mining, or whether it be to reward a more romantic and mystery-seeking impulse. Whatever the motivation, this Penwith landscape in particular offers not just a depth of time but a range of experience, from hard-core field science to 'New Age' emotionalism. It certainly embodies remarkable archaeological landscapes; but it is 'cultural' too in being to some just as ideographic as any 'indigenous' landscape in, say, northern Australia or western north America.

Quite different visually and in nature are estuarine landscapes. One example illustrates the variety within them. Overlooking Portsmouth Harbour, more or less in the centre of the southern English coast, is a whole series of 'Defence of the Realm' installations. They range from a Roman fort at Portchester to relatively high-tech military structures of the very recent past; while out to sea are known wrecks - one, the Mary Rose, has been lifted and landed but others submerged can still be protected and are part, therefore, of a cultural landscape. Beyond to the SW is Southampton Water and the Isle of Wight, the latter with expanses of inter-tidal mud flat forming a special sort of landscape with artefacts both on it and in it. Similarly, the unattractive mud flats of the west side of the Severn estuary also conceal a well-preserved late prehistoric and Roman landscape, complete with organic survivals such as wooden structures. Single artefacts and structures do not, of course, a landscape make; but, however unappealing aesthetically such areas may look, once extents of manmade features in and below the mud can be revealed, and relationships in vertical and horizontal dimensions demonstrated, then the essential elements of landscape created by the interaction of people and Nature would seem to exist. Such must, then, be taken seriously in terms of cultural landscape.

The Lowlands

We move inland now and into perhaps more familiar terrain. Essentially we shall continue to look at landscape situations rather than cultural or chronological themes, or types of archaeological site complexes; though in truth there are but two main divisions to our remaining discussion, lowland and upland. In British terms, a crude line between the two is at about 250-300 m, above sea level. Another, more traditional line is that between, roughly, Exeter in the south west and Lincoln in the north east, with the lowlands east of the line and the 'highland zone' to its west. A number of situations, and therefore of cultural landscape sub-types, occur throughout both zones. In the lowlands, clearly important landscapes along river valleys and across or along relatively high ground can be identified but the lack of sharp topographical distinctions calls for a certain subtlety in perception. Particularly rich and scientifically-valuable areas of archaeological significance stretch, for example, not only along the higher ground around the Middle Thames of the Oxford area where some sites and monuments visibly survive but also across what is visually the very ordinary-looking countryside of the gravel terraces of the river valley itself. Indeed, this phenomenon is common in Britain. This is not to say that stretches of countryside with visibly surviving archaeological sites are unimportant; of course, they are, not least for their act of survival which often itself is of considerable historical interest. But what study of landscape has now brought to the fore is that, if we wish to understand, and through understanding, wish to conserve, then we should look at the workings of past landscapes. To understand and conserve and demonstrate how they evolved, we need to look at the system of which they were a part, at its workings which produced what we now see, and not just at the bits of land where monuments survive and buildings sag in ruination.

This means in topographical terms that we need to look at 'bottom lands', to use the Americanism, and valley sides as well as the plateaux and hill-tops where, because of their marginal nature in land-use terms since prehistoric times, archaeological structures such as burial mounds and hill-forts survive. A classic example is provided by the Avebury area, already a World Heritage Site, in Wiltshire. Practically every nearby hill-top and whole stretches of surrounding downland bear the marks of former occupation, activity and structures. A Neolithic causewayed enclosure, for example, crowns Windmill Hill to the NW of the great (and much later) henge monument at Avebury itself; burial mounds of c 3000 BC dot that landscape of early farmers, with many more burial mounds on the skylines and plateaux of the 2nd millennium BC. A large hill-fort developed on a hill-top to the SW during the 1st millennium BC, while to the east of the now-derelict henge, a farming landscape was organised and developed on the rolling downland of Fyfield and

Figure 2. Air photograph from the north of Iona Abbey, its *vallum monasterium* and their environs, Scotland, a cultural landscape with visible archaeological and physical evidence of many phases of farming and construction over the last two millennia and, overall, a Christian Saint, Columba (Crown Copyright, Royal Commission of the Ancient and Historical Monuments of Scotland).

Overton Downs. These Downs are designated a National Nature Reserve for their geological interest but they also now constitute a rare tract of grassland surrounded by a sea of arable. This preserves a series of agrarian landscapes from the Neolithic up to the present, their lineaments remarkably surviving as earthworks and stone structures of settlements, fields, tracks and funerary monuments.

Yet in and on what is now the plough-zone of the slopes down to and immediately around Avebury, there used to be similar survivals, some of them recorded from the 16th to the 19th centuries and others into this century. To understand this present and former extent of the evidence of land-use over the millennia, however, we have also to take into account the invisible evidence of the valley floor. Certainly the archaeology of Fyfield and Overton Downs can only be understood as the product of processes by looking down below. Chance exposures in service trenches and road-widening, and archaeological excavation proper, have shown glimpses of the 'invisibles' there, for example a series of enclosures forming an elaborate complex right beside the River Kennet just to the east of Silbury Hill, c 2 km south of and contemporary with Avebury henge itself.

Such 'new' evidence does not just fill up the landscape distributionally; much more importantly for present purposes, it helps explain the workings of a whole series of contemporary and successive landscapes in **functional** terms. In other words, cultural landscapes like that around Avebury do not merely contain a marked density of archaeological sites and other manmade features such as the garden of the Manor and a splendid thatched barn (indeed such do not need to be visibly present at all); they also embrace a variety of resources, natural as well as anthropogenic - 'bottom lands' and hill-tops, water and woodland, and so on, and the evidence of their interaction. So while the Marlborough Downs, an area of pleasing high chalkland rolling away to the east of Avebury towards the River Thames, are designated an Area of Outstanding Natural Beauty by the Countryside Commission, any suggestion of their designation as an outstanding cultural landscape could be challenged.

Of course, in one sense the Marlborough Downs are not even 'natural' in that their present appearance is markedly anthropogenic, not God-given. That we can see the sinuous contours of rounded chalk spurs and dry valleys is because the post-glacial tree cover has been cleared away by farmers since c 5000 BC. Beautiful the countryside of the Marlborough Downs may be but 'natural' the landscape most certainly is not. But the objection to their being a high-class 'cultural landscape' is something else. The history of the Downs, the development of their 'culture', can only be understood in relationship to what was happening around them, notably in the Thames and Kennet valleys - and around Avebury. So we would argue that the environs of Avebury, embracing a range of topography, resources and archaeology, more properly constitute a 'cultural landscape' than the Marlborough Downs as a whole. The latter area is primarily a topographical one, attractive to look at and with a good archaeology, explicable perhaps as a unit in functional terms up to c 3000 BC but thereafter economically and functionally fragmented and related to other places off the Downs.

The former, the Avebury area, is also attractive, not least for its downland backdrop; it also has an impressive archaeology of a density and monumentality comparable to that of Orkney. And like that archipelago, it can be explained by looking, not for its topographical homogeneity but for its variety. The landscape has become, in both cases, a cultural landscape, deep, distinctive and value-laden, no longer remaining just any landscape and certainly far more than scenery. A cultural landscape might indeed be defined as one which not only contains the evidence of its development but one which explains itself in eco-historical terms.

The Avebury region must represent other outstanding lowland cultural landscapes in Britain which we cannot explore here. We would be less than fair, however, if we did not even mention the Somerset Levels and the Norfolk Broads as - very different, - wetland exemplars; and the New Forest and Hatfield Forest as the two outstanding examples of extensive ancient woodland with a well-documented archaeology and history making them cultural landscapes - and, thankfully, 'continuing' ones too. We have to mention the sadly reduced and demeaned, but still existing, lowland heath of Thomas Hardy's 'Egdon' in Dorset, part 'continuing', part 'relict' and part 'associative'; and the 'associative' landscape of John Constable in Suffolk. The vast skies over, and high scientific value under, the flatness of the Fens characterise a sub-region not to everyone's liking by any means but it is one of the most distinctive landscapes in Britain, virtually man-created and certainly man-maintained.

So too, though of a different scale and aesthetic effect, are the deliberately-created parkland landscapes sculpted and planted around some of the great English country houses such as Blenheim, Stourhead and Stowe. Parks of this type are such a feature of the

Figure 3. A cultural landscape on Mountsland Common, Dartmoor, England, showing a typical but outstandingly preserved rectilinear field system of the later 2nd millennium bc surrounded by poorly-drained moor (top-right), and woodland of various dates in what is now an area of marginal farming (Copyright, Cambridge University Collection of Air Photographs).

English landscape that the best one thousand of them occupy 1,5% of the country's surface area. Blenheim already is a World Heritage Site; Stourhead or Stowe would probably be the first 'Parks' nomination from England as a subset of the new category of 'Cultural Landscape'.

Historic gardens usually go with parks and country houses, physically and often bureaucratically too. Can a single garden be a landscape? - if it is big enough, yes. Can one constitute a cultural landscape of gardens? - again, yes. These slightly rhetorical questions serve to emphasise that gardens, within parks or on their own, are another marked feature of the British landscape - and 'British', not just 'English'. Some wonderful gardens flourish, for example, in the Scottish 'Gulf Stream' counties of Dumfries and Galloway, and the remains of one of the most ambitious of 'Picturesque' landscapes dotted with various gardens are currently being attended to at Hafod in the Ystwyth valley, west Wales. Indeed, it could well be argued that Britain gave gardening to the western world and now, in England anyway, historic gardens have been catalogued with a view to their conservation. One, somewhere, probably ought to be a World Heritage Site.

Characteristic though gardens may be in Britain, perhaps what many visitors come for most of all is not one of the great landscapes on the hills or large parks in the lowlands but just a 'typical' piece of English/Scottish/Welsh countryside. In England it could be a quiet mosaic of lanes, village, trees and hedges, nothing dramatic but projecting qualities of tranquillity, timelessness, permanence. Given the dynamics of landscape, some of those qualities may be scientifically unreal; but that which is sought and perceived, the subjective not fact, is the significant element. It is clearly difficult to define and name such landscapes but they would probably be in the lowland zone, a bit off the beaten track perhaps in Norfolk, Kent, Shropshire, Somerset or Dorset.

The Uplands

In many respects, the uplands of Britain are very different from the lowlands. What, after all, have the Lake District or the Scottish Highlands in common with the flatness of the Fens or the modulated gentility of classical Stowe? To ask the question is to fall victim to an imagined priority for visibility and to forget the sort of criteria already discussed. Different the landscapes of the uplands may well look but, if we are looking for evidences of time-depth, process and evolution, then eye-catching grandeur in a cloud-capped mountain peak is not of itself very relevant; it is diverting rather than significant, unless our ancestors have given it 'meaning' which we wish to respect.

By world standards, none of Britain's uplands are very high; much of even the most mountainous countryside lies between only 1000-1300 m. above sea level whereas Europe's top eight mountains are all above 3300 m. high. Yet, **relatively**, much of the upland is high, whether it be the North Yorkshire Moors in relation to the Tees valley, Snowdonia in contrast to the Conwy valley, or the Grampians compared to the fertile coast of east Scotland between Dundee and Aberdeen. In much of the mountainous area, especially in Scotland and Wales, it is often quite difficult to detect the impact of people on a scenery dominated by geology and harsh climate; and why should we? - the uplands of Britain, like the Swiss Alps and the Colorado Rockies (though on a different scale) are sufficient unto themselves as spectacular views, with physical challenges and interesting geologies, plants and bird-life. And in truth, though people have sometimes lived in the

British uplands and often passed through, searching for ore perhaps, transhuming or shepherding, the anthropogenic effects, even when detectable, have not necessarily been significant.

In certain places, however, the impact has been crucial. Locally in many a now bleak upland, industry has had a major impact, may be for a short time but nevertheless first attracting in lots of workers and then leaving the landscape changed and littered with workings and waste. Stone itself has of course often been the quarry; but frequently upland industry has been out to extract the minerals in the stone. In the Lake District, over the longer term, land-clearance and stone-quarrying in the 4th millennium, and further land clearance and land enclosure in medieval and early modern times, both major phases of impact, have very much contributed to what we see - and value, - today. But this anthropogenic dimension alone, any more than the scenery *per se*, would not qualify the Lake District as an outstanding cultural landscape. What makes it different, and of universal significance, is not in what we see on it but the very way in which we look at it. For it was here, through the eyes and then the mind, first of Wordwsworth and then of Ruskin, that the revolutionary concept of the aesthetic of landscape appreciation was conceived and developed. It could indeed be argued that the fact of UNESCO's support for landscapes as World Heritage Sites goes back to what was theorised in the Lake District between one and two hundred years ago. The 20th century's contributions have been the origins of the National Trust - and Peter Rabbit: truly a landscape of iconography.

Just as the Lake District meant a lot to Peter Rabbit's only begetter, Beatrix Potter, similarly though without the literary overtones tracts of upland in Caithness and Sutherland, north of Inverness in north Scotland, exert a strong pull on countless other, less famous, people. This is the country of the 'clearances' of the 19th century when landlords pushed their tenants off the land to make way for sheep. The hurt of this lives on. It is perhaps worth remarking that a similar change in the Midlands of Tudor England now arouses no emotional reaction at all. Could there be a major cleft in group psychology between 400 years and 150 years ago? - if so, the point is of considerable significance in considering the designation of 'cultural landscape'.

The Highland clearances have left a characteristic landscape of low-density, rough pasture for sheep, scattered with the ruinous remains and earthworks of abandoned settlements, their fields and related features of what was a working landscape - and a home. The later 20th century sees a steady trickle of third and fourth generation emmigrants to the 'New World' returning to the field and the archive office questing their roots. The search, for the lucky ones, is bound to lead to a bit of wall, some humps and bumps in the bracken, undistinguished features in perhaps a visually unremarkable landscape; but obviously, to the returning great-grand child, it means a very great deal, probably far more than just being 'interesting'. Historically, the 'clearances' were important too, in North America and other parts of the world as well as in Scotland, and there would undoubtedly be a strong argument for designating a 'clearance landscape' as a 'cultural landscape' in World Heritage terms.

Like the lowlands throughout Britain, most of the uplands are privately owned. Paradoxically, certainly in the eyes of those from countries where the national government becomes legal owner of the land in various types of Park, most of the British National Parks are in the uplands - where land values are low and competition for space is less acute than in the lowlands. One thinks by association of the vast expanses of the USA National Parks in the 'unwanted' West. The National Parks in England and Wales primarily have a twofold purpose: conservation and recreation, particularly through access. The lack of legal ownership means that Park management requires consultation and co-operation with local interests in pursuing national as well as local priorities. So three major areas of potential difficulty, perhaps even conflict, are immediately identifiable: over proprietorial rights, over national and local priorities, and over Park objectives.

A tract of upland northern England, for example, is already a World Heritage Site for cultural reasons; part of it is in a National Park. The Site contains not just Hadrian's Wall but is a Roman military zone, some 120 kms long and of undefined, but certainly many kilometres, width. It was the NW frontier of the Roman Empire in the early centuries AD, a frontier zone which cut across a landscape already 'old' i.e. markedly modified by people. Now the remains of the Wall, often most unspectacular though partly in spectacular landscape, with its earlier and later military accoutrements, survive in a countryside deeply affected in post-Roman times by its former status as a military frontier. Visually, for example, fortified towers and defensive houses witness the continuation of the frontier role in medieval times up to the 17th century; and many a farmstead and kilometres of 19th century field wall are built of stones quarried for Hadrian's Wall and subsequently recycled into a recent agrarian landscape.

The frontier mentality, however, goes rather deeper than that. Now, much of the most striking landscape belongs to the National Trust which manages it as its Hadrian's Wall Estate. The whole of the Wall and much of its associated frontier archaeology is protected under Ancient Monuments legislation. The landscape and its contents could hardly be more designated and it is a landscape already enjoyed by many. A few want to make it enjoyed by more; and hence a serious clash in the 1990s between conservation and recreation.

The elements are familiar: a duty on the part of the statutory body to make the National Park more accessible, in this case by creating a National Trail; the routing of the Trail on, along and across the archaeology of a World Heritage Site; enthusiasm for, and serious doubts about the desirability of, doing anything to make the Wall country more attractive and accessible to more and more people; financial incentives from officialdom, elements of local 'Nimbyism' ('Not in my Back Yard'-ism); farmer's fears about damage to gates and stock, archaeologists' fears about potential damage and erosion to earthworks; and so on, but here played out on relatively remote uplands, not in the more familiar surroundings for such public controversy of more crowded lowlands.

It is an important case which World Heritage will suffer from if the Trail goes through despite the landscape's 'universal values'. There are several other equally important upland cultural landscapes in Britain, not yet designated as of World Heritage status but of that class. Their nomination might be seen as pointless if the Roman military Zone is impaired by a badly conceived Trail. This would be a pity, for some British upland areas are of world quality as cultural landscapes. This applies to some quite remarkable landscapes of the 2nd and 1st millennia BC in general, and to the five hundred years or so specifically around 1200 BC. The latter was a time of considerable upheaval throughout much of the Old World and not just on the increasingly impoverished soils of the British uplands, Bodmin Moor, Dartmoor, the Peak District, the northern Pennines, the Cheviots, and several areas in the Scottish uplands - all such display remarkable agrarian landscapes remarkably preserved and, by and large, without later, damaging intrusions. There are other, later agrarian landscapes too of similar outstanding qualities: while prehistoric elements are often present within them, it is the stone-walled fields of the 18th and 19th centuries which make the limestone landscapes of the Peak District and the Yorkshire Dales so visually attractive. But they are far more than pretty pictures because here, with important floristic, technological and land management implications, the traditional ways in which the land was worked continue in at least some degree, and can be encouraged with financial incentives through various conservation schemes.

Discussion

Much has not been said, not just about individual examples named here but also about many not even mentioned. The topographical approach works in some ways but constrains thematic development. Industrial landscapes, for example, have been created from the Neolithic period onwards - the Neolithic flint mines at Grimes Graves in Norfolk produced a landscape of disturbance and waste heaps repeated a thousand times thereafter; while at the other extreme are the 'continuing' landscapes of 18th and 19th century industries like coal-mining and ship-building which at this very moment are changing into 'relict' landscape as their *raisons d'être* disappear.

Britain already boasts two industrial World Heritage Sites - Ironbridge and New Lanark - but it is worth stressing that there is as much variety in industrial as there is in agrarian landscapes. Manufacturing, power generation, transport - they all produce different landscapes; and the landscapes of each change through time, for example as technology changes. Britain's role as world-wide generator of the 'industrial revolution' in the 18th century is widely recognised and, to an extent, the significance is acknowledged in designation and protection; but there are many more landscapes that ought to be considered, not least from very recent times. The problem, and the opportunity, here is that change is happening so fast that, before we have realised it, the familiar has become the past. With the deep coal-mining industry on the point of extinction in most regions of Britain, for example, should an attempt be made to 'keep' a whole coal-mining landscape *in situ* rather than afford the future the sole option of re-creating one in a museum context? Should we preserve a 'motor car factory landscape' at, for example, Cowley or Dagenham? And what about the power generation industry? - we can feel good about a folksy landscape of windmills in Norfolk and even get romantic about those wonderful old gasometers outside St. Pancras Station; but at what point does a redundant nuclear power station become cuddly? Dounreay on the north coast of Scotland is available - and a landmark if ever there was one. The interesting point about all such questions dealing with recent time and items not yet in the conservationist canon is when you try to answer the question with another one: why NOT?

We have also used 'landscape' entirely in a rural sense, though we are of course well aware that it can be an umbrella word covering urban too. Cityscape and townscape are subdivisions of landscape; conversely, landscape is not a synonym for 'countryside'. Britain of course contains some great urban landscapes. A characteristic of them is often the setting for the urban core. Contrast is vital, as three World Heritage Sites illustrate: the open space of Parliament Square to one side, and of the Thames beyond St. Stephen's Green, around Westminster Abbey; the similar interplay of bulky buildings and open space (which, ridiculously, is not part of the designation) at Durham Cathedral and Castle; the vistas to the surrounding hills from the streets of Georgian Bath. Other examples spring to mind: the Backs at Cambridge, the contrast between Old and New Towns and the green, railway-filled valley in between at Edinburgh, the 'buffer' of the green space between cathedral and the medley of houses in the Close at Salisbury.

Urban parks, another form of green space but deliberately designed as such for public recreation were virtually invented in Britain and given to the world. Obviously some of the great metropolitan ones like Hyde Park, London, belong to the international class along with Central Park, New York, and Parc du Champ de Mars, Paris. But most provincial cities have their own too, perhaps anonymous to the world in general but valued landscapes to the citizens. The first municipal park specifically laid out for public use was

Figure 4. Near-vertical view of The Parks, Oxford, a different sort of cultural landcape near an historic city centre with all sorts of iconographic values for generations of students, an historic cricket ground (centre bottom), 17th century civil war earthworks and, beneath the grass of a public park, crop-marks of many different features of Anglo-Saxon, Roman and prehistoric date, typical of the gravel terraces of the region (Copyright, Cambridge University Collection of Air Photographs).

Birkenhead Park in 1843 by Joseph Paxton. Jesmond Dene, Newcastle upon Tyne, bought by Lord Armstrong and given in to the City in 1883, is a classic, or rather 'rustic', example of the *genre*. Less mannered but equally manmade, and equally enjoyed as urban open spaces, are those traditional grazing areas just outside some medieval cities: Port Meadow, Oxford, Clifton Downs, Bristol, and the Town Moor, Newcastle, are outstanding examples.

Such provide not just recreational space but distinctiveness, a sense of place. British people seem to like that, even to need it. Many of them think of a particular landscape as 'home', even as 'theirs' without any presumption to legal ownership. It may not be particularly distinguished by its architecture, its history or archaeology, or even by its scenery; it just has to be recognisable in a meaningful way to a person. The experts talk about the 'personality of landscape', meaning how they can categorise it scientifically; but perhaps we would do well to remember that most bits of landscape probably mean something to somebody and that most people have their own favourite landscape. It would seem especially important to think of such layers and levels of perception when we look at the landscapes of a whole country with a view to evaluating them, and even more so when we presume to grapple at global level with 'universal values' of a relatively new concept, 'cultural landscapes'.

Bibliographic Notes

Britain is extremely rich in its topographical literature, a cultural phenomenon which has developed since the writings of the Venerable Bede in the early 8th century and flourished, at both local and national levels, since the 16th century. This literature has itself given a 'cultural overlay' to many landscapes in Britain. It is easily accessed, so no specific, in-text references have been given here in such a general essay.

Basic information about the cultural landscape throughout England, Scotland and Wales is available from the Royal Commissions on the Ancient/Historical Monuments of each of the three countries of England, Scotland and Wales. Each of them maintains as a public archive for each country a voluminous and detailed National Monuments Record. Their numerous publications from early in the 20th century include Inventories on a county basis and, more recently, volumes such as *North-East Perth an archaeological landscape* (1990, HMSO Edinburgh) and the English Commission's study of *Bodmin Moor* (1994).

No one book, however, covers our attempted field, so the following titles, highly select but carefully selected, provide both background and introduction, not least through their own bibliographies:

References

Birks, H.H., Birks, H.J.B., Kaland, P.E. and Moe, D. (eds.) (1988). *The Cultural Landscape - Past, Present and Future*, Cambridge University Press, Cambridge.

Coones, P. and Patten, J. (1986). *Guide to the Landscape of England and Wales*, Penguin, Harmondsworth.

Cosgrove, D. and Daniels, S. (ed.) (1988). *The iconography of landscape. Essays on the symbolic representation, design and use of past environments*, Cambridge University Press, Cambridge.

Darvill, T. (1987). *Ancient Monuments in the countryside. An archaeological management review*, English Heritage, London.
Devereux, P.(1992). *Symbolic Landscapes. The Dreamtime Earth and Avebury's Open Secret*, Gothic Image, Glastonbury.
Fleming, A. (1989). *The Dartmoor Reaves*, Batsford, London.
Fowler, P.J. (1983). *The Farming of Prehistoric Britain*, Cambridge University Press, Cambridge.
Fowler, P.J. (1992). *The Past in Contemporary Society: Then, Now*, Routledge, London.
Fowler, P.J. and Sharp, M. (1990). *Images of Prehistory*, Cambridge University Press, Cambridge.
Hoskins, W.G. (1995). *The Making of the English Landscape*, Hodder and Stoughton, London.
Jacques, D. (1983). *Georgian Gardens. The Reign of Nature*, Batsford, London.
Rackham, O. (1990). *Trees and Woodland in the British Landscape*, Dent, London.
Salway, P. (1981). *Roman Britain*, Clarendon Press, Oxford.
Simmons, I.G. (1989). *Changing the Face of the Earth. Culture, Environment, History*, Blackwell, Oxford.
Ucko, P.J. et al. (1991). *Avebury Reconsidered. From the 1660s to the 1990s*, Unwin Hyman, London.
Woodell, S.R.J. (ed.)(1985). *The English Landscape, Past, Present and Future*, Oxford University Press, Oxford.

Peter Fowler is Professor of Archaeology at the University of Newcastle upon Tyne, England.

David Jacques is a Landscape Historian. He lectures at the University of York and has recently finished the restoration of the Privy Gardens at Hampton Court, England.

Chapter 31

The Cultural Landscape of Markim/Orkestra

Kerstin Riessen

Introduction

The landscape discussed in this paper is situated in the parishes of Markim and Orkesta in the middle of Sweden. Together with 1,700 other objects in Sweden it has been designated as an Area of National Importance, and has also been nominated for the tentative list for the World Heritage List as an important example of an agriculture landscape with a thousand year old continuity.

The Central Board of National Antiquities has therefore allocated special funding for an information project, conjointly with the Stockholm County Administration, the local municipal council and other local institutions, for the purpose of identifying and describing the heritage values of the area and informing the inhabitants and the local politicians of its cultural values.

Geography

The actual region is situated 35 kilometers north of Stockholm in the municipality of Vallentuna and measures approximately 60 square kilometers. The terrain is representative for the Lake Malar Valley, with open agricultural areas divided by dells and hills. The farms and the hamlets together with the prehistoric burial grounds are, in this part of the country, located on the hills and the fields in the valleys.

Geologically the region is partly flat and exposed, disintegrated by systems of rift valleys and subject to a land elevation which has been going on since the Glacial Period. The elevation here is still of the order of 0.3-0.4 meter per century. At the end of the Stone Age, large parts were still under water. During the Bronze Age and up to the time when the sea was about 15 meters higher than today, large areas resembled an archipelago, with narrow channels and creeks between rocky and moraine landparts and only small, grass-covered fields in the clay covered valleys. It is not until the Iron Age that we can regard this part of Uppland as a continuous mainland, and even at the beginning of the Middle Ages there were inlets and channels of the open sea.

Prehistory

The parishes of Markim and Orkesta contain the largest concentration of prehistoric remains such as burial grounds and settlements in the County of Stockholm. The oldest remains are found in the Orkesta area. Here we find a couple of burial grounds and some isolated graves from the Bronze Age (1800 BC-500 BC).

Colonization seems to have expanded a great deal in the early Iron Age (550 BC-400 AD). From this period there are about ten burial grounds, nearly half of them very large, with more than 150 graves. The largest has more than 270 graves. Most of the remains from this period are to be found in the Orkesta district. Other remains from the early Iron Age are the so-called stone fences. These are the remains of boundaries between the infields and surrounding land (forests and grazing lands) from the early Iron Age.

The Markim area does not seem to have been colonized until the later part of the Iron Age (400 AD-1050 AD). A typical feature for the area of Markim/Orkesta is the separation of the burial grounds from the early part of the Iron Age from those dated to the late part. However, some exceptions can be found, as the Vaxtuna burial ground where the whole Iron Age seems to be represented. The later burial grounds are located in the more central parts of the area, the older ones in the outer parts. This indicates a shift of settlement from the outskirts to the more central parts of this area in about 500 AD.

Burial grounds from the late part of the Iron Age could be found close to nearly all of the present-day farms/hamlets. They mostly consist of five to eighty graves. The largest one, with 170 graves, is situated at the hamlet of Orkesta, just north of the parish church.

The administrative centres in this period of the Iron Age were probably Husby and Vaxtuna. This assumption is supported both by the place-names and by the rather special grave fields. The "Husby"-names are usually connected with the royal power like the "Tuna"-named sites where one often find large burial mounds in the neighborhood, otherwise known as "king mounds", like those of ancient Uppsala.

Runes

More than 3,500 inscriptions are known from Sweden. The oldest one might be from about 200-300 AD, but the majority date from the late Iron Age, the Viking era (800 AD-1050 AD). Those inscriptions are often marked with a cross, i.e. Christian. Geographically they are concentrated in central eastern Sweden, in the Lake Malar Valley, and above all in the Province of Uppland.

The runic inscriptions are our first written documents and make a very important contribution to Swedish history. Here we also find the first named Swedish artists, as many of the rune masters signed their work. The inscriptions have a great deal to tell us of the social and cultural life of the area.

The rune stones were often memorials to a deceased person, and they tell us his (or her) name and the name of the farm where he lived. They were also a kind of legal document, serving the important purpose of indicating land ownership. And so, as confirmation of the heritage, the names of a family or kinship can be recited for several generations back in time.

The rune stones sometimes tell a great deal about Viking expeditions to eastern and western countries. The country most mentioned is Greece, but the name England often occurs in the inscriptions.

But also more peaceful and local public actions are told: the clearing of roads, bridge building, mostly causeways and establishing of "thing-places". The locations of the rune stones are important. They were meant to be seen and are therefore placed along roads and at "thing-places", for example, as a memorial of the benefactor.

In the municipality of Vallentuna we have 109 known runic inscriptions, eight from the parish of Markim and fourteen from Orkesta. Almost half the rune stones in Markim/Orkesta are still in situ. But some have been moved to other places, destroyed or used as building material. Rune stones often turn up in the mended walls of medieval churches.

Churches

When Christianity became the leading religion in the 11th century a period of church building ensued. A church was built in every parish . We know from archeological excavations that the first ones were wooden buildings. Later, in the 12th century, these were replaced by stone-built churches. The heathen village burial grounds were abandoned and replaced by common cemeteries located round the churches.

The two churches at Markim and Orkesta are typical of early 12th century church buildings in the Province of Uppland. They had a very simple layout to begin with: nave,

Figure 1. The church of Markim at its special location not in a village, but in the centre of an broad agricultural basin (Photo Jan Norrman).

chancel and apse. During the 15th century the flat wooden inner roofs were replaced by vaults. The interiors were painted and additions were made - vestries and church porches, for example. In the 18th century many of the medieval paintings were white-washed or plastered and bigger windows were inserted, and exteriors were similarly treated.

The church in the parish of Orkesta was erected at the end of the 12th century in a typical Romanesque style with nave, chancel and apse. During the 15th century a vestry and a small porch were added, as well as a western section intended as the base of a tower. Inside the church, vaulting was constructed throughout and the walls and ceilings painted with biblical themes and floral decorations; these were white-washed over in the 18th century but have now been restored. The pulpit and the altar date from the Roccoco period and, unusually, are in the chancel. The wooden bell belfry, separate from the church, probably dates from the end of the 17th century.

There are four rune stones here, two inside the church and two outside. The latter have some very interesting inscriptions. They tell us about Ulf from Borresta who three times went to England to collect the Danagald, i. e. the tribute which the English had to pay, from the end of the 10th century onwards, to buy off the Viking marauders. This helps us to date the rune inscription, because the last "Danagald" was paid in about 1018. Ulf was also a rune-master and has signed other rune stones. The farm of Borresta still exists, visible from the church.

Figure 2. The church of Orkesta with surrounding farms (Photo Jan Norrman).

The church was placed in the village of Orkesta, and the naming of the church after the village, where it was built, was common practice in southern Sweden.

The church at Markim is one of the two best preserved Romanesque churches in Uppland, as the exterior additions have been fairly small. The church was erected in the beginning of the 13th century, the church porch and vestry were added in the 15th. Here again the walls were white-washed and the only medieval paintings to been restored are in the church porch. As in the church of Orkesta the altar and the pulpit are placed in the chancel. The entrance door to the church porch is from the 13th century and has very interesting wrought-iron ornaments, featuring a ship similar to the Viking ships of Oseberg in Norway. The wooden bell-tower is from the early 18th century.

In the cemetery is a rune stone which was found during repairs to the church. The stone is very large but the inscription is traditional: It is marked with a cross and commemorates a father and his relatives.

The church of Markim is located, not in a village but in the centre of a broad, mainly agricultural basin. The farms/hamlets of the parish occupy the higher hill, surrounding the plain with the church in the centre. There is no village named Markim and the name refers to the whole area. This way of naming is typical for northern Sweden.

Farms and Hamlets

The Markim/Orkesta area is a typical farming district. Today you find three hamlets and seven farms in the parish of Orkesta and six hamlets and six farms in Markim, all of them dependent on agriculture. Nearly all the farms or hamlets occupy the same sites as in the Iron Age; this is confirmed by the nearby placed burial grounds from the same period. Most of the farm houses are from the late 19th century. There are just a few from earlier periods. Some houses have been modernized or enlarged, but the farm complexes are still kept in a traditional style and in the old locations. Specially well-preserved dwelling houses are to be found in the farms of Bergby, Snottsta and Husby in the parish of Markim, and Granby, Husby, Vaxtuna and Borresta in the parish of Orkesta Many of the farming buildings, barns for example, were built or modernized in this century, but there are still some well-preserved outbuildings like those at Vaxtuna Farm and Bergby Windmill (built 1868). Out of the hamlets are several crofts and share-croppers cottages, many of them now second homes for town dwellers. Most of them are not modernized or enlarged but kept as earlier.

Some examples of the most interesting farmsteads in the Markim/Orkesta area include the following.

At Granby the remains of an almost complete Viking era homestead are located on the heights behind the present-day settlement. To the east there is a well preserved burial ground with about 85 graves from the later part of the Iron Age. Immediately to the west are house foundations and terraces from buildings of the same period. The largest house foundation is about 35 meters long with an visible entrance ramp. That house has been partly excavated and is dated to late Viking Age and early Middle Ages. The farm, for which the name Hyppinge has been suggested, was probably abandoned in the Middle Ages and the place has been used as grazing or meadow land ever since. Within the perimeter of the homestead is one of Sweden's largest runic slabs, bearing a remarkable inscription by the well known rune-master Visate. Close to the hamlet are some well-preserved crofts from the 19th century.

Figure 3. The village of Granby (Photo Jan Norrman).

Vaxtuna is a small-scale well-preserved agrarian environment. West of the farm, in wooded pasture, is a large burial ground with about 150 graves. The geometry and form of the graves suggest that this burial ground was in continuous use from the early till the late Iron Age. Immediately to the south of Vaxtuna is a large burial mound which, through excavations already undertaken 1724, has been dated about 600 AD. The old "Vasa Road", the road linking the central settlements of Vallentuna with the "thing" and market-place of Attundaland, north of the Markim I Orkesta area, also passed this way. The prehistoric remains are still visible, close to the grave-field.

Snottsta has a outstandingly well-preserved settlement environment. The burial grounds and the runic inscriptions, as well as the name of the place, tell us that the hamlet dates back to the late Iron Age. Inga, who commissioned four runic inscriptions in the hamlet during the 11th century is also mentioned on a rune stone in Svartsjolandet.

Husby has a farmstead environment of outstanding historic interest, consisting of a corps de logis from the 18th century with two timbered wings. There is also a farmstead museum here, illustrating the home of the owner at the turn of the century. Another unique feature is the share-cropper building/croft nicknamed "Tratten" (The Funnel), which is square in shape with a porch on each side, built for four families during the second part of the l9th century. Not far from the hamlet there is a couple of small burial grounds from the late Iron Age. There is also a rune stone near the road, and some very interesting stone fence-systems from the early Iron Age.

Figure 4. The viking homestead at Granby with burrial ground, house foundations and runic slab (Photo Jan Norrman).

Landscape

Remains from the Bronze Age are confined to a few burial places. From the early phase of the Iron Age we find burial grounds and fence-systems, which indicate a different settlement structure than in the late Iron Age.

During the late part of the Iron Age the settlements were more firmly established, placed on the moraine hills with the arable fields close to the farms, often on the hill-slopes. The meadows laid in the moist valleys. Those infields, together with the farms, were fenced from the pasture lands and woods.

The Middle Ages (1050 AD-1550 AD) brought no great visible changes in farming. Churches were erected, the old hamlet burial grounds were deserted for the central cemeteries and a stricter administration system was established. But the division between infields and outfields remained the same and so did the tools which were used.

In the 18th century, the Swedish government issued new partition and redistribution orders with a view to agriculture improvement. There had been no survey of this organization since the so called "Sun Partition" in the Middle Ages. Due to partly inheritance, arable holdings were dotted about all over the villages in long strips. This was an ineffective system of cultivation and yielded smaller harvests than desired. The partition or redistribution orders were in this area introduced in the years of 1760 until 1820, and again between 1830 and 1870.

In many parts of Sweden, where the villages were large, this had the effect of splitting the villages up and transferring single farms to new areas outside the village. In Markim/Orkesta, however, the villages were small, and so the effect of the various partition orders had little effect. Most farms remained in the same place as before and the hamlets were left fairly intact. So the maps from this period are the most permanent material from these partition orders and nowadays make very important documents for research works.

The industrial revolution in the mid-19th century also influenced the farming system. The improvement of the plough made it possible to cultivate new areas as the rich but heavy clay soils in the valleys, used previously as meadows and pasturage. By the end of the l9th century almost all the meadow lands had been turned to arable land. The invention of the fertilizers superseded the cattle manure. Demand for new fields were also due to the experiments with lowering the lakes, mostly without success. Rational forestry became more important. In earlier periods the wood lands were mostly used for solid fuel, building and fencing materials, and as grazing land. Crofter holdings or share-croppers' houses were built, especially at the larger farms or manors. The area has only a few such houses, because the farms were rather small. From the mid-19th century we know of about 20 crofts or share-croppers buildings in Markim and 15 in Orkesta. The system with agriculture workers was abolished in 1943.

Agriculture has been much more highly mechanized since the end of the Second World War. Bigger, more efficient machines have led to new field boundaries and the construction, for example of covered drains. The old croft rotation systems have been replaced by new systems and other crops with different demands have been introduced.

Place-names

The area's place names are typical for this part of Sweden. Place-names experts tell us that names ending with -inge are from the early part of the Iron Age and those ending -sta and -by from the late Iron Age. All three suffixes mean a site or settlement. The prefix to the -by names often refers to topography: Bergby, for example, means "the site of the mountain", Ekeby "the site with oaks" and so on. The prefix of -sta names are more difficult to analyze but are supposed to be personal names. Orkesta, for example, being the place where Oreka (man's name) lived. The name Markim consists of two parts, Mark = wood, and -im = heim, homestead. Husby and Tuna were, as I said before, probably administrative centres in the kingdom of Svealand.

Discussion

In Sweden we have an agricultural surplus which we have been selling at very low prices on the international market. To stop this, the Government has decided that parts of the cultivated acreage is to be used for other purposes, principally for forestry. As an incentive, the farmers are paid for this change.

But on the other hand the Swedish farmers can be compensated for keeping the landscape open in order to preserve special cultural values. For the 1991/92 fiscal year, the Stockholm County Administration allotted 7 million Swedish crowns for this purpose, and farmers in this small area received no less than 24% of the allocation (1.7 million crowns).

The buildings, and especially their position in the landscape, form an essential part of the cultural heritage. But the Plan and Building Law allows people to do many things outside the town centres or densely populated areas without building permission being necessary. Farm buildings, for example, do not require planning permission, and so nothing can be done to influence their positioning or design.

Preservation suggestions

In Markim/Orkesta there are no regulations, except general ones. The masterplan for Vallentuna municipality has only recommendations and is not legally binding.

We have a very strong law protecting ancient monuments and remains. Where buildings are concerned we have fairly good possibilities of establishing rules by detailed planning. For the area as a whole there are legal possibilities of preservation under to the National Resources Act, but the consequences of compensation claims, for example, are uncertain. To protect the area, building permit stipulations will have to be tightened up to create the opportunity for a dialogue between the house owner and the building committee before a building project is put into effect.

But the most effective course of action is to increase and improve the information to all concerned - local politicians, farmers in the area and all municipal residents. Since the information project started in 1992, we have noticed an increasing interest among the inhabitants and we have also observed a growth of pride living in this part of Sweden. To round off the discussion I have been summarizing, I find that the best way is, step by step, to try to inform and influence all people concerned, both the politicians and the residents, and make them see that the consequences of placing this area on the World Heritage List are positive and not negative, although some restrictions will be necessary.

Conclusions

The uniqueness of this man-made landscape lies in its very rich and well preserved content. Here you can find numerous relics from the prehistoric periods, many well-preserved and interesting rune stones, two well-preserved early medieval churches and a very well-preserved structure of settlement and land use. We also have several farms and hamlets with well preserved typical buildings, showing the agricultural activities. The area has been untouched by urban influences such as industries and suburbs, and no big communication or road systems have intruded on the old roads from ancient times. Altogether this forms a cultural landscape of outstanding quality with a continuity from early Iron Age to the present day, easy to describe and make understandable in a educational manner. Lastly, this is still a living landscape and not just a museum.

References

Ambrosiani, B. (1964). *Fornlamningar och bebyggelse*. Uppsala.
Dyhlen-Tackman, I. (1986). *Kulturminnesvardsprogram for Vallentuna kommun*. Stockholm.
Gustavsson, H. (1991). *Runstenar i Vallentuna*. Stockholm.
Hoglin, S. (1991). *Gardar och gardesgardar i Markim*. Stockholm.
Kallman, R. (1992). *Markim och Orkesta - tva socknar i Malardalen*. Stockholm.
Tollin, C. (1991). *Attebackar och odegarden*. Stockholm.

Kerstin Riessen works at the Central Board of National Antiquities, Stockholm, Sweden.

Chapter 32

Nature and Culture – Two Aspects of the Same Story. Norwegian Landscape Management in the 1990s

Tonte Hegard

Norway, lying between 57° and 71° N, has a very varied topography. It also has a varied climate through these 14 degrees of latitude, which has imposed a variety of conditions on habitation and the exploitation of natural resources. Besides agriculture, fishing has traditionally been a major occupation along the country's 21,000 km coastline, and not unsurprisingly fishing has been a determining factor in settlement in the northern part of the country.

There are some four and a quarter million people living in Norway today. Divided among the 324,000 km^2 of the Norwegian land surface, the result is fourteen inhabitants per km^2. Consequently, there is much "landscape" in Norway! Some 27.5% of the population live in sparsely inhabited areas. In 1992 there were 92,000 farms and smallholdings in the country, providing a total of 92,400 man/year in agriculture. For approximately 30% agriculture was the only source of income.

In a European context, the term "wilderness" is often used in connection with the Norwegian landscape. This is understandable, considering the high population density in other countries and the exploitation of nature there. Nonetheless, such a description belies the fact that Norway's forests, mountains and wild open country have provided major areas of occupation throughout the country, of both a primary and a secondary character. As a result, this so-called "undisturbed landscape" contains numerous traces of human activity from the 10,000 years of the country's history. Norway's areas of wilderness today are in fact important cultural landscapes when seen in a historical perspective. For example, large tracts of Norway are still actively used for reindeer herding, with the various effects that such an activity has on the landscape. Reindeer herding in Norway is particularly associated with the Saami population (the Lapps), who are an indigenous people with their own cultural heritage management in Norway. This has led to an emphasis not only on Man in the landscape and all the traces of human impact, but also on the landscape in Man and the different ways in which various cultures regard the landscape.

The conditions imposed by Nature and by the historical development have meant that there has always been a close association between people and the surrounding landscape. The environmental authorities in Norway state categorically that the physical surroundings must be regarded as an entity - that cultural heritage and nature must be considered in relationship to each other. As a consequence of this approach, the Directorate for Cultural Heritage and the Directorate for Nature Management are both placed under the Ministry for the Environment.

The administration of the landscape takes place within a total environmental perspective. The value of this has been confirmed politically in the handling of the 1987 report from the World Commission on Environment and Development (Our Common Future): the Norwegian Parliament has emphasized that "natural resources and the cultural heritage together constitute the major part of the management of the environment and resources" (translation by the author).

In Norway this perspective is covered by the term "cultural landscape". It is the sum of all aspects of the environment, both those given by Nature and those created by Man - in other words, the interaction between ecological and cultural processes which has formed and which continues to uphold the various types of landscape. It should be emphasized that in Norwegian administration the term "cultural landscape" covers all kinds of cultural landscape from the extensively exploited, the reindeer pastures of the Saami and the high mountain pastures used by dairy cattle in the summer, to the urban landscape of the cities.

A determining factor for being able to implement this total view of environmental management is the close collaboration which was established at the beginning of the 1990s between the cultural heritage and the nature conservancy authorities. This is based on the acceptance that the conditions imposed by Nature and the effects of Man cannot be separated from one another in the landscape as it appears today: both are present everywhere, and consequently affect the management of the landscape.

The natural sciences and the humanities both play a part in the public administration of the landscape - in their different ways of looking at the question, their different kinds of competence, their different methods of analysing and dealing with the areas. The collaboration between natural scientists and specialists in the humanities in public administration is a precondition for securing a satisfactory total approach to caring for the landscape. A joint administrative effort presupposes a similar interdisciplinary collaboration in the fields of research and education. How to achieve this is still under consideration.

An essential consequence of the World Commission report is that environmental policy has become an interdepartmental responsibility. This means that other sectors of society have an independent responsibility for paying due regard to the environment within their own areas. Before new plans are put into effect, they must be analysed and their consequences considered. Any doubts about the consequences must be settled in favour of the environment. Since 1990 this principle has been incorporated in the Planning and Building Act. A general awareness and acceptance of responsibility are of course fundamental concepts here.

Interdepartmental activity has advanced, especially with regard to the cultural landscape. The collaboration between the agricultural and the environmental authorities is vital here. Whereas agriculture previously focused single-mindedly on agricultural products, the production of environmental benefits has now been included as a supplementary objective. This development has been stimulated by extensive grants from public funds, and the environmental authorities participate actively in the disbursement of these grants.

There is also a strong democratic element in the management of the landscape in Norway. It will always be that specific governmental intervention, protection through the law and the use of public funds can only be used for specially selected and valuable landscapes, whereas landscape management must also deal with land areas which do not fulfill such narrow selection criteria. It is the total landscape that comprises what both local people and visitors regard as characteristic for the district, the region or the country.

The environment is a common responsibility. Local involvement and local responsibility for the environment are accepted policy, and this is also an important ingredient in the administration of the landscape. Not least, great attention has been focused during the past ten years on sensitive areas which form the transition between built-up areas and the open countryside beyond. The strong tradition in Norway of indulging in outdoor activities is a driving force here: walking in the countryside, through the forests and over the mountains has been a pursuit widely practised by town-dwellers for over a century, and teaching children the joys of experiencing the countryside is given high priority in the political programme for children and youth in the welfare state.

The chief means for securing the formal protection of the cultural and natural values of the landscape is legislation. A central problem in the administration of the landscape is the implementation of a sensible and reasonable division of responsibility between local and national authorities - in other words, the correlation between general planning policy and the imposition of a protection order on a particular area. The question of imposing a protection order - with various degrees of restriction - is, among other things, tied to the desire to give certain areas special protection as representatives of ordinary types of landscape in different parts of the country. But it is also related to the fact that a protection order is imposed through a specific Act of Parliament, administered through national government, whereas the local municipality deals with the whole of the municipal area as an entity through its planning regulations under the Planning and Buildings Act.

The particular legislation in Norway concerning the cultural heritage has undergone a conceptual development which is parallelled in the other Scandinavian countries. The earliest act of parliament dealing with the cultural heritage, the Preservation and Protection of Antiquities Act, dates from 1905. It gave automatic protection to archaeological sites or monuments proved to be older than AD 1537 (the date of the Reformation in Norway). In 1920 the Protection of Buildings Act was passed, through which a protection order could be placed on any standing building of architectural or historical interest more than 100 years old. In 1951 the Antiquities Act was extended to include a limited zone around prehistoric and medieval sites, but this had no effect on the administration of cultural landscapes. In the late seventies, a new Cultural Heritage Act, which combined the previous two acts, allowed for the establishment of a protected zone around any site or monument, whether under a protection order or automatically protected because of its date. Nevertheless, there still had to be an object of special value such as a building or an archaeological site at the centre and the extent of the area was limited. The criterion was that it should help to safeguard the effect of the object in the landscape.

The great breakthrough with regard to the protection of cultural landscapes came with the revision of the Cultural Heritage Act in 1992. This now makes it possible to place a protection order on a cultural landscape, large or small, based on its qualities as a cultural landscape. The Act uses the term "cultural environment", which is defined as "any area where a monument or site forms part of a larger entity or context". This implies that the monument or site does not need to be worthy of protection in itself.

With this move, parallel regulations for the protection of the landscape now exist in the two relevant pieces of legislation, the Nature Conservancy Act from 1970 and the Cultural Heritage Act of 1992.

This milestone is the result of a conscious - and escalating - emphasis on the collaboration of the cultural heritage and nature conservancy authorities over the past four of five years. It has been made possible by the fact that they both come under the same

> **Box 1.** Extract from the Cultural Heritage Act
> (Act No. 50 of 9 June 1978 Concerning the Cultural Heritage with Amendments of 3 July 1992)
>
> **Chapter I**
> **Purpose and Scope**
>
> **§ 1 Purpose of the Act**
>
> The purpose of this Act is to protect archeological and architectural monuments and sites, and cultural environments in all their variety and detail, both as part of our cultural heritage and identity and as an element in the overall environment and resource managment. It is a national responsibility to safeguard these resources as scientific source material and as a permanent basis for the experience, self-awareness, enjoyment and activities of present and future generations. (...)
>
> **§2 Monuments and sites, and cultural environments - definition of terms**
>
> The term 'monuments and sites' is defined here as all traces of human activity in our physical environment, including places associated with historical events, beliefs or traditions.
> The term 'cultural environment' is defined here as an area where a monument or site forms a part of a larger entity or context. (...)

section in the Ministry for the Environment. The two bodies, the Directorate for Cultural Heritage and the Directorate for Nature Management, share the responsibility of reporting on cultural landscape.

So, as you have seen, nature and culture are two sides of the same story in the management of the cultural landscape in Norway. The Norwegian authorities believe in the synergetic effect of a joint effort and the results so far have been more than promising.

References

Current legislation:
Nature Conservancy Act of 19 June 1970, with amendments of 8 June 1990.
The Cultural Heritage Act of 9 June 1978, with amendments of 3 July 1992.
Planning and Building Act of 14 June 1985, with amendments of 26 June 1990.

Earlier Acts:
The Preservation and Protection of Antiquities Act of 13 July 1905.
Nature Conservancy Act of 25 July 1910.
Protection of Buildings Act of 3 December 1920.
The Preservation and Protection of Antiquities Act of 29 June 1951.
Nature Conservancy Act of 1 December 1954.
Building Act of 18 June 1965.

Tonte Hegard is working as a Senior Advisor in Riksantikvaren – Directorate for Cultural Heritage – in Oslo.

Conserving Cultural Landscapes: Elements for a Strategy of Protection through Development

Cultural Landscapes: an IUCN Perspective
Adrian Phillips

Functional Criteria for the Assessment of Cultural Landscapes
Harald Plachter

Principles for Protecting Endangered Landscapes: The Work of the IUCN-CESP Working Group on Landscape Conservation
Bryn H. Green

Conservation of Landscapes in Post-Industrial Countries
David Jacques and Peter Fowler

Tentative Lists as a Tool for Landscape Classification and Protection
Sarah Titchen and Mechtild Rössler

Chapter 33

Cultural Landscapes: an IUCN Perspective

Adrian Phillips

Introduction

Cultural landscapes are to be found in every part of the populated world. They represent a rich and almost infinitely varied part of the human heritage. Although often much changed from their natural state, such landscapes are important to the conservation of nature and biodiversity - many of the ecosystems within them have evolved, and continue to survive, because of human intervention. As large areas of undisturbed land become more scarce, due to rising human numbers and intensified land use, the value of these places as repositories of biological richness seems bound to increase.

Such landscapes also contain evidence of human history - from archaeological structures to vernacular buildings - and reveal traces of past land use practices. They contribute importantly to the physical and mental health of people, especially those subject to the stresses of modern urban living. They continue to inspire writers and artists. They provide places for enjoyment and learning.

Finally, cultural landscapes often reflect living models of sustainable use of land and natural resources. Many reflect the presence of indigenous peoples and local communities maintaining durable systems of land use, providing sustenance and economic livelihood. But the landscapes which these people create and manage are also in harmony with nature, are aesthetically pleasing and preserve the cultural identities of communities.

This paper recognises, therefore, that there are many values in cultural landscapes. However, it specifically addresses the particular interests which IUCN - the International Union for Conservation of Nature and Natural Resources, known as the World Conservation Union - has in the subject. To do so, it analyses IUCN's mission statement, identifies the relationship between cultural landscapes and the conservation of biological diversity, discusses the relevance of the protected landscape approach to protected areas, and offers some thoughts on the selection of cultural landscapes for the World Heritage Convention.

IUCN and the World Heritage Convention

Under the terms of the World Heritage Convention, IUCN advises the World Heritage Committee on all aspects of the convention relating to natural sites. As the leading international body for the conservation of nature and natural resources, IUCN is clearly uniquely qualified to fulfil this role, and it has indeed done so to good effect for many years. Nonetheless, it also takes a very close interest in the question of cultural landscapes, and plans to work closely with ICOMOS in this area, including in the assessment of possible World Heritage Sites put forward as Cultural Landscapes of "outstanding, universal value". In order to understand IUCN's interest here, it is necessary to appreciate the nature of IUCN and its mission; and to recognise the important natural qualities present in many cultural landscapes.

IUCN's mission

IUCN has just held the nineteenth General Assembly of its governmental and non-governmental members in Buenos Aires, Argentina (January 1994). The session was largely devoted to the development of a strategy for the Union, at the core of which was agreement on a new mission for IUCN, thus:

"to influence, encourage and assist societies throughout the world to conserve the integrity and diversity of nature and to ensure that any use of natural resources is equitable and ecologically sustainable"

This mission statement, the product of a long and serious debate, has some important messages which bear on the question of cultural landscapes:

– IUCN sees conservation of nature being achieved *through* societies, recognising that many communities follow land use practices which work for conservation. The outward expression of a society's ability (or otherwise) to live in harmony with nature is the landscape. By concerning ourselves with landscape, we concern ourselves also with ways of life of those who live in the landscape, and help shape it;
– IUCN places great emphasis on the *diversity* of nature. Such diversity is often reflected in, and an expression of, diversity in the cultural landscape. By concerning ourselves with landscape diversity, we concern ourselves also with biological diversity;
– IUCN sees the need to use natural resources for the purposes of human welfare but recognises that *social and ecological principles* should guide this use. Landscapes can tells us whether such principles are being followed; the cultural landscapes which we value most highly are often those where social and ecological principles underlie the management of land and other natural resources.

However, there is a semantic difficulty with the term "cultural landscapes". It is now recognised that nearly all landscapes bear the imprint of past or present human activity or influence. The more that we learn about the evolution of landscapes, the more apparent it has become that human influences are very widespread indeed, and often of great antiquity - many landscapes, which had previously been considered to be "natural", turn out to have been modified by humans over centuries, even millennia. Indigenous peoples have harvested the tropical forests and subtly altered their structures; herdsman have burnt the pastures of the African savannas, thus changing the ecology; and the aboriginal people of Australia have done likewise to their environment. Often, indeed, the assertion that a landscape is natural is a by-product of an imperialistic view of the world which found it hard to recognise the influence of cultures which came before those of the Europeans.

If the influence of people on landscapes has indeed been so universally pervasive, then the adjective "cultural" ought correctly to be applied so widely that it is of little value. Susan Buggey quotes the all-embracing definitions of cultural landscapes used by Parks

Canada in 1990 ("any geographical area that has been modified or influenced by human activity") and the US National Parks Service in 1992 ("a geographic area, including both cultural and natural resources, and the wildlife and domestic animals, associated with an historic event, activity or persons, or exhibiting other cultural or aesthetic values"). She concludes that "most of the earth's land surface would qualify as cultural landscapes"(see Buggey in this volume). In effect, then, we are dealing only with *landscapes*, where there is a spectrum of human impacts varying from negligible to comprehensive. Nonetheless, the term "cultural landscapes" has been adopted by the World Heritage Committee, and it has helpfully identified three types of such landscape. In the remainder of this paper, the term is used in the way in which the Committee has interpreted it.

Cultural Landscapes and Biodiversity

A central concern of IUCN is the conservation of biological diversity. This is usually taken to mean conservation of ecosystems, species and the variation within species. Cultural landscapes often contain important resources of biodiversity. However, the relationship between cultural and natural values in the cultural landscape is complex. Sometimes the two set of values share the same scale (eg. high cultural values are found in association with high natural values); but there are also many cases where the scales operate independently (eg. places of high cultural value are not always of great importance for the conservation of biodiversity).

In examining each of the three categories of cultural landscapes in the operational guidelines adopted by the World Heritage Committee in Santa Fe (December 1992) we find as follows:

- in *intentionally designed landscapes* (such as great parks and gardens), natural qualities are usually present only by design, such as the introduction of exotic species of trees, flowers, birds or mammals. As in the case of botanic gardens or zoos, such areas may therefore be important for *ex situ* conservation. However, in this category, the factors that would normally be used to determine suitability for World Heritage status are most likely to be those concerned with artistic achievement or influence on landscape design.
- in the case of *associative landscapes*, natural values may be of the highest order - or not present at all. Examples of the former would be Tongariro National Park (New Zealand) or Uluru Rock (Australia). Both are culturally very important places to the indigenous peoples concerned; but both also have outstanding, universal natural qualities which have already been recognised under the World Heritage Convention. But there will be other places, such as sites of some former battlefields or places associated with great religious events, where there is effectively little or no natural interest.
- many *organically evolved landscapes*, and especially those which continue to evolve to the present day, are important for nature conservation. Often such places have been subject to non-intensive forms of land use which create very favourable conditions for biodiversity. However, there are also organically evolved landscapes where there is little biodiversity; examples might be some terraced vineyards or rice terraces, which may produce dramatic scenery but where intensive forms of production have largely destroyed the wildlife and natural qualities of the landscape. (Further consideration of this category is developed below).

From this analysis one can conclude that, while many cultural landscapes put forward for inclusion on the World Heritage List will be very important from a biodiversity perspective, this will not always be the case. Thus each landscape must be assessed for its individual merit, and experts from both the cultural (ie ICOMOS) and the natural (ie IUCN) disciplines should be involved.

The Conservation of Biodiversity in Organically-evolving Cultural Landscapes

It is clear that the greatest challenge will arise in interpreting the new criteria in the organically evolved cultural landscapes, especially those which continue to develop.

A continuing, evolving landscape, (as defined in para. 33 of the new operational guidelines), is one that retains an active social role in contemporary society, is closely associated with the traditional way of life, and where the evolutionary process is still in progress. As Henry Cleere has noted, this concept (like that of cultural landscapes generally) could apply "to much of the surface of the globe" (Cleere, 1993). Yet a concern for cultural landscape has, at least until recently, been seen as predominantly the preoccupation of long settled and farmed parts of the world, and notably Europe.

This almost certainly reflects the greater attention which has been given to the evolution of rural landscapes in Europe in particular; these have been subject to detailed analysis by cultural historians, geographers and environmental experts. But it would be a fundamental misconception to see cultural landscapes as an exclusively Euro-centric phenomenon. There is much evidence, (for example among the papers presented to the Schorfheide-Chorin experts' meeting on cultural landscapes (see eg:Amoaka-Atta, O'Donnell and Wager in this volume)), of the existence of cultural landscapes of great cultural and natural value throughout the developing world. What has often been lacking, however, in such countries is an awareness of the significance of landscape issues and a well-researched analysis of national landscape types and their evolution.

However, it seems likely that during the next few years there will be an awakening of interest in cultural landscape issues in the developing world. The inclusion of cultural landscapes under the World Heritage Convention should help promote greater awareness of this kind. A more far-reaching influence is the growing appreciation that cultural landscapes often reflect systems of *sustainable* land use. As recognised in *Agenda 21* (especially chapter 10) from the Rio Conference, and *Caring for the Earth* (IUCN, UNEP, WWF, 1991), these systems need to be identified, supported and publicised.

The organically-evolving cultural landscapes which are of greatest value to the conservation of biodiversity are based on traditional or low-intensity land-use systems. Many of these systems are operated by human communities who have great knowledge of the natural world with which they are in contact (McNeely 1992, Kemf 1993). Often these land-use systems create or help maintain valuable semi-natural habitats. For example, low density grazing regimes provide habitats which are shared with wild plants and animals. Likewise, traditional forest and woodland management can co-exist with the survival of wild species; for example, coppiced woodlands in many parts of Europe provide ideal conditions for woodland flora. Management systems of many wetlands (eg the regular harvesting of reeds) maintain open water areas and encourage wetland species. Mountain pastures, managed through seasonal grazing regimes, are rich in flora the world over.

However, many cultural landscapes are not so much made up of single land uses but of a complex mosaic of uses. While parts of the landscape may be farmed - or worked for other purposes - these are often interwoven with other areas where semi-natural habitats survive. Small areas of woodland, hedgerows, ponds and so forth thereby provide a network within the farmed landscape which favours the survival of wildlife. Even the farmed areas, such as the rice paddies in South East Asia or the water meadows of Europe, are often well suited to the requirements of certain birds and amphibia.

Throughout these various kinds of cultural landscapes, the survival of biodiversity, and indeed the continued presence of healthy life-support systems (clean water, clean air, productive soils etc.) in the rural environment, depends upon maintaining a relatively low-intensity form of land use. Land use systems are characterised by limited reliance on artificial inputs like chemicals and large machinery. However, once inputs begin to be applied in large amounts to increase production, the natural qualities of the area will almost always decline. Even if the appearance of the landscape maintains - for a while at least - a superficial similarity to that which was produced through less intensive farming methods, its value from the perspective of biodiversity conservation will be eroded. A similar process will occur where rural populations may persist in traditional land use practices but be forced by increased human numbers to work the land more intensively, removing remaining pockets of natural vegetation or adopting shorter cycles of fallow or forest regrowth.

Herein lies the central dilemma of conserving cultural landscapes. Since they are by definition the product of a particular human society living in a particular way at a particular population density, changes in that society, (and especially in the land use practices which it follows), will inevitably bring about changes in the landscape itself, and thus often affect its value for biodiversity. It is not enough therefore to attempt to protect the landscape as such: attention must be given instead to the ways of life of those who are the architects of the landscape, and upon whom the survival of the biodiversity within it depends.

This is not an argument for seeking to fossilise the way in which communities use the land. Rather the aim should be to encourage them to adopt more sustainable patterns of living, so that rural communities can both improve their prospects of economic and social progress, and continue to maintain the landscape that they have created. There can be little doubt that this will be the challenge facing many of the cultural landscapes recognised under the World Heritage Convention, especially those which are living, dynamic and organically evolving landscapes.

A great deal has been written and studied on the techniques of sustainable rural development which can help in the management of such landscapes. One area of IUCN's experience is however directly relevant to the aims of the World Heritage Convention, the category of protected areas known as Protected Landscapes/Seascapes.

Protected Landscapes/Seascapes

The Commission on National Parks and Protected Areas of IUCN (CNPPA) has recently completed a thorough review of the international system of protected area management categories. As a result, the following definition of a protected area (which accepts the probability that many will contain important cultural values), has been adopted by IUCN:

"an area of land and/or sea especially dedicated to the protection and maintenance of biological diversity, and of natural and cultural resources, and managed through legal or other effective means".

The CNPPA guidelines identify a number of different categories of protected area, according to the objectives of management. These are listed in Box 1 below:

Box 1. Categories of protected areas (Source: IUCN 1994)

I	Strict Nature Reserve/Wilderness Area: protected area managed mainly for science or wilderness protection
II	National Park: protected area managed mainly for ecosystem protection and recreation
III	Natural Monument: protected area managed mainly for conservation of specific features
IV	Habitat/Species Management Area: protected area managed mainly for conservation through management intervention
V	Protected Landscape/seascape: protected area managed mainly for landscape/seascape conservation and recreation
VI	Managed Resource Protected Area: protected area managed mainly for the sustainable use of natural resources.

Though World Heritage Cultural Landscapes might occur under several categories (for example associative landscapes may well be sites already recognised by IUCN as Category II or III areas), in the case of continuing, organically-evolving landscapes, Category V - Protected Landscapes/Seascapes - is especially relevant.

The definition of a Protected Landscape/Seascape is as follows:

"an area of land, with coast and sea as appropriate, where the interaction of people and nature over time has produced an area of distinct character with significant aesthetic, ecological and/or cultural value, and often with high biological diversity. Safeguarding the integrity of this traditional interaction is vital to the protection, maintenance and evolution of such an area"

The *values* contained within protected landscapes include the following:
- conserving nature and biodiversity
- buffering more strictly controlled areas
- conserving human history in structures and land use patterns
- maintaining traditional ways of life
- offering recreation and inspiration
- providing education and understanding
- demonstrating durable systems of use in harmony with nature (Lucas, 1992).

The objectives of management, guidance for selection and notes on the organisational responsibility for their administration are given in Box 2 below. It is immediately apparent that the inclusion of phrases such as "harmonious interaction of nature and culture", supporting "lifestyles ... in harmony with ... the preservation of the social and cultural fabric of the communities concerned", and "manifestations of unique or traditional land-use patterns and social organisations as evidenced in human settlements and local customs, livelihoods and beliefs" all speak to a rounded view of culture and nature in harmony, this being expressed through the landscape. Or, put another way, the kinds of places which IUCN would recognise as Category V protected landscapes will often be potential candidates for Cultural Landscape World Heritage Sites, of the organically-evolving kind.

It is also the case that there is a close parallel between much of the thinking behind protected landscapes and that which underlies biosphere reserves designated under the MAB programme of UNESCO. Like protected landscapes, biosphere reserves must have adequate long-term legal protection, be large enough to be effective conservation units, include representative examples of natural biomes and be examples of harmonious

---

Box 2. Guidance on protected landscapes/seascapes (Source: IUCN 1994)

Objectives of Management

- to maintain the harmonious interaction of nature and culture through the protection of landscape and/or seascape and the continuation of traditional land use, building practices and social and cultural manifestations
- to support lifestyles and economic activities which are in harmony with nature and the preservation of the social and cultural fabric of the communities concerned
- to maintain the diversity of landscape and habitat, and of associated species and ecosystems
- to eliminate where necessary, and thereafter prevent, land uses and activities which are inappropriate in scale and/or character
- to provide opportunities for public enjoyment through recreation and tourism appropriate in type and scale to the essential qualities of the area
- to encourage scientific and educational activities which will contribute to the long term well-being of resident populations and to the development of public support for the environmental protection of such areas, and
- to bring benefits to, and to contribute to the welfare of, the local community through the provision of natural products (such as forest and fisheries products) and services (such as clean water or income derived from sustainable forms of tourism)

Guidance for Selection

- the area should possess landscape and /or coastal and island seascape of high scenic quality, with diverse associated habitats, flora and fauna along with manifestations of unique or traditional land-use patterns, and social organisations as evidenced in human settlements and local customs, livelihoods and beliefs
- the area should provide opportunities for public enjoyment through recreation and tourism within its normal lifestyle and economic benefits

Organisational Responsibility

The area may be owned by a public authority, but is more likely to comprise a mosaic of private and public ownerships operating a variety of management regimes. These regimes should be subject to a degree of planning or other control, and supported, where appropriate, by public funding and other incentives, to ensure that the quality of the landscape/seascape and the relevant local customs and beliefs are maintained in the long term.

landscapes dependent upon traditional land use patters. It is therefore not surprising that a number of Category V areas are also biosphere reserves (two examples are the Pinelands National Reserve in New Jersey, USA, and Ngorongoro Conservation Area in Tanzania).

There are some 2,273 Protected Landscapes/Seascapes recognised by IUCN in the 1994 UN List of National Parks and Protected Areas. Their distribution between the regions of the world is shown in Box 3.

Box 3. Distribution of protected landscapes/seascapes (from data compiled by the World Conservation Monitoring Centre (1994)

CNPPA region	Category V sites:		% of land surface
	Number	Area (ha)	
N. America	507	25,793,725	1.10%
Europe	1307	33,748,761	6.61%
N. Africa and Middle East	54	5,111,744	0.39%
East Asia	72	4,297,156	0.36%
N. Eurasia	10	151,217	0.01%
Sub-Saharan Africa	20	2,299,947	0.10%
South Asia	56	799,052	0.09%
Pacific	7	14,571	0.03%
Australia	32	48,273,354	6.28%
Antarctic/New Zealand	1	1,000	<0.01%
C. America	4	6,671	0.01%
Caribbean	28	708,257	2.97%
S. America	175	19,886,467	1.10%
Total	**2273**	**141,091,932**	**0.95%**

While these figures confirm that there are many such areas in Europe, it also shows that there are protected landscapes in many other countries around the world. There is also a particular concentration in Australia (IUCN 1987, Lucas 1992, "Lake District Declaration" 1987); most of this is accounted for by the Great Barrier Reef, which is clearly a special case.

Over the years, IUCN has taken a growing interest in protected landscapes. This stems from the convergence of two lines of thought: that conservation of species and habitats cannot be achieved in nature reserves and national parks alone; and that conservation depends upon the involvement of people, and therefore places where people co-exist with nature are worthy of special attention.

At its General Assembly in 1988 in Costa Rica, IUCN adopted a resolution on protected landscapes. This stressed the importance of the approach, and recognised that such places are important from an economic, environmental, social and cultural point of view. It called for IUCN to give advice on the concept of protected landscapes. It also recommended that IUCN work with UNESCO and ICOMOS "to develop criteria for the consideration of sites with mixed natural and cultural values for the World Heritage list"; and that the World Heritage Committee adopt the principle "that selected protected areas possessing significant harmonious associations of cultural and natural features can be considered of outstanding universal value and worthy of inscription on the World Heritage list".

At the Fourth World Congress on National Parks and Protected Areas (Caracas, February 1992), planned by CNPPA and convened by IUCN, a workshop was organised on cultural landscapes. This too stressed the need for the connections to be drawn between landscapes and the World Heritage Convention. It specifically recommended that:

"the World Heritage Criteria be amended to take account of protected/cultural landscapes/seascapes and living cultures which are an harmonious blend of nature and culture".

There is thus a direct linkage from the Costa Rica General Assembly, via the Caracas Congress, to the World Heritage meetings at la Petite Pierre, Santa Fe and Schorfheide-Chorin. IUCN now fully recognises the importance of "lived-in" landscapes, and commits itself to working with ICOMOS to bringing about the proper recognition of such places within the World Heritage Convention.

Some Concluding Thoughts on Selecting Cultural Landscapes for World Heritage Status

It would seem that the most difficult questions facing the World Heritage Committee, and its advisers ICOMOS and IUCN, in assessing Cultural Landscapes for World Heritage status will be these:

- the need for a *typology* of landscapes
- the need for methods of *evaluating* landscapes
- the need to find ways to *manage* landscapes

Comments follow on these points.

Typology: The development of a typology is essentially the result of a descriptive and analytical process. It identifies and classifies landscapes by their types, taking account of such factors as those listed in Box 4. Such an exercise, leading to the development of a landscape typology, is desirable as the first stage in identifying individual landscapes for their "universal, outstanding value". The resulting categorisation of the different landscape types can be used to identify and compare individual landscapes. At its simplest, this exercise is analogous to the classification of cultural monuments (so that gothic cathedrals can be distinguished from hindu temples) or natural sites (eg wetlands and mountains).

To develop a universal, world-wide landscape typology for use in identifying suitable candidates for World Heritage status in all countries, using factors such as those in Box 4, would be a daunting task. However, a number of countries have undertaken national studies of their landscape resources in a comprehensive way (eg Australia and Sweden), and these offer an excellent starting point for the consideration of candidate areas for World Heritage status put forward by those countries.

> **Box 4.** Factors contributing to the identification of landscapes types
>
> *Physical factors*
> eg   geology
>   landform
>   drainage
>   soils
>
> *Human use of land*
> eg   farming systems
>   forestry and other land uses
>   settlements
>   transport systems
>
> *Natural Factors*
> eg   ecosystems
> species (fauna and flora)
>
> *Cultural factors*
> eg   aesthetic (visual etc.)
>   associations (historic, artistic)

Within Europe, there is an interesting effort to develop a broader, regional typology which could be used in identifying places which deserve World Heritage status. This is being done as part of the follow-up to the European Environment Ministers Conference in Lucerne (1993). The report called for by the Ministers, (European Agency Task Force 1995), contains a chapter on landscapes. This identifies some 30 "pan-European" landscape types, ranging from Arctic Tundra to Atlantic Bocage; and Polder to Terraced Landscapes. Although this report is not a policy document, it will provide the foundation upon which the next meeting of European Environment Ministers (Sofia, 1995) will develop a pan-European environmental programme. The report on Europe's Environment will ensure that landscape issues receive greater attention at the Sofia meeting that they have hitherto been accorded at international environmental meetings.

It will be easier for ICOMOS and IUCN to advise the World Heritage Committee on candidate cultural landscapes for World Heritage status where a national landscape analysis has been undertaken; and even more so where a regional analysis also exists. IUCN and ICOMOS should develop guidance to countries on landscape typologies as a basis for the submission of cultural landscapes for World Heritage recognition.

Evaluating landscapes: While the development of a typology is descriptive and analytical, the evaluation of landscapes involves the exercise of value judgement. It is here that the World Heritage Convention is so demanding by setting forth the required standard of outstanding, universal value.

Much experience already exists within IUCN and ICOMOS on the evaluation of sites for their natural or cultural qualities, and this will be of great use in evaluating cultural landscapes as well. However, landscape evaluation involves the exercise of judgment which differs in two important respects from that for natural or cultural qualities alone:

– the subject matter is landscape, which has its own set of qualities which are *independent* of the cultural and natural resources it contains; and

– landscape evaluation should be concerned with the *interrelationship* between cultural and natural elements, as well as with the value of these elements in their own right.

Some suggestions, derived from work done in the UK (Land Use Consultants 1991, Cobham Resources Consultants 1993), of the factors which might be taken account of in evaluating cultural landscapes for World Heritage status quality, are set out in Box 5.

> **Box 5.** Check list of items for evaluating cultural landscapes for world heritage status
>
> *Landscape as a Resource*
> the landscape should be a resource of world importance in terms of rarity and representativeness
>
> *Scenic Quality*
> the landscape should be of the highest scenic quality, with pleasing or dramatic patters and combinations of landscape features, and important aesthetic or intangible qualities
>
> *Unspoilt character*
> the landscape within the area should be unspoilt by large scale, visually intrusive or polluting industrial or urban development, or infrastructure
>
> *Sense of place*
> the landscape should have a distinctive and common character, including topographic and visual unity
>
> *Harmony with Nature*
> the landscape should demonstrate an outstanding example of a harmonious interaction between people and nature, based upon sustainable land-use practices, thereby maintaining a diversity of species and ecosystems
>
> *Cultural Resources*
> the landscape should contain buildings and other structures of great historical and architectural interest; the integrity of these features should be apparent
>
> *Consensus*
> there should be a consensus among professional and public opinion as to the world importance of the area; reflected, for example, through associations with writings and paintings about the landscape which are of international renown.

This check list is not exhaustive. Nor are the items on it to be interpreted as elements which *must* be present. For example, as noted above there are some important, organically evolving cultural landscapes whose natural qualities are very limited; also the World Heritage Committee may wish to give World Heritage status to landscapes that have been scarred by industrial or semi-urban developments because of their cultural associations.

In their approach to cultural landscapes, ICOMOS and IUCN will need to develop guidance and assessment criteria. Initially it will be possible to develop only broad guidelines, backed up by illustrative examples. However, as experience in the operation of the World Heritage Convention with landscapes accumulates, more precise advice and clearer assessment criteria should emerge. While it is in the nature of evaluations of landscape that there will always be a large element of subjective judgement, the extent to which that is an *informed* judgement should increase over time.

The Management of Landscapes: Inscription on the World Heritage list carries with it the obligation to maintain those outstanding, universal qualities which gave rise to the site's designation. This is hard enough in the case of many natural and cultural sites; it will be even more challenging in the case of cultural landscapes, for the reasons discussed above. However, there are certain requirements and principles which can be identified - at least as regards organically evolving cultural landscapes.

> **Box 6.** Requirements for management of cultural landscapes
>
> - sound legal basis for the management of the area, based in national law, but reflected also in site specific regulations
> - a national authority with expertise and resources to oversee policy and implementation for the protection of cultural landscapes
> - a managing body at the local level, able to call on a range of professional expertise
> - ways of providing two-way communication between the people living in, and/or working within the cultural landscapes,; other interests such as visitors and commercial concerns; and the managing body
> - a continuing monitoring and feed-back process which ensures that policies are kept under review at the national land local levels - and revised should this be required

> **Box 7.** Principles to guide management of organically-evolving cultural landscapes
>
> - Landscape protection requires the presence of a vital and sound local economy. It is also true that landscape resources are needed to ensure that development can be sustainable. Thus the management of an organically-evolving cultural landscape is, in fact, the management of the local economy and of change
> - Landscape protection requires the support and involvement of the local people. Thus protection must be seen to be in their interests, using educational and financial incentives, and local powers of decision
> - The basic resources of the area (natural and cultural) should be recorded, examined and protected
> - Planning and management in the area should involve the public discussion of options
> - Regulatory measures are necessary, but they should be flexible and respect the rights, interests and needs of local people
> - The traditional knowledge of local people in sustainable land use should be respected and supported
> - No cultural landscape can survive in isolation from the areas around it

It is necessary to distinguish between the *requirements* for effective management (Box 6) and the *principles* of landscape management (Box 7) in cultural landscapes. The ideas are derived from several sources, notably Lucas (Lucas,1992). Although the challenge of managing cultural landscapes will be difficult, there is much experience to draw on already, particularly in well-managed protected landscapes. An early task for IUCN and ICOMOS should be to draw on this experience to develop guidance on the management of cultural landscapes recognised under the World Heritage Convention.

Summary of future action: Three areas have been identified for possible collaboration between IUCN and ICOMOS in the matter of advice:

– guidance on how to identify types of cultural landscapes,
– guidance and criteria on the evaluation of cultural landscapes, and
– guidance on the management of cultural landscapes.

In all three cases, ICOMOS and IUCN should - subject to the availability of resources - draw liberally on the available examples of good practice, and broadcast these.

Conclusion

The inclusion of cultural landscapes under the World Heritage Convention marks an exciting development in the operation of the convention itself. It will raise awareness at the international level of landscape issues and it should encourage a closer partnership between ICOMOS and IUCN. The task is complex, however, especially in the case of organically-evolving landscapes. This paper has highlighted the existence of relevant experience which can be drawn on from Category V Protected Landscapes.

The decision to expand the scope of the Convention in this way has a wider significance. It is recognition of a central theme of the Earth Summit: that sustainable development will only come about through the involvement and participation of communities, and by drawing on the wisdom and knowledge of those groups which do live in some kind of harmony with nature. Cultural landscapes are often the outward expressions of such a positive relationship. By seeking to identify and protect the best of these, the Convention will be making a much needed contribution to the search for sustainable development.

References

Cleere, H. (1993). *Cultural Landscapes and World Heritage*; paper to the International Scientific Conference on Cultural Landscape-Historic Landscape-Monument Protection (Budapest 7-11 June 1993).

Cobham Resource Consultants (1993). *Landscape Assessment Guidance*, Countryside Commission.

European Agency Task Force (European Commission) (1995). *Europe's Environment – The Dobris Assessment;* Stanners, D. and Bordeau, P. (eds.) European Environment Agency, Copenhagen.

IUCN (1987). *Protected Landscapes: Experience Around the World*, IUCN.

IUCN, UNEP, WWF (1991). *Caring for the Earth - A Strategy for Sustainable Living*, IUCN.

IUCN (1994). *Guidelines for Protected Area Management Categories*, IUCN, Cambridge.

IUCN (1994). *1993 United Nations List of National Parks and Protected Areas*, prepared by the World Conservation Monitering Centre and the Commission on National Parks and Protected Areas. IUCN, Gland, Switzerland and Cambridge, UK.

Kemf, E. (ed.) (1993). *The Law of the Mother*, Sierra club.

Land Use Consultants (1991). *Landscape Assessment: Principles and Practice*, Countryside commission for Scotland.

Lucas, P.H.C. (1992). *Protected landscapes: a Guide for Policy-makers and Planners*, Chapman and Hall.

Mc Neely, J. (1992). *Nature and Culture: Conservation needs them both*, Nature and Resources, vol. **28** no. 3, pp 37-43.

"The Lake District Declaration" (1987). Countryside Commission, Cheltenham, UK.

UNESCO (1992). *Operational Guidelines for the Implementation of the World Heritage Convention: Revised Version of Cultural and Natural Criteria* as Adopted by the World Heritage Committee in Santa Fe, December 1992. Paris.

Adrian Phillips is a geographer, and planner by training. He teaches at the University of Wales, Cardiff and is the Chair of the Commission on National Parks and Protected Areas (CNPPA) of IUCN.

Chapter 34

Functional Criteria for the Assessment of Cultural Landscapes

Harald Plachter

Introduction

Landscape protection has three basic prereqisites: a typology, methods of evaluation and ways of management (Philipps 1995). As landscapes are distinct entities on a specific hierarchic level of the biosphere, their characterisation, evaluation and protection needs specific methodologies which are different from those used for the protection of single monuments or ecosystems (cf. Haber 1995). This is especially obvious for cultural landscapes. In a broad definition almost all landscapes of the world can viewed as "cultural landscapes", regarding the fact that man even in historic times has more or less influenced all regions of the world, including tropical forests, savannas and high mountain regions (Bourlière 1983, di Castri 1989, Jelinek 1967, Remmert 1985, Schüle 1992). Therefore the simple alternative of presence or absence of man's influence on nature is not valid as a basic criterion for the evaluation of landscapes.

In view of the complexity, variability and dynamic change of landscapes a holistic approach to describe and evaluate landcapes is not appropriate. Indicators are necessary, which reflect specific characteristics or values of distinct landscapes. These indicators can be of a tangible quality like the set and distribution of species and ecosystems or buildings and settlements or they can be intangible like landuse systems or aesthetic features. The existing drafts for typology and evaluation schemes primarily refer to the material features of landscapes and to their aesthetic qualities. Other intangible criteria are neglected or at best used on a very general descriptive level.

Cultural landscapes are defined to be the result of the interaction of man and nature (McNeely and Keeton 1995, Rössler 1995). Although interaction normally leads to specific material features it originally belongs to the immaterial part of landscapes. Interaction clearly refers to functional qualities. This leads to two basic questions: How far functional criteria or parameters serve as indicators, and whether functional qualities generally determine cultural landscapes much more fundamentally than material ones. If this is true, the protection of cultural landscapes should take much more a functional than a material approach. This paper discusses the significance of functional criteria for the comparative evaluation of cultural landscapes with restriction to so-called "organically evolved cultural landscapes" (cf. Rössler 1995), emphasizing ecological features in particular. The results may also be applicable to other types of landscapes like gardens or sacred localities. But there, of course, cultural functions will be more in the centre of interest.

A Functional Definition for Cultural Landscapes

Cultural landscapes or seascapes might be defined as those areas on earth, where man exposed a substantial influence on nature and thereby changed its image significantly. But this definition turns out to be insufficient as a valid characterization, especially with respect to practical reglementations and measures. Obviously, urban landscapes would fall under this definition as well as many landscapes which had been looked upon as being natural in the past. Recent data increasingly prove that man's influence on nature not only dates back much further than once believed, but also that this influence has caused substantial changes in natural ecosystems in nearly all regions settled by man. Many of those ecosystems still look perfectly "natural", but they are not. The structure of vegetation and the distribution of species is heavily influenced by man due to fire, shifting cultivation or merely the transport of seeds. This has been documented for example for parts of tropical rainforests in Western Africa or for the landscape surrounding Uluru in Australia (Bridgwater and Hooy 1995, Layton and Titchen 1995).

"Interaction" always means a two-way approach. Thus, only those parts of the earth's surface should be looked upon as cultural landscapes (cf. Plachter 1995), where:

1) man's culture and nature really shapes or has shaped each other
2) where man is or was conscious of this influence in terms of defined aims, so that the material structure of the landscape reflects an overall creative principle of man with respect to a specific culture or a certain span of time of this culture, and
3) ecological mechanisms of control, reconstruction and decomposition are still at work and man's interaction with nature makes use of these mechanisms.

Urban landscapes, at least those of the type of a modern metropolis, clearly do not meet those additional criteria. It is true that there are still considerable remnants of nature and well defined urban associations of plants and animals. The overall biodiversity in urban areas can be higher than in natural areas (Sukopp 1983, Sukopp et al. 1990). Thus from a material point of view, towns do not differ fundamentally from other parts of the earth's surface. But there man has emancipated himself totally from the limits of nature through his buildings, techniques and the import of resources from the outside. Achieving this, man is no longer urged to take advantage of natural ecological mechanisms. In urban areas he also determines structure and internal function of the remaining parts of nature, with results reflecting defined cultural lines or attitudes. And through gardens and parks he still makes use of nature as an important aesthetic element of his environment. But the functional welfare of natural processes is minimized, restricted to some sectors like climatic improvements or waste water management, which are fairly independent of ecosystem structure and species composition. In cities man treats nature much more like an abiotic environmental factor than as an integrated element.

In principle the same is true for many of the modern, "industrialized" agricultural and forestry landscapes. The flux of substances is no longer balanced. Man-made ecosystems depend on the import of resources and energy to a very high degree and the structure of the landscape is much more formed by these impacts than by the local qualities. Those landscapes poorly reflect the local or regional features of nature and those of the regional climate or rough types of soil. In their overall image they do not clearly reflect a distinct culture, but rather the application of some global landuse technique. And - similar to urban landscapes - man no longer is urged to care for the natural functions and limits of the landscape. Severe violations of ecological principles are no longer a direct threat to survival, but only require reclaiming new land or changing the job. Therefore modern agricultural and forestry landscapes not only tend to be very similar in different parts of the world, but actually enhance the process of uniformization of local cultures to a monotonous and mobile "international civilization".

On the other hand, landscapes should only be defined as cultural, if the overall image not only reflects specific qualities of a culture but also the conscious interaction with nature. Again this can not be restricted to material qualities alone. For example many steppe ecosystems of the world are obviously heavily influenced by man. And he of course used fire there in the persecution of a concious goal, to hunt animals, to create open space for settlement or, in some other regions, to support his livestock. If there had not been any awareness of the functional entity on a landscape level, if there is no intellectual idea or concept which is consciously transferred to the landscape, if the distinct impact was carried out for one specific and restricted reason only, regardless of eventual ecological consequences and countereffects, the result should not be called cultural landscape. From this point of view, even some fundamentally changed landscapes, like opencast mining landscapes or landscapes spoilt by environmental catastrophies, are not cultural ones. Thus, it is not the extent of change that counts, but the degree of insight in the qualities of a certain landscape and in the framework of a certain culture.

Of course the limits of such a definition are somewhat vague. Are ecosystem structures produced by shifting cultivation cultural landscapes? Do they meet the definition only if local cultural qualities can be correlated with specific features of the resulting ecosystems? Are grassland ecosystems cultural landscapes because they are facultatively used by livestock or are additional signs of goal directed management required, such as stone fences or community reglementations for use. It should be noted, that again those reglementations are primarily functional, which often but not necessarily result in structural features.

Some Basic Considerations on Evaluation

Any evaluation requires a characterization of the object(s) in question with regard to specific qualities. In many cases of everyday evaluation the selection and application of those qualities is not too big a problem. There is a common methodological system which is understandable and acceptable to everyone, although it might lead to diverging indivual conclusions. The continuous and successful application confers on those everyday evaluation schemes the character of "natural laws". But these are everything but "natural laws". Methodologies as well as evaluation parameters are social conventions depending on intellectual and common attitudes, reflecting the history and spiritual framework of the culture to which they belong.There are in principle no "natural" qualities beyond human society which inevitably determine any evaluation. Therefore it is always from a mere anthropocentric point of view, which leads to any assessment. Natural scientists in particular sometimes have problems with this - or better: the public, which seeks for "true" answers from them.

As most objects of our environment are too complex for a detailed holistic description only a very limited selection of qualities can be analysed in view of pragmatic considerations. The basic question arises: what are the most appropriate and valid parameters that indicate more general qualities of the object? For the analytic description of objects and conditions science logically derives the answer to this question from gaps in the theoretical scientific modell. It is a common misunderstanding, that the most appropriate parameters for evaluation can be unequivocally and inevitably selected from the known structure of those scientific models. But attributing "value" to any natural or cultural element is neither a part nor an aim of such models. "Value" is basically – a human attribution which depends on and changes with the human view of the object or condition in question. Thus evaluation always has a scientific *and* a social component. It becomes clear, that the solution of any evaluation problem requires a convention on methodology and evaluation indicators between representatives of sciences and society (Plachter 1994).

The latter is essential, because the parameters which describe an object best according to the scientific model are not necessarily the best indicators of "value". For example, the analysis of the material used for building a monument might be of outstanding importance for its scientific description. But this parameter might be a poor indicator of value, which might perhaps arise from the overall visual image. Or, for the description of a natural area, the volume and naturalness of interactions between species might be important. But society considers the occurence of a single threatened species or the recreational potential of much higher value when it comes to protect this area.

This means that we need two independent systems of methodology and indicators for analytic scientific description and evaluation. This does not exclude a distinct parameter being appropriate for description or classification and for evaluation. It means furthermore, that any system of classification, which is a scientific tool, is not easily applied for evaluation, although it might be one of the prerequisites. We do not inevitably need a complete and elaborated classification to evaluate a single object out of a set of objects. For example, for the identification of objects to be priorly protected a screening scheme, consisting of logical, consecutive key questions might be as useful as a consistent and detailed classification. Those screening schemes will need some classification of objects as well, but very rough classification procedures may then be sufficient.

This is especially important for cultural landscapes. Landscapes are among the most complex and variable units of the biosphere. It is extremely difficult to identify the proper parameters for description and classification. As a result, a consistent classification scheme for landscapes is still lacking and even the question whether landscapes can be classified at all is still under discussion in sciences (cf. Bankson and Green 1991, Lucas 1992). On the other hand, there is an actual need to decide over management alternatives as well as development and protection of landscapes. This ultimately can only be done on the basis of evaluating decisions. The development of screening schemes might be a solution to this problem.

Of course then we need valid indicators for the evaluation procedure. The value of any object depends on qualities on two levels. On the one hand, the value obviously depends on the affiliation to a certain type of object ("type-value"). For example a building differs in value because it belongs to the type "gothic church" or "modern concrete business building". Accordingly a nature reserve differs in value depending on whether it is a tropical rainforest, a coral reef or a desert.

On the other hand the objects within one type differ in value depending on their specific condition ("object-value"). Cultural monuments of one type can be ranked in value along the quality of certain frescos. Accordingly natural areas could be ranked along the degree of human encroachment. For general concepts and the setting of priorities for protection within an overall strategy value on the type level might be given special emphasis. In order to achieve successful evaluation however, the meaning of a "type" must be sufficiently defined. For example: are "forests", "rainforests" or "temperate rainforests of the Rocky Mountains" one type? If this is clarified, we can decide to protect rainforests prior to beech forests in Central Europe or any types of rain forests prior to others.

Parameters that are most commonly used in evaluation procedures are for example naturalness, integrity or authenticity. These are not indicators in the sense defined above, but already complex conditions which had to be defined by one or a series of more precise indicators. Generally, they are applicable only on the object level of evaluation, defining the state of a specific object. It should be noted, that indicators on the object level are not inevitably applicable for all types to be evaluated. For example "naturalness" and the precise indicators associated with it might be very appropriate for the evaluation within the type "rainforest" but might be rather poor for the evaluation of anthropo-zoogenic grassland ecosystems; or the number of species might be a very valid parameter to compare different conditions of rainforest ecosystems but this parameter is not very useful in the comparison of low biodiversity ecosystems, such as certain kinds of temperate and boreal bogs. Here, human encroachment can increase the number of niches and thus cause the invasion of additional species. A disturbed area would then be more valuable than a natural one according to biodiversity. Therefore every type of object needs its specific set of evaluation indicators on the object level or at least a specific interpretation of these (cf. Plachter 1991).

Functional Criteria for the Evaluation of Landscapes

The discussion concerning the comparative evaluation of landscapes is still in a very premature state, being far from a unanimously accepted methodological convention. Therefore the following considerations should only be seen as a contribution to this discussion, not substituting other criteria that might be applicable too, but just stressing the significance of functionality. A special emphasis is given to natural functional criteria (for additional informations see Farina 1995) and cultural aspects are only mentioned if they have direct influence on the state of natural functionality. Presumably there will be additional cultural criteria for functionality which should also be discussed in this context.

Biodiversity

The diversity of living creatures in an area is a very important parameter indicating basic qualities of a landscape. Biodiversity is defined on three levels: genetic diversity within one species, species diversity and diversity of habitats or ecosystems (Mc Neely et al. 1990). For the evaluation of landscapes the latter two levels might be given emphasis, but genetic diversity is important, too. There is a global trend towards a few types of very uniform landscapes, caused by application of the same landuse techniques, treatment with the same machines and vehicles and overall eutrophication. This narrows the spectrum of environments for animal and plants significantly, not only in a general perspective, but within one type of landscape as well. Indirectly, this might lead to diminished genetic diversity, for many genotypes will no longer find appropriate habitats in those landscapes. Thus it might be relevant for the assessment of a specific landscape, whether specific environmental conditions, which had been typical in former times but had become rare, now still exist. Those could be specific states of wide-spread ecosystems such as lack of nutrients and extraordinarily high insolation or the persistence of natural stochastic events such as flooding, fire or draught (cf. Picket and White 1985).

Here again it should be mentioned, that "biodiversity" as an evaluation criterion has to be defined separately for every type of ecosystem and landscape. Generally used in the sense "more biodiversity means a higher value" it is often misleading. The reference has to be the average or optimal state of the specific type of ecosystem or landscape.

For the purposes of evaluation the criterion "biodiversity" is normally used in a material and not in a functional sense. Then it is often restricted to certain groups of organisms, usually higher animals and flowering plants and among those the more attractive ones. But from a functional point of view biodiversity is much more linked to very inconspicuous groups of organisms: to soil dwelling and limnic organisms and in the oceans to algae and invertebrates. Not only do they make up most of the biomass of the ecosystems, but they also are crucially responsible for its state. Without those organisms there would be no fertile soil on earth and there would be no natural cleaning in freshwater ecosystems. In light of the global shortcomming of fertile soil, which is the natural resource that is presumably going to limit future development of mankind, this fact should not be underestimated.

To what extend the present landuse supports and makes use of natural processes is therefore an important factor for the assessment of cultural landscapes. In general ecosystems are not only characterized by their elements but by the interactions between them as well. These interactions are the basis for self-regulation and for flexibility in case of internal or external disturbance. It is argued, whether the amount and strength of those interactions corresponds to the age of an ecosystem type (cf. Begon et al. 1990). Anyway, some of those interactions are changed whenever man uses a natural or semi-natural ecosystem and they are more or less substituted by technical control mechanisms in man-made ecosystems like fields or urban habitats. Thus, use of nature inevitably causes change normally a reduction in natural processes within the system. But the encroachments can be of a different quality. They can be smooth, regarding the natural limits of a stand and conserving natural ecological functions to the utmost, thus being economical in the use of energy and resources. Or they can be "technical", substituting a high amount of natural functions by human control mechanisms. This always requires additional expenditure of energy and resources. And those "industrial" landuse systems bear a greater danger of ecosystem conditions going out of control (i.e. pests). Decisions about a specific landuse system are not solely a question of intensity. High population densities require intensive landuse. This is not only the case nowadays. One of the most intensive types of landuse are the terraced rice fields in South-East Asia, dating back more than 2,000 years (Villalon 1995). It is much more the question how far a landuse system - within the framework and in support of present human needs - considers or ignores the natural functions.

Conductivity

The analysis of intrinsic and external stochastic incidents resulted in fundamentally new concepts for population dynamics. According to this local extinctions are "normal" events in the life history of animals and plants, caused by the random variation of the demographic, genetic and enviromental constitution of the specific population. The probability of such an event per time unit is inversely correlated to the size of the population. Small populations are therefore exposed to a high risk of local extinction. This led to the concept of "minimum viable populations" which is defined to be the population size necessary to achieve a given risk of local extinction in a given period of time (Schaffer 1981, 1987).

The effect of local extinction would inevitably lead to a progressive impoverishment of ecosystems and landscapes respectively, if there was no balancing countereffect. This is either recolonization or first colonization of recently developing habitats. Many species seem to exist not in isolated local populations but in regional nets of adjacents populations, so-called "metapopulations", linked together by the occasional exchange of individuals (Fahrig and Merriam 1985, Gilpin and Hanski 1991, Hansson 1991).

Natural ecosystems might look static concerning their set of species but they are obviously not. There is rather a more or less balanced equilibrium between extinction and colonization. Man influences this equilibrium in different ways. On one hand he reduces the average size of natural and semi-natural habitats in cultural landscapes, thus raising the risk of local extinction. On the other hand he reduces the frequency of individual exchange by creating barriers for migration and dispersal respectively, such as roads, fields or settlements. It is documented that the loss of species in modern, "industrialized" cultural landscapes is extensively caused by these effects of fragmentation and isolation (cf. Burgess and Sharpe 1981, Opdam 1991, Saunders et al. 1991). And the space unit, where these effects act, is, of course, the landscape and not a single, isolated ecosystem, which might be protected as a reserve. Thus again, modern landuse practices effect nature on a functional level, reducing the conductivity of the landscape.

In many parts of the world artificial corridors and "stepping stones" for the migration of animals and plants are built up as a measure of nature conservation, hoping to lower the effects of isolation (Henein and Merriam 1990, Hobbs and Saunders 1993). But what is built up follows a human idea of suitability of landscape structures for migration. And it is a static and segregative concept for landscapes which are fixed concerning shaping and use. The biological functions are attached to the areas which are most unsuitable for production, just to be free of limitations to production on the remaining area.

This concept is in clear contrast to what happened in most of the traditional cultural landscapes which are known to be rich in species. The type of use changed frequently on a considerable part of the area and many used areas periodically turned to fallow land, in order to "recreate" the soil or to accumulate nutrients. The fallow land could serve as an occasional habitat for many species and even the conductivity of regularily used areas was much higher, due to the lower level of impacts. Thus traditional landuse systems often maintained a high level of dynamics whereas the structure of use is extensively fixed in "planned" and "industrialized" landscapes. Keeping in mind the crucial significance of dynamic change for the persistance of natural ecosystems (cf. Picket and White 1985, Remmert 1991) this is surely one of the most fundamental differences between traditional and modern landscapes. Thus the degree of dynamics in use and habitat pattern might be an important indicator for the natural condition of a landscape, although it must be taken into account, that many natural and semi-natural ecosystems need a long time for development and therefore should be excluded from such rapid turnover.

Coevolution

We know that natural ecosystems need considerable periods of time to gain a state of equilibrium (normally as balanced dynamic; see above). These periods of time range from some decades to several thousands of years. Even longer should be the periods required to reach equilibrium states on the level of landscapes. This is, for example, demonstrated for marine archipelos as a result of "island biogeography" (Williamson 1981). So time plays a major role for the development of any natural system.

Indeed we can see that there is a fundamental difference between the set of species and the ability of natural self-regulation between traditional cultural landscapes and those created during the past few decades, even if both were and are used on a comparable level of intensity. Mixed crop cultivations spread out in many region of the tropics during the past decades. The level of impact is not very high compared with other systems of landuse. Nevertheless biodiversity is normally very low in those systems. The same is true for some European landuse systems which have been transferred to other regions of the world. Biodiversity and stability are often lower in the "new" landscapes abroad, compared with the "old" ones in Europe.

The reasons for this are not yet sufficiently understood. But there are strong indications that the period of time for development as well as the appropriate adaptation of human landuse techniques to the specific natural qualities of the stand by "trial and error" may play a substantial role. The latter takes time. Historic landuse systems normally developed very slowly. The starting point for any improvement was not scientific analysis but the experience of the results of techniques in use. Mistakes and inadequancies in techniques caused pressure on the culture using this system and thereby gave rise to counterreactions. This process of optimization has not inevitably led to "ideal" landuse techniques. Undesirable development which resulted in sweeping and irreparable degradation of nature can be found all over the world and in all historic periods. But on the other hand there are very fine examples of landuses, which have persisted over centuries.This is especially the case, where one natural resource exclusively dominates the whole system and determines the limits of production, like water in rice cultivation or in many Andean agrosystems, or the seasonal change of climate in many mountain regions.

Modern science strives to find more optimized landuse techniques by causal analysis of the ecological systems and the human influence acting on them. For this experimental methods are increasingly applied. Undoubtedly sciences have contributed a good deal to the improvement of landuse techniques. But experimental science excludes systematically one factor, which may be of crucial importance for the success or failure of any landuse system in the long-term, the factor of stochastic events. No one can experimentally imitate the effects on rice fields caused by a combination of a series of dry years, the impact of any pest and very low temperatures for some weeks during one of these years. It are the rare and stochastic coincidences which determine the structure and condition not only of natural systems but the applicability of specific human landuse techniques as well. Thus, seeking better techniques, science alone can not give ultimate answers. We need the experience of traditional cultures as well, which sum up all environmental events over a long period of time.

Input/output bilances

Apart from specific environmental qualities, nutrients and energy have generally been the determining factors for production in historic cultural landscapes. The rational use and the saving of nutrients and energy were of prominent interest. The goal was the establishment of more or less closed cycles where input was limited to the fixation of sun energy by assimilation and the output to soil erosion and the translocation of waste by rivers and streams. It is worth to mention that this strategy is very similar to that of many mature ecosystems like tropical rainforests on oligotrophic soils or coral reefs (cf. Begon et al. 1990).

In cultural landscapes this goal, of course, has never been perfectly reached. Often there was additional import of energy sources like charcoal or of animal stock. European agriculture had to fall back on natural ecosystems to cover the nutrient supply by the way of grazing and withdrawal of litter. The towns of the region had to be supplied and they demanded a considerable proportion of the net production. Some cultural landscapes evolved even only to guarantee the supply of the historic cities. But anyway the principle is kept to save nutrients and energy wherever possible.

Modern agricultural landscapes are in sharp contrast to this strategy. Nutrients and energy seem to be available without limits on the local level. The input now vastly exceeds the output. Under the industrialized conditions of European and Anglo-American agriculture only 10 to 40 per cent of the overall energy invested by man is available in harvested food at the end. In a global view the expenditure of fertilizers to produce any additional ton of yield has grown continuously for decades. This not only demonstrates the limits of modern agriculture. The droping of former limits of production, which ultimately shaped the associated landscapes must have consequences on the basic structure and function of the agro-ecosystems. There are very few valid data on this. But we know that the frequency of nutrient demanding plants grows in many parts of the world. The growing mechanical impact by machines causes fundamental changes of the epigaic fauna (Heydemann and Meyer 1983). Effects on soil biocoenoses by overfertilization are probable at least for poor soils with low buffer capacity. This all happens independently of eventual changes in the visual image or the habitat spectrum of the landscape and often long before these become obvious. And it directly effects the functional "services" of nature for man's welfare in cultural landscapes.

Conclusions

We normally describe and evaluate landscapes by their material feature. But the elements which constitute a landscape are not isolated from one another. Only functional interaction between these elements makes a part of the earth's surface worthy of being "landscape". If man acts and shapes a landscape, we might call it a "cultural landscape" and, of course, he then is integrated in the functional networks.

Nearly all landscapes of the world comprise a similar spectrum of basic material elements: natural or semi-natural ecosystems, fields and pastures, roads and human settlements. The variety of these basic elements is vast and mixed together in an irregular pattern in a specific landscapes. Thus is it very difficult to classify landscapes on the basis of these material elements. But there are functional criteria which show a clear gradient from natural landscapes to urban areas. Some of these are:

In <u>natural and semi-natural landscapes</u> man may have changed structure fundamentally, but the natural qualities of self-regulation and self-development are fairly pristine. Man depends fully on those ecological functions. His culture reflects the natural qualities of the region. There is normally no awareness of what we call a "landscape" but only of selected important resources of the environment. In <u>traditional cultural landscapes</u> man is still fully integrated in and dependent on the functional services and limits of the natural system, although he directed many of these functions for his own purpose. The natural functions of competition, predation and regulation are still at work and man is a part of these. The ecological functions of the region and the stand respectively clearly determine the appropriate landuse techniques and limit the yields. The limiting factors are well known within the associated culture. The development of landuse techniques strives to maximize the consumption of resources not by import but by the change of functional pathways. This so far resembles the strategy of animal and plants in natural ecosystems. There is awareness within the local cultures of "their" surrounding landscape, leading to the goal of shaping it in line with specific technical, visual or religious concepts. Changes in human population and culture confirm in changes of the landuse and habitat pattern. Thus, these landscapes still have a very distinct dynamic to which plants and animals can adapt. In contrast to this, <u>modern agricultural landscapes</u> depend on huge imports of resources and energy. Although often ignored, there is still a considerable dependence of man on natural qualities. The image of landscapes is no longer shaped by the knowledge of the local nature and the long-term experiences of the local culture. It is determined by international principles for production and an international market and thus at best reflects the attitude of a "global culture". Man believes himself to be emancipated from the limits of nature. In view of the importance of stochastic events, this substitution of long-term experience of local populations by short-term scientific results rises the risk of failures considerably, as even in those landscapes natural processes ultimately determine development. This is no longer the case in <u>urban landscapes</u>. There indeed man is fully emancipated from the limits of nature. An even higher import of resources and energy as well as refined techniques for distribution and regulation enable this. Towns often reflect much more cultural authenticity than our modern agricultural landscapes, and nature is not at all without meaning. Why then not consider towns and cities as "cultural landscapes"? There is no real "interaction" between man and nature because man acts like a dominating abiotic factor. But the local population is no longer functionally dependent on urban nature. The ecological interdependence is more or less completely substituted by other forms of "interaction", for example in the field of visual qualities or in the expression of artistic or philosophical attitudes. Those interactions might be as "valuable" as those in organically evolved cultural landscapes, but they are of a fundamentally different quality.

Summing up, a functional approach may therefore be a key for better understanding cultural landscapes. Comparing traditional, historic cultural landscapes with those created by the modern, globally standardized agriculture and forestry, the functional changes are clearer and more fundamental than material ones. Functional criteria might be particularly appropriate to define different types of cultural landscapes and to evaluate them.

In relict cultural landscapes the material structure persists but the culture is more or less gone and characteristic functional features with it. Often there is no other option but to conserve a given state by planning concepts and management from outside. But the long-term goal should be to restore functional characteristics of the landscape as well, which will inevitably require the integration of the local population.

Acknowledgement

I wish to thank Martin Dieterich and Alison Semple for the stylistic revision of the English manuscript.

References

Begon, M., Harper, J.L. and Townsend, C.R. (1990). *Ecology.* – 2nd ed., 945 pp.; Boston (Blackwell Sci.Publ.).

Blankson, E.J. and Green, B.H. (1991). *Use of landscape classification as an essential prerequisite to landscape evaluation.* – Landscape and Urban Planning **21**, 149–162.

Bourlière, F. (ed.) (1983). *Tropical savannas.* – Ecosystems of the world **13**, 730 pp.; Amsterdam (Elsevier Publ.).

Bridgewater, P. and Hooy, T. (1995). *Outstanding cultural landscapes in Australia, New Zealand and the Pacific: the footprint of man in the wilderness.* – In von Droste, B., Plachter, H. and Rössler, M. (eds.): *Cultural landscapes of universal value*; Jena (G.Fischer Verl.) (in this volume).

Burgess, R.L. and Sharpe, D.M. (1981). *Forest island dynamics in man-dominated landscape.* – New York (Springer Verl.).

di Castri, F. (1989). *History of biological invasions with special emphasis on the Old World.* In Drake, J.A., Mooney, H.A., di Castri, F., Groves, R.H., Kruger, F.J., Rejánek, M. and Williamson, M. (eds.): *Biological invasions. A global perspective*, pp. 1–30; Chichester (J.Wiley).

Fahrig, L. and Merriam, G. (1985). *Habitat patch connectivity and population survival.* – Ecology **66**, 1762–1768.

Farina, A. (1995). *Cultural landscapes and fauna.* – In von Droste, B., Plachter, H. and Rössler, M. (eds.): *Cultural landscapes of universal value*; Jena (G. Fischer Verl.) (in this volume).

Gilpin, M. and Hanski, I. (eds.) (1991). *Metapopulation dynamics: empirical and theoretical investigations.* – 336 pp.; London (Acad.Press).

Hansson, L. (1991). *Dispersal and connectivity in metapopulations.* – Biol. J. Linnean Soc. **42**, 89–103.

Henein, K. and Merriam, G. (1990). *The elements of connectivity where corridor quality is variable.* – Landscape Ecology **4**, 157–170.

Heydemann, B. and Meyer, H. (1983). *Auswirkungen der Intensivkultur auf die Fauna in den Agrarbiotopen.* – Schr.R. Deutscher Rat f. Landespfl. **42**, 174–191.

Hobbs, R.J. and Saunders, D.A. (eds.) (1993). *Reintegrating fragmented landscapes. Towards sustainable production and nature conservation.* – 332 pp.; Berlin (Springer Verl.).

Jelinek, A.J. (1967). *Man's role in the extinction of Pleistocene faunas.* – Proc.VII Congr. Int. Ass. Quarternary Res. 6, 193–200; New Haven (Yale Univ. Press).

Layton, R. and Titchen, S. (1995). *Uluru: an outstanding Australian aboriginal cultural landscape.* – In von Droste, B., Plachter, H. and Rössler, M. (eds.): *Cultural landscapes of universal value*; Jena (G. Fischer Verl.) (in this volume).

Lucas, P.H.C. (1992). *Protected landscapes. A guide for policy-makers and planners.* – 297 pp.; London (Chapman & Hall).

McNeely, J. and Keeton, W.S. (1995). *The interaction between biological and cultural diversity.* – In von Droste, B., Plachter, H. and Rössler, M. (eds.): *Cultural landscapes of universal value*; Jena (G. Fischer Verl.) (in this volume).

McNeely, J.A., Miller, K.R., Reid, W.V., Mittermeier, R.A. and Werner, T.B. (1990). *Conserving the world's biological diversity.* – 193 pp.; Gland and Washington, D.C. (IUCN, WRI, GI, WWR-US, The World Bank).

Opdam, P. (1991). *Metapopulation theory and habitat fragmentation: a review of holarctic breeding bird studies.* – Landscape ecology **5**, 93–106.

Philipps, A. (1995). *Cultural landscapes: an IUCN Perspective.* – In von Droste, B., Plachter, H. and Rössler, M. (eds.): *Cultural landscapes of universal value*; Jena (G. Fischer Verl.) (in this volume).

Picket, S.T.A. and White, P.S. (eds.) (1985). *The ecology of natural disturbance and patch dynamics.* – 472 pp.; Orlando (Acad.Press).

Plachter, H. (1991). *Naturschutz.* – 463 pp.; Stuttgart (G. Fischer Verl.).

Plachter, H. (1994). *Methodische Rahmenbedingungen für synoptische Bewertungsverfahren im Naturschutz.* – Z. Ökologie u. Naturschutz (ZÖN) **3**, 87–106.

Plachter, H. (1995). *Ecological aspects of Central European cultural landscapes.* – In Villalon, A. (ed.): *Rice culture in South-East Asia and its terraced rice landscapes*; Manila (in press).

Remmert, H. (1985). *Der vorindustrielle Mensch in den Ökosystemen der Erde.* – Naturwissenschaften **72**, 627–632.

Remmert, H. (ed.) (1991). *The mosaic-cycle concept of ecosystems.* – Ecol. Studies **85**; Berlin (Springer Verl.).

Rössler, M. (1995). *UNESCO and cultural landscape protection.* – in: von Droste, B., Plachter, H. and Rössler, M. (eds.): *Cultural landscapes of universal value*; Jena (G. Fischer Verl.) (in this volume).

Saunders, D., Hobbs, R.J. and Margules, C.R. (1991). *Biological consequences of ecosystem fragmentation: a review.* – Conserv. Biol. **5**, 18–32.

Shaffer, M.L. (1981). *Minimum population sizes for species conservation.* – Bioscience **31**, 131–134.

Shaffer, M.L. (1987). *Minimum viable populations: coping with uncertainty.* – In Soulé, M.E. (ed.): *Viable populations for conservation*, pp. 69–87; Cambridge (Univ. Press).

Schüle, W. (1992). *Vegetation, megaherbivores, man and climate in the Quarternary and the genesis of closed forests.* – In Goldammer, J.G. (ed.): *Tropical forests in transition*, pp. 45–76; Basel (Birkhäuser Verl.).

Sukopp, H. (1983). *Ökologische Charakteristik von Großstädten.* – Grundriß der Stadtplanung; Akad. Raumforschung Landesplanung, 554 pp.; Hannover.

Sukopp, H., Hejny, S. and Kowarik, I. (eds.) (1990): *Urban ecology. Plants and plant communities in urban environments.* – Den Haag (SPB Acad.Publ.).

Villalon, A. (1995). *The cultural landscapes of the Philippine Cordilleras rice terraces.* – In von Droste, B., Plachter, H. and Rössler, M. (eds.): *Cultural landscapes of universal value*; Jena (G. Fischer Verl.) (in this volume).

Williamson, M. (1981). *Island populations.* – 286 pp.; Oxford (Oxford Univ. Press).

Harald Plachter has a Ph.D. for biology. He is professor for nature conservation at the University of Marburg, Germany.

Chapter 35

Principles for Protecting Endangered Landscapes: The Work of the IUCN-CESP Working Group on Landscape Conservation

Bryn H. Green

Introduction - What Are Landscapes ?

It is increasingly realised that few, if any, environments are free of human intervention and, moreover, that in many environments such intervention is a key element in generating and maintaining biodiversity. In many parts of the world human intervention has created and maintained environments which are arguably richer and more diverse in species, scenic beauty, historical interest and recreational opportunity than the natural forest and other ecosystems they have replaced. These cultural environments, ranging from the mixed farm and forestlands of Europe and Eastern North America, through the pasture lands and savannahs of the Middle East and Africa to the paddylands of the Pacific Rim, are usually the product of relatively low-level, sustainable exploitation of the environment over long periods of time.

The concept of landscape gives expression to the products of this spatial and temporal interaction of people with the environment. A landscape may be conceived as a particular configuration of topography, vegetation cover, land use and settlement pattern which delimits some coherence of natural and cultural processes and activities.

This is a definition of a modern concept of landscape, concerned more with process than pattern. It is rather different from the origins of landscape as a word describing the visual impression of a tract of scenery. Landscape as defined in this modern sense has great utility, both as a framework for the study of ecological processes operating at a larger scale than the species, population, community or ecosystem, and, particularly, as the appropriate scale for studying the impact or influence of human activities on the environment. This has been the impetus of the new and flourishing discipline of landscape ecology.

Landscape Conservation

As arenas which frame the interaction of people and nature, landscapes can be an important analytical mechanism for development planning and management. Both Caring for the Earth and the UNCED Agenda 21 programme for sustainable development place considerable emphasis on an integrated approach to the planning and management of land resources, the latter clearly recognizing the role of landscape ecology in achieving this:

> Governments should ... adopt planning and management systems that facilitate the integration of environmental components, such as air, water, land and other natural resources using landscape ecological planning (LANDEP)....

As natural units, landscapes are not only potentially a very useful means of approaching sustainable development and ecological and conservation enterprises, but are worthy of maintenance in their own right. More intensive agricultural and forestry practices are now replacing the traditional ones, many rural communities are in decline, and cultural landscapes are everywhere threatened. They merit conservation, not only for their intrinsic values, but because they may be useful as models of harmonious human interaction with the environment which can be applied in both the developed and developing world. Such landscapes commonly form the matrix in which protected areas are set and their wellbeing is vital to the conservation of such protected areas. Some cultural landscapes are themselves designated as National Parks or as other categories of protected area. This has been acknowledged by the recognition of a Protected Landscapes Category (V) of designated areas by IUCN (Lucas 1992).

The Challenges of Landscape Conservation

As products of socio-economic systems now changing through rural depopulation, urban expansion and new technologies, landscape protection poses particular problems. It is usually highly undesirable, indeed often impossible, to constrain the evolution of socio-economic systems which have created and maintained cherished landscapes. Many of them involve impoverished and difficult ways of life which younger generations of people are no longer prepared to tolerate. Alternative livelihoods or other means may have to be found to maintain communities and desired landscape characteristics (Figure 1).

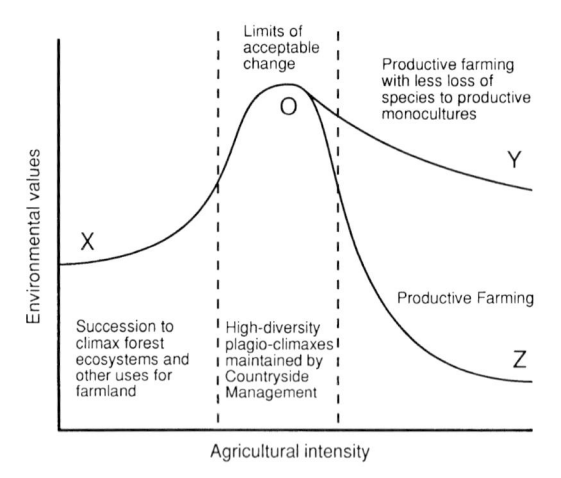

Figure 1. Cultural Landscape Dynamics. A model based upon Grimes (1979) data relating species density in herbaceous communities to above ground standing crop and Connell's (1979) model relating species diversity in rainforests and tropical reefs to disturbance events. Agriculture may be considered a combination of these factors. It has diversified the environment by creating new biotopes such as grasslands and heathlands, often richer in species than the climax forest they replaced. Modern intensive agriculture however leads to loss of biotopes and species diversity (from Green 1993). Overcapacity in agriculture offers the opportunity to : a) take land out of production which could be used for forestry, recreation and other purposes (0 -X), b) manage the countryside by traditional farming (Z - O), c) develop more environmentally-benign systems of productive agriculture (O-Y).

There has also been some reluctance on technical grounds to accept the landscape as a natural unit. The use of landscape as a natural unit is seen as having three major difficulties: whether landscape units with a clear identity can be recognised; whether such units are unique, or repeatable, and at what scales landscapes should be defined.

These issues are linked. Few would be prepared to quarrel with the idea of natural areas defined largely by topography and geology. (Many countries have produced maps of such areas). But when it comes to grouping such areas into like kinds, into a classification of natural areas, strong reservations quickly begin to arise in most peoples' minds. Yet if one adopts very generalised large scale natural area units, such as mountains, estuaries, valleys, scarplands or plateaux, then the very existence of these words testifies to their acceptance as genera of natural area types.

Some landscape classifications of practical utility have begun to be made which introduce land use into this topographical framework. European landscapes have been broadly classified into thirteen types (Meeus et al. 1990). In Britain a quantitative methodology has been used to classify landscapes into thirty-two classes (Benefield and Bunce 1982). The protection of wildlife and natural areas would be difficult to envisage in the absence of accepted classifications of species and biotopes. The artificiality of such classifications does not detract greatly from their practical utility. Neither should it with landscapes (Blankson and Green 1991).

Once recorded, described and classified landscape types should be amenable to evaluation in a similar way to species and biotopes using criteria such as threat, rarity, diversity, scenic beauty and historical and literary associations to decide priorities for protection. To protect them an understanding will be needed of the processes creating and maintaining them and of how such process can be continued or simulated. These are formidable challenges to scientists, policymakers and practitioners. (Green 1985)

The Working Group's Programme

The IUCN-CESP Working Group on Landscape conservation, in collaboration with The International Association of Landscape Ecologists (IALE), brings together scientists, policymakers and practitioners to respond to these challenges. Its broad purpose is to refine and promote landscape approaches in environmental planning as a tool for sustainable development. To do this it will develop work on threatened landscapes and serve overall as a basis for IUCN's landscape activities.

The Working Group has 30 members from many different countries, mainly European and North American, and many more correspondents all over the world. It has held two Workshop meetings; in Montecatini Italy in April 1992 and Wye, England in April 1993. Three major work areas have emerged from these meetings.

The listing of endangered valued landscapes (EVLs)

Since so many landscape-types are now subject to rapid change, particularly through agricultural and forestry activities and social factors leading to either intensification or abandonment, the first priority must be to identify what kinds of landscape are both most valuable and most threatened and give them some preliminary recognition.

It is proposed that this will be undertaken through the preparation of **Red Lists of Threatened Landscapes**.

To aims of this activity will be to:

i) gain some assessment of the nature and numbers of endangered valued landscapes in different countries and regions, in order to measure the magnitude of the conservation task overall and define priorities for promoting their designation as protected areas;

ii) record and register for posterity the nature and range of cultural landscapes. (There is the very real risk that some landscapes may be lost, or subject to irreversible change, before measures to conserve them can be brought into effect).

iii) by drawing attention to them as **Endangered Landscapes (EL)**, help to provide immediate initial protection for threatened landscapes and their biological, ecological, visual and cultural values until the appropriate level of protection is determined and given to the area;

iv) create a professional and organizational methodology and expertise that will help expedite the protection of threatened landscapes.

Ideally this process of listing should be preceded by a major exercise of survey, recording and analysis to describe, classify and evaluate landscapes which are potential candidates for inclusion in the list, using standard methodologies and criteria. It will be one of the functions of the Working Group to promote the development of such methodologies. However, in practice it is clear that if the listing is to be effective, and that means rapid, it cannot await the development of these methodologies. It must begin and be a dynamic process which is modified as it progresses to make use of new methodologies as they come to be available.

It is therefore proposed that the listing process will start with the preparation of a simple selection rationale and checklist questionnaire to characterise EVLs and report on any protection strategies for them. This initially will be drafted as the minimum necessary for participants to understand and undertake the recording. Local national and regional experts will then be sent the questionnaires and invited to submit preliminary lists of EVL candidates. Much of this may be done initially from existing information and expertise as a desk exercise. Finally those EVLs submitted to be registered on the Red List will be selected by an International Expert Panel using selection rationale criteria. In an iterative procedure local experts will be sent copies of the Red List to upgrade their entries and benefit from creative ideas for rescue and management strategies. This last activity will be closely linked with the second main work area to be promoted by the Working Group.

The Conservation of Endangered Valued Landscapes

The ultimate objective of the Red Listing process is to move a representative selection of EVLs from an endangered to rescued status. Some are already safeguarded in various categories of protected area; the World Heritage Convention has also recently been re-interpreted to embrace them. More EVLs need to be thus protected and additional means of safeguarding them through information, incentives and regulation are required.

The Working Group will promote the development and adoption of educational, legislative and other mechanisms of EVL protection.

The aims will be to :

i) increase awareness of endangered valued landscapes and ways to protect them through collaboration, co-operation, information exchange publicity and training;
ii) assist, guide and encourage local, regional, national and international bodies in their efforts to protect threatened landscapes by providing professional support and creating an atmosphere that may attract political and financial support;
iii) facilitate and expedite the preparation of sustainable landscape conservation and development strategies and support systems;
iv) promote the development of legislation, conventions and other means of giving national and international recognition to EVLs.

Their large size, widespread distribution and their generation and maintenance by socio-economic systems commonly in flux makes EVLs unusually difficult to protect. To do so usually means finding ways of supporting the local communities and the traditional practices which maintain them.

Governments should ...strengthen management systems for land or natural resources by including appropriate traditional and indigenous methods; examples of these practices include pastoralism. Hema reserves (traditional Islamic land reserves) and terraced agriculture. (Agenda 21)

It has to be accepted that only very rarely will traditional systems be able to remain unchanged. New livelihoods and systems of management compatible with the maintenance of desired landscape characteristics will have to be identified with local people, developers, planners and politicians and means found to make them economically viable. This will not be possible everywhere and alternative strategies for landscapes moving out of a cultural to either more natural or more technolgical phases will need to be developed. Acceptable limits of change may be able to be defined.

The application of Landscape Ecology in Sustainable Development

The wider application of the principles and practice of landscape ecology into land planning and management policy and decision-making will greatly facilitate sustainable development and landscape conservation. This and, more specifically, the EVL red listing process will necessitate the description, classification and evaluation of endangered landscapes, the identification of threats to them and the elaboration of planning and management strategies to help protect them. All this, particularly the latter, will require research to gain a better understanding of EVLs and the transmission of its results to policy-makers, planners and managers.

The Working Group will promote this through encouraging the collaboration of scientists and practitioners in research and through meetings and networking.

The aims will be to :

i) develop standardised methodologies for the survey, recording, description, monitoring and classification of landscapes;
ii) develop criteria for the assessment and analysis of both the value and threats to landscapes which can be used for Red List and Protected Area selection;

iii) promote the application of these methodologies in endangered landscape studies and research to characterise and understand natural and cultural systems and structures and their trends.
iv) transmit this information to policymakers and planners in an accessible format.

Descriptive studies to characterise EVLs are relatively straightforward compared with the more difficult task of preparing prescriptions for their planning and management. These require an understanding of natural and socio-economic processes which interact to maintain them. The study of endangered landscapes to provide this information is still a relatively new and developing discipline. We have little real understanding of the processes of interaction between people and the land which have created and maintained many endangered valued landscapes. These processes are often complex, subtle and dynamic. Their study requires the collaboration of natural and social scientists in order that landscapes can be addressed in an integrated, holistic manner. This requires the bringing together of two academic and institutional cultures and represents a major challenge.

The Working Group has already begun these activities through meetings and the preparation of **Green Book Case Studies of Endangered Valued Landscapes.** These are intended to serve as one of the key practical tools for bridging the gaps between researchers and practitioners. A number of pilot studies have been undertaken and they are being developed into a standard integrative methodology for holistic landscape conservation based on advances in landscape ecology. The elaboration of a standard format for the recording and description of landscapes is in progress.

Collaboration and Development

These three main work areas of the Working Group's programme are closely inter-related and the success of each is very much contingent on that of the others. They abut other activities elsewhere. The Working Group on Landscape Conservation is in contact with **IUCN-CNPPA, WCMC** and a number of other international and national programmes related to its work through some of its members also being associated with these other organisations. There are a number of such related initiatives with which links are being established. These include :

i) The incorporation of **Cultural Landscapes of Outstanding Universal Value** into the **UNESCO World Heritage Convention** and the development of criteria for their selection.
ii) A chapter on landscape classification and protection in the **EC State of the Environment Report.**
iii) A proposal for a **European Convention for the Protection of Europe's Rural Landscapes** as part of the emerging **IUCN Action Plan for Protected Areas in Europe.**
iv) A research proposal by the **Permanent European Conference for the Study of Rural Landscape** for **An Atlas of the European Cultural Landscape.**
v) The identification of **Natural Areas** by **English Nature** and of landscape-types by the **Countryside Commission** in their **New Map of England** project.
vi) A proposal from the **University of Zurich** to establish a **European Federation for the Protection and Management of the Landscape.**

It would seem to be desirable that co-ordinated, mutually compatible approaches are made. The Working Group would be pleased to hear of any other similar initiatives.

The Landscape Dimension in the Work of IUCN

These parallel initiatives serve to emphasize the relevance and urgency of the work of landscape conservation. This is not new to the work of IUCN. In its former manisfestation CESP promoted a project to produce a **Green Book of Outstanding Landscapes**. The preliminary results were published in 1978 as **Some Outstanding Landscapes**, but the project did not proceed further. Current perceptions of the need to address conservation problems in a much wider context than species and site protection give this approach new impetus. We need to define how landscape relates to other approaches which circumscribe coherent tracts of territory and living systems, eg catchments, bioregions, laboratory regions, living heritage zones, biosphere reserves etc, and demonstrate the particular contribution that landscape ecology can make in both developed and developing countries. These are formidable challenges for the Working Group.

Acknowledgements

This paper is closely based on a statement of the activities of the Working Group on Landscape Conservation to be published in Environmental Strategy, the IUCN-CESP Newsletter.

I am greatly indebted to a number of colleagues, particularly to Adrian Phillips, Zev Naveh, Ted Trzyna and Almo Farina for valuable discussion, suggestions and help in drafting this paper. It draws upon material presented at the Wye workshop, especially the paper on Red Listing proposed by Yoav Sagi.

References

Benefield, C.B. and Bunce R.G.H. (1982). *A preliminary visual presentation of land classes in Britain.* Merlewood Res & Dev Paper 91, ITE, Grange-over-Sands. 37pp.

Blankson, E.J. and Green, B.H. (1991). *Use of landscape classification as an essential prerequisite to landscape evaluation.* Landscape and Urban Planning **21**, 149-162.

Connell, J.H. (1979). *Tropical rain forests and coral reefs as open, non-equilibrium systems.* In Anderson, R. et al. (eds.): *Population Dynamics.* Blackwell, Oxford. pp 141-63.

Green, B. (1985). *Countryside conservation: the protection and management of amenity ecosystems.* Unwin-Hyman, London. 253 pp.

Green, B. (1993). *Towards a more sustainable agriculture: time for a rural land-use strategy?* Biologist **40**, 81-5.

Green, B. H. (1993): *The challenges of landscape conservation: a work plan for IUCN.* Environmental Strategy **1**, 11–15.

Grime, J.P. (1979). *Plant strategies and vegetation processes.* Wiley, Chichester.

Lucas, P.H.C. (1992). *Protected landscapes: a guide for policy-makers and planners.* Chapman & Hall, London. 314pp.

Meeus, J.H.A., Wijermans, M.P. and Vroom, M.J. (1990). *Agricultural landscapes in Europe and their transformation.* Landscape and Urban Planning **18**, 289-352.

Bryn H. Green teaches at Wye College, University of London

Chapter 36

Conservation of Landscapes in Post-Industrial Countries

David Jacques and Peter Fowler

Background

Many formerly "industrialized" countries are now post-industrial, economically and sociologically. Whilst many traditional differences between them remain, there is often social fragmentation within each of them, for example as a result of multiculturalism. At the same time, sophisticated information and communication is now accessible to most. These factors have profound consequences for attitudes to the past, to landscapes as "heritage", and to cultural landscapes. No longer can the heritage be viewed as something fixed and common to all. Instead attitudes towards heritage are becoming complex; they are both diverse and dynamic.

Many important cultural landscapes are experiencing rural desertion, and meanwhile the increasing proportion of the population living in cities, towns and suburbia is lessening its links with the land and its understanding of its ways of life. The identification of individuals and communities with specific landscapes is thus less common, but other forms of value remain strong and are increasing. Tourists' enjoyment of the aesthetic value of the landscape expands continuously, whilst the role of landscapes as icons of lost values for an urban population seeking a more environmentally friendly way of life is an old quest given fresh impetus in recent years.

A third background point is that the age of the expert as dictator is over. Consultation is essential, both in principle and in practice. In spite of rural communities declining or being taken over by formerly urban people with no connection to the land, consultation with them before designation of landscape is de rigueur. Afterwards, a continuing sensitivity to the people who already manage the land is not just practical, but a political aim too.

An underlying philosophy

The rise of interest in cultural landscapes amongst professionals over the last few years has been marked, leading to a consensus in the recognized types of cultural landscape (see box). To some extent cultural landscapes are the beneficiary of spill-over from abutting disciplines. Archaeologists realize that they can understand ancient cultures better if they look at the wider scene. Ecologists recognize that an area's ecology is often critically determined by human intervention. Anthropologists listen to the oral traditions of native peoples celebrating the landscape. And so on.

> **Box 1.** Types of cultural landscape:
>
> I ornamental
>   A gardens/public spaces
>   B parks
>
> II functional (or evolved)
>   A continuing
>   B relict (or "fossil")
>
> III associated with
>   A belief systems (sacred places)
>   B aesthetic preferences
>   C writers, poets, painters
>   D events, battles
>
> IV settings to monuments or ensembles

However there are deeper reasons underlying the rise of cultural landscapes. The lack of a widely accepted religious dogma that ordains answers to questions such as "what is humankind's place on this planet?" impels a search for a new way to make sense of it all. The loss of ultimate certainty is a crisis that can be faced only by humankind taking more responsibility for its own destiny. This can best be achieved by behaving rationally, i.e. using judgement informed by the practical knowledge of what consequences are likely to flow from a defined set of decisions. This encourages the idea that the landscape is an archive of value systems as they have interacted with their physical environments. It is the record of the human race's struggle, intellectual and physical, etched upon the Earth's surface, of historical interest and an irreplaceable aid to shaping the future.

The second reason is similar, in that the landscape is seen as a source of knowledge about processes, but is couched in ecological terms. The Earth's limited resources must be husbanded carefully for the sake of future generations. A management plan for the planet is needed. Of course this is not attainable instantly, but in the meantime a conceptual framework for sustainable living worldwide can be built up through study of the various forms of landscape management, and their consequences as far as resources are concerned. This is the philosophy underlying the Protected Landscapes movement within IUCN.

There are problems with interpreting the experience of ancient systems in terms that are useful to projections for life in the 21st century. The most sustainable systems yet found are primitive in material terms. Sustainability will not be politically attractive if it offers a return to the Middle Ages, and the benefits of technology, particularly sanitation and communications, will have to form part of a sustainable future. Nevertheless, the point remains that the landscape is a vast database with many valuable lessons to give, if interpreted intelligently.

The aspects of landscape value

The more common arguments for existing forms of landscape protection are:
   I. the natural aesthetic
  II. the interplay of natural and man-made
 III. the man-made aesthetic
  IV. associations
   V. archaeological value

Aesthetic motivation is behind most of the earliest forms of protection of cultural landscapes. Sometimes the landscape concerned was clearly one modified by humans, and in other cases it has been the absence of human intervention, and the pristine state of nature, that has been the focus of interest. Although the World Heritage Criteria classify natural beauty as one of the natural criteria, an aesthetic judgement is a matter of cultural values. Arguably, then, landscape beauty is more sensibly a cultural criterion.

The first National Park, Yellowstone, was protected for its natural beauty (which was emphasized more than its nature conservation value), and an American precursor of the National Trust for England and Wales, the Massachusetts Trustees for Reservations, was set up in order to protect beauty spots from development. The French, the Germans, and many European nations remain keen on protection of landscape for its qualities of natural beauty.

A slightly different twist to the rhetoric emerged in the United Kingdom, where there is hardly any truly natural landscape as a result of extensive human exploitation throughout the post-glacial era. Wordsworth's perception of landscape was not just a love of the grandeur of scenery. He had a fascination for the interplay of the wild, untameable, unforgiving forces of nature on the one hand, and the indomitable human spirit that sought to find a niche for humankind even in the most inhospitable conditions on the other. When, in the 1890s, the National Trust was set up initially to protect the scenery of Wordsworth's Lake District, the visual image was inseparable from the reputation of the simple, hardy hill folk. The English National Parks, set up in the late 1940s, were defined on the basis of "natural beauty". This concept needed translating into the English context, and everyone understood that the term was a shorthand for beauty that was derived mostly from natural factors, but was embellished by the handiwork of humankind.

Nowadays the effects of human intervention are recognized almost everywhere. There are those who point out that even Yellowstone has a claim to be a cultural landscape, since the suppression of burning has interrupted the sequence of periodic conflagration that beforehand happened naturally. Today, the rigid division between natural and man-made beauty is dissolving, and acceptance of the value of interplay between human intervention and nature is on the ascendancy. For example the Hungarians are proud of the Fertorakos region where lakes, mountains and architecture enhance each other visually. Some monuments already on the World Heritage List, like Mont St Michel, Meteora and Mesa Verde, gain their interest from their unusual and spectacular topographical situations which have come to symbolize religious or national values.

Designed landscapes, where the "natural beauty" is the result of careful manipulation, should not be omitted. Capability Brown "will be least remembered where he has been most successful". Gardens are slightly off the subject as they are already recognized, for the purposes of the World Heritage List, as monuments, but landscape parks would appear not to be.

It is quite common to find houses protected because they have associations. Indeed this was a principal route for Americans and Canadians into the conservation of their built heritage. With several houses of ex-presidents, like Monticello, come designed landscapes. Battlefields have been purchased and commemorated. In the USA and Australia landscapes have been protected for their associations with the belief systems of native peoples. In England, painters' and writers' landscapes are found to be of interest, with, for example, the local planning authority nudging "Constable Country", the area painted by William Constable in the early nineteenth century, more to how it was in his day.

Waymarking national histories by commemoration through places is harmless enough, but this process can be abused in the name of national or ethnic identity by keeping alive the memory of devisive events. Battlefields are an obvious example, triumphalism by the victors, and an unnecessary reminder of an unfortunate episode in the history of the losing side. There can be a dark side of associationism.

A further, and more common, reason for protection of cultural landscapes has been archaeological, particularly of those derived from industry. In Canada, the area of interest at the 8,000 year old Head-Smashed-in Buffalo Leap (inscribed on the World Heritage List in 1981) was shown to be the herding area above the leap (where the bison were tricked into thinking that cairns were humans), as well as the leap itself. In the United Kingdom, an area of prehistoric flint mines at Grimes Graves is an Ancient Monument. In the USA and the UK, power generation and/or manufacturing complexes from the eighteenth and nineteenth centuries, extensive enough to be classified as industrial landscapes, are protected; Ironbridge, inscribed on the World Heritage List in 1986, is a well-known example. At such places, and at the prehistoric religious sites like Stonehenge (inscribed on the World Heritage List in 1986), it is not just the great structures that are protected, but also their context of a supporting landscape that can amount to extensive swathes of the surrounding countryside.

The view of the existing managers of the land

Conservation of cultural landscapes has been coming more to the fore. When this happens, the issues familiar to conservationists of all forms emerge, chiefly that of public versus private interest. Economic arguments eventually overwhelm all others, but there may also be resistance to the loss of local pastimes and traditions which happen to be deleterious when seen in a wider context, such as the shooting of migratory birds in some parts of Southern Europe. There is no doubt that the creation of National Parks is resented by the locals everywhere. They are expelled, bought out, or at least constrained in their activities, for reasons that they may think are inadequate, and there is also a fear of loss of autonomy to a conservation-driven, bureaucratic oligarchy. "Why us?" Heritage conservation and tourism impinges upon locals in the developing world and post-industrial countries alike.

It was unfortunate that when the English National Parks, for example, were created, largely for the sake of the town-dweller, the farmers were not compensated for the fall in viability deriving from a range of new restrictions, for example on the erection of new buildings and the use of materials. This burden fell upon a class of farmers who were least able to afford it. However the cooperation of the owner is vital to successful conservation, and financial considerations naturally weigh heavily. There seem, then, to be two prerequisites for further intervention in "continuing" landscapes: grants or subsidies that are in excess of the losses that landowners will sustain, and very clear reasons why the intervention is desirable.

Why and how to conserve

In thinking about conservation measures for cultural landscapes, it helps to start with this last question: what purpose is served by conservation? The answer will help in sorting out priorities. If landscapes are to be retained as a database on human activity, is aesthetic value of relevance? Should the simple and clear examples that anyone can understand be protected, or the evidence of more complex interactions that require sophisticated interpretation? It could also be asked what role recording may have. Is it a cheaper and more effective way of capturing the information than preservation in situ? Is it the only practical approach in fast-changing "continuing" landscapes?

Meanwhile most systems of conservation developed for cultural landscapes are borrowed from those for cultural monuments, or those for nature conservation. Considerable strains are placed on regulatory systems developed for historic fabric as the subject spills over into more subjective questions of natural value and associative value. There is considerable variability in opinion as to what should be classed as cultural landscape for the purposes of legislation. An example from the UK is the current unwillingness by English Heritage to expand the scope of their work on cultural landscapes into associative landscapes. The reasoning is eminently practical; under any system of regulation, efficient protection requires that the resource and its value are precisely described, so that owners and regulators know where they stand. Whilst this can be achieved with the objective evidence, i.e. the "fabric" of walls, hedges, ditches etc., it is not possible with intangible qualities such as associations.

Regulation in a landscape associated with a poet or a painter, or which is said to be beautiful, would require acquiescence to an ad-hoc "professional judgement", something which is under attack the world over, and is increasingly contentious. As an example, a few years ago local planning authorities in the UK were told that they should no longer exercise aesthetic judgements.

There would also be problems with nominations of associative landscapes to the World Heritage List. Who prevails if one country cannot accept the universal significance of another nation's greatest poet? On the other hand, the Australians are keen on promoting the aboriginal view of landscape. This is almost purely "in the mind", and rests upon the continuance of an oral tradition that gives history and folk meaning to features of the landscape. To a European a landscape may look like just another tract of the outback, but to the aboriginal it may be sacred ground associated with stories about his ancestors. The fabric in this case is almost nothing, but the case put forward for protection is that the belief system retained by the aborigines is of outstanding universal significance. Further problems then arise; does the value of the landscape evaporate as fewer aborigines find value in their own oral tradition? Bearing in mind these problems, it is not surprising that existing conservation measures for associative landscapes are few.

The reverse is true, though, for conservation measures for nature conservation, which are found everywhere in industrialized countries. Eastern European legislation for cultural landscape tends to be an offshoot of that protecting its aesthetic value, and that tends to be an offshoot of legislation protecting natural value. In the UK, at least, there is one great potential benefit of conservation in this tradition, which is the heavy emphasis upon management issues. Whilst relict landscapes, typically on upland, can often be managed by sheep, continuing landscapes are sensitive to external influences like market demand and government policy, and any attempt to conserve historic features would require skill, persuasiveness and financial incentive from the public official. Some people question whether it is at all possible to conserve living, evolving, landscapes.

There are calls for cultural landscapes to be recognized in their own right, which might imply that protection should be shifting to a unified system of specifically cultural landscape protection. The wide scope of cultural landscape is, however, a major obstacle to this. The strands of the subject come together only at a high level of conceptualization, i.e. when considering some definition such as "cultural landscapes are the product of the interaction of human values with the physical environment", and appropriate legislation for one type of cultural landscape may have more in common with another aspect of the heritage than with other types of cultural landscape.

There is no doubt that the conservation of associative landscapes, to give the chief example, will require a very different approach to, say, that for relict landscapes. Relict landscapes, in turn, will require quite a different approach to continuing landscapes. Hence a sensible form of protection for relict landscapes may well look a lot more like archaeological protection, than measures to conserve continuing landscapes, which may come to have much in common with nature conservation.

Public control and incentives

The main prerequisite to cultural landscape conservation mentioned earlier was to avoid putting the local population at an economic disadvantage. This introduces the question of the current nature and scope of public control of land.

Forms of protection fall into three categories: acquisition, regulation and nationalization of development rights. Acquisition is the only feasible means of protection when private property rights are inviolable, and is the traditional route in capitalist societies. Historically this was the US National Park and the UK National Trusts approach, clean-cut but potentially heavy-handed. The Shenandoah National Park was created by purchase of the land and removal of the inhabitants, and the National Trust of England and Wales bought property for demolition at Avebury until the 1960s. The dangers were that merely holding the land could be claimed as success, whereas active management is generally required (nowadays means are devised to give a greater emphasis upon agreements and management). The acquisition of covenants over the land by purchase, agreement or gift, is an alternative to outright acquisition, but its success depends in practice upon the goodwill of the owner and efficient policing by the conservation body.

A second form of protection is the regulation of private rights. Most western countries except the United Kingdom operate on this basis for environmental protection. In the United States the system is fairly basic; regulation may be introduced on the grounds of health, safety and welfare only. Zoning maps are drawn up which are (theoretically anyway) fairly rigid in application. Elsewhere, in Western Europe, regulation is relatively complex.

The socialist solution is that development rights are vested in the State as representative of the interests of the population as a whole. Owners then became mere occupiers, and either may not develop, or need permission to develop. This became the British system in 1947, since when a fairly sophisticated town and country planning system has emerged, based not on rigid maps, but on published policies which are interpreted flexibly in each case. This made it easier to conserve the National Parks in England and Wales, and subsequently to operate legislation protecting the character of towns and landscapes.

Some people consider that the various forms of protection that could be applied to landscape to stop the owner doing something will ultimately be less successful than forms of incentive to persuade the owner to do the right thing. This is because the owner's freedom to manage land is largely an illusion. Most Governments have good overall control of the use of rural land, through farming and forestry subsidies, price control and other mechanisms.

In the United Kingdom the drive for productivity after the Second World War seriously depleted the complexity and beauty of the countryside. Now there are agricultural surpluses, the Government, spurred on by the Countryside Commission, regards the land and farmers in a new and interesting way. Instead of them being just the operatives of one large food factory, diversity of aims is welcomed, and farmers are regarded as multi-purpose managers who should be serving recreational and aesthetic demands as well as growing food.

There is an experimental scheme called "Countryside Stewardship", which gives incentives to owners to replace hedges, repair walls, plant trees, convert arable land into pasture, and generally reverse the ravages of the last 40 years. The possibility of hanging the protection of historic landscape on this hook is already being explored. Meadows, parkland, and orchards are amongst the categories of historic landscape for which schemes are already running. In summary, the future for historic landscapes conservation looks more like being a system of incentives operated flexibly and face-to-face between farmer and official, than new laws.

The French have an interesting system for protecting certain historic landscapes which uses a form of "appellation controllée" for the agricultural products of an area. This device seeks to protect the local economy that formed the landscape as much as the landscape itself. It may help those communities and landscapes that are marginal economically, but there must be doubt as to whether this will be an effective long-term strategy. For example the technology of production may change without the product changing, thus rendering some landscape features redundant. Ultimately there may be no short cut to measures that address the conservation of the fabric directly.

Subsidiarity

At what level should decisions be made? All good Europeans are now supposed to subscribe to the principle of subsidiarity: that decisions should be made at the lowest feasible level. The idea that local communities should be democratically involved in protection sounds attractive. The logic of devolving decision making to local level is that it can decide upon its own priorities. These may bear no relation, though, to the values of the areas themselves as perceived from a national viewpoint. Hence they can be unprotected simply because local politicians are more concerned about, say, the local tourist industry. So what happens when local views differ from the general view? Should they be allowed to thwart the goals of society as a whole?

Historically, most measures for landscape protection have been generated from the higher levels of government. The argument for continuing with this are the rationality that can be brought to bear, and the distinct dangers of misguided or introspective attitudes held by local politicians. The dangers of high level decisions, on the other hand, are that the people being affected feel powerless, and the them-and-us syndrome easily develops. The process easily becomes irrational anyway if the public relations aspect is ignored. There is no simple solution to this puzzle of how to balance the local versus the national or European view.

Usually, in practice, the broad policy decisions on landscape protection are retained by national or regional government, though their application is delegated to local level. The balance reached often depends upon how much the national or regional government cares, i.e. it tends to depend upon importance. Hence there is a hierarchy of national, regional and local reserves or parks in many countries, with nationally important areas being protected by national government, and locally important areas by local government.

This issue of local democratic involvement becomes redundant when landscape protection is handled by incentives rather than by regulation. Incentives are generated at national or European level, and usually work by intermediaries negotiating voluntary agreements between individual owners and national government or its agencies. Local representatives are seldom a party to them. This approach appears to be gaining ground where right-of-centre governments operate on the basis that issues can be settled through the cheque book and with little patience for local Government. Whether it could flourish under more left-of-centre regimes with a belief that the "will of the people" should be sought, and a preference for regulation over inducement, is yet to be tested.

Conclusion

"Industrialized" countries have much experience, and well-tested methodologies and organizational structures. Countries where landscape protection is being newly considered can observe past mistakes and successes in them. Designation will not be enough. Successful, long-term protection of value depends upon management, and good management will depend upon collaboration with those who already manage the land. Industrialized countries have much experience of the consequences of uncontrolled tourism. It is essential for cultural landscapes that the tourist industry addresses conservation concerns; this is potentially a task for the World Heritage Centre.

Finally, if only to reiterate, major social and intellectual changes are occurring in many countries, especially in Western Europe and North America, as they face up to a post-industrial future. No-one knows what the ultimate consequences will be, least of all for conservation, but our emerging attitudes to cultural landscapes will be amongst the more interesting of the indicators.

David L. Jacques is a Landscape Historian. He lectures at the University of York and has recently finished the restoration of the Privy Gardens at Hampton Court, England.

Peter Fowler is Professor of Archaeology at the University of Newcastle upon Tyne, England.

Chapter 37

Tentative Lists as a Tool for Landscape Classification and Protection

Sarah M. Titchen and Mechtild Rössler

Introduction

As the World Heritage Convention moves into its third decade of implementation two particular issues continue to cause difficulty and confusion for those identifying and assessing cultural heritage of "outstanding universal value" for inclusion in the World Heritage List. The issues to which we refer are the inclusion of cultural landscapes in the World Heritage List and the preparation of Tentative Lists to include cultural properties, and now to also include cultural landscapes.

At the "International Expert Meeting on "Cultural Landscapes of Outstanding Universal Value"" held at the UNESCO Biosphere Reserve of Schorfheide/Chorin in Templin, Germany in 17 October 1993 two workshops addressed these issues: "First suggestions towards the classification and evaluation of cultural landscapes based on the La Petite Pierre recommendation" and "Survey of Tentative Lists submitted by State Parties".

In exploring the important role that Tentative Lists will play in the future inclusion of cultural landscapes of "outstanding universal value" in the World Heritage List the deliberations and outcomes of these two workshops have been used to prepare this paper. Importantly this paper also acknowledges the preparation of an "Action Plan for the Future (Cultural Landscapes)" by those attending the Templin meeting and the outcome of the June 1994 "Expert Meeting on the "Global Strategy" and thematic studies for a representative World Heritage List" held at UNESCO Headquarters in Paris.

What is a Tentative List?

Following the references made to "inventories submitted by States" in Article 11 of the World Heritage Convention, the inclusion of a cultural property in a Tentative List has become a pre-condition to its evaluation by ICOMOS for inclusion in the World Heritage List. ICOMOS and the World Heritage Committee and its Bureau have repeatedly stated and reiterated that they will not consider a cultural property for inclusion in the World Heritage List unless it is included in a Tentative List.

Article 1 of the Convention and Paragraphs 7 and 8 and Annex 1 of the Operational Guidelines for the Implementation of the World Heritage Convention provide some guidance as to what Tentative Lists are, who prepares them and for what purpose they are prepared. Box 1 below provides a summary of this guidance.

> **Box 1.** Guidance concerning Tentative Lists provided by Article 11 of the World Heritage Convention and Paragraphs 7 and 8 and Annex 1 of the Operational Guidelines for the Implementation of the World Heritage Convention (adapted from UNESCO 1972 and UNESCO 1994b: Paragraph 7 and 8 and Annex 1). A Tentative List will constitute the "inventory" provided for in Article 11 of the World Heritage Convention.
>
> - Tentative Lists are to be prepared by State Parties to the World Heritage Convention and submitted to the World Heritage Committee.
> - The standard format to be used by State Parties to submit their Tentative Lists is included in Annex 1 of the Operational Guidelines.
> - A Tentative List should include a list of cultural and natural properties which a State Party intends to nominate for inscription to the World Heritage List during the following 5 to 10 years.
> - A Tentative List should include the cultural and natural properties situated within the territory of each State Party and which it considers suitable for inclusion in the World Heritage List.
> - A Tentative List should not be considered to be exhaustive.
> - The Tentative List should include an indication of who drew up the Tentative List, the name of the country and date on which the Tentative List was drawn up.
> - A Tentative List should include documentation about the name of the properties (and if possible the order in which they will be nominated for inclusion in the World Heritage List), the geographical location of the properties and brief descriptions of the properties.
> - The Tentative List should include justification of the "outstanding universal value" of the properties included in the Tentative List in accordance with the criteria and conditions of authenticity or integrity set out in Paragraphs 24 and 44 of the Operational Guidelines taking account of similar properties both inside and outside the boundaries of the State Party concerned.
> - Natural properties included in the Tentative List should be grouped according to biogeographical provinces.
> - Cultural properties included in the Tentative List should be grouped according to cultural periods or areas.
> - The purpose of a Tentative List is to enable the World Heritage Committee and its Bureau, ICOMOS and IUCN to evaluate within the widest possible context the "outstanding universal value" of each property nominated to the List.
> - The World Heritage Committee will not consider cultural nominations unless a Tentative List of cultural properties has been submitted.

Despite the existence of the guidance included in the World Heritage Convention and Operational Guidelines as outlined above, many State Parties have found it difficult to prepare Tentative Lists.

Recent revisions to the cultural heritage criteria to include cultural landscapes of "outstanding universal value" in the World Heritage List

Cultural landscapes represent the "combined works of nature and of man" designated in Article 1 of the Convention (UNESCO 1994b: 10, Paragraph 36).

In recent years a number of significant changes have been made to the cultural and natural heritage criteria used to justify nominations of properties for inclusion in the World Heritage List. Changes to the cultural heritage criteria have ensured the accommodation of cultural landscapes of outstanding universal value in the World Heritage List while changes to the natural heritage criteria have limited the possibility of recognizing human/environment interactions when nominating properties for inclusion in the World Heritage List.

An expert meeting was convened in the village of La Petite Pierre near Strasbourg in France in October 1992 to review the cultural and natural heritage criteria presented in the Operational Guidelines for the Implementation of the World Heritage Convention. The review of the criteria was undertaken to ensure the future inclusion of cultural landscapes of outstanding universal value in the World Heritage List. Modifications to the cultural heritage criteria devised at La Petite Pierre were adopted by the Sixteenth Session of the World Heritage Committee meeting in New Mexico in the United States of America in December 1992 (UNESCO 1992). The modified cultural heritage criteria are included in the February 1994 edition of the Operational Guidelines for the Implementation of the World Heritage Convention (UNESCO 1994b).

Recommendations for new interpretative or guiding paragraphs to replace the previously existing Paragraph 34 of the Operational Guidelines were made at La Petite Pierre and adopted by the Sixteenth Session of the World Heritage Committee in December 1992 (UNESCO 1992). These 12 new paragraphs provide guidance for the inclusion of three categories of cultural landscapes in the World Heritage List. The three categories used to classify cultural landscapes are included in the Operational Guidelines for the Implementation of the World Heritage Convention. They are shown in Box 2.

Box 2. The three categories of cultural landscapes to be used for classifying cultural landscapes of "outstanding universal value" (adapted from UNESCO 1994b: 11, Paragraph 39).

(i) the **clearly defined landscape** designed and created intentionally by humans;
(ii) the **organically evolved landscape**, whether it be a **relict or fossil landscape** or a **continuing landscape**; and,
(iii) the **associative landscape**.

In the first twenty years of implementation of the World Heritage Convention it has been possible to nominate a property for inclusion on the World Heritage List as a cultural, natural or "mixed" cultural and natural property. While it has been possible to nominate properties for inclusion on the World Heritage List according to these three categories, it is now possible to use five categories of cultural and natural heritage. With the introduction of the new cultural landscape categories it is now possible to nominate a property as a cultural property, natural property, "mixed" cultural and natural property, cultural landscape or "mixed" natural and cultural landscape inclusion.

The December 1992 adoption of revisions to the natural heritage criteria

The World Heritage Committee also considered proposed revisions to the natural heritage criteria during its Sixteenth Session. Reference to "man's interaction with his natural environment" and "exceptional combinations of natural and cultural elements" formerly included in natural criteria (ii) and (iii) respectively were removed at the December 1992 Committee meeting (UNESCO 1992: 54).

It is important for State Parties to recognize that while the revised cultural heritage criteria and the new guiding principles concerning cultural landscapes included in the Operational Guidelines for the Implementation of the World Heritage Convention (UNESCO 1994a) provide new opportunities for nominating cultural landscapes of "outstanding universal value" for inclusion in the World Heritage List, the natural heritage criteria now have limited application for justifying the nomination of properties exhibiting human/environment interactions of "outstanding universal value".

The Action Plan for the Future (Cultural Landscapes)

Following the development of cultural landscape categories at La Petite Pierre, the UNESCO World Heritage Centre requested that all State Parties submit a new Tentative List to include cultural landscapes (Circular Letter Number 4 of 10 February 1993). New Tentative Lists were to be submitted by August 1993. The modest response to this Circular Letter is discussed in Rössler's chapter earlier in this volume.

Recognizing the modest response to the Circular Letter those meeting at Templin in Germany in October 1993 at the "International Expert Meeting on "Cultural Landscapes of Outstanding Universal Value"" devised an "Action Plan for the Future (Cultural Landscapes)". The Action Plan was adopted by the Seventeenth Session of the World Heritage Committee meeting in Cartagena, Colombia in December 1993 (UNESCO 1994a). The Action Plan called for the difficulties encountered by State Parties in developing Tentative Lists to be identified and addressed. Furthermore it was recommended that additional information, guidance and advice be provided to State Parties on the subject of cultural landscapes and their inclusion in Tentative Lists. It was recommended that this could best be achieved with the preparation of an explanatory illustrated booklet on cultural landscapes. Additional strategies concerning the identification, assessment, nomination and management of cultural landscapes for inclusion in the World Heritage List were included in the Action Plan (see annex). Most importantly the Action Plan identified the need for State Parties to review the cultural criteria and the boundaries for which properties have been included in the World Heritage List. Although this recommendation focused on the revision to the cultural heritage criteria as providing the catalyst for such a review we suggest that it is equally applicable given the recent revisions to the natural heritage criteria.

Acknowledging the general lack of experience and understanding concerning the identification, assessment, nomination and management of cultural landscapes of "outstanding universal value" the Action Plan also called for the development of a Thematic Study on Cultural Landscapes to be initiated by the UNESCO World Heritage Centre in association with ICOMOS and IUCN possibly as part of the broader initiative known as the Global Study, now renamed the Global Strategy (UNESCO 1994c). It was noted that the completion of this Thematic Study should not delay the inscription on the World Heritage List of unquestionably outstanding landscapes. It was envisaged that comparative thematic studies, such as those suggested for cultural landscapes, would form components of the Global Study. Tentative Lists would provide both the foundation working documents for comparative thematic studies. In addition Tentative Lists would be generated by or derived from these thematic comparative studies. For this reason Tentative Lists can be seen to be one of the central elements in the process of identifying and assessing cultural landscapes for inclusion in the World Heritage List.

Within the context of the discussions held in the workshops at Templin a number of potential topics for studies of cultural landscapes were proposed. A small list of topics that might be addressed by the working group(s) proposed by the Action Plan are shown in Box 3. These topics tend to be limited by the definition of property type rather than being broad and open thematic groupings. The opportunity to explore broader themes inclusive of cultural landscapes will be discussed later with reference to the June 1994 "Expert Meeting on the "Global Strategy" and thematic studies for a representative World Heritage List" (UNESCO 1994c).

Box 3. Potential Topics for Studies of Cultural Landscapes proposed by Workshop 1 at the "International Expert Meeting on "Cultural Landscapes of Outstanding Universal Value" (UNESCO 1994a).

- Rice terraces in South-East Asia
- Maize cultivation landscapes in the Andean Region
- Traditional industrial landscapes
- Irrigation systems in Asia, Oceania and America
- Windmill landscapes
- Alpine and other mountain landscapes
- River valley landscapes
- Bocage landscapes of Northern Europe

The Action Plan also provides the opportunity for the working group(s) to study a number of issues of a methodological and technical nature (see annex). Most importantly the proposed thematic study working group(s) were requested to give careful consideration to the relevant definitions in the Operational Guidelines, and to make recommendations for their revision with the object being to clarify the definitions of the three categories of cultural landscapes making them more comprehensive and of greater use to State Parties.

With reference to the Action Plan's mention of thematic methodologies for the development of Tentative Lists prepared by some State Parties it is interesting to note that in Australia a group of consultants recently devised a framework for the assessment of Australia's cultural heritage sites against the World Heritage criteria to enable the Australian Government as signatory to the World Heritage Convention to prepare a Tentative List of cultural properties (Domicelj et al. 1992).

The conceptual framework (Domicelj et al. 1992) is dependent on three clearly defined steps. The first step is to identify significant prehistoric and historic themes manifested in Australia. Each theme is then assessed in its global context to determine whether it is of "outstanding universal value". Once themes of "outstanding universal value" have been identified, prehistoric and historic places representative of these themes of outstanding universal value are identified. It is these places that are then assessed as being either *essential*, *integral* or *peripheral* to the representation of the theme. *Essential* and *integral* places are then eligible for inclusion on a Tentative List for future individual or serial nomination for inclusion in the World Heritage List (Domicelj et al. 1992: 37-40).

Cultural Landscapes and the June 1994 "Expert Meeting on the "Global Strategy" and thematic studies for a representative World Heritage List"

In June 1994 an "Expert Meeting on the "Global Strategy" and thematic studies for a representative World Heritage List" was held at UNESCO Headquarters in Paris (see von Droste in this volume). In addition to making suggestions for further revisions to the cultural heritage criteria the meeting presented a new enlightened vision for the development of a "representative, balanced and credible" World Heritage List (UNESCO 1994c: 8) in accordance with the goals of the Strategic Guidelines for the Future adopted by the World Heritage Committee in 1992 (UNESCO 1992).

The Global Strategy Expert Meeting desired to ensure that the unacceptably narrow interpretation of the cultural heritage as architectural monuments be broadened to encompass "cultural groupings that were complex and multidimensional, which demonstrated in spatial terms the social structures, ways of life, beliefs, systems of knowledge, and representations of different past and present cultures in the entire world" (UNESCO 1994c: 3). The Global Strategy Expert Meeting called for "each individual piece of evidence" to be considered "not in isolation but within its whole context and with an understanding of the multiple reciprocal relationships that it had with its physical and non-physical environment" (UNESCO 1994c: 3). This new anthropological articulation of the definition of cultural heritage of "outstanding universal value" will provide an essential foundation from which to move towards the inclusion of cultural landscapes in the World Heritage List.

The Global Strategy Expert Meeting proposed the adoption of a thematic methodology to help redress the "geographical, temporal, and spiritual imbalances" in the World Heritage List (UNESCO 1994c: 8). The Expert Meeting sought to develop a non-typological approach to be called the "Global Strategy for the Implementation of the World Heritage Convention" (UNESCO 1994c: 8). The Expert Meeting recommended that Tentative Lists could be prepared as working documents for regional meetings to discuss themes as well as properties already inscribed in the World Heritage List. The Expert Meeting provides no further guidance on the relationship between the preparation of Tentative Lists and regionally based thematic comparative studies.

The Expert Meeting also recommended that the cultural heritage criteria be modified in order "to encourage inscriptions of properties that would fill gaps in the List" (UNESCO 1994c: 10). The text of the suggested modifications are shown in Box 4.

> **Box 4.** Suggested revisions to the cultural heritage criteria made at the June 1994 "Expert Meeting on the "Global Strategy" and thematic studies for a representative World Heritage List" (UNESCO 1994c: 10).
>
> | | |
> |---|---|
> | Criterion (ii) | Re-examine this criterion so as to reflect better the interaction of cultures, instead of the present formulation, which suggests that cultural influences occur in one direction only; |
> | Criterion (iii) | Remove "which has disappeared", since this excludes living cultures; |
> | Criterion (iv) | Remove the phrase "especially when it has become vulnerable under the impact of irreversible change," since this favours cultures that have disappeared; |
> | Criterion (vi) | Encourage a less restrictive interpretation of this criterion. |

The suggested modifications to cultural heritage criteria (ii), (iii) and (v), and most particularly their strengthened approach to the recognition of living cultures, will most certainly help in fulfilling initiatives to include cultural landscapes of "outstanding universal value" in the World Heritage List.

The Global Strategy report and the recommendations to further revise the cultural heritage criteria were examined at both the World Heritage Bureau and Committee meetings in 1994.

Two thematic studies were carried out by expert meetings in 1994: A conference on Heritage Canals was organized by Canadian authorities in October 1994 and made suggestions for changes of the Operational Guidelines both in the paragraphs on the criteria and in a separate paragraph on a definiton for a canal. Furthermore, a meeting on "Itineraries" was hosted by the Spanish authorities which focussed on recommendations for the eighteenth World Heritage Committee session. The texts of both expert meetings figure in the annex of this book. As the World Heritage Committee had not enough time to discuss the recommendations, it was suggested that the World Heritage Bureau at its nineteenth session should look into both thematic studies.

While the Global Strategy Expert Meeting acknowledged that work is under way to prepare comparative thematic studies of industrial heritage, 20th century architecture and cultural landscapes the report of the Meeting does not include particular comment as to the method that has been proposed for the Thematic Study of Cultural Landscapes. When compared to the methodology and philosophy of the thematic comparative evaluations that are proposed by the Global Strategy Expert Meeting, the Thematic Study on Cultural Landscapes is overtly typological.

It is to be expected that the thematic studies proposed by the Global Strategy Expert Meeting will identify and assess the full diversity of cultural expression according to designated themes and that new cultural landscapes will be included in Tentative Lists and the World Heritage List as a result or by-product. For this reason the proposed Global Strategy thematic studies will be useful tools in the identification and assessment of cultural landscapes of "outstanding universal value" for inclusion in the World Heritage

List. Acknowledgment of the methodological and anthropological insights provided by the Global Strategy Expert Meeting might also lead to the adoption of a less typological approach than that proposed in the Thematic Study on Cultural Landscapes. It will be important to ensure the use of a methodology that seeks to openly explore cultural landscapes as expressions of living cultures, ethnographic and archaeological landscapes (see UNESCO 1994c: 8).

References

Domicelj, J., Halliday, H. and James, P. (1992). *Australia's Cultural Estate. Framework for the assessment of Australia's cultural properties against the World Heritage criteria*. Volume I. Commonwealth of Australia, Canberra, Australia.

UNESCO (1972). *Convention Concerning the Protection of the World Cultural and Natural Heritage*. Adopted by the General Conference at its seventeenth session, Paris, 16 November 1972. Paris, France.

UNESCO (1992). *World Heritage Committee Sixteenth Session* [Santa Fe, United States of America (7-14 December 1992)]. Report. WHC-92/CONF.002/12. 14 December 1992.

UNESCO (1994a). *World Heritage Committee Seventeenth session* (Cartagena, Colombia, 6-11 December 1993). Report. WHC-93/CONF.002/14. 4 February 1994.

UNESCO (1994b). *Operational Guidelines for the Implementation of the World Heritage Convention*. WHC/2/Revised February 1994.

UNESCO (1994c). *Report of the Expert Meeting on the "Global Strategy" and thematic studies for a representative World Heritage List*, UNESCO Headquarters, Paris.

Sarah M. Titchen has recently completed her doctoral thesis on World Heritage in the Department of Archaeology and Anthropology, at the Australian National University, Canberra.

Mechtild Rössler is a programme specialist at the UNESCO World Heritage Centre, Paris.

Annexes

I   *Action Plan for the Future (Cultural Landscapes)
adopted by the seventeenth session
of the World Heritage Committee in December 1993*

II   *Extract of the Operational Guidelines
for the Implementation of the World Heritage Convention*

III   *Extract from the report of the expert meeting on
"Heritage Canals" (Canada, September 1994)*

IV   *Extract from the report of the expert meeting on
"Routes as Part of Our Cultural Heritage"
(Spain, November 1994)*

V   *Extract from the report of the
"Regional Thematic Study Meeting on Asian Rice Culture
and its Terraced Landscapes"
(Philippines, March/April 1995)*

VI   *Extract from the report of the
"Asia-Pacific Regional Workshop
on Associative Cultural Landscapes"
(Australia, April 1995)*

VII   *World Heritage Convention (1972)*

ANNEX I

Action Plan for the Future (Cultural Landscapes) adopted by the seventeenth session of the World Heritage Committee in December 1993

Guidance to state parties on the identification, assessment, nomination and management of cultural landscapes for inclusion in the World Heritage List

(a) that the difficulties encountered by State Parties in developing Tentative Lists be identified and addressed;

(b) that additional information, guidance and advice be provided to State Parties on the subject of cultural landscapes and their inclusion on Tentative Lists; this should include an explanatory illustrated booklet on cultural landscapes;

(c) that the opportunity for applying for preparatory assistance for the development of Tentative Lists should again be communicated to State Parties;

(d) that State Parties that have not yet submitted revised Tentative Lists, to include cultural landscapes, be urged and encouraged to do so within the next two years;

(e) that in light of the recent revisions to the cultural criteria that State Parties be made aware of the opportunity to review properties that are already on the World Heritage List with the object of reassessing the criteria and the boundaries for which the property was included. It was noted that this was at the discretion of State Parties;

(f) that specific guidelines for the management of cultural landscapes, including both conservation and development, be incorporated in the existing "Guidelines for the Management of World Heritage Properties" taking into account successful management experiences;

(g) that an exchange of information, case studies and management experiences on the level of regional and local communities for the protection of cultural landscapes between State Parties be encouraged;

(h) that the expert groups and NGOs (ICOMOS, IUCN/CNPPA, IFLA, ILAA, IALE) be encouraged to promote a broader understanding of cultural landscapes and their potential for inclusion of the World Heritage List;

(i) that the World Heritage Centre be asked to facilitate all of the above.

Thematic study on cultural landscapes

(a) that a working groups(s) be convened to initiate a cultural landscape(s) thematic study. This group(s) should be established by the World Heritage Centre in association with ICOMOS and in consultation with IUCN;

(b) it was noted that a number of State Parties had developed thematic methodologies for the preparation of Tentative Lists. It was suggested that the working group(s) investigate how these thematic frameworks could be applied to the development of Tentative Lists to include cultural landscapes;

(c) that the completion of this thematic study should not delay the inscription of cultural landscapes of unquestionable outstanding universal value on the World Heritage List;

(d) that the proposed working group(s) be requested to give careful consideration to the definitions and categories of cultural landscapes included in the Operational Guidelines. That the "Model for Presenting a Tentative List" (Annex 1 of the Operational Guidelines), the nomination form, and the format of the World Heritage List, be reviewed to insure the visibility of cultural landscapes;

(e) that paragraph 14 of the Operational Guidelines be redrafted in response to the changes to the cultural criteria to provide appropriate information to the public during the nomination process.

ANNEX II

Extract of the Operational Guidelines for the Implementation of the World Heritage Convention

WHC/2/Revised
February 1995

[...]

24. A monument, group of buildings or site - as defined above - which is nominated for inclusion in the World Heritage List will be considered to be of outstanding universal value for the purpose of the Convention when the Committee finds that it meets one or more of the following criteria <u>and</u> the test of authenticity. Each property nominated should therefore:

(a) (i) represent a masterpiece of human creative genius; or

(ii) exhibit an important interchange of human values, over a span of time or within a cultural area of the world, on developments in architecture, monumental arts or town-planning and landscape design; or

(iii) bear a unique or at least exceptional testimony to a cultural tradition or to a civilization which is living or which has disappeared; or

(iv) be an outstanding example of a type of building or architectural ensemble or landscape which illustrates (a) significant stage(s) in human history; or

(v) be an outstanding example of a traditional human settlement or land-use which is representative of a culture (or cultures), especially when it has become vulnerable under the impact of irreversible change; or

(vi) be directly or tangibly associated with events or living traditions, with ideas, or with beliefs, with artistic and literary works of outstanding universal significance (the Committee considers that this criterion should justify inclusion in the List only in exceptional circumstances or in conjunction with other criteria cultural or natural);

<u>and</u>

(b) (i) meet the test of authenticity in design, material, workmanship or setting and in the case of cultural landscapes their distinctive character and components (the Committee stressed that reconstruction is only acceptable if it is carried out on the basis of complete and detailed documentation on the original and to no extent on conjecture).

(ii) have adequate legal and/or traditional protection and management mechanisms to ensure the conservation of the nominated cultural property or cultural landscapes. The existence of protective legislation at the national, provincial or municipal level or well-established traditional protection and/or adequate management mechanisms is therefore essential and must be stated clearly on the nomination form. Assurances of the effective implementation of these laws and/or management mechanisms are also expected. Furthermore, in order to preserve the integrity of cultural sites, particularly those open to large numbers of visitors, the State Party concerned should be able to provide evidence of suitable administrative arrangements to cover the management of the property, its conservation and its accessibility to the public.

[...]

35. With respect to <u>cultural landscapes,</u> the Committee has furthermore adopted the following guidelines concerning their inclusion in the World Heritage List.

36. Cultural landscapes represent the "combined works of nature and of man" designated in Article 1 of the Convention. They are illustrative of the evolution of human society and settlement over time, under the influence of the physical constraints and/or opportunities presented by their natural environment and of successive social, economic and cultural forces, both external and internal. They should be selected on the basis both of their outstanding universal value and of their representativity in terms of a clearly defined geo-cultural region and also for their capacity to illustrate the essential and distinct cultural elements of such regions.

37. The term "cultural landscape" embraces a diversity of manifestations of the interaction between humankind and its natural environment.

38. Cultural landscapes often reflect specific techniques of sustainable land-use, considering the characteristics and limits of the natural environment they are established in, and a specific spiritual relation to nature. Protection of cultural landscapes can contribute to modern techniques of sustainable land-use and can maintain or enhance natural values in the landscape. The continued existence of traditional forms of land-use supports biological diversity in many regions of the world. The protection of traditional cultural landscapes is therefore helpful in maintaining biological diversity.

39. Cultural landscapes fall into three main categories, namely:

   (i) The most easily identifiable is the clearly defined landscape designed and created intentionally by man. This embraces garden and parkland landscapes constructed for aesthetic reasons which are often (but not always) associated with religious or other monumental buildings and ensembles.

   (ii) The second category is the organically evolved landscape. This results from an initial social, economic, administrative, and/or religious imperative and has developed its present form by association with and in response to its natural environment. Such landscapes reflect that process of evolution in their form and component features. They fall into two sub-categories:

   – a relict (or fossil) landscape is one in which an evolutionary process came to an end at some time in the past, either abruptly or over a period. Its significant distinguishing features are, however, still visible in material form.

   – a continuing landscape is one which retains an active social role in contemporary society closely associated with the traditional way of life, and in which the evolutionary process is still in progress. At the same time it exhibits significant material evidence of its evolution over time.

   (iii) The final category is the associative cultural landscape. The inclusion of such landscapes on the World Heritage List is justifiable by virtue of the powerful religious, artistic or cultural associations of the natural element rather than material cultural evidence, which may be insignificant or even absent.

40. The extent of a cultural landscape for inclusion on the World Heritage List is relative to its functionality and intelligibility. In any case, the sample selected must be substantial enough to adequately represent the totality of the cultural landscape that it illustrates. The possibility of designating long linear areas which represent culturally significant transport and communication networks should not be excluded.

41. The general criteria for conservation and management laid down in paragraph 24.(b).(ii) above are equally applicable to cultural landscapes. It is important that due attention be paid to the full range of values represented in the landscape, both cultural and natural. The nominations should be prepared in collaboration with and the full approval of local communities.

42. The existence of a category of "cultural landscape", included on the World Heritage List on the basis of the criteria set out in paragraph 24 above, does not exclude the possibility of sites of exceptional importance in relation to both cultural and natural criteria continuing to be included. In such cases, their outstanding universal significance must be justified under both sets of criteria.

ANNEX III

Extract from the report of the expert meeting on "Heritage Canals" (Canada, September 1994)

Information Document on Heritage Canals Experts Meeting, 15–19 September 1994

Chaffeys Lock, Ontario, Canada

Purpose of the meeting

Canada, following a World Heritage Committee decision in December 1992, hosted a meeting of experts on heritage canals in September 1994 to explore the nature and extent of canals, and to examine the components of significance. The results of the deliberations are herein presented to the World Heritage Committee for consideration.

I. Definition

A canal is a human-engineered waterway. It may be of outstanding universal value from the point of view of history or technology, either intrinsically or as an exceptional example representative of this category of cultural property. The canal may be a monumental work, the defining feature of a linear cultural landscape, or an integral component of a complex cultural landscape.

II. Value and ares of significance

The significance of canals can be examined under technological, economic, social, and landscape factors.

A. Technology

Canals can serve a variety of purposes: irrigation, navigation, defence, water-power, flood mitigation, land-drainage and water-supply.

The following are areas of technology which may be of significance:
1. The line and waterproofing of the water channel
2. The engineering structures of the line with reference to comparative structural features in other areas of architecture and technology
3. The development of the sophistication of constructional methods
4. The transfer of technologies.

B. Economy

Canals contribute to the economy in a variety of ways, e.g. in terms of economic development and the conveyance of goods and people. Canals were the first man-made routes for the effective carriage of bulk cargoes. Canals played and continue to play a key role in economic development through their use for irrigation. The following factors are important:
1. Nation building
2. Agricultural development
3. Industrial development

4. Generation of wealth
5. Development of engineering skills applied to other areas and industries
6. Tourism.

C. Social factors

The building of canals had, and their operation continues to have, social consequences:
1. The redistribution of wealth with social and cultural results
2. The movement of people and the interaction of cultural groups.

D. Landscape

Such large-scale engineering works had and continue to have an impact on the natural landscape. Related industrial activity and changing settlement patterns cause visible changes to landscape forms and patterns.

Note: There are potentially some additional areas of significance discussed in other sections of the Operational Guidelines for the Implementation of the World Heritage Convention that deal with historic towns (paragraph 29) and with the natural criteria (in particular paragraph 44 a, points iii and possibly iv).

III. Authenticity and integrity

A. Authenticity depends holistically upon values and the relationships between these values.
B. One distinctive feature of the canal as a heritage element is its evolution over time. This is linked to how it was used during different periods and the associated technological changes the canal underwent. The extent of these changes may constitute a heritage element.
C. The authenticity and historical interpretation of a canal encompass the connection between the real property (subject of the Convention), possible movable property (boats, temporary navigation items) and the associated structures (bridges, etc) and landscape (SEE APPENDIX).

IV. Management

A. The concepts of monumental work, corridor and cultural landscape are essential management considerations.
B. Management mechanisms for canals require participation by many partners - public administrations, associations and individuals - and a co-ordinating body is therefore essential. This body must be given strong encouragement and the question of its governance must be examined at the national or international level.
C. Management of a canal corridor involves renewing its components and the cultural landscapes comprising it. By nature, it is dynamic over a span of time (see III.B).
D. Management must develop an information policy aimed at making the public and the partners aware of the authenticity and historical value of the heritage resource. Efforts to promote the canal must have an educational component aimed at fostering an understanding of the canal corridor.
E. Any tourist development must tie in the aspects of authenticity with the history of the heritage resource, in a dynamic perspective unique to the canal. In this regard, the fragility of the sites must be made apparent and given attention by the public, as well as by the management partners.
F. Management bodies should consider the possibility of reinvesting a portion of the tourism revenues in maintenance and conservation.

Changes proposed to operational guidelines

14   Delete sentence 1 since it contradicts sentence 2. Sentence 2 may be understood to supersede sentence 1 and to more accurately reflect the current public circumstances of nomination.

24 (a) (i) reinforce current recommendation of Global Strategy Report for deletion from English version of "represent a unique artistic achievement"
 (ii) add "or technology" after "landscape design"
 (iii) no change
 (iv) add "or technological ..." ie "architectural or   technological ensemble"
 (v) no change
 (vi) no change

Proposed Addition after paragraph 40

A canal is a human-engineered waterway. It may be of outstanding universal value from the point of view of history or technology, either intrinsically or as an exceptional example representative of this category of cultural property. The canal may be a monumental work, the defining feature of a linear cultural landscape, or an integral component of a complex cultural landscape.

Appendix

It was felt important to seek methodological means to improve and clarify to the degree possible the application of the test of authenticity to canals and to their associated landscapes. In this endeavour, it was felt useful to expand the aspects of authenticity examined from the four currently noted in the Operational Guidelines, to associate these with criteria or indicators which could suggest how authenticity of canals might best be measured in relation to each of the aspects considered and to examine these within a time continuum including project planning, execution and ongoing use. It was felt important to stress that the resulting matrix was not meant to be used in a directive or mechanistic fashion, but to provide a guiding framework for consideration of a range of evidently interdependent factors, and ultimately to provide an integrated overview of these various factors.

The proposed table is to take the criteria of 24b(i), expand on them, and suggest new criteria. For this purpose, we have provided an outline for approaching authenticity. One of the first distinguishing features is their evolution over time: design, then construction, then uses.

We have chosen the format of key words and explanatory subcriteria. This outline is not exclusive; it is basically indicative and is intended to facilitate an exploration of the authenticity. It is a guide for examining possible questions. The result should not be an arithmetic sum of the positive responses in a table, but a harmonious whole representing a synthesis of elements of authenticity of a canal.

	Plan	Execution	Use
1. Intentions - Objectives - decipherable - documentation - intellectual context			
2. Know-how - transmissions - technological context			
3. Environment - physical surroundings - validity of canal - environment links - implications of know-how (2) - implications of materials (4)			
4. Materials - conservation			
5. Design - restoration - periods decipherable - influences - documentation			
6. Uses and functions - continuity of uses - congruence - interruptions in uses and functions			

Annex IV

Extract from the report of the expert meeting on "Routes as Part of Our Cultural Heritage"

Madrid 24–25 November 1994

1. Aim of the meeting

When the Pilgrim's Route to Santiago de Compostela was added to the World Heritage list in Cartagena in 1993, Spain announced its intention of bringing together experts to discuss the question of "cultural routes" in more depth.

The World Heritage Committee Board approved this initiative at its meeting held in July 1994 in Paris. The following conclusions of the meeting of experts which took place in Madrid on 24 and 25 November 1994 are submitted to the World Heritage Committee and the Director General of UNESCO for their consideration.

2. A rich and fertile concept for today's world

a) The concept of heritage routes is shown to be a rich and fertile one, offering a privileged framework in which mutual understanding, a plural approach to history and a culture of peace can all operate. It is based on population movement, encounters and dialogue, cultural exchanges and cross-fertilization, taking place both in space and time.

b) The nature of the concept is open, dynamic and evocative, bringing together the conclusions of the global strategic study striving to improve the recognition within Heritage "of the economic, social, symbolic and philosophical dimensions and constant and countless interactions with the natural environment in all its diversity".

3. A wide range of initiatives

a) The experts noted numerous initiatives based on the idea of movement and dialogue. They are being carried out by UNESCO (e.g. the Silk Route and the slave route), the Council of Europe (European cultural routes) and by other groups and organisations.

b) These initiatives fall within the scope of a global vision of exchanges, which includes material, cultural and spiritual ones, combining tangible and intangible elements, culture and nature.

c) The acceptance of these cultural heritage routes leads to research work on the importance of the exchanges they have generated, prompts study expeditions, opens up the way for cultural tourism and - another very important aspect - public awareness programmes and youth training schemes.

d) The protection and promotion of these cultural heritage routes require skilled management and, more particularly, careful control of the level of tourism affecting them, as well as the participation of the inhabitants living in the lands over which the routes cross. Reference is also made to a land planning policy within a framework of lasting development.

e) The experts recommend that the World Heritage Committee and the Director General of UNESCO ask countries to implement this new approach, on a nationwide, regionwide and worldwide basis.

4. Inclusion of cultural routes as part of World Heritage

a) The requirement to hold <u>exceptional universal worth</u> should be recalled.
b) The concept of heritage routes:
   - is based on the dynamics of movement and the idea of <u>exchanges</u>, with <u>continuity</u> in space and time;
   - refers to a <u>whole</u>, where the route has a worth over and above the sum of the elements making it up and through which it gains its cultural SIGNIFICANCE;
   - highlights exchange and dialogue <u>between countries or between regions</u>;
   - is <u>multi-dimensional</u>, with different aspects developing and adding to its prime purpose which may be religious, commercial, administrative or otherwise.
c) A heritage route may be considered as a <u>specific, dynamic type of cultural landscape</u>, just as recent debates have led to their acceptance within the Operational Guidelines.
d) <u>The identification</u> of a heritage route is based on a collection of strengths and <u>tangible elements</u>, testimony to the significance of the route itself (see reference document in annex 3).
e) <u>The authenticity test</u> is to be applied on the grounds of its significance and other elements making up the heritage route. It will take into account the duration of the route, and perhaps how often it is used nowadays, as well as the legitimate wishes for development of peoples affected. These points will be considered within the natural framework of the route and its intangible and symbolic dimensions.
f) The experts propose the following addition to <u>the Operational Guidelines</u>. The new paragraph would follow paragraph 40. This proposal is put forward at the same time as the suggestions made by the other meeting of experts held in Canada on the question of canals.

Proposed new paragraph

A heritage route is composed of tangible elements of which the cultural significance comes from exchanges and a multi-dimensional dialogue across countries or regions, and that illustrate the interaction of movement, along the route, in space and time.

5. Reference note on identification and delimination criteria

The World Heritage Conference's acknowledgement of the concept of routes is an important step forward on the path to recognition of the diverse nature of mankind's heritage. One specific merit of such a step is that it will mean nomadic communities can now aspire to gain a degree of cultural recognition which was previously only open to sedentary peoples. This is particularly important in all those areas of the world (Africa, Asia, America) where the level of productivity (poor and uncertain) offered by the natural environment means that its natural resources cannot be exploited on a continued and long-lasting basis and effectively prevents man from establishing a permanent presence there. These areas cover vast (between 30 and 40%) expanses of the three continents and the human communities affected are many and varied (Moors, Touareg, Teda, Peul, etc. in Africa). With this new situation, these nomadic peoples may gain recognition for the role that they have played. This does not only include their development of adapted strategies for the temporary exploitation of resources which have only limited availability (and thus cannot be used on a permanent basis) but also the knowledge they have acquired about an area and a masterly command of routes, linking up sedentary communities. They play a part in this either by providing experts (guides), by ensuring the logistical elements required (beasts of burden, caravan personnel), or by guaranteeing the safety of the convoys (nomadic communities are often the first societies to have developed their economy based on services and not on the primary sector).

1. Typology: defining elements

From waggon trains to the mechanised rallies seen in the twentieth century, countless kinds of spatio-temporal routes have made their mark on mankind throughout its prehistory and history. Nevertheless, these routes do not all have the same cultural heritage worth (in this context, cultural is used as opposed to natural, to mean anything produced by man and not just limited to cultural manifestations in the narrow sense of the term as exemplified by art, literature and architecture).

The cultural worth of a route can be measured both by the dynamics (commercial, philosophical, religious) which it may have generated or favoured (transfer of goods, knowledge, know-how) and by the symbolic significance it represents for anyone using it (or for anyone who may have used it, or for anyone referring to it).

There are so many different kinds of routes that some type of classification needs to be established to ensure a better understanding of the subject. Without conducting any specific research the following are some examples of routes which regularly come up in our daily lives: the Odyssey, the silk route, the salt route, the rum trade route, the spice trade route, the waggon trail, the pilgrim's way to Santiago de Compostela, the hadji pilgrimage to Mecca, the slave route, intercontinental rallies, the crusades, Hannibal's alpine crossing, Napoleon's route, and Roman ways.

These different examples given above can immediately be divided up into religious events (pilgrimages, crusades), trade activities (silk, salt, spices), military campaigns (crusades, Napoleon's route, Hannibal's alpine crossing), sports events (the rum race, Paris-Peking rally, Paris-Dakar rally), etc.

It is also possible to pick out those routes which describe specific moments or events in history (taking place just once but leaving their mark: the Odyssey, the Russian campaign) and those which are regular routes (repeated time and time again over centuries and millennia).

Some of the routes can be classified as having strengthened cohesion and exchanges between different peoples (silk, salt, pilgrimages) and others clearly signified aggression and imperialism (slaves, crusades, etc.).

Some routes have a universal worth, whereas the scope of impact of others is more limited (national or local).

Within the context of World Heritage, our idea is to consider routes as a social phenomenon (time needs to go by before any of mankind's creations actually become part of cultural heritage and not simply something in fashion or representing a particular moment or event in history) rather than as an expression of one particular exceptional incident or moment. Even if they did make an impression at the time, routes like Hannibal's trek from North Africa to Rome, crossing the Alps on the way, or the route followed by Napoleon (from the island of Elba to Paris) cannot fall under this category. The same can be said about modern-day events that can be likened to treks: early twentieth century intercontinental races and other mechanised rallies (Paris-Peking, Paris-Dakar, etc). They cannot be regarded either as a cultural practice or as having a notable diachronic cultural or commercial effect. They are really just technological tests and/or sporting feats, even if they do generate passion and considerable financial income at a given moment in time.

We intend to consider routes which combine **exchanges and journeys** and exclude those which are limited to representing a **physical way used for travelling**: Roman ways would not be classified under this idea of routes although they could still be included on the basis of their architectural or technological interest (for instance).

We could propose considering a route as having exceptional universal cultural heritage worth on the basis of its:

spatial characteristics - the length and diversity (varying) of a route reflect the interest of the exchange and the complexity of the links that it maintains (or maintained).

temporal characteristics - how long it has been in existence and the frequency of use, which could be multiannual, annual, seasonal. It must have established its identity through diachronic practice over sufficient time to leave its imprint on mankind.

cultural characteristics - the fact that it includes cross-cultural aspects (or effects), e.g. it links remote ethnic and cultural groups and fosters their mutual progress through exchange. Its capacity to bring together different peoples.

role or purpose - the fact that it has been used to exchange spiritual goods (religious or philosophical) or basic necessities for the survival of communities or has contributed to their development (trade in foodstuffs, minerals, manufactured goods, etc.).

The criteria set out above certainly enable us to distinguish different categories of routes, but beyond these categories it is also necessary for the use of a route to have had some kind of repercussion for civilisation, even if (or when) any exchanges produced now no longer take place or have been modified. The Silk Route, to quote an example, has not lost its cultural heritage worth simply because ships have taken over from caravans in the transport of silks.

On the contrary, this very fact has granted a mythological or symbolic value to the route which it never acquired simply through its material use, turning it into an almost legendary phenomenon.

2. Material nature:

Any site considered part of World Heritage must be perfectly identified for it to take advantage of suitable protection and development measures which may be implemented as a result. A route, therefore must be correctly identified together with any important heritage components linked to it.

Delimiting the route

It is important (if only for the record) to accurately define the routes followed: recognised overland routes, river and sea routes. The many and substantial modifications mankind has made to the environment over recent decades have meant that this task is not as simple as it may seem on the surface. To take an example, it is not so easy to accurately retrace the 17th century caravan routes used in Anatolia, despite the rather detailed documentation which does exist (e.g. Jean-Baptiste Tavernier's texts).

Political events (wars, coup d'états, diplomatic hazards) or natural disasters (floods, droughts) have wrought great changes on routes and this is something we should realise and take into account.

Identifying important heritage components

Throughout history, up to the twentieth century, journeys included:
concentration points (departure, arrival);
lodging places (on overland journeys there are often reception points every 40 km) (caravanserais, hostels etc);
watering holes (for animals and men, such as wells, springs and fountains);
compulsory passing places: fords, bridges, mountain passes, ports, etc.

All of these components which marked out the routes have consequently left architectural remains or signs on the landscape. We should acknowledge these different elements and protect them by incorporating them into the description of the site forming part of our Heritage.

Furthermore, every long journey needed some kind of specific organisation beforehand (caravan leader, travel and protection agreements), experts to take part (guides, navigators), and documents to be held (safe-conducts, passports, visas, bills of exchange, etc.).

It is important too for us to compile documentation on all these services which enabled the journey to take place along the route.

Another original feature of routes, compared with any other category of site forming part of World Heritage, is certainly the fact that they are not limited to the elements making up their material nature (the physical way itself). We have to add to this aspect specific interactions between human groups over and beyond political barriers. This does not only include the objects, products, or the results of direct exchange (i.e. elements researched and declared as such, e.g. silk), themselves, but also any indirect, subsequent products, which often have had more important cultural consequences, such as the introduction of Buddhism into China. Consequently, the acceptance of routes as part of World Heritage should generate significant and varied research work in this field to bring out all their different dimensions and the impact they may have had on the peoples and cultures involved.

Such work may also lead to the preparation and implementation of the strategy to signpost the site as part of World Heritage: route boards, specific milestones, gateways to entrance and exit points or to important crossroads, etc.

Routes and natural heritage

Owing to their importance, certain routes have had an impact on natural resources, on the landscape or countryside (deforestation, track erosion), which should be noted in an inventory and taken into account. In fact, some routes have really only been able to develop because the ecosystems crossed allowed travel to take place (by providing resources). It would be useful to consider the present condition of this natural heritage and to preserve the elements which even now may still indicate the conditions of usage which existed when these routes were in intensive use.

3. Inventory method:

If we consider that one of the strengths of routes lies in their capacity to bring together communities and to facilitate exchanges inventories should be set up on a regional basis, aided by existing core elements in the field of human sciences in the regions under consideration [e.g, in the arid African region: Dakar (IFAN), Niamey (IRSH)]. A working group should be set up in each region to consider this concept and to take stock of available knowledge in this field. In certain cases, we will discover that existing knowledge deserves to be researched in greater depth. This concept may then usefully help to develop theses and to train those experts working on this heritage category.

4. Delimitation criteria:

[I have problems differentiating identification criteria and delimitation criteria.] Three categories of criteria could be used to delimit a route: spatial and temporal criteria to establish its exact material nature and cultural criteria to define the effects and consequences arising from its use.

Spatial criteria
the route followed, sites, monuments, constructions, buildings, ways, area of influence.

Temporal criteria
its beginning, end, frequency of use; intensity of use and variations

Cultural criteria
Impact. The purpose of the route and its limits, meaning the type of exchange (spiritual or material). Its impact on mankind's memory or experience (introduction of new practices). The volume and the nature of the exchanges (men, goods, technologies).

5. Submission procedures:

Routes constitute original cultural heritage (concepts) in their definition and their material nature. Most routes with a universal heritage value are spread over several countries. Consequently, it is important to set out the procedures for submitting this new type of site for inclusion as part of World Heritage.

The most desirable method is for the relevant request to be made with the agreement of all the countries concerned which would make a joint application. However, the inherent risk in this procedure is that it may be blocked by differences in appraisal of priorities, for a particular country may believe it is more urgent to submit a site that is wholly located in its national territory than to collaborate on the recognition of a route.

In the case of transnational routes, the problem of legislation (management, protection, ownership, financial aid) will also arise.

Can we imagine registration requests being made, for example, by a country anxious to preserve a particular route crossing its territory without all the other countries concerned participating in the initiative? Would total acceptance of the route only take place as and when the other countries concerned subscribed to the application?

ANNEX V

Extract from the report of the "Regional Thematic Study Meeting on Asian Rice Culture and its Terraced Landscapes"

Manila (Philippines) 28 March to 4 April 1995

1. Purpose of the meeting

Following a decision by the World Heritage Committee at its seventeenth session in December 1993 to undertake regional thematic studies on cultural landscapes, the Philippine National Commission for UNESCO, the Department of Foreign Affairs, the Department of Tourism and the National Commission for Culture and the Arts, hosted the expert meeting "Regional Thematic Study Meeting on the Asian Rice Culture and its Terraced Landscapes".

The meeting was held in Manila and Banaue from 28 March to 4 April 1995. The results of this meeting are here presented to the World Heritage Bureau for consideration. The full report will be made available to the nineteenth session of the World Heritage Committee.

2. Introduction

Throughout the Asia-Pacific region mountainous terrain has been, over the centuries, shaped into landscapes of terraced pond fields for the cultivation principally of rice, but also of taro and other crops. These landscapes exist, both as archaeological sites and as living landscapes which continue to be used and maintained by the people who created them. It is essential to conserve outstanding representative examples of these landscape that are found in almost all Asian countries, both for their intrinsic value and for what they can teach about enduring systems of human-nature interaction. However, it is not only the physical structure of the sites that must be conserved. It is necessary to analyze the different factors that are integrated in these structures. Over the centuries, traditional culture has developed a sophisticated support system of cultural, socio-economic, ecological, agricultural, hydraulic and other practices that continue to exist up to the present day in order to maintain these sites. To preserve the life of these sites, including wild living organisms (biodiversity) and their specific habitats, it is necessary to continue the delicate interrelationship between the culture and its traditional systems.

These are monuments to life itself. These landscapes celebrate the traditional lifestyle of the Asian people. They represent this particular regional culture's special imprint on and relationship with nature manifested with significant aesthetic and harmonic values. They are landscapes that are being renewed daily and will continue to exist for as long as the unbroken line of this lifestyle continues.

Asians celebrate rice as an important staple and as the basis for many of their traditional practices, myths and beliefs.

It is appropriate that any cultural heritage conservation program be inter-agency, multi-disciplinary, and inter-governmental in nature. This regional meeting examined the special Asian relationship to rice as expressed in the rice-growing landscapes found all over the region.

3. Case studies and regional comparative overview

19 delegates from Asia made presentations about rice culture in their countries (China, Korea, India, Indonesia, Japan, Myanmar, Philippines and Thailand). Cultural landscape studies from other parts of the world (Australia, Europe, South America) provided an additional context for discussions. In addition, a number of theoretical papers were presented, on both cultural and natural aspects including the importance

of community involvement. Presentations by UNESCO, IUCN-CNPPA, and ICOMOS outlined the Global Strategy within which the identification, evaluation and conservation of specific regional landscape types are to be considered.

There was an in-depth examination of the Ifugao rice terraces of the Philippine Cordillera, including a field visit to the terraces themselves, which have been nominated by the Philippine Government for inclusion on the World Heritage List as a continuing cultural landscape. The Ifugao Terraces Commission established by Philippine President, Fidel Ramos, in 1994 presented its master plan for the conservation and development of the site. During the course of the meeting, this case study of the Ifugao terraces served as a "type-site" against which propositions of the experts were tested and evaluated.

This wide-ranging background on both the ecology of rice landscapes and the diverse cultural manifestations of terraced pond-field agriculture underscored for the experts the complexity of the relationship between nature and human cultures which has shaped the distinctive terraced pond-field agricultural landscapes of Asia and the Pacific. It was noted that, in addition to the case-studies presented at the Manila meeting, terraced pond-fields are characteristic of the Himalayas, central and south China, Java, Sumatra and Sulawesi, many of the high islands of Polynesia and Melanesia, as well as many other areas of the Asia-Pacific region. A substantial body of ethnographic, archaeological and ecological literature is available on the various aspects of this landscape type, as a result of decades of research by scholars. The experts felt that it would be important for the Committee to consider the full body of this interdisciplinary scholarly research in its evaluation of future nominations of specific terraced pond-field agricultural landscapes.

4. Issues considered by the experts

4.1 Asian Terraced Landscapes

4.1.1 Definition

The Asian rice culture and its terraced landscape should be seen as a component in a wider series of those landforms transformed by human action through agricultural practices. The entire Asia-Pacific region is characterized by the technique of pond-field agriculture, which modifies and shapes the landscape. The application of the technique to mountainous terrain has created a cultural landscape of terraces. These terraces provide habitats modified by humankind. Archaeological evidence indicates that the earliest terraces may have been used for the cultivation of root crops (e.g. taro), which continue to be important staples for some parts of the region. The development of this technique has been widely applied to the cultures of the region for the production of rice. These relationships are explained in the following diagram:

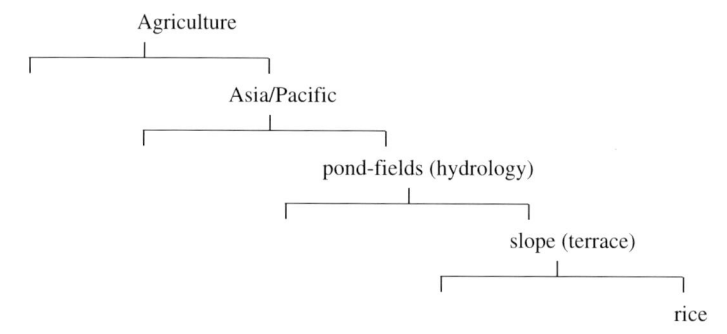

```
Agriculture
     |
 ┌───┴───┐
     Asia/Pacific
         |
     ┌───┴───┐
         pond-fields (hydrology)
                 |
             ┌───┴───┐
                 slope (terrace)
                         |
                     ┌───┴───┐
                             rice
```

There are two broad categories of Asian rice-production landscapes: wet and dry rice cultivation. Irrigation and water management is a key issue in both types of cultivation. The typical, lowland rice paddied landscape is commercially viable, producing most of the Asian requirement for rice.

The most spectacular terraces are found in the mountainous areas of the region, where the difficult terrain demands a very laborious method of terrace construction. In response to the harsh environmental conditions for rice growing and maintaining a lifestyle in the mountains, strong cultural traditions have evolved, governing all aspects of daily life and agriculture. These factors are essential in maintaining the terraces and the lifestyle of its inhabitants and ensure an enduring relationship with nature itself.

The meeting therefore focused on high-altitude, pond-field cultivation rather than the lowland rice agriculture landscape.

Four types of terrace wall construction are to be found in the Asian rice landscapes. In the gently sloping topography of the lowlands, the paddy walls are constructed of packed earth to an average height of approximately 0.50 meters. When the slopes are steeper, the lower part of the paddy wall is constructed of stone and topped with a low packed earth wall. Both wall types are also found in terraces on the gentler slopes of the highlands. The terracing on steeper slopes is more visually spectacular and more difficult to construct. The steep terrain no longer allows the use of packed earth walls and so two types of stone construction are employed. The first is a vertical wall constructed of stone; the second is a canted wall for steeper slopes. Since the ponds are constantly flooded, the lips of walls are constructed to contain the water, considerably higher than the water level or concave to prevent water spillage.

4.1.2 Evaluation of terraced landscapes

4.1.2.1 Specific attributes of terraced pond-field agriculture

Some kinds of modification and transformation of the natural surroundings that are significant for evaluating pond-field terraced agricultural landscapes in the Asia-Pacific region, with emphasis on their cultural and ecological integration in relation to continuing evolving local systems of knowledge and technology, include:

Climatically-related (water)
- watershed management (in particular forest protection and rehabilitation);
- irrigation works (weirs, dams, sluices, canals, tunnels, reservoirs);
- heavy engineering works especially for drainage (free-standing stone walls, deep channels);
- hydraulic controls of internal as well as external water flow;
- hydraulic transportation of rock, soil, earth and organic material from higher sources.

Edaphically-related (soil)
- major earthworks in mountainous terrain (excavation, leveling, filling, dyking of terraces);
- embankment walling and buttressing with boulders, stone;
- devices used for repairing damaged terraces (due to avalanches, earthworm-induced seepage, earthquakes, cloudbursts, river flooding);
- recycling of soil nutrients by field-to-field transport.

Biotically-related (biomass, biodiversity)
- organic residue management of weeds including water ferns, aquaculture of fish and other edible fauna (snails, shell-fish, mole crickets, etc), blue-green algae, and various forms of edible flora other than the principal cultivars (rice and taro);
- transport and distribution of organic fertilizers of domestic and wild origin (including green manure);
- intercropping of legumes and other vegetables, root crops, spices, and other plants of food and medicinal value;
- development and maintenance of adjacent woodlots;
- routinely selected and appropriately placed varieties of major cultivars (rice, etc).

Ethnoecologically-related (in general)
- fine-tuning, synchrony, and interlocking of cropping cycles and resource flows with the organization of labour;
- linkages and integration of religious and social traditions and adaptations with the modifications and transformations of the landscape noted above.

4.1.2.2 General evaluation indicators

In addition, the following broad indicators were defined, on the basis of the study of terraced landscapes, as being among those that should be taken into consideration in the evaluation of specific examples of continuing cultural landscapes in general:

- Traditional knowledge and technology and cultural-ecological integration.
- Involvement of local people in active maintenance and modification of the landscape.
- Degree of transformation of the natural landscape.
- Evolution and survival over time.
- Completeness of physical unit.
- Cultural tradition/identity.
- Comparative value within region.
- Significance in cultural, economic, social, and/or religious development of region.
- Representative nature of landscape type.
- Degree of enhancement of biodiversity (fauna, flora, domesticated livestock, and cultivated crops).
- Authenticity/integrity.
- Necessary management and support conditions in place.

4.1.3   Management and conservation

4.1.3.1   Objectives of conservation policies for Asian Rice Terrace Landscapes

An overriding principle of conservation is the sustainability and continuity of the balanced cultural and ecological integration between humanity and nature which gives rise to the landscape. In particular the following objectives should be pursued:

- environmental sustainability (in space and time), i.e. the protection of natural processes and cycles and the ecological system in place (including the protection of soils, water and biodiversity in fauna, flora and domesticated crops);
- protection of characteristic landscape features, including technological aspects such as water channels, irrigation and terracing;
- maintenance and strengthening of living cultural traditions, including increased awareness of the value of these traditions;
- maintenance of the economic viability of farming and traditional landuse systems using traditional knowledge-based technology;
- strengthening the capacity of the local community to cope with external pressures and forces.

4.1.3.2   Means and mechanisms for conservation planning for Asian Rice Terrace Landscapes

It is particularly important to develop policies in the following key issues:

- Greater community empowerment, so that local and indigenous communities, especially those people directly involved in the evolution and maintenance of the shaped landscape, are able to determine to the maximum extent possible the content of the conservation plan and to participate in its implementation;
- Awareness building of the potential impacts of tourism on the local community, the landscape and the environment; community determination of the form of tourism which takes place; redistribution of tourism revenues so that the local community benefits; and information to, and education of, visitors about the significance of the culture and the landscape of rice terraces;
- Determination of appropriate zones (including buffer zones) and their boundaries which identify the outstanding features themselves, ensure the protection of the ecosystem upon which the landuse system depends and recognize also the interactions between cultural, social and administrative factors.

In addition, the following organizational principles should be followed as far as possible:

- The presence of a strong body, representative of and responsive to the local community, responsible for overseeing the conservation of the area;
- This body should ensure a partnership and dialogue between all interests involved, including arrangements for participation by the private sector, NGOs and international organizations;

- The body should be responsible for developing programmes of financial and other support for the conservation of the landscape, policies for the control and regulations of incompatible activities, and arrangements for monitoring, feedback and review of the effectiveness of the conservation plan.
- All sectors of public policy need to be integrated and coordinated to achieve the objectives of the conservation of the cultural landscape.

4.2   General considerations on Continuing Organically Evolved Landscapes

Asian rice terrace landscapes are representative of a living culture. If one or more such areas are to be inscribed on the World Heritage List, this will be under the category of "continuing, organically-evolved landscapes" (Operational Guidelines, para. 39 (ii)). A number of more general questions arise from the Asian case studies, which will be relevant to the assessment of other continuing, organically-evolved landscapes.

This category of cultural landscapes presents particular challenges. Whereas intentionally-designed landscapes, "relict" organically-evolved landscapes and associative landscapes are, by their nature, more likely to be confined to a relatively few areas of limited geographical extent, continuing organically-evolved landscapes are very widespread : all agrarian landscapes can be considered in that light, and some other landscapes which have been fashioned by humanity (e.g. managed by fire regimes) can be similarly regarded.

> The first challenge, therefore, is to find an approach to the classification or typology of such landscapes so that a basis for selecting from such a potentially vast field can be made.
>
> The second major challenge is to develop meaningful guidance for comparative evaluation of the quality of such landscapes. Without such guidance, which will need to be based on the agreed criteria in the Operational Guidelines, it will not be easy to establish whether or not a particular site has outstanding, universal values.
>
> The third challenge is perhaps the most daunting of all. Because the essence of this type of cultural landscape is its dependence on a living culture, the management of such landscapes has to be through the community, rather than of the landscape as such (see section 4.1.3).

Consideration on Typology
Rather than trying to develop a world-wide categorization of cultural landscapes, a more pragmatic approach is suggested. This would involve recognition that relatively few organically evolved cultural landscapes are likely to exhibit outstanding universal qualities and that the World Heritage community should concentrate its attention upon these. The indicators which might be looked for in selecting priority types of landscape include the following examples: the demonstration of outstanding techniques for coping with extreme environmental conditions (e.g. steep slopes, low rainfall), the excellent examples of the adaptation of cultural and land use to the natural conditions, the sustainability of land use over a long period of time, and the enhancing or sustaining of biodiversity in fauna, flora and cultivated crops and domesticated livestock.

Evaluation of Continuing, Organically-evolved landscapes
Within any one priority landscape, there will be certainly be a number of potential sites worthy of nomination. The task of choosing which satisfy the World Heritage criteria will require the development of a set of evaluation indicators. It is desirable that these be standard (i.e. apply to all nominated continuing organically evolved landscapes). Examples are given under section 4.1.2.

5. Recommendations

5.1 In order to complement and further extend the valuable discussion and results of the Expert Meeting in Manila it is recommended that an interdisciplinary, technical paper be commissioned to provide as wide a context as possible for the evaluation of future nominations of terraced pond-fields. This paper, which should consist of a search of the wide body of already published literature on the subject, would extend the context to include the entire Asia-Pacific region in which terraced pond-fields are widespread. Such a widening will serve both the Bureau and the Committee in their deliberations on the nominations of cultural landscapes.

5.2 It is recommended that as soon as possible a **small** interdisciplinary and intercultural meeting be held under the auspices of UNESCO, and advised by ICOMOS and IUCN, to address the typology and evaluation tasks, and more specifically to develop a list of criteria for the selection of priority landscape types of a continuing, organically-evolved nature, to draw up a list of such priority landscape types for the attention of the Committee, and to prepare indicators for assessing individual nominations under these priority landscape types.

5.3 It is recommended that the World Heritage Committee invite ICOMOS and IUCN to develop draft principles and guidelines on the management of continuing, organically-evolved cultural landscapes based on the initial ideas generated through the meeting on Asian rice terrace landscapes, which need to be elaborated further and made general to all continuing, organically evolved cultural landscapes.

6. Acknowledgement

The experts commended the World Heritage Committee, the UNESCO National Commission of the Philippines, the Department of Foreign Affairs, the Department of Tourism, the National Commission for Culture and the Arts and the Ifugao Terraces Commission for their support.

ANNEX VI

Extract from report of the "Asia-Pacific Regional Workshop on Associative Cultural Landscapes"

A Report by Australia Icomos to the World Heritage Committee
"Where the physical and spiritual unite"

Carmen Añon Feliu

Sydney Opera House and Jenolan Caves, Blue Mountains, New South Wales, Australia
27–29 April 1995

1. Summary and Recommendations

The adoption of the concept of cultural landscapes by the World Heritage Committee at its sixteenth session in 1992 made the World Heritage Convention more applicable to a wider international audience. More specifically, in the Asia-Pacific region, the Convention's potential application was extended, both culturally and geographically, by the inclusion of this category of heritage. These developments are recognised as having the potential to broaden the representativeness of the World Heritage List.

The Asia-Pacific Regional Workshop on Associative Cultural Landscapes held in Australia in April 1995 endorsed the findings of two recent UNESCO/ICOMOS meetings - the June 1994 Expert Meeting on the Global Strategy and Thematic Studies for a representative World Heritage List and the November 1994 Nara Expert Workshop on Authenticity. These workshops recognised that the consideration of properties of outstanding universal value needs to be contextual (recognising a place in its broader intellectual and physical context) rather than specific (as in the limited approach to viewing heritage solely as monuments or wilderness). The incorporation of the cultural landscape concept in the Operational Guidelines is a positive move in this direction. A cultural landscape, in reflecting the interactions of people and their environment, is defined by its cultural and natural elements which may be inseparable.

The Workshop further endorsed the Global Strategy and the Nara Document on Authenticity as being particularly apt for the Asia-Pacific region because of the continuity of living traditions in relation to land and water within this region. The Global Strategy and the December 1993 Action Plan for the Future (Cultural Landscapes) emphasised the need for regional workshops and educational programs to increase awareness of cultural landscapes among States Parties. To allow such programs to take place the Workshop recommended that an extension of time be granted to States Parties to incorporate cultural landscapes in their tentative lists (see the Action Plan for the Future (Cultural Landscapes)).

The World Heritage Committee at its sixteenth session in December 1992 revised the Operational Guidelines for the Implementation of the World Heritage Convention to allow for the inclusion of cultural landscapes on the World Heritage List. The Operational Guidelines identify associative cultural landscapes as one of the categories of cultural landscapes. Paragraph 39 (iii) of the Guidelines states:

The inclusion of such landscapes on the World Heritage List is justifiable by virtue of the powerful religious, artistic or cultural associations of the natural element rather than material cultural evidence which may be insignificant or even absent.

The Asia-Pacific Regional Workshop on Associative Cultural Landscapes examined the definition, evaluation, management and monitoring of associative cultural landscapes with particular reference to the Asia-Pacific region.

The associative cultural landscape category has particular relevance to the Asia-Pacific region where the link between the physical and spiritual aspects of landscape is so important. This is especially so given workshop by Mr Tumu Te Heuheu and those of Uluru Kata-Tjuta were represented by Mr Yami Lester, Chair of Uluru's Board of Management.

The celebration was enhanced by the presentation by the Director-General of the UNESCO Picasso Gold Medal to the Uluru Kata-Tjuta Board of Management. This Board includes representatives of the traditional Aboriginal custodians of Uluru Kata-Tjuta and of the Australian Nature Conservation Agency. The traditional owners have majority representation on the Board of Management.

The award of the UNESCO Picasso Gold Medal to the Uluru Kata-Tjuta Board of Management was a clear demonstration of the international recognition of associative cultural landscapes as an important category of heritage environment and of the value of traditional management practices in caring for them.

In his opening address to the Workshop, the Director-General of UNESCO, Dr Federico Mayor, stressed that "man and nature are indeed inseparable" and pointed to the all-encompassing features of the World Heritage Convention. For too long in international fora the environment has been compartmentalised into the "natural" and the "cultural". In the Asia-Pacific region there has sometimes been a further division between indigenous and non-indigenous cultural environments. There is a growing recognition that these distinctions are artificial and there is a need for a more integrated approach as reflected in the cultural landscape concept.

The recognition of associative cultural landscapes is particularly relevant to the Asia-Pacific region where a diversity of traditional cultures both depend on and have influenced the landscape for their corporal and spiritual well being.

Working sessions - understanding

Some thirty of the experts present at the Opera House travelled to the Jenolan Caves, a world-famous karst site in the Blue Mountains to the west of Sydney, for further workshop sessions on the World Heritage Convention and associative cultural landscapes. Regional participants came from Fiji/Tonga, The Philippines, Taiwan, New Zealand and Australia. Representing ICOMOS, Carmen Añon Feliu, a Spanish specialist in cultural landscapes, stressed the need for recognition of the link between the physical and spiritual aspects of landscapes.

Bing Lucas, representing the International Union for the Conservation of Nature and Natural Resources (IUCN), outlined the evolution of the concept of World Heritage cultural landscapes. Augusto Villalon brought from the Philippines the experience of the recent and related expert workshop on rice terraces as organically evolved cultural landscapes.

Participants discussed definitions, evaluation, management and monitoring, with particular emphasis on associative cultural landscapes in the Asia-Pacific region. Outcomes of the Workshop were discussed in relation to a traditional cultural landscape and an inspirational landscape to gauge the relevance of the cultural and natural criteria and the conditions of authenticity, integrity and management requirements in the Operational Guidelines to each case.

3. Defining associative cultural landscapes

In discussing the definition of associative cultural landscapes within the Operational Guidelines, and the range of types of landscapes implied within it, the Workshop considered it useful to suggest the amplification or qualification of specific terms included in Paragraph 39 (iii) of the Guidelines .

These suggestions were as follows:

The term "artistic" in Paragraph 39 (iii) of the Guidelines encompasses all forms of artistic expression, including "literary".

The term "cultural" in Paragraph 39 (iii) includes associations with historic events and with traditions of indigenous and non-indigenous cultures.

The term "landscape" in Paragraph 39 (iii) includes seascapes, so important to island and maritime people and environments. An example cited is the fisheries culture of the indigenous inhabitants of Taiwan's offshore islands. It was noted that the ICOMOS International Scientific Committee on

Underwater Cultural Heritage examines marine environments in terms of shipwrecks and other material evidence and that a useful addition to its work would be the consideration of the associative values linked to the marine environment.

The Workshop discussed traditional or indigenous, and inspirational or artistic associative cultural landscapes.

Associative cultural landscapes may include large or small contiguous or non-contiguous areas and itineraries, routes or other linear landscapes - these may be physical entities or mental images embedded in a people's spirituality, cultural tradition and practice. Examples important to the Asia-Pacific region include Aboriginal dreaming tracks in Australia, the spread of Polynesian culture across the Pacific Ocean and the Silk Road from China to the West. Another example would be slave routes such as those by which indentured labourers were brought from the Pacific Islands to Queensland in Australia to work in the sugar industry.

The Workshop agreed that the attributes of associative cultural landscapes also include the intangible, such as the acoustic, kinetic (eg. air movements) and olfactory, as well as the visual (eg. patterns of light, colours and shapes in the landscape). The acoustic dimension is vital to many cultures, for example those in Papua New Guinea which are tuned to the songs of birds or the sounds of waterfalls.

It was pointed out that in Pacific and other cultures in this region, some landscapes have been created by women or carry "religious, artistic or cultural" traditions specific to women rather than men. Therefore, in identifying associative cultural landscapes, gender should be taken into account.

In this region it is vital to recognise that geographical features may have cultural significance without there being any visible archaeological evidence (see Paragraph 39 (iii) of the Operational Guidelines). In the absence of cultural fabric, the evidence may exist through words (eg. poetry, songs), photography or paintings - "the landscapes of memory".

Inspirational landscapes may become familiar to people through their depiction in paintings such as those of the strong nineteenth century landscape tradition in Australia exemplified by the works of Conrad Martens which had their European counterparts in the paintings of artists such as Turner.

Sydney Harbour has inspired not only local artists from the early colonial Port Jackson painters to the recent creations of Lloyd Rees, Brett Whiteley and Ken Done, but also the designers of the Harbour Bridge and the Sydney Opera House. These latter tangible inspirational responses have added to the cumulative mix of cultural and natural features in the landscape which, in turn, inspire new associative responses.

The inspirational photographs of Tasmania's Franklin River by Olegas Truchanas, Peter Dombrovskis and others have become a symbol for the wilderness movement in Australia just as Ansell Adams' evocative photographs of the landform Half Dome in America's Yosemite National Park have become a symbol for the wilderness movement in the United States.

4. Evaluating associative cultural landscapes

The Workshop endorsed the findings of two recent UNESCO/ICOMOS meetings - the June 1994 Expert Meeting on the Global Strategy and the November 1994 Nara Expert Workshop on Authenticity. These workshops recognised that the consideration of properties of outstanding universal value needs to be contextual (recognising a place in its broader intellectual and physical context) rather than specific (as in the limited approach to viewing heritage solely as monuments or wilderness). The incorporation of the cultural landscape concept in the Operational Guidelines is a positive move in this direction. A cultural landscape, in reflecting the interactions of people and their environment, is defined by its cultural and natural elements which may be inseparable.

The Workshop recommended that:

The Workshop noted the need for an integrated approach to the evaluation of associative cultural landscapes, combining the skills and expertise of natural and cultural heritage experts. ICOMOS should continue to be the lead agency for the evaluation of cultural landscapes but, where appropriate, the evaluation of all categories of landscape should be undertaken jointly by ICOMOS and IUCN to link their areas of expertise.

On the question of evaluation the workshop participants addressed the following questions:

Which of the natural and cultural criteria in the Operational Guidelines are relevant to associative landscapes?

What constitutes the authenticity, both in character and components, and integrity required by the Operational Guidelines in relation to associative cultural landscapes?

How should boundaries of associative cultural landscapes be determined in relation to both functionality and intelligibility, as required by the Operational Guidelines?

Criteria

The Workshop recommended that, in evaluating any associative cultural landscape for World Heritage listing the criteria in Paragraphs 24 and 44 of the Operational Guidelines be considered comprehensively. Tongariro National Park and Uluru Kata-Tjuta National Park, the two places in this region now listed as associative cultural landscapes, were found to meet both cultural and natural criteria.

Cultural criteria in Paragraph 24 (a) of the Operational Guidelines, relating to "unique or exceptional testimony to a cultural tradition or to a civilisation" (cultural criterion iii) and "associated with ... artistic and literary works of outstanding universal significance" (cultural criterion vi) were clearly applicable to associative cultural landscapes. It was noted that cultural criterion (vi), according to the Guidelines should not be used in isolation except "in exceptional circumstances or in conjunction with other criteria, cultural or natural".

Cultural criterion (iv) dealing with "landscape which illustrates significant stages in human history" and (v) relating to "an outstanding example of a traditional land-use which is representative of a culture (or cultures), especially when it has become vulnerable under the impact of irreversible change", may also apply to associative cultural landscapes.

The Workshop recommended that in applying cultural criterion (vi) a broader rather than a narrower interpretation be used, and that in particular, oral traditions not be excluded.

The Workshop considered that the natural criterion defined in Paragraph 44 (a) (iii) may be relevant for an associative cultural landscape. The criterion highlights "superlative natural phenomena", "areas of exceptional natural beauty" and "areas of exceptional aesthetic importance". It is important that any nomination for World Heritage listing clearly specify how and why the landscape is seen as having these qualities, which may well be by cultural association.

There are management implications arising from the specific criteria used to evaluate associative cultural landscapes. The criteria in Paragraphs 44 (a) (ii) and (iv) for evaluating natural properties for World Heritage listing may, for the purposes of integrity, require the maintenance of biological diversity. While changes to Paragraph 38 have emphasised the potential for traditional cultural practices to assist the maintenance of biological diversity, management problems may arise if traditional land-use practices are seen to conflict with other nature conservation strategies.

The Workshop, noting that communities which are stakeholders in properties of World Heritage significance may not always be aware of the criteria and the listing process, supported the requirement for educational programs and full consultation with all communities which are culturally associated with the properties. It is recognised that in some instances cross-cultural differences may lead to conflicts concerning evaluation, listing and management of properties.

Authenticity and Integrity

The Workshop endorsed the wording of Paragraph 11 of the November 1994 Nara Document on Authenticity which states that :

All judgements about values attributed to cultural properties as well as the credibility of related information sources may differ from culture to culture, and even within the same culture. It is thus not possible to base judgements of value and authenticity on fixed criteria. On the contrary, the respect due to all cultures requires that heritage properties must be considered and judged within the cultural contexts to which they belong.

While the Workshop participants agreed that Paragraph 24 (b) (i) of the Operational Guidelines is relevant to associative cultural landscapes, they considered that for regional applications the definition of authenticity needed to clarify the interactions between culture and the natural environment.

Authenticity, related to the criteria for which a place was nominated, should encompass the continuation of cultural practices which maintain the place. This authenticity, however, must not exclude cultural continuity through change, which may introduce new ways of relating to and caring for the place.

Because of the particular characteristics of associative cultural landscapes, authenticity may not refer to the maintenance of the fabric of a place, or its reconstruction to an earlier or original configuration. Instead, authenticity may mean the maintenance of a continuing association between the people and the place, however it may be expressed through time. This may on occasion necessitate the need for acceptance of some change to the landscape as well as a change in attitude to it.

The Workshop accepted the need to fulfil the conditions of integrity set out under Paragraph 44 (b) of the Operational Guidelines. It would seem that Paragraph 44 (b) (iii) may most often be relevant, through its reference to sites of 'outstanding aesthetic value".

An example discussed in regard to authenticity and integrity was Mount Fuji in Japan. In addition to its natural values, Mount Fuji has undoubted spiritual, artistic and inspirational values. However, a range of landuses, protective mechanisms and management regimes for the surrounding areas have affected integrity and made boundary determination difficult.

Boundaries

World Heritage listing requires determination of property boundaries with reference to a clearly defined geocultural region and the capacity to illustrate the essential and distinct cultural and natural elements of such regions or cultures.

The Workshop found that it can be difficult to specify boundaries for associative cultural landscapes because of the difficulties in quantifying the values and in delineating where they are expressed. However, it found that boundaries could be sought for each defined value and that the overall boundary incorporating all values could be presented by maps based on overlays for each.

For traditional indigenous associative cultural landscapes, it is necessary to define boundaries with reference, for example, to spirituality, cultural tradition and practice, language, kinship and social relationships and/or the interactions (including use and care of plant and animal species) that exist between people and their natural environment.

The boundary requirements for properties with natural values set out in Paragraphs 44 (b) were seen to be relevant for associative cultural landscapes where the nomination depended on any of the criteria in Paragraph 44 (a).

5. Managing associative cultural landscapes

Management

The Workshop endorsed the management requirements set out under Paragraphs 24 (b) (ii) and 44 (b) (v) of the Operational Guidelines, including those related to integrity and control of visitation to the property nominated. Paragraph 14 of the Operational Guidelines was perceived to be somewhat ambiguous in intent, offering some potential for secrecy and conflict rather than the open process considered desirable.

Paragraph 24 (b) (ii) of the Operational Guidelines regarding the adequacy of legal and/or traditional protection and management mechanisms applies to associative cultural landscapes. Paragraph 24 (b) (ii) appears to presuppose the arrest of change whereas what will often be needed is a mechanism to manage change appropriately. A management plan, or other conservation arrangement, should provide people with the framework and mechanisms to manage change, whilst conserving the stated values of the property.

Linkages between the evaluation and management of associative cultural landscapes need to be recognised. Close involvement of traditional custodians, as in the case of Tongariro National Park in New Zealand and Uluru Kata-Tjuta National Park in Australia should be a prerequisite in the assessment of appropriate management regimes for such landscapes.

With reference to the management of associative cultural landscapes, it should be recognised that indigenous peoples make an important and ongoing contribution to the maintenance and care of the values of the place.

The Workshop recommended that:

Interpretation programs for World Heritage associative cultural landscapes need to promote the traditional and/or inspirational values for which the places were nominated. For traditional indigenous landscapes, this interpretation program should be developed in consultation with, and with the agreement of, the appropriate traditional owners/custodians.

Education programs and information services need to be made available to State Party governments and the general public to encourage a greater feeling of ownership and respect for World Heritage properties.

Monitoring

Inspirational places such as artistic associative cultural landscapes are particularly difficult to monitor due to the lack of an effective gauge. One measure of success is whether or not the values for which the landscape was noted are still appreciated by the community and respected by visitors. Another measure of success is whether or not the place itself continues to inspire creative works.

With reference to the monitoring of traditional cultural landscapes, the need to involve indigenous peoples must be recognised.

There is a need to protect all associative cultural landscapes, not only from neglect but also from the excesses of presentation and visitor overuse. The impact of heritage management regimes must therefore be monitored regularly, and appropriately controlled.

The Workshop accordingly endorsed the efforts of the World Heritage Committee to establish effective monitoring systems and to consider a cooperative regional approach to monitoring.

6. Community involvement

The Workshop participants considered community involvement and participation to be an important part of the identification, management and monitoring of associative cultural landscapes for World Heritage listing.

7. Testing the workshop outcomes

To test the outcomes of the Workshop, and particularly the relevance of the criteria in the Operational Guidelines to the inclusion of associative cultural landscapes in the World Heritage List, two associative cultural landscapes of World Heritage potential were discussed. One of the landscapes chosen had cultural associations to indigenous peoples, and the other, artistic associations. A simple testing methodology involving the consideration of the following questions in relation to each of the cultural landscapes was used:

Does the property fit the definition of associative cultural landscape in the Operational Guidelines?

If so, which criteria does it satisfy?

Does it satisfy the requirements concerning authenticity and integrity?

Does the associative cultural landscape have adequate management arrangements in place?

Is it of outstanding universal value?

How would you identify the boundaries?

The example of the indigenous cultural landscape was found to satisfy a range of both natural and cultural criteria. The example of the inspirational landscape met several cultural criteria and possibly some natural criteria. Boundary definition for both examples was not possible given the constraints of information available to Workshop participants. Nonetheless, the exercise served to confirm the Workshop findings on definitions, evaluation and management.

8. Implications for the Asia-Pacific region

The adoption of the concept of cultural landscapes by the World Heritage Committee at its sixteenth session in 1992 made the World Heritage Convention more applicable to a wider international audience. More specifically, in the Asia-Pacific region, the Convention's potential application was extended, both culturally and geographically, by the inclusion of this category of heritage. These developments are recognised as having the potential to broaden the representativeness of the World Heritage List.

The Asia-Pacific Regional Workshop on Associative Cultural Landscapes held in Australia in April 1995 endorsed the findings of two recent UNESCO/ICOMOS meetings - the June 1994 Expert Meeting on the Global Strategy and Thematic Studies for a representative World Heritage List and the November 1994 Nara Expert Workshop on Authenticity. These workshops recognised that the consideration of properties of outstanding universal value needs to be contextual (recognising a place in its broader intellectual and physical context) rather than specific (as in the limited approach to viewing heritage solely as monuments or wilderness). The incorporation of the cultural landscape concept in the Operational Guidelines is a positive move in this direction. A cultural landscape, in reflecting the interactions of people and their environment, is defined by its cultural and natural elements which may be inseparable.

The Workshop further endorsed the Global Strategy and the Nara Document on Authenticity as being particularly apt for the Asia-Pacific region because of the continuity of living traditions in relation to land and water within this region. The Global Strategy and the December 1993 Action Plan for the Future (Cultural Landscapes) emphasised the need for regional workshops and educational programs to increase awareness of cultural landscapes among States Parties. To allow such programs to take place the Workshop recommended that an extension of time be granted to States Parties to incorporate cultural landscapes in their tentative lists (see the Action Plan for the Future (Cultural Landscapes)).

In this vital United Nations Year of Tolerance, in culturally diverse areas such as the Asia-Pacific region, it is important to encourage people to share what can be shared of their values, traditions and places; to care for that which cannot be shared; and to respect places reflecting different values and practices from their own. World Heritage listing of associative cultural landscapes and their ongoing management should reflect these values.

ANNEX VII

World Heritage Convention (1972)

Convention for the Protection of the World Cultural and Natural Heritage

The General Conference of the United Nations Educational, Scientific and Cultural Organization meeting in Paris from 17 October to 21 November 1972, at its seventeenth session,
Noting that the cultural heritage and the natural heritage are increasingly threatened with destruction not only by the traditional causes of decay, but also by changing social and economic conditions which aggravate the situation with even more formidable phenomena of damage or destruction,
Considering that deterioration or disappearance of any item of the cultural or natural heritage constitutes a harmful impoverishment of the heritage of all the nations of the world,
Considering that protection of this heritage at the national level often remains incomplete because of the scale of the resources which it requires and of the insufficient economic, scientific and technical resources of the country where the property to be protected is situated,
Recalling that the Constitution of the Organization provides that it will maintain, increase and diffuse knowledge, by assuring the conservation and protection of the world's heritage, and recommending to the nations concerned the necessary international conventions,
Considering that the existing international conventions, recommendations and resolutions concerning cultural and natural property demonstrate the importance, for all the peoples of the world, of safeguarding this unique and irreplaceable property, to whatever people it may belong,
Considering that parts of the cultural or natural heritage are of outstanding interest and therefore need to be preserved as part of the world heritage of mankind as a whole,
Considering that, in view of the magnitude and gravity of the new dangers threatening them, it is incumbent on the international community as a whole to participate in the protection of the cultural and natural heritage of outstanding universal value, by the granting of collective assistance which, although not taking the place of action by the State concerned, will serve as an effective complement thereto,
Considering that it is essential for this purpose to adopt new provisions in the form of a convention establishing an effective system of collective protection of the cultural an natural heritage of outstanding universal value, organized on a permanent basis and in accordance with modern scientific methods,
Having decided, at its sixteenth session, that this question should be made the subject of an international convention,
Adopts this sixteenth day of November 1972 this Convention.

I. Definitions of the Cultural and the Natural Heritage

Article 1

For the purposes of this Convention, the following shall be considered as "cultural heritage":
monuments: architectural works, works of monumental sculpture and painting, elements or structures of an archaeological nature, inscriptions, cave dwellings and combinations of features, which are of outstanding universal value from the point of view of history, art or science;
groups of buildings: groups of separate or connected buildings which, because of their architecture, their homogeneity or their place in the landscape, are of outstanding universal value from the point of view of history, art or science;
sites: works of man or the combined works of nature and of man, and areas including archaeological sites which are of outstanding universal value from the historical, aesthetic, ethnological or anthropological points of view.

Article 2

For the purposes of this Convention, the following shall be considered as "natural heritage";
natural features consisting of physical and biological formations or groups of such formations, which are of outstanding universal value from the aesthetic or scientific point of view;
geological and physiographical formations and precisely delineated areas which constitute the habitat of threatened species of animals and plants of outstanding universal value from the point of view of science or conservation;
natural sites or precisely delineated natural areas of outstanding universal value from the point of view of science, conservation or natural beauty.

Article 3

It is for each State Party to this Convention to identify and delineate the different properties situated on its territory mentioned in Articles 1 and 2 above.

II. National Protection and international Protection of the Cultural and Natural Heritage

Article 4

Each State Party to this Convention recognizes that the duty of ensuring the identification, protection, conservation, presentation and transmission of future generations to the cultural and natural heritage referred to in Articles 1 and 2 and situated on its territory, belongs primarily to that State. It will do all it can to this end, to the utmost of its own resources and, where appropriate, with any international assistance and co-operation, in particular, financial, artistic, scientific and technical, which it may be able to obtain.

Article 5

To ensure that effective and active measures are taken for the protection, conservation and presentation of the cultural and natural heritage situated on its territory, each State Party to this Convention shall endeavour, in so far as possible, and as appropriate for each country:

(a) to adopt a general policy which aims to give the cultural and natural heritage a function in the life of the community and to integrate the protection of that heritage into comprehensive planning programmes;
(b) to set up within its territories, where such services do not exist, one or more services for the protection, conservation and presentation of the cultural and natural heritage with an appropriate staff and possessing the means to discharge their functions;
(c) to develop scientific and technical studies and research and to work out such operating methods as will make the State capable of counteracting the dangers that threaten its cultural or natural heritage;
(d) to take the appropriate legal, scientific, technical, administrative and financial measures necessary for the identification, protection, conservation, presentation and rehabilitation of this heritage; and
(e) to foster the establishment or development of national or regional centres for training in the protection, conservation and presentation of the cultural and natural heritage and to encourage scientific research in this field.

Article 6

1. Whilst fully respecting the sovereignty of the States on whose territory the cultural and natural heritage mentioned in Articles 1 and 2 is situated, and without prejudice to property rights provided by national legislation, the States Parties to this Convention recognize that such heritage constitutes a world heritage for whose protection it is the duty of the international community as a whole to co-operate.
2. The States Parties undertake, in accordance with the provisions of this Convention, to give their help in the indentification, protection, conservation and preservation of the cultural and natural heritage referred to in paragraphs 2 and 4 of Article 11 if the States on whose territory it is situated so request.

3. Each State Party to this Convention undertakes not to take any deliberate measures which might damage directly or indirectly the cultural and natural heritage referred to in Articles 1 and 2 situated on the territory of other States Parties to this Convention.

Article 7

For the purpose of this Convention, international protection of the world cultural and natural heritage shall be understood to mean the establishment of a system of international co-operation and assistance designed to support States Parties to the Convention in their efforts to conserve and identify that heritage.

III. Inergovernmental Committee for the Protections of the World Cultural and Natural Heritage

Article 8

1. An Intergovernmental Committee for the Protection of the Cultural and Natural Heritage of Outstanding Universal Value, called "the Wolrd Heritage Committe", is hereby established withing the United Nations Educational, Scientific and Cultural Organization. It shall be composed of 15 States Parties to the Convention, elected by States Parties to the Convention meeting in general assembly during the ordinary session of the General Conference of the United Nations Educational, Scientific and Cultural Organization. Thr number of States members of the Committee shall be increased to 21 as from the date of the ordinary session of the General Conference following the entry into force of theis Convention for at least 40 States.
2. Election of members of the Committee shal ensure an equitable representation of the different regions and cultures of the world.
3. A representative of the International Centre for the Study of the Preservation and Restoration of Cultural Property (Rome Centre), a representative of the International Council of Monuments and Sites (ICOMOS) and a representative of the International Union for Conservation of Nature and Natural Resources (IUCN), to whom may be addend, at the request of States Parties to the Convention meeting in general assembly during the ordinary sessions of the General Conference of the United Nations Educational, Scientific and Cultural Organization, representatives of other intergovernmental or non-governmental organizations, with similar objectives, may attend the meetings of the Committee in an advisory capacity.

Article 9

1. The term of office of States members of the World Heritage Committee shal extend from the end of the ordinary session of the General Conference during which they are elected until the end of its third subsequent ordinary session.
2. The term of office of one-third of the members designated at the time of the first election shall, however, cease at the end of the first ordinary session of the General Conference following that at which they were elected; and the term of office of a further third of the members designated at the same time shall cease at the end of the second ordinary session of the General Conference following that at which they were elected. The names of these members shall be chosen by lot by the President of the General Conference of the United Nations Educational, Scientific and Cultural Organization after the first election.
3. States members of the Committee shall choose as their representatives persons qualified in the field of the cultural or natural heritage.

Article 10

1. The World Heritage Committee shall adopt its Rules of Procedure.
2. The Committee may at any time invite public or private organizations or individuals to participate in its meetings for consultations on particular problems.
3. The Committee may create such consultative bodies as it deems necessary for the performance of its functions.

Article 11

1. Every State Party to this Convention shall, in so far as possible, submit to the World Heritage Committee an inventory of property froming part of the cultural and natural heritage, situated in its territory and suitable for inclusion in the list provided for in paragraph 2 of this Article. This inventory, which shall not be considered exhaustive, shall include documentation about the location of the property in question and its significance.
2. On the basis of the inventories submitted by States in accordance with paragraph1, the Committee shall establish, keep up to date and publish, under the title of "World Heritage List", a list of properties forming part of the cultural heritage and natural heritage, as defined in Articles 1 and 2 of this Convention, which it considers as having outstanding universal value in terms of such criteria as it shall have established. An updated list shall be distributed at least every two years.
3. The inclusion of a property in the World Heritage List requires the consent of the State concerned. The inclusion of a property situated in a territory, sovereignty or jurisdiction over which is claimed by more than one State shall in no way prejudice the rights of the parties to the dispute.
4. The Committee shall establish, keep up to date and publish, whenever circumstances shall so require, under the title of "List of World Heritage in Danger", a list of the property appearing in the World Heritage List for the conservation of which major operations are necessary and for which assistance has been requested under this Convention. This list shall contain an estimate of the cost of such operations. The list may include only such property forming part of the cultural and natural heritage as is threatened by serious and specific dangers, such as the threat of disappearance caused by accelerated deterioration, large-scale public or private projects or rapid urban or tourist development projects; destruction caused by changes in the use or ownership of the land; major alterations due to unknown causes; abandonment for any reason whatsoever; the outbreak or the threat of an armed conflict; calamities and cataclysms; serious fires, earthquakes, landslides; volcanic eruptions; changes in water level, floods, and tidal waves. The Committee may at any time, in case of urgent need, make a new entry in the List of World Heritage in Danger and publicize such entry immediately.
5. The Committee shall define the criteria on the basis of which a property belonging to the cultural or natural heritage may be included in either of the lists mentioned in paragraphs 2 and 4 of this article.
6. Before refusing a request for inclusion in one of the two lists mentioned in paragraphs 2 and 4 of this article, the Committee shall consult the State Party in whose territory the cultural or natural property in question is situated.
7. The Committee shall, with the agreement of the States concerned, co-ordinate and encourage the studies and research needed for the drawing up of the lists referred to in paragraphs 2 and 4 of this article.

Article 12

The fact that a property belonging to the cultural or natural heritage has not been included in either of the two lists mentioned in paragraphs 2 and 4 of Article 11 shall in no way be construed to mean that it does not have an outstanding universal value for purposes other than those resulting from inclusion in these lists.

Article 13

1. The World Heritage Committee shall receive and study requests for international assistance formulated by States Parties to this Convention with respect to property forming part of the cultural or natura situated in their territories, and included or potentially suitable for inclusion in the lists referred to in paragraphs 2 and 4 of Article 11. The purpose of such requests may be to secure the protection, conservation, presentation or rehabilitation of such property.
2. Requests for international assistance under paragraph 1 of this article may also be concerned with identification of cultural or natural property defined in Articles 1 and 2, when preliminary investigations have shown that further inquiries would be justified.
3. The Committee shall decide on the action to be taken with regard to these requests, determine where appropriate, the nature and extent of its assistance, and autorize the conclusion, on its behalf, of the necessary arrangements with the government concerned.

4. The Committee shall determine on order priorities for its operations. It shall in so doing bear in mind the respective importance for the world cultural and natural heritage of the property requiring protection, the need to give international assistance to the property most representative of a natural environment or of the genius and the history of the peoples of the world, the urgency of the work to be done, the resources available to the States on whose territory the threatened property is situated and in particular the extent to which they are able to safeguard such property by their own means.

5. The Committee shall draw up, keep up to date and publicize a list of property for which international assistance has been granted.

6. The Committee shall decide on the use of the resources of the Fund established under Article 15 of this Convention. It shall seek ways of increasing these resources and shall take all useful steps to this end.

7. The Committee shall co-operate with international and national governmental and nongovernmental organizations having objectives similar to those of this Convention. For the implementation of its programmes and projects, the Committee call on such organizations, particulary the International Centre for the Study of the Preservation and Restoration of Cultural Property (the Rome Centre), the International Council of Monuments and Sites (ICOMOS) and the International Union for Conservation of Nature and Natural Resources (IUCN), as well as on public and private bodies and individuals.

8. Decisions of the Committee shall be taken by a majority of two-thirds of its members present and voting. A majority of the members of the Committee shall constitute a quorum.

Article 14

1. The World Heritage Committee shall be assisted by a Secretariat appointed by the Director-General of the United Nations Educational, Scientific and Cultural Organization.

2. The Director-General of the United Nations Educational, Scientific and Culturtal Organization, utilizing to the fullest extent possible the services of the International Centre for the Study of the Preservation and the Restoration of Cultural Property (the Rome Centre), the International Council of Monuments and Sites (ICOMOS) and the International Union for Conservation of Nature and Natural Resources (IUCN) in their respective areas of competence and capability, shall prepare the Committee's documentation and the agenda of its meetings and shall have the responsibility for the implementation of its decisions.

IV. Fund for the Protection of the World Cultural and Natural Heritage

Article 15

1. A Fund for the Protection of the World Cultural and Natural Heritage of Outstanding Universal Value, called "the World Heritage Fund", is hereby established.

2. The Fund shall constitute a trust fund, in conformity with the provisions of the Financial Regulations of the United Nations Educational, Scientific and Cultural Organization.

3. The resources of the Fund shall consist of:

    (a) compulsory and voluntary contributions made by the States Parties to this Convention,

    (b) contributions, gifts or bequests which may be made by:

       (i) orter States;

       (ii) the United Nations Educational, Scientific and Cultural Organization, other organizations of the United Nations system, particularly the United Nations Development Programme or other intergovernmental organizations;

       (iii) public or private bodies or individuals;

    (c) any interest due on the resources of the Fund;

    (d) funds raised by collections and receipts from events organized for the benefit of the Fund; and

    (e) all other resources authorized by the Fund's regulations, as drawn up by the World Heritage Committee.

4. Contributions to the Fund and other forms of assistance made avialable to the Committee may be used only for such purposes as the Committee shall define. The Committee may accept contributions to be used only for a certain programme or project, provided that the Committee shall have decided on the implementation of such programme or project. No political conditions may be attached to contributions made to the Fund.

Article 16

1. Without prejudice to any supplementary voluntary contribution, the States Parties to this Convention undertake to pay regularly, every two years, to the World Heritage Fund, contributions the amount of which, in the form of a uniform percentage applicable to all States, shall be determined by the General Assembly of States Parties to the Convention, meeting during the sessions of the General Conference of the United Nations Educational, Scientific and Cultural Organization. This decision of the Ceneral Assembly requires the majority of the States Parties present and voting, which have not made the declaration referred to in paragraph 2 of this Article. In no case shall the compulsory contribution of States Parties to the Convention exceed 1% of the contribution to the Regular Budget of the United Nations Educational, Scientific and Cultural Organization.

2. However, each State referred to in Article 31 or in Article 32 of this Convention may declare, at the time of the deposit of its instruments of ratification, acceptance or accession, that it shall not be bound by the provisions of paragraph 1 of this Article.

3. A State Party to the Convention which has made the declaration referred to in paragraph 2 of this Article may at any time withdraw the said declaration by notifying the Director-General of the United Nations Educational, Scientific and Cultural Organization. Hewever, the withdrawal of the declaration shall not take effect in regard to the compulsory contribution due by the State until the date of the subsequent General Assembly of States Parties to the Convention.

4. In order that the Committee may be able to plan its operations effectively, the contributions of States Parties to this Convention which have made the declaration referred to in paragraph 2 of this Article, shall be paid on a regular basis, at least every two years, and should not be less than the contributions which they should have paid if they had been bound by the provisions of paragraph 1 of this Article.

5. Any State Party to the Convention which is in arrears with the payment of its compulsory or voluntary contribution for the current year and the calendar year immediately preceding it shall not be eligible as a Member of the World Heritage Committee, although this provision shall not apply to the first election.
The terms of office of any such State which ist already a member of the Committee shall terminate at the time of the elections provided for in Article 8, paragraph 1 of this Convention.

Article 17

The States Parties to this Convention shall consider or encourage the establishment of national public and private foundations or associations whose purpose is to invite donations for the protection of the cultural and natural heritage as defined in Articles 1 and 2 of this Convention.

Article 18

The States Parties to this Convention shall give their assistance to international fund-raising campaigns organized for the World Heritage Fund under the auspices of the United Nations Educational, Scientific and Cultural Organization. They shall facilitate collections made by the bodies mentioned in paragraph 3 of Article 15 for this purpose.

V. Conditions and Arrangements for International Assistance

Article 19

Any State Party to this Convention may request international assistance for property forming part of the cultural or natural heritage of outstanding universal value situated within its territory. It shall submit with its request such information and documentation provided for in Article 21 as it has in its possession and as will enable the Committee to come to a decision.

Article 20

Subject to the provisions of paragraph 2 of Article 13, sub-paragraph (c) of Article 22 and Article 23, international assistance provided for by this Convention may be granted only to property forming part of the cultural and natural heritage which the World Heritage Committee has decided, or may decide, to enter in one of the lists mentioned in paragraphs 2 and 4 of Article 11.

Article 21

1. The World Heritage Committee shall define the procedure by which requests to it for international assistance shall be considered ans shall specify the content of the request, which should define the operation contemplated, the work that is necessary, the expected cost thereof, the degree of urgency and the reasons why the resources of the State requesting assistance do not allow it to meet all the expenses. Such requests must be supported by experts' reports whenever possible.
2. Requests based upon disasters or natural calamities should, by reasons of the urgent work which they may involve, be given immediate, priority consideration by the Committee, which should have a reserve fund at its disposal against such contingencies.
3. Before coming to a decision, the Committee shall carry out such studies and consultations as it deems necessary.

Article 22

Assistance granted by the World Heritage Committee may take the following forms:

(a) studies concerning the artistic, scientific and technical problems raised by the protection, conservation, presentation and rehabilitation of the cultural and natural heritage, as defined in paragraphs 2 and 4 of Article 11 of this Convention;
(b) provision of experts, technicians and skilled labour to ensure that the approved work is correctly carried out;
(c) training of staff and specialists at all levels in the field of identification, protection, conservation, presentation and rehabilitation of the cultural and natural heritage;
(d) supply of equipment which the State concerned does not possess or is not in a position to acquire;
(e) low-interest or interest-free loans which might be repayable on a long-term basis;
(f) the granting, in exceptional cases and for special reasons, of non-repayable subsidies.

Article 23

The World Heritage Committee may also provide international assistance to national or regional centres for the training of staff and specialists at all levels in the field of indentification, protection, conservation, presentation and rehabilitation of the cultural and natural heritage.

Article 24

International assistance on a large scale shall be preceded by detailed scientific, economic and technical studies. These studies shall draw upon the most advanced techniques for the protection, conservation, presentation and rehabilitation of the natural and cultural hertiage and shall be consistent with the objectives of this Convention. The studies shall also seek means of making rational use of the resources available in the State concerned.

Article 25

As a general rule, only part of the cost of work necessary shall be borne by the international community. The contribution of the State benefiting from international assistance shall constitute a substantial share of the resources devoted to each programme or project, unless its resources do not permit this.

Article 26

The World Heritage Committee and the recipient State shall define in the agreement they conclude the conditions in which a programme or project for which international assistance under the terms of this Convention is provided, shall be carried out. It shall be the responsibility of the State receiving such international assistance to continue to protect, conserve and present the property so safeguarded, in observance of the conditions laid down by the agreement.

VI. Educational Programmes

Article 27

1. The States Parties to this Convention shall endeavour by all appropriate means, and in particular by educational and information programmes, to strengthen appreciation and respect by their peoples of the cultural and natural heritage defined in Articles 1 and 2 of the Convention.
2. They shall undertake to keep the public broadly informed of the dangers threatening this heritage and of activities carried on in pursuance of this Convention.

Article 28

States Parties to this Convention which receive international assistance under the Convention shall take appropriate measures to make known the importance of the property for which asistance has been received and the role played by such assistance.

VII. Reports

Article 29

1. The States Parties to this Convention shall, in the reports which they submit to the General Conference of the Unidet Nations Educational, Scientific and Cultural Organization on dates and in a manner to be determined by it, give information on the legislative and administrative provisions which they have adopted and other action which they have taken for the application of this Convention, together with details of the experience acquired in this field.
2. These reports shall be brought to the attention of the World Heritage Committee.
3. The Committee shall submit a report on its activities at each of the ordinary sessions of the General Conference of the United Nations Educational, Scientific and Cultural Organization.

VIII. Final Clauses

Article 30

This Convention is drawn up in Arabic, English, French, Russian and Spanish, the five texts being equally authoritative.

Article 31

1. This Convention shall be subject to ratification or acceptance by States members of the United Nations Educational, Scientific and Cultural Organization in accordance with their respective constitutional procedures.
2. The instruments of ratification or acceptance shall be deposited with the Director-General of the United Nations Educational, Scientific and Cultural Organization.

Article 32

1. This Convention shall be open to accession by all States not members of the United Nations Educational, Scientific and Cultural Organization which are invited by the General Conference of the Organization of accede to it.
2. Accession shall be effected by the deposit of an instrument of accession with the Director-General of the United Nations Educational, Scientific and Cultural Organization.

Article 33

This Convention shall enter into force three months after the date of the deposit of the twentieth instrument of ratification, acceptance or accession, but only with respect to those States which have deposited their respective instruments of ratification, acceptance or accession on or before that date. It shall enter into force with respect to any other State three months after the deposit of its instrument of ratification, acceptance or accession.

Artricle 34

The following provisions shall apply to those States Parties to this Convention which have a federal or non-unitary constitutional system:

(a) with regard to the provisions of this Convention, the implementation of which comes under the legal jurisdiction of the federal or central legislative power, the obligations of the federal or central government shall be the same as for those States Parties which are not federal States;
(b) with regard to the provisions of this Convention, the implementation of which comes under the legal jurisdiction of individual constituent States, countries, provinces or cantons that are not obliged by the constitutional system of the federation to take legislative measures, the federal government shall inform the competent authorities of such States, countries, provinces or cantons of the said provisions, with its recommendation for their adoption.

Article 35

1. Each State Party to this Convention may denounce the Convention.
2. The denunciation shall be notified by an instrument in writing, deposited with the Director-General of the United Nations Educational, Scientific and Cultural Organization.
3. The denunciation shall take effect twelve months after the receipt of the instrument of denunciation. It shall affect the financial obligations of the denouncing State until the date on which the withdrawal takes effect.

Article 36

The Director-General of the United Nations Educational, Scientific and Cultural Organization shall inform the States members of the Organization, the States not members of the Organization which are referred to in Article 32, as well as the United Nations, of the deposit of all the instruments of ratification, acceptance, or accession provided for in Articles 31 and 32, and of the denunciations provided for in Article 35.

Article 37

1. This Convention may be revised by the General Conference of the United Nations Educational, Scientific and Cultural Organization. Any such revision shall, however, bind only the States which shall become Parties to the revising convention.
2. If the General Conference should adopt a new convention revising this Convention in whole or in part, then, unless the new convention otherwise provides, this Convention shall cease to be open to ratification, acceptance or accession, as from the date on which the new revising convention enters into force.

Article 38

In conformity with Article 102 of the Character of the United Nations, this Convention shall be registered with the Secretariat of the United Nations at the request of the Director-General of the United Nations Educational, Scientific and Cultural Organization.

Done in Paris, this twenty-third day of November 1972, in two authentic copies bearing the signature of the President of the seventeenth session of the General Conference and of the Director-General of the United Nations Educational, Scientific and Cultural Organization, which shall be deposited in the archives of the United Nation Educational, Scientific and Cultural Organization, and certified true copies of which shall be delivered to all the States referred to in Articles 31 and 32 as well as to the United Nations.